M000315221

California Family Law
for Paralegals

EDITORIAL ADVISORS

Deborah E. Bouchoux, Esq.
Georgetown University

Therese A. Cannon
Executive Vice President
Western Association of Schools and College Accrediting Commission
for Senior Colleges and Universities

Katherine A. Currier
Chair, Department of Paralegal and Legal Studies
Elms College

Susan M. Sullivan
Director, Graduate Career Programs
University of San Diego

Laurel A. Vietzen
Professor Emeritus
Elgin Community College

ASPEN COLLEGE SERIES

California Family Law for Paralegals

Sixth Edition

Marshall W. Waller, CFLS*
Member, California Bar

*Certified Family Law Specialist Board of Legal Specialization
State Bar of California

Wolters Kluwer
Law & Business

Copyright © 2012 Marshall W. Waller.

Published by Wolters Kluwer Law & Business in New York.

Wolters Kluwer Law & Business serves customers worldwide with CCH, Aspen Publishers, and Kluwer Law International products. (www.wolterskluwerlb.com)

No part of this publication may be reproduced or transmitted in any form
or by any means, electronic or mechanical, including photocopy, recording,
or utilized by any information storage or retrieval system, without written permission
from the publisher. For information about permissions or to request permissions online, visit us at www.wolterskluwerlb.com, or a written request may be faxed to our permissions department at 212-771-0803.

To contact Customer Service, e-mail customer.service@wolterskluwer.com,
call 1-800-234-1660, fax 1-800-901-9075, or mail correspondence to:

> Wolters Kluwer Law & Business
> Attn: Order Department
> PO Box 990
> Frederick, MD 21705

Printed in the United States of America.

1 2 3 4 5 6 7 8 9 0

ISBN 978-0-7355-9871-3

Library of Congress Cataloging-in-Publication Data

Waller, Marshall W.
 California family law for paralegals / Marshall W. Waller. — 6th ed.
   p. cm. — (Aspen college series)
Includes bibliographical references and index.
ISBN 978-0-7355-9871-3 (alk. paper)
 1. Domestic relations — California.   2. Legal assistants — California — Handbooks, manuals, etc.
I. Title.
KFC115.W345 2012
346.79401'5 — dc23

                                                        2012005343

Certified Chain of Custody
Product Line Contains At Least
20% Certified Forest Content
www.sfiprogram.org
SFI-00756

About Wolters Kluwer Law & Business

Wolters Kluwer Law & Business is a leading global provider of intelligent information and digital solutions for legal and business professionals in key specialty areas and respected educational resources for professors and law students. Wolters Kluwer Law & Business connects legal and business professionals as well as those in the education market with timely, specialized authoritative content and information-enabled solutions to support success through productivity, accuracy, and mobility.

Serving customers worldwide, Wolters Kluwer Law & Business products include those under the Aspen Publishers, CCH, Kluwer Law International, Loislaw, Best Case, ftwilliam.com, and MediRegs family of products.

CCH products have been a trusted resource since 1913 and are highly regarded resources for legal, securities, antitrust and trade regulation, government contracting, banking, pension, payroll, employment and labor, and healthcare reimbursement and compliance professionals.

Aspen Publishers products provide essential information to attorneys, business professionals, and law students. Written by preeminent authorities, the product line offers analytical and practical information in a range of specialty practice areas from securities law and intellectual property to mergers and acquisitions and pension/benefits. Aspen's trusted legal education resources provide professors and students with high-quality, up-to-date, and effective resources for successful instruction and study in all areas of the law.

Kluwer Law International products provide the global business community with reliable international legal information in English. Legal practitioners, corporate counsel, and business executives around the world rely on Kluwer Law journals, looseleafs, books, and electronic products for comprehensive information in many areas of international legal practice.

Loislaw is a comprehensive online legal research product, providing legal content to law firm practitioners of various specializations. Loislaw provides attorneys with the ability to quickly and efficiently find the necessary legal information they need, when and where they need it, by facilitating access to primary law as well as state-specific law, records, forms, and treatises.

Best Case Solutions is the leading bankruptcy software product to the bankruptcy industry. It provides software and workflow tools to flawlessly streamline petition preparation and the electronic filing process, while timely incorporating ever-changing court requirements.

ftwilliam.com offers employee benefits professionals the highest quality plan documents (retirement, welfare, and nonqualified) and government forms (5500/PBGC, 1099, and IRS) software at highly competitive prices.

MediRegs products provide integrated health care compliance content and software solutions for professionals in healthcare, higher education, and life sciences, including professionals in accounting, law, and consulting.

Wolters Kluwer Law & Business, a division of Wolters Kluwer, is headquartered in New York. Wolters Kluwer is a market-leading global information services company focused on professionals.

This book is dedicated to my parents, Charles W. Waller and Fern A. Waller. Their constant support and love throughout my life have taken me many places, not the least of which is this book. I also dedicate this book to my wife and partner, Mary Ellen Waller.
Her support and dedication has been an invaluable resource and a keystone in our success in life.

Summary of Contents

Contents

List of Figures

Preface

The purpose of this book is to provide a source of reference and explanation on the material discussed in a class in family law. It is also intended to be a starting point for those not necessarily pursuing this particular course of study but nonetheless interested in the area and searching for a treatise that is written neither for certified specialists nor for completely untrained laypersons. Hopefully this book will fill that need.

As I so often caution my students, this particular study of law, second only perhaps to taxation, is one of the most rapidly evolving areas of law. Of course, all of "the law" changes significantly over time. This results from previously unanticipated necessity to meet the ever-changing dynamics of our society and often simply to satisfy the demands of a particular interest group.

Whatever the reason, change is inevitable. In family law, it is both inevitable and *quick*. Thus the reader is cautioned to bear in mind that what is correct today may very likely be incorrect tomorrow. This book will be updated periodically to keep up with significant changes in the law, but nothing in this book should be relied upon in an actual legal setting without first undertaking extensive research regarding the particular legal question or consulting a trained professional. No book can substitute for legal advice given by a professional after evaluating all the pertinent facts.

The reader must also be aware that by its very nature this book cannot serve to fully explain the many mysteries of family law. Indeed, this book will be a success if it is able to shed a guiding light on the vast panoply of family law and clearly illuminate the "tip of the iceberg" of the various subjects covered. To presume to fully cover all of the areas referenced in this book does justice to neither the author nor the many fine authors of extensive, detailed treatises in this area.

This book is not a casebook, although where appropriate cases are mentioned and discussed. Nor is this merely a reference book to the various statutes used in family law, although they too are discussed as appropriate. Indeed, California family law is a creature of statute. The general common law, while incorporated for the most part into the Family Code, plays little active role in the current resolution of disputes in this area. Case law, too, for the most part only interprets and refines the statutory system. Many is the family court that defers to the legislature to remedy problems in the law.

Accordingly, the plain focus of this book is on the "heart" of the law in this area: the Family Code. This book will thus integrate the two concepts of statutory law and judicial interpretation into a cohesive general discussion of family law and its various aspects. Reference to figures and diagrams are made periodically to help explain the ideas under consideration, and there is a rather detailed discussion of many of the various judicial council forms used in family law practice.

A final note regarding the judicial council forms is appropriate. The forms shown in this book were current as of the date this book went to print. However, as with all other aspects of the law, the Judicial Council regularly revises these forms, sometimes as often as twice a year. As such, care should be taken when reviewing the forms in the book to ensure that the most current one is being studied. Fortunately, although revisions are common, they are typically ministerial and do not reflect significant changes in the substance or content of the form.

Should the reader be so interested, a complete set of judicial council forms can be obtained from any county courthouse at minimal cost. For purposes of this text, the learning process will, in this author's opinion, be unaffected should any of these forms be modified between the time the book goes to print and the time it ends up in the reader's hands.

This book has been a work in progress over the past 17 years. I have seen the area of family law change dramatically over this time, and this book in its various editions has sought to keep up with these changes. This new sixth edition has seen a substantial overhaul of this book, both substantively and in format, because as the law in this area grows and develops there is simply more to write about. Changes in the law have given rise to a restructuring of this book into separate chapters devoted to custody, visitation, spousal support, and child support. Truth is, there is simply too much going on in these areas to keep them grouped together. This restructuring has allowed these areas of family law to be addressed in greater detail in their individual chapters while at the same time maintaining the general flow and consistency between these admittedly related topics.

Additionally, Chapter 11 (formerly Chapter 8), titled "Selected Issues," has been expanded to include discussion in the areas of collaborative divorce, same-sex marriage, and limited scope representation. These issues represent "hot topics" in California right now and will no doubt remain so for years to come.

Marshall Waller

February 2012

Acknowledgments

I would like to recognize the help and support of the many people who have assisted me in this endeavor. Inasmuch as the development of this book over its six separate editions has spanned over seventeen years and required many, many long nights, I feel that the first to receive my sincerest thanks should be, and is, my family: my wife, Mary Ellen, and my children, Ryan and Lauren, all of whom have been patient and understanding throughout its development. I also thank my various assistants who have typed the several different incarnations of this book: Cathy Avery, Michele Lazaro, Sam Cesar, Courtney Stensvold, and Doina Gallion. Of my colleagues at work, attorney Sandra Salinas has provided insights and suggestions that have found their way into this book over time, for which I am sincerely grateful.

I also wish to thank the various editors who have worked diligently on this book to ensure that it is grammatically sound and substantively readable. A lot goes into producing a book like this, and one would be amazed to see the many gaffes, inconsistencies, misspellings, and non sequiturs that survive the author's initial draft. These people make these books readable, and they deserve much praise for doing so. To the extent that I look good between these two covers, I have them to thank.

I am very appreciative of and wish to recognize the efforts put into this book by Lisa Crowder, the project manager for this book. To say that she has been diligent and dedicated to the success of this project would be to understate her hard work and attention to detail and her focus on the completion of this project on time and within guidelines. She has been instrumental in bringing this project to completion and has done so with tact, patience, and understanding. Finally I wish to thank Betsy Kenny, my developmental editor at Aspen Law and Business. Betsy has been patient, kind, caring, and tolerant of me for over twelve years and frankly deserves a promotion, a raise, and a medal for putting up with me for so long. Without her input and guidance throughout this process this project would have been nearly impossible to put together. I thank her for her time, her efforts, and her support, and I look forward to working with her on the next five editions!

California Family Law
for Paralegals

CHAPTER 1

Introduction to Family Law

A. The Approach to Family Law
B. Jurisdiction; Service of Process; Venue
C. Ethics and the Paralegal
D. The Family Code
E. Validity of Marriage

CHAPTER OVERVIEW

Family law is one of the most challenging and rapidly evolving areas of law today. It involves elements of psychology, taxation, mathematics, accounting, and, of course, law, to name but a few. In addition, the accomplished practitioner in this field must excel at legal research and writing, trial advocacy, and human relations. It has often been said that family law is an area in which it is relatively easy to do poorly and difficult to do well.

This exciting area of the law involves virtually every aspect of the human condition; never will the practitioner see, hear, and experience the range of human emotion as in family law. When one catches a person involved in a marital dissolution, one is not seeing him at his best. Any unpleasant behavior is forgotten, though, the first time a parent thanks you for literally saving her child's life. Believe it; it happens.

This chapter will introduce some of the general concepts used in family law. You will review some basic aspects of civil procedure and study in some depth concepts of jurisdiction, service of process, and venue. You will be exposed to some of the ethical aspects of the practice of law in general and the practice of family law in particular. Finally, there is a general discussion and overview of the fundamental basis for family law in California: the Family Code.

A.   The Approach to Family Law

The term "family law" is somewhat of a euphemism in that it is more accurately described, in many respects, as "unfamily law." Indeed, for the most part, when one thinks of family law, the first thought to come to mind is that of divorce or, more accurately from a California perspective, marital dissolution. However, divorce is only one aspect of a very complex and diverse study.

When the subject of family law is examined in any detail, it becomes apparent that this moniker is an umbrella encompassing many diverse and complex areas of study including juvenile law, adoption, guardianship and conservatorship (typically under the major heading "probate"), legal separation, and marital dissolution, to name but a few.

Due to the sheer volume of material, attempting to address all of these subjects would fail to do justice to any of them. Discussion of these subjects sufficient to do more than merely mention their major aspects would exceed the scope of most school terms. The focus of this work, then, is the termination of marital and quasi-marital relationships and post-judgment modifications of these matters. This study will emphasize division of property, child custody and visitation, issues of spousal and child support, and procedural considerations in the application of these concepts to everyday situations.

Because this book is designed primarily for a course of study leading to a career as a paralegal, this author combines a strong belief in the concept of "learn by doing" with a heavy emphasis on the conceptual aspects of the study of family law. This combination provides a strong foundation for the student to enter the workplace with a familiarity with the basic concepts involved and a working knowledge of the preparation and utilization of the various judicial council forms that are the cornerstone of everyday family law practice.

This book is divided into several main sections, each of which provides more detailed insights into the myriad of subjects encompassed by the general category. The major categories include a general introduction to the legal system and the legal process, the nature and origins of the community property system in use in California, the procedural aspects of family law (that is, *marital dissolution*) practice, child custody and visitation, spousal support ("alimony"), child support, enforcement of orders, and selected procedural and substantive issues, including a brief discussion of nonmarital relationships, discovery, registered domestic partnerships, marital settlement agreements, and paternity.

As you approach the study of family law, keep in mind that the law is a constantly changing creature. Family law is no exception. In fact, along with taxation, family law is one of the most rapidly evolving areas of law at this time. As such, the *concepts* become every bit as important as the specific code sections and case law in use at any given moment. Accordingly, the memorization of code sections and certain cases, while not necessarily disadvantageous, should not be the student's primary focus. Instead, that focus should be directed to a thorough understanding of the ideas underlying the statutes. In this way, as the statutes change (and they *will*), the student will be able to change and adapt along with them.

Second, and of equal importance, is the concept that the law, in many respects, represents not always the study of what things *are*, but what they *should* be. Very often the student will not necessarily be expected to know the right answer, but *will* be expected to be familiar enough with the concepts in question to fully address and argue both (that is *all*) sides of the question presented. The student is thus cautioned not to rely entirely on an assessment of the right answer because in the next breath she may be called upon to challenge what she *knows* to be right, and vigorously argue the opposite position. The ability to do so represents a true command of the subject.

A working knowledge of these concepts is important in our context for several reasons. Foremost is the absolute requirement of understanding the environment into which the student is about to enter (here, of course, family law). Along a similar vein, an understanding of the general process of our court system will assist in the study and practice of *all* areas of law because, for the most part (and with apologies to Gertrude Stein), "a lawsuit is a lawsuit is a lawsuit." As the reader will soon discover, in many respects there is very little procedural difference between a termination of marriage proceeding and most other civil lawsuits. A brief review of these concepts of general civil litigation is thus recommended.

Most people are probably familiar, through personal experience or television, with what is known as a *personal injury* lawsuit (for example, one typically arising out of an automobile accident). Some may have been involved in a dispute over a broken promise or a product that failed to perform as expected. If so, then they most likely saw a *Complaint*, which started the lawsuit, an *Answer*, which responded to the complaint, and then various other documents involving pretrial requests for information from either or both parties or from the court. Then, ultimately, they may have participated in a trial, which typically resolved the matter, and some even may have participated in an appeal following trial.

With some general exceptions, this is exactly the same type of procedure that a participant in a marital termination proceeding will follow (with certain changes in the names of documents and the designation of the parties). As such, a working knowledge of the structure of the court system and some of its basic procedures will assist you in your study of family law.

In most counties, the population is so numerous and the workload so great that the separate departments of the superior court (criminal, probate, family law, and so forth) are often characterized not simply by their own courtroom, but by their own section of the building. Indeed, in downtown

Los Angeles the criminal caseload is so high that, even though the criminal cases are handled by a separate department of one superior court, they are heard in their own building, which is over 15 stories tall. Similarly, the family law department of the downtown Los Angeles Superior Court occupies multiple floors of the courthouse with over 20 departments (courtrooms) devoted to family law.

From a procedural standpoint, the *branch court* concept bears mention. Each county in each state typically has its own headquarters or central office. Just as each state has its capitol, and each city has its city hall, each county has *its* center of government. Although the label may not be in current fashion, this concept is generally referred to as the *county seat*. While there is little need for such distinction in a small county where one courthouse will typically suffice, in the larger counties this concept is indeed present. In Los Angeles County, for example, the county seat is in downtown Los Angeles. In Orange County, the county seat is in Santa Ana. In San Francisco County, the county seat is San Francisco.

To meet the needs of a large population, and to obviate a trip downtown just to use the court system, most counties have adopted the use of a series of branch courts, sprinkled liberally throughout the county, to make the courts easily accessible to all areas in the region. In Los Angeles, for example, there are 50 separate courthouse locations and 12 branch courts: Central (downtown Los Angeles and surrounding areas), East (Pomona and surrounding areas), North (Lancaster), North Central (Burbank, Glendale), North Valley (Chatsworth, San Fernando), Northeast (Pasadena and surrounding communities), Northwest (Van Nuys), South (Catalina, Long Beach and San Pedro), South Central (Compton), Southeast (Norwalk, Whittier and surrounding areas), Southwest (Torrance and nearby communities), West (Beverly Hills, Malibu, Santa Monica and related areas). The various branches are defined geographically, with the county being split up (generally by known cities or areas of the county) by territory. As a rule, in each of these branch courts you will find all the basic court services available in the county seat. There are various local rules that have been adopted by these many courts (including the county seat), especially in the context of a family law proceeding, and adherence to them is a requirement.

From a statutory standpoint, there are literally *thousands* of laws (code sections) in California that have been enacted over the years and are *still* operative. Fortunately, this course of study concerns itself with only a few. In general, however, there is a large amount of legislation on the subject of family law. The following is a basic list of those laws and their location in the code[1]:

- **Abandonment and neglect of children:**
  Pen. C. §§270 et seq.

- **Adoptions:**
  Fam. C. §§8500 et seq.
- **Child support:**
  Fam. C. §§3900 et seq.
- **Spousal support:**
  Fam. C. §§4300 et seq.
- **Custody of children:**
  Fam. C. §§3000 et seq.
- **Division of property:**
  Fam. C. §§2500 et seq.
- **Conservatorships:**
  Prob. C. §§1400 et seq.
- **Dissolution, Nullity and Legal Separation of marriage:**
  Fam. C. §§2000 et seq.
- **Enforcement of Family Law Act judgments:**
  C.C.P. §683.310
- **Enforcement of support orders:**
  Fam. C. §4500
- **Guardianships:**
  Prob. C. §§1400 et seq.
- **Juvenile Court Law:**
  W.&I.C. §§200 et seq.
- **Marital agreements:**
  Fam. C. §§1500 et seq.
- **Parent and child relationships:**
  Fam. C. §§7500 et seq.
- **Uniform Reciprocal Enforcement of Support Act (URESA):**
  Fam. C. §§4800 et seq.
- **Spousal abuse:**
  Pen. C. §§273.8 et seq.
- **Uniform Parentage Act:**
  Fam. C. §§7600 et seq.
- **Uniform Child Custody Jurisdiction and Enforcement Act:**
  Fam. C. §§3400 et seq.
- **Uniform Premarital Agreement Act:**
  Fam. C. §§1600 et seq.
- **Void or voidable marriage:**
  Fam. C. §§2200 et seq.
- **Wage assignment for support:**
  Fam. C. §§5200 et seq.
- **Withholding order for support:**
  C.C.P. §§706.030, 706.051, 706.052

Along with those listed, there are other statutes throughout the California codes that pertain to or mention family law subjects. They will be discussed as required throughout this book.

In addition to case opinion and statutory law, there is (in California, at least) a panoply of treatises dealing with the subject of family law. Some of the more popular include:

- Witkin, Summary of California Law
- Witkin, California Procedure
- California Family Law Service (Bancroft Whitney)
- Hogoboom & King, Family Law (The Rutter Group/Thomson West)
- Markey, California Family Law (West's Publishing Co.)
- Stephen Adams, California Family Law Practice (CFLR/Thomson West, CA)

There are also numerous other works available including seminar materials, weekly and monthly update services (notably those provided by CFLR on a weekly and monthly basis), a quarterly update service put out by Bancroft Whitney as part of the above-mentioned California Family Law Service, and the many fine publications of the California Continuing Education of the Bar [CEB].[2] Additionally, the Los Angeles County Bar Association provides to its members in an electronic format (by e-mail) daily "e-briefs," wherein a brief mention of all published cases is provided.

B. Jurisdiction; Service of Process; Venue

Of paramount importance regarding basic litigation procedure are the concepts of *jurisdiction* (over what (and when) is the court empowered to render decisions), *service of process* (how does the court *obtain* this jurisdiction), and finally, *venue* (where should the action be filed and heard). In addition to these concepts is the related question of the *residence* of the parties.

Before a family law court can appropriately hear a family law case, it must first ensure that it has the *power* to hear that case. Contrary to what may be thought by the reader, the court does not automatically have jurisdiction (that is, power) over a particular case simply because it has been filed. Certain procedural hurdles and safeguards, involving questions of jurisdiction over the subject matter of the lawsuit and jurisdiction over the people and property of the marriage,[3] must first be met to ensure that the exercise of that power by the court is fair and appropriate under all the facts and circumstances.

Always ask two questions: (1) Does the court have subject matter jurisdiction, and (2) does the court have personal jurisdiction? The answer to these questions must always be "yes" for the matter to proceed. If the answer is yes, the subject matter jurisdiction must come from some statute; some specific source of statutory law must have given the court the power to hear the case.[4]

1. Subject Matter Jurisdiction

The term *subject matter jurisdiction* means just that: Does the court have power over the *subject matter* of the case (for example, the dissolution of the marriage) and the issues to which that is related? Or, perhaps stated somewhat more specifically, *which* court has jurisdiction over the subject matter of a marital dissolution proceeding? And when is it appropriate to *exercise* this jurisdiction?

In California, pursuant to Family Code sections 200 and 2010, the superior court has exclusive jurisdiction to hear all issues arising out of a marital dissolution (or other Family Code) matter. Thus one will never see a family law matter in the municipal or small claims court.[5] Specifically stated, all issues in the following matters shall be decided (at the trial level) in the superior court:

- child custody
- child visitation
- child support
- spousal support
- property division
- issues related to or arising out of the above
- status of the parties as married persons

Although there are many "wrinkles" to these general concepts, for our purposes the above can be accepted as the general rule. There are also various other provisions of the Family Code that confer specific subject matter jurisdiction over certain issues to the superior court. For example, Family Code section 2060 refers to jurisdiction over pension plans, section 3100 deals with visitation rights of parents, and sections 3101, 3103, and 3104 address visitation rights of stepparents and grandparents.

Every once in a while, two different states may be competing for subject matter jurisdiction over a dissolution of marriage. Although not common, it does occur, typically where one of the spouses has moved out of state and subsequently decides to file for dissolution. Because subject matter jurisdiction is generally appropriate in the state of *domicile* of *either* spouse, there can be instances of both parties filing for dissolution at or about the same time, thus vesting subject matter jurisdiction in two different jurisdictions at the same time. This is easily resolved, however: The state that is first to acquire jurisdiction over the other party by service of process will be the forum for ultimate resolution of the case, regardless of which case was filed first. It is the first to *serve*, not the first to file, that controls.

2. Residence and Domicile

The concept of *domicile* is mentioned above and involves the *permanent* location of a party within the state. The exercise of subject matter jurisdiction conferred by Family Code section 2010 is not available in all circumstances. There is an additional requirement that at least one of the parties be *domiciled* within California. This means that at least one of the parties, either husband or wife, must be living in California with the intention of making it his or her *permanent* home. This is not as clear a test as may first be assumed. In fact, it is almost defined in the negative.

By definition, a person can have only one domicile. This will continue to be that person's domicile until he leaves the state and establishes a presence in some other state, with the intent to remain there indefinitely. Mere absence from the state does not destroy a person's status as being domiciled there. Temporary absences, even if they add up to a majority of the time, will not destroy domicile. A person's *residence*, on the other hand, is not thought of in terms so permanent in nature. A residence can be any location where a person lives for any period of time. Indeed, one can have several residences, but only one domicile. It should also be noted that a person's nonimmigrant alien status (i.e., one visiting this country on a temporary visa) will not in and of itself preclude a finding by the court that they satisfy the domicile requirements of California.

The concept of domicile, as might be imagined, is not very clear cut, nor is it defined simply by referring to some time formula. To establish domicile, one must establish intent, and that is never easy, especially if the other party is fighting it. How then *is* it proven? It is proven by examining the details of a person's life. This requisite intent can very often be established by employing evidence of the following factors: home (or other property) ownership, voter registration, location of tax filings, where an individual pays state taxes; all of these can help to establish one's "intent to remain indefinitely" in a particular state.

The importance of the question of domicile is significantly noticeable when analyzing the effect of decisions made in violation of the domicile requirements. Generally, there is little the court can do if the only basis for asserting jurisdiction is the petitioner's domicile.[6] In fact, the only matter to be adjudicated under these circumstances is the status of the marriage. All other aspects of the dissolution proceeding (for example, property division, support) are deemed to be personal in nature, and exercise of the court's power over these issues is appropriate only when personal jurisdiction has been established over the *responding party*. If that party is not subject to California's jurisdiction, then California can make few decisions that affect that person. Of significant exception to this rule is the ability of the court to adjudicate a nullity proceeding, even if *neither* party is domiciled in California, so long as they both personally appear.

The legal effect of a judgment entered in California when neither party is domiciled here is that it is *void;* that is, it is not subject to recognition at all and is of no force and effect whatsoever; it is not entitled to full faith and credit (that is, recognition) by other states, and it is susceptible to being challenged either directly by a motion to dismiss, or indirectly by challenging any attempt to enforce its provisions.

Family Code section 2320 sets forth the residency requirement that must be met before entry of a decree of dissolution. This section requires that at least one of the parties to the marriage must be a resident of this state for six months and of the county in which the action is pending for three months immediately before commencement of the dissolution action. This requirement does not apply in actions for legal separation or nullity. Accordingly, if a party is new to the state and must initiate an action immediately,[7] the next step is to commence an action for legal separation,[8] wait the six-month period mandated in Family Code section 2320 to establish residency, and then amend the Petition to change the request from "legal separation" to "dissolution of marriage." Because California is a "no-fault" state (an idea that is discussed below), this request will always be granted. In fact, this procedure is specifically provided for in Family Code section 2321.

In contrast to an order entered by a court lacking subject matter jurisdiction, this residency requirement is not *jurisdictional.* That is, failure to meet the requirement does not make the order void. Further, such an order is not subject to collateral attack once the order has been made. Failure to meet the residency requirement, however, can be raised in a *motion to quash the proceeding,* which is (more or less) the family law equivalent of a demurrer.[9]

3. Personal Jurisdiction

The next step in this inquiry is the establishment of the court's appropriate exercise of personal jurisdiction over the parties in question.[10] Just as the court must have power over the subject of a particular case, it must also be in a position to exercise power over the parties themselves, for without this power the orders made against these parties are not susceptible to enforcement.

The basis of the personal jurisdiction requirement has its genesis in the United States Constitution, and, concomitantly, the California State Constitution. The due process clause of these documents (the California Constitution is substantially similar to the United States Constitution in this area) is the enabling clause that mandates the presence of such jurisdiction before the state (through its courts) will be able to make an order against someone affecting their personal rights (including orders regarding money, property division rights, and so on).[11]

In California this requirement is not hard to meet. This state's exercise of personal jurisdiction will be deemed to be consistent with due process requirements so long as "it does not violate 'traditional notions of fair play and substantial justice.'" These "traditional notions of fair play and substantial justice" allow a court to exercise personal jurisdiction on either of the following bases:

- physical presence in the state (this assumes personal service of process);
- domicile in the state when the action is commenced;
- consent to the exercise of personal jurisdiction by the respondent; or
- "minimum contacts" with the forum state.

Mere physical presence in the state is sufficient to establish personal jurisdiction. California Code of Civil Procedure section 410.10 is the statute that defines the basis of personal jurisdiction. It says little more than words to the effect that *any* exercise of personal jurisdiction is appropriate as long as it comports with the United States Constitution. These bases are listed in C.C.P. section 410.10:

- presence in the state
- domicile in the state
- residence in the state
- citizenship in the state
- doing business in the state
- causing an *effect* in this state
- consent of the person in question
- ownership of property within the state
- any other such relationship with the state which makes the exercise of personal jurisdiction reasonable

As can be seen, it does not take much for California to grant its courts power over someone. This concept is typically thought of as the *minimum contacts* rule: So long as a person has certain *minimum* contacts with the state, and *purposefully* avails himself of the benefits and protection of California's law, then personal jurisdiction is appropriately exercised. As stated above, although subject matter jurisdiction is something the court either has or does not have, regardless of the actions of the parties, personal jurisdiction can be conferred on the court simply by a party's *appearance* and consent to it.[12] Of course, court orders made in violation of this requirement are void.

For an excellent discussion of these concepts in the context of a California family law proceeding, the reader is invited to read the case of Burnham v. Superior Ct., 495 U.S. 604, 110 S. Ct. 2105 (1990). The question presented and the facts of this case as it presented to the United States Supreme Court are set forth by that Court as follows:

> The question presented is whether the Due Process Clause of the Fourteenth Amendment denies California courts jurisdiction over a non-resident, who was personally served with process while temporarily in that State, in a suit unrelated to his activities in the State.
>
> Petitioner Dennis Burnham married Francie Burnham in 1976 in West Virginia. In 1977 the couple moved to New Jersey, where their two children were born. In July 1987 the Burnhams decided to separate. They agreed that Mrs. Burnham, who intended to move to California, would take custody of the children. Shortly before Mrs. Burnham departed for California that same month, she and petitioner agreed that she would file for divorce on grounds of "irreconcilable differences." In October 1987, petitioner filed for divorce in New Jersey state court on grounds of "desertion." Petitioner did not, however, obtain an issuance of summons against his wife and did not attempt to serve her with process. Mrs. Burnham, after unsuccessfully demanding that petitioner adhere to their prior agreement to submit to an "irreconcilable differences" divorce, brought suit for divorce in California state court in early January 1988. In late January, petitioner visited southern California on business, after which he went north to visit his children in the San Francisco Bay area, where his wife resided. He took the older child to San Francisco for the weekend. Upon returning the child to Mrs. Burnham's home on January 24, 1988, petitioner was served with a California court summons and a copy of Mrs. Burnham's divorce petition. He then returned to New Jersey. Later that year, petitioner made a special appearance in the California Superior Court, moving to quash the service of process on the ground that the court lacked personal jurisdiction over him because his only contacts with California were a few short visits to the State for the purposes of conducting business and visiting his children. The Superior Court denied the motion, and the California Court of Appeal denied mandamus relief, rejecting petitioner's contention that the Due Process Clause prohibited California courts from asserting jurisdiction over him because he lacked "minimum contacts" with the State. The court held it to be "a valid jurisdictional predicate for in personam jurisdiction" that the "defendant [was] present in the forum state and personally served with process." App. to Pet. for Cert. 5. We granted certiorari.

In affirming the Appellate Court's exercise of jurisdiction over this admitted nonresident, the Supreme Court gave great deference to the benefits and protections afforded to people who visit a state (use of the roads and the related infrastructure inherent in virtually all of the states) and the effect voluntarily taking advantage of these benefits and protections will have on that nonresident.

4. Service of Process

The other concept fundamental to this discussion is that of notice and opportunity to be heard. One simply cannot go forward with a lawsuit without giving notice to the other side that it is pending, and allowing them an opportunity to come to court, tell their version of the facts and argue their position. Of course, very often parties to a lawsuit will choose to allow the proceeding to go forward in their absence, but even then, until and unless proper service and notice has been given to them of the specifics of the dispute, the court will not proceed.

The notice requirement is satisfied by properly *serving* the papers involved in the lawsuit on the opposing party. Code of Civil Procedure section 413.10 sets out the service requirements to be met in California. There are many ways in which to accomplish service, including personal service, substituted service, service by mail, and service by publication.[13]

The main principle of service of process is to advise one's adversary of the exact details of what is being requested in the lawsuit. This not only affords the adversary an opportunity to appear and respond or defend, but it also fully apprises them of the exact nature of the dispute so they can make an intelligent decision whether to appear and contest the litigation or not.

Assume, for example, that John owes Mary $500 and for whatever reason has not yet paid this debt even though the money is due. If Mary serves John with her complaint for money indicating that she is asking for $5,000, John may very well want to respond to the complaint and argue that the actual amount is really only $500. The only way John learns about this difference between what is claimed by Mary and what is actually owed to her is because of the notice requirement, which acts to protect John.

If Mary had asked for the actual amount owed of $500, John, realizing that he did in fact owe the money, might simply have decided not to appear and contest the lawsuit and thus would have allowed Mary to win, by default,[14] an award of $500. The requirement of notice has given John sufficient information with which to make an intelligent decision whether to appear and defend.

Mary cannot, however, simply state in her lawsuit "John owes me money" without being more specific as to the amount and expect to be awarded any amount she asks for at the subsequent court hearing. By framing her request in this vague fashion, she has not fully advised John of its specifics. Since the court cannot give Mary anything in excess of what she notified John she would be seeking, by leaving the amount sought subject to speculation, the court cannot make an award in Mary's favor even though John has not even appeared. This is because John did not receive *notice* of exactly what Mary was seeking and is exactly the reason why certain matters must be pleaded (that is, set out in the requesting papers) completely and specifically.

This situation can arise in family law matters with some regularity and embarrassment. An "uncontested dissolution" is not all that unusual. When a relationship ends many people find any continuing dialogue with their former mate, especially in the context of litigation, painful and wish to avoid it. As such (and this is most common when there is little to resolve and divide) a responding party who is either resigned to the concept of getting divorced or wants it as well may simply choose to ignore the service of summons and Petition and allow the matter to proceed without him.

If this is the case, whether by chance or by design, care must be taken to ensure that the petition that has been served on the respondent contains all the specifics of the request. If not, the petitioner (and her lawyer) may be placed in the unenviable position of having to amend the petition to reflect the missing specifics and re-serve the papers all over again. Not only does this delay the process significantly, but serving the respondent again may be difficult or even impossible (which will even *further* delay the proceedings, to say nothing of causing the attorney embarrassment, extra costs, and potential exposure to claims of malpractice).

In marital dissolution litigation, the California Rules of Court (CRC) provide a detailed discussion of the various documents that must be served in this context. In general, judicial council forms are mandated for use in Family Law Act matters. These are preprinted "fill in the blanks"-type forms, designed to make the process more accessible and intelligible for the public. In general, the bulk of these forms can easily be found online at a variety of sources. A good starting point is the official Web site for the California courts. The URL for the judicial council forms is http://www.courtinfo.ca.gov/forms/. Many of these forms will be discussed in greater detail later in this book.

5. Venue

Of final consideration in this procedural section is the question of venue or, in other words, the question of *where* the action should be entertained. This can be an issue of international, interstate, or intrastate (that is, between counties) venue. Also considered hand in hand with the question of venue is that of *forum non conveniens*, or "inconvenient forum." Inasmuch as this simply deals with the best location for trial and is not jurisdictional, an improper court (from a venue perspective) *can* render an otherwise enforceable order (assuming venue is not challenged).

In California the venue rules in family law matters are relatively simple: Pursuant to Code of Civil Procedure section 395(a), venue in a marital dissolution proceeding is appropriate in the county where one of the parties has resided for three months immediately preceding the commencement of the action. As such, a petition for dissolution can be filed by the petitioner in the county where she has resided for at least three months prior to filing the petition, or in the county where the respondent has resided for at least three months prior to the commencement of the action. The same is true of *nullity* and *legal separation* actions, except there is no minimum time period for residence. In other words, in a nullity or legal separation action, the action may be commenced in such county as either of the parties make their residence, regardless how long (or short) they have been so residing.

For good cause, the court may relocate the proceedings to a different venue if it would serve the interests of justice by being more convenient for all concerned. For example, if an action is properly commenced in Los Angeles County but would be more conveniently tried in Ventura County (due to location of witnesses, for example), upon proper motion the court can order that the action be moved to Ventura. This objection based on inconvenient forum is waived if not raised at the first opportunity. Further, an order made by the court that is made in violation of the rules of venue is just as enforceable as if those rules had been followed because they are not jurisdictional and have no effect on the validity of the order.

Sometimes a situation arises where, after separation, the spouses relocate to different counties, and then each start their own dissolution actions. In this case, the first person to serve the other will have the benefit of having the matter heard in the county in which they filed the petition. Note that it is not the first to file—it is the first to serve. Also note that if the parties both file in the same county, it is no longer a "race to serve"; rather, the case that is filed first will be the lead case in which the matters will be decided.

6. Attacking the Judgment

Generally speaking, once a judgment in any civil action (which of course includes a family law matter) becomes final, it becomes subject only to *modification* and *enforcement*. This is not to say that a final judgment is immune from attack so much as it is generally not susceptible to attack. In the context of attacking a judgment, there are two types of "attacks" to be mentioned: *collateral* and *direct*.

A direct attack is raised in the context of the proceeding in which the offensive judgment was rendered; for example, a motion for a new trial or an appeal. A collateral attack, on the other hand, is raised in a separate proceeding whose goal is to demonstrate that the previous judgment is void based on (usually) some jurisdictional basis. A collateral attack is raised in one of two ways: an action filed to declare the judgment void or by asserting the invalidity of the judgment as a defense to its enforcement.[15]

The grounds upon which a judgment is generally attacked include lack of subject matter jurisdiction, lack of personal jurisdiction, lack of notice given to the respondent, a judgment entered in excess of the court's jurisdiction, and other due process violations. Conversely, there are two basic theories of law that will operate to defeat an attack on a judgment: *res judicata* and *collateral estoppel*.

Res judicata essentially prohibits any attack on a judgment if the claimed defect has already been litigated in prior proceedings between the same parties. Thus, if the attacking party participated in the earlier proceedings and had an opportunity to litigate the issue that forms the basis of the attack in that proceeding, then for all practical purposes there is nothing left to litigate in the subsequent proceeding, since that issue has already been decided. The reader should note that actual participation in the earlier proceeding is not required. All that is required is the *opportunity* to participate.

Collateral estoppel is similar to res judicata in that it will prevent a party from, essentially, "re-litigating" an issue under circumstances in which it would be inequitable to do so. In other words, a party will be denied the opportunity to re-litigate an issue if he participated in its earlier determination, or in some other way, by his action or inaction, allowed the situation to exist in the first place. In these circumstances, the courts look to the equities of the situation and seek to determine whether the objecting party is entitled to the relief he seeks. If he has somehow contributed to his situation, or undertaken a course of conduct that would require doing an inequity to the other party, the courts will deny his request.[16]

C.   Ethics and the Paralegal

Many and various rules are assigned to govern and regulate the behavior of licensed attorneys in California. These rules have been codified as the California Rules of Professional Conduct (CRPC) and are published as part of the California codes. It is highly recommended that any individual interested in the legal system and its operations read these rules in their entirety. For the paralegal, knowledge of these rules is an absolute must.

These rules, generally referred to as "ethical considerations," are designed to ensure that the public receives legal services that are competently, conscientiously, and fairly performed by the attorney of their choosing. The rules tend to be somewhat uniform in all jurisdictions and are typically enforced by the licensing agency of the state in which the attorney practices. In California, for example, the State Bar of California is assigned this task. Since this organization is comprised of all active members of the state bar, it can be said that the attorneys for this state are self-policing.

The sanctions for violating these rules can result in punishment including public reproval, suspension, and, if the offense is serious enough or if the attorney has a long record of ethical violations, disbarment. Disbarment is the most serious punishment available and is meted out only under the most extreme circumstances. Its effect is, after all, to deprive the offending attorney of his or her license to practice law and, with that, the ability to earn a living in that chosen vocation.

In general, the ethical rules governing attorneys regulate the level of competence that the attorney must possess in order to practice law, the type and amount of fees charged for legal services, the manner in which the attorney maintains certain office records, and the manner in which the attorney accounts for monies held on behalf of her clients. The California Rules of Professional Conduct are organized into the following major topic areas:

Chapter 1:	Professional Integrity in General	Rule 1-100
Chapter 2:	Relationship among Members	Rule 2-100
Chapter 3:	Professional Relationship with Clients	Rule 3-101
Chapter 4:	Financial Relationship with Clients	Rule 4-100
Chapter 5:	Advocacy and Representation	Rule 5-100

As of this writing, there are no such rules to govern and regulate the conduct of paralegals. In this author's opinion, however, this will change in the near future. And, inasmuch as those rules will no doubt be based in no small part on the existing rules governing an attorney's behavior, a review of those rules will prove helpful.

For the most part, the Rules of Professional Conduct deal with the attorney's relationship with his clients. Paralegals by definition are not attorneys licensed to practice law and thus are not allowed to give legal advice to clients. Therefore one might wonder why the paralegal should become familiar with rules regulating the behavior of attorneys. Generally speaking, the paralegal's role in a family law practice will focus on research and preparation of some of the basic documents used in dissolution matters, including preparation and review of discovery (interrogatories, document production requests, for example), and deposition summaries. Some paralegals may also find themselves joining in client interviews with the attorney and acting as a "liaison" between the attorney and the client (being careful, of course, not to dispense any legal advice, even if requested). Even in this somewhat restricted capacity, however, and due in part to the lack of definition of the role of the paralegal in the law office, strict adherence to the CRPC, if not in letter then in spirit, is well advised.

While paralegals are not (for the time being) held to the same standard of conduct as attorneys, there are certain situations that are somewhat unique to the practice of family law and about which the paralegal working in that field should be familiar. These typically involve representation by the attorney of both sides to a family law matter, as well as the avoidance of conflicts of interest that may arise in the course of a marital dissolution proceeding.

The mandates found in CRPC 3-310 provide a wide basis for potential problems for the family law attorney. That section, divided into specific subsections, generally provides:

3-310(B): If an attorney has or had a relationship with another party in the litigation or is interested in the subject matter of the litigation, that attorney cannot accept or continue the representation without first obtaining the client's *informed written consent*.

3-310(C): No dual representation of both sides to a proceeding where their respective interests conflict is allowed without first obtaining *both* of their *informed written consents*.

3-310(C)(3): An attorney must not undertake representation adverse to the interests of a former client (that is, must not represent someone who is suing a former client of the lawyer's) if, by virtue of the former representation that lawyer has obtained *confidential information* pertinent to the current subject matter of the representation, without first obtaining the former client's *informed written consent*.

3-310(A): This section defines "informed" as used above in the context of consent as *disclosure and advice* to the client as to *any* actual or likely adverse effects to the client. Any client who is in the position of signing such an *informed written consent* must first be referred to some other attorney to advise him as to the consequences of that act.

In addition to the rules mentioned above, litigation guidelines adopted by the Los Angeles County Bar Association Board of Trustees expand the professional code of conduct to be adhered to by members of that association. With particular focus on family law practitioners, the following list sets forth a brief listing of these new rules. A review of this list will not only provide guidance to the reader in her work in this area, but it will also give an interesting insight into the general condition of the Bar and the sheer necessity for its evolution:

1. Family Law Attorneys (FLAs) should not engage in churning a case. This refers to the practice of unnecessarily running up fees in order to either gain an advantage in the litigation (by "burying" the opposition with paper, discovery, motions, etc.) or to simply run up the attorney's fees to his own advantage, in the absence of any legal necessity for his actions.
2. The FLA should not engage in economic warfare of harassment of the opposing party simply to gain a litigation advantage over an unsophisticated or underfunded litigant.

3. The FLA should not participate in vindictive litigation, such as litigation where the primary goal is simply to cause the other party harm, as opposed to solving a legitimate problem for the client.

4. The FLA should not take any action that will unnecessarily exacerbate the emotional level of a family law dispute.

5. The FLA should actively participate in preparing his client for the mediation process so as to make it more meaningful.

6. The FLA should, as soon as possible, disclose the existence of any preexisting social or professional relationship between herself and any expert witness appointed by the court or obtained pursuant to stipulation of the parties.

7. The FLA should not participate in a child custody or visitation dispute motivated primarily by harassment, coercion, or vindictiveness.

8. The FLA should not communicate ex parte with a child custody evaluator or court-appointed witness.

9. The FLA should never make a personal attack on opposing counsel.

10. The FLA should utilize the ex parte process with restraint—only when the circumstances truly warrant emergency judicial intervention.

11. The FLA should promptly return her telephone calls to opposing counsel, or, if that is not possible, have someone else return the calls for her.

12. The FLA should not harass the opposing counsel through the use of unnecessary motions, faxes, etc. (in other words: "don't play games!").

13. The FLA should cooperate with the opposing counsel to ensure an effective and efficient resolution of family law matters.[17]

Perhaps one of the most frequent situations directly impacted by these rules is where a husband and wife go to an attorney together and declare: "We agree on everything—we just want you to write up the agreement and make it official." Clearly there is a conflict, unless the only issue to be decided is the termination of marital status. But that is quite rare. Often there are issues of property division, support, and child custody to be resolved as well.

Even though the parties may "agree," more often than not such agreement is the product of overreaching or undue pressure being brought to bear upon the "agreeing" spouse by the "insisting" spouse. Perhaps the agreement is based upon an incorrect understanding of the law. Indeed, an agreement can easily fall apart once the parties are fully informed of the law and what the options available to them may be. How then can an attorney effectively advocate for the rights of one party when she also represents the other party? Indeed, she cannot, and should not place herself in that position.

This representation conflict also occurs when one spouse, for example, the husband, requests an attorney to represent him in a dissolution proceeding notwithstanding the fact that the attorney had, in the past, represented the wife in an unrelated business matter. While not as blatant, the conflict is just as present.

In both of the above situations, representation by one attorney, while not necessarily technically prohibited (assuming both spouses agree), is a big mistake and should be avoided. Access to certain confidential information as well as the foolish attempt to advocate on behalf of both sides to a contested issue seriously compromises the attorney's duty of loyalty to *each* client.

This prohibition against conflicting representation even extends to *prospective* clients of the attorney. For example, if a wife goes to an attorney, discloses the facts of her situation, discusses with the attorney the rules of law and her options in the dissolution, and then decides to retain some other lawyer, then the lawyer with whom she first spoke is precluded from representing the husband.

The potential for conflict extends beyond what might seem to be the obvious situations mentioned above. For example, what about the attorney who has represented both husband and wife in business dealings, or the purchase of a home, or in an automobile accident? What about the attorney who drafts mutual wills or performs other estate-planning services? When a wife then comes to this attorney and asks for representation against her husband in a dissolution proceeding, should the attorney accept this representation? Should an attorney agree to represent a husband (or wife) when the attorney has a *social* relationship with either or both of them? In all of these cases, the answer is "no."

These potential conflict problems can also extend to situations in which the attorney has (or had) a confidential relationship with opposing *counsel*. For example, a father and daughter should never represent opposite sides in the same lawsuit.

In addition to the matters discussed above, there are regulations governing the nature of the relationship between the attorney and the client, for example, avoidance of acquiring any interest adverse to one's client, avoidance of a sexual relationship with one's client (unless the sexual relationship preceded the attorney-client relationship) and things of a similar nature.[18]

What then are the *practical* aspects of this discussion?[19] If a case comes to an attorney under these circumstances and it is contested in any aspect, or if litigation of any kind arises, the attorney *cannot* represent both spouses. As a matter of law, it has been held that under those circumstances, even if consent was obtained, that consent was neither intelligent nor informed.

As such it is prohibited. Where there is no *actual* conflict present, although not a good idea, the court will generally permit dual representation. This situation arises where the parties have, in fact, resolved all of their differences and are in agreement on all issues. In this occurrence, after a full disclosure by the attorney of the conflict, coupled with an intelligent and informed waiver of the conflict of interest, the attorney may proceed to represent both sides. However, if any actual conflict arises, that lawyer must withdraw immediately from representation of both of them and cannot continue to represent either of them.

Generally in uncontested proceedings the attorney advises the clients *up front* that he cannot actually represent both of them. The attorney should select one of the clients to be the subject of the representation (usually the one who was initially referred to the attorney) and advise the other that once the preparation of the documentation necessary to conclude the matter is complete, she (the other [unrepresented] party) will be required to have all that documentation reviewed and explained to her by an attorney of her choosing.

This party will then sign a statement incorporated into the agreement acknowledging that the preparing attorney does not represent her, has not given her any advice or answered any questions upon which she relied in entering into the agreement, and finally that she has been advised to seek independent counsel to review the documents and their legal effect and that she has either done so or intelligently chosen not to. If at all possible, it is wise to have the reviewing attorney "sign off" on the agreement as well.[20]

A word about malpractice is prudent at this point. Almost everyone knows or has heard of the concept of malpractice. That is the name given to the cause of action one pursues when claiming that a professional (in this case, an attorney) made mistakes in the representation that could have been avoided had the attorney not been negligent. As might be imagined, these lawsuits are not uncommon in a situation where the attorney was not necessarily negligent, but where the client was not happy with the outcome.[21]

In situations such as this, it is not unusual for a plaintiff in a malpractice case to sue everybody having anything to do with his file (from a decision-making standpoint). Due to the "gray" nature of the paralegal's role in the law office, the suit might well include the paralegal. Accordingly, it would behoove the paralegal to ensure that his interests in this regard are adequately protected in the workplace. Whether this extends to the acquisition of Errors and Omissions Insurance is an undecided question, but these are issues that should be addressed at the employment level.[22]

Many paralegals have heard that as long as they are working for an attorney when their alleged malpractice took place they need not worry about their own liability. This is not the case, however. The concept at the source of this confusion is known as *respondeat superior*, which operates to hold an employer liable for the negligence of their employees so long as the employees were working within the course and scope of their employment when the negligent act occurred. Respondeat superior will not, however, shield the offending employee; it merely *expands* the pool of persons liable for the negligence. Typically the potential plaintiff will pursue the attorney in cases of this type because the attorney is usually insured and also the party most likely to have money. To rely on a plaintiff choosing in this manner is an invitation to disaster, however. It is far easier to protect oneself simply by putting out a good work product and adhering to the ethical considerations discussed in this chapter.

D. The Family Code

Historically, California has placed the basic framework of its family law in the Family Law Act located in Division 4 (General Provisions), Part 5 of the California Civil Code (C.C.), commencing at section 4000 with Title 1, "Marriage." Effective January 1, 1994, however, this structure was radically changed by the California legislature. Recognizing that the statutes impacting on family law matters were spread out over no less than five separate codes, the legislature undertook the task of gathering most (if not all) of the statutes that pertain to family law matters and reorganized and updated them in the context of a separate code devoted exclusively to family law. Hence, the Family Code was enacted.

The creation of this Code took over five years to complete, the first incarnation of it seeing light in 1989. Careful attention was paid to reorganizing the existing laws and eliminating conflicts in the laws that pre-existed this effort due to the fact that this subject matter was previously treated in so many different places in California's laws.

The Family Code is divided into 17 Divisions,[23] each containing various subdivisions, called "Parts," which are further subdivided into "Chapters," with the final level of division being called "Articles," depending on the breadth of the subject covered and the need for such detail. Division 20, for example, has but one level of subdivision, contained in its "Part 1." Division 9, on the other hand, is divided into five separate Parts, containing 27 separate Chapters and 44 different Articles. The Divisions of the Family Code are as follows:

Division 1:	Preliminary Provisions and Definitions (§1)
Division 2:	General Provisions (§200)
Division 2.5:	Domestic Partner Registration (§297)
Division 3:	Marriage (§300)
Division 4:	Rights and Obligations During Marriage (§700)
Division 5:	Conciliation Proceedings (§1800)

Division 6:   Nullity, Dissolution, and Legal Separation (§2000)
Division 7:   Division of Property (§2500)
Division 8:   Custody of Children (§3000)
Division 9:   Support (§3500)
Division 10:   Prevention of Domestic Violence (§6200)
Division 11:   Minors (§6500)
Division 12:   Parent and Child Relationship (§7500)
Division 13:   Adoption (§8500)
Division 14:   Family Law Facilitator Act (§10000)
Division 16:   Family Law Information Centers [Repealed]
Division 17:   Support Services (§17000)
Division 20:   Pilot Projects (§20000)

An example of the manner in which a division is further subdivided into parts, chapters, and articles is seen in Division 9, "Support":

Division 9:   Support (§3500)
   Part 1:   Definitions and General Provisions (§3500)
      Chapter 1:   Definitions (§3500)
      Chapter 2:   General Provisions (§3550)
      Chapter 3:   Support Agreements (§3580)
         Article 1:   General Provisions (§3580)
         Article 2:   Child Support (§3585)
         Article 3:   Spousal Support (§3590)
      Chapter 4:   Spousal and Child Support During
                 Pendency of Proceedings (§3600)

And so on. A complete table of these divisions of the Family Code and their related subdivisions showing their placement and organizations within the Code is included in the appendices of this book. This detailed organization of the law is done to distill the subject matter down to a manageable level for ease of use. As can be seen by even a cursory review of the Family Code, family law is primarily a creature of statute: Most everything needed to be known in family law has its genesis either in these code sections or in the cases that have interpreted them.

Of particular note in the Family Code are some of its explanatory provisions, which sections help orient the reader to the fundamental concepts underlying the laws and provide a theoretical base for the other more specific statutes. With a thorough comprehension of the concepts, extrapolation in the absence of specific statutes is possible. For example, by understanding that a primary concern of the Family Code is to provide for the best interests of minor children, we are able to make a decision, in a situation not precisely covered by the Code, guided by the expressed principle of achieving what is in the best interests of the minor child.

A brief example of some of these provisions follows:

- **Family Code §3900: Equal Duty of Parents to Support Child**
  Subject to this division, the father and mother of a minor child have an equal responsibility to support their child in the manner suitable to the child's circumstances.

- **Family Code §4400: Duty of Adult Children to Support Parents**
  Except as otherwise provided by law, an adult child shall, to the extent of his or her ability, support a parent who is in need and unable to maintain himself or herself by work.

- **Family Code §300: Consent; Issuance of license and solemnization**
  Marriage is a personal relation arising out of a civil contract between a man and a woman to which the consent of the parties capable of making that contract is necessary. Consent alone does not constitute marriage. Consent must be followed by the issuance of a license and solemnization as authorized by this division. . . .

- **Family Code §2300: Effect of Dissolution**
  The effect of a judgment of dissolution of marriage when it becomes final is to restore the parties to the state of unmarried persons.

- **Family Code §3020: Legislative Findings and Declarations [Custody]**
  The Legislature finds and declares that it is the public policy of this state to assure that children have frequent and continuing contact with both parents after the parents have separated or dissolved their marriage, or ended their relationship, and to encourage parents to share the rights and responsibilities of child rearing in order to effect this policy, except where the contact would not be in the best interests of the child, as provided in Section 3011.

- **Family Code §3100(a): Visitation Rights**
  . . . in making an order pursuant to [Section 3080], the court shall grant reasonable visitation rights to a parent unless it is shown that the visitation would be detrimental to the best interests of the child. In the discretion of the court, reasonable visitation rights may be granted to any other person having an interest in the welfare of the child. . . .

- **Family Code §2550: Manner of Division of Community Estate**
  Except upon the written agreement of the parties, or on oral stipulation of the parties . . . the court shall . . . divide the community estate of the parties equally.

- **Family Code §2310: Grounds for Dissolution or Legal Separation**
  Dissolution of the marriage or legal separation of the parties may be based on either of the following grounds, which shall be pleaded generally:
  (a) Irreconcilable differences, which have caused the irremedial breakdown of the marriage.
  (b) Incurable insanity.

These are but a few of the many sections expressive of legislative policy and intent with regard to family law. They can be summed up in more simplistic terms as follows:

California is a "no-fault" state when it comes to dissolving marriages. This basically means that all one needs to do to obtain a divorce[24] in California is to *ask* for it. This is in contrast to the states in which fault (or the reason for the divorce) must be pleaded and proven by the requesting party. The most common grounds for divorce in those states are adultery, mental cruelty, and insanity.

In California, Family Code section 2310 codifies this no-fault concept by providing that dissolution of marriage (or legal separation) is available if "irreconcilable differences" exist, which have caused an "irremedial breakdown" of the marriage. These are the magic words, and so long as one of the parties is prepared to testify to the existence of these facts, the marriage will be dissolved.[25] California formerly required fault as grounds for marital dissolution, but this was changed in 1970 when no-fault became the new grounds for dissolution.[26] This change coincided with the establishment and adoption of the Family Law Act, which became operative on January 1, 1970. That act completely overhauled the concept of marital dissolution in California and was carried over into the Family Code.

The basic rules regarding the division of property, set out in sections 2500 et seq. of the Family Code, provide for an equal division of all marital property *and* debts upon dissolution of marriage or legal separation. As simple as this may sound, this particular area of family law practice is actually one of the most complex. Dozens of statutes and hundreds (if not thousands) of appellate opinions have been devoted to the many nuances contained in this rather simple statement.

The same can be said of Family Code section 3020's seemingly innocent statement that child custody is to be determined by evaluating the best interests of the minor child and the requirement to ensure the minor child's frequent and continuing contact with both parents. This legislative declaration has produced a seemingly endless series of opinions and editorial comment on how best to interpret and provide for these requirements.

It should be clear by now that this field of law, even limited to the area of termination of marriage (and other areas of the Family Law Act), is detailed and complex. It is by no means an insurmountable task to grasp and understand its concepts, however, as the following pages will show.

E.   Validity of Marriage

1.   Generally

Even though this text is primarily devoted to the law surrounding termination of a marital relationship, a few words on the subject of *creating* a valid marriage are appropriate to begin. This subject is addressed in Division 3 of the Family Code. That division is further divided into five parts, covering most every aspect of issues surrounding the creation of a valid marital union.

As seen earlier in the text, section 300 of the Family Code establishes the basic nature of the marital relation as one of consent and contract between a man and a woman. Consent alone, however, will not validate the union. There is also a requirement of the issuance of a license and certain acts of "solemnization." The consent required prior to being able to enter into a marriage is the same as that required for entering into any other contract: The parties to the marital contract must both be at least 18 years of age, or entering into the marriage with their parent's consent unless a minor is an "emancipated minor" (discussed later in this book), in which event he is treated as an adult for these purposes.

The concept of solemnization of the marriage literally refers to the ceremony involved. It is not enough to simply get married in California; there must be some "ceremony" involved. The Family Code, at section 420, provides the essential elements of solemnization as follows: "No particular form for the ceremony of marriage is required for solemnization of the marriage, but the parties shall declare, in the presence of the person solemnizing the marriage and necessary witnesses, that they take each other as husband and wife. . . . "

A person authorized to solemnize marriages must be a "priest, minister or rabbi of any religious denomination . . . a judge or retired judge, commissioner of civil marriages or retired commissioner of civil marriages . . . a judge or magistrate who has resigned from office. . . . " or one of miscellaneous other federal and state judges, justices, magistrates, and retired judges, justices and magistrates. The duties imposed upon the person solemnizing the marriage include conducting the service, insuring the correctness of the facts set out in the marriage license, issuance of the marriage certificate, and returning the license, endorsed with the fact of the marriage, to the county recorder of the county in which the marriage ceremony was performed.

The Family Code also establishes various provisions for the issuance and registration of the marriage license, which are found at sections 350 through 360, and generally discuss the ministerial aspects related to the license. Generally, the marriage license must state the names of the parties, their ages, and their place of residence. Once issued, the bride and groom must also obtain from the county clerk a certificate of registry of marriage. The person solemnizing this certificate then returns it to the county recorder where it is subsequently recorded.

2.   Confidential Marriages

The basic condition for obtaining a confidential marriage is that the applicants have been living together prior to their marriage. If this is the case, a health certificate is not necessary.

All that is required to obtain the issuance of a confidential marriage license is that the applicants appear personally, pay the required fees, and complete the appropriate application and affidavit. Once issued, the confidential marriage license is treated basically the same as a "normal" marriage license except that the county recorder maintains these confidential licenses in a special location, and the public is not allowed to inspect them. Further, the county clerk is allowed to search these records to establish the existence of the marriage, but no other information (date of marriage, for example) will be made available except upon court order.

Summary

Family law is primarily a creature of statute. Previously located throughout various portions of the codes, in 1994 the California legislature gathered and codified over 18 Divisions of this vast body of law under the umbrella of the Family Code. The Family Code is designed to provide guidance in virtually every aspect of marital relations: the relationship of parent and child, the division of property upon marital dissolution or legal separation, and aspects of the regulation of behavior between parties who are "at war" with each other.

Subject matter jurisdiction over Family Code (marital) proceedings is vested in the superior court. In addition, in order to completely adjudicate the rights and obligations of the parties incident to a family law proceeding, it is necessary that the court also exercise personal jurisdiction over the parties. Such jurisdiction is typically achieved through service of process of the litigation on the responding party. Further, under appropriate circumstances, a judgment entered in a family law action may be subject to either direct or collateral attack.

Anyone practicing in this field should pay significant attention to the subject of ethics. In a family law context, it is very easy to become drawn into the personal problems of the clients. It is only natural to empathize with a client who is going through an arduous ordeal. Care must be taken, however, to maintain a professional distance; sympathize, perhaps; empathize, never. Care must also be taken to ensure that the interests of the client are served and are not jeopardized by dual representation. Finally, be aware of the ever-present threat of malpractice. The best preventative is thorough preparation, competence, and a readiness to communicate.

The study of family law is primarily the study of the Family Code, although explanatory judicial interpretation and explanation of those statutes abound. We have seen that in order to be legally married in this state, the parties must (normally) be at least 18 years of age, have received a license to marry and undergone a premarital medical examination, and have participated in a ceremony sufficient to satisfy the solemnization requirement of the Family Code. Finally, the Family Code makes provision for a "confidential marriage" under certain, rather limited, circumstances.

Key Terms

The following is a list of key terms and phrases that you should be able to define and use in context. Only then will you have demonstrated a command of the material in this chapter.

- county seat
- statutory law
- common law
- California Rules of Professional Conduct
- informed written consent
- errors and omissions insurance
- full disclosure
- confidential information
- jurisdiction
- service of process
- venue
- subject matter jurisdiction
- domicile
- residence
- residency requirement
- personal jurisdiction

- due process
- notice and opportunity to be heard
- minimum contacts
- forum non conveniens
- change of venue
- trial court jurisdiction
- Family Code
- titles
- articles
- chapters
- divisions
- no fault
- irreconcilable differences
- irremedial breakdown
- res judicata
- collateral estoppel

Questions for Discussion

1. To what extent is it necessary or advisable for the paralegal to adhere to the rules of ethics, which govern attorney conduct?

2. Where there is no actual conflict, explain the circumstances, if any, under which it would be appropriate to represent both sides to a marital dissolution proceeding.

3. In what way are the concepts of notice and due process important in American jurisprudence?

4. Compare and contrast the concepts of residence and domicile, discussing the manner and degree of proof for each. What is the significance of these concepts in a family law context?

5. What is meant by the term "venue," and what is its significance, if any, to a family law proceeding?

ENDNOTES

1. Most references will be made to the Family Code (Fam. C.). Other abbreviations used in this book include C.C. (Civil Code), C.C.P. (Code of Civil Procedure), W.&I.C. (Welfare and Institutions Code), Pen. C. (Penal Code), and Prob. C. (Probate Code).

2. The list of publications, seminars, update materials, and computer-assisted research and analysis software is too extensive for this author to list in complete detail. My sincerest apologies to those who read this and feel that their work was unfairly omitted from the above discussion.

3. The reader should note that this discussion will be very limited. A more thorough treatment of this subject is deferred to a treatise on civil procedure.

4. Note that the court must possess both subject matter and personal jurisdiction to hear a case.

5. One exception to this rule is found in the Municipal Court's power to issue a temporary restraining order in the context of domestic violence in cases where the Superior Court cannot do so "in a timely manner." (See generally Family Code sections 240 et seq.)

6. In other words, little can be done when the court does not possess *personal* jurisdiction.

7. This might occur if, for example, temporary orders as to custody, support or injunctive relief (to name but a few) are desired.

8. As will be discussed further below, actions for nullity are very rare and typically not available to the average litigant.

9. The procedure is discussed below in the section dealing with the respondent's alternatives when filing a response.

10. The exercise of personal jurisdiction is typically only a question regarding the respondent. Since the petitioner is the party commencing the proceedings, their submission to the court's exercise of personal jurisdiction is evident.

11. The constitutions of both California and the United States provide, among other things, that each person is entitled to certain fundamental rights vis-à-vis their dealings with the state. Three of these are the right to *due process*, the right to *notice*, and the *opportunity to be heard*. Whenever a court makes an order against someone that affects their *personal* rights (for example, when someone is sentenced to jail or ordered to pay money), it is generally taking something of value to him away (for example, the right to liberty or property). The states look upon this as a serious matter (as does the federal government) and so before the state *gives* that kind of power to the court, the court must first satisfy the state that the exercise of this jurisdiction (i.e., power) is fair and appropriate.

12. When child custody is in issue, the question becomes one of the *child's* relationship to the state rather than the parties'. This concept is discussed in greater detail later

in this book in the section dealing with the Uniform Child Custody Jurisdiction and Enforcement Act (UCCJEA).

13. All of these methods are discussed in detail in the Code of Civil Procedure and elsewhere, and this book will defer to those sources. This material must be mastered, either in a civil procedure class or on one's own, if one plans on working in this field.

14. If someone is served with a lawsuit and chooses to ignore the warnings on the summons (one of the papers served) and not appear to defend, the court will go ahead and rule without him.

15. The reader should also note that there are some special rules regarding attacks on foreign judgments (judgments entered outside of California). These tend to be rather hyper-technical and are outside the scope of this discussion. The reader is thus directed to research this specific area thoroughly before undertaking such a task.

16. These concepts of res judicata and collateral estoppel are the bane of many a law student, and this brief mention barely does them justice. There are many, many permutations, exceptions, and technicalities associated with the application of these rules. Should the reader find herself encountering these issues in the future, it is strongly recommended that she supplement her analysis by referring to a civil procedure textbook.

17. That guidelines such as these even had to be adopted is, in this author's opinion, a sad commentary on the current state of affairs of the practicing bar.

18. As will be stated often throughout this book, the above comments are merely the tip of the iceberg in this area. From a paralegal's standpoint, you are not required to police the attorney for whom you work. For the most part these rules impact upon the attorneys and are not directed toward paralegals. Adherence to their intent, however, and the swift disassociation from those who do not follow it, is, in this author's opinion, sound advice.

19. Because, as a practical matter, very often attorneys *do* represent both spouses in a dissolution proceeding.

20. That is, sign a statement incorporated into the agreement to the effect that the attorney has reviewed the agreement and advised his client accordingly.

21. This is not so unusual. As stated before, there are usually no winners in family law. Rarely does a litigant to a dissolution proceeding leave the process with a sense of happiness. It is an extremely emotionally upsetting time in a person's life. Also, regardless of what amount of property the client owns going into a marital termination proceeding, he or she generally comes out of that proceeding with one-half of that amount.

22. Errors and Omissions Insurance is insurance that is purchased by the professional in the event he is sued for malpractice. This is a cause of action based on concepts of negligence, which seek to assign fault to the attorney for some problem that has arisen in the proceedings and caused the client harm (typically financial) on the theory that

had the attorney not been negligent, the loss would not have occurred. The paralegal should inquire of her employer whether or not she is named as an insured on their insurance policy. If no such coverage is present (or available), then the paralegal may wish to discuss with her employer some other arrangement (for example, indemnification) in the event of a lawsuit by a disgruntled client.

23. Note that the third division is labeled "Division 2.5," the fifteenth division is labeled "Division 17" (the number 15 was simply skipped and the old Division 16 was recently repealed) and the eighteenth Division is labeled "Division 20" rather than "Division 18."

24. This is technically known as a dissolution of marriage.

25. This section also provides that incurable insanity is a ground for dissolution or legal separation, but this does not come up too often. The reader should also note that in this context, the idea of dissolving a marriage includes marital dissolution *and* legal separation, a distinction discussed later in this book.

26. This is not to say the idea of fault has been completely abandoned. For the most part it has, although its concepts seem to creep back into the practice every once in a while.

CHAPTER 2

Parents and Children

A.   Introduction
B.   Minors
C.   Parent and Child Relationship

CHAPTER OVERVIEW

In this chapter we will discuss the many aspects of the relationship between parents and their children, including the role of the paternity action, both to establish paternity and to provide a mechanism for the assessment of child support and the establishment of custody and visitation (timeshare), the manner in which parental rights can be terminated, and, briefly, adoptions.

A.   Introduction

As mentioned earlier, with the advent of the Family Code in 1994 came a restructuring of the many various code sections dealing with the area of family law. In the course of this reorganization, the new Family Code was divided into multiple Divisions. Four of those Divisions are discussed in this and the following chapters: Division 11, "Minors" (sections 6500 to 7143), Division 12, "Parent and Child Relationship" (sections 7500 to 7952), Division 8, "Custody of Children" (sections 3000 to 3465), and Division 13, "Adoption" (sections 8500 to 9340).

Division 11, "Minors," and Division 12, "Parent and Child Relationship," generally define the statutory framework of the treatment of minors by the law, their general rights and obligations in our society as they are related to civil (generally business) matters, and the circumstances under which they can request (and obtain) emancipation. Division 12, "Parent and Child Relationship," seeks to define certain parental rights vis-à-vis their children, the general statutory scheme related to the establishment of paternity, and the circumstances under which a child may be declared to be free from parental custody and control.

Division 13, "Adoption," sets forth the statutes that regulate adoption proceedings in California, including the adoption of unmarried minors, married minors, and adults. Division 8, "Custody of Children," establishes the manner in which the court in contested family law matters will determine custody and visitation. This chapter will first review the Division devoted to minor children, then explore the relationship of parent and child, will next move on to a review of custody and visitation statutes (including the Uniform Child Custody Jurisdiction and Enforcement Act), and will close with a brief overview of adoption proceedings.

Division 14, "Family Law Facilitator Act," establishes, on a statewide basis, the office of the family law facilitator. This office is designed to assist persons to obtain and enforce orders for support of minor children as well as spousal support. Division 17, "Support Services," is also designed to provide an avenue of assistance for litigants involved in support-related proceedings. These two divisions will be discussed in greater detail in the section of this book discussing support.

We will also discuss the expanding law related to frustration of the parent-child relationship. This includes issues as simple as one parent interfering with visitation by the other parent, and as complex as parental kidnapping of a minor child.

B. Minors

At various times in this course of study, which is admittedly intended to be focused primarily on matters arising out of and pertaining to dissolution of marriage, in order to obtain a full understanding of that context it is (in this author's opinion) worth spending some time on matters that relate to and impact upon such a discussion. In this immediate context, this includes a brief entree into some general rules and procedures relating simply to "minors" in *all* contexts, and not simply as defined by the context of the termination of a family relationship. As stated above, Division 11 of the Family Code, found at sections 6500 to 7143, contains statutes unique to the circumstance of dealing with minors, most notably in the areas of civil liability exposure, contracts, medical treatment, enlistment in the armed forces, and emancipation. The Division starts out with some obvious definitions: An *adult* is anyone who is 18 years or older, and a *minor* is anyone who is under 18 years of age. It is specifically expressed that the state, in its position of *parens patriae*, is charged with a continuing interest in the welfare of minor children within its borders. *Ex parte Barents*, 99 Cal. App. 2d 748, 222 P.2d 488 (1950). As such, in California, a significant body of case law has developed to "flesh out" this rather simple expression of majority, and the rationale surrounding it. It is also the expressed policy of the law to protect a minor against himself and his indiscretions and immaturity as well as against the "machinations of other people and to discourage adults from contracting with an infant." Niemann v. Deverich, 98 Cal. App. 2d 787, 793, 221 P.2d 178 (1950). The law is designed to shield minors from their "lack of judgment and experience and under certain conditions vests in them the right to disaffirm their contracts." *Id.*

The law has also been found to be "scrupulously careful to protect the interests of minor children and incompetent persons who are incapable of looking after their own affairs." *In re Guardianship of Carlon's Estate*, 43 Cal. App. 2d 204, 110 P.2d 488 (1941). The purpose of these statutes is to facilitate computation of the date on which the child's period of minority ends. This date marks a "legally important event by which all persons lose privileges and disabilities of minors and assume rights and duties of adults." Justus v. Atchison, 139 Cal. Rptr. 97, 19 Cal. 3d 564, 565 P.2d 122 (1977).

Under the so-called "birthday rule, a person obtains a certain age on the first minute of his or her birthday." Tran v. Fountain Valley Community Hospital, 51 Cal. App. 4th 1646, 60 Cal. Rptr. 2d 91 (1997), citing *In re Harris*, 5 Cal. 4th 813, 855 P.2d 391 (1993). Further, the California Supreme Court recently held that "absent an expression of contrary legislative intent, [this rule] generally applies to all statutory calculations of age." *Id.*

1. Civil Liability Exposure

In the context of civil actions, a minor can prosecute a civil action to enforce her rights, the only proviso being that the action must be maintained by the minor's parent or adult guardian. A minor can also be held civilly liable for a wrong she may have done (for example, a tort such as vandalism), but she is only liable for punitive damages if at the time she did the act she knew (or was capable of knowing) that what she was doing was wrong (Family Code sections 6500 to 6602). It may seem difficult to imagine that anyone would want to sue a minor. Yet, in this age of vandalism and gang activity (much of which is committed by minors), not only can parents be liable for the torts of their children, but the children themselves can be liable too.

Even though minors can be (and very often are) sued civilly, there is a general limitation on the imposition of punitive damages against them. The reasoning behind a limitation on the availability of *punitive* damages against a minor is due to the very nature of punitive damages. These damages are over and above the actual damages suffered by a plaintiff in a tort action. They are designed to *punish* the wrongdoer and to act as an example to other potential wrongdoers. It is for this reason that punitive damages are sometimes called *exemplary damages*. Obviously, if the minor who committed the act giving rise to the liability was not capable of understanding that his act was wrong, it makes very little sense to punish this person under such circumstances. These statutes are merely codifications of the common-law rule that seeks to ensure that a minor or person of unsound mind should be liable in compensatory damages for his tortuous conduct, regardless of whether or not he was capable of knowing the "wrongful character" of his act at time that he committed it. Ellis v. D'Angelo, 116 Cal. App. 2d 310, 253 P.2d 675 (1953). The *Ellis* court, citing recognized treatises in this area, recognized that:

> [l]iability of an infant in a civil action for his torts is imposed as a mode, not of punishment, but of compensation. If property has been destroyed or other loss occasioned by a wrongful act, it is just that the loss should fall upon the estate of the wrongdoer rather than on that of a guiltless person, and that without reference to the question of moral guilt. Consequently, for every tortious act of violence or other pure tort, the infant tort-feasor is liable in a civil action to the injured person in the same manner and to the same extent as an adult. . . . Infancy, being in law a shield and not a sword, cannot be pleaded to avoid liability for frauds, trespasses, or torts. . . . A child of tender years may be held liable for acts of violence, and liability has often been imposed for the injuries caused by such acts, although committed in play and without the intent to inflict substantial injury. Of course, if the injury was an accident, or the acts of the child were only the natural activity of friendly play, there is no liability.

It has further been determined that for a minor to be liable for his torts, he must possess the state of mind necessary for the commission of the particular wrong with which he has been charged. Of course, a determination of this state of mind is a question of fact to be decided by the court.

A related inquiry is that of parental liability, if any, for torts committed by their children. Generally speaking, before parents may be held responsible for damages caused by one of their children, "it must be shown that the parents as reasonable persons previously became aware of habits or tendencies of the infant which made it likely that the child would misbehave so that they should have restrained him in apposite conduct and actions." Weisbart v. Flohr, 67 Cal. Rptr. 114, 260 Cal. App. 2d 281 (1968). That is, "the evidence must show that they had a duty as reasonable persons to restrain the child from the use of the implements in question." *Id.* Mere parenthood alone will not make the parent liable for torts committed by their children, even while in the parent's control and custody. Of course, the conduct of the parent in the totality of the circumstances will be reviewed by the trier of fact and, if that conduct is found to be negligent, then the parent himself will face potential liability for his own actions.

2. Contracts

In the context of contracted relationships, the minor has a distinct advantage over his adult counterpart. While the law recognizes a minor's right to enter into contracts that are legally binding on both the minor and the other party (Family Code section 6700), the minor is given the right to *disaffirm* that contract, thus terminating his obligation for further performance (Family Code section 6710). The general purpose behind this legislation is to protect minors from themselves, due to their assumed lack of experience as well as the perceived tendency of adults to take advantage of minors. As one court rather succinctly put it: "A person dealing with an infant does so at his peril. The law shields minors from their lack of judgment and experience and confers upon them the right to avoid their contracts in order that they may be protected against their own improvidence and the designs and machinations of other people, thus discouraging adults from contracting with them." Sparks v. Sparks, 101 Cal. App. 2d 129, 225 P.2d 238 (1951). The contract must, however, be disaffirmed before the minor reaches the age of 18 or "within a reasonable time afterwards." The Code also gives the minor's heirs or personal representative the right to disaffirm a contract on behalf of the minor following his death.

As with most everything else, there are exceptions to this rule of "disaffirmance." A minor is not allowed to disaffirm an obligation that is entered into under the express authority of a statute, and a minor cannot disaffirm a contract for the "necessities of life." This is generally meant to include food, clothing, shelter, and health services. Interestingly (probably because most laws are written and interpreted by lawyers[1]) it has also been held that attorney's fees fall into the category of "necessaries." That exception is found in Family Code section 6712, which states as follows:

> A contract, otherwise valid, entered into during minority, may not be disaffirmed on that ground either during the actual minority of the person entering into the contract, or at any time thereafter, if all of the following requirements are satisfied:
>
> (a) The contract is to pay the reasonable value of things necessary for the support of the minor or the minor's family.
>
> (b) These things have been actually furnished to the minor or the minor's family.
>
> (c) The contract is entered into by the minor when not under the care of a parent or guardian able to provide for the minor or the minor's family.

A special group of statutes has been established to regulate minors' contracts in the areas of art, entertainment, and professional sports. Because of the nature of these contracts and the potential for exploitation of children in these businesses, this is a heavily regulated subject. Indeed, the statutes contained in these sections are merely the tip of the iceberg. The types of contracts governed by these laws are described in section 6750, a portion of which is included herein:

> (a) This chapter applies to the following contracts entered into between an unemancipated minor and any third party or parties on or after January 1, 2000:
>
> (1) A contract pursuant to which a minor is employed or agrees to render artistic or creative services, either directly or through a third party, including, but not limited to, a personal services corporation (loan-out company), or through a casting agency. "Artistic or creative services" includes, but is not limited to, services as an actor, actress, dancer, musician, comedian, singer, stunt-person, voice-over artist, or other performer or entertainer, or as a songwriter, musical producer or arranger, writer, director, producer, production executive, choreographer, composer, conductor, or designer.
>
> (2) A contract pursuant to which a minor agrees to purchase, or otherwise secure, sell, lease, license, or otherwise dispose of literary, musical, or dramatic properties, or use of a person's likeness, voice recording, performance, or story of or incidents in his or her life, either tangible or intangible, or any rights therein for use in motion pictures, television, the production of sound recordings in any format now known or hereafter devised, the legitimate or living stage, or otherwise in the entertainment field.
>
> (3) A contract pursuant to which a minor is employed or agrees to render services as a participant or player in a sport.

Contracts that fall within this definitional statute are not subject to the disaffirmance statute discussed above, assuming the superior court has *approved* that contract, a standard procedure in these situations, obtained by petitioning the court for such approval. Further, in the context of that petition, the court has the power to require a portion of the minor's net earnings to be placed in a trust fund or similar savings plan, so long as the amount set aside does not exceed one-half. Finally, the court has continuing jurisdiction over that savings account to modify or terminate the account.

3. Medical Treatment

Next, Division 11 examines medical treatment associated with minors. These sections primarily address the grant of consent by an adult or guardian of a minor, as well as a minor's ability to consent to certain medical treatment. Section 6910 provides: "The parent, guardian, or caregiver of a minor who is a relative of the minor and who may authorize medical care and dental care under Section 6550, may authorize in writing an adult into whose care a minor has been entrusted to consent to medical care or dental care, or both, for the minor." Of course, this is not unexpected. The more interesting aspects of this portion of the Code are those related to a minor's ability to obtain certain medical treatment *without* his parent's consent.

In general, and subject to certain statutory exceptions, a minor is allowed to consent to medical or dental care without first obtaining the consent of a parent or guardian (Family Code section 6920). This consent is also specifically *not* subject to disaffirmance. Before a minor is capable of giving the consent contemplated in these sections, however, he or she must:

- be 15 years old or older
- be living separate and apart from parents or legal guardians (regardless of the duration of the separate residence and with or without parents' consent)
- be the sole manager of his or her financial affairs, regardless of the source of those funds

Accordingly, a 15-year-old, living on an allowance provided by his parents, could move out of the house with or without his parents' consent, and as long as he is the sole manager of his finances and he has established a separate residence (for example, moved in with a friend), he is free to consent to medical and dental care and treatment. Under these circumstances, however, the minor's parents (or legal guardians) are not financially liable for his medical or dental care, but the doctor is free to contact and advise them if treatment is given (Family Code section 6922).

A minor 12 years of age or older is statutorily allowed to consent to either outpatient mental health treatment and counseling or residential shelter services provided both of the following conditions are met (Family Code section 6924):

> (1) The minor, in the opinion of the attending professional person, is mature enough to participate intelligently in the outpatient services or residential shelter services, [and]
> (2) The minor (A) would present a danger of serious physical or mental harm to self or to others without the mental health treatment or counseling treatment or residential shelter services, or (B) is the alleged victim of incest or child abuse.

If a minor presents himself for this treatment, however, the health care provider is expected to make every effort to notify the minor's parents or guardians and, if possible and appropriate, involve them in the counseling.

Under this section a minor is allowed to consent to medical care related to birth control or prenatal care, but she cannot consent to be sterilized or receive an abortion without her parents' consent or otherwise provided by law. Specifically, Health and Safety Code section 123450 provides that, even though an unemancipated minor cannot consent to an abortion, she is free to petition the juvenile court for permission to undergo an abortion without advising her parents of the petition. She is free to petition under an assumed name as well, so the parents cannot learn of the proceeding. The court will then consider all the evidence, and if it finds that the minor is "sufficiently mature and sufficiently informed to make the decision on her own regarding an abortion, and that minor has, on that basis, consented thereto, the court shall grant the petition."[2]

A 12-year-old minor may consent to treatment of a communicable disease (a sexually transmitted disease, for example) without first obtaining his parents' consent; further, he may consent to diagnosis and treatment of a medical condition brought about by rape or a sexual assault committed against him. Finally, the Family Code authorizes a minor child 12 years of age or older to consent to treatment for drug or alcohol abuse. For the most part, then, this chapter is designed to allow a minor child of older years unfettered access both to routine medical and dental care as well as medical or counseling services in what might be considered extreme or emergency circumstances: rape, sexual assault, communicable disease, teenage pregnancy, and things of this nature. It is usually *expected* that the providing physician will attempt to contact the minor's parents, but the physician is not required to do so. The basic purpose for this is to get these minors the medical and counseling treatment they require as soon as possible, without worrying about the effects of this action on the parents once the needed care has begun. The reader should note that a minor cannot simply walk into a doctor's office and demand unnecessary treatment; the doctor makes the final decision as to whether such treatment is necessary.

4. Emancipation of Minors

Sections 7000 to 7143 address the concept of emancipation as it relates to minors. The purpose of the Emancipation of Minors Law is expressed in Family Code section 7001:

> It is the purpose of this part to provide a clear statement defining emancipation and its consequences and to permit an emancipated minor to obtain a court declaration of the minor's status. This part is not intended to affect the status of minors who may become emancipated under the decisional case law that was in effect before the enactment of Chapter 1059 of the Statutes of 1978.

In order to become an emancipated minor, one of three circumstances must be present: the minor has entered into a valid marriage, is on active duty in the armed forces, or has received a declaration of emancipation pursuant to the Emancipation of Minors Law. As such, a minor can become emancipated either by requesting this status from the court or by taking a direction in life (marriage or enlistment) that will result in emancipation.

The effect of emancipation is that the minor is now, for all practical purposes, treated as an adult. An emancipated minor is free to sue in her own name, consent to virtually all aspects of medical care, and control all other aspects of her life, including her finances, without first obtaining parental consent. In turn, an emancipated minor's parents are free from their obligation to support their child, and they cannot be held vicariously liable for their child's torts.[3]

The procedure for obtaining emancipation is rather straightforward. A petition for emancipation is prepared and served upon the minor's parents (or legal guardians), thus giving them notice of the minor's desire to become emancipated. The minor is the petitioning party, and the petition must allege that the minor (1) is at least 14 years old, (2) is living "separate and apart" from his parents, *with their consent*,[4] and (3) is managing his own finances. If any of these elements are missing (or not proven), the court will deny the petition. If the facts are adequately proven, however, the court will issue its declaration of emancipation, which becomes *conclusive evidence* that the minor is emancipated.

Of course, the decree of emancipation (as well as its denial) can be appealed, and, under appropriate circumstances (such as fraud in the petition), a separate action to rescind the declaration can also be maintained by the parents. This is also accomplished by a noticed petition procedure.

C. Parent and Child Relationship

In the context of the rights of parents and children, Division 12 of the Family Code primarily concentrates on the rights of parents vis-à-vis their minor children. It also addresses the issues of paternity and determining the parent–child relationship. The Division concludes by discussing the termination of parental rights.

Somewhat confusingly, Division 12 recites a noninclusive list of parental rights. For example, Family Code section 7500 clearly grants the parents of a minor entitlement to his "services and earnings." Section 7502, however, denies parents the right to control their child's property. Section 7503 instructs a minor's employer to pay a minor's earnings to the minor, "until the parent . . . entitled to the earnings gives the employer notice that the parent . . . claims the earnings."[5]

One of the more interesting sections in this statutory scheme has to do with parental abuse. Section 7507, entitled "Abuse of parental authority; remedy" provides as follows:

> The abuse of parental authority is the subject of judicial cognizance in a civil action brought by the child, or by the child's relative within the third degree, or by the supervisors of the county where the child resides; and

when the abuse is established, the child may be freed from the dominion of the parent, and the duty of support and education enforced.

This code section (or its predecessor sections) has been used as authority to allow an impoverished and indigent minor child to maintain an action to declare herself free from "dominion of the parent for abuse of parental authority," and to obtain support and education, notwithstanding that her custody had been previously awarded to a guardian. Fagan v. Fagan, 43 Cal. App. 2d 189 (1941). In addition, section 7507 enables an impoverished and indigent minor to enforce a support order directed against his parent. Franklin Life Ins. Co. v. Kitchens, 249 Cal. App. 2d 623 (1967). The legislature has instructed that the state has a duty to protect children from abuses of parental authority; the rights of parenthood are not absolute and are subject to the superior right of the state to intervene and protect the child against the misuse of parental authority, subject to the caveat that the state may not constitutionally interfere with the "natural liberty of parents to direct the upbringing of their children." Odell v. Lutz, 78 Cal. App. 2d 104 (1947).

1. The Paternity Action

The question of a child's *paternity*, or identity of the father, has been a difficult area of law for hundreds of years. Over time various statutes, rules, and procedures have evolved to quickly and accurately identify a child's parents. At best, these rules and regulations ensure that fathers meaningfully participate in their children's lives; at the very least, they ensure that fathers pay their share of child support if the circumstances so warrant. Part 2 of Division 12 presents a detailed examination of current rules and regulations in this area.

The Code commences this inquiry into paternity by recognizing a "conclusive presumption" of paternity in the husband of a cohabiting wife[6] who, while living with him, gives birth to a child (assuming the husband is neither impotent nor sterile). Interestingly, then, if a wife who is living with her husband enters into an extramarital relationship, becomes pregnant from the affair, and gives birth, her husband will *conclusively* be deemed to be that child's father, regardless of the reality of the situation. This situation can have devastating results for both the husband *and* the natural father.[7]

The nature of this presumption is to preserve the "sanctity of the marital relationship and the unified family." The concept is generally perceived as being substantively related to the "fact" that the child is conceived and "brought into" an existing marriage. Of course, the courts are not unmindful of the potentially drastic consequences operation of this presumption can have on all four people involved: the mother, the biological father, the marital "father," and the child. One appellate court has examined this situation, the facts and judicial analysis of which are very instructive (and entertaining) as to warrant a thorough review by any reader genuinely interested in learning more about this area. The case is Brian C. v. Ginger K., 77 Cal. App. 4th 1198 (2000).

In *Brian C.*, Ginger (the mother) married William (the husband) in March of 1994. She met Brian (the father) in December of 1994. Ginger and Brian commenced an affair that month. In late January, 1995, the two of them had sex in a Las Vegas hotel room, and it was about that time that Ginger's daughter, Kennedy, was conceived. However, during this period of time (that is, late January and early February 1995) Ginger also continued to live with her husband, William, and had sex with him too. In March, Ginger left her husband and moved into an apartment which she rented with Brian. Kennedy (the child) was born in October 1995. Brian was present at Kennedy's birth, and his name appears as her father on her birth certificate and on her baptismal records.

Brian doted on Kennedy: feeding, holding, bathing, rocking, walking, and soothing her, and "tending to her every need" (as he put it in his declaration in opposition to the summary judgment motion). In a letter from Ginger written soon after Kennedy's birth, he was described as doing a "great job as a Dad." Ginger and Brian "broke up" in November 1996. However, Brian continued to see Kennedy after work each day and had custody on weekends until May 1997, when Ginger unilaterally "cut off all contact" because she and her husband William were reconciling. Brian continued to "try" to see Kennedy, calling Ginger and leaving messages "all to no avail." Brian was injured on the job and could not work, so he had no income; he tried to be "patient and wait" rather than immediately institute litigation. Eventually, though, he filed his paternity action, prompting Ginger's response: a motion for summary judgment, contending that since Kennedy was conceived while Ginger was living with and married to William, she was conclusively presumed to be William's child.

The trial court found that Ginger and her husband William were indeed cohabiting at the time of Kennedy's conception and that William was not impotent or sterile. The trial court granted the summary judgment motion based on the fact that cohabitation at the time of conception would trigger the conclusive presumption. For the trial court, the facts that the child was conceived while the mother was cohabiting with her husband and that her husband was neither impotent nor sterile were absolutely dispositive.

The appellate court reversed. As a group of California Supreme Court and United States Supreme Court cases demonstrate, there are times when the due process clause of the federal Constitution precludes states from applying substantive rules of paternity law which have the effect of terminating an existing father-child relationship. This case is one of them. In particular, because the child was not "born into" an extant marital union (in any meaningful sense) and because the plaintiff developed a substantial parent-child relationship with the child immediately upon her birth and for one and a half years thereafter, he could bring an action to be declared the legal father of the child. The appellate court's ruling did not ultimately resolve this question, however. Rather, that court simply held that the trial court should not have granted summary judgment. The case was sent back to the trial court for further proceedings consistent with this ruling (i.e., a full trial on these issues).

This father–child presumption can generally be rebutted in two ways:

1. The husband may use biological tests to rebut the presumption if he brings the case within two years of the child's birth; or
2. The wife may use biological tests to rebut the presumption if the case is brought within two years of the child's birth and the wife provides an affidavit stating the identity of the actual biological father.

The courts are also typically willing to ignore this presumption when they think that they "should." Most typically, courts rely on the child's constitutional right to know the identity of its biological father; in this context, courts are willing to ignore the "conclusive" presumption. The most practical test to be gleaned from the cases in this regard is as follows: Which decision by the court will leave the following family intact: Mother, Child, and Mother's chosen man? If Mother has chosen to form a firm family unit with her husband, regardless of the child's biology, the court will probably respect that decision. Similarly, if she has chosen to form a union with the biological father, the court will probably respect that decision as well.

Section 7541 of the Code seems to provide some relief in these circumstances. This section authorizes the court to ignore this presumption if the evidence produced by the use of blood tests demonstrates that the husband is not the child's father. There are restrictions on the use of this statute, however. There are very strict time limitations, for example. The husband must file his notice of motion for blood tests under this section within two years of the child's birth. If he waits beyond this period, he will always be the child's *presumed father* and will be treated accordingly (just as the child's "natural father").

The wife may also avail herself of this Code section, typically to refute a natural father's attempt to gain recognition or to refute the child's father. She, too, must bring this motion before the child's second birthday. Section 7541 is the second presumption in this section of the Code, and is not nearly as powerful as section 7540. This presumption generally states that the child of a mother who was married to the husband within the 300 days preceding the birth of the child (following divorce) is presumed to be the child of that husband. Note that this presumption does not have any cohabitation requirement.

In regards to these presumptions, the reader should note that the term "impotent" or "sterile" under section 7540 has been interpreted narrowly. Courts have held that if there is even *one* live sperm, there cannot be a finding of sterility. The courts do their very best, however, to see this exception is *not* used. How then are situations involving artificial insemination handled? Assuming artificial insemination occurs with the husband's consent, and occurs during the marriage, and is performed by a doctor, the child will be deemed in law to be the husband's child.

Another conclusive presumption of paternity is found in Family Code sections 7570 to 7577, which describe the procedure known as establishing paternity by voluntary declaration. Sections 7570 and 7571 clearly establish the legislature's thinking in this area:

§7570 Legislative Declaration
The Legislature hereby finds and declares as follows:

(a) There is a compelling state interest in establishing paternity for all children. Establishing paternity is the first step toward a child support award, which, in turn, provides children with equal rights and access to benefits, including, but not limited to social security, health insurance, survivors' benefits, military benefits, and inheritance rights. Knowledge of family medical history is often necessary for correct medical diagnosis and treatment. Additionally, knowing one's father is important to a child's development.

(b) A simple system allowing for establishment of voluntary paternity will result in a significant increase in the ease of establishing paternity, a significant increase in paternity establishment, an increase in the number of children who have greater access to child support and other benefits, and a significant decrease in the time and money required to establish paternity due to the removal of the need for a lengthy and expensive court process to determine and establish paternity and is in the public interest.

§7571 Voluntary Declaration of Paternity; liability of
health care provider; payment[8]
(a) On and after January 1, 1995, upon the event of a live birth, prior to an unmarried mother leaving any hospital, the person responsible for registering live births under Section 102405 of the Health and Safety Code shall provide to the natural mother and shall attempt to provide, at the place of birth, to the man identified by the natural mother as the natural father, a voluntary declaration of paternity together with the written materials described in Section 7572. Staff in the hospital shall witness the signatures of parents signing a voluntary declaration of paternity and shall forward the signed declaration to the Department of Child Support Services within 20 days of the date the declaration was signed. A copy of the declaration shall be made available to each of the attesting parents.

§7576 Presumption

(a) Except as provided in subdivision (d) [rebuttal provisions], the child of a woman and a man executing a declaration of paternity under this chapter is conclusively presumed to be the man's child. The presumption under this section has the same force and effect as the presumption under Section 7540.

The declaration of paternity contemplated by the above sections is very detailed and must meet several specific requirements, too numerous to mention here. They are set out in their entirety in Family Code section 7574. The presumption created by this declaration can also be rebutted, within three years of its making, but only by persons contemplated in section 7541, that is, the husband and wife. Section 7576 of the Family Code also recognizes that the presumption created by these sections shall not override a section 7540 presumption.

An additional presumption of paternity is found in Family Code section 7611, which recognizes a man as the presumed father of a child if he is found to be so under section 7540 or if he meets any of the following criteria:

§7611 Status as natural father; presumption; conditions[9]

A man is presumed to be the natural father of a child if he meets the conditions provided in Chapter 1 (commencing with Section 7540) or Chapter 3 (commencing with Section 7570) of Part 2 or in any of the following subdivisions:

(a) He and the child's natural mother are or have been married to each other and the child is born during the marriage, or within 300 days after the marriage is terminated by death, annulment, declaration of invalidity, or divorce, or after a judgment of separation is entered by a court.

(b) Before the child's birth, he and the child's natural mother have attempted to marry each other by a marriage solemnized in apparent compliance with law, although the attempted marriage is or could be declared invalid, and either of the following is true:

(1) If the attempted marriage could be declared invalid only by a court, the child is born during the attempted marriage, or within 300 days after its termination by death, annulment, declaration of invalidity, or divorce.

(2) If the attempted marriage is invalid without a court order, the child is born within 300 days after the termination of cohabitation.

(c) After the child's birth, he and the child's natural mother have married, or attempted to marry, each other by a marriage solemnized in apparent compliance with law, although the attempted marriage is or could be declared invalid, and either of the following is true:

(1) With his consent, he is named as the child's father on the child's birth certificate.

(2) He is obligated to support the child under a written voluntary promise or by court order.

(d) He receives the child into his home and openly holds out the child as his natural child.

(e) If the child was born and resides in a nation with which the United States engages in an Orderly Departure Program or successor program, he acknowledges that he is the child's father in a declaration under penalty of perjury, as specified in Section 2015.5 of the Code of Civil Procedure. This subdivision shall remain in effect only until January 1, 1997, and on that date shall become inoperative.

The presumption created by section 7611 is merely "rebuttable" (not "conclusive"), however, and cannot operate to defeat any of the other presumptions discussed above. The section 7611 presumption is, in essence, the general starting point in the paternity examination and sets forth several different means by which a person may seek to establish paternity. Invariably, however, that inquiry will turn on the results of the blood tests.[10]

These tests to determine paternity have been evolving over the years and actually constitute far more than simple blood tests. They now include actual genetic testing of the DNA of the pertinent parties. Under these circumstances, the question of determining paternity has become almost automatic when it comes to determining the correct person (or eliminating the wrong person). In the absence of such effective testing, the parties were left to litigate over the specific facts and circumstances of the instant of conception, the amount of intercourse the parties engaged in during the probable period of conception, and other factors arising out of their sexual relationship such as might bear upon the probability that the person involved in the litigation was in fact the father of the child. With the new level of testing, however, such an inquiry has become almost obsolete.[11]

Specifics of the actual *action* to determine paternity are contained in Chapter 4 of the Uniform Parentage Act, found in Family Code sections 7630 to 7650. Virtually all parties to the transaction are entitled to bring an action to determine paternity under this chapter: the child, the child's natural mother, or a presumed father. The purpose of that action is to obtain a finding of paternity (or no paternity) of the presumed father.

The reader must note that the designation of "presumed father" contained in Family Code section 7611 is very important. Without such designation, a man will be precluded from bringing a paternity action, regardless of his actual paternal status. Because of the restrictions of section 7611, it is possible for a man who is not the child's natural father to achieve presumed father status—and thereby prevent the natural father from seeking to establish his own paternity. It is only when the presumed father dies that the natural father will be allowed to bring his own action to establish paternity. An exception to this rule is found in section 7631, which provides that a man who is *not* the presumed father *may* bring a paternity action (to obtain a judgment of paternity in his favor) if the child's mother takes steps to place the child up for adoption. The time limitations imposed upon this man are, however, very strict: He must file his action within 30 days after (1) he is served with notice required on a natural father prior to the commencement of adoption proceedings or (2) the birth of the child, whichever is later.

The paternity action contemplated by this chapter may be commenced by the mother, any presumed (or potential) father, the child, or (under certain circumstances) the district attorney. The court is empowered to make additional orders in this context, including custody, visitation, and support. The court may also order that the child's name be changed if requested in the petition and appropriate under the circumstances. The court may also allocate attorney's fees, expert fees, and other court costs between the parties in a proportion deemed appropriate by the court (a subject discussed in greater detail later in this book).

The Uniform Parentage Act is the subject of form pleadings. Family Law Rules form FL-200 titled Petition to Establish Parental Relationship is set forth on pages 50 and 51 in Figure 2-1. Finally, form FL-220 (Figure 2-2, pages 52 and 53) establishes the form "answer" to a complaint to establish parental relationship. These forms have been *approved* by the judicial council rather than adopted and thus their use is discretionary. However, for all practical purposes, their use is recommended by virtue of the fact that they are simple, self-explanatory, and the court is accustomed to them.

2. Termination of Parental Rights

As we discussed immediately above, the Code has established a category of parents known as a "presumed fathers." The rights of a presumed father can supersede those of the biological father under circumstances specified by the Code. Under certain circumstances, if the mother wishes to place her child up for adoption she must, among other things, notify any individuals who either qualify as presumed fathers or who could in fact be the father of the child prior to allowing the child to be given up for adoption. Chapter 5 of the Uniform Parentage Act addresses the rights and concerns of potential fathers under these circumstances.

Section 7660 of the Uniform Parentage Act instructs that before a mother can place her child up for adoption, assuming there is a presumed father under section 7611 or a father "as to whom the child is a legitimate child under the law of [California] or under the law of another jurisdiction," she must first notify that father of the adoption proceeding, thus giving him the opportunity to object or in some other way participate. Similarly, if the father proposes to relinquish his parental rights to the child, the mother shall be given notice of the adoption proceeding and she shall also have the right to participate in that proceeding, unless of course her relationship with the child has been previously terminated either by operation of law or by her consent to adoption.

This chapter of the Code is primarily devoted to an assessment of the manner in which the parental rights of a potential or presumed father can be terminated so as to "free up" the child from any undue restraints prior to it being placed up for adoption. As discussed above, sections 7660 and 7661 of the Code require notice to the parents prior to the commencement of adoption proceedings to give them an opportunity to interpose any objections that they may have to those proceedings and to in any other way establish and confirm their parental rights. However, under certain circumstances the mother is not always aware of the identity of the natural father, or in some cases the mother is not able to locate the natural father. It is under these circumstances that this aspect of the Uniform Parentage Act comes into play. When the identity or whereabouts of the natural father is unknown, the legislature has deemed that this should not, in and of itself, prevent an adoption proceeding from going forward. Accordingly, the Code has laid out specific procedures to be followed with regard to attempting to identify and locate the natural father and to terminate that individual's parental rights so that the adoption can go forward. Thus, Family Code section 7662 establishes the statutory parameters for commencing a petition to terminate the parental rights of the father.

Family Code section 7663 instructs either the Department of Social Services, any licensed county adoption agency, or the specific licensed adoption agency to which the child has been relinquished for adoption to question the mother and any other appropriate person regarding the identity of the natural father. The inquiry is to include whether the mother was married at the time the child was conceived (or at any time thereafter), whether the mother was cohabiting with a man at either the conception or birth of the child, whether the mother has received any support payments or promises of support regarding the child or in connection with her pregnancy, or whether any man has acknowledged, either formally or informally, his possible paternity of the child. If the identity of the natural father has been ascertained to the satisfaction of the court or if more than one man has been identified as a possible father, then each is given notice of the proceeding in accordance with section 7666 of the Family Code (which describes the manner in which notice is to be given), basically apprising them that an adoption proceeding is pending. That individual (or individuals) has the opportunity to assert his parental rights at which time the court will make a determination if he is the father. Once the court makes that determination, it determines whether it is in the best interest of the child that this man retain his parental rights, or if, in the court's opinion, the adoption of the child should be allowed to proceed. In this situation, the court is empowered to consider any evidence it finds relevant to the inquiry, including any effort made by the father to obtain custody himself. If the father has chosen not to be a part of this child's life in any way, shape, or form, the court is not going to invest in him a tremendous amount of credibility if he later turns up and attempts to contest these adoption proceedings.

Figure 2-1
Form FL-200—Petition to Establish Parental Relationship

FL-200

ATTORNEY OR PARTY WITHOUT ATTORNEY *(Name, state bar number, and address):*	FOR COURT USE ONLY
TELEPHONE NO. *(Optional):* FAX NO. *(Optional):* E-MAIL ADDRESS *(Optional):* ATTORNEY FOR *(Name):*	

SUPERIOR COURT OF CALIFORNIA, COUNTY OF
STREET ADDRESS:
MAILING ADDRESS:
CITY AND ZIP CODE:
BRANCH NAME:

PETITIONER:

RESPONDENT:

PETITION TO ESTABLISH PARENTAL RELATIONSHIP ☐ **Child Support** ☐ **Child Custody** ☐ **Visitation** ☐ **Other** *(specify):*	CASE NUMBER:

1. Petitioner is
   - a. ☐ the mother.
   - b. ☐ the father.
   - c. ☐ the child or the child's personal representative *(specify court and date of appointment):*
   - d. ☐ other *(specify):*

2. The children are
   - a. <u>Child's name</u>   <u>Date of birth</u>   <u>Age</u>   <u>Sex</u>

   - b. ☐ a child who is not yet born.

3. The court has jurisdiction over the respondent because the respondent
   - a. ☐ resides in this state.
   - b. ☐ had sexual intercourse in this state, which resulted in conception of the children listed in item 2.
   - c. ☐ other *(specify):*

4. The action is brought in this county because *(you must check one or more to file in this county):*
   - a. ☐ the child resides or is found in the county.
   - b. ☐ a parent is deceased and proceedings for administration of the estate have been or could be started in this county.

5. Petitioner claims *(check all that apply):*
   - a. ☐ respondent is the child's mother.
   - b. ☐ respondent is the child's father.
   - c. ☐ parentage has been established by Voluntary Declaration of Paternity *(attach copy).*
   - d. ☐ respondent who is child's parent has failed to support the child.
   - e. ☐ *(name):*   has furnished or is furnishing the following reasonable expenses
     of pregnancy and birth for which the respondent as parent of the child is obligated:
     <u>Amount</u>   <u>Payable to</u>   <u>For *(specify):*</u>

   - f. ☐ public assistance is being provided to the child.
   - g. ☐ other *(specify):*

6. A completed *Declaration Under Uniform Child Custody Jurisdiction and Enforcement Act (UCCJEA))* (form FL-105) is attached.

Page 1 of 2

Form Approved for Optional Use Judicial Council of California FL-200 [Rev. January 1, 2003]	**PETITION TO ESTABLISH PARENTAL RELATIONSHIP** **(Uniform Parentage)**	Family Code, § 7630 www.courtinfo.ca.gov

Figure 2-1 (continued)

PETITIONER:	CASE NUMBER:
RESPONDENT:	

Petitioner requests the court to make the determinations indicated below.

7. **PARENT-CHILD RELATIONSHIP**
   a. ☐ Respondent   b. ☐ Petitioner
   c. ☐ Other *(specify):*   is the parent of the children listed in item 2.

8. **CHILD CUSTODY AND VISITATION**   Petitioner   Respondent   Joint   Other
   a. Legal custody of children to   ☐   ☐   ☐   ☐
   b. Physical custody of children to   ☐   ☐   ☐   ☐
   c. Visitation of children:
      (1) ☐ None
      (2) ☐ Reasonable visitation.
      (3) ☐ Petitioner ☐ Respondent   should have the right to visit the children as follows:

      (4) ☐ Visitation with the following restrictions *(specify):*

   d. Facts in support of the requested custody and visitation orders are *(specify):*
      ☐ Contained in the attached declaration.
   e. ☐ I request mediation to work out a parenting plan.

9. **REASONABLE EXPENSES OF PREGNANCY AND BIRTH:**
   Reasonable expenses of pregnancy   Petitioner   Respondent   Joint
   and birth be paid by   ☐   ☐   ☐
   as follows:

10. **FEES AND COSTS OF LITIGATION**   Petitioner   Respondent   Joint
    a. Attorney fees to be paid by   ☐   ☐   ☐
    b. Expert fees, guardian ad litem fees, and other costs
       of the action or pretrial proceedings to be paid by   ☐   ☐   ☐

11. **NAME CHANGE**
    ☐ Children's names be changed, according to Family Code section 7638, as follows *(specify):*

12. **CHILD SUPPORT**
    The court may make orders for support of the children and issue an earnings assignment without further notice to either party.

13. I have read the restraining order on the back of the *Summons* (FL-210) and I understand it applies to me when this Petition is filed.

I declare under penalty of perjury under the laws of the State of California that the foregoing is true and correct.

Date:

▶

_____   _____
(TYPE OR PRINT NAME)   (SIGNATURE OF PETITIONER)

A blank *Response to Petition to Establish Parental Relationship* (form FL-220) must be served on the Respondent with this Petition.

> **NOTICE:** If you have a child from this relationship, the court is required to order child support based upon the income of both parents. Support normally continues until the child is 18. You should supply the court with information about your finances. Otherwise, the child support order will be based upon information supplied by the other parent.
> Any party required to pay child support must pay interest on overdue amounts at the "legal" rate, which is currently 10 percent.

FL-200 [Rev. January 1, 2003]   **PETITION TO ESTABLISH PARENTAL RELATIONSHIP**   Page 2 of 2
                                       (Uniform Parentage)

Figure 2-2

Form FL-220—Response to Petition to Establish Parental Relationship

FL-220

ATTORNEY OR PARTY WITHOUT ATTORNEY *(Name, State Bar number, and address):*	*FOR COURT USE ONLY*
TELEPHONE NO.: FAX NO. *(Optional):* E-MAIL ADDRESS *(Optional):* ATTORNEY FOR *(Name):*	

SUPERIOR COURT OF CALIFORNIA, COUNTY OF
    STREET ADDRESS:
    MAILING ADDRESS:
    CITY AND ZIP CODE:
    BRANCH NAME:

PETITIONER:

RESPONDENT:

RESPONSE TO PETITION TO ESTABLISH PARENTAL RELATIONSHIP (Uniform Parentage)	CASE NUMBER:

1. The children are *(name each):*

   a. <u>Child's name</u>   <u>Date of birth</u>   <u>Age</u>   <u>Sex</u>

   b. ☐ A child who is not yet born

2. The petitioner is

   a. ☐ the mother of the children listed above.

   b. ☐ the father of the children listed above.

   c. ☐ not certain whether he or she is the biological parent of the children listed above.

   d. ☐ the child or child's representative *(specify court and date of appointment):*

   e. ☐ other *(specify):*

3. The respondent

   a. ☐ lives in the State of California.

   b. ☐ was in California when the listed children were conceived.

   c. ☐ neither a nor b

   d. ☐ other *(specify):*

4. The children

   a. ☐ live or are in this county.

   b. ☐ are children of a parent who is deceased, and proceedings for administration of the estate have been or could be started in this county.

5. The respondent is

   a. ☐ the father of the children listed in item 1 above.

   b. ☐ the mother of the children listed in item 1 above.

   c. ☐ not certain if he or she is the parent of the children listed in item 1 above.

   d. ☐ not the parent of the children listed in item 1 above.

   e ☐ other *(specify):*

6. Additional statements

   a. ☐ Parentage has been established by a Voluntary Declaration of Paternity *(attach copy).*

   b. ☐ Parentage has been established in another case ☐ governmental child support ☐ other *(specify):*

   c. ☐ Public assistance is being provided to the children.

Form Approved for Optional Use
Judicial Council of California
FL-220 [Rev. January 1, 2006]

RESPONSE TO PETITION TO ESTABLISH PARENTAL RELATIONSHIP
(Uniform Parentage)

Family Code, § 7600
www.courtinfo.ca.gov

Figure 2-2 (continued)

PETITIONER:	CASE NUMBER:
RESPONDENT:	

The respondent requests that the court make the orders listed below.

7. Parent-child relationship *(check all that apply)*:

a. ☐ Respondent ☐ Petitioner ☐ Other *(specify)*: is the parent of the children listed in item 1.

b. ☐ Respondent ☐ Petitioner ☐ Other *(specify)*: is not the parent of the children listed in item 1.

c. ☐ Respondent requests genetic (blood) tests to determine whether the ☐ petitioner ☐ respondent is the parent of the children listed.

8. Child custody and visitation

a. If ☐ Petitioner ☐ Respondent ☐ Other is found to be the parent of the children in listed in item 1:

	Petitioner	Respondent	Joint	Other
b. Legal custody of the children should go to	☐	☐	☐	☐
c. Physical custody of the children should go to	☐	☐	☐	☐

d. Visitation of the children should be as follows:

(1) ☐ None

(2) ☐ Reasonable visitation

(3) ☐ Petitioner ☐ Respondent should have the right to visit the children as follows *(specify)*:

(4) ☐ Visitation should occur with the following restrictions *(specify)*:

(5) ☐ I request mediation to work out a parenting plan.

9. Reasonable expenses of pregnancy and birth

	Petitioner	Respondent	Both
Reasonable expenses of pregnancy and birth should be paid by	☐	☐	☐

10. Fees and costs of litigation

	Petitioner	Respondent	Both
a. Attorney fees should be paid by	☐	☐	☐
b. Expert fees, guardian ad litem fees, and other costs of the action or pretrial proceedings should be paid by	☐	☐	☐

11. Name change. ☐ The children's names should be changed, according to Family Code section 7638, as follows *(specify old and new names)*:

12. Other orders requested *(specify)*:

13. Child support. The court may make orders for support of the children and issue an earnings assignment without further notice to either party.

I have read the restraining order on the back of the *Summons* (form FL-210) and I understand it applies to me.

I declare under penalty of perjury under the laws of the State of California that the foregoing is true and correct.

Date:

▶

_____ _____
(TYPE OR PRINT NAME) (SIGNATURE OF RESPONDENT)

NOTICE: If you have a child from this relationship, the court is required to order child support based upon the income of both parents. Support normally continues until the child is 18. You should supply the court with information about your finances. Otherwise, the child support order will be based upon information supplied by the other parent. Any party required to pay child support must pay interest on overdue amounts at the "legal" rate, which is currently 10 percent.

FL-220 [Rev. January 1, 2006] **RESPONSE TO PETITION TO ESTABLISH PARENTAL RELATIONSHIP** Page 2 of 2
(Uniform Parentage)

If, after the inquiry on these matters, the court finds that it is in the best interest of the minor child that the father be allowed to retain his parental rights, then the father's consent is necessary before the child can be adopted by some other party. If the court finds that the man claiming parental rights is not the child's father, or if he is the father but it is in the child's best interest that the adoption be allowed to proceed, then the court will order that that person's consent is not required for the adoption. The court's findings in this regard will terminate all parental rights and responsibilities with respect to this child. In some circumstances, the court is not able to ascertain the identity of the father despite the use of blood and other tests. If the court cannot identify any possible natural father and no one has presented themselves to the court claiming to be the natural father, then the court will simply enter an order terminating the unknown father's parental right, thus allowing the adoption proceeding to go forward.

The laws regarding termination of parental rights tend to be somewhat complex. Therefore, they are applied with the utmost care to ensure that everyone's rights are preserved and protected in all respects. As the reader can no doubt imagine, the court does not take the termination of parental rights lightly. Furthermore, when one parent seeks to place her child up for adoption (thus effectively denying her natural parent's rights to that child), great care must be taken to ensure that all relevant parties are notified of these proceedings and are given an opportunity to participate. By so doing, the court is able to consider all factors pertinent to the best interest of this minor child, which may or may not allow the matter to proceed as an adoption.

The Uniform Parentage Act also provides for temporary protective and restraining orders, both in the summons (the automatic temporary restraining orders discussed later in this text) and also in the availability of ex parte protective restraining orders (discussed generally earlier in this section). Related to the foregoing discussion are the statutes contained in the Uniform Parentage Act, which pertain not only to termination of the father's parental rights, but termination of the parental rights of either or both parents prior to placing the child up for adoption. Family Code sections 7800 and 7801 establish the purpose of Part 4 of the Uniform Parentage Act entitled Freedom from Parental Custody and Control:

§7800
    The purpose of this part is to serve the welfare and best interest of a child by providing the stability and security of an adoptive home when those conditions are otherwise missing from the child's life.

§7801
    This part shall be liberally construed to serve and protect the interests and welfare of the child.

The purpose of a declaration under this part of the Uniform Parentage Act is to in fact declare the child free from all parental custody and control and to terminate all parental rights and responsibilities with regard to the child. The circumstances under which this type of proceeding would most likely be brought are those concerning: an abandoned child (Family Code section 7822), neglect or cruel treatment of a child (Family Code section 7823), a parent disabled due to alcohol or controlled substances or "moral depravity" (Family Code section 7824), a parent convicted of a felony (Family Code section 7825), a parent declared developmentally disabled or mentally ill (Family Code section 7826), a parent found to be mentally disabled (Family Code section 7827), a situation in which the child has been placed in supervised out-of-home placement for a period of at least one year (Family Code section 7828), or a situation where the child has been found to be a "dependent child" and reunification services have been deemed inappropriate (Family Code section 7829).

The procedure for terminating these parental rights is commenced by a petition, which is filed by either a private or public adoption agency, including a state or county agency. The petition will seek a judgment declaring the child free from the custody or control of either or both of its parents and may be filed by any "interested person" who seeks such a declaration. The county is instructed to undertake an extensive investigation of the circumstances related to this child and to report back to the court with findings and recommendations. The court has the power to appoint independent counsel to represent the child in these proceedings and can (and must) appoint counsel for a parent unable to afford it. The hearing on the Petition to Terminate Parental Custody and Control of the Child takes precedence over virtually all other matters and will be continued only under extreme circumstances. Of course, the court has the power to compel the attendance of certain individuals to the hearing on this matter and can hold a person who has been personally served with a citation to appear in the hearing in contempt of court if he fails to appear.

At the hearing, the fundamental consideration of the court is the determination of the best interests of the minor child. Keeping in mind the age of the child, the court may consult with the child in chambers (in private), provided that he is at least ten years of age, in an attempt to determine the child's wishes and feelings with respect to this matter.

At the conclusion of the hearing, the court either will make a finding declaring the child free from the custody and control of a parent or both parents or it will not. Interestingly, once the court makes its findings and order in this regard, it no longer has the power to set aside, change, or modify that judgment. This policy is clearly set forth in unambiguous language in section 7894 of the Family Code. Once the court makes its finding, it must then consider appropriate placement for the minor child. Part 5 of the Uniform Parentage Act, Family Code sections 7900 to 7910, addresses this subject under the auspices of the Interstate Compact on Placement of Children. This Interstate Compact is basically a statement adopted by various states concerning the placement of children following termination of parental rights and control. Its provisions are too lengthy to quote in detail here; however, should the reader be interested in this type of detailed information with regards to this document, he is best referred to Family Code section 7901. In essence, this part of the Uniform Parentage Act establishes the propriety of the utilization of the Interstate Compact on the placement of children to matters such as are under consideration herein. Part 6 of the Uniform Parentage Act considers the order of placement preference with regard to placing children in foster care. As this reader should be aware, once parental care and control of the minor child has been terminated, that child must be placed in a foster home or some other suitable placement. Part 6 of the Uniform Parentage Act stresses the priorities of preference with regard to placement.

Section 7950 of the Family Code establishes these priorities as follows:

(a) With full consideration for the proximity of the natural parents to the placement so as to facilitate visitation and family reunification, when a placement in foster care is being made, the following considerations shall be used:

(1) Placement shall, if possible, be made in the home of a relative, unless the placement would not be in the best interest of the child. Diligent efforts shall be made by an agency or entity to which this subdivision applies, to locate an appropriate relative. Before any child may be placed in long-term foster care, the court shall find that the agency or entity to which this subdivision applies has made diligent efforts to locate an appropriate relative and that each relative whose name has been submitted to the agency or entity as a possible caretaker, either by himself or herself or by other persons, has been evaluated as an appropriate placement resource.

(2) No agency or entity that receives any state assistance and is involved in foster care placements may do either of the following:

(A) Deny to any person the opportunity to become a foster parent on the basis of the race, color, or national origin of the person or the child involved.

(B) Delay or deny the placement of a child into foster care on the basis of the race, color, or national origin of the foster parent or the child involved.

(b) Subdivision (a) shall not be construed to affect the application of the Indian Child Welfare Act (25 U.S.C. Sec. 1901 and following).

(c) Nothing in this section precludes a search for an appropriate relative being conducted simultaneously with a search for a foster family.

Once these considerations have been met, the court is free, in the context of those considerations, to make the appropriate placement.

3. Adoption

By virtue of the sheer volume of law on adoption, both statutory and judicial, we can only touch upon some of the more salient aspects of those laws as they are outlined by the Family Code. Concepts arising out of and pertaining to adoption are pertinent inasmuch as they can drastically affect the rights and obligations of natural parents and minor children. However, anything other than the following general reference to these proceedings is best left to any one of the many fine treatises on this subject.

The superior court has exclusive jurisdiction over an adoption proceeding, the end result of which is to designate a nonparent third party as the minor child's parent. An individual who adopts a minor child quite literally takes the place of the child's natural parents and assumes all the rights and obligations pertinent to that relationship. For all practical purposes, the natural parent who was replaced by the adoptive parent takes on a status equivalent to a third-party stranger. The child's relationship with the natural parent is severed, and that parent's rights are terminated fully and finally forever. Similarly, once an adoption has taken place the natural parent has no further duty, obligation, or right to provide support, care, or any other aspect of upbringing to the minor child.

Adoption proceedings can be commenced by one or both of the natural parents; or, such proceedings can be instituted by the court (or other governmental agency) by its own motion to terminate parental rights. Those proceedings are generally undertaken in the dependency court and follow a finding that placement in the home of either or both parents would be detrimental to the minor child and that placement away from the natural parents would be in the child's best interests. The natural parents have many rights with regard to these types of proceedings, and no placement can take place until all of the natural parents' rights to appeal this decision have been exhausted. The process can be very lengthy, but it is designed to protect and preserve the relationship between the natural parent and his or her child as much as is humanly possible.

Division 13 of the Family Code entitled "Adoption" and found at sections 8500 to 9340 is divided into three basic sections. The first, Part 1, is laid out in sections 8500 to 8548. This part concerns itself with the various definitions used in the context of this Division. Part 2 of Division 13 deals with the adoption of unmarried minors and is set out in sections 8600 to 9210. Finally, Part 3 of Division 13, set out in sections 9300 to 9340, deals with the adoption of adults and married minors. The definitional sections are unremarkable and are easily understood. This text will step directly into Part 2 of Division 13, "Adoption of Unmarried Minors."

Part 2 of Division 13, "Adoption of Unmarried Minors," is broken down into ten distinct chapters, each dealing with a specific aspect of this topic. The first chapter, "General Provisions," establishes some interesting ground rules with regard to the adoption of unmarried minors. For example, Family Code section 8601 mandates that a prospective adoptive parent (or parents) must be at least ten years older than the child sought to be adopted. Additionally, and contrary to what many believe, if the child is over the age of 12 years, she must consent to the adoption before the court will allow it to go forward. (Family Code Section 8602). Family Code section 8603 provides that "a married person, not lawfully separated from the person's spouse, may not adopt a child without the consent of the spouse, provided that the spouse is capable of giving that consent."

This chapter also instructs that if a child has a presumed father (as that term is used in Family Code section 7611) that child may not be adopted without the consent of the mother and this presumed father. Interestingly, Family Code section 8604 goes on to stress:

(b) If one birth parent has been awarded custody by judicial order, or has custody by agreement of both parents, and the other birth parent for a period of one year willfully fails to communicate with and pay for the care, support and education of the child when able to do so, then the birth parent having sole custody may consent to the adoption, but only after the birth parent not having custody has been served with a copy of a citation in the manner provided by law for the service of a summons in a civil action that requires the birth parent not having custody to appear at the time and place set for the appearance in court under [Family Code section citations omitted]. . . .

(c) Failure of a birth parent to pay for the care, support, and education of the child for the period of one year or failure of a birth parent to communicate with the child for a period of one year is prima facie evidence that the failure was willful and without lawful excuse.

These concepts, painful enough in the context of a disputed custody matter, become even more relevant in the context of an adoption of a child unwanted by one of the birth parents. As might be expected, if the child does not have a presumed father pursuant to section 7611, an adoption may be effected simply by obtaining the consent of the mother, assuming she is alive.

Under certain circumstances, consent by the birth parent for an adoption is not necessary. Family Code section 8606 sets forth five separate categories in which the consent of the birth parent will not be necessary prior to adoption of their minor child:

Notwithstanding Sections 8604 and 8605, the consent of a birth parent is not necessary in the following cases:

(a) Where the birth parent has been judicially deprived of the custody and control of the child (1) by a court order declaring the child to be free from the custody and control of either or both birth parents pursuant to Part 4 (commencing with Section 7800) of Division 12 of this code, or Section 366.25 or 366.26 of the Welfare and Institutions Code, or (2) by a similar order of a court of another jurisdiction, pursuant to a law of that jurisdiction authorizing the order.

(b) Where the birth parent has, in a judicial proceeding in another jurisdiction, voluntarily surrendered the right to the custody and control of the child pursuant to a law of that jurisdiction providing for the surrender.

(c) Where the birth parent has deserted the child without provision for identification of the child.

(d) Where the birth parent has relinquished the child for adoption as provided in Section 8700.

(e) Where the birth parent has relinquished the child for adoption to a licensed or authorized child-placing agency in another jurisdiction pursuant to the law of that jurisdiction.

Of course, there are many other rules and regulations that must be adhered to when adopting a minor child, including required medical forms and reports, accounting reports, and similar documents that must be prepared and given to the court as a means of providing an accounting of the circumstances surrounding this adoption. Ultimately there will be a hearing pursuant to the requested adoption at which time the court will examine virtually all persons who have an interest in the proceeding, including the prospective adoptive parents. If the court is satisfied, following this inquiry, that the best interest of the minor child will be served by the adoption, then the court, in its discretion, will enter an order of adoption substituting the adoptive parents as the lawful parents of the minor child.[12]

Part 2 of the Division of the Family Code dealing with adoptions then moves on to discuss with specificity *agency adoptions*. Under circumstances in which an agency adoption takes place, the parents of a minor child typically relinquish custody and control of that child to a licensed adoption agency, which will then undertake the placement of that child in an appropriate home. The Family Code specifically grants birth parents the right to relinquish their child for adoption to a licensed adoption agency or adoption department. The birth parents also have the right to name the person or persons with whom placement by the department or licensed adoption agency is intended. In this regard, Family Code section 8700 instructs:

(g) If the relinquishment names the person or persons with whom placement by the department or licensed adoption agency is intended and the child is not placed in the home of the named person or persons or the child is removed from the home prior to the granting of the adoption, the department or agency shall mail a notice by certified mail, return receipt requested, to the birth parent signing the relinquishment within seventy-two (72) hours of the decision not to place the child up for adoption or the decision to remove the child from the home.

(h) The relinquishing parent has 30 days from the date on which the notice described in subdivision (g) was mailed to rescind the relinquishment.

(1) If the relinquishing parent requests rescission during the 30-day period, the department or licensed adoption agency shall rescind the relinquishment.

(2) If the birth parent does not request rescission during the 30-day period, the department or licensed adoption agency shall select adoptive parents for the child.

(3) If the relinquishing parent and the department or licensed adoption agency wish to identify a different person or persons during the 30-day period with whom the child is intended to be placed, the initial relinquishment will be rescinded and a new relinquishment identifying the person or persons completed.

(j) The filing of the relinquishment with the department terminates all parental rights and responsibilities with regard to the child, except as provided in subdivisions (g) and (h).

Clearly put, therefore, Family Code section 8700 recognizes that when the birth parents of a minor child place the child up for adoption with a licensed adoption agency, they are entitled to designate the intended parties to receive the child as the adoptive parents. If, however, after investigation the adoption agency determines that such placement would be inappropriate or unwarranted as not being in the best interests of the minor child, then the agency has the right to terminate that placement and/or remove the child from the adoptive parents' home as the circumstances may warrant. However, notwithstanding the fact that the original relinquishment of their child to the adoption agency for adoption terminates all parental rights of the birth parents, in the event that the adoption agency makes the determination to remove the child from the intended adoptive parents' home or simply not to place the child with the intended adoptive parents, the birth parents are then given notice of this intent and are once again allowed to redesignate an adoptive home. This redesignation takes the form of a new relinquishment, which, once again, follows the signing of the relinquishment and terminates all of the birth parents' rights and responsibilities with regard to the child, thus starting this process all over again.

As might be imagined, there are several "hoops" that must be "jumped through" in order to render the relinquishment of parental rights effective.

There is a significant amount of information of which the adoption agency must apprise the birth parents prior to their signing the relinquishment. Not the least of this includes the birth parents' right to, at any time in the future, request from the agency any known information about the status of the child's adoption. The only exception is that the birth parents will not be allowed to obtain any personal identifying information about the adoptive family. Accordingly, the birth parents will be able to learn whether or not the adoption was successful and the general nonspecific status of the child's well-being.

The birth parents must also be advised that it is of the utmost importance to keep the adoption agency advised of their address and whereabouts at all times in order to allow the adoption agency to respond to any inquiries related to medical or social history that might prove a necessity to the adopted child. This information also becomes extremely important in the context of section 9203 of the Family Code, which allows an adopted person who has turned 21 years old to request the adoption agency to disclose the name and address of her birth parents. Inasmuch as the birth parents themselves will have the ultimate say as to whether this information will be released to the child, it is important that the birth parents keep their address on record with the adoption agency to facilitate such inquiry. A similar notice is required to be delivered not only to birth parents who voluntarily relinquish their child for adoption, but also to those whose parental rights were involuntarily terminated pursuant to operation of Chapter 5 of Part 3 of Division 12 discussed above.

As might be expected, the Family Code invests in the department or adoption agency to which the child has been given for adoption, either by voluntary relinquishment or by termination of parental rights, all responsibilities for care of the child, including exclusive custody and control, until such time as an Order of Adoption is granted. The process of petitioning the court for adoption is actually not commenced by the adoption agency, notwithstanding the fact that it, following relinquishment or termination of parental rights, maintains the exclusive custodial right over the child. Instead, the petition to adopt a child who is relinquished to a department or licensed adoption agency is brought by the prospective adoptive parents with whom the child has been placed. In this regard, the adoption agency will typically place a "to be adopted" child in the home of prospective adoptive parents for purposes of determining whether this placement will be appropriate and suitable for all concerned. Later the prospective adoptive parents will petition the court for adoption as indicated in the Code section.

The department or licensed adoption agency maintains primary control over the custody and responsibility for the child. The agency in fact may remove the child from the home of the prospective adoptive parents with the court's approval upon motion filed by it after notice to the potential new parents, setting forth the grounds on which it seeks to remove the child. The department or licensed adoption agency may also refuse to consent to the adoption by the individuals provided this refusal is in the child's best interests. If the court finds that such refusal was not in the child's best interests, it may order the adoption over the objection of the licensed adoption agency. It should be noted, however, that pursuant to statutory and decisional law it is generally understood that the longer the child has been in foster care, the more substantial are the emotional ties to his foster parents (or parent), thus making the cause for removal from the foster parents' home subject to strict scrutiny.

As we discussed earlier, there are specific placement preferences regarding ethnic, religious, and racial background with regard to placement of the child for adoption. These preferences are set forth in Family Code section 8710 as follows:

> (a) If a child is being considered for adoption, the department or licensed adoption agency shall first consider adoptive placement in the home of a relative. . . . However, if a relative is not available, if placement with an available relative is not in the child's best interest, or if placement would permanently separate the child from other siblings who are being considered for adoption or who are in foster care and an alternative placement would not require the permanent separation, the foster parent or parents of the child shall be considered with respect to the child along with all other prospective adoptive parents where all of the following conditions are present:
>> (1) The child has been in foster care with the foster parent or parents for a period of more than four months.
>> (2) The child has substantial emotional ties to the foster parent or parents.
>> (3) The child's removal from the foster home would be seriously detrimental to the child's well-being.
>> (4) The foster parent or parents have made a written request to be considered to adopt the child.
>
> (c) This section does not apply to a child who has been adjudged a dependent of the juvenile court pursuant to Section 300 of the Welfare and Institutions Code.

The department is statutorily mandated to adopt rules governing the diligent search required by the above-referenced code section. It must be able to establish to the court's satisfaction that a diligent search for families meeting the criteria set forth in these relevant sections was in fact undertaken prior to placement.

The specific procedural aspects of filing a petition for adoption are set forth in Family Code section 8714. That section basically provides that a person (or persons) who wishes to adopt a child may file a petition in the superior court containing her name and the adoptive child's name. The identifying information regarding the child is limited to the child's sex and date of birth. The department or licensed adoption agency is then instructed to submit a complete report of all the facts of this case to the court and to make a recommendation as to the propriety of the contemplated adoption. A motion on the petition is subsequently heard at which time the court will make its determination as to the propriety or impropriety of granting the adoption petition.

4. Independent Adoptions

In contrast to the agency adoptions discussed above, Family Code sections 8800 to 8823 set forth the statutes designed to regulate the so-called *independent adoptions*, which are becoming more common in our society. These independent adoptions are arranged and handled outside the context of the intervention and oversight by a county department or agency; rather, they are typically handled by an attorney. Basically, an independent adoption starts with the birth parents' selection of prospective adoptive parents who are *personally known to them*. This important aspect of independent adoption cannot be delegated to an attorney or an agent of the birth parents; it must be undertaken by the parents themselves.

Even though this is an independent adoption, it is not entirely outside of the watchful eye of the county. The appropriate county adoption agency is statutorily mandated to investigate the proposed independent adoption and submit to the court a complete report containing the facts disclosed by their inquiry along with a recommendation regarding the granting of the petition. The county adoption agency will conduct a thorough investigation of the prospective adoptive parents, including an investigation of the adoptive parents' criminal record, if any.

Family Code sections 9000 to 9007 specifically discuss the propriety of a stepparent adoption. Family Code section 9000 grants to a stepparent desiring to adopt a child of his spouse the right to file a petition in the superior court. The court, operating under statutory mandate, will instruct a qualified court investigator, the welfare department, or a probation officer in the county in which the adoption proceedings are pending to make a complete and thorough investigation of each case of stepparent adoption. The court is not allowed to make an order on the adoption until such time as it has received and reviewed this investigation report. The costs of the investigation are borne by the prospective parents but cannot exceed $700. In a stepparent adoption, the consent of the birth parents is necessary and, once signed, cannot be revoked or redrawn without court approval. With these exceptions there is very little to distinguish a stepparent adoption from many other adoptions.

Under certain circumstances, an adoption can be vacated after the fact. Such an attempt to vacate an adoption must be commenced within one year at the earliest and five at the latest of entry of the court's order of adoption. Procedurally, that matter will be undertaken pursuant to a petition upon which there will ultimately be a hearing and ruling.

5. Adoption of Adults and Unmarried Minors

The adoption of an adult or a married minor is a much less complicated procedure primarily because the prospective adopted "child" is capable of consenting to the adoption himself. Of course, as with other adoptions, the prospective adoptive parent must also obtain the consent of his spouse prior to adopting an adult or a married minor. Similarly, the person to be adopted must also obtain consent from his or her spouse, in the event either is married, prior to being adopted. After the adoption, the adopted child and the adoptive parent will maintain the legal relationship as parent and child and have all the rights and be subject to all of the duties of that relationship from then on.

The procedure for an adult adoption generally commences with the preparation of an adoption agreement which is executed by the prospective adoptive parent and the prospective adoptee, and which establishes the nature of the adoption and the consent of all parties thereto. Thereafter, the prospective adoptive parent and the prospective adoptee will file a petition for approval of the adoption in the superior court. The matter is then set for hearing, notice is given to all interested parties, the prospective adoptive parent and the proposed adoptee attend the hearing, and the court is free to examine the facts and circumstances surrounding this adoption and either approves the adoption or not. The court also has the power and the discretion to require an investigative report with regard to this adoption procedure. That is somewhat unlikely in these circumstances, however, because of the legal status of all the parties involved. Finally, section 9340 of the Family Code sets forth the right of a person who has been adopted pursuant to this adult adoption procedure, upon notice given to the adoptive parent, to file a petition terminating that relationship with parent and child. At the hearing on that petition, the court will examine the propriety of entering such an order.

6. Child Abuse

Recent legislative changes have focused on the increasing prevalence in our society of child abuse. The definition of "child abuse" has been expanded, as have the child abuse reporting requirements, to ensure swift intervention on behalf of the child who is being abused or where abuse is reasonably suspected.

As a general rule, situations involving suspected child abuse are referred to and fall within the exclusive jurisdiction of the juvenile court, sometimes referred to as the *dependency court*. The statutory authority for the inquiry and proceedings in this court is found in Welfare and Institutions Code sections 300 et seq. Welfare and Institutions Code section 300 establishes the grounds upon which the juvenile court may exercise jurisdiction in situations involving suspected child abuse, with the end result of the exercise of such jurisdiction being to have the child declared a ward of the court and thus subject to the court's decision-making power pertinent to issues typically reserved to the legal and physical custodians.

Specifically, Welfare and Institutions Code section 300 sets forth the requirements for finding that a minor is subject to the jurisdiction of the juvenile court, which will result in the minor being made a dependent child of the court (that is, a *ward*). Subsection (a) of Welfare and Institutions Code section 300 provides that the minor may be declared to be a ward of the court if:

> (a) The minor has suffered, or there is a substantial risk that the minor will suffer, serious physical harm inflicted non-accidentally upon the minor by the minor's parent or guardian.

Section 300 continues to provide additional jurisdictional bases to declare a child a dependent child of the court:

> (b) The minor has suffered, or there is a substantial risk that the minor will suffer, serious physical harm or illness as a result of the failure or inability of his or her parent or guardian to adequately supervise or protect the minor, or the willful or negligent failure of the minor's parent or guardian to adequately supervise or protect the minor from the conduct of the custodian with whom the minor has been left, or by the willful or negligent failure of the parent or guardian to provide the minor with adequate food, clothing, shelter or medical treatment, or by the inability of the parent or guardian to provide regular care for the minor due to the parent's or guardian's mental illness, developmental disability, or substance abuse.
>
> (c) The minor is suffering serious emotional damage, or is at substantial risk of suffering serious emotional damage, evidenced by severe anxiety, depression, withdrawal, or untoward aggressive behavior toward self or others, as a result of conduct of the parent or guardian or who has no parent or guardian capable of providing appropriate care.
>
> (d) The minor has been sexually abused, or there is a substantial risk that the minor will be sexually abused, as defined in Section 1165.1 of the Penal Code, by his or her parent or guardian or a member of his or her household or the parent or guardian has failed to adequately protect the minor from sexual abuse when the parent or guardian knew or reasonably should have known that the minor was in danger of sexual abuse.
>
> (e) The minor is under the age of five years and has suffered severe physical abuse by a parent, or by any person known by the parent, if the parent knew or reasonably should have known that the person was physically abusing the minor. For the purposes of this subdivision, "severe physical abuse" means any of the following: any single act of abuse which causes physical trauma of sufficient severity that, if left untreated, would cause permanent physical disfigurement, permanent physical disability or death; any single act of sexual abuse which causes significant bleeding, deep bruising or significant external or internal swelling; or more than one act of physical abuse, each of which causes bleeding, deep bruising, significant external or internal swelling, bone fracture, or unconsciousness; or the willful, prolonged failure to provide adequate food.
>
> (f) The minor's parent or guardian has been convicted of causing the death of another child through abuse or neglect.

(g) The minor has been left without any provisions for support; the minor's parents have been incarcerated or institutionalized and cannot arrange for the care of the minor; or a relative or other adult custodian with whom the child resides or has been left is unwilling or unable to provide care or support for the child, the whereabouts of the parent is unknown, and reasonable efforts to locate the parent have been unsuccessful.

(h) The minor has been freed for adoption from one or both parents for 12 months by either relinquishment or termination of parental rights or an adoption petition has not been granted.

(i) The minor has been subjected to an act or acts of cruelty by the parent or guardian or a member of his or her household, or the parent or guardian has failed to adequately protect the minor from an act or acts of cruelty when the parent or guardian knew or reasonably should have known that the minor was in danger of being subject to an act or acts of cruelty.

(j) The minor's sibling has been abused or neglected . . . and there is a substantial risk that the minor will be abused or neglected, as defined in those subdivisions.

As can be seen from the foregoing, Welfare and Institutions Code section 300 is indeed a powerful tool for the protection of children who are in an abusive situation. The ultimate goal of the dependency court, assuming a basis for taking jurisdiction has been found, is to prevent the recurrence of the abuse, to eliminate the existence of abusive conditions in the home, and to provide a reunification of the family and the child. The court has sweeping authority, however, to terminate parental rights, place children for adoption, and place children outside of parental care and custody and into foster homes should the circumstances so require.

The focus of the dependency court is, of course, to protect the child, and there are significant jurisdictional protections for both the child and the parent in these circumstances. However, it is this author's experience and opinion that once a petition has been filed under the provisions of Welfare and Institutions Code section 300, rare indeed is the circumstance in which the dependency court does not find a jurisdictional basis. In other words, in this author's opinion, once the dependency court becomes involved in a proceeding, the chances are nearly 100 percent that the child will be found to be a dependent child of the court and will be placed in alternate care, if not a foster home; further, this situation will continue until and unless the parents have complied with the requirements of the Department of Social Services as mandated by the juvenile court.

Dependency court proceedings are generally conducted in two stages: the *jurisdictional phase* (when the determination is made whether to take jurisdiction over the minor child), and the *disposition phase* (the time at which the court decides what to do with the minor child once it has taken jurisdiction over him or her). The level of proof as to whether a child falls within the jurisdiction of the dependency court is simply that of a "preponderance of the evidence" or 51 percent in favor versus 49 percent against. This is a relatively low standard of proof and can be stated as follows: whether it is more likely than not that one of the enumerated conditions of Welfare and Institutions Code section 300 is present.

The burden of proof at the disposition phase is much more stringent. "Clear and convincing evidence" is required to remove a child from the parent or guardian's physical custody and cannot be based upon speculation that future harm will come to this child. For all practical purposes, however, at the disposition phase the minor child will typically be placed back in the home under strict supervision by the Department of Social Services subject to an order that the offending parent (depending upon the abuse) seeks treatment, relocates out of the minor child's residence, or participates in restricted or monitored visitation only. If this is unrealistic under the circumstances, the court can order that a child be placed in a foster home pending termination of parental rights and be placed up for adoption.

In addition, recent amendments to the California Penal Code have expanded the scope of persons who are required by law to report any reasonable suspicion that a minor child with whom they have contact has been the victim of child abuse. Penal Code section 11166(a) provides:

> Any child care custodian, health practitioner, or employee of a child protective agency who has knowledge of or observes a child in his or her professional capacity or within the scope of his or her employment whom he or she knows or reasonably suspects has been the victim of child abuse shall report the known or suspected incident of child abuse to a child protective agency immediately or as soon as is practically possible by telephone and shall prepare and send a written report thereof within 36 hours of receiving the information concerning the incident.

Section 11166.05 makes it discretionary for these individuals to report a reasonable suspicion that "mental suffering has been inflicted on the child or the child's emotional well being is endangered in any other way." Further, Section 11166 (e) requires a commercial film and photographic print processor to report to a law enforcement agency evidence of any film, photograph, videotape, negative, or slide obtained within the scope of their professional capacity or employment depicting a child under the age of 14 years engaged in an act of sexual conduct. *Sexual conduct* in this context is statutorily defined to include sexual intercourse (in all its permutations), masturbation, sado-masochistic abuse, genital exhibition, and similar items of a prurient nature.

These reporting requirements are serious, and Penal Code section 11172(b) provides a shield from liability for any individual who makes a report in accordance with the provisions of these code sections. There is even a provision that an individual who is sued as a result of making a report under these Code sections and who prevails in that lawsuit is entitled to recover attorney's fees against the individual(s) who sued him.

Finally, Penal Code section 11166 (c)provides: "Any mandated reporter who fails to report an incident of known or reasonably suspected child abuse or neglect as required by this section is guilty of a misdemeanor punishable by up to six months confinement in a county jail or by a fine of one thousand dollars ($1,000) or by both that imprisonment and fine. If a mandated reporter intentionally conceals his or her failure to report an incident known by the mandated reporter to be abuse or severe neglect under this section, the failure to report is a continuing offense until an agency specified in Section 11165.9 discovers the offense." As such, this duty is not looked upon lightly by individuals who fall within the definitional provisions of this Code section.

Summary

The relationship of parent and child is perhaps one of the most heavily codified, and litigated, areas of the law. This is an emotion-packed arena in which parents are rarely satisfied with the result. From an initial standpoint, the relationship of parent and child is influenced in no small part by the statutes relating to emancipation of minors.

There is a statutory scheme whereby, under certain limited circumstances, a minor who is at least 14 years of age can petition the court for a declaration of his emancipation. This declaration, if granted, will have the effect of allowing the minor to be treated as an adult for virtually all purposes. Interestingly, under certain equally limited circumstances, the declaration of emancipation can be set aside, thus returning the minor to his original, unemancipated status.

The paternity action is typically brought either by the natural mother or by the county, usually on behalf of a welfare agency. It is not uncommon, however, for this procedure to be used by a natural father, not married to the mother, to seek judicial (and thus "legal") recognition of his status as father to the child in question. This generally comes up in situations where the natural mother does not want anything to do with the natural father and feels equally as strong regarding the child.

The purpose of the paternity action is, to the extent possible, to render a determination regarding the identity of the natural father of a child. Along with this determination, of course, come all the rights, duties, and obligations incident to the status as "father," including custodial and visitation rights as well as obligations of child support.

Key Terms

The following is a list of key terms and phrases that you should be able to define and use in context. Only then will you have demonstrated a command of the material in this chapter.

- juvenile court
- dependency court
- paternity action
- Emancipation of Minor
- termination of parental rights
- adoption
- stepparent adoption
- disaffirmance of contract
- presumed father

Questions for Discussion

1. Describe the circumstances under which a county agency would be interested in bringing a paternity action against a presumed father.
2. Under what circumstances may a minor petition for emancipation? If granted, what will the effect of such a declaration be? (Be thorough; do not simply say "he will be treated like an adult.")
3. Under what circumstances will the court terminate a parent's parental rights?
4. Describe the circumstances under which the Department of Social Services will intervene on a child's behalf. What is the mechanism of this intervention? Where are these issues heard, and how (if at all) does this differ from the "Family Law" Department?
5. Under what circumstances can a minor enter into a legally binding contract?

ENDNOTES

1. An admittedly cynical observation.

2. The reader should note that this statutory scheme is very detailed and not nearly as clear as it would appear from this select passage. Although available, an abortion for an unemancipated minor without the consent of her parents is very difficult to obtain.

3. Family Code §7050 presents a laundry list of the areas in which a minor will be considered an adult following emancipation, too lengthy to be repeated here. The reader is recommended to review this section for further details on this subject.

4. The statute actually requires that the minor's parents acquiesce to the minor living separate and apart. This is not exactly the same as consenting to it. Acquiescence, in its literal sense, implies that the parents are not complaining about the living situation of their child. This, of course, is not the same as actually consenting to it.

5. There are other statutory rights set out in this division of the Code, but in this author's opinion their inclusion adds little to this section of the Code. It is anticipated that future revisions and amendments of this Code will either relocate or expand upon these few sections.

6. That is, living together in the same home as "husband and wife."

7. Note, however, that in its practical application (as discussed below) this conclusive presumption is what could be better described as a "soft" presumption, since the courts have of late been trying to respect the wishes of the mother relative to the desired family unit in their application of this presumption.

8. The entirety of this section is not quoted in the interest of economy of space. Only the portions relevant to the declaration itself are cited. The portions regarding support of the child (which is the fundamental underpinning of this section) are deferred to a later chapter.

9. Note that part of this section has been held to be unconstitutional by the California Appellate Court in In re Jerry P., 95 Cal. App. 4th 793. The Supreme Court granted review, however that grant was subsequently dismissed. The moral of this story is to read this decision and this statute carefully before citing either for any proposition. The Legislature has yet to repeal or amend this section, so extreme caution must be exercised in using this section as authority for anything. Its inclusion here is as a teaching tool and nothing else.

10. An interesting aside to this discussion is the presumption dealing with artificial insemination. Under those circumstances, the husband (not the sperm donor) must consent to the procedure in writing, and certain other conditions must be met that, if done properly, will give rise to the treatment of the husband as if he were the natural father of the child. This will be deemed conclusive as against the biological father (the donor of the sperm) if done in accordance with statute. If not, the biological father may prove successful in a subsequent paternity action.

11. The Uniform Act on Blood Tests to Determine Paternity, Family Code §§7550-7557, discusses these tests in greater detail.

12. The following Code does not discuss the various procedural aspects of this area of adoption practice nor will this book. If the reader is interested in pursuing the subject of adoption in greater detail, the reader is invited to review the many fine treatises on this subject.

CHAPTER 3

Child Custody

A. Introduction
B. Custody

CHAPTER OVERVIEW

In this chapter we will continue our discussion of the relationship between parents and their children, focusing on issues surrounding the custody of a child, that is, who will make the important decisions relating to the child's health, education, and welfare. The reader should note that issues related to children of same-sex relationships will be raised in the context of registered domestic partnerships and same-sex marriages as presented in Chapter 11 of this book.

A. Introduction

No area of family law brings to the courtroom the tension, anxiety, hostility, volatility, and simple raw emotion as child custody litigation. Rare indeed is the family in transition that is able to sidetrack the personal differences that exist between husband and wife and devote energy to the singular goal of ensuring what is best for their children. Of course, all parents pay lip service to this lofty ideal and would be appalled at the suggestion that they thought otherwise. However, as experience in the family courts has demonstrated, quite often it is the children who are the real victims of divorce, while their parents, in the name of what is "good for the children," heap previously unknown misery, accusations, and character assassination upon each other. Imagine how that must make these children feel.

Most often a judge will take great pains to get parents themselves to come to a mutually acceptable custody agreement rather than placing the issue into the hands of the judge, a total stranger. As these judges recognize, more often than not a decision reached by a stranger will be palatable neither to the father, the mother, nor the children. The family court system has several levels of mediation, counseling, and conciliation to attempt to bring warring parents together to help them resolve the issues of custody and visitation as a family rather than as combatants, whose primary goal is to "win." As is stated throughout this book, there are no winners in family court. Indeed, many have argued that there are, in fact, only losers. While this is not a position to which this author adheres, I most certainly accept the premise that there are no winners. Divorce is a difficult time for any individual, made more so when the question of custody of children, and the effect that the divorce will have on their lives, is considered.

This chapter will explore the procedural and substantive aspects of the murky waters known as custody litigation. Custody litigation is the last bastion of "fault" in the California family courts. As the reader will recall, California is a "no-fault" state. Who is right, who is wrong, who is good, who is bad, and all of the related judgmental opinions of the people involved in a divorce case and their conduct are utterly irrelevant in nearly all aspects of family law with the major exception of that related to custody and visitation. Issues related to children require inquiry into *all* aspects of the litigants' behavior, the only limitation being the requirement that the inquiry must focus upon a determination as to what is in the best interests of the children. It is hard to imagine what factor would not be relevant when trying to make that determination.

B. Custody

1. Preliminary Considerations

Family Code section 2010 vests the superior court with subject matter jurisdiction to determine issues related to the custody of the children and make orders that are appropriate concerning the status of the marriage, and the custody and support of minor children of the marriage as well as children for whom support is authorized. Of course, litigation under the Family Code is not the exclusive venue for determination of custody disputes. Issues relating to the custody and visitation of children can arise in family law proceedings, guardianship proceedings, dependency court, and other similar matters.[1]

It should be noted that the existence of a valid marriage bears absolutely no relationship to the propriety of a determination as to custody and visitation of minor children. There is certainly no requirement that individuals be married prior to bringing children into this world. Accordingly, the issue of child custody (in the family law context, at least) is ripe for resolution whether in the context of a dissolution of marriage, legal separation, nullity, or even a paternity action (which presupposes that the parents are not married to each other). Similarly (and as will be discussed later in the chapter dealing with child support) issues of child support are completely unrelated to the nature of the relationship between the father and mother.

When determination of custody is fully litigated it involves many different phases. At the outset, the parties must decide whether a request for temporary custody by way of an order to show cause or an *ex parte* application for custody is required. The court, of course, has the power to entertain such requests, and the automatic temporary restraining orders built into the family law summons (listed on the back of the summons) prevent both parties from removing their minor children from the state without the prior written consent of the other party or a court order. Further, Family Code section 3064 provides that although custody orders cannot generally be made or modified on an *ex parte* basis, if the party requesting such an order is capable of showing immediate harm to the child or an immediate risk that the child will be removed from the state, such orders can be granted under those circumstances. Typically, the phrase "immediate harm to the child" includes situations involving domestic violence or child abuse.

The next phase in the custody dispute typically involves mediation, counseling, and child custody evaluation/investigation. This process is discussed in greater detail in the sections of this book involving mediation and conciliation. Generally, however, it entails a series of referrals to court-appointed mediators or family counseling professionals working under the auspices of the *conciliation court*, who provide counseling and mediation services to the litigants free of charge. This is done, of course, to facilitate the parties working together to bring about a mutual agreement as to custody, which will almost always be better than one imposed by the court.

Child custody evaluation/investigation comes about in one of two ways: (1) The court on its own motion may appoint a mental health professional and experienced child custody evaluator to investigate the situation and report his findings back to the court as an aid in making a child custody determination, or (2) one or both of the parties may unilaterally or mutually hire such an expert witness to investigate and evaluate the situation and report back to the court on their behalf. Naturally, a joint evaluation is preferable from the court's perspective inasmuch as it represents the parents working together with the evaluator to produce a unified position on the issue of custody and visitation.

The child custody evaluator typically will interview the parents individually, together, together with their children, individually with their children, at their offices, and at their home; generally, the evaluator will also conduct interviews with the children independent of the parents (depending, of course, on the child's age). Additionally, most child custody evaluators will interview friends, neighbors, teachers, pediatricians, and similar persons who are in a position to shed insight on the family situation as a whole, review school and medical records, and consider such other factors as might impact upon the respective parents' ability to participate in the custody situation. Upon completion, the results are prepared in written form and submitted to the court for review. Most experienced child custody evaluators will produce reports that are on the average approximately 25 to 50 pages in length. The court then has this available as additional evidence to assist it in making the final determination as to custody and visitation.

2. Jurisdictional Considerations

As stated earlier, Family Code section 2010 provides that the superior court is vested with subject matter jurisdiction over the issue of child custody and visitation. Family Code section 3120 grants the superior court the jurisdiction to adjudicate the request of a husband or a wife to obtain custody of a child of a marriage without the necessity of bringing a dissolution or legal separation action. Such action would, in fact, constitute an action independent from any required dissolution or legal separation proceedings.

Interestingly, the Code does not require that the court be possessed of personal jurisdiction over the parents to determine a custody dispute. The Uniform Child Custody Jurisdiction Act establishes the bases for exercising jurisdiction in a child custody dispute when other jurisdictions are competing for the same power and generally focuses on the child.

The juvenile court (operating generally under the mandate of Welfare and Institutions Code section 300) is a separate yet equal (some would say more equal) branch of the superior court whose functions generally take precedence over family law matters and, in the event of a conflict between the juvenile court and the family law court, will take precedence in making determinations as to custody. These proceedings fall generally within the category of what is referred to as the *dependency court*. Matters involving the dependency court typically originate when the child is taken out of the home by the County Department of Public Social Services (DPSS) as a result of being advised either by a teacher, a doctor, a police officer, or an otherwise concerned individual that a situation exists that constitutes a danger to a child, which is not being addressed adequately in the family home (or, as is often the case, is a result of dysfunction within the family home).

Generally, a DPSS social worker will respond to a complaint regarding child abuse or child endangerment by instituting an investigation of the allegations and formulating an opinion as to whether DPSS intervention is required. In this author's experience and opinion, the decision of the DPSS to intervene is almost always made in the affirmative. The DPSS social worker will contact the local law enforcement and appear at the location of the child (usually the family home) with the police officer and actually take the child into physical custody. Within a very short period of time, the matter is called before the court much like an arraignment in a criminal court proceeding at which time the court makes a preliminary determination as to whether sufficient facts exist to justify the intervention of DPSS and to justify a petition being filed to have the child declared to be a ward of the court pursuant to the provisions of Welfare and Institutions Code section 300(a). Those petitions are almost always granted.

Assuming the court finds that sufficient facts and circumstances exist to have the child declared to be a ward of the court pertinent to the referenced Welfare and Institutions Code section, then the matter will shift to what is known as the disposition phase. At that time, the court makes a determination as to whether the child should be returned to the family home or placed in some other suitable placement (for example, a foster home). The court will then maintain jurisdiction over this child and will maintain the child's status as a ward of the court for a specific period of time (usually at least one year) and will require that all of the parties return to the court to reevaluate the situation at that time. Assuming the offending situation has been removed from the home or the child has been taken out of danger by virtue of the court's intervention, and assuming further that the court sees no reason to continue the child in its status as a ward of the court, the child will be released back to its parents.

In certain cases, the juvenile court has authority to terminate the parental rights of the natural parents and put the child up for adoption. This is an extreme remedy, but it is one that is used with some frequency in the dependency court.

From a jurisdictional standpoint, the family law court is not empowered to entertain issues related to custody of stepchildren. Bear in mind that we are talking about subject matter jurisdiction. Accordingly, even though other sections of the Family Code (most notably Family Code sections 3020 et seq.) paint a wide brush of empowering language allowing the court discretion to make such orders as are necessary in the best interests of the children, this language cannot create subject matter jurisdiction. Similarly, although Family Code section 3102 contains language that supports a grandparent's request for visitation with minor children, there is no statutory authority to support a grandparent's independent request for custody.[2]

Personal jurisdiction over the parents is not required in a child custody proceeding. As discussed in greater detail below, child custody jurisdiction is based upon the relationship of the state to the *child*, not to the parents. Assuming the child is present in the state where the matter is being adjudicated (or the state has satisfied one of the other jurisdictional bases of the Uniform Child Custody Jurisdiction Act), the court is fully empowered to make whatever orders it deems necessary and in the best interests of the minor child whether or not the parents are subject to the state's personal jurisdiction.

3. The Uniform Child Custody Jurisdiction and Enforcement Act and Related Statutes

Family Code sections 3400 through and including 3465 contain the text of the Uniform Child Custody Jurisdiction and Enforcement Act (UCCJEA). This statutory scheme sets forth a uniform (hence the name) system of resolving custody disputes between competing jurisdictions (county to county, state to state, or country to country). The general purpose of the Act was formerly set forth in section 3401 of the Family Code. This particular section was repealed, however, in 1999, with the enactment of the Uniform Child Custody Jurisdiction *and Enforcement* Act. While substantially similar to the Uniform Child Custody Jurisdiction Act (the UCCJA), it is not identical. The UCCJEA applies to cases commenced on or after January 1, 2000 and to motions (or other requests) to modify custody brought after January 1, 2000, regardless of when the case itself was commenced.

Generally speaking, cases interpreting the UCCJA are not only instructive authority, but dispositive as well to situations involving the UCCJEA, except in those instances where the terms of the old Act conflict with those of the new. In this context, a good recitation of the general purpose of this legislation can be found in several cases that have interpreted it over the years. One such court has stated it thus:

> The purposes of the UCCJA [now the UCCJEA] include avoiding competition and conflict for jurisdiction between courts of different states; promoting cooperation with courts of other states so that a custody decree is rendered in the state that can best decide the case in the interest of the child; assuring that litigation concerning child custody take place in the state with the closest connection to the child and child's family; discouraging continuing controversies over child custody; deterring abductions and other unilateral removals of children undertaken to obtain custody awards; avoiding relitigation of custody decisions of other states; facilitating enforcement of other states' custody decrees; and promoting the exchange of information and mutual assistance between courts concerned with the same child.

Brossoit v. Brossoit, 31 Cal. App. 4th 361 (1995).

The UCCJEA in its current state as that enacted by California has, as of January 2004, been enacted in 35 U.S. jurisdictions and is pending in 3 others. Practically speaking, however, virtually every state in the United

States and many foreign countries have enacted legislation substantially similar to the provisions of the UCCJEA. Generally speaking, the UCCJEA, like the UCCJA, is designed to avoid competition between jurisdictions and conflicts between courts of different states in the resolution of child custody disputes. This is designed to keep the parties from bouncing their children all over the country or all over the state in an attempt to obtain a favorable ruling, and to promote cooperation between courts of the various states with the ultimate goal that a child custody decree be rendered in the state best equipped to deal with the particular case. The basic "difference" (if it can be so called) between the UCCJA and the UCCJEA is seen in the UCCJEA's intention to bring its provisions more in line with the Federal Parental Kidnapping Prevention Act (FPKPA), discussed below, and to clarify and strengthen the basic jurisdictional standards employed by the courts in this context.

The UCCJEA is also designed to assure that the litigation concerning custody takes place in the state where the child and the family have the most significant contacts (typically where the child lives) concerning the child's care, protection, training, and personal relationships. It discourages continuing controversies in the area of child custody litigation that might otherwise occur if the parties could run from state to state or from jurisdiction to jurisdiction with impunity and attempt to relitigate the same issues over and over again.

The UCCJEA (or some similar version thereof) has been adopted by virtually all states, the District of Columbia, and the Virgin Islands. Notwithstanding this "uniform" adoption of the Act, there is still some room for interpretation by the courts of the specific jurisdiction applying its provisions. As such, the decisions of those courts will be viewed by California courts as persuasive (albeit not controlling) authority here. The UCCJEA is not, however, reciprocal. Its provisions will *control* in any California case dealing with its subject matter regardless of the Act's adoption (or not) by some other court claiming jurisdiction, even when the foreign court is a different country. Put another way, if a sister-state or foreign jurisdiction claims jurisdiction over a child custody dispute based on its laws, and a California court also claims jurisdiction, the California court will apply the provisions of the UCCJEA in making its decision and will disregard any provision of the law of the sister-state or foreign jurisdiction that conflicts with its provisions.

The UCCJEA is one of the few examples of a law that will be applied against an individual in the absence of personal jurisdiction. The UCCJEA concerns itself only with subject matter jurisdiction over the issue of child custody; personal jurisdiction over the parents is not a prerequisite to its application. In fact, it is not even necessary that the child in question be physically present in the state for the state to exercise its jurisdiction over him (although that is nevertheless preferable).

The UCCJEA applies in all child custody proceedings, including proceedings under the Family Code and juvenile court and dependency proceedings. It does not apply, however, in adoption or juvenile delinquency proceedings. It will also not apply to custody disputes involving Indian (Native American) children. Those issues are governed by a separate statutory scheme, the Indian Child Welfare Act (ICWA) found at 25 U.S.C. sections 1901 et seq. Any conflict between the Family Code and the UCCJEA will be resolved in favor of strict adherence to the requirements of the UCCJEA. Indeed, when it comes to child custody determinations, the UCCJEA is subject only to the provisions of the Federal Parental Kidnapping Prevention Act (FPKPA) found at 28 U.S.C. sections 1738A et seq. This federal act is substantially similar to the UCCJEA and primarily makes matters involving parental kidnapping a question of "overriding federal policy."

As mentioned above, another child custody oriented statutory scheme is found in the Federal Parental Kidnapping Prevention Act (FPKPA). While similar to the UCCJEA in many respects, it is nevertheless a unique act. Like the UCCJEA, this Act seeks to minimize jurisdictional disputes on the issue of child custody jurisdiction and further provides a basis upon which conflicting jurisdictions can find ground for the recognition of sister-state judgments on this subject. Further, to the extent any of the provisions of the FPKPA conflict with the UCCJEA, the doctrine of federal preemption instructs that the FPKPA shall control (since it is a federal law, and the UCCJEA is a state law).

Interestingly, the federal court does not automatically have jurisdiction to hear these child custody disputes simply because the FPKPA is a federal law. As mentioned earlier in this book, the issues arising out of a family law dispute are typically the exclusive domain of the state courts. The Act itself speaks of the obligations of the state courts in applying its directives on this subject. Of course, this is not to say that the federal court will never interject itself into this arena; however, generally speaking, the application of the FPKPA will be left to the state court that is exercising subject matter jurisdiction over the child in question.

Like the UCCJEA, the FPKPA also provides guidelines for the exercise of subject matter jurisdiction over child custody. Under the UCCJEA, the fundamental basis for exercising such jurisdiction is determined by the home state of the subject child. This is known as the *home state preference* of the FPKPA. As such, if two states assert conflicting and arguably equal jurisdictional claims, under the FPKPA (for example, *home state* and *significant contacts* [explained in detail below]) this conflict will be resolved by application of the FPKPA in favor of the state that is found to be the child's home state.

In addition to the FPKPA, there are other statutory schemes on this (or closely related) subjects. For example, the Federal International Parental

Kidnapping Crime Act of 1993 makes it a felony to remove or detain a child under the age of 16 outside of the United States with the intent to obstruct parental rights. The defenses to a charge of violating this Act include acting pursuant to a valid court order, fleeing to avoid child abuse, and things of this nature. The Missing Children Act compels the FBI to maintain an extensive database of information related specifically to missing children. This database will be made available to any parent who has reported a missing child. The Federal Fugitive Felon Act authorizes the issuance of a federal warrant for the apprehension of a parent who takes a child in violation of any state's felony child-abduction laws and who then crosses state lines with the child to avoid prosecution.

In California, the issuance of a state warrant for violation of Penal Code section 278 is a prerequisite to utilization of this procedure. That section provides as follows:

> Every person, not having a right to custody, who maliciously takes, entices away, keeps, withholds, or conceals any child with the intent to detain or conceal that child from a lawful custodian shall be punished by imprisonment in a county jail not exceeding one year, a fine not exceeding one thousand dollars ($1,000), or both that fine and imprisonment, or by imprisonment in the state prison for two, three, or four years, a fine not exceeding ten thousand dollars ($10,000), or both that fine and imprisonment.

Additionally, the Family Code provides for an action by the District Attorney in assisting in locating missing children.

Family Code section 3130 provides as follows:

> If a petition to determine custody of a child has been filed in a court of competent jurisdiction, or if a temporary order pending determination of custody has been entered in accordance with Chapter 3 (commencing with section 3060), and the whereabouts of a party in possession of the child are not known, or there is reason to believe that the party may not appear in the proceedings although ordered to appear personally with the child pursuant to section 3430, the district attorney shall take all actions necessary to locate the party and the child to procure compliance with the order to appear with the child for purposes of adjudication of custody. The petition to determine custody may be filed by the district attorney.

Similarly, Family Code section 3131 provides:

> If a custody or visitation order has been entered by a court of competent jurisdiction and the child is taken or detained by another person in violation of the order, the district attorney shall take all actions necessary to locate and return the child and the person who violated the order and to assist in the enforcement of the custody or visitation order or other order of the court by use of an appropriate civil or criminal proceeding.

On an international level, the *Hague Convention on the Civil Aspects of International Child Abduction* (generally referred to as the "Hague Convention") provides guidance when confronted with these issues and problems across national boundaries. The Hague Convention was adopted by the United States in 1988. Each country that has joined this Convention has agreed to establish and maintain a central authority to receive and process requests for assistance in the areas of child custody and visitation. To date, the following countries are signatories to the Convention: Albania, Australia, Austria, Belarus, Belgium, Brazil, Bulgaria, Canada, Chile, China, Cyprus, Czech Republic, Denmark, Ecuador, Finland, France, Germany, Greece, Hungary, India, Ireland, Israel, Italy, Latvia, Luxembourg, Mexico, Netherlands, Norway, Panama, Peru, Philippines, Poland, Portugal, Romania, Russian Federation, Slovakia, Slovenia, Spain, Sri Lanka, Sweden, Switzerland, Turkey, United Kingdom of Great Britain and Northern Ireland, United States of America, Uruguay, and Venezuela. Other nations are also currently working on adoption of the Convention as well. It is hoped that the Convention will someday apply worldwide.

The Hague Convention generally provides a mechanism of uniformity in resolving child-related disputes across international boundaries, much as the UCCJEA seeks to achieve across state lines. To invoke the Convention, the aggrieved parent or interested party files an application for assistance with the "central authority" of the member country that establishes compliance with the Convention's procedures and an appropriate basis for invocation of its provisions. In the United States, the U.S. State Department's Office of Citizens Consular Services has been designated as this nation's central authority. Once the application has been accepted by the central authority it will then take all available steps to locate, protect, and ensure the safe return of the child. As a general rule, the Hague Convention will use the child's "habitual residence" as the basis for its jurisdiction. This is very similar to the "home state" analysis under the UCCJEA and the FPKPA (discussed below).

Simply put, the Hague Convention is an international treaty signed by many countries to provide for the return of a child wrongfully taken from its place of "habitual residence." The purpose of the statute is not to determine the merits of who should have custody. Rather, it simply is to determine *where* that determination should be made. The fundamental question in this context is "where is the habitual residence of the child?" This is a factual determination and will be made by the court, whose discretion will not generally be overturned in the absence of facts that are simply so persuasive as require such a result.

The Hague Convention applies to children under 16 years of age only since these older children have a strong voice to determine where they wish to live in any event. The action must be brought within one year of the child's removal, unless the facts show the child's whereabouts had been deliberately concealed during that year.

The defenses to a Hague Convention Case are generally as follows:

1. The petitioner has failed to exercise his or her custodial rights.
2. The petitioner consented to the taking.
3. There is a grave risk that return would expose the child to physical or psychological harm or place the child in an intolerable situation.
4. The return would simply shock the conscience and violate fundamental principles of the country where the child has been taken relative to human rights.

When analyzing the defenses, counsel must be prepared to discuss their existence and their general application. The most common defense is that of grave risk of harm to the child. There is also an interesting question where the parent resisting return claims that she or he was the victim of domestic violence in the other country and that is why they left. The court will have to analyze who the victim was, whether there is a system in place in the country from which the child was removed to address these issues, and other related issues.

The fundamental analysis of a Hague Convention Case follows these lines:

1. Was there a taking
2. Of a child
3. Under the age of 16
4. From his/her habitual residence
5. In derogation of a custodial right of the other parent
6. Where enforcement is sought within one year

Once all of these questions have been answered with an ultimate "yes," the analysis turns to an examination of whether there are any available defenses to a return to that country:

1. Has there been a failure of the parent who is seeking the petition to return to exercise his/her custodial right? Note that the party who has removed the child from the jurisdiction cannot undertake such an act and then make the claim that the other parent is not exercising visitation. In other words, you can't interfere with visitation and then claim that the other party isn't exercising it.
2. Is there in fact grave harm going to befall the child? This is a factual determination, and cannot be bootstrapped by the taking

parent. For example, the taking parent cannot bring the child back to California and then claim that it would constitute grave harm to return the child to the country of origin because they are now "settled" in California.

Once these Hague standards are determined by the court, and the court determines that the defenses don't apply, a decision to return the child to that jurisdiction will be made.

The interpretive cases include Friedrich v. Friedrich (Friedrich II), 78 f.3D 1060 (1996): In this case, the child was born in Germany. Mother took the child to the USA. Father claimed that the child should be returned to Germany pursuant to the Hague Convention. Mother claimed that Father was not exercising his custodial rights because he did not have a paper granting him custody. The court held that custodial rights are inherent of a parent, and a parent does not need a "piece of paper" in order to be operating under the color of custodial rights.

Mother then claimed that grave harm would befall the child because the child was now 5 years of age and had become accustomed to living in the United States. The court rejected that argument claiming that, since Mother (the taking parent) had created this "grave harm," she could not then use that as a reason to keep the child in the United States.

Another useful case for review is that of Wipranik v. Superior Court of Los Angeles (1998), 63 Cal. App. 4th 315. In this case, the child was born in the United States. A dissolution was later filed, but before it could be concluded the parties reconciled and moved to Israel. Three years later the mother returned to the United States with the child, and the father filed a Hague petition in California for an order compelling the return of the child to Israel. The mother opposed, claiming that the time in Israel was "temporary" and the habitual residence was in fact the United States. This argument was rejected by the court as a matter of a factual determination.

Next, the mother claimed that grave harm would befall the child due to the turmoil and violence in Israel. The court found that substantial evidence supported a finding that the child was not at grave risk such as would warrant not returning it to Israel.

The California Legislature has enacted legislation designed to provide further clarity in this sometimes confusing area. Family Code section 3048, effective July 2003, imposes specific requirements on the courts regarding the findings they must make in cases involving children, just so the disputes and issues raised in the context of competing jurisdictions can be planned for and dealt with according to an organized plan. This section reads as follows (and is worth reading and understanding in its entirety):

§3048. Required contents for custody or visitation orders; risk of child abduction; risk factors and preventative measures; notation of preventative conditions on minute order of court proceedings; Child Abduction Unit; child custody order forms

(a) Notwithstanding any other provision of law, in any proceeding to determine child custody or visitation with a child, every custody or visitation order shall contain all of the following:

(1) The basis for the court's exercise of jurisdiction.

(2) The manner in which notice and opportunity to be heard were given.

(3) A clear description of the custody and visitation rights of each party.

(4) A provision stating that a violation of the order may subject the party in violation to civil or criminal penalties, or both.

(5) Identification of the country of habitual residence of the child or children.

(b) (1) In cases in which the court becomes aware of facts which may indicate that there is a risk of abduction of a child, the court shall, either on its own motion or at the request of a party, determine whether measures are needed to prevent the abduction of the child by one parent. To make that determination, the court shall consider the risk of abduction of the child, obstacles to location, recovery, and return if the child is abducted, and potential harm to the child if he or she is abducted. To determine whether there is a risk of abduction, the court shall consider the following factors:

(A) Whether a party has previously taken, enticed away, kept, withheld, or concealed a child in violation of the right of custody or of visitation of a person.

(B) Whether a party has previously threatened to take, entice away, keep, withhold, or conceal a child in violation of the right of custody or of visitation of a person.

(C) Whether a party lacks strong ties to this state.

(D) Whether a party has strong familial, emotional, or cultural ties to another state or country, including foreign citizenship. This factor shall be considered only if evidence exists in support of another factor specified in this section.

(E) Whether a party has no financial reason to stay in this state, including whether the party is unemployed, is able to work anywhere, or is financially independent.

(F) Whether a party has engaged in planning activities that would facilitate the removal of a child from the state, including quitting a job, selling his or her primary residence, terminating a lease, closing a bank account, liquidating other assets, hiding or destroying documents, applying for a passport, applying to obtain a birth certificate or school or medical records, or purchasing airplane or other travel tickets, with consideration given to whether a party is carrying out a safety plan to flee from domestic violence.

(G) Whether a party has a history of a lack of parental cooperation or child abuse, or there is substantiated evidence that a party has perpetrated domestic violence.

(H) Whether a party has a criminal record.

(2) If the court makes a finding that there is a need for preventative measures after considering the factors listed in paragraph (1), the court shall consider taking one or more of the following measures to prevent the abduction of the child:

(A) Ordering supervised visitation.

(B) Requiring a parent to post a bond in an amount sufficient to serve as a financial deterrent to abduction, the proceeds of which may be used to offset the cost of recovery of the child in the event there is an abduction.

(C) Restricting the right of the custodial or noncustodial parent to remove the child from the county, the state, or the country.

(D) Restricting the right of the custodial parent to relocate with the child, unless the custodial parent provides advance notice to, and obtains the written agreement of, the noncustodial parent, or obtains the approval of the court, before relocating with the child.

(E) Requiring the surrender of passports and other travel documents.

(F) Prohibiting a parent from applying for a new or replacement passport for the child.

(G) Requiring a parent to notify a relevant foreign consulate or embassy of passport restrictions and to provide the court with proof of that notification.

(H) Requiring a party to register a California order in another state as a prerequisite to allowing a child to travel to that state for visits, or to obtain an order from another country containing terms identical to the custody and visitation order issued in the United States (recognizing that these orders may be modified or enforced pursuant to the laws of the other country), as a prerequisite to allowing a child to travel to that county for visits.

(I) Obtaining assurances that a party will return from foreign visits by requiring the traveling parent to provide the court or the other parent or guardian with any of the following:

(i) The travel itinerary of the child.

(ii) Copies of round trip airline tickets.

(iii) A list of addresses and telephone numbers where the child can be reached at all times.

(iv) An open airline ticket for the left-behind parent in case the child is not returned.

(J) Including provisions in the custody order to facilitate use of the Uniform Child Custody Jurisdiction and Enforcement Act (Part 3 (commencing with Section 3400)) and the Hague Convention on the Civil Aspects of International Child Abduction (implemented pursuant to 42 U.S.C. Sec. 11601 et seq.), such as identifying California as the home state of the child or otherwise defining the basis for the California court's exercise of jurisdiction under Part 3 (commencing with Section 3400), identifying the United States as the country of habitual residence of the child pursuant to the Hague Convention, defining custody rights pursuant to the Hague Convention, obtaining the express agreement of the parents that the United States is the country of habitual residence of the child, or that California or the United States is the most appropriate forum for addressing custody and visitation orders.

(K) Authorizing the assistance of law enforcement.

(3) If the court imposes any or all of the conditions listed in paragraph (2), those conditions shall be specifically noted on the minute order of the court proceedings.

(4) If the court determines there is a risk of abduction that is sufficient to warrant the application of one or more of the prevention measures authorized by this section, the court shall inform the parties of the telephone number and address of the Child Abduction Unit in the office of the district attorney in the county where the custody or visitation order is being entered.

(c) The Judicial Council shall make the changes to its child custody order forms that are necessary for the implementation of subdivision (b). This subdivision shall become operative on July 1, 2003.

(d) Nothing in this section affects the applicability of Section 278.7 of the Penal Code.

This statute is a relatively new portion of the Family Code that imposes specific requirements on family law courts. These requirements basically require that, in any proceeding to determine child custody or visitation, every custody or visitation order shall contain the following:

1. Basis for the court's exercise of jurisdiction
2. The manner in which notice and opportunity to be heard were given
3. A clear description of the custody and the visitation rights of each party
4. A provision stating that a violation of an order may subject the party to criminal penalties
5. Identification of the country of habitual residence

The statute goes on to provide that, in cases in which the court becomes aware of "facts" that may indicate a risk of abduction, the court shall determine whether additional measures are needed to prevent the abduction of the child. The factors that the court will consider are detailed in the Code and include:

1. Previous abductions
2. Threats or previous abductions

3. Whether a party lacks "strong ties" to this state
4. Whether a party has ties "elsewhere"
5. Whether the party is "financially footloose." Bad intent is not necessary here; someone who is financially independent, able to work anywhere, things of this nature, will trigger this factor.
6. Whether there have been any "removal activities" on the part of one of the parties. This could include quitting a job, terminating a lease, selling a house, closing a bank account; a whole variety of otherwise innocent things.
7. Whether there has been any domestic violence
8. Whether there is any history of crime

If the court is persuaded by its determination relative to these factors, it can impose a variety of remedies against this party, including:

1. Supervised parenting time
2. Posting a bond
3. Restrictions on removal of the child
4. Restrictions on relocation
5. Removal of passports
6. Mandated registration at the local consulate during trips
7. Mandated registration of a custody order in some other jurisdiction
8. Denial of the right to purchase tickets for international travel

Some California courts have adopted a policy of *not* analyzing these factors if it can be at all avoided, primarily due to the Draconian nature of the inquiry and the possibility that an otherwise innocent parent my end up being punished for otherwise innocent behavior (changing banks, for example). The important thing to remember about this section is that the findings required in it are *mandatory*, and the factors are *discretionary*. Many of these factors are innocent and don't require any kind of evil intent. There are much broader factors, and we must wonder how this statute may affect people who are not from the United States, where we admittedly enjoy a much more "free-thinking" approach to these kinds of factors. The reader must note, however, that the fact that a person is a foreign national, or has strong familial ties in a foreign country will not be a sufficient factor all by itself to authorize the court to invoke one of the various remedies. Any of the others standing on their own would suffice, but this one alone will not be sufficient.

a) *Jurisdictional Bases under the UCCJEA*

Four jurisdictional tests are set forth in the UCCJEA to determine the propriety of the exercise of jurisdiction by any given state. Any one of these tests (but at least one), if met by the state attempting to exercise jurisdiction over the child custody dispute, will be sufficient to allow that state to go forward. There is no other basis upon which child custody jurisdiction can be exercised. Simply the presence of the parties or the children in the jurisdiction is insufficient, nor can the parties stipulate or consent to the state taking jurisdiction. The only manner in which a state may appropriately take jurisdiction over a child custody dispute is if it meets one of the four alternate tests set forth in the UCCJEA.[3]

The first such test is known as the *home state test*. Family Code section 3421(a)(1) provides that if, at the time the proceedings are commenced, California is the home state of the child in question, it is appropriate for the court to exercise jurisdiction under the UCCJEA and determine the child custody dispute. The child must be present (for example, California must have been the child's home state) for at least six months immediately preceding the date of filing the petition.

In the event the child was not present in the state for the entire six-month period immediately preceding the filing, but was absent from the state because of his or her removal (or retention) outside the state by a person claiming custody, then the period of time the child has been removed or inappropriately retained from the state will be included within the calculation of the six-month period. Temporary absences (holidays, vacations) will not defeat this six-month requirement.

Under the FPKPA, absolute priority is given to jurisdiction in the home state by allowing the exercise of jurisdiction on alternate bases ("significant connection" or "best interests") only when no other state has home state jurisdiction. The UCCJEA also extends this absolute preference to home state jurisdiction, unlike the former UCCJA. Under the UCCJA, this was merely one of four alternatives, any one of which could be used to satisfy the jurisdictional requirements in child custody matters. This declaration of absolute preference for home state jurisdiction found in the UCCJEA is but one example of the new law's attempt to achieve conformity with the FPKPA.

Application of this test is quite simple: Whenever two states (or other competing jurisdictions) assert jurisdiction in a custody dispute, the state that falls within the definition of home state as discussed above is the appropriate one to determine custody. As will be explained below, in the event one state satisfies one test under the UCCJEA and another state satisfies a different test under the UCCJEA, jurisdiction is appropriate in the state that exercised jurisdiction first. Under the FPKPA, however, even if the state exercising an alternate basis of jurisdiction does so first, home state jurisdiction will still be deemed appropriate.

The second test under the UCCJEA is found in section 3421(a)(2)(A) and (B) and is known as the *significant connection/substantial evidence test*. This Code section presumes that it is in the child's best interest for this state to assume jurisdiction provided the child and parents have a significant connection with the state and there is substantial evidence available in this state concerning the child's present or future care, protection, training, and personal relationships. The FPKPA, at 28 U.S.C. section 1738A(c)(2)(B), contains a similar provision, which is conditioned, however, on the *absence* of home state jurisdiction.

It has been determined that the purpose of the UCCJEA is to limit the exercise of jurisdiction rather than to expand it. As such, the significant connection test is construed very conservatively. In contrast to the personal jurisdiction requirements discussed earlier in this book, which contemplated *minimum* contacts with the state for the exercise of jurisdiction, the opposite is true in making determinations under the significant connection test: *maximum* contacts with the state are required rather than minimum. The factors examined when making determinations under this test include the length of time that the litigants have resided in the jurisdiction, the availability of evidence concerning the educational progress of the child, the relationship of the child to the community in which the court is located, and similar factors that revolve around the availability of significant and substantial evidence to facilitate a child custody determination following a full and complete examination of all relevant factors.

The third test contained in the new statutory scheme is a departure from that contained in the UCCJA. Under the UCCJA the third test was referred to as the *emergency protection of the child test*. Under the UCCJEA, however, this third test (found at Family Code section 3421(a)(3)) for jurisdiction reads as follows: "All courts having jurisdiction under paragraph (1) or (2) have declined to exercise jurisdiction on the ground that a court of this state is the more appropriate forum to determine the custody of the child under section 3427 or 3428."

The final basis upon which a state may exercise jurisdiction over a child custody situation is sometimes called *vacuum* or *default jurisdiction*. Simply stated, if no other state satisfies any of the other jurisdictional bases for assertion of child custody jurisdiction, and it is in the child's best interests, then the court in question may assume such jurisdiction. This provision is found in Family Code section 3421(a)(4). This statute has been interpreted to provide that if another state could exercise jurisdiction on one of the bases but determines that the state attempting to exert jurisdiction is the more appropriate forum to determine the custody issue, then the court may assume jurisdiction if it is believed to be in the best interests of the child. The child must, however, be physically present in the state attempting to exercise such jurisdiction.

Determination of jurisdiction under the vacuum jurisdiction test is a two-step process. For California to assert jurisdiction in this regard, the court must find that there is no other state that could exercise UCCJEA jurisdiction or that another state that could exercise UCCJEA jurisdiction has declined. The California court must also determine that it is in the best interests of the child to take jurisdiction. Assuming this two-part test is met, jurisdiction will be appropriate under this provision.

It is not uncommon for more than one state to satisfy multiple bases of jurisdiction under the UCCJEA. When this happens, determination must be made as to which state will be allowed to maintain the jurisdiction that it has previously asserted.

Jurisdiction in the context of an emergency related to the welfare and well-being of the subject child is also available under this statutory scheme. Family Code section 3424(a) provides that child custody jurisdiction is appropriate if "[a] court of this state has temporary emergency jurisdiction if the child is present in this state and the child has been abandoned or it is necessary in an emergency to protect the child because the child, or a sibling or parent of the child, is subjected to, or threatened with, mistreatment or abuse." Such threatened abuse includes circumstances in which the child's parent is a victim of domestic violence. The FPKPA contains a similar provision in 28 U.S.C. section 1738(A)(c)(2)(C), using the language "mistreatment or abuse." The full text of section 3424 is instructive in this area:

> (a) A court of this state has temporary emergency jurisdiction if the child is present in this state and the child has been abandoned or it is necessary in an emergency to protect the child because the child, or a sibling or parent of the child, is subjected to, or threatened with, mistreatment or abuse.
>
> (b) If there is no previous child custody determination that is entitled to be enforced under this part and a child custody proceeding has not been commenced in a court of a state having jurisdiction under Sections 3421 to 3423, inclusive, a child custody determination made under this section remains in effect until an order is obtained from a court of a state having jurisdiction under Sections 3421 to 3423, inclusive. If a child custody proceeding has not been or is not commenced in a court of a state having jurisdiction under Sections 3421 to 3423, inclusive, a child custody determination made under this section becomes a final determination, if it so provides and this state becomes the home state of the child.
>
> (c) If there is a previous child custody determination that is entitled to be enforced under this part, or a child custody proceeding has been commenced in a court of a state having jurisdiction under Sections 3421 to 3423, inclusive, any order issued by a court of this state under this section must specify in the order a period that the court considers adequate to allow the person seeking an order to obtain an order from the state having jurisdiction under Sections 3421 to 3423, inclusive. The order issued in this state remains in effect until an order is obtained from the other state within the period specified or the period expires.
>
> (d) A court of this state that has been asked to make a child custody determination under this section, upon being informed that a child custody

proceeding has been commenced in, or a child custody determination has been made by, a court of a state having jurisdiction under Sections 3421 to 3423, inclusive, shall immediately communicate with the other court. A court of this state which is exercising jurisdiction pursuant to Sections 3421 to 3423, inclusive, upon being informed that a child custody proceeding has been commenced in, or a child custody determination has been made by, a court of another state under a statute similar to this section shall immediately communicate with the court of that state to resolve the emergency, protect the safety of the parties and the child, and determine a period for the duration of the temporary order.

(e) It is the intent of the Legislature in enacting subdivision (a) that the grounds on which a court may exercise temporary emergency jurisdiction be expanded. It is further the intent of the Legislature that these grounds include those that existed under Section 3403 of the Family Code as that section read on December 31, 1999, particularly including cases involving domestic violence.

Just what does or does not constitute an "emergency" is broadly construed under the UCCJEA, unlike the UCCJA. Indeed, the UCCJEA does not define "mistreatment or abuse." But the Legislature has declared its intent to expand the grounds upon which a court may exercise temporary emergency jurisdiction, and it has also stated that those grounds shall include those that existed under the UCCJA, in particular cases arising out of instances of domestic violence. This expression of legislative intent is a significant departure from the earlier language of the cases interpreting the UCCJA's "emergency jurisdiction" provision narrowly, so as to apply only in cases of "imminent peril" to the child. Instances of child abuse and domestic violence are still within the penumbra of this statutory scheme, just as was the case under the UCCJA.

These temporary orders under the UCCJEA's emergency jurisdiction provisions are, however, just that: temporary. They will not ordinarily rise to the stature or, perhaps put more accurately, statutory authority as would otherwise be the case pursuant to original jurisdiction under the UCCJEA. If a custody order from some other state is already in effect at the time California exercises jurisdiction pursuant to a perceived emergency, those temporary orders will only remain in effect long enough to abate the emergency and allow the court of original jurisdiction to take over. These emergency orders are required to specify a period of time that the court considers appropriate to allow the party seeking the temporary order to obtain an order from the state having UCCJEA jurisdiction, with the temporary orders remaining in effect until this court of "original jurisdiction" issues its orders in this regard.

Section 3443 of the UCCJEA requires that California recognize a preexisting out-of-state custody order, provided said order was entered in compliance with the UCCJEA and FPKPA. Assuming that such out-of-state order is enforceable, the issue before the California court is whether it may modify the order entered by another state—not whether it may assert initial jurisdiction.

Statutorily, there can be no *concurrent* jurisdiction with the issuing state because the issuing state remains the state of appropriate jurisdiction (unless, of course, the child and all of the parties have moved away, at which time the issuing state would have *issuing jurisdiction* and the new state would also have jurisdiction). This doctrine of continuing jurisdiction is supported both in the UCCJEA and the FPKPA. It essentially provides that whatever state made the initial custody decree continues to maintain subject matter jurisdiction so long as at least one party to the litigation remains in that state, even when the children have moved from the state and established a jurisdictional basis consistent with some other state. Once the party who has remained in the initial state relocates from that state, however, such continuing jurisdiction ends.

Assume two states have exercised jurisdiction essentially at the same time. For example, the determination of jurisdiction under the home state test occurs at the time the action is filed and jurisdiction under the significant connection test occurs at the time the hearing is held; thus, it is possible that the home state appropriately takes jurisdiction and a significant connection state *also* appropriately takes jurisdiction. In this situation, the Act's intent to limit rather than expand jurisdictional conflicts provides resolution of this dispute in favor of the home state (in keeping with the UCCJEA's preference and the FPKPA's priority for home state jurisdiction). If the custody order to be modified is from another state, the California court must first determine whether that state continues to have jurisdiction to modify its own decree. If it does not, California may assert jurisdiction under the UCCJEA, assuming it fulfills at least one of the required jurisdictional bases.

If both states appropriately exercised jurisdiction, the general rule is that the first court to assert its jurisdiction (that is, issue an order) will be the state of continuing jurisdiction in that matter. This tends to create a situation of a jurisdictional determination being nothing more than a "race to the courthouse," which is generally frowned upon by the courts. In that regard, the notes to Civil Code section 5155 (the predecessor to the UCCJA) instruct that the statute is intended to apply only if (1) no other state has determined initial custody; (2) the state of the initial decree has declined to exercise its continuing jurisdiction; or (3) continuing jurisdiction has ended because all parties concerned have relocated to another state.

Family Code sections 3427 and 3428 give courts the opportunity to decline jurisdiction in a custody matter notwithstanding the fact that it would otherwise be appropriate under the UCCJEA. Grounds for this rejection of jurisdiction include inconvenient forum, unclean hands, and the existence of simultaneously pending proceedings.

Under the concept of *inconvenient forum*, if the court determines (either on its own motion or on the motion of one of the parties) that it is an inconvenient location to entertain the dispute, and the court makes a finding that some other location (or forum) is more appropriate to make the determination, California can decline to exercise its jurisdiction. For example, in Clark v. Superior Court, 140 Cal. Rptr. 709 (1977), the court determined that once the child had been living for five years in another state, jurisdiction was inappropriate in California—even though California exercised continuing jurisdiction under the UCCJEA because one of the parties remained in the state. The court based its decision on the fact that, for all practical purposes, California was no longer the most appropriate, or most convenient, forum. 73 Cal. App. 3d 298 (1977).

Some of the relevant factors in making this determination include how long it has been since the issuing state was the child's home state, whether another state has a closer connection with the child and family or witnesses, and whether substantial evidence concerning issues pertinent to child custody (the child's present care, protection, training, and personal relationships, and so on) is more readily available in some other jurisdiction. As a general rule, California will not apply this test unless there is in fact some other forum that is deemed to be more appropriate. There is no such limitation in the Code, however, and it is possible that even though no other state has taken jurisdiction over this issue or has presented itself as a contender for taking jurisdiction, California *could* decline to exercise jurisdiction under this doctrine, however unlikely that might be. This is, of course, a case-by-case determination made after examination of all relevant facts.

It should also be noted that if the home state test is satisfied in California due to a recent relocation, it will not override application of the doctrine of inconvenient forum if another jurisdiction is, for all practical purposes, the jurisdiction with the majority of facts and evidence pertinent to resolution of the dispute.

The next situation in which the court may choose to decline exercise of its jurisdiction typically concerns the refusal to render an initial custody decree if the person petitioning for the court to take jurisdiction has done something wrong (for example, kidnapped the child and relocated him to another state just to create home state jurisdiction in that state). This long-standing common law concept of equity wherein the courts have maintained the power to deny the request of someone who comes to the court asking for relief yet has manipulated the situation to the detriment of others and to their own benefit is known as the doctrine of *unclean hands.*

The final circumstance under which a court may decline to exercise otherwise appropriate UCCJEA jurisdiction is that in which there are proceedings currently pending in another state. Obviously, it would violate the letter and spirit of the UCCJEA if two states could exercise jurisdiction over the same child at the same time. Thus, if California is informed at any time during the course of its proceedings that another state is also exercising child custody jurisdiction in compliance with the UCCJEA, the California court must stay its proceedings and communicate with the other court to determine which court is a more appropriate forum. Of course, the reverse would be true as well: If the other state learns of California's appropriate exercise of jurisdiction, and that state has adopted the UCCJEA, then that court must contact the California judge to determine who should have jurisdiction.

One aspect of analysis that is of paramount importance in the context of UCCJEA (or, for that matter FPKPA) cases is that of "continuing exclusive jurisdiction" (CEJ). This concept is relatively simplistic on its face, but its importance cannot be overstated. Put simply, once a jurisdiction has laid claim to the determination of custody in a given matter (typically through a finding that it is the child's "home state"), that jurisdiction will hang onto that jurisdiction as long as at least one of the original parties remains in that jurisdiction. The issuing state will retain CEJ until the issuing state decides that there are no significant contacts and no substantial evidence, or the issuing state or the modifying state determines that the child and the parents have all moved away.

4. Definitions

a) *Legal and Physical Custody*

California Family Code sections 3011 et seq. establish the basic legislative understanding and instruction on the subject of determination of child custody and visitation. In the context of those sections, and those that follow, certain terms are used to describe both the legal and physical custodial arrangement imposed upon the parties (either through their agreement or by judicial fiat). These include references to legal custody and physical custody, and several variations upon that theme regarding joint and sole (primary) custody, which will be discussed below.

The concept of *legal custody* pertains to the right and responsibility of the legal custodian to make decisions relating to the child's health, education, and welfare. This is a broad grant and is liberally construed to include most of the significant decisions in the child's life. The reader is forewarned, however, that the grant of legal custody, in addition to the enormous responsibilities relative to raising children in general, carries with it certain legal consequences, which cannot be ignored by the party fighting to obtain such custody.

For example, Penal Code section 490.5(b) makes a parent who exercises legal custody over a child jointly and severally liable with the child for certain criminal activity of the minor child in the context of shoplifting or the theft of library books. Similarly, Civil Code section 1714.1 makes a parent who exercises legal custody and control over a minor liable for up to $10,000 in damages resulting from acts of the minor that caused death, physical injuries, property damage, or defacement of property with paint (that is, graffiti). There is also an attempt to expand criminal liability for a child's acts to include the parents on the theory that they have failed to supervise a child over whom they have been deemed to have legal custody: to wit, control and supervision of that child's actions. A potential legal custodial parent must understand this inasmuch as it may have an impact on whether or not that person desires to share in the legal custody of the minor child.

Physical custody refers to where the child will reside. The parent exercising physical custody over the child will generally be considered the *custodial parent* while the other parent is commonly referred to as the *visiting parent*.[4] An award of physical custody is often considered much more significant than an award of legal custody because the parent with whom the child is residing typically makes the lion's share of decisions pertaining to the child's health, education, and welfare. Indeed, the court will not contemplate an award of physical custody without a concomitant award of legal custody, either "sole" or held jointly with the other parent.

However, legal custody can be divided jointly between the two parties, while physical custody can be vested exclusively in one parent, leaving the other to be the visiting parent. In this situation, it is not uncommon for the visiting parent to find himself excluded from many decisions that one would ordinarily consider to be within the purview of legal custody. Under these circumstances, the visiting parent may find his status as joint legal custodian to be frustrating at best.

b) *Joint and Sole Custody*

Now that we have touched upon the concepts of legal and physical custody, we turn to the manner in which these concepts are applied to everyday custody orders. Family Code sections 3000 et seq. list certain terms pertinent to this discussion, including joint custody, sole physical custody, joint physical custody, sole legal custody, and joint legal custody. How are these terms used in everyday application?

Sole physical custody means that the child will primarily reside with and be supervised by one particular parent, while the other parent will simply visit. The right to make decisions regarding the child's residence, health, education, and welfare will be shared by both parents if an award of *joint legal custody* exists. A parent may be granted sole physical custody even if she is not granted exclusive legal custody.

Sole legal custody means that one parent alone is the decision-making parent when it comes to issues regarding the child's health, education, and welfare.

The concept of *joint custody* can be broken down into three basic categories: pure joint custody, joint legal custody, and joint physical custody. In *pure joint custody* neither parent exercises exclusive control over legal or physical custodial rights. All decisions relating to the child's health, education, and welfare are shared jointly by both parents, and the child does not reside at any one parent's house for significantly more than 50 percent of the time.

Under *joint legal custody*, parents equally share the rights and responsibilities to make decisions regarding their child's health, education, and welfare. They do not, however, necessarily share the right to the child's physical presence. Such a situation would contemplate that one parent is the physical custodial parent and the other is the visiting parent; however, both parents have equal decision-making power over significant issues affecting the child.

Joint physical custody contemplates that each parent has a significant period of physical custody. This is typically thought of as *shared physical custody*, and under these circumstances the child will roughly split her time between the parents' respective homes. For example, the child will live one week with Mother, the next week with Father, the next week with Mother, and so on. Other parents may choose to have their child live six months with one parent, then six months with the other parent. Either way, the concept is that the child's physical presence is divided roughly equally between the parents. Note that it is not essential to divide joint legal custody in this fashion. Note also that the child's time does not need to be divided absolutely equally between the parents under a joint physical custody order. Rather, all that is necessary is that the custody must be shared in such a way as to assure "frequent and continuing contact" of the child with both parents.

5. Statutory Considerations

California Family Code sections 3020 through 3031 establish the primary statutory scheme pertinent to resolving custody disputes. It has been referred to as the "heart" of custody legislation in California, and its sweeping grant of discretionary authority to the court makes virtually any inquiry fair game when it comes to resolving custody disputes. Family Code section 3020 sets forth the express public policy of the State of California as codified by the legislature in this area of law. Its content is worth restating here in its entirety:

(a) The Legislature finds and declares that it is the public policy of this state to assure that the health, safety, and welfare of children shall be the court's primary concern in determining the best interest of children when making any orders regarding the physical or legal custody or visitation of children. The Legislature further finds and declares that the perpetration of child abuse or domestic violence in a household where a child resides is detrimental to the child.

(b) The Legislature finds and declares that it is the public policy of this state to assure that children have frequent and continuing contact with both parents after the parents have separated or dissolved their marriage, or ended their relationship, and to encourage parents to share the rights and responsibilities of child rearing in order to effect this policy, except where the contact would not be in the best interest of the child, as provided in Section 3011.

(c) Where the policies set forth in subdivisions (a) and (b) of this section are in conflict, any court's order regarding physical or legal custody or visitation shall be made in a manner that ensures the health, safety, and welfare of the child and the safety of all family members.

Some of the words used in this Code section are worth highlighting. The legislature makes it clear that when it comes to awarding custody of a minor child a fundamental aspect of this public policy is to assure *frequent and continuing contact* of that child with *both parents*. This mandate may be disregarded only upon a finding that its compliance would be detrimental to the *best interests of the minor children.* "Frequent and continuing contact." "Both parents." "Best interests of the minor children." These are the fundamental concepts that control virtually every aspect of child custody litigation in California.[5]

By specific reference to Family Code section 3011, section 3020 grants the court authority to consider virtually all relevant factors concerning child custody. Section 3011 does, however, compel the court to examine four specific categories or factors bearing upon child custody:

- he health, safety, and welfare of the child
- any history of abuse by one parent against the child or against the other parent
- the nature and amount of contact with both parents
- the habitual or continual illegal use of controlled substances or habitual or continual abuse of alcohol by either parent

It is noteworthy that section 3011(b), which mandates inquiry into the history of abuse by one parent against the child, also indicates that a relevant factor pertinent to the child custody determination is the history of abuse by one parent against the other parent. It is not uncommon that the breakup of a family involving legal proceedings pertinent to custody of minor children is preceded by some form of serious dysfunction in that family. Such dysfunction quite often takes the form of abusive conduct by one parent toward the other parent. Often a combative parent will vent hostilities and anger upon his spouse, secure in the belief that such behavior will not necessarily impact upon his chances to obtain custody, inasmuch as he "loves his children" and would "never do anything to harm them." Such belief is misplaced. The history of abuse by one parent against the other parent is a significant factor in the court's eye in making determinations as to child custody, for reasons which this author hopes are obvious to the reader.[6]

There are also specific provisions requiring inquiry into allegations of substance abuse by either parent. Family Code section 3011 expands upon this requirement:

> (d) Before considering these allegations, the court may first require independent corroboration, including, but not limited to, written reports from law enforcement agencies, courts, probation departments, social welfare agencies, medical facilities, rehabilitation facilities, or other public agencies or nonprofit organizations providing drug and alcohol abuse services. As used in this subdivision, "controlled substances" has the same meaning as defined in the California Uniform Controlled Substances Act, Division 10 (commencing with Section 11000) of the Health and Safety Code.
>
> (e) (1) Where allegations about a parent pursuant to subdivision (b) or (d) have been brought to the attention of the court in the current proceeding, and the court makes an order for sole or joint custody to that parent, the court shall state its reasons in writing or on the record. In these circumstances, the court shall ensure that any order regarding custody or visitation is specific as to time, day, place, and manner of transfer of the child as set forth in subdivision (b) of Section 6323.

Family Code section 3040 describes the statutory order of preference with respect to the legislature's interpretation of the mandate of Family Code section 3011 (that is, making a custody award that is in the best interests of the minor child). This preference is expressed as follows:

> (a) Custody should be granted in the following order of preference according to the best interest of the child as provided in Sections 3011 and 3020:
>
> (1) To both parents jointly pursuant to Chapter 4 (commencing with Section 3080) or to either parent. In making an order granting custody to either parent, the court shall consider, among other factors, which parent is more likely to allow the child frequent and continuing contact with the noncustodial parent, consistent with Section 3011 and 3020, and shall not prefer a parent as custodian because of that parent's sex. The court, in its discretion, may require the parents to submit to the court a plan for the implementation of the custody order.

(2) If to neither parent, to the person or persons in whose home the child has been living in a wholesome and stable environment.

(3) To any other person or persons deemed by the court to be suitable and able to provide adequate and proper care and guidance for the child.

(b) This section establishes neither a preference nor a presumption for or against joint legal custody, joint physical custody, or sole custody, but allows the court and the family the widest discretion to choose a parenting plan that is in the best interest of the child.

Note that this Code section does not provide a breakdown as to how custody should be divided *between* parents. Rather, it simply states that custody should *first* be awarded to either parent (or, ostensibly, both parents, as the circumstances may allow). The Code does express preference for the parent who may be most likely to allow the other parent "frequent and continuing contact" with the child.

The Family Code also provides alternatives pertinent to custody in the event that the parents are not appropriate custodians of the children. However, this section 3041 makes it clear that the court *cannot* award custody to a person other than a parent, without the consent of the parents, until and unless it makes a finding "that granting custody to a parent would be detrimental to the child and that granting custody to a nonparent is required to serve the best interest of the child." Note that this is a two-prong test: The court must specifically find that awarding custody to the parent would be detrimental to the child *and* awarding custody to a nonparent would serve the mandate of Family Code section 3011 in the minor child's best interests. This is a difficult test to meet.

The determination is based upon all of the relevant factors and circumstances surrounding a particular case. In making the decision to award custody to a nonparent, the court will generally give greater consideration to keeping the child in the home in which the child has been living in a suitable and stable environment. The court will, of course, give serious consideration to the nomination of a guardian by a parent and will then look to willing family members before awarding custody to a complete familial stranger. That choice is, however, open to the court under the appropriate circumstances.

Interestingly, in an almost side note tenor, Family Code section 3042 debunks the myth prevalent in this society that there is a specific age at which a minor child can choose which of his or her parents will be the custodial parent. Family Code section 3042(a) provides: "If a child is of sufficient age and capacity to reason so as to form an intelligent preference as to custody or visitation, the court shall consider, and give due weight to, the wishes of the child in making an order granting or modifying custody or visitation."

Recently, the Family Code was amended to indicate that the wishes of children age 14 or older warrant special consideration, at least in regards to their custodial arrangements. (In August 2010 Family Code section 3042 was amended, with changes to take effect on January 1, 2012.) As amended, section 3042(c) states: "If the child is 14 years of age or older and wishes to address the court regarding custody or visitation, the child shall be permitted to do so, unless the court determines that doing so is not in the child's best interests. In that case, the court shall state its reasons for that finding on the record." Thus, a child age 14 or older has a statutory right to voice his opinion to the court regarding his custodial arrangement—subject of course to the court's determination that such action is in the child's best interests. Note that a child *under* 14 is not necessarily prohibited from voicing his opinion regarding custody to the court; section 3042(d) states: "Nothing in this section shall be interpreted to prevent a child who is less than 14 years of age from addressing the court regarding custody or visitation, if the court determines that is appropriate pursuant to the child's best interests."

There is an age at which a child may decide with whom he or she wishes to live: In California (for the time being at least), that age is 18 (that is, the date at which that child is no longer a minor). That is not to say that the child's wishes are ignored; the above-cited language makes it clear that they are not. However, the court must simply evaluate those wishes in accordance and in conjunction with all of the other evidence produced at the time of hearing on the custody issue.

As might be expected, the opinion of a teenage child will carry much greater weight with respect to this issue than that of a child under ten. It is generally thought that by the age of 12 a child can form and express an intelligent, reasoned opinion on the subject of with whom he or she wishes to live. Although the child does not have the unfettered decision-making power on this issue, the courts will start to give greater weight to the child's preference at this more than at any earlier age.

Along a similar vein, notwithstanding the court's policy of encouraging parents to arrive at their own child custody plan in order to bring them back into this decision making process as much as possible, parents' discretion is not without limitations. Family Code section 3011, which requires courts to assure that the best interests of the minor child are met, is of paramount importance in fashioning any custody order. It compels the court to review and approve a custodial plan proposed by the parents by their mutual agreement. That said, however, unless the parents provide a plan that contemplates the bizarre, the court will typically defer to the judgment of the parents in making these decisions. Most judges are reluctant to impose their will over that of a parent unless specific, articulable cause exists in the judge's opinion to reject the plan as not in the child's best interests. This preference for parenting plans arrived at by mutual agreement of the parents is actually codified in Family Code section 3040(b), which allows "the court *and the family* the widest discretion to choose a parenting plan which is in the best interest of the children."

Family Code section 3040(a) establishes the legislative preference to award custody to both parents jointly pursuant to section 3080 over and above custody in any other fashion. Family Code sections 3080 et seq. expand upon this concept and define the many permutations that this term "joint custody" can entail. Specifically, Family Code sections 3002, 3003, 3004, 3006, and 3007 set forth these definitions as follows:

> **section 3002:** "Joint Custody" means joint physical custody and joint legal custody.
>
> **section 3003:** "Joint Legal Custody" means that both parents shall share the right and responsibility to make the decisions relating to the health, education and welfare of a child.
>
> **section 3004:** "Joint Physical Custody" means that each of the parents shall have significant periods of physical custody. Joint physical custody shall be shared by the parents in such a way so as to assure a child of frequent and continuing contact with both parents.
>
> **section 3006:** "Sole Legal Custody" means that one parent shall have the right and responsibility to make the decisions relating to the health, education and welfare of a child.
>
> **section 3007:** "Sole Physical Custody" means that a child shall reside with and under the supervision of one parent, subject to the power of the court to order visitation.

Family Code section 3080 provides that upon mutual agreement of the parties to an award of joint custody, either in open court or by written stipulation, there shall exist a presumption affecting the burden of proof that joint custody is in the best interests of the minor child. This is not to say that one parent acting alone cannot *request* that the court enter an award of joint custody. Under those circumstances, there simply will be no presumption that such an award is in the best interests of the minor child. Assuming both parents make this request, however, there does exist such a presumption and the court is thus spared any further inquiry into compliance with section 3011 save and except for such inquiry as is necessary to implement the joint custody award.[7]

The implementation of a joint custody award is not, however, as easy as it may at first appear. Inasmuch as any aspect of joint custody[8] involves some form of cooperation between parents, this is not always the easiest thing to achieve in the context of splitting up a family. Indeed, cases dispositive on this issue have in essence determined that the inability of parents to cooperate with respect to the day-to-day decisions pertinent to their children makes a joint custody arrangement impractical at best and detrimental to the child's interests at worst. The court has a statutory directive to attempt to head these problems off as found in Family Code section 3083, which provides:

> In making an order of joint legal custody, the court shall specify the circumstances under which the consent of both parents is required to be obtained in order to exercise legal control of the child and the consequences of the failure to obtain mutual consent. In all other circumstances, either parent acting alone may exercise legal control of the child. An order of joint legal custody shall not be construed to permit an action that is inconsistent with the physical custody order unless the action is expressly authorized by the court.

Section 3084 expands upon this concept as follows:

> In making an order of joint physical custody, the court shall specify the rights of each parent to physical control of the child in sufficient detail to enable the parent deprived of that control to implement laws for relief of child snatching and kidnapping.

Even these sections, however, do not provide adequate assurance or instruction with regard to the implementation of a joint custody award. Theoretically, these statutes could provide (at least on the issue of legal custody) that the court's failure to specify any circumstances under which *mutual* consent is required is in essence a mandate that the party who exercises physical control of the child (assuming legal custody is jointly held) may unilaterally make decisions pertinent to the child's health, education, and welfare without input from the "non-controlling" parent; according to this interpretation, if the non-controlling parent does not agree with a decision made by the controlling parent, the non-controlling parent's redress is through the judicial system.

The bottom line is if custody is to be awarded jointly in any of its statutory permutations, parents must cooperate with each other when it comes to the child's medical care (including surgery, both emergency and elective), the child's education (and the parents' willingness to participate in that education), the child's religion (and the ability of the parents to arrive at an acceptable compromise in this area in the event they do not share similar religious beliefs), the child's residence, and other issues regarding the child's day-to-day life.

> If the court finds that joint custody is not in the best interests of the minor child, it must choose between the two parents in awarding custody. Statutorily, the best interests of the child continue to be the overriding public policy. When making the determination as to which of the two parents will be more appropriate as the custodial parent (either legal, physical, or both), the court must be vigilant to ensure that it is in full compliance with the mandate of Family Code section 3011. In this regard, there have been dozens of cases that have attempted to enumerate the various factors that the court must consider in arriving at its

decision. Of particular note, however, are In re Marriage of Carney, 24 Cal. 3d 725 (1979), and Burchard v. Garay, 42 Cal. 3d 531 (1986). Both of these cases contain an excellent discussion of the factors arising out of and pertaining to this type of determination. In its often-quoted decision, the *Carney* court offers this general overview of the essence of making this type of important decision: Contemporary psychology confirms what wise families have perhaps always known—that the essence of parenting is not to be found in the harried rounds of daily carpooling endemic to modern suburban life, or even in the doggedly dutiful acts of "togetherness" committed every weekend by well-meaning fathers and mothers across America. Rather, its essence lies in the ethical, emotional, and intellectual guidance the parent gives to the child throughout his formative years, and often beyond. The source of this guidance is the adult's own experience of life; its motive power is parental love and concern for the child's well-being; and its teachings deal with such fundamental matters as the child's feelings about himself, his relationships with others, his system of values, his standards of conduct, and his goals and priorities in life.

In *Carney*, Father had de facto custody of his sons from their infancy for five years. One year before trial, an accident left him with paralyzed legs and severely impaired use of his hands and arms. An expert testified on Father's behalf at the custody trial as to his successful parenting skills. Nevertheless the trial judge awarded custody to Mother, basing this decision largely on Father's disability. Interestingly, up until only a few days prior to trial, Mother had no physical contact with her sons for over five years, she had only minimal telephone and written contact, and she had failed to provide any child support. The Supreme Court reversed the trial court's ruling, finding that the trial judge had not properly considered whether Father's disability would have a substantial and lasting effect on the children. The court's thoughts in this context are worth quoting in their entirety:

> We do not mean, of course, that the health or physical condition of the parents may not be taken into account in determining whose custody would best serve the child's interests. In relation to the issues at stake, however, this factor is ordinarily of minor importance; and whenever it is raised—whether in awarding custody originally or changing it later—it is essential that the court weigh the matter with an informed and open mind.
>
> In particular, if a person has a physical handicap it is impermissible for the court simply to rely on that condition as prima facie evidence of the person's unfitness as a parent or of probable detriment to the child; rather, in all cases the court must view the handicapped person as an individual and the family as a whole. To achieve this, the court should inquire into the person's actual and potential physical capabilities, learn how he or she has adapted to the disability and manages its problems, consider

how the other members of the household have adjusted thereto, and take into account the special contributions the person may make to the family despite—or even because of—the handicap. Weighing these and all other relevant factors together, the court should then carefully determine whether the parent's condition will in fact have a substantial and lasting adverse effect on the best interests of the child. . . . [I]t has at last been understood that a boy need not prove his masculinity on the playing fields of Eton, nor must a man compete with his son in athletics in order to be a good father: their relationship is no less "normal" if it is built on shared experiences in such fields of interest as science, music, arts and crafts, history or travel, or in pursuing such classic hobbies as stamp or coin collecting. In short, an afternoon that a father and son spend together at a museum or the zoo is surely no less enriching than an equivalent amount of time spent catching either balls or fish.

In examining the factors enumerated both by the Code and the cases, several stand out. For example, Family Code section 3040 specifically precludes preference of one parent over the other simply on the basis of gender. Neither can race nor religion, in and of themselves, be the basis for accepting or rejecting a parent as the custodial parent of a minor child. Similarly, a parent's economic status will not be the determinative factor in the child custody arena. A parent's particular sexual preference will not necessarily brand him or her as an unsuitable custodial parent nor will a physical or mental handicap act in this fashion. Finally, a decision by one parent to cohabit (live in a nonmarital union with a lover) will not be deemed a per se basis for disqualification as a custodial parent. The focus is on the child's needs for emotional stability and the parent's ability to love the child and give the child ethical, emotional, and intellectual guidance.

Courts have considered the following factors, among others, in making custody and visitation awards:

- abuse of alcohol or drugs
- change in the child's residence
- the child's preference
- issues of nonmarital cohabitation
- conduct of the parents in general
- daycare issues
- history of domestic violence
- ethical and emotional guidance
- expert recommendations (child custody evaluators, mental health professionals, etc.)
- finances
- frequent and continuing contact
- frustration of visitation
- future relationships of the parents

- gender of the parents
- homosexuality/sexual orientation
- past criminal activity
- physical or emotional handicap
- psychological issues
- race and ethnicity issues
- religion
- schooling
- status quo
- unconventional lifestyle
- work-related issues

As has been stressed throughout this chapter, paramount in the court's consideration is the examination of what is in the best interests of the child. Even though none of the above-cited situations are necessarily grounds to disqualify a person from being a custodial parent, they can (and very often do) constitute relevant factors and circumstances, which must be examined as part of the child custody determination process. This examination is confined, however, only to a review of the extent to which, if at all, such a situation impacts on the best interests of the minor child. To the extent that the court makes a finding that any one of those factors will in fact operate against the best interests of the minor child, then such factor will play a role in the custodial decision making. The mere *existence* of such a factor, however, cannot so dictate the outcome of the custody determination.

The emphasis of the court in these circumstances is to provide stability and continuity of environment for the minor child. The case of Burchard v. Garay cited above recognized that stability, continuity, and a loving relationship are the most important criteria for determining a child's best interests. As such, there is an almost overriding preference of the courts to consider the existing status quo and to take great pains to preserve that status quo in making their custody determinations. Thus, an early determination of custody pending trial can be of utmost importance to a parent who ultimately desires to obtain an award of permanent custody.

6. Mediation and Conciliation[9]

Family Code sections 3160 et seq. establish the statutory scheme for the mediation of contested child custody and visitation disputes. The reader should note that the directive of these Code sections is *mandatory*. The parties do not have a choice as to whether to go to mediation. The Code is quite clear that in any contested custody matter "the court *shall* set the contested issue for mediation." Indeed, the failure of a parent to participate in this legislatively mandated mediation may operate to terminate that parent's right to be heard on the issue of custody.[10]

Section 3161 describes the purposes of mediation as follows: "(a) To reduce acrimony that may exist between the parties, (b) To develop an agreement assuring the child close and continuing contact with both parents that is in the best interest of the child, consistent with Sections 3011 and 3020, and (c) To effect a settlement of the issue of visitation rights of all parties that is in the best interest of the child." To fulfill these legislatively decreed goals, the statute conveys upon the mediator a rather broad range of authority. The mediator may meet and confer with the parties; meet with the children in question (if appropriate); exclude counsel from the proceedings if that is deemed by the mediator to facilitate the mediation process; report back to the court with recommendations on the issues of custody or visitation of the children; and suggest to the court that it should enter restraining orders.

The reader should note, however, that with the exception of appearing for, cooperating with, and participating in a mediation process, nothing that occurs in mediation is binding upon the parties. The mediator can only help to *affect an agreement* and is not empowered to make any orders on these issues of any kind. The entire process is designed to facilitate communication, cooperation, and agreement of the parties, nothing more.[11] The proceedings are held privately, and confidentiality is maintained with respect to the mediation sessions. The mediation process is provided free of charge through the superior court and is usually undertaken at the courthouse.

Along a similar vein, Family Code sections 3110 to 3116 provide for the preparation of a written confidential report by a "court-appointed investigator" (a probation officer, domestic relations investigator, or a court-appointed evaluator) based upon his custody investigation and evaluation. These Code sections empower the probation department of the superior court to conduct the investigation and to issue a report to the court. The report must be made available to the parties at least ten days before any hearing on the issue of custody. At that hearing, the court may receive the report in evidence upon the stipulation of all interested parties. The purpose of this report is to give the judge an objective evaluation of the situation coupled with the evaluator's recommendations on the subject to assist in the task of determining custody. This is very similar to the function provided by private child custody evaluators who will investigate the situation and testify in court as expert witnesses on the subject of child placement and custody.

The mediation process is an invaluable tool in arriving at a resolution of child custody disputes. A child custody evaluation report very often can tip the scales in favor of settling a bitterly disputed custody battle and can help parents who are at war with each other see, from an objective standpoint, the absolute necessity of working together ensure that the best interests of their children are maintained. Indeed, the Family Code compels mediation under circumstances where the court finds a "reasonable possibility of reconciliation" in cases involving minor children. Section 1841 provides as follows:

> If a petition for dissolution of marriage, for nullity of marriage, or for legal separation of the parties is filed, the case may be transferred at any time during the pendency of the proceeding to the family conciliation court for proceedings for reconciliation of the spouses or amicable settlement of issues in controversy in accordance with this part if both of the following appear to the court:
>
> (a) There is a minor child of the spouses, or of either of them, whose welfare may be adversely affected by the dissolution of the marriage or the disruption of the household or a controversy involving child custody.
>
> (b) There is some reasonable possibility of a reconciliation being effected.

7. Temporary Custody Awards; Modification of Custody Awards

As mentioned above, courts view the status quo of the minor child as one of the most fundamental determinative factors when approaching custody and visitation disputes. Coming from a family that has achieved the state of dysfunction resulting in divorce, the very foundation upon which a child's sense of security, family, and even identity are based is threatened. The breakup of the home, the relocation of one or both parents, and the potential relocation of the child can have devastating consequences upon the psyche of a young child. It is for this reason that courts stress above all things the ability to achieve and maintain stability in the child's environment. One of the best ways to achieve this stability is by maintaining the status quo.

It is absolutely imperative that a parent seeking permanent custody of his child take all steps necessary to obtain an award of temporary custody, or *pendente lite* (pending litigation) custody. Such a parent must begin work on the status quo as quickly as possible. The courts simply will not want to change the child's living situation once that situation has been established post-separation.[12] Therefore, the parent who is first able to establish a stable and loving living environment for the child is in a much better position than the other parent to obtain permanent custody.

Custody determinations are typically not made *ex parte*. Indeed, section 3064 of the Family Code clearly states:

> The court shall refrain from making an order granting or modifying a custody order on an ex parte basis unless there has been a showing

of immediate harm to the child or immediate risk that the child will be removed from the State of California. "Immediate harm to the child" includes having a parent who has committed acts of domestic violence, where the court determines that the acts of domestic violence are of recent origin or are part of a demonstrated and continuing pattern of acts of domestic violence.

However, if one party obtains a "kick out" order (that is, an order for exclusive use of the family home) against the other party, she is in effect establishing a de facto order of temporary custody *ex parte* inasmuch as she is now the parent with whom the child is exclusively living.[13] Thus, a parent seeking permanent custody should get an order to show cause concerning custody on file as soon as possible and file a request for exclusive use of the family home. If circumstances warrant a kick out order, the attorney representing the parent who wants permanent custody can take advantage of that fact to obtain the kick out order, thus also receiving an "order" for de facto custody.

In addition to favoring the status quo with regard to entering initial custody awards, the *modification* of a custody award can be even more difficult. Relatively recent case law makes it clear that once an initial custody determination has been made, a party seeking to change that custody determination must carry the burden of proof that a substantial change in circumstances has transpired that warrants reevaluating the earlier custody determination, thus making a new determination based upon the best interests of the child necessary. However, the desire to reevaluate the best interests of the child alone will not be sufficient to warrant a change in custody. A "substantial change of circumstances" must also be shown before the change will be warranted, notwithstanding the fact that such a change would be in the best interests of the minor child.[14]

There are several situations in which the court will consider whether a sufficient change in circumstances has transpired to warrant the reopening of the initial custody determination. One of the most common situations is that of the custodial parent desiring to relocate to another area of the state or country and take the minor child with her. This will of course have the effect of seriously curtailing (if not essentially destroying) the noncustodial parent's visitation rights. Under these circumstances, the noncustodial parent may very well request that the court reevaluate the original custody determination on the basis that a change in circumstances has occurred (or is about to occur), namely the anticipated move.

Another situation that may give rise to a finding of a change in circumstances is a marked change in the child's performance at school. Sometimes even the passage of time may be sufficient, provided it is coupled with some other significant effects of that passage of time. The remarriage of a custodial (or noncustodial) parent may also provide a basis for a finding of changed circumstances, but this is a factual determination made on a case-by-case basis. It is easy to see, however, how almost any event or factor, depending upon its impact on the minor child, can potentially rise to the level of constituting a change in circumstances.

The case of Burchard v. Garay, 42 Cal. 3d 531 (1986), essentially recognized this standard of a required change in circumstances in order to modify an existing custody arrangement, but in a somewhat roundabout manner. In *Burchard*, a three-year-old child had been raised from birth by Mother. Although Father initially denied paternity, he later supported and visited with Child. When Child was almost two years old, both parties filed motions seeking exclusive custody. Father contended, among other things, that Mother had interfered with his visitation. With no prior custody order, the trial court awarded custody to Father primarily due to his superior financial condition and the presence of his current wife, who could care for Child in their home as opposed to Mother's reliance on daycare since she worked, and also on Mother's prior frustration of visitation. On appeal, Mom argued that the trial court committed reversible error when, before ordering the change in custody (from Mom to Dad), it did not require proof of a change in circumstances from the time the current custody scenario had commenced.

The Supreme Court held that when there has been no prior judicial determination on the issue of custody, evidence of a change in circumstances is not required before modifying a preexisting custodial scheme that has been in effect without a court order:

> We conclude that [the changed circumstance rule] cannot apply. The rule requires that one identify a prior custody decision based upon circumstances then existing which rendered that decision in the best interest of the child. The court can then inquire whether alleged new circumstances represent a significant change from preexisting circumstances, requiring a reevaluation of the child's custody. Here there is no prior determination; no preexisting circumstances to be compared to new circumstances. The trial court has no alternative but to look at all the circumstances bearing upon the best interests of the child.

The Court continued, adding that although a change in circumstances need not be proven in the absence of a prior custody order, the benefit to the child of a stable custodial arrangement cannot be ignored:

> [I]n view of the child's interest in stable custodial and emotional ties, custody lawfully acquired and maintained for a significant period will have the effect of compelling the noncustodial parent to assume the burden of persuading the trier of fact that a change is in the child's best interest. That effect, however, is different from the changed-circumstance rule, which not only changes the burden of persuasion but also limits the evidence cognizable by the court.

The *Burchard* court also emphasized the need, when the changed-circumstances rule did apply, for proof of both changed circumstances *and* proof that change of custody was in the best interests of the child:

> In deciding between competing parental claims to custody, the court must make an award "according to the best interests of the child"[citation]. This test, established by statute, governs all custody proceedings. [Citation.] The changed-circumstance rule is not a different test, devised to supplant the statutory test, but an adjunct to the best-interest test. It provides, in essence, that once it has been established that a particular custodial arrangement is in the best interests of the child, the court need not reexamine that question. Instead, it should preserve the established mode of custody unless some significant change in circumstances indicates that a different arrangement would be in the child's best interest. The rule thus fosters the dual goals of judicial economy and protecting stable custody arrangements.

Although this decision was met with some trepidation by the family law community when it was issued, as a practical matter it does little to alter existing law. It recognizes, for example, that emphasis must be placed on maintaining the status quo and on acting in the best interests of the child in establishing custody. It simply refuses to apply the change in circumstances rule to a de facto custody arrangement, deferring instead to a more detailed analysis of the situation in cases where there is no prior court order—probably a good idea in any event. And, by reaffirming the importance of a stable custody situation, the Supreme Court placed the burden on the party seeking to modify that arrangement to show not only that, everything being equal, the child would be better off with him but that the change would be beneficial enough to offset the disruption caused by the modification of custody. As a practical matter, if one can meet this burden, most likely one could have met the changed circumstances burden as well.

The change in circumstances rule has been employed in many cases to frustrate the desires of an unusually combative parent to continually harass and annoy the other parent (and, unfortunately, the children) with repeated requests for a reevaluation of the custody order. It is a difficult decision to make in the first place, and the court is reluctant to reopen the issue every time one of the parents decides that such a reopening is appropriate. This would entirely defeat the court's overriding interest in establishing stability for the minor child and, perhaps even more important, *maintaining* that stability.[15]

In the general "back and forth" between the requirement of a change in circumstances prior to a change in custody versus maintenance of the status quo, 2000 saw some interesting and instructive decisions. One of the more recent decisions comes to us from the Appellate Court and involves a thorough discussion of most of the more important aspects of this area of the law. In Lester v. Lenane, 84 Cal. App. 4th 536 (2000), the court was presented with the following general facts: A baby was conceived when a wealthy, married businessman from Florida who had business and family ties in California spent two nights with an unmarried woman who lived in California. While still pregnant, the mother filed an action seeking child custody and support for the unborn child. The father sought physical custody of the child in Florida. The child was born premature and the mother commenced breast-feeding. Shortly after the birth, the trial court adopted a mediator's recommendation that the father have one hour of visitation per day as a *pendente lite* custody order. After a court-appointed psychologist recommended that the father receive sole physical custody, the trial court ordered increased visitation with the father. At trial, psychologists retained by the mother criticized the court-appointed psychologist's report.

The trial court awarded primary physical custody to the mother and entered judgment accordingly. The court was faced with the conflict between adherence to a standard of stability and status quo of the minor child versus an examination of changes in the child's life as he grew as constituting a change of circumstances from the initial orders, thus warranting a review of the prior custody orders. Interestingly, this father (having the financial means to do so) sought judicial intervention at virtually every phase of this young child's life, starting when he was an infant and continuing virtually unabated through kindergarten. The court also discussed issues of gender bias and frustration of visitation as they were alleged to be related to this determination. Although lengthy, the timeliness of this opinion, coupled with its detailed and thorough discussion and analysis of the law in this area as well as the procedural aspects of custody litigation makes it essential reading for the student of this subject. It also provides an excellent discussion and recitation of the manner in which these cases are presented to the court from an evidentiary basis.

One of the fundamental issues dealt with by the *Lester* court centered upon the court's adherence to notions of stability and maintenance of the status quo in determining the best interests of a minor child in this context of visitation and modification of custody, as opposed to recognition of the continuing changes in a child's life as they occur over time, and a recognition of these changes in making these determinations. These issues were raised by Dad almost immediately upon learning of the pregnancy, resulting in the judge's decision that these determinations were premature. Once the baby was born, Dad requested a "bird nesting" order. This order contemplated the baby staying in one house, while the parents moved in and out in accordance with their custodial time. The court rejected this plan, and instead ordered a custody evaluation. Father was opposed to this plan because it contemplated delays in this determination, delays that inevitably work against the noncustodial parent, since they are part and parcel of the creation of the status quo.

Thereafter, a trial was held that amounted in no small way to a "battle of the experts," with Dad's expert recommending a custodial plan that contemplated significant time with Father, and Mom's expert recommending essentially sole physical custody with Mother during the child's first several months of life. This refers to Father's arguments against just this type of custodial arrangement on the grounds that it constitutes little more than "gender bias" and should thus be rejected by the court. At trial, the court awarded primary physical custody to Mom. On appeal, the appellate court affirmed this ruling, based on what it believed to be two "simple" facts: First, Mother intended to breast-feed the baby,[16] and second, the court was concerned about unnecessary transportation of a newborn baby. Although the court dealt with these issues in an apparently rather straightforward manner, this case has opened the door for further argument and examination on a variety of factors that are dispositive of issues relating to custody and visitation.

Montenegro v. Diaz, 26 Cal. 4th 249 (2001) provides an excellent discussion of the concepts involved in resolving the conflict between the best interests of the child rule and the change in circumstances rule. In *Montenagro*, Father, who had been an aggressive litigant in the arena of custody over his son,[18] sought yet another opportunity to change custody from the child's mother to him. He based this attack on allegations that Mother was frustrating his access to the child.[19] This case shows how these issues are raised and sometimes blown out of proportion by the litigants. The trial court found that Father's allegations of frustration of visitation were well founded, and determined that, based thereon, it would be in the best interests of the child that custody be changed from Mother to Father. Not unexpectedly, Mother appealed. The appellate court held that there must first be a change of circumstances present before a modification/ change in custody as was requested by Father could be awarded. Finding that no such change of circumstances had been shown, the appellate court reversed the trial court. Perhaps most interesting was the appellate court's finding that Mother's frustration of visitation (which they apparently believed was taking place) was not a change in circumstances, because the evidence showed that she had been frustrating father's visitation since the child's birth.

On these facts, the California Supreme Court unanimously reversed the appellate court, holding that the trial court correctly applied the best interest standard instead of the change in circumstances rule. The court found that the parties' prior stipulations did not constitute "final decrees" to which the change in circumstances rule applies. Specifically, the stipulations did not unambiguously state that they were final judgments, and it was not clear that the minute orders confirming the stipulations were final; further, the parties' conduct strongly indicated that they did not intend for the minute orders to be final custody judgments. In essence, the court stated that a stipulated custody order should not be considered a final judicial custody order in regards to the change in circumstances rule unless the parties have given clear, affirmative indications that they intended such an outcome.

The State Supreme Court ultimately did not reach the issue of whether the change in circumstances rule should be reevaluated. It did state that the rule should be flexible and able to accommodate children's changing needs. In addition, the court drew on its earlier decisions (including Buchard v. Garay, 42 Cal. 3d 531 (1986)) in stating that the change in circumstances rule is not intended to displace the best interests of the child test; rather, the tests should be applied in conjunction with each other. The court concluded by advising that in order to encourage judicial economy and protect the stability of custody arrangements, once the court determines that a specific custody arrangement is in the child's best interest, the court should maintain that arrangement unless a change in circumstances demonstrates that a new custody arrangement is in the child's best interests.

One would think that the court would have taken this opportunity to "soften" the application of the change in circumstances rule, since to do so would require adherence to a determination of the child's best interests, a concept that makes intrinsic sense in any event. However, the change in circumstances rule is one that has been with us for nearly 30 years and been consistently upheld. Nevertheless, the landscape in this arena is rapidly changing. More and more courts are recognizing the role of both parents in the bonding and raising of children. Under the appropriate factual circumstances, it is not hard to envision a court awarding a 50/50 timeshare of a newborn infant. Time will tell how this issue will ultimately be resolved. It is this author's opinion, however, that the most important determination in this context is that of the best interests of the child. Nothing more, nothing less.

Summary

One of the most litigated aspects of this sub-area of family law is general custody litigation. Perhaps the most difficult thing for divorcing parents to do is accept less than "full time" contact with their children. However, in circumstances of dissolution and legal separation (and others involving children), that is exactly what must be done. Of paramount concern to the court in making a custody determination is making an order that will be in the minor's best interests, and one that will promote the statutorily decreed mandate that children have "frequent and continuing" contact with *both* parents. This determination, both as to custody and visitation, is left up to the sound discretion of the trial court, guided by the various factors set out in the Code.

Custody and visitation disputes are the subject of both mediation and conciliation procedures, which are designed to help parents work together to formulate a plan for the custody and visitation of their children, and also to ease some of the burdens an already congested court system is experiencing. From a jurisdictional perspective, interstate as well as intrastate custody battles are governed by the Uniform Child Custody Jurisdiction and Enforcement Act. This Act is a set of laws, enacted in substantially similar form throughout all 50 states and various territories of the United States, the purpose of which is to provide uniformity and predictability in the resolution of these disputes.

Key Terms

The following is a list of key terms and phrases that you should be able to define and use in context. Only then will you have demonstrated a command of the material in this chapter.

- Uniform Child Custody Jurisdiction and Enforcement Act
- Federal Parental Kidnapping Prevention Act
- continuing exclusive jurisdiction
- home state test
- significant connection; substantial evidence test
- emergency protection of the child test
- vacuum jurisdiction test
- legal custody
- physical custody
- sole v. joint custody

Questions for Discussion

1. Discuss the various bases considered by the court in making an award of custody and visitation.
2. What are the jurisdictional bases described by the Uniform Child Custody Jurisdiction and Enforcement Act? Discuss and give an example of each one in operation.
3. Compare and contrast legal custody and physical custody.
4. Define, compare, and contrast sole and joint custody.
5. What are the factors considered by the court when making custody determination? What are the fundamental concerns of the court in making a determination of custody?
6. List the factors that the court cannot consider when making a child custody determination.

ENDNOTES

1. Inasmuch as this text concentrates on the Family Code, that will be the focus of this discussion relative to custody and visitation.

2. It should also be noted that the entire statutory scheme of allowing for nonparent rights in this context has been thrown into question by the United States Supreme Court decision in Troxel v. Granville, discussed later in this book.

3. The reader must note that these jurisdictional tests are determinative for an initial custody award. In a situation where a jurisdiction is being asked to modify an out-of-state custody order, additional tests must also be met.

4. Note, however, that the term "visiting parent" is being rapidly usurped in the statutes with the concept of that parent possessing "secondary custody."

5. Historically, the mandate of former Civil Code §4600 (the predecessor to Family Code §3020) was applied to virtually all proceedings involving child custody. Such is no longer the case. Specifically, juvenile court dependency, guardianship, and parental termination proceedings expressly preempt this section in custody disputes being decided in those forums. In those circumstances the legislature has provided specific statutes dealing with these custody matters. Probate Code §§1500 et seq. control in guardianship proceedings, while Welfare and Institutions Code §§300 et seq. have application in juvenile dependency proceedings. Invariably, these Code sections tend to be somewhat more restrictive in regard to the court's discretion to make a custody award than Family Code §3020. This is fundamentally due to the nature of those proceedings. Very often they arise as a result of grave consequences involving child abuse, child abandonment, and the like, wherein there is virtually a prima facie finding that the family unit as a whole has become seriously dysfunctional. A review of the child custody statutes found in the Family Code makes it clear that it is the desire of the legislature to impose a statutory scheme of child custody determination that will approximate an unbroken, fully functional family as much as possible.

6. The court is primarily interested in placing children in stable, loving, nurturing environments. Such environments usually do not include individuals who abuse others, including a spouse or co-parent.

7. In other words, before a court makes a custody order it must meet certain tests to ensure that the order fulfills the requirements of the Code. One of those tests is the specific finding that joint custody is, in fact, in the child's best interests. This is a question of fact to be decided by the judge and for which specific reasons must be stated. The judge cannot simply declare that joint custody is in the child's best interests. The judge must also explain why that statement is true.
    Per this Code section, however, if both parents request an order of joint custody, the inquiry ends right there. The law establishes a presumption that the best interests of the child will be met, thus making it unnecessary for the judge to list the reasons in support of this finding. Of course, if both parents do not join in a request for joint custody, there is no presumption and, if the judge is going to make such an award anyway, the reasons for that order must then be listed.

8. "Pure" joint custody: All major decisions as well as the child's residence are shared equally; joint "physical" custody: the child's residence is shared equally; and joint "legal" custody: important decisions pertinent to the child are shared between the parents.

9. The subject of mediation and conciliation is discussed in detail in Chapter 8. Their basic concepts are discussed in this section in general only.

10. Mediation is also mandatory for issues arising out of or pertaining to visitation. It is not simply reserved for the resolution of custody disputes.

11. This "benign" nature of mediation may be changing a bit, however. For years, judges have tended to place a good deal (if not too much) weight on the opinion of the mediator in this context. This has taken the next step, however, with the advent of "reporting" and "non-reporting" jurisdictions. In some counties (for example, Ventura), the court directs that the mediators shall formally report to the judge and make themselves available for questioning as to their thoughts and recommendations following the conclusion of the mediation process. Other counties, such as Los Angeles, are not "officially" reporting jurisdictions, but it is leaning that way in the context of the so-called "fast track" custody evaluation. This is an evaluation undertaken by the court-appointed mediator at the courthouse, typically followed by a court session at which time the mediator shall appear and testify on his thoughts and opinions.

12. That is assuming that such a situation is functioning well.

13. This is not to say that an *ex parte* custody order is impossible to obtain. Quite the contrary. Family Code §§6321 and others make provision for an *ex parte* order granting a parent temporary custody of the minor child. Such custody orders are typically dependent upon a showing of immediate harm to the child or an immediate risk that the child will be removed from the jurisdiction. Unless those factors are present, it is unlikely that the court will simply grant an award of temporary custody on an *ex parte* basis.

14. As a practical matter, it is most unlikely that a court would deny a change in custody simply on the grounds that there was not a sufficient change in circumstances to warrant the change if all the other findings pointed to the fact that such a change would be in the best interests of the minor child.

15. A more detailed discussion of the availability of temporary orders and the procedures related thereto is found in Chapter 6 of this book.

16. Somewhat of a "de facto" gender bias, but one that neither the court nor the parties could do anything about. This author perceives this as an issue that will be revisited by the appellate courts in the future as there is now authority for this issue being seriously considered as one of the factors weighing on "stability" in an infant's life.

17. Put charitably.

18. An otherwise appropriate basis on which to seek a modification of custody, or so it would seem.

CHAPTER 4

Child Visitation

CHAPTER OVERVIEW

In this chapter we continue our discussion of the relationship between parents and their children, focusing on matters related to the custody that a child spends with each parent, typically referred to as *visitation*. Concepts related to interference with custodial and visitation rights are also explained. The reader should note that issues related to children of same-sex relationships will be raised in the context of registered domestic partnerships and same-sex marriages as presented Chapter 11 of this book.

Note that it is intended that this chapter will be read in conjunction with Chapters 2 and 3 since these all bear on the parent-child relationship.

A. Child Visitation

Family Code section 3100 mandates that whenever a custody order pertinent to section 3080 is made, "the court *shall* grant reasonable visitation rights to a parent unless it is shown that the visitation will be detrimental to the best interest of the child." The use of the word "shall" makes it clear that visitation must be ordered. Assuming that visitation is not detrimental to the best interests of the child, the noncustodial parent will be allowed such visitation as is deemed "reasonable" under the circumstances, keeping in mind that the Code mandates as much contact with both parents as is reasonably practical. This is not to say that visitation under the Family Code is completely unfettered: quite the contrary. Family Code section 3100(b) provides the court the authority to order that such visitation be supervised or monitored by a third person so as to ensure that the visiting parent is not in a position to harm or abuse the child or take such actions as might deprive the custodial parent of his custodial rights. The Code in general provides that all orders made in this regard should be tempered by a finding of what is reasonable given the circumstances.

B. Visitation Plans

The Code is basically silent on the specifics of a visitation plan, deferring instead to the concept of "reasonable visitation" to the noncustodial parent. As might be expected, the courts have wide discretion in interpreting and applying this mandate. The fundamental requirement in this regard, however, is the instruction of Family Code section 3020 to ensure that the children maintain "frequent and continuing contact" with both parents. This has generally been interpreted by the courts to contemplate that "reasonable visitation" is the maximum possible visitation time available to the noncustodial parent, with the proviso that such visitation must be in the best interest of the minor child and must not interfere with the custodial parent's time with that child. The ideal, of course, is for a 50/50 split of time. However, to the extent that this would interfere in the child's development or schooling, or provide similar obstacles to establishing stability and continuity in the child's life, the goal of a 50/50 split is not artificially imposed for the sake of achieving mathematical equality of time.

One case has established what many judges and lawyers have adopted as the standard, basic visitation order, sometimes called a *Freeman order*, named after the judge who created it. That order contemplates visitation by the noncustodial parent as follows:

1. alternating weekends from Friday at 6:00 p.m. to Sunday at 6:00 p.m.;
2. one mid-week dinner (or sometimes overnight) visit;
3. equal division of holidays (for example, father gets the child for Thanksgiving in even-numbered years, mother has the child during odd-numbered years, and so on as to the other holidays);
4. two uninterrupted weeks during the summertime for each parent; and,
5. equal division of school vacations (Christmas and spring week, for example).

According to the Freeman plan, the noncustodial parent has the child approximately 20 percent of the time. This schedule of visitation is not carved in stone, however, and the parties and the court have great flexibility in working with this schedule as an initial framework in arriving at an ultimately workable (and reasonable) visitation schedule. In fact, in recent years the trend has been to ensure greater visitation for the noncustodial parent and thus the Freeman order has for all practical purposes moved from the realm of being the standard order to being the starting point for discussion when creating a visitation plan.

Certain noteworthy situations frequently arise in the context of a noncustodial parent visiting with his child. For example, what kind of decision-making power does the noncustodial parent possess when the child is in that person's care and custody? The answer to that question is rather simple: He possesses such decision-making power as is consistent with the award of legal custody, the custodial parent's award of physical custody, and as is in the best interest of the child. On more subjective topics, such as religious preferences, the visiting parent is free to instruct the minor child on the religion of that parent's choice when that child is in the noncustodial parent's physical care and custody, subject again to the admonition that the practices observed during the visitation period cannot be detrimental to the best interests of the child.[1]

C. Visitation Restrictions

There are a variety of circumstances in which a restriction can and should be placed on visitation, ranging from financial misconduct to domestic violence. Some of the areas in which the California courts have expressed an opinion or guidance are discussed below. As might be expected, the party seeking to restrict visitation has the burden of proof on this point, and visitation will not be restricted or denied absent finding a good cause. Further, as might also be expected, the inquiry into any restriction on visitation has at its core a "common sense" approach to the analysis, with the essence of the inquiry being the determination of the appropriateness of making the restriction, with a desire to provide as minimal a restriction as possible. In this regard, the appellate court, in reversing a trial court's termination of a father's visitation (following his prior lack of visitation and payment of support), stated:

> [i]n this type of proceeding the best interest of the child must also be given paramount consideration. [Citations.] However, it must also be remembered that the father has a right, subservient only to the best interest of the child, to visit reasonably with his child. "Such right ensues from parenthood and should not be denied without cause."[Citations.][¶] Because of

the importance of the parent-child relationship and the likely benefits to the child as it grows up from reasonable (and, where necessary, supervised or restricted) visits with the parent who does not have custody, the courts should not deprive such a parent of all visitation privileges absent a clear showing that any contact with such parent would be detrimental to the child. It would follow that any diminution of visitation privileges contained in the interlocutory and final divorce decrees should be no greater than necessary to serve the best interests of the child. Where it is possible to serve such interests by an order providing for less than full deprivation of visitation privileges, the court should make such an order and no more.

When appropriate and necessary, however, the appellate court will not hesitate to uphold a visitation restriction. For example, in a piece of litigation that seems destined to haunt the legal system for years to come, one court has ruled that a parent's financial misconduct will provide the basis for restricting his visitation, primarily because the court found that such misconduct evidenced a potential for violating the custody orders and running away with the children.

In re The Marriage of Economou (*Economou I*), 224 Cal. App. 3d 1466 (1990), the husband had amassed an enormous amount of community wealth. He attempted to hide this wealth and repeatedly violated the trial court's discovery orders regarding the parties' substantial community property, In addition, he misappropriated and hid millions of dollars in assets outside the country. The trial court originally granted the husband extensive periods of physical custody with the parties' two sons. But when the court learned of his financial escapades, it modified its order, to give sole custody to the wife and severely restrict the husband's visitation. For example, the court required that in order to exercise his visitation, the husband needed to surrender his passports during periods of visitation. The trial court stated that it believed the husband's devious attempts to deprive his wife of her share of the community property was likely to carry over with regard to his children. He had a Greek passport, owned real property in Greece, and transferred millions of dollars out of the country. His wife testified that he had threatened to take the children to Greece and not return them. The court found Mr. Economou to be "deceitful, untrustworthy and likely to detain the children." It stated: "[Husband] cannot be trusted; his word is worthless. He is more than a cad and a bounder, he is a con and a thief. . . . " It should be noted that it is not often that the court will go to these lengths in its opinion; however, Mr. Economou presented an interesting (and, more important, provable) insight into the lengths one may go to gain an advantage in a nasty divorce. The reader is invited to read this opinion (and the many others Mr. Economou's dissolution has spawned) in its entirety for a cold, harsh glimpse into the level of dissolution-related hostilities sometimes encountered in this practice.

Other examples of judicial inquiry into this area include restriction requests based on religion (typically denied); homosexuality/lifestyle (typically denied); transportation disputes (usually "fine tuned" to bring into line with common sense; supervised visitation (typically granted in situations where harm to the child is likely, such as domestic violence; sexual assault/molestation; and likelihood to flee the jurisdiction with the child, etc.). Again, this is essentially a "common sense" analysis, balanced with the rights of the parents and best interests of the child.

D. Interference with Custody and Visitation

Interference with custodial and visitation rights can take shape in many ways. One parent, for example, frustrated with the court orders, or the entire process leading up to those orders, may take it upon himself to leave the state, taking the minor child with him. However this may appear on its face, there is little more one individual can do to another that carries with it the same devastation of depriving her of contact with and supervision over her children. Of course, not every act of interference with custody rises to the level of parental kidnapping, but that event is always a concern in situations involving troublesome custody awards. Similarly, it is not at all unusual for a custodial parent, frustrated over nonpayment of child support or some other aspect of the relationship with the former spouse, to extract revenge or gain leverage over that person by withholding visitation. Either way, these are serious concerns shared by tens of thousands of parents throughout this country.

Along the same lines are cases dealing with the problem of visitation by one parent unhappy with the custody or visitation award. This typically involves a custodial parent who, having difficulty securing child support from the noncustodial parent, unilaterally takes it upon herself to deny visitation until the noncustodial parent comes current on the child support payments. Again, this may seem like a logical approach to the situation since the logic underlying its implementation is rather simple and straightforward: "If he does not want to pay for the care of the child, then why should he be allowed to visit with the child?" This logic is flawed, however, and this attitude is no less insidious than an outright act of parental kidnapping. It is simply more passive-aggressive.

Another situation arises when the minor child himself, rather than a custodial parent, is reluctant to visit. Under these circumstances, the extent to which the noncustodial parent may extract some form of "punishment" against the custodial parent for non-delivery of the child for his regularly scheduled visitation generally depends upon the child's age. If the child is a teenager or poses some other actual physical impediment to the custodial parent's ability to exercise sufficient control over that child to ensure that visitation proceeds as scheduled, then the custodial parent will generally not be held accountable for the child's failure and refusal to visit.

On the other hand, if it is a relatively small child over whom the custodial parent continues to exercise substantial parental control, the custodial parent will not escape liability for refusing to permit visitation. In fact, a custodial parent who refuses visitation when the child is otherwise inclined to visit runs a very serious risk of losing custody of that child inasmuch as it is the express policy of the legislature to place physical custody of the child with the parent who is more likely to allow visitation to take place.

Sometimes interference with custodial or visitation rights occurs innocently. For example, when a custodial parent desires to relocate to another area for a legitimate reason: to obtain a better job or a better environment for herself and her children. Sometimes the decision is completely outside the parent's control. For example, he is transferred to a new location by his employer and the real decision is to move or lose his job. In these difficult economic times these are concerns not easily put aside.

There is little doubt that, as a general rule, the custodial parent has a right to change the child's residence to the extent that the parent deems either necessary or in the best interests of the child. This right is not unfettered, however, and is subject to the court's authority to prevent relocation if it would not serve the child's best interests or if it would prejudice or adversely impact upon the rights of the noncustodial parent. As is discussed later, one of the automatic restraining orders that goes into effect upon filing a petition in a Family Code case and serving it on the other side is an order restraining both parents from taking the minor children out of California without the written consent of the other or a prior court order. As such, restraints on relocation and removal are not only common in family law proceedings, in the circumstances described above they are automatic.

E. Relocation

When faced with a relocating custodial parent, the court generally will require that parent to give the other parent a minimum amount of notice prior to the anticipated move. This notice gives the noncustodial parent an opportunity to go to court and seek orders restraining the relocation of the child. This concept is codified in Family Code section 3024, which provides that:

> In making an order for custody, if the court does not consider it inappropriate, the court may specify that a parent shall notify the other parent if the other parent plans to change the residence of the child for more than 30 days, unless there is prior written agreement to the removal. The notice

shall be given before the contemplated move, by mail, return receipt requested, postage pre-paid, to the last known address of the parent to be notified. A copy of the notice shall also be sent to that parent's counsel of record. To the extent feasible, the notice shall be provided within a minimum of 45 days before the proposed change of residence so as to allow for time for mediation of a new agreement concerning custody. . . . [2]

The so-called "move away" cases have gone back and forth on allowing or disallowing a move by the custodial parent with the children for over 20 years. While the best interests of the child has always been at the heart of the discussion, each case seemed to put its own spin on this issue and, as cases were distinguished but not necessarily overruled, the waters became murky indeed. In the previous editions of this book it was perceived that we had received a definitive statement on this issue from the California Supreme Court in the form of the *Burgess* decision (discussed below). To the delight of many practitioners in this area, however, the somewhat unsettling aspects of the *Burgess* decision were recently re-visited by the California Supreme Court in the *La Musga* (pronounced "la mushay") decision, a case that dramatically altered the landscape of this area of the law. To fully appreciate and understand this area of custody and visitation, however, a historical review and analysis of these various cases is necessary.

1. Marriage of Ciganovich, 61 Cal. App. 3d 289 (1976)

After obtaining dissolution of marriage in California, Wife (who had been awarded primary physical custody) moved to Nevada. The court found no reason for that move, except to frustrate her husband's visitation. She changed her residence several times, gave incorrect or misleading addresses to her husband, and basically disregarded his visitation rights. Once he was able to catch up with her and bring her into court on this issue, she argued to the trial court that she had an absolute constitutionally protected right to travel, regardless of its impact on her ex-husband's visitation rights. Although the trial court agreed with her and refused to change custody to husband, the appellate court reversed that decision and ordered the trial court to consider the issue of frustration of visitation as it related to husband's request for custody. The appellate court stated:

As a general rule a parent having child custody is entitled to change residence unless the move is detrimental to the child. [Citations.] That the child's removal from the state practically deprives the father of his visitation rights is "generally" insufficient to justify restraint on the mother's free movement. [Citations.][¶] The general rule does not govern when the mother acts with an intent to frustrate or destroy the father's visitation right. . . . Confronted with such a situation, a trial court should be concerned with the child's welfare as the paramount consideration. The court should bear in mind that preservation of parental relationships is in the best interest of the child as well as the parent. [Citations.] The court should also bear in mind that a custodial parent's attempt to frustrate the court's order has a bearing upon the fitness of that parent.

2. Marriage of Rosson, 178 Cal. App. 3d 1094 (1986)

In *Rosson*, Mother and Father shared joint legal custody according to a stipulated judgment. Eight years later, in order to advance her career, Mother planned to move from Napa (the residence of the children's father and place of dissolution) to San Francisco. Father brought an action in court to prevent Mother from taking the children with her. The court took testimony from the parents and a court mediator. The mediator testified that the children, ages 10 and 13, were mature and had good reasons for their preferences. One child had no strong preference but the other expressed a strong preference to stay with his father in Napa. The trial court modified its prior order and awarded custody to Dad, finding that the Mom's move constituted a change in circumstances supporting the modification. The appellate court affirmed this decision. This ruling has since been disapproved by the court in *Burgess* (discussed below), but only to the extent that it may increase the burden of proof on the relocating parent over that imposed by *Rosson*. The decision itself, however, was approved, although it was criticized as having been arrived at for the wrong reason. The change was appropriate, said the *Burgess* court, not due to the mom's desire to move, but due to the children's desire to remain with their father; additionally, the change furthered the children's best interests.

3. Marriage of Fingert, 221 Cal. App. 3d 1575 (1990)

In this case, the parties divorced in 1983 in Ventura County, when their child was one year old. They shared legal custody, with Mom having physical custody. Subsequently, Mom and Child relocated to a different county (San Mateo). In 1988, when the child was about to start first grade, Mom filed a motion to modify visitation to accommodate the child's school schedule. In this context, the parties met with a mediator, who recommended that Mom move back to Ventura so Dad could spend more time with the child; the mediator made this recommendation notwithstanding the fact that Mom and Child had not lived in Ventura County for over three years and that Child had significant contacts with San Mateo, including school, soccer, Sunday school, and friends. The trial court nevertheless adopted this recommendation and ordered Mom either to move back or give up physical custody. In its ruling, the trial court found such a "move back" in the child's best interests, due in no small part to Dad's superior financial position. Mom appealed, and the appellate court reversed, essentially basing that decision on their opinion that, absent evidence of Mom frustrating Dad's access to the child, there was no justification for an order that she relocate or lose custody. It seems the *Fingert* court placed a very high value on a party's right to relocate, unless relocation would frustrate visitation. The reader will note that such a view focuses the analysis not on the best interests of the child but instead on the "best interests" of the relocating parent, so long as those interests do not conflict with the child's. That is, in fact, at the core of this periodic "flip-flop" by the courts in this area: whether the focus is on the child or the relocating parent.

4. Marriage of Carlson, 229 Cal. App. 3d 1330 (1991)

During their marriage, the Carlson's lived alternatively in Pennsylvania and California, but at the time of their dissolution, they lived near Father's family in California. Mom decided that she wanted to move with their children (ages 6 and 8) to Pennsylvania to attend college and live closer to her family. Both parties had close, loving relationships with their children. The trial court awarded the parties joint legal custody with primary physical custody to Mom; further, the court restrained each party from removing the children from California. The court of appeal affirmed, stressing that its primary consideration was to ensure that every reasonable effort was made to preserve the relationship of the children with *both* parents:

> [W]e do not make the noncustodial parent's ability to exercise visitation the sole or preeminent factor in cases such as this. We do, however, call attention to it as one of the significant considerations the trial court must take into account in evaluating the best interests of the child in light of all the evidence before the court.

Clearly, the concerns of the *Carlson* court were focused on the children, and the preservation of that relationship with both parents. In that regard, the court specifically found that the parties simply did not have the financial wherewithal to sustain a long-distance relationship between the father and the children had they been allowed to relocate to Pennsylvania.

5. Marriage of McGinnis, 7 Cal. App. 4th 473 (1992)

In *McGinnis*, the appellate court expressed an unwillingness to allow relocation of minor children without a very extensive investigation into the facts and circumstances surrounding the move, the motivation of the parties in their respective positions, and a thorough analysis of the best interests of the children. This case illustrates that a custodial parent who desires to relocate with the children bears a very difficult burden indeed.

In *McGinnis*, a 1990 Santa Barbara dissolution judgment gave Mom and Dad joint custody of their three young children. Dad remained in the family residence, where the children spent three days per week. The joint custody arrangement was working well. Then the parties remarried. Mom, who was a part-time waitress, married a man who was a football coach at a local school. In August of 1991, Mom told Dad that her new husband had accepted a coaching job in Los Angeles and they intended to relocate there, taking the children (then four, five, and nine) with them. Dad filed a request with the court that Mom be restrained from making this move pending the completion of a child custody evaluation. The trial court denied both requests and made findings in support of its decision, including that it would be in the best interests of the children to remain with Mom. The appellate court reversed, holding that the trial court should have frozen the status quo until after Dad had an opportunity to obtain a child custody evaluation and gather evidence in support of his request that the children remain with him. The appellate court instructed that the trial court should have then held a proper hearing wherein Dad would have been permitted to present live testimony. Then custody should have been changed only for an "imperative reason." The court stated:

> In "move away" cases where a shared parenting arrangement is working, an order changing custody should be made only after adequate notice, a meaningful mediation, and the parents have been given the opportunity for an outside evaluation. [A] change of custody is the exception, not the rule. It can be made only for an "imperative reason."

The appellate court further placed the burden of proof squarely on the shoulders of the party wishing to move the children to establish that the move is appropriate under all the circumstances:

> The State of California has a strong public policy "in . . . protecting stable custody arrangements"[Citation.]" 'It is well established that the courts are reluctant to order a change of custody and will not do so except for imperative reasons; that it is desirable that there be an end of litigation and undesirable to change the child's established mode of living.'[Citation.]"[Citation.] We hold that these same rules apply to a "move away" when a shared parenting arrangement is working. [¶] In such a situation, the burden of proof is upon the "move away" parent to demonstrate that the move is in the best interests of the children, i.e. that it is "essential and expedient" and for an "imperative reason."[Citations.]

6. Marriage of Burgess, 13 Cal. 4th 25 (1996)

The *Burgess* case used to be the pivotal judicial exposition on this subject. What made it significant was that it was a decision of the California Supreme Court and thus constituted a reconciliation of all these above-cited appellate level cases to the effect that any such opinion contrary to this case was disapproved (and not controlling authority).

In May of 1992, Mr. and Mrs. Burgess separated. Mrs. Burgess left the family home in Tehachapi and moved into a nearby apartment. Both Mr. and Mrs. Burgess were correctional officers in a nearby prison. After separation, Mrs. Burgess expressed a desire to transfer to a new prison being built in Lancaster, 40 miles away. In July of 1992, the trial court entered a "Stipulation and Order" dissolving the marriage and providing for temporary custody and visitation in accordance with a mediation agreement worked out between the parties. The temporary order provided that Mom would have sole physical custody of the children (ages three and four), the parties would have joint legal custody, and Dad would enjoy significant visitation. The mediation agreement expressly stated that Dad's visitation schedule would have to be revisited if Mom moved.

At the February 1993 custody hearing, Mom testified that she had accepted the job transfer to Lancaster and planned to relocate after her kids completed preschool that June. Mom's reasons for the move included career advancement and greater access to medical care, extracurricular activities, private schools, and daycare facilities for her children. Even though the distance between Tehachapi and Lancaster was only 40 minutes by car, Dad testified that he would not be able to maintain his current visitation schedule if the children were moved there. He also asked for physical custody of the children if Mom relocated. The trial court found that it was in the children's best interest that they be permitted to move to Lancaster with Mom, but Dad should be granted liberal visitation. The appellate court reversed the trial court, but the supreme court then reversed the appellate court. The California Supreme Court held that the custodial parent has the right to change a child's residence, subject to the court's power to restrain a removal that would prejudice a child's rights or welfare; no other or additional burden may be placed on relocating parent.

The supreme court instructed that when immediate or eventual relocation of children is an issue, the trial court must consider Family Code section 7501 and the presumptive right of a custodial parent to change the residence of the minor children, so long as the removal would not be prejudicial to their rights or welfare. Thus, in considering all the circumstances bearing on the best interests of the minor children, it may consider any effects of such relocation on their rights or welfare.

The court noted that in various appellate decisions over the preceding several years (many of which are discussed immediately above), the appellate court had imposed many additional burdens on the parent wishing to relocate to prove that the move was "necessary," "expedient," "essential," or "imperative." To the extent that these cases imposed any such burdens over and above that contemplated in the *Burgess* decision, they were disapproved. The court stated:

> In an initial custody determination, a parent seeking to relocate with the minor children bears no burden of establishing that the move is "necessary." The trial court must—and here did—consider, among other factors, the effects of relocation on the "best interest" of the minor children, including the health, safety and welfare of the children and the nature and amount of contact with both parents. [Citation.] We discern no statutory basis, however, for imposing a specific additional burden of persuasion on either parent to justify a choice of residence as a condition of custody.

The court rejected the appellate court's reliance on its authority to restrict the right of the custodial parent to move with the children, stating:

> The policy of section 3020 in favor of "frequent and continuous contact" does not so constrain the trial court's broad discretion to determine, in light of all the circumstances, what custody arrangement serves the "best interest" of minor children. [¶] . . . Moreover, construing section 3020 by implication to impose an additional burden of proof on a parent seeking to relocate would abrogate the presumptive right of a custodial parent to change the residence of the minor child.

The court was equally unimpressed with the distinction imposed by some appellate decisions in the context of modifying a permanent custody awards:

> The same allocation of the burden of persuasion applies in the case of a custodial parent's relocation as in any other proceeding to alter existing custody arrangements: "[I]n view of the child's interest in stable custodial and emotional ties, custody lawfully acquired and maintained for a significant period will have the effect of compelling the noncustodial parent to assume the burden of persuading the trier of fact that a change [in custody] is in the child's best interests."[¶] Similarly, the same standard of proof applies in a motion for change in custody based on the custodial parent's decision to relocate with the minor children as in any other matter involving changed circumstances: "[O]nce it has been established [under a judicial custody decision] that a particular custodial arrangement is in the best interests of the child, the court need not reexamine that question. Instead, it should preserve the established mode of custody unless some significant change in circumstances indicates that a different arrangement would be in the child's best interest."[¶] The showing required is substantial.

Thus, the focus is not on why one parent is moving, but rather on whether custody should be changed: "The dispositive issue is accordingly, not whether relocating is itself 'essential or expedient' either for the welfare of the custodial parent or the child, but whether a change in custody is 'essential or expedient for the welfare of the child.'"

Of course, many of the appellate level observations and rulings survive this decision. For example, the supreme court recognized that each case must still be evaluated in the context of its own facts and circumstances:

> Although the interests of a minor child in the continuity and permanency of custodial placement with the primary caretaker will most often prevail, the trial court, in assessing 'prejudice' to the child's welfare as a result of relocating . . . may take into consideration the nature of the child's existing contact with both parents—including de facto as well as de jure custody arrangements—and the child's age, community ties, and health and educational needs. Where appropriate, it must also take into account the preferences of the child. [Citation.]

The supreme court also recognized that the analysis must be flexible enough to accommodate all types of custody sharing arrangements. For example, in the context of a true joint custody arrangement:

> A different analysis may be required when parents share joint physical custody of the minor children under an existing order and in fact, and one parent seeks to relocate with the minor children. In such cases, the custody order "may be modified or terminated upon the petition of one or both parents or on the court's own motion if it is shown that the best interest of the child requires modification or termination of the order."[Citation.] The trial court must determine de novo what arrangement for primary custody is in the best interest of the minor children.

Finally, the court recognized that an exception must exist where a move is simply to frustrate the noncustodial parent's contact with the minor children. In such a case, the custodial parent's conduct may itself be grounds for changing custody. Even if the custodial parent is otherwise "fit," such bad faith conduct may be relevant to a determination of what permanent custody arrangement is in the minor children's best interest.

7. Montenegro v. Diaz, 26 Cal. 4th 249 (2001)3

Montenegro, the State Supreme Court's fifth ingress into this area, changed the rules set forth above. In this case, the child was born in 1994. Two years later father filed for paternity action, claiming that Mother was frustrating his access to the child. Pursuant to a variety of stipulations between the parties, primary physical custody was awarded to Mother. At the 1999 trial, Mother was still frustrating access, and Father requested custody. The question in this case was "does Dad have to show a change of circumstance or can the court simply go straight to the best interests tests when deciding this issue?" The trial court said that because there was no initial order yet in place, it could go straight to a best interests analysis; in that context, it changed custody away from Mother to Father due to her frustration.

The appellate court reversed, holding that a change of circumstance was required pursuant to *Burchard*, because the previous "stipulations" were "final judgments" on the issue of custody. (One of the stipulations used the word "judgment.")

The California Supreme Court reversed, finding that the best interests of the child test was proper. Specifically, there was no need to show a change of circumstance because the previous stipulations were *not* clearly and affirmatively labeled "final" orders. This is an important aspect of the case: A showing of changed circumstances is only necessary when it is demonstrated that custody stipulations were intended to be "final."

Stated another way, has the upstream order or paperwork "clearly and affirmatively indicated finality," or does it leave the door open and acknowledge the need to revisit best interests in the future? The burden is on the party claiming finality to show that the clear and affirmative intent test has been met.

The *Montenegro* case has essentially established that it is in the interests of children to have the court able to assess their needs by a best interests tests, unless the prior order, agreement or decision clearly and affirmatively labels that decision as something that they intend to be a final order that will not be modified in the absence of a change of circumstance showing. The magic words for *Montenegro* are: Does the upstream order or paperwork clearly and affirmatively indicate finality? A summary of the post-*Montenegro* law shows that the best interests of the child will be the determining factor at each stage of custody litigation *until* such time as a final order for that particular stage is entered. Stipulations *are* included in the finality analysis; further, the label "judgment" does not, by itself, qualify a document as final. The courts are *influenced* by stability, but they are not locked into a change of circumstance test in all situations. Thereafter, at a modification proceeding where there is an order in place that meets the clear expression of finality test, that order will not be modified absent a showing of change of circumstances.

What are the implications of *Montenegro*?

In light of the *Montenegro* case, what do lawyers now tell their clients at an initial court custody hearing? If we want to require a change in circumstances test for any further modifications, we'd better have some sort of finality language from *Montenegro* in the stipulation or order. Lawyers are now in the business of negotiating as to the *label* that is placed on orders. We must also watch out for labels of "sole" or "joint" parent. These labels are extremely important from the perspective of the *Burgess* case, since the label of "sole" will open the door for a move away. What is the downstream effect on move away cases? In other words, what happens when *Burgess* conflicts with *Montenegro*?

Somebody comes into court with a classic *Burgess* argument: "I am the primary custodial parent, so I have the right to change the child's residence." *Burgess* says I must show a change of circumstances in order to change custody in the face of a move-away, but *Montenegro* indicates that the change of circumstance requirement is not necessary if the underlying threshold is not met. This set the stage for the *La Musga* case, which is (at least for now) the definitive word on these issues.

8. In re Marriage of LaMusga, 32 Cal. 4th 1072 (2004)

The *LaMusga* case reads like a definitive treatise on the subject of custody determinations in general and move-away cases in particular. The author cannot stress enough how important it is to review the case. Although too long to be reprinted here in its entirety, key sections are included below.

> Susan and Gary LaMusga married on October 22, 1988, and had two children: Garrett, who was born on May 5, 1992, and Devlen, who was born two years later to the day on May 5, 1994. The mother filed an amended petition for dissolution of marriage on May 10, 1996, and requested sole physical custody of the children, who were living with her in the family residence. The father objected and requested joint legal and physical custody.
>
> The parties were unable to agree on a visitation schedule and, pursuant to a court order, stipulated to the appointment of Philip Stahl, Ph.D., a licensed psychologist, to conduct a child custody evaluation. Pending this evaluation, the parties agreed to a visitation schedule under which the children would be with their father every Wednesday from 3:30 p.m. to 7:30 p.m. and Sunday from 10 a.m. to 5 p.m. The mother asserted that even this limited visitation with the father was detrimental to the children, causing Garrett to become overly aggressive, disorganized, unfocused, and to regress in toilet training, and causing Devlen to develop a facial tick, a stutter, and a squint.
>
> In a report dated October 10, 1996, Dr. Stahl observed that "there has been a great deal of verbal hostility between Mr. and Mrs. LaMusga for years, at times escalating to some pushing and shoving between them. . . . Both acknowledge that communication has deteriorated completely and that there is no trust between them. Mrs. LaMusga is concerned that Mr. LaMusga lives in an unsafe environment, doesn't take adequate care of

the boys and is not responsive to their needs. She would prefer that his time be even more limited."

"Additionally, Ms. LaMusga has expressed a desire to move with the boys to the Cleveland, Ohio, area. . . . [¶] In contrast, Mr. LaMusga is quite upset that she wants to take the boys to Cleveland, and describes the environment there as hostile to him. He believes that Ms. Musga has attempted to alienate him from both the boys and . . . is quite concerned that, if she does get to move, he'll end up having no relationship with his boys whatsoever."

Dr. Stahl opined that, in general, both the mother and the father were "good enough parents," but noted that the mother was "struggling with supporting and encouraging frequent and continuing contact between" the children and their father. Dr. Stahl believed that "each parent has different positive qualities to give to the children and that it is in the children's best interest to maintain a relationship with each of them as they continue to grow." But he noted his concern "about the dynamic of conflict between Mr. and Ms. LaMusga and its impact on the children. They don't speak to one another, their conflict does filter down to the children, and the children do show some evidence of anxiety related to this. Additionally, their charges and counter-charges reflect the extent to which both parents are willing to go to make the other look bad, something that is clearly detrimental to Garrett and Devlen. . . . [T]he conflict level between the parents is the single-most significant problem, and it has been going on for years."

Dr. Stahl stated that the mother's desire to move to Cleveland "must be balanced with the children's apparent need for frequent and continuing contact with their father and looked at in the context of the parental hostility. As we already observe, it appears that Ms. LaMusga has been reluctant to support additional time or overnight time with the boys and their father, even though they live less than five miles apart. She has been reluctant to support consistent phone calls, as well. As indicated, Ms. LaMusga has concerns about the boys and their functioning and she has chosen to respond to these concerns with efforts at keeping Mr. LaMusga's time rather limited. Additionally, it is this examiner's observation that Ms. LaMusga sees little or no negative impact on the boys at the potential distance in their relationship with their father. While the likelihood of parental conflict will be significantly reduced on a day-to-day basis if Ms. LaMusga is in Cleveland (and that will likely benefit the boys), it is this examiner's observation that we must be concerned about Ms. LaMusga's willingness to follow through on regular and consistent visitation if she is half a country away. [¶] It is this examiner's opinion that the attachment between Garrett and Devlen and their father is strong. However, the children have not reached an age where they can maintain this attachment if they are away from him over long distance and time. . . . Thus, it is this examiner's observation that a move at this time would be difficult for the boys given their developmental needs. If we add the concern regarding Ms. LaMusga's follow through associated with the current level of conflict, a move might be difficult for the boys."

Following a hearing on November 14, 1996, the superior court awarded the parties joint legal custody of the children, with the mother having "primary physical custody." With the mother's agreement, the father's visitation was increased over a period of months to a final schedule of every Tuesday and Wednesday from 4 p.m. to 7:30 p.m. and every other weekend from Friday at 5 p.m. to Sunday at 6 p.m. Judgment subsequently was entered dissolving the marriage as of December 31, 1997.

On July 6, 1998, the parties stipulated that during the summer, the father would have custody of the children from July 9-15 and August 21-27, 1998, and the mother would have custody of the children from July 17-23 and August 13-19, 1998. The preexisting custody and visitation schedule would apply at all other times. On November 15, 1998, the father filed an order to show cause to have the court establish a holiday visitation schedule, which it did by an order issued on December 8, 1998.

The mother subsequently married Todd Navarro and, on September 16, 1999, gave birth to a daughter. The father also remarried. His wife, Karin, has a daughter from her prior marriage.

On February 13, 2001, the mother filed an order to show cause to modify the visitation order to permit her to relocate with the children to Cleveland, Ohio. She alleged that she had family in the Cleveland area and her husband had received an offer for a more lucrative job there. She noted in her supporting declaration that Dr. Stahl had been reappointed and was conducting an evaluation to determine whether the father's visitation should be increased.

The father objected to the mother's plan to move the children to Ohio and asked that primary custody of the children be transferred to him if the mother moved to Ohio. The father declared that the mother had attempted to alienate him from their sons since their separation and feared that moving the boys to Ohio would result in his "being lost as their father."

On February 26, 2001, Dr. Stahl submitted a supplemental report that did not address the mother's proposal to move to Ohio, which she had made less than two weeks earlier. Dr. Stahl stated that the parents were "at a continued impasse"; the father wanted "equal joint custody of the boys" while the mother wanted to discontinue the boys' midweek visits with their father. He reported some disturbing aspects of the boys' relationship with their father, noting that the boys were very critical of their father, but almost always in rather vague terms. Dr. Stahl observed, however, that the children "seemingly had a good time at their father's home." Once, Dr. Stahl "observed Devlen being affectionate with his dad, but he later denied it."

Dr. Stahl concluded that the boys were "alienated and split in their feelings toward their parents," in part because "[t]hey appear to be very aware of the conflicts between the parents" and appeared to take the mother's side. Dr. Stahl further concluded the children seemed to be "somewhat overindulged," stating: "With their extreme polarization and with their overindulged emotions, both Garrett and Devlen run the risk of having significant struggles emotionally, especially with their peers, and with authority figures. In addition, it is this examiner's impression that both the boys also struggle a bit with difficulties in self-image and feelings of inadequacy in comparison to others." He blamed this, in part, on "their parent's high conflict divorce." Dr. Stahl noted that the mother "does appear to be contributing to the alienation of the boys," although this alienation tended to be "covert" and "unconscious." He observed that the father was "somewhat self-centered and doesn't seem to deal with the boys' feelings that well."

Dr. Stahl recommended that the father be awarded longer periods of visitation and raised the possibility of transferring primary physical custody of the children to their father if the situation did not improve, stating: "Research suggests that alienated children do better with longer rather than shorter blocks of time with each parent, and also that it's helpful if fathers participate with children in the schooling. . . . I would recommend a schedule in which they are with their father every other week from Thursday after school until return to school on Monday morning and every other week from Thursday after school until Friday morning. Not only does this reduce the number of transitions that need to take place with the parents together, but it also broadens the blocks of time that they are with their dad. It also keeps mother as the primary parent, which is consistent for them." Dr. Stahl noted that if the situation did not improve, he might recommend either "a truly joint custody arrangement" or giving "primary custody" to the father.

Following a hearing on March 19, 2001, the father's visitation was increased as recommended by Dr. Stahl. The court again reappointed Dr. Stahl "to provide a focused evaluation on the issue whether the relocation of the parties' two minor children is in the best interest of said children."

Dr. Stahl's June 29, 2001, supplemental report notes that the mother has wanted to move ever since the divorce but waited, at Dr. Stahl's urging, until the children were older. The move would improve her family's "economic standard of living, and . . . inherent quality of life. . . . " The mother "believes that she will have no difficulty supporting the boys in their relationship with their dad," asserting "that she has always supported the boys in their relationship with their dad, and that she is not a contributor to any alienation that the boys might feel. [¶] Not surprisingly, Mr. LaMusga doesn't see things the same way. . . . He is opposing the move, especially at this time, because he worries that the boys will regress in their relationship with him, especially after making tremendous progress in their work with Dr. Tuggle [the boys' therapist]. . . . He feels strongly that a disruption now will break the bond that is developing."

Dr. Stahl was concerned "that the boys might not maintain any positive relationship with their dad if they move," noting that such a loss "would be significant." But he added that this "must be balanced with the potential losses that the boys might experience if their mother moves, and they stay," observing: "They have been in the primary care of their mother since the parents' divorce and they will likely have a significant loss [if] she moves without them. They also have a very close relationship with their sister Aisley, as well as Todd, and they will feel those losses as well. Third, they have their own desire to move. . . . if they don't move, they're likely to feel that their wishes aren't being heard." Dr. Stahl also observed that forcing the children to remain in California could cause them to further reject their father.

Dr. Stahl opined that if the boys were permitted to move to Ohio: "The primary loss for the boys will be related to the growing and improving relationship with their dad. I suspect that they'll have few problems adjusting to a new school, friends, or activities, but it may be hard for them to deal with the emerging change in their relationship with their dad. The relationship currently is tenuous at best, for all of the reasons I outlined in the original update, and it is unlikely that there will be no impact to their relationship. . . . [¶] The underlying risk, however, is that, with absence, they will regress to a more detached and disconnected state with their father. With regular and somewhat increased contact, there is improvement in the relationships. However, this improvement is tenuous, and I am concerned that the move will interrupt any progress that might be occurring at the present time."

Although the mother stated that she wanted to move to Ohio because that "is where she is originally from and where she has family support," Dr. Stahl suggested an additional motive: "Underneath, however, it has always appeared that [the mother] has wanted to move so that she can remove herself and take the boys from the day-to-day interactions with [the father]. She has difficulty dealing with him and prefers to have as little communication with him as possible."

"I am concerned about ways that she might inadvertently or unconsciously provoke loyalty conflicts, as the children are all too aware of her negative dealings toward their father. Her contribution to the conflict is a major contribution to the boys' loyalty conflicts and alienation."

Acknowledging that there was "no good solution in this matter," Dr. Stahl observed that "there is a risk that both moving or not moving may create a significant change" in the children's relationship with their father, stating, "It's difficult to predict which way this will go. Mother believes that the boys will be less rejecting of their dad if they move and father believes that a move will put the nail in the coffin of their relationship. I suspect that neither of them is accurate and the actual reaction of the boys will be based on how the parents handle their issues over time.

"In fact, in my opinion, the critical issue will be mother's 'real' behavior after the move takes place. If she acts as she says she will, the boys will talk with their father two or three times per week, and these conversations and communications will be substantive and not superficial. If she acts as she says she will, the boys will enjoy their father's periodic visits to Ohio. If she acts as she says she will, they will get on the plane and come to California for dad's custodial time, and they'll be ready to have a good time with their dad. If she acts as she says she will, it could be that the boys will actually improve in their relationship with their dad, and the gains being made now can continue. [¶] However, the risk is that she won't act as she says she will. If dad is correct, and mother's sister is going to foment the anger, there won't be any support in Ohio for her to act as she says she will. If that's the case, once they get to Ohio, he'll be correct that his relationship with the boys will regress."

On August 23, 2001, a hearing was held in the superior court on the mother's request to move the children's residence to Ohio. The mother declared that her husband had accepted a position as sales manager at a Toyota dealership in Cleveland, Ohio in March 2001 and had been living in Cleveland with her family since then.

Dr. Stahl testified and responded to a question by the mother's counsel why the mother should not be permitted to move the children to Ohio, stating: "I think the reasons would be twofold: [¶] One, there is no evidence that I've seen in the five years that I've known this family that [the mother] will really do what she said she will do. In terms of being supportive of the boys' relationship with their father in a way that truly will reduce the loyalty conflicts and truly will help them, um, feel better about things with him. [¶] That would be one reason. [¶] The other is it is still a tenuous relationship. And in that it's a tenuous relationship, I'll stick with what I said in 1996: It makes it very difficult to—to predict that it's likely to get better rather [than] stay tenuous or get worse if the move is allowed."

Dr. Stahl acknowledged that the father also bore some of the responsibility for his strained relationship with his sons, stating: "He gets frustrated and impatient sometimes." Dr. Stahl added that the father contributes to the children's alienation to the extent he perpetuates his conflict with the mother.

The superior court ruled as follows: "The issue is not whether either of these parents are competent and qualified to be custodial parents, I think the evidence indicates that they are. That is not the question. [¶] The question is whether there is sufficient evidence at this point to determine, one, that the best interests of the children is served by relocating with Mother to Ohio, or whether the best interests are served by the—a change of physical custody if [the mother] is to relocate."

The court acknowledged that the mother is not purposely trying to alienate the children from their father, but noted that the mother's inability to "let go" of her anger toward the father caused her to project those feelings onto their children and to reinforce the children when they expressed negative feelings toward their father. "That aligns the children with one parent and results in a strained or hostile relationship with the other parent." The court also acknowledged that this was not "a bad faith move away. I don't think this is an instance where [the mother is] attempting to relocate with the children for the specific purpose of limiting their contact or relationship with their father. I think it's far more subtle than that."

"The primary importance, it seems to me at this point, is to be able to reinforce what is now a tenuous and somewhat detached relationship with the boys and their father. . . . [¶] I think the concerns about the relationship being lost if the children are relocated at this time are realistic. . . . [¶] Therefore, I think that a relocation of the children out of the State of California, the distance of 2000 miles is—would inevitably under these circumstances be detrimental to their welfare. It would not promote frequent and continuing contact with the father, and I would deny the request to relocate the children. [¶] If [the mother] wishes to relocate to the state of Ohio, certainly she is entitled to do that. Should she choose to do so, then I would implement the recommendations contained in Dr. Stahl's supplemental report of June 29th of 2001 which would provide for the primary physical custody of the children, at least during the school year, to Mr. LaMusga. . . . [¶][I]f [the mother] decides not to relocate, then the existing custodial arrangement will remain."

The mother appealed and the Court of Appeal reversed the judgment. The Court of Appeal applied the deferential abuse of discretion standard of review we recognized in *In re* Marriage of Burgess, supra, 13 Cal.4th 25, 32, 51 Cal. Rptr. 2d 444, 913 P.2d 473: "The precise measure is whether the trial court could have reasonably concluded that the order in question advanced the 'best interest' of the child." But the appellate court concluded that "although the [superior] court referred several times during the hearing to 'best interest' as the applicable standard, its order was not truly based on that criterion as it applies in the context of this custodial parent's relocation." The Court of Appeal concluded that the superior court "neither proceeded from the presumption that Mother had a right to change the residence of the children, nor took into account this paramount need for stability and continuity in the existing custodial arrangement. Instead, it placed undue emphasis on the detriment that would be caused to the children's relationship with Father if they moved." We granted review.

Shortly after we granted review, the mother filed a notice of abandonment of her appeal, supported by a declaration stating that she no longer intended to move to Ohio, but intended to move to Arizona instead. She asked this court to dismiss the appeal. The father objected. We denied the mother's motion to dismiss the appeal. The mother's counsel later sent to this court a copy of a letter dated July 8, 2003, informing the father that the mother and their children had moved to Arizona. Upon the request of the mother, and without objection by the father, we have taken judicial notice of an order of the superior court filed on August 29, 2003, permitting the children to live with the mother in Arizona "temporarily" pending our ruling in the present proceedings.

Despite the fact that it appears that the mother no longer intends to move to Ohio, the matter under review is not moot. It remains possible that the mother could choose to move to Ohio, and she has changed the residence of the children to Arizona. Accordingly, the issue of whether it is in the children's best interests to modify the custody order if the mother changes the residence of the children is not moot. In any event, we may decline to dismiss a case that has become moot "where the appeal raises issues of continuing public importance. [Citations.]" (Lundquist v. Reusser (1994) 7 Cal. 4th 1193, 1202, fn. 8, 31 Cal. Rptr. 2d 776, 875 P.2d 1279.) This appeal certainly does.

Simply put, and as codified by the California Legislature post-*Burgess* in Family Code section 7501: custodial parents have a presumptive right to change the residence of a child in their custody. Post-*Burgess*, the custodial parent did not need to show that the move was necessary as long as there was no bad-faith reason or motivation for the move (such as to deny the noncustodial parent contact with the child). The California Supreme Court, however, felt that the trial court should look beyond the presumption of Family Code section 7510 to preserve the existing custody arrangement unless the noncustodial parent shows a significant change of circumstances indicating that a custody change is in the child's best interests. Therefore, the trial court must look beyond the moving parent's motive to any possible detriment to the child that the move might cause, placing greater emphasis on the detriment than on the motive.

The supreme court essentially found that flexibility is needed in adhering to presumptions created by *Burgess* and its statutory progeny. The fundamental inquiry in this context is the best interests of the minor child, plain and simple.

> The foregoing cases, many of which involve heart-wrenching circumstances, remind us that this area of law is not amenable to inflexible rules. Rather, we must permit our superior court judges—guided by statute and the principles we announced in *Burgess* and affirm in the present case—to exercise their discretion to fashion orders that best serve the interests of the children in the cases before them. Among the factors that the court ordinarily should consider when deciding whether to modify a custody order in light of the custodial parent's proposal to change the residence of the child are the following: the children's interest in stability and continuity in the custodial arrangement; the distance of the move; the age of the children; the children's relationship with both parents; the relationship between the parents including, but not limited to, their ability to communicate and cooperate effectively and their willingness to put the interests of the children above their individual interests; the wishes of the children if they are mature enough for such an inquiry to be appropriate; the reasons for the proposed move; and the extent to which the parents currently are sharing custody.

The rule in this area of custody litigation is now quite clear (in an unclear and unpredictable way): The primary focus must be on the child—not the parents, not the motivation for their move, not their good faith or bad faith. The court recognizes that the burden of proof is on the parent who opposes the relocation to show that the move is not in the child's best interests, but they also granted the trial court great discretion in its ultimate rulings. The moving party need not prove necessity for the move either. Again, however, the focus will be on the child: his stability, his relationship with both parents, and his risk of detriment. There are a variety of factors that the *LaMusga* court has announced as being probative to this inquiry, and it is likely, especially given the supreme court's recognition of the need to be "flexible" in this context, that we haven't heard the final word on these issues.

As a general rule, custody evaluators' opinions and reports have a significant impact on relocation cases. This individual is in a much better position than is the court to judge all aspects of the intended move and discuss its consequences with the parties, the child, and the other individuals in the child's life. Prior to even starting the relocation proceedings, any custodial parent desiring to relocate with a minor child who anticipates opposition from the noncustodial parent should sit down with the noncustodial parent, explain the situation, and attempt to work out an amicable resolution and plan for the future. If this is not feasible, then the parents should sign a stipulation to hire a child custody evaluator who will investigate the situation and report back on his or her findings.

If the parties still cannot agree to act in accordance with the child custody evaluator's recommendations, then court intervention is the only avenue. At least, however, the parties will have already obtained a child custody report.[4]

F. Remedies for Frustration of Visitation

A variety of remedies are available to provide relief to the noncustodial parent who is in the unhappy position of having his visitation rights frustrated. For example, the noncustodial parent can commence an order to show cause concerning contempt in an attempt to have the court levy a monetary fine against the custodial parent if not imprison him altogether for violating the court's order pertinent to visitation.[5] Much thought must be given to this alternative, however, since the act of one parent "arranging for" the imprisonment of the other parent, especially the custodial parent, cannot possibly leave a good impression on the minor child.

The court also has the authority to terminate or refuse to enforce spousal support payments (not child support, only spousal support) being received by the custodial parent in the event the custodial parent continues to frustrate visitation. Again, great thought must be given to employment of this remedy since it has the effect of creating a hardship for the minor child once the custodial parent's household income is reduced by termination of spousal support.

The noncustodial parent could also ask the court to order the custodial parent to post a monetary bond (in some significant amount, for example, $10,000) to secure performance and compliance with the visitation orders. This bond could then be forfeited upon a showing of a frustration of visitation and turned over to the noncustodial parent; the bond would thus act as a fine against the custodial parent for denial of visitation, while at the same time providing a legal fund for the noncustodial parent to secure judicial relief. Such a request will generally not be granted the first time that the parties find themselves in court on this issue. Usually, the noncustodial parent must demonstrate a history of frustration of visitation before the court will require the custodial parent to post such a bond.

Perhaps the most effective—albeit most extreme—method of enforcing visitation rights under these circumstances is to request a modification of custody based on the argument that the mandate of the Family Code is to provide frequent and continuing contact of the minor child with both parents;further, the Code is based on the principle that preference should generally be given to the parent more likely to allow visitation by the other parent. Upon a showing of extreme and habitual frustration of visitation, the court has all that it needs to make a finding that the custodial parent is not meeting these goals and it would be in the best interests of the minor child to give custody to the other parent.

As mentioned above, the noncustodial parent may request an order terminating or temporarily suspending the payment of spousal support until such time as visitation is restored. Let there be no mistake, however, that such a request will not be considered pertinent to child support. Unjustified interference with visitation, no matter how deliberate or malicious, will not excuse the withholding of child support. Visitation interference is not a defense to an action for nonpayment of child support (for example, contempt), and it cannot provide a basis for modification or termination of child support.

Many noncustodial parents have fallen into this trap, however, and have paid stiff penalties for contempt of court (including in some cases imprisonment) for violating the court's order and directive that support be paid on a regular basis. These parents generally believe that they have the right to withhold support to force the custodial parent's cooperation in allowing visitation. The logic of this reasoning seems clear on its face: "If I withhold child support, then the custodial parent will have no other alternative but to give in and allow me the visitation to which I am entitled." This reasoning is flawed, however; the only one who is harmed and who pays the price for the sins of the parent in these circumstances is the child. This prohibition against the trade-off between child support and visitation finds support in Family Code section 3556, which provides:

> The existence or enforcement of a duty of support owed by a noncustodial parent for the support of a minor child is not affected by a failure or refusal by the custodial parent to implement any rights as to custody or visitation granted by a court to the noncustodial parent.

There are some situations, however, that may prevent the custodial parent from taking action to collect child support arrearages if the cause of the arrearages has been the custodial parent's intentional frustration of visitation, coupled with "active concealment" of herself and the minor child. While it will not justify a wrongful withholding of child support, if a custodial parent is actively concealing the whereabouts of the minor child, then attempts to enforce a support order, she essentially comes to court with unclean hands; consequently, the court may find that she has *waived* collection of this child support. Of course, the noncustodial parent must first assert this defense to the collection of child support arrearages by claiming that such a finding is appropriate for the period during which the child was actively concealed and the payment of support was thus, for all practical purposes, impossible.

Some courts allow noncustodial parents to actively conceal their children as a defense to a child support enforcement action; other courts are just as certain in their rejection of this defense. Perhaps the best course of action for a noncustodial parent who does not know the whereabouts of the custodial parent and the child is to make payments into a trust or escrow account until the custodial parent or the child make their presence known. In so doing, the noncustodial parent will be able to demonstrate a good faith attempt to segregate the appropriate amount of child support for the benefit of the child. Moreover, the noncustodial parent will have established a fund necessary to bring these payments current if the court so orders.

Parents whose visitation is being frustrated have additional remedies, including: a general civil lawsuit for emotional distress, a lawsuit charging interference with the relationship between parent and child, and other torts of a similar nature. Of course, frustration of visitation is not always a function of the custodial parent actively interfering with the rights of the noncustodial parent. Sometimes it is the other way around, and it is the noncustodial parent who refuses to visit. In this situation, two basic questions arise: What can be done to force the parent to exercise his visitation, and what kind of monetary relief is available under the circumstances?

The first question—can a parent be forced to visit with the minor child— must be answered in the negative. This question has been entertained by the court in the case of Louden v. Olpin, 118 Cal. App. 3d 565 (1981), which concluded that there is simply no authority, either in the Code or as defined by cases, that allows it to force an unwilling parent to visit with a child. There is some remedial action available to the custodial parent, however, in circumstances such as these. Family Code section 3028 provides that the court can order a parent who refuses to assume "caretaker responsibilities" to reimburse the other parent for the "reasonable expenses incurred for, or on behalf of, a child, resulting from the other parent's failure to assume caretaker responsibility."

As such, to the extent the custodial parent incurs additional expenses "for or on behalf of the child" resulting from the noncustodial parent's refusal to visit, these costs can be recovered, together with attorney's fees.

This remedy is rather strictly construed, however, and should probably not be viewed as a device designed to force visitation. The harsh reality of the situation is that if a noncustodial parent truly wants nothing to do with the minor child, then he simply is not going to visit. Section 3028 provides a similar action by a noncustodial parent to recover these same costs incurred as a result of his visitation being thwarted by the custodial parent.

The concepts of parental kidnapping and frustration of visitation go hand in hand, inasmuch as frustration of visitation is part and parcel of parental kidnapping (although the opposite is not true). The most common example of frustration of visitation is found, as stated above, when a custodial parent uses visitation with the minor child to extract leverage over the noncustodial parent. This typically occurs when the custodial parent is not receiving child support. It can, however, arise in many other circumstances, becoming a potential problem whenever the custodial parent tries to obtain the noncustodial parent's cooperation.

When frustration of visitation extends to actual kidnapping of the child by the parent, the remedies, as might be expected, become much more serious. California Penal Code section 278.5 makes the wrongful taking and concealment of a minor child a crime:

> (a) Every person who takes, entices away, keeps, withholds, or conceals a child and maliciously deprives a lawful custodian of a right to custody, or a person of a right to visitation, shall be punished by imprisonment in a county jail not exceeding one year, a fine not exceeding one thousand dollars ($1,000), or both that fine and imprisonment, or by imprisonment in the state prison for 16 months, or two or three years, a fine not exceeding ten thousand dollars ($10,000), or both that fine and imprisonment.
>
> (b) Nothing contained in this section limits the court's contempt power.
>
> (c) A custody order obtained after the taking, enticing away, keeping, withholding, or concealing of a child does not constitute a defense to a crime charged under this section.

Similarly, Penal Code section 278 provides:

> Every person, not having a right to custody, who maliciously takes, entices away, keeps, withholds, or conceals any child with the intent to detain or conceal that child from a lawful custodian shall be punished by imprisonment in a county jail not exceeding one year, a fie not exceeding one thousand dollars ($1,000), or both that fine and imprisonment, or by imprisonment in the state prison for two, three, or four years, a fine not exceeding ten thousand dollars ($10,000), or both that fine and imprisonment. Penal Code section 278.5 applies to *"every person"* who wrongfully takes or conceals a child—and thus applies to those who have legal custodial rights over the child; Section 278, on the other hand, applies only to persons *"not having a right to custody."*

Penal Code section 278.7 offers protection from the harsh punishments of sections 278.5 and 278. Section 278.7 provides that sections 278 and 278.5 do not apply to persons who "with a good faith and reasonable belief that the child, if left with the other person, will suffer immediate bodily injury or emotional harm." Section 278.7 also protects persons who have "a right to custody of a child who has been a victim of domestic violence." Section 278.7 requires such individuals to file, within a reasonable time (at least 10 days), a report with the district attorney that includes their contact information and the reasons why they took or concealed the child. Additionally, such persons must, within a reasonable time (30 days), commence a custody proceeding consistent with the federal Parental Kidnapping Prevention Act or the Uniform Child Custody Jurisdiction Act.

In addition to these statewide statutes dealing with parental kidnapping, several federal statutes also address the situation. Specifically, the Missing Children Act, 28 U.S.C. section 534, sanctions the Attorney General to collect and exchange information in order to help authorities identify unidentified deceased persons and locate missing persons, including children. In accordance with the Act, the FBI to compiles reports of missing children, which are made available to local law enforcement agencies in situations involving parental kidnapping (among others). Additionally, the FBI will quite often assist in locating minor children who have been wrongfully abducted in violation of either state or federal statute, once the violation has warranted issuance of a state felony warrant.

The Federal Fugitive Act, found at 18 U.S.C. section 1073, provides penalties for individuals who cross state lines to avoid child abduction prosecution in a particular state. Under those circumstances, federal law intercedes to facilitate either the extradition of the individual back to the state of the offense, or prosecute the individual directly in federal court for violation of the Act.

Finally, the Hague Convention is an international treaty designed to facilitate legal relations between signatory nations. It was signed in 1965 and is now in effect between the United States and most of the so-called Western countries, including Australia, Austria, Canada, China, France, Norway, Portugal, Spain, Sweden, Switzerland, and the United Kingdom. The Hague Convention as it relates to this particular topic is designed to ensure cooperation between nations on the subject of parental kidnapping and the swift return of children who have been wrongfully removed from the jurisdiction of the custodial parent. The initiation and prosecution of proceedings under the Hague Convention are much more complicated, and no action in that regard should be undertaken without first reviewing the full text of the Convention. Its provisions are, in spirit and intent at least, substantially similar to the statewide provisions discussed above.

G. Nonparent Access to Children

Author's Note: The following discussion of nonparent access to children has been dramatically impacted by recent court decisions, most notably the United States Supreme Court decision Troxel v. Granville, 530 U.S. 57 (2000). In *Troxel*, there was no custody action pending. The grandparents requested access to their grandchildren, and the trial court in Washington gave it to them. The Washington statute under review stated that "any person" could ask for visitation, and imposed a best interests of the children standard. The U.S. Supreme Court found the statute to be unconstitutional and threw it out.

Troxel involved the right of a natural parent to keep everybody else out of the affairs of his children. The *Troxel* case did NOT involve a constitutional right on the part of a grandparent to visit with the child. The U.S. Supreme Court found significant problems with the Washington statute: it was breathtakingly overbroad because it authorized *any person* at *any time* to petition for visitation. No special weight was given to the parents' views. No weight was given to the parents' authorization of limited access.

In its plurality decision the U.S. Supreme Court determined that there was no need for a remand. The statute was simply found to be unconstitutional and stricken. We should note that in *Troxel* the mother said to the grandparents: "I will give you some time, but I will be the one to decide when and how long." It is important to note that the mother was at least trying to work with the grandparents.

In Marks v. United States, 430 U.S. 188 (1977), the Supreme Court of the United States explained how the holding of a case should be viewed where there is no majority supporting the rationale of any opinion: "When a fragmented Court decides a case and no single rationale explaining the result enjoys the assent of [the majority], the holding of the Court may be viewed as that position taken by those Members who concurred in the judgments on the narrowest grounds." *Marks*, 430 U.S. at 193.

Troxel is binding on California because it was decided by the United States Supreme Court. Yet, *Troxel* is a plurality opinion, or one that garnered more support than any other opinion written by a justice, but did not garner the support of at least half the justices. This means that the *reasoning* of the opinion does not control. The decision simply reflects the reasoning of the *single justice* who authored the opinion. Thus, in the future, the appropriate case, with the appropriate facts, could result in a different decision. In other words: "When a fragmented Court decides a case and no single rationale explaining the result enjoys the assent of [the majority], the holding of the Court may be viewed as that position taken by those Members who concurred in the judgments on the narrowest grounds." Marks v. United States, 430 U.S. 188 (1977).

For this reason, I have elected to keep the text of the section of this book dealing with nonparent access to children in this current edition. As a practical matter, most of the California statutes cited in this section (specifically Family Code sections 3101, 3102 and 3104) have been found unconstitutional by recent California cases. The chance of further review, however, and the historical significance of the content and analysis of these sections do, however, justify their continued inclusion in this book. Be advised, however, that reliance on the following section's analysis for anything other than a general understanding of this area of the law is not recommended.

Post-*Troxel*, then, any statute that creates a right adverse to the desires of the parent will probably need to include the following elements to survive a constitutional challenge:

1. A prior relationship existing with the child
2. A presumption favoring the parents' views
3. There should be no burden placed on the parent in this context.

Additional factors that might help the statute survive:

1. There is a custody determination pending.
2. There is evidence of harm or detriment to the child.
3. There has been a complete denial of any contact or visitation by the parent.
4. The statute will not adversely impact other people.

Some of the more fundamental questions involved in a *Troxel*-type case revolve around the following issues:

1. What are "family values?"
2. Do they include grandparents visiting with grandchildren?
3. Do family values include the nuclear family only, or do they include the grandparents too?
4. Who is best equipped to make decisions: biological relatives or psychological parents?
5. Estoppel: should a mother who allowed a relationship to grow, or even fostered it, be allowed to later deny it using *Troxel*?
6. Are the children being harmed or at risk of harm?
7. Can the state interfere with parental rights? Sometimes it is okay (child labor laws, vaccination rules, etc.); sometimes it is not okay (a parent denying a grandparent visitation with the child).

In light of *Troxel*, certain California statutes have been held unconstitutional. They are as follows:

1. Section 3101: allowed stepparents to visit if such contact was in the child's best interests.
2. Section 3102: allowed "close relatives" of a deceased parent to visit if such contact was in the child's best interests.

Section 3103 has not yet been held unconstitutional, but that could be as much a matter of lack of current opportunity as it could be the statutory construction. This section allows a grandparent to petition in an existing custody matter for access to the child, and is thus distinguishable from 3104 (which allowed grandparents to initiate their own petition, even against the wishes of the parent).

(As noted above, the following discussion, which was included in earlier editions of this book, is no longer legally viable. It is included as historical background and to provide the reader with a general understanding of this area of law.) Family Code section 3100 also grants the court discretion to allow reasonable visitation rights to a *nonparent*, provided simply that such nonparent has "an interest in the welfare of the child." This determination is entirely within the court's discretion. Sections 3101 and 3104 cover visitation for stepparents or grandparents. Bear in mind, however, that these individuals have the opportunity and right only to *request* visitation. Nothing in the Code mandates that they be given such visitation. Also, as with virtually all other determinations in this area, the primary inquiry will focus upon what is in the best interests of the minor child.[6]

This subject of "nonparent" visitation can be divided into three basic areas: grandparents, stepparents, and nonparents. The Family Code and the cases cited thereunder provide instruction in all three areas. The state of the law in this area is presently in a state of flux, however, with decisions affecting the constitutionality of this statutory scheme being decided even as this book goes to print. In fact, one statute that is part of this legislative scheme has recently been ruled unconstitutional by the California Appellate Court. No doubt for a valid reason, that Court did not strike down the entire statutory scheme as contained in sections 3101 through 3104. Nevertheless, this author can see the day coming when these statutes are, if not ultimately stricken down by the courts or the legislature, certainly overhauled in significant respect, so as to bring them in line with the current thinking in this area.

The following text provides a discussion of the law as it has existed in this area for the past many years. Next, it provides a discussion of recent cases that have completely changed the way we examine this subject. Without the original (now historical) statutory framework, this review would be at best difficult, and at worst impossible, to understand. The reader should note that, unless specifically stated, as of the time this text went to print, the statutes discussed in this section continue to be "good" law. That is, they have not been modified by the courts or the legislature. This does not, however, imply their continuing viability. These matters change over time as the issues are ultimately presented to the appellate court or the legislature. If the issues requiring interpretation of a particular code section have not yet been brought to the court's attention, the statute will remain unchanged until that day occurs.

1. Grandparent Visitation

The current Family Code significantly expanded the provisions for grandparent visitation. Section 3103 addresses grandparent visitation in the context of a dissolution of marriage (or related) proceeding between parents. Section 3103 provides that in any proceeding involving child custodial rights, upon petition by the child's grandparent(s), the court may grant them reasonable visitation if it finds that to be in the best interests of the child. If the child's parents agree that the grandparent should not be granted visitation rights, then there is a presumption that grandparent visitation is not in the best interests of the minor child.

Visitation rights may not be ordered under this section if such visitation conflicts with the custody or visitation rights of a birth parent who is not a party to the proceeding.

If the issue of grandparent visitation arises during the marriage of the parents (i.e., no divorce pending), section 3104 provides that the court may grant a grandparent's petition for reasonable visitation rights if: (1) there is a *preexisting relationship* between the grandparent and child that has engendered a bond such that visitation is in the best interest of the child, *and* (2) the child's interest in visitation with the grandparent outweighs the parents' right to exercise parental authority. This petition may not be filed while the parents are married unless the parents are currently living separate and apart on a permanent or indefinite basis, one of the spouses has been absent with his/her whereabouts unknown for over a month, the child is not residing with a parent, or a parent joins in the petition. Should the court grant visitation and the condition ceases to exist, the court must terminate visitation upon petition of *either* parent.

There is a presumption that grandparent visitation is not in the best interest of the child if both parents agree that the grandparent should not be granted visitation rights or the parent with whom the child is living or who has been granted sole legal and physical custody objects to grandparent visitation.

The court cannot order grandparent visitation rights under this section if such visitation would conflict with the custodial or visitation right of a birth parent who is not a party to the proceeding. Under both statutes, grandparent visitation cannot create a basis for or against a change of residence of the child, but it is one factor for the court to consider in ordering a change of residence. Additionally, a parent's child support obligation can be affected by an order for grandparent visitation if such visitation significantly alters the amount of time the parent spends with the child. As explained in the next chapter, time spent with one's children directly affects the amount of support one must pay on their behalf.) Both statutes also provide for the payment of child support by or to a grandparent and parent for the support of the minor. This support is limited, however, to transportation and basic expenses of the child or grandchild, such as medical and daycare costs.

2. Stepparent Visitation

Family Code 3101 provided as follows in the context of stepparent visitation:

> (a) Notwithstanding any other provision of law, the court may grant reasonable visitation to a stepparent, if visitation by the stepparent is determined to be in the best interest of the minor child.
> (b) If a protective order, as defined in section 6218, has been directed to a stepparent to whom visitation may be granted pursuant to this section, the court shall consider whether the best interest of the child requires that any visitation by the stepparent be denied.
> (c) Visitation rights may not be ordered under this section that would conflict with a right of custody or visitation of a birth parent who is not a party to the proceeding.
> (d) As used in this section:
>> (1) "Birth parent" means "birth parent" as defined in Section 8512.
>> (2) "Stepparent" means a person who is a party to the marriage that is the subject of the proceeding, with respect to a minor child of the other party to the marriage.

In *Marckwardt v. Superior Court (Soto)*, these concepts were taken to an interesting extreme in the context of an adoption. 150 Cal. App. 3d 417 (1984). In *Soto*, Mom's second husband adopted the children that Mom conceived with her first husband (presumably with the first husband's consent). Mom's first husband (the natural father) sought visitation, citing his right to visit as a *stepparent*. Mom moved to dismiss that proceeding for lack of subject matter jurisdiction. The trial court denied her motion and ordered the parties to undergo psychiatric evaluation. Mom's second husband appealed, alleging that upon entry of the adoption decree, the family law court lost jurisdiction over the minor children.

The appellate court granted Second Husband's request. The court noted that historically, adoption proceedings terminated the visitation rights of a parent who was replaced in the adoption. The court then examined whether the (then) recently enacted stepparent visitation statute (later Family Code section 3101) would allow such visitation. The court stated:

> A "stepfather" is defined . . . as "a man who succeeds one's father as the husband of one's mother."[Citation.]"[S]tepparent"[is defined] as "[t]he mother or father of a child born during a previous marriage of the other parent and hence, not the natural parent of such child."[Citation.] Under any such definition, [the natural father] is not the stepparent of his natural children, for he is not and never has been simultaneously the husband of their mother while not their legal father.

The court's opinion is an interesting (and creative) approach to First Husband problems. *Soto* is a good example of the many ways stepparent visitation and adoption issues can arise.

The reader should note that, unless specifically stated, as of the time this text went to print, the statutes discussed in this section continue to be "good" law. That is, they have not been modified by the courts or the legislature.

3. Other Visitation

From 1994 to 2002, Family Code section 3102 acted as a "catch-all" section, addressing everybody else who desired, but nevertheless might not otherwise be entitled to, visitation. Family Code section 3102 provided as follows[7]:

> (a) If either parent of an unemancipated minor is deceased, the children, siblings, parents, and grandparents of the deceased parent may be granted reasonable visitation with the child during the child's minority upon a finding that the visitation would be in the best interest of the minor child.
> (b) In granting visitation pursuant to this section to a person other than a grandparent of the child, the court shall consider the amount of personal contact between the person and the child before the application for the visitation order.

These concepts were explored by the appellate court in *Huffman v. Grob*, 172 Cal. App. 3d 1153 (1985). In this case, an infant child was adopted by Mother Number 1. After her death, with the adoptive father's consent, the child was adopted by Mother Number 2. Subsequently, the mother, sister, and brother of Mother 1 filed a petition seeking visitation with the child. The trial court denied the petition, finding that it did not have jurisdiction to order such visitation. The court of appeal affirmed, holding:

> When a child is adopted, the law creates a parent-child relationship between the adopting parent(s) and the child and severs the child's relationship with his or her natural family. [Citations.]"In an adoption proceeding the child receives a 'substitute' parent, and although he loses his right to look to the natural parent for support, he can now look to the adoptive parent."
>
> The purpose of the laws severing old family ties after adoption is to permit the new, adoptive family ties to solidify and to confer upon the new parent(s) discretion to provide for the best interests of the adopted child without interference from the former relatives.

The *Huffman* court concluded that the adoption cut off any visitation rights that Mother 1's family members might have had. This situation is somewhat atypical, however, due to the operation of the adoption proceedings and the desire of the court to ensure the stability of the newly created adopted family. Query the extent to which the court would grant visitation rights to family members outside of the context of a marital dissolution (or related) proceeding. Probably not much, if any at all.

4. Current State of the Law

As indicated at the beginning of the nonparent visitation section, recent case law has made sweeping changes to this statutory scheme. For example, Family Code section 3102 has been found unconstitutional, as being in violation of Due Process for (essentially) substituting the court's decisions regarding the best interests of a child for that of a parent. That decision (Punsly v. Ho, 969 P.2d 21 (2001)) was made by the California Appellate Court, and was based upon the decision of the United States Supreme Court in *Troxel v. Granville*. In *Troxel*, the Court was asked to strike down as unconstitutional a Washington state statute that had an impact similar to the California statutory scheme being discussed here.[8] The *Punsly* court succinctly summarized the effect of *Troxel*:

> The Court prefaced its analysis of the Washington statute with its recognition that all 50 states have enacted grandparent visitation statutes in some form in an attempt to protect the vital role grandparents often play in children's lives. However, it noted "the State's recognition of an independent third-party interest in a child can place a substantial burden on the traditional parent-child relationship." *Troxel*, supra, 530 U.S. at p. 64 [120 S. Ct. at p. 2059].)

With these competing interests in mind, the Court directed its attention to the 'sweeping breadth' of the Washington statute, focusing on the effect of the statute's language"[footnote omitted]. It stated, "[t]hus, in practical effect . . . a court can disregard and overturn any decision by a fit custodial parent concerning visitation whenever a third party affected by the decision files a visitation petition, based solely on the judge's determination of the child's best interests." (*Troxel*, supra, 530 U.S. at p. 57 [120 S. Ct. at 2061] italics in original.)

The Court then addressed the facts of the case and made three important determinations. First, the Court noted the grandparents did not allege, nor did the trial court find, that the mother was an unfit parent. This fact ran contrary to the presumption that fit parents act in the best interests of their children. (*Troxel*, supra, 530 U.S. at p. 58—[120 S. Ct. at 2061], citing Parham v. J.R. (1979) 442 U.S. 584, 602 [99 S. Ct. 2493, 2504, 61 L. Ed. 2d 101].)

Second, the trial court in the case gave no special weight to the mother's determination of her children's best interests. Rather, the findings of the trial court indicated it effectively placed the burden on the mother to disprove a presumption that visitation with the grandparents was in her children's best interests. (*Troxel*, supra, 530 U.S. at p. 58—[120 S. Ct. at 2062].)

Third, the [c]ourt emphasized the trial court's failure to give any weight to the fact the mother voluntarily agreed to allow visitation with her children's grandparents. The dispute at hand arose because the grandparents wanted more than the mother willingly offered. (*Troxel*, supra, 530 U.S. at p. 58 [120 S. Ct. at 2063].)

Based on these factors, the [c]ourt determined the Washington statute, as applied, was unconstitutional. The [c]ourt concluded "this case involve[d] nothing more than a simple disagreement between the Washington Superior Court and [the mother] concerning her children's best interest." (*Troxel*, supra, 530 U.S. at p. 58 [120 S. Ct. at 2063].) It further explained, "the Due Process Clause does not permit a State to infringe on the fundamental right of parents to make childrearing decisions simply because a state judge believes a 'better' decision could be made." (*Id*. at p. 58 [120 S.Ct. at p. 2064).

Because of the significance of this decision by the Supreme Court, , it is strongly recommended that the reader review this opinion in its entirety, including the concurring as well as dissenting opinions.[9]

The *Troxel* court went to great lengths, in the main, concurring, and dissenting opinions, to discuss and analyze these very important issues. Of course, this is due to the far-reaching implications of this decision, and the effect it has on a wide range of constitutional issues, only one of which has to do with children. *Troxel* is now the lead case in this area of the law, in all jurisdictions. As indicated earlier, one California appellate court has used *Troxel* to strike down the California equivalent of the Washington statute that was at issue in *Troxel*. The Supreme Court's approach to this Washington statute essentially focused on its breadth of application, and the effect its application would have on parental rights. In fact, they felt so strongly about the defects in this law that they struck it down in its entirety, without remand to the lower court for further review and action in light of their opinion.[10]

In California, as stated above, the statutory scheme presented by Family Code sections 3100 through 3104 is now at risk for being held unconstitutional, with the possible exception of 3104, which is actually cited by the Supreme Court as an example of how to properly draft this type of law. Section 3100, granting visitation rights to (essentially) "any person" is very similar to the Washington law and will most likely be struck down. Section 3101, addressing stepparent visitation with a best interest of the child standard of review, also probably violates *Troxel*. In fact, in 2003, it was found unconstitutional as it applied to a particular case for failing to expressly require "the court to presume that a parent's decision is in the best interest of the child" and for "violat[ing] a parent's right to raise his or her children free of excessive judicial interference if applied without such a presumption." *In re Marriage of W*, 114 Cal. App. 4th 68 (2003). Section 3102, addressing relatives of a deceased parent, is even more removed and, as we know, has been ruled unconstitutional.

Perhaps the best and most significant lesson to be learned in this context is as follows: This is a rapidly evolving area of the law, and it is only barely keeping up with the changes in our culture and our family structure. As a matter of fact, these days it is not just the parents of a child that are involved in the child-rearing process. Grandparents, stepparents, nonmarital partners, relatives of deceased parents, and other members of an extended family can be and very often are central players in a child's life. The courts and the legislature seem to recognize this, but it is indeed difficult to craft laws that will satisfy the concerns of so broad a range of players. Paramount in this determination are concepts of the best interests of the child. We have seen, however, that even this standard will be rejected in favor of the status quo, even if the status quo is not, in many people's opinion, otherwise in the best interests of the child. We have also seen that, absent some unusual circumstances, the rights of any of these extended family members will not be preserved or upheld against the wishes of the child's parent, even as to relatives of a deceased parent. Look for this area of the law to continue to evolve.

Summary

One of the most litigated aspects of this subarea of family law is general custody litigation. Perhaps the most difficult thing for divorcing parents to do is accept less than "full time" contact with their children. However, in circumstances of dissolution and legal separation (and others involving children), that is exactly what must be done. Of paramount concern to the court in making a custody determination is making an order that will be in the minor's best interests, and one that will promote the statutorily decreed mandate that children have "frequent and continuing" contact with *both* parents. This determination, both as to custody and visitation, is left up to the sound discretion of the trial court, guided by the various factors set out in the Code.

Custody and visitation disputes are the subject of both mediation and conciliation procedures, which are designed to help parents work together to formulate a plan for the custody and visitation of their children, and also to ease some of the burdens an already congested court system is experiencing. From a jurisdictional perspective, interstate as well as intrastate custody battles are governed by the Uniform Child Custody Jurisdiction and Enforcement Act. This Act is a set of laws, enacted in substantially similar form throughout all 50 states and various territories of the United States, the purpose of which is to provide uniformity and predictability in the resolution of these disputes.

Key Terms

The following is a list of key terms and phrases that you should be able to define and use in context. Only then will you have demonstrated a command of the material in this chapter.

- visitation
- *Freeman* order
- relocation
- "move away" cases
- *Troxel*

Questions for Discussion

1. At what age may a child decide for himself/herself where to live?
2. Describe a *Freeman* order (concerning visitation) in detail.
3. Under what circumstances will a custodial parent be allowed to relocate her residence (and that of the minor child)?
4. Explain the circumstances under which grandparents would be allowed to request orders of the court relating to their grandchildren.

ENDNOTES

1. In this regard, it is this author's opinion that the court would think long and hard before instructing noncustodial parents on what theycan or cannot do with respect to their chosen religion vis-à-vis their children; in fact, the court would only take such steps in situations in which the practice of the noncustodial parent's religion constituted a grave and imminent threat or danger to the child.

2. The reader should note that such a contemplated move will not necessarily constitute a "change in circumstances" as is necessary to effect a change in an existing custody order. However, Family Code §3024 seems to indicate to the contrary without actually coming out and saying it. It is this author's opinion that this Code section can be read either way. Most likely the Code section provides for mediation not as an indication of a legislatively created change in circumstances justifying a custody order; rather, the required mediation is more likely simply designed to help the parents work out a compromise so that further court proceedings will not be necessary.

3. Not directly a "move away" case, but a case seeking to modify an existing custody arrangement (which a relocation case typically, out of necessity, does, and thus is of importance here).

4. Child custody reports are expensive. They typically run anywhere between $2,500 to $7,500, depending on who performs the evaluation and how many people are interviewed. If the parties decide to obtain a joint child custody report before litigation, they may save money, but they may also, inadvertently, affect (perhaps adversely) subsequent court proceedings on this matter. Further, what if one parent is so unhappy with the evaluator's recommendation that he decides to go to court anyway? A new expert will then be hired by the unhappy parent and a new one might be required (or desired) by the other parent. So much for saving money!
    Additionally, the parties may be bound by the findings and conclusions of the first evaluator if the stipulation regarding the expert's hiring is not handled correctly. The moral of this story is that these situations should be approached with an attitude of cooperation between the parties, but certainly with eyes wide open. In other words, prior to privately engaging an expert to evaluate and make recommendations in this area, each parent should consult with an attorney to determine the current state of the effect this privately hired expert will have on the outcome of this matter and what other options are available.

5. As discussed later in this book, one of the options a court has after finding a person to be in contempt of court is to put him in jail for up to five days for every count of contempt the citee is found to have committed.

6. Interestingly, Family Code §3103(d) contains a rebuttable presumption that visitation by a grandparent is not in the child's best interests if the parents of the child both agree that the requesting grandparent should not be awarded visitation rights. Such mutual parental agreement on the subject of depriving an individual of visitation is typically the only circumstance in which such person would be denied rights to visit with the minor child. Indeed, in the face of the objection of both parents to visitation by a nonparent, such nonparent visitation can only be allowed upon the court making a finding that such visitation would be in the best interests of the child, as well as a separate and independent finding that denial of nonparent visitation would be detrimental to the child.

7. Section 3102 was ruled unconstitutional in Punsly v. Ho, 87 Cal. App. 4th 1099 (2001).

8. The Washington statute provides in pertinent part: "Any person may petition the court for visitation rights at any time including, but not limited to, custody proceedings. The court may order visitation rights for any person when visitation may serve the best interest of the child whether or not there has been any change of circumstances." (Wash. Rev. Code, §26.10.160, subd. (3).)

9. When reviewing decisions of the U.S. Supreme Court, it is not unusual to find that the dissenting opinion presents a more compelling, or perhaps better reasoned, approach to the issues. This is because the Supreme Court is not just a decisional "court"; it is a policymaking branch of the government. The Court is not required to hear all cases presented; instead, it may choose which ones to review. It chooses cases primarily: (1) to resolve conflicts that it perceives as "worthy" of resolution (in its sole discretion and opinion), or (2) to make policy. As such (and because the makeup of the Supreme Court changes over time as sitting justices retire and new justices are appointed) over time, different policy agendas become relevant that were not so when the original decision was made. Very often, at those times, the dissenting opinion become the basis for the "new" majority opinion. That is fundamentally why the Justices make the effort to write these opinions, and why we must make the effort to read them.

10. A somewhat unusual move. Typically, when the Supreme Court indicates its preference to strike or modify a law or some decisional law they will remand the proceedings back to the lower court for further proceedings based upon and consistent with their opinion. Here, they simply struck it down as unconstitutional and called it a day.

CHAPTER 5

Child Support

CHAPTER OVERVIEW

The question of support, both child and spousal, has been the subject of considerable debate over the years. Spousal support, for example, is not even considered in some states, while in California it is a frequent component to marital termination proceedings. Child support, on the other hand, is virtually uniformly awarded in all jurisdictions but is computed in nearly as many ways as there are jurisdictions awarding it.

The next chapters will explore the circumstances and bases considered in awarding and calculating child and spousal support. The circumstances arising out of modifying and terminating these support awards will also be reviewed.

A.   Introduction

The blanket term *support* as used in the family law context contemplates three basic categories: child support, spousal support, and family support. Each of these concepts will be discussed in greater detail below. Generally, however, they represent exactly what they appear to be on their face. *Child support* refers to the monetary contributions made by one parent of a child (or children) to the other parent. Typically, the noncustodial parent pays support to the custodial parent. This is not always the case, although such an occurrence is rare absent a significant difference in income between the custodial and noncustodial parent. The existence of a valid marriage is completely irrelevant to the assessment and collection of child support, which can arise in many proceedings including dissolution, legal separation, nullity, and paternity.

Spousal support refers to monies paid by one spouse to the other following dissolution of marriage or legal separation. In contrast to child support, spousal support *is* dependent upon the existence of a valid marriage for its assessment and collection. In other words, one cannot receive spousal support unless one is (or was) a *spouse.* The only exception to this rule is found in nullity actions wherein a "putative spouse" may sometimes collect "spousal" support as a result of the circumstances arising out of and pertaining to the action for nullity.

Family support represents a "hybrid" of spousal support and child support. It is primarily designed for tax purposes and takes advantage of the fact that while child support is not tax-deductible, spousal support *is.* Support is often paid *by* an individual who has a greater need for a tax deduction *to* an individual who has a lesser concern for the inclusion in income of the amounts referenced by the support. Thus, family support was devised to allow certain tax advantages to flow back and forth between these individuals, and in doing so (ideally) generate more money for support all together. This is a rather complicated subject and will be covered in greater detail below.

The structure of the Family Code on the subject of support is quite straightforward. Split into five parts, it encompasses 27 separate chapters and is organized as follows:

Part 1: Definitions and General Provisions (sections 3500-3830)
Part 2: Child Support (sections 3900-4253)
Part 3: Spousal Support (sections 4300-4360)
Part 4: Support of Parents (sections 4400-4414)
Part 5: Enforcement of Support Orders (sections 4500-5616)

Part 1, as its name predicts, discusses the statutory definitions and certain general provisions unique to the subject of support. For example, Family Code section 3550 defines the terms *obligee* and *obligor* as the person to whom a duty of support is owed and the person who owes that duty, respectively. Section 3552 provides that in support proceedings the tax returns of the parties, usually *not* available to the other side, *must* be produced on demand for inspection and consideration by the court (and the other party).

Part 1 also discusses selected issues related to child and spousal support, such as expedited child support, support agreements, and modification and termination of support. These concepts will also be discussed later in this chapter.

Part 2 addresses issues related to child support, including the duty to pay and the manner of calculating the amount. Parts 3 and 4 entertain a similar discussion on the subject of spousal and parental support, while Part 5 examines the methods and procedures to enforce these orders.

At the conclusion of this (and the following) chapter, the reader should have a firm grasp of the structure of the Family Code as it relates to support, both child and spousal. The student will understand the manner in which child support is calculated and the circumstances under which those calculations are necessary. Further, there are several special circumstances related to child support (such as the *Duke* order), which will be examined in this chapter.

Similarly, the student will understand the nature of spousal support and will have examined several cases that have grappled with its application. Ideally, after this review the student should become quite conversant on the subject of spousal support, both as to the initial award, the amount, modification, and termination.

B.   Child Support

1.   Duty to Provide Support

As discussed in earlier chapters, the statutory obligation for parental support of minor children is found in several locations in the Code. Generally, however, Family Code sections 3900 et seq. describe the general obligation of both parents to support their child "in the manner suitable to the child's circumstances." This duty extends to all minor children of the parents, whether legitimate or illegitimate, natural or adopted. The obligation to support a child is not dependent upon the existence of a valid marriage. Further, one might interpret Family Code section 3900 as restricted in scope to "minor children." This reading is not correct, although when speaking of the concept of child support in the family law context, the focus is almost always on the support of minor children.

Family Code section 3900 specifically refers to "minor" children. Family Code section 3901 states: "The duty of support imposed by section 3900 continues to an unmarried child who has attained the age of 18 years, is a full time high school student, and who is not self-supporting, until the time the child completes the 12th grade or attains the age of 19 years, whichever occurs first." This section expands upon the earlier statutory termination of child support, which was tied to reaching the age of majority.

Another Code section of interest to this inquiry is Family Code section 4400, which provides: "Except as otherwise provided by law, an adult child shall, to the extent of his or her ability, support a parent who is in need and unable to maintain himself or herself by work."

This Code section is found in Part 4 of Division 9 of the Family Code, "Support of Parents." Division 9 provides general authority for the support not only of minor children but of spouses and parents as well. Many people do not realize that a statute exists for the continuing obligation between parents and children to support each other. This is a reciprocal obligation, which could provide the basis for an action by a county agency providing support to an adult parent or on behalf of the adult parent himself who is "in need" as that term is used throughout the Code.

The reader should also take note of Family Code section 3900, which imposes "equal responsibility" upon both parents to support their children. The parents are, of course, free to agree between themselves as to who will have primary responsibility to support their minor children, but this agreement will not restrict the court's power to enter a contrary order, or to deny the minor child an action to compel support from either one or both of his parents in the event the agreed-upon primary payor of support ignores his responsibilities. If one parent provides child support voluntarily, that parent will generally be denied an action for reimbursement from the other parent absent some agreement or court order. There is, however, statutory authority for the court to order financial compensation for periods when a parent fails to assume the caretaker responsibility contemplated by a custody order. Such authority is generally found in Family Code section 3028.

This mutual duty of support imposed by Family Code section 3900 will not be affected by a court judgment that imposes a child support obligation on one parent alone. Such a judgment will establish the relationship between the *parents*, but it does not terminate the statutory duty of both parents to support their minor children. Thus, if the mother is ordered to provide support for the minor children but fails to do so, Family Code section 3900 provides a vehicle by which the court (or the minor child) can pursue an action against the *father* for payment of support of those children. Father would, of course, have an action against mother by virtue of the allocation of the support duty as between them by the family law court; this does not, however, eliminate father's responsibility to provide support for his minor children in the event he is the only source available for such support.

Perhaps the Code sections cited most often in the context of a family law proceeding pertinent to the support of minor children are Family Code sections 4000 et seq. Family Code section 4000 provides as follows: "If a parent has the duty to provide for the support of the parent's child and willfully fails to so provide, the other parent, or a child by a guardian ad litem, may bring an action against the parent to enforce the duty."

Family Code section 4001 states: "In a proceeding where there is at issue the support of a minor child or a child for whom support is authorized under Section 3901 or 3910, the court may order either or both parents to pay an amount necessary for the support of the child."

And Family Code section 3910 provides: "(a) The father and mother have an equal responsibility to maintain, to the extent of their ability, a child of whatever age who is incapacitated from earning a living and without sufficient means."

These sections extend the reciprocal duty of father and mother to support all of their children, including adult children, notwithstanding the authority to discontinue the payment of support provided by section 3900 as set forth in Family Code section 3901. These sections clearly establish a reciprocal duty of parents to child and child to parents to continue to maintain each other, without reference or regard to termination due simply to the passage of time. This duty does not, of course, extend to anything other than payment for the "necessaries of life." Therefore, the parent does not have a statutorily imposed continuing duty to pay for college expenses, or even living expenses, of an adult child who is capable of working and who simply chooses not to. These statutes are read narrowly rather than liberally and are construed to provide for support under only the most extreme circumstances. The statutory scheme found in sections 4000 et seq. ("Court Ordered Child Support") provides the refinements on these themes and the basic obligation for the parents to do more than simply provide for their children's bare necessities.

These Code sections are also used to provide for the support of a disabled adult child through use of the language, "who is unable to maintain himself by work." These statutory rights are not limited to actions brought by an adult child; they have also been recognized by the appellate courts as providing for an action between the parents who wish to sue each other for the support of an incapacitated adult child.

Although statutes pertinent to the reciprocal duties of the parents find typical application in actions *between* the parents for support of their children, such is not always the case. Indeed, there is an entire line of cases that interprets these statutes vis-à-vis the obligation of the parents to reimburse third parties who provide support for the children following the parent's failure to do so. The third party typically involved in these proceedings is a county or similar welfare agency who has stepped in to provide support for the children in the absence of parental support. When that happens, this "third person" is entitled to be reimbursed under certain circumstances.

As regards third parties providing the child with the "necessities of life," Family Code section 3950 provides: "If a parent neglects to provide articles necessary for the parent's child who is under the charge of the parent, according to the circumstances of a parent, a third person may in good faith supply the necessaries and recover their reasonable value from the parent."

This duty does not extend to children who have abandoned their parents, however. Family Code section 3951 states: "(a) A parent is not bound to compensate the other parent, or a relative, for the voluntary support of the parent's child, without an agreement for compensation, (b) [nor to] compensate a stranger for the support of a child who has abandoned the parent without just cause."[1]

The term "abandonment" is subjective and depends on a review of the facts and circumstances of a particular case. It is generally thought, however, to contemplate a child's permanent relinquishment of submission to parental control.

Finally, although there is some general speculation that stepparents may become liable for child support, such is simply not the case, at least not in a direct sense. Liability for child support rests upon a relationship between the parent and the child either through biological means or through adoption. A stepparent (unless that person has adopted the child) maintains neither relationship. However (as will be explained in the chapters dealing with marital property), certain Family Code sections do provide for a continuing child or support obligation arising from a previous marriage to be treated as a debt incurred "before marriage." This debt is susceptible to collection by resort to the current community property. Inasmuch as the stepparent shares an interest in that community property, to the extent that such property is used to satisfy these premarital obligations, the stepparent could be seen as having some liability for child support. However, it is simply derivative of the marital relationship and the existence of community property that makes the stepparent *appear* to be liable. There is in fact no direct liability under these circumstances. Furthermore, additional provisions of the Family Code provide a right of reimbursement to the stepparent against the biological or adoptive parent in the event community property is used to satisfy a premarital child support obligation.

As with virtually all other Family Code proceedings, the superior court has exclusive jurisdiction to determine child support pursuant to Family Code section 2010. This jurisdiction can only be exercised, however, incident to a marital dissolution, a nullity or legal separation proceeding, an independent proceeding to adjudicate the duty of support, reimbursement or enforcement issues, a modification of an already established support obligation, or a paternity proceeding. Further, jurisdiction extends to support in regards to minor children and to adult children whom the parents have agreed to support.

Inasmuch as child support orders affect the personal rights and obligations of the payor and recipient of child support, the state must have personal jurisdiction over the parents who are being ordered to pay child support. Thus, such person must either be a resident of California, have entered a general appearance in the action, or have in some other way satisfied the "minimum contacts" test pertinent to in personam jurisdiction. Note, however, that Family Code section 3550 clearly states that *every* obligor resident of this state is required to adhere to the duty of support as defined in sections 3900, 3901, 3910, 4300, and 4400, regardless of the obligee's presence or residence.

It can be argued that even an unborn child is owed a duty of support. The court has the authority to assess support payments against the father while the mother is still pregnant. This is law, which dates back over 50 years. Additionally, the father can be compelled to share in the prenatal and birth costs of the minor child.

2. Obtaining an Award of Child Support—Statutory Considerations

A child support award (order) can be obtained basically two different ways: (1) the parties can agree on entry of an order, or (2) the court can order payment of support in those situations where the parties do not agree. Certainly the latter method is by far the most common—not so much because parties are recalcitrant to *pay*, but because the parties cannot agree on an *amount* to be paid (more on that later).

The parties are of course free to agree on an award of child support, and the Family Code recognizes this fact. Chapter 3 of Division 9, Part 1, entitled "Support Agreements," addresses this situation. Section 3585 clearly recognizes such an agreement and charges the superior court with the power to enter an order for support thereon. Section 3587 even authorizes the court to give effect to an agreement between parents that contemplates the continuation of support after the child attains the age of majority by entering its order for such support.

The above pertains, of course, to the establishment of an order for child support in general. The amount of that award is susceptible to even greater scrutiny by the court. Family Code section 4065 provides that the parties are free to stipulate to a child support amount, but that amount is subject to court approval. The section further directs the court to withhold its approval unless the parties declare:

(1) They are fully informed of their rights concerning child support.
(2) The order is being agreed to without coercion or duress.
(3) The agreement is in the best interests of the children involved.
(4) The needs of the children will be adequately met by the stipulated amount [, and]
(5) The right to support has not been assigned to the county pursuant to Section 11477 of the Welfare and Institutions Code and no public assistance application is pending.

There are other protections as well, typically involving situations where welfare is being paid on behalf of the minor child(ren), and of course the court is always free to refuse to accept the parties' stipulation. The calculation of child support has become an extremely rigid process. Deviation from the statutory guidelines, even pursuant to a stipulation of both parents, is not easy to come by.

The most common method used for obtaining an award of child support is based on Family Code section 4001. Indeed, most all child support awards stem from a proceeding under this Division of the Family Code. Section 4001 states that "in any proceeding where there is at issue the support of a minor child, or a child for whom support is authorized under section 3901 or 3910, the court may order either or both parents to pay any amount necessary for the support of the child." Section 4001 also provides authority for the award of child support to certain adult children who are "in need" and unable to maintain themselves through employment.

In addition to section 4001, several other sections of the Family Code provide generally for the support of children, including, sections 2010, 3029, 3587, and 3621. Additionally, a general civil suit may be brought on behalf of a minor child (or by an adult child who qualifies for support) to obtain support. This chapter also allows a child (or the county on the child's behalf) to sue to enforce a parental support obligation. Finally, Family Code section 4000 specifically provides for an independent action by either the recipient parent or the child (through a guardian ad litem) against a parent who has the duty to provide for child support and "willfully fails to so provide." Plainly, this chapter of the Code is drawn very broadly to provide for payment of the statutorily imposed support through whatever avenue necessary.

In addition, government agencies have several avenues to collect support payments either on behalf of the child and the recipient parent or on behalf of the county itself in welfare situations. For example, the district attorney for any county that is providing Aid to Families with Dependent Children (AFDC) may maintain an independent action to obtain reimbursement from the noncustodial parent for amounts paid on behalf of the child under the authority of Family Code section 17400.

Similarly, if the minor child is taken out of the home (typically under the auspices of the juvenile dependency court) and placed in foster care, the court may maintain an action against the child's parents for the "reasonable costs of support" for the minor while the minor child is "placed, or detained in, or committed to, any institution or other place pursuant to Section 625 or pursuant to an order of the juvenile court." The authority for this action is found in Welfare and Institutions Code sections 625 and 903. Family Code section 4012 further provides that, upon a showing of good cause, the court has authority to require any parent who is obligated to pay child support to post security to ensure that such payments are in fact made when due. Section 3651 also contains authority for the modification (or revocation, as the court may deem necessary) of preexisting child support awards. Section 3653 provides that an award (or modification) of child support may be made retroactive to the date of filing the notice of motion or the order to show cause requesting the change. Finally, section 3652 includes a provision for the recovery of attorney's fees and court costs to the prevailing party in these matters.[2] The Family Code also addresses "indirect" aspects of child support. Section 3028 contains provisions for the court to order "financial compensation for periods when a parent fails to assume the caretaker responsibility, or when a parent has been thwarted by the other parent when attempting to exercise visitation or custody rights." This Code section limits the ability to recover such compensation as follows:

> (b) The compensation shall be limited to (1) the reasonable expenses incurred for or on behalf of a child, resulting from the other parent's failure to assume caretaker responsibility or (2) the reasonable expenses incurred by a parent for or on behalf of a child resulting from the other parent's thwarting of the parent's efforts to exercise custody or visitation rights. The expenses may include the value of caretaker services but are not limited to the cost of services provided by a third party during the relevant period.
>
> (c) The compensation may be requested by noticed motion or an order to show cause, which shall allege, under penalty of perjury, (1) a minimum of one hundred dollars ($100) of expenses incurred or (2) at least three occurrences of failure to exercise custody or visitation rights or (3) at least three occurrences of the thwarting of efforts to exercise custody or visitation rights within the six months before filing of the motion or order.
>
> (d) Attorney's fees shall be awarded to the prevailing party upon a showing of the nonprevailing party's ability to pay as required by Section 270.

Thus, section 3028 provides relief for the parent with primary physical custody when the other parent simply refuses or is uncooperative in exercising his physical custodial rights. As any parent can attest, arranging and paying for child care, especially at the last minute, is very expensive and anxiety-producing. If a custodial parent has scheduled a vacation, for example, and the other parent fails to exercise his physical custodial rights, thousands of dollars can be lost on the cancelled vacation. This section provides some aspect of relief to the custodial parent in this situation.

Obtaining and enforcing these orders can prove somewhat intimidating, however. In recognition of this fact, the legislature has enacted laws designed to facilitate these efforts. These laws have undergone a variety of incarnations, the most recent of which can be found in Family Code sections 17000 et seq.

In the past, the local district attorney held responsibility for state-sponsored enforcement of child support, and acted pursuant to authority of the State Department of Social Services and the Attorney General. That system proved to be less than adequate for addressing these concerns, thus prompting the legislature to create a new State Department of Child Support Services (DCSS). DCSS is charged with the duty to "administer all services and perform all functions necessary to establish, collect, and distribute child support." The local district attorney enforces criminal laws related to delinquent child support obligations.

It is not necessary that the child support recipient also be a recipient of public assistance. DCSS has authority to both establish and enforce child support orders. Basically, its duties include: obtaining an initial order for child support "by civil or criminal process"; obtaining a temporary child support order effective during the pendency of the action; collecting child support arrearages from a delinquent obligor; initiating a motion or OSC to increase an existing child support order; responding to an obligor parent's motion or OSC to decrease an existing child support order; initiating a motion or OSC to obtain a medical support order; responding to an obligor parent's motion or OSC to decrease or terminate an existing medical support order; and transferring of accounts receivable for management of child support delinquencies to the Franchise Tax Board.

The parents are free to participate in these proceedings, but they are not required to do so. Additionally, for the most part, the only issues that will be addressed in these proceedings are those related directly to child support. Generally, custody and visitation and related issues will not be heard in this context. As is the case with all new legislation, Family Code sections 17000 et seq. will be subject to much fine-tuning over the years as they are used and interpreted. The reader is advised, however, to become very familiar with these concepts and the manner in which the legislature approaches problems associated with issues of child support.

3. Amount of the Award

a) *Historical Perspectives*

Without a doubt, the most heavily litigated issue in the context of child support does not concern the *liability* for support, but rather the *amount* of support. The law in this area has undergone a rather significant evolution over the years. Historically, the establishment of the amount of child support was primarily left to the discretion of the trial court. The court would examine factors related to the needs of the children as presented by both parties, the income and earning abilities of both parties, and other factual circumstances that had a bearing on the child's standard of living, both pre- and post-separation. As might be expected, these child support awards varied widely from county to county and even from courtroom to courtroom within the same county. A common complaint was that the same parties could get three different rulings on the amount of child support from three different judges on any given day.

This lack of uniformity and predictability led to a tremendous amount of confusion and made settlement in this area extremely difficult. There was also the problem of how to reimburse the county welfare agencies for amounts that had been "advanced" by them on behalf of an absent parent of a minor child who was not receiving support from that parent. While the welfare agencies (especially those operating under federal mandate) were forced to pay a uniform and specific amount per month per child, their chances for recovering the same amount from the noncustodial parent were haphazard at best. Furthermore, even where a preexisting court order for support was simply disobeyed by the noncustodial parent, it was not at all uncommon for that court order to be in an amount far less than the amount paid by the welfare agency.

In 1984, in an attempt to close this gap between the amounts being paid by the welfare agencies and the amounts being ordered by the court as child support, the Agnos Child Support Standards Act of 1984 came into effect, set out at (then) Civil Code sections 4720 et seq. The Agnos Act established a two-level system of child support guidelines, which included both a mandatory minimum statewide component and a discretionary component for making awards that were higher than the minimum amount. The Agnos guideline was essentially designed to establish the noncustodial parent's percentage of liability for welfare reimbursement, and to ensure that the support awarded by the court did not fall below that minimum amount. In so doing, it was reasoned that the welfare agency would at least be able to recover the amounts expended on behalf of the minor child and appropriately attributable to the noncustodial parent when pursuing their reimbursement rights for amounts paid to a custodial parent under the various welfare programs, most notably AFDC.[3]

The concept of using guidelines for the establishment of support was not created in 1984. Indeed, Santa Clara County had already established a basic and uniform schedule of proposed child support awards based on a comparison of the relative net income of the noncustodial parent versus the custodial parent. These guidelines gradually spread throughout California counties and by 1984 were in regular (albeit unpublished) use throughout many of the more populated counties. The guidelines were primarily based upon various research studies that attempted to establish exactly how much it costs the average family to raise the average child on a per month basis. A comparison was made of the income earned by both parents, and then a determination was made as to what percentage of that entire pool of income (or pie) was devoted to the support, care, and maintenance of the children in the family. These various concepts were algebraically strung together in a formula, which (arguably) would produce a predictable guideline (that is, proposed) amount for child support.

The Agnos Act fine-tuned this concept and created a statewide system of guidelines based upon the ideas discussed above in an attempt to provide the uniformity and predictability so badly needed in child support awards. However, the Agnos Act's guidelines merely established a mandatory *minimum* amount and left the rest (which constituted well in excess of 90 percent of the child support awards being made in the state) entirely up to the discretion of the judge.

Parallel to this development was an increased awareness on a federal level of the wide disparity in child support awards from state to state and county to county. Accordingly, it became a matter of federal priority for each state to establish guidelines for child support that would be applied *uniformly* throughout the state. This federal directive is found at 42 U.S.C. section 667(a), (b)(2) and is known as the Family Support Act of 1988. The federal legislature made it clear that if California (and other states) wished to continue to obtain federal funding for its public assistance programs then it had better comply with this federal mandate and establish uniform statewide guidelines.

Effective March 1, 1991, the California legislature did just that. California Rule of Court 1274 was enacted, which purported to adopt certain components of the Agnos Act that the legislature found attractive and to incorporate into those concepts statewide uniformity through the establishment of its guidelines for child support. The intention was to take away from the courts the discretion that was traditionally exercised by them in awarding child support and to provide uniformity of awards on a statewide basis. The Agnos Act was thus repealed and superseded by CRC 1274.[4]

The child support calculation promulgated by CRC 1274 was designed simply as an interim guideline, however, while work progressed on a permanent formula for the establishment of uniform statewide guidelines. After much fine-tuning and several urgency bills extending the effective date of application, July 1, 1992, a permanent mandatory statewide child support guideline came into effect pursuant to the provisions of Civil Code section 4721. These changes (from the interim child support guidelines of California Rules of Court section 1274) were designed to actually increase the effective amount of child support being generated under the formula set forth in CRC 1274.[5]

b) *Current Law Concerning Guideline Child Support*

With the enactment of the Family Code, effective January 1, 1994, the guidelines found in Civil Code section 4721 were once again fine-tuned, with the result being the current statutory scheme for the calculation of guideline child support found at sections 4050 et seq. of the Family Code. The changes enacted by the Family Code legislation were minimal, thus continuing the basic statutory structure from its enactment as Civil Code section 4721 in July 1992.

Article 2, "Statewide Uniform Guidelines," takes great pains to define the legislature's intent and specifies that its primary goal is to comply with federal guidelines. The introductory sections mandate application of this formula and allow for deviation only under the specific "special circumstances" discussed in the article. The basic legislative intent and directive on this area is spelled out in Family Code section 4053. Due to the clarity with which the legislature has articulated these fundamental concepts related to the issue of child support, that code section is reprinted below in its entirety:

§4053 Mandatory adherence to principles

In implementing the statewide uniform guideline, the courts shall adhere to the following principles:

(a) A parent's first and principal obligation is to support his or her minor children according to the parent's circumstances and station in life.

(b) Both parents are mutually responsible for the support of their children.

(c) The guideline takes into account each parent's actual income and level of responsibility for the children.

(d) Each parent should pay for the support of the children according to his or her ability.

(e) The guideline seeks to place the interests of children as the state's top priority.

(f) Children should share in the standard of living of both parents. Child support may therefore appropriately improve the standard of living of the custodial household to improve the lives of the children.

(g) Child support orders in cases in which both parents have high levels of responsibility for the children should reflect the increased costs of raising the children in two homes and should minimize significant disparities in the children's living standards in the two homes.

(h) The financial needs of the children should be met through private financial resources as much as possible.

(i) It is presumed that a parent having primary physical responsibility for the children contributes a significant portion of available resources for the support of the children.

(j) The guideline seeks to encourage fair and efficient settlements of conflicts between parents and seeks to minimize the need for litigation.

(k) The guideline is intended to be presumptively correct in all cases, and only under special circumstances should child support orders fall below the child support mandated by the guideline formula.

> (l) Child support orders must ensure that children actually receive fair, timely, and sufficient support reflecting the state's high standard of living and high costs of raising children compared to other states.

After reading section 4053, there should be little doubt left in the mind of the reader that the establishment of an appropriate award of child support is one of (if not the) most important directives of the Family Code. Section 4054 mandates that the judicial council monitor the effectiveness and viability of these guidelines and make recommendations in that regard to the legislature on a periodic basis.

The actual algebraic formula for the calculation of guideline child support is contained in Family Code section 4055. That formula is expressed as follows: $CS = K [HN - (H\%)(TN)]$. In this formula, the symbols set forth below (and used in the formula) make reference to the following definitions:

CS = child support amount
K = amount of both parents' income to be allocated for child support
HN = high earner's net monthly disposable income
H% = higher earner's approximate time of physical responsibility for the children
TN = the parties' total monthly net income

This formula will produce an amount of support per minor child. When more than one child is involved, the end result (CS) is then multiplied by a specific factor depending upon the number of children. For example, for two children, the multiplier is 1.6; for three children, the multiplier is 2; for four children, the multiplier is 2.3; for five children, the multiplier is 2.5; for six children, the multiplier is 2.625, and so on, up to a factor of 2.86 for ten children.

The K factor (the amount of both parents' income to be allocated for child support) is also computed by application of a mathematical formula contained in section 4055(b)(3), which fluctuates based on the total net disposable monthly income. It was in fact the upwards adjustment of this K factor that produced the desired result of increasing overall guideline child support awards.

These calculations can become rather complicated until they are actually seen in operation. Fortunately, section 4055 provides an example of calculating at least one part of the formula. Recall that formula is as follows:

$$CS = K [HN - (H\%)(TN)].$$

Algebraically, then, child support (CS) is equal to the amount of both parents' income to be allocated to child support (K), multiplied by the result obtained when the *product* of the approximate percentage of time the high earner spends with the child(ren) (H%), multiplied by the total net monthly disposable income of the parties (TN), is *subtracted* from the high earner's total net monthly disposable income (HN).

All this is still quite confusing, especially since many of these terms need to be further defined. The K factor, as well as gross and net income, are prime examples. Fortunately, the Code provides these definitions.

The K factor is defined in 4055 (b)(3) as a function of the amount of time the high earner spends with the child(ren) multiplied by a statutorily determined fraction. If the high earner spends 50 percent or less time with the children, then the multiplier is calculated one way, and if the amount of time is greater than 50 percent, then the multiplier is calculated another way.

If the percentage of time is 50 or less, the multiplier is equal to one plus that percentage. For example, if the amount of time is equal to 20 percent, then the multiplier is equal to 20 percent plus 1, or .20 + 1 = 1.20. If the amount of time is equal to 85 percent, then the multiplier is equal to 85 percent *subtracted from* 2, or 2 − .85 = 1.15.

As should be evident, the more time the high earner spends with the children, the lower the multiplier will be, which (as will be seen below) will have the effect of lowering the guideline amount of child support. This result is due to the statutorily recognized (and common-sense) conclusion that the more time the children spend with the high earner, the more it will cost to provide the day-to-day needs of those children, and the less it will cost the other parent (since she doesn't have the children as much). The language supporting this idea is found in Family Code section 4053(g), which states: "Child support orders in cases in which both parents have high levels of responsibility for the children should reflect the increased costs of raising the children in two homes and should minimize significant disparities in the children's living standards in the two homes."

Sections 4058 and 4059 define gross and net disposable income, respectively, and address these concepts as they relate to child support calculations. Conceptually, they provide that *gross income* includes income (as that term is generally construed by the IRS) from all sources; *net disposable income* is gross income less all allowable deductions (usually state and federal taxes, union dues, mandatory retirement benefits, health insurance deductions, and items of a similar nature).

One of the more interesting provisions related to the calculation of gross income is contained in Family Code section 4057.5. Resolving a controversy that provided no clear guidelines and many disparate results (depending upon the specific judge involved), the legislature, in this section, put to rest (for the time being at least) the question of whether the income of a new spouse, or a live-in partner, will be included in the determination of the obligor or obligee's income: it will not. Naturally, there is an exception to this rule, but that exception is rather limited: only where excluding that income will "lead to extreme and severe hardship to any child subject to the child support award" will that income be considered.

Getting back to calculation of the K factor, the discussions above account only for determination of the *multiplier*: (1 + H%[≤50], or 2 − H%[≥50]). What of the other half of the equation, the *multiplicand*? Section 4055(b)(3) expresses the multiplicand in terms of a predetermined fraction that varies according to the total net disposable monthly income of both parties (TN). The chart containing this list is as follows:

Total Net Disposable Income per Month	K Equals
$0–800	.20 + TN/16,000
$801–6,666	.25
$6,667–10,000	.10 + 1000/TN
Over $10,000	.12 + 800/TN

For example, if total monthly income (TN) is $750, then the multiplicand is equal to .20 + (750/16,000), or .20 + .0486 = .2468. If the total net monthly disposable income (TN) is $8,500, then the multiplicand would be equal to .10 + (1000/8500), or .10 + .118 = .218.

Using the numbers derived above, if the H% factor is 20, and TN is $750, then K = (1 + 0.20) × .2468 => 1.20 × .2468 = .296.

In the same example, if TN equals $8,500, then K = (1 + 0.20) × .218 => 1.20 × .218 = .261.

Using the example from the Code, if TN equals $1,000, and assuming an H% factor of 20, then K = (1 + 0.20) × .25 => 1.20 × .25 = .30.

An interesting phenomenon takes place when H% is significantly changed. One would expect that the K factor would decrease significantly as H% exceeded 50. Due to the structure of the formula, however, this is not the case. In fact, assuming a constant TN, there is no real decrease until H% exceeds 80 because, as written, the formula for calculating the H% does not reflect a lower number until the 80% threshold is reached. At H% = .20 and H% = .80 the K factor is the same. Thus, for the high earner to realize a noticeable decrease in the K factor, he must have primary responsibility over the minor children for at least more than 80 percent of the time. In fact, if the high earner has the children 75 percent of the time, the K factor is actually *higher* than if he only had them 20 percent of the time (.31 versus .30).

Now that the K factor is easily determined, the rest is simply plugging numbers into the formula. Let us assume, then, that the high earner's net monthly disposable income is $8,000 and the other party's net monthly income is $2,500. The high earner also has primary responsibility over the minor child 20 percent of the time. Based on these facts, the K factor equals $(1 + 0.20) \times (0.10 + [1000/10,500])$, or, $1.20 \times .195 = .234$.

Plugging this number into the formula yields the following result:

$$CS = K[HN - (H\%)(TN)]$$
$$CS = .234 [8500 - (.20)(10,500)]$$
$$CS = .234 [8500 - 2100]$$
$$CS = .234 \times 6400 = \$1,497.60$$

The guideline child support award under these facts is thus $1,497.60 per month, which the high earner will pay to the low earner.

Adding one more level of complexity to this analysis, let's assume the same facts as above, only now we are calculating support not for one child, but for four. The result is simple to obtain. Section 4055(b)(4) establishes a chart of multipliers to be employed when there is more than one child. The multiplication factor for four children is 2.3. To arrive at the appropriate amount of child support we merely multiply the result obtained for one child ($1,497.60) by 2.3 to arrive at a monthly child support award, for four children, of $3,444.48.

The final piece of business to be accomplished to fully satisfy the requirements of Family Code section 4055 in our example is to allocate this $3,444.48 amount among the four children, providing a specific dollar amount for each. Section 4055(b)(8) instructs that this is accomplished by allocating *at least* the amount of support allocable to one child (under these circumstances $1,497.60) to the *youngest* child, with the next youngest being allocated the difference between that amount and the amount allocated for two children. In this case, the amount allocated for just two children would have been $2,396.16, so this "next youngest" child is allocated $898.56 of the $3,444.48. The remaining two children are allocated a support amount in a similar fashion: child number 2 receives the difference between $2,396.16 (two children) and $2,995.20 (three children), or $599.04. The oldest child is thus left with an allocation of $449.28. The total child support award of $3,444.48 is thus allocated among these children as follows:

youngest child:	$1,497.60
next youngest:	898.56
third youngest:	599.04
oldest child:	449.28

By allocating the child support in this manner, the highest portion of the support is allocated to the youngest child. By so doing, as the older children reach the age of majority and no longer receive child support payments, not only will the parties know by how much the award will drop, but the drop-off will be the lowest possible amount, thus ensuring that the remaining children continue to receive the amount required by the guidelines.[6]

When arriving at the various numbers to be plugged into the formula above, care must be taken to ensure that the determination of net monthly income as referenced in the formula comports with the requirements of the Code. As mentioned briefly above, gross income refers to any gross income from any source, including bonuses, rents, workers' compensation benefits, unemployment and disability insurance benefits, royalties, and pensions. From this figure, then, certain deductions are allowed in order to arrive at the net figure. Examples of eligible deductions include state and federal taxes accruing to the parties and actually payable, and other deductions generally allowable pursuant to generally accepted accounting principles with regard to the establishment of net income from a tax perspective. Once the annual net income is determined, that amount is divided by 12 to obtain the monthly net income.[7]

The reader should note that the court will not turn a blind eye to the earning capacity of the parties as opposed to what they are actually earning. For example, an individual who is a doctor may have the earning capacity of several hundred thousand dollars per year, yet choose to work at a grocery store, and thus earn only $24,000 per year. The court has authority to look beyond the plain mathematical calculation referenced above to determine income in this case and to impute to the payor parent (that is, pretend as if that person was in fact earning) income from the higher paying "earning capacity" employment (see generally Family Code section 4058(b)). The purpose behind this is to discourage parents with an otherwise high earning capacity from deliberately suppressing their income by taking a low-paying job in an attempt to deprive their children of adequate and reasonable child support.

c) Statutory Add-Ons and Deductions

There is a statutory presumption that the amount determined pursuant to the guidelines is, in fact, the correct order. The court can, however, deviate from the guideline amount upon a finding that rebuts the statutory presumption that the amount arrived at pursuant to the guidelines is correct and should be ordered in all cases. Such deviation will be allowed in situations, for example, in which: the parties have stipulated to a different amount under Family Code section 4065[8]; the sale of the family residence has been deferred pursuant to Family Code sections 3800 to 3810 (a "*Duke* order," discussed below); a party is not contributing to the children's needs commensurate with that party's time share (that is, he is spending so little time with his child that he should be paying more); the extraordinarily high income of the paying parent would result in an award under the guidelines that was in excess of the child's needs; the application of the guideline formula would be unjust in any particular case. These provisions allowing for deviation from the guideline amount set forth above are established at Family Code section 4057.

Once the calculation of net income has been determined to the court's satisfaction as regards an "earning capacity" analysis, there are certain mandatory and discretionary add-ons and reductions to the net income as provided by statute that may act to increase (or decrease) net income and in so doing lower the amount of the child support award. Section 4059(g) of the Code states that under appropriate circumstances, when computing net income, there shall be a deduction from gross income "for *hardship* as defined by sections 4070 to 4073, inclusive, and applicable published appellate court decisions." This section further instructs that the amount of the hardship is deducted not from the child support itself; rather, it operates to lower the income of the party claiming the hardship (which in most cases will in fact operate to lower the award). What then is a hardship deduction?

The concept of a *hardship deduction* is defined by statute at sections 4070 and 4071 of the Code. Those sections provide that the hardship deduction will be allowed only in cases of "extreme financial hardship," arising from the following statutorily defined circumstances:

(1) Extraordinary health expenses for which the parent is financially responsible, and uninsured catastrophic losses.
(2) The minimum basic living expenses of either parent's natural or adopted children for whom the parent has the obligation to support from other marriages or relationships who reside with the parent.

There are, of course, limits to the amount of a hardship deduction allowed for basic living expenses of another child living with the parent. These limits require that the deductions can be equal to, but not greater than, the support to be awarded to each child who is the subject of the child support award so that child will not be prejudiced by the presence of the other child.

The allowance of these hardship deductions is entirely discretionary with the court, and the Code specifically directs the court to state, in writing or on the record, the reasons it had found in support of the deduction, document the amount of the deduction and the manner in which it was calculated, and, if possible, to specify the duration of the hardship. Additionally, in considering allowance of a hardship deduction, section 4073 of the Code requires that the court "be guided by the goals set forth in this article [related to calculation of minimum child support awards] when considering whether or not to allow a financial hardship deduction, and, if allowed, when determining the amount of the deduction."

In addition to *deductions* from income, the Code also provides that certain items either *shall* or *may* be added to the child support award. These are listed in section 4062:

Mandatory add-ons:
(1) Child care costs related to employment or to reasonably necessary education or training for employment skills.
(2) The reasonable uninsured health care costs for the children as provided in section 4063.

Discretionary add-ons:
(1) Costs related to the educational or other special needs of the children.
(2) Travel expenses for visitation.

Generally, to the extent the above items exist and are added on to the child support calculation, the court will apportion them equally between the two parents unless the court finds the existence of good cause to apportion them differently.

d) Computer-Assisted Support Calculations

These child support calculations of income, add-ons, deductions, and the resulting guideline amount of support are performed for both the payor parent and the recipient parent and are primarily a function of the numbers set forth on the income and expense declaration (described in the various sections above). The actual mechanical employment of the formula in an attempt to obtain a "preview" of the probable child support award under the circumstances can be a time-consuming and confusing task if done by hand. Fortunately, however, a variety of computer software programs are preprogrammed with these formulas and are designed to take a gross income figure as to each parent and apply the various add-ons and deductions to that amount to determine ultimate net income for each parent. The program will then apply those figures to the child support formulas discussed above, perform all the calculations, and present a guideline child support amount.[9]

There is little doubt that calculation of the guideline amount of child support in California is an increasingly complex process. As a general rule, almost uniform reliance has been placed upon computer-assisted support software. The mathematical calculations can become quite cumbersome. Fortunately, courts are very receptive to the use of these software programs in arriving at child (and spousal) support calculations. In fact, Family Code section 3830 provides that no court may use any of these computer software programs to compute support unless it conforms to the rules of court adopted by the judicial council prescribing standards for these programs.

These rules essentially codify an existing practice of most (if not all) family law judges and make provision for a standard of quality and accuracy to which these programs must adhere. The recognition of this use and the implied acceptance of this by the Legislature have provided a clear resolution to promote the use of these programs, provided they meet with the specific requirements of the Code.

4. Additional Aspects of Child Support

It is generally thought that once an amount of child support has been established, payment of that amount will (for the most part) relieve an obligor parent of the duty to pay additional sums for the support or maintenance of the child. There are, however, exceptions to this rule. Of particular note are the provisions found at Chapter 7 of Division 9, entitled "Health Insurance," and those found at Chapter 8 of that Division entitled "Deferred Sale of Home Order." Of course, there are many varying circumstances under which a court may require an obligor parent to contribute more than a simple monthly payment of cash for the support of a minor child. Most of these instances, however, are confined to the unique facts and circumstances of any given case. These concepts of health insurance coverage and those related to the deferred sale of the family home, however, have been recognized by the legislature and codified in very specific legislation.

a) *Mandatory Health Insurance*

One of the fundamental concerns of the California legislature in recent years has been the apparent lack of concern (or action, at least) on the subject of providing effective health care for minor children. Indeed, the controversy over health care coverage for the public in general has recently become a topic of significant debate. In recent years, in an attempt to remedy this situation and to provide certain statutorily decreed protections for minor children in the context of health insurance coverage, the legislature has enacted legislation addressing these concerns, and, perhaps most importantly, tying this legislation to certain court orders defining child support in general. The rationale is that if the legislature cannot reach all children residing in this state with regard to health insurance coverage legislation, it can at least reach those children who are before the court as a result of child support proceedings.

In this regard, Family Code section 3751 established mandatory provisions requiring maintenance of health insurance coverage for a supported child. Family Code section 3750 defines health insurance coverage, as used in this specific article, to include all of the following items:

(a) Vision care and dental care coverage whether the vision care or dental care coverage is part of existing health insurance coverage or is issued as a separate policy or plan.

(b) Provision for the delivery of health care services by a fee for service, health maintenance organization, preferred provider organization, or any other type of health care delivery system under which medical services could be provided to a dependent child of an absent parent.

Family Code section 3751 implements these mandates with regard to health insurance coverage as follows:

(a)(1) Support orders issued or modified pursuant to this chapter shall include a provision requiring the child support obligor to keep the agency designated under Title IV-D of the Social Security Act (42 U.S.C. Sec. 651 et seq.) informed of whether the obligor has health insurance coverage at a reasonable cost and, if so, the health insurance policy information.

(2) In any case in which an amount is set for current support, the court shall require that health insurance coverage for a supported child shall be maintained by either or both parents if that insurance is available at no cost or at a reasonable cost to the parent. Health insurance coverage shall be rebuttably presumed to be reasonable in cost if it is employment-related group health insurance or other group health insurance, regardless of the service delivery mechanism. The actual cost of the health insurance to the obligor shall be considered in determining whether the cost of insurance is reasonable. If the court determines that the cost of health insurance coverage is not reasonable, the court shall state its reasons on the record.

(b) If the court determines that health insurance coverage is not available at no cost or at a reasonable cost, the court's order for support shall contain a provision that specifies that health insurance coverage shall be obtained if it becomes available at no cost or at a reasonable cost. Upon health insurance coverage at no cost or at a reasonable cost becoming available to a parent, the parent shall apply for that coverage.

(c) The court's order for support shall require the parent who, at the time of the order or subsequently, provides health insurance coverage for a supported child to seek continuation of coverage for the child upon attainment of the limiting age for a dependent child under the health insurance coverage if the child meets the criteria specified under Section 1373 of the Health and Safety Code or Section 10277 or 10278 of the Insurance Code and that health insurance coverage is available at no cost or at a reasonable cost to the parent or parents, as applicable.

Naturally, not all parents will have this type of insurance available to them "at no or reasonable cost." However, the reader would be surprised how many obligor parents seek to increase their cash flow after support payments have been computed by canceling what they feel to be "discretionary" items of expense, including health care coverage. The Code sections referenced above seek to ensure that an obligor's post-support cash flow problems are not softened at the expense of health care coverage for minor children. The reader should note, however, that Family Code section 3751 does not limit its application to obligor parents. That Code section specifically requires that such health insurance coverage shall be maintained by "either or both parents."

Moreover, Article 1 of Chapter 7 contains additional Code sections designed to ensure implementation of child support orders.Article 2 of Chapter 7 is entitled "Health Insurance Coverage Assignment" and is found at sections 3760 to 3773 of the Family Code. These Code sections are also what might be deemed *enabling Code sections* inasmuch as they provide a mechanism through which health insurance can be secured and maintained without the cooperation of the employee parent. Family Code section 3761 provides:

> Upon application by either a party or local child support agency in any proceeding where the court has ordered one or both parents to maintain health insurance coverage . . . the court shall order the employer of the obligor parent or other person providing health insurance to the obligor to enroll the supported child in the health insurance plan available to the obligor through the employer or other person and to deduct the full cost of the premium or costs, if any, from the earnings of the obligor unless the court makes a finding of good cause for not making the order.

Section 3761 also provides certain procedural criteria with regard to the issuance of this assignment, as do Code sections 3762 to 3764. Code section 3765 provides the procedure by which an obligor parent may move the court to quash a health insurance coverage assignment under circumstances enumerated in that section, including: the amount withheld for premiums is greater than that authorized by Family Code section 3750, the amount of the increased premium is unreasonable, and the employer's selection of health plan is inappropriate.

In this regard, Family Code section 3766 requires the employer (or other person providing health insurance) to provide health insurance coverage consistent with the court's order within thirty days of being served with the assignment order. In addition, Family Code section 3766(c) provides that "if the obligor has not enrolled in an available health plan, there is a choice of coverage, and the court has not ordered coverage by a specific plan, the employer or other person providing health insurance shall enroll the child in the plan that will reasonably provide benefits or coverage where the child resides." By so doing, the legislature essentially shifted the obligation to obtain appropriate health care coverage for a supported child away from the obligor and placed it on the shoulders of the employer in situations where multiple choices for health insurance coverage exist. In most cases, the obligor parent already participates in an employer-provided health plan, and it is not necessary for the employer to select from a smorgasbord of plans; instead, the employer may simply enroll the child in the existing health insurance plan, then deduct the enrollment costs from the obligor's paycheck. It should be noted that these legislatively mandated requirements placed upon the employer are not without "teeth." Family Code section 3768, entitled "Failure to Comply with a Valid Assignment Order; Liability," provides as follows:

> (a) An employer or other person providing health insurance who willfully fails to comply with a valid health insurance coverage assignment entered and served on the employer or other person pursuant to this article is liable to the applicant for the amount incurred in health care services that would otherwise have been covered under the insurance policy but for the conduct of the employer or other person that was contrary to the assignment order.
> (b) Willful failure of an employer or other person providing health insurance to comply with a health insurance coverage assignment is punishable as contempt of court under Section 1218 of the Code of Civil Procedure.

Clearly, then, not only can an employer be held liable for the costs of medical services provided, it can also be held in contempt of court—and face the fines and penalties associated with such a finding.

b) *Deferred Sale of Home Order*

Another relatively common and significant aspect to "additional" child support is detailed in Chapter 8 of Division 9, the "Deferred Sale of Home Order," sometimes known as a *Duke* order.

In somewhat rare cases, as part of a child support order, the court will allow the recipient parent to remain in the family home with the minor child for so long as the child remains a minor or continues to live with that parent. This can be both a very valuable award from the recipient parent's standpoint and a very troubling award from the obligor parent's standpoint.

Very often, the most significant asset in a family is its residence. It is not at all uncommon for a family to remain in its home for upwards of five or ten years (even longer for individuals who purchased homes 15 to 20 years ago). As such, by the time the parties commence a dissolution or legal separation proceeding, they may find that there is significant equity in their home,[10] equity which the supporting parent (the so-called *out spouse*) would like to obtain so that alternate housing can be purchased. Unfortunately, as is most often the case, the custodial parent and child are not able to obtain comparable housing post-dissolution because the cost is prohibitive. Furthermore, the courts and child and family counselors are generally in agreement that to the extent a minor child has bonded with his home, neighborhood, and friends, a relocation from that source of stability and security, especially during the difficult times of dissolution, might not be in the child's best interests.

Naturally, this discussion becomes irrelevant if there are sufficient community assets to simply award the entire family residence to the custodial parent and provide the noncustodial parent with an equal amount of "offsetting" assets. However, if this is economically unfeasible (for example, if the custodial parent is unable to "cash out" the noncustodial parent's interest in the house) then the discussion turns to a consideration of whether the sale of the family residence should be deferred until the occurrence of certain events related to the minor child. Such an order is called a *Duke order*, now referred to as the *deferred sale of home order*. Historically, an order deferring the sale of the family home as an additional component of child support was first established by a judicial opinion rather than statute. *Marriage of Bozeman*, 31 Cal. App. 3d 372 (1973) was the first case to define and work with these concepts. That case, together with *Marriage of Herrmann*, 84 Cal. App. 3d 361 (1978), established the basic guidelines for deferring the sale of a family home under circumstances where it is "economically unfeasible" to award the house to either parent.

The case of Marriage of Duke, 101 Cal. App. 3d 152 (1980), compelled these awards in the context of additional child support under the specific circumstances established by that court. The *Duke* court established the rationale of the deferred sale of family home award as follows: "Where adverse economic, emotional and social impacts on minor children and the custodial parent which would result from an immediate loss of a long-established family home are not outweighed by economic detriment to the non-custodial party, the court shall, upon request, reserve jurisdiction and defer sale on appropriate conditions."

While the *Duke* court did not create or carve out any additional factors or circumstances to be considered with respect to deferred sale awards, it did provide that courts are *required* to reserve jurisdiction on this issue and in fact order that the sale of the family home be deferred if the circumstances warrant. These orders later became to be known as *Duke* orders as a result of this directive.

In 1985 *Duke* orders were made part of the Family Law Act and labeled "Family Home Awards." They were contained in Civil Code section 4800.7. That Code section was ultimately repealed and a new statute, which contains clear guidelines, has taken its place. Family Code sections 3800 to 3810 statutorily establish the Deferred Sale of the Family Home Order and require that the court, upon the request of a party to the action, determine whether it is economically feasible for the custodial parent (the so-called *in spouse*) to continue making all required payments on that property and, assuming that threshold is met, make a determination of the existence or nonexistence of certain factors set forth in the statute that would warrant the deferral of the sale of the family home as an additional component of child support.

The determination of the propriety of entering a Deferred Sale of Home Order is basically a two-step process: (1) determine the economic feasibility of the order, and (2) consider the various factors pertinent to granting that order once economic feasibility has been found. Preliminary to even those inquiries, however, are certain definitional concepts, which are spelled out in section 3800 of the Code.

> (a) "Custodial Parent" means a party awarded physical custody of a child.
> (b) "Deferred sale of home order" means an order that temporarily delays the sale and awards the temporary exclusive use and possession of the family home to a custodial parent of a minor child or child for whom support is authorized under Sections 3900 and 3901 or under Section 3910, whether or not the custodial parent has sole or joint custody, in order to minimize the adverse impact of dissolution of marriage or legal separation of the parties on the welfare of the child.
> (c) "Resident parent" means a party who has requested or has already been awarded a deferred sale of home order.

In determining the economic feasibility of granting a party's request for a deferred sale of home order, the court must consider whether it is economically feasible to "maintain the payments of any note secured by a deed of trust, property taxes, insurance for the home during the period the sale of the home is deferred, and the condition of the home comparable to the time of trial." Family Code section 3801 requires the court, in making this determination, to consider *all* of the following factors:

(1) the resident parent's income
(2) the availability of spousal support, child support, or both spousal and child support
(3) any other sources of funds available to make those payments

Further, Family Code section 3801 expressly describes the legislature's intent in defining these requirements:

(1) avoid the likelihood of possible defaults on the payments of notes and resulting foreclosures
(2) avoid inadequate insurance coverage
(3) prevent deterioration of the condition of the family home
(4) prevent any other circumstance which would jeopardize both parents' equity in the home

In this regard, the legislature is aware that it is, for all practical purposes, balancing the equities between the needs of the in spouse and the property rights of the out spouse. This is a fine line for the court to walk, and the legislature seeks to give it guidance by, essentially, ensuring that these orders will not be granted unless every reasonable effort is made to protect the asset in question, with specific attention to the equity positions of the parties.

The court has discretion to enter a deferred sale of home award. However, section 3802 requires the court to consider several factors in exercising that discretion:

(1) the length of time the child has resided in the home

(2) the child's placement or grade in school

(3) the accessibility and convenience of the home to the child's school and other services or facilities used by and available to the child, including child care

(4) whether the home has been adapted or modified to accommodate any physical disabilities of a child or a resident parent in a manner such that a change in residence may adversely affect the ability of the resident parent to meet the needs of the child

(5) the emotional detriment to the child associated with a change in residence

(6) the extent to which the location of the home permits the resident parent to continue employment

(7) the financial ability of each parent to obtain suitable housing

(8) the tax consequences to the parents[11]

(9) the economic detriment to the nonresident parent in the event of a deferred sale of home order

(10) any other factors the court deems just and equitable

After considering these factors, the court has discretion to order that the sale of the family home be deferred pending the child reaching the age of majority (or the occurrence of some other particular event directly related to the child). The court also may reconsider this award upon proper application by the noncustodial parent. Typical reasons for such reconsideration are a rapid devaluation of property values, or a change in the tax laws that affect a deferral of the sale of the family home.

These cases are of course determined on a case-by-case basis, and, as can be seen from a review of the factors set forth above, especially number 10, the court has wide discretion in approaching a request for a deferral of the sale of the family home. Assuming that such an award is made, the court will also consider the financial impact of this order on the noncustodial supporting parent; the court has authority to make adjustments to the amount of child support ordered to compensate for that financial impact.

The custodial in spouse will, of course, be required to maintain all mortgage payments, including principal and interest, property taxes, maintenance, and the like. Upon a showing that this parent is either unwilling or unable to maintain the property in this fashion, the court has can rescind the *Duke* order and order that the house immediately be placed for sale. Whenever a *Duke* order is made, the court is required by Family Code section 3809 to reserve jurisdiction over these and other issues that can arise in this context until such time as the house is sold or the *Duke* order otherwise expires.

Generally, it is very difficult to obtain a *Duke* order. There are essentially four inquiries that must be successfully met before this order will be granted:

1. Eligibility—that is, no other assets are available except the house (otherwise an equalizing division could be made); and
2. Economic feasibility—the court must make a finding that the sales proceeds from the house are not actually needed by the out spouse; and
3. There must be other subjective factors—the kids "can't live without this house," etc.; and
4. The order must be "necessary to minimize" the adverse impact of the divorce (for example, the house has been modified out for a disabled child in a wheel chair, things of this nature.

After all of these factors have been considered, it remains a discretionary decision for the court. Those of us who have faced this issue typically advise our clients that the chances of obtaining a *Duke* order are extremely slim.

c)   *Expedited Child Support Order*

Once the amount of support has been established, several other issues can arise, including: manner and method of court-ordered child support payments, alternatives to cash child support payments, security for child support payments, collection of child support payments, duration and termination of child support pending court proceedings, special statutory procedures for obtaining expedited support, and modification and termination of child support. Most of these issues will be discussed later in this chapter because they have application to both child *and* spousal support. One topic appropriate here is the statutory procedure outlined in Chapter 5 of Part 1, entitled "Expedited Child Support Order."

Federal legislation calls for expedited processes regarding the establishment and enforcement of child support orders. In response to this call for action, the legislature enacted the statutory scheme set out in Family Code sections 3620 et seq. These Code sections provide a mechanism by which a party may apply ex parte for an order requiring payment of child support during the pendency of the underlying action. The amount ordered by the court will be the amount as would be appropriate by virtue of application of the formula set forth in Family Code section 4055; or, if the income of the obligated parent (or parents) is not known to the applicant, then the minimum amount of support as provided in section 11452 of the Welfare and Institutions Code is used. The applicant for one of these expedited child support orders need not be a parent. Indeed, more often than not, the district attorney or some similar governmental agency will be the party taking advantage of this new procedure in order to obtain relatively immediate child support orders to offset welfare being paid on behalf of unsupported minor children.

Procedurally, the process is quite simple. On court forms promulgated by the judicial council, the applicant applies for the order by setting forth the minimum amount required to be paid by the obligated parent pursuant to Family Code section 4055 or Welfare and Institutions Code section 11452. The applicant also submits an Income and Expense Declaration for both parents to the extent that the information is available at the time of application. Additionally, the applicant must supply the court with a worksheet that sets forth the basis of the support requested, as well as a proposed "expedited child support order."

Pursuant to Family Code section 3624, unless a response to the application under Family Code section 3625 is filed by the proposed obligated parent, the order requested will automatically become effective 30 days after service of the application on the obligated parent. No further action by the court is required unless a response to the application has been filed. However, if no such response is filed, then the order is automatically entered.

Family Code section 3625 provides the appropriate procedure for responding to an Application for Expedited Child Support. Pursuant to that section, a response to the application for the order, together with the obligated parent's Income and Expense Declaration, may be filed with the court "at any time before the effective date of the expedited support order and, on filing, shall be served upon the applicant by any method by which a response to a notice of motion may be served." Contrast the manner of service of the responding papers with that required for service of the application. As indicated in section 3625, the responding papers need only be served pursuant to "any method by which a response to a notice of motion may be served." This generally is effected simply by mailing the responsive documents to the applicant party. Section 3624(b), however, requires that service of the application and other documents on the obligated parent "be by personal service or by any method available under

Sections 415.10-415.40, inclusive, of the Code of Civil Procedure [which sections generally provide for either personal or an acceptable manner of substituted service]."

Once the responsive papers have been filed and served, the obligated parent must arrange with the court clerk for a hearing on the application; such hearing will take place between 20 and 30 days after the responsive documents are filed. Additionally, the obligated parent is required to give notice of the hearing to the other parties by first class mail not less than 15 days before the hearing. The responding party can delay the effective date of this order by 50 to 60 days: he can wait 30 days after the application is served to file his response, and he can schedule a court hearing on the application between 20 and 30 days following the filing of the response. If for some reason the obligated parent fails to give the notice required by the Code of the hearing date, then the order will simply become effective forthwith, or 30 days after service, whichever first occurs.

Pursuant to Family Code section 3629, at the hearing on the application, all parties who are parents and subjects of the application procedure are required to produce copies of their most recently filed federal and state income tax returns; these documents may be reviewed by other parties to the action and the court. To the extent that any party fails to submit these documents as required by the Code, they shall be denied the relief that they have requested. In other words, if the applicant party fails to submit the required tax returns, the application will be denied. Similarly, if the responding party fails to submit appropriate tax documents, then her objection to the application will be denied.

d)   *Application of Case Law to Child Support Awards*

One might be led to conclude that as a result of the enactment of the statewide uniform child support guidelines discussed above, the extensive body of case law establishing precedent in the area of child support would become obsolete at best and misleading at worst. However, even the current guidelines grant the courts discretion in certain areas, most notably adjustments to income, adjustments related to a disparity in time-sharing, and examinations and determinations of the standard of living for children and parents . Family Code section 4053(f) provides authority for investigation into a child's standard of living: "Children should share in the standard of living of both parents. Child support may therefore appropriately improve the standard of living of the custodial household to improve the lives of the children."

Additionally, as discussed above, the court has authority to consider the cost of child care as an element of the child's needs. Indeed, this is an add-on specifically provided for in the Code, as expressed in Family Code section 4062. That code section lists several items that can be ordered by the court as additional child support.

In determining the standard of living that a child enjoyed when his family was intact, the court is guided by the concept that the child is allowed to participate in the "good fortune" of both parents, regardless of the fact that he does not necessarily live with both anymore. Indeed, case law has clearly established that a child is entitled to be maintained in a style and condition consistent with both parents' position in life. Simply providing for necessities is not enough if the parents can afford more. As such, a noncustodial paying parent may find himself paying well in excess of not only the guideline amount, but also that which this person may believe to be sufficient to satisfy the child's "basic support requirements" (assuming he is financially capable of paying more). Admittedly this will have the effect of allowing the custodial parent to enjoy a higher standard of living than he or she might otherwise be entitled to enjoy as a result of the receipt of this extra money; however, the policy to allow children to participate in the good fortune of their parents is so significant that the courts are willing to allow such situations to occur.

Another controversial area is the obligor parent's "ability to pay" the child support award. Obligor parents often argue that the court should reexamine their income, usually in an effort to lower their child support payments. In that regard, it is not at all unusual for legal proceedings involving the determination of child and spousal support to be accompanied by a rather radical, "unexpected" shift in the obligor's ability to earn income. This can take the form of willful suppression of income, a new "change of heart" by the paying parent to leave a high-paying job and undertake employment in a low-paying job, or some other similar chicanery.

The court, however, is vested with wide authority to investigate all aspects of both parties' income positions; and if one parent can show that the other parent is deliberately depressing his or her income to avoid financial responsibilities vis-à-vis their children, the court may base its orders for child support on the parties' ability to earn rather than their *actual* earnings. The case authority for this proposition dates back well over 35 years.[12]

C. Modification; Termination of Child Support

In order to modify an award for child support, one must show that a significant change in circumstances has taken place since the prior order was issued.[13] Many child support orders are based on agreements, however, rather than on orders issued by the court after a court proceeding. When child support is based on an agreement, the court does not need to make a finding of change of circumstances to support a modification. The reader should note, however, that (especially in child support proceedings) it is not difficult to show that a change of circumstances has occurred. Indeed, some courts have held that the passage of time alone can, under appropriate circumstances, constitute a change of circumstances. A modification based solely on the passage of time would, however, no doubt be the least likely way to satisfy the change in circumstances rule.

As a result of this limitation on modification of child support awards, it is prudent to include a detailed recital of the parties' circumstances at the time they signed the agreement to provide for support. This recital should include circumstances related to the parties' standard of living, the parties' income and expenses, and the child's particular monetary needs (for example, private school tuition or special medical costs).

1. Age of Majority

As a general rule, a Family Code child support order terminates when the child reaches the age of majority. On March 4, 1972, the age of majority in California became 18. Thus, subject to various exceptions, the duty to pay child support, which generally extends only to minor children, will terminate when a child turns 18. Similarly, the court loses jurisdiction to award child support to adult children (except in the various exceptional circumstances already discussed) once the child turns 18.

Interestingly, the California age of majority rules are not controlling over child support orders made by other states. It is the law of the state in which the original order is made that is determinative on the issue of the age of majority. As such, it is possible for an out-of-state order that terminates at the age of 21 or 25 to remain in existence and be susceptible to enforcement in California beyond the child's eighteenth birthday.

The Family Code contains a number of exceptions to the rule that terminates child support at age 18. Section 3901 provides that if a child is over 18 but is not married and is attending high school full-time and residing with a parent, he is still entitled to child support. This child will continue to receive support until he turns 19 or graduates from high school, whichever first occurs.

Family Code section 3910 provides another exception and states that any children, including adult children who are "incapacitated from earning a living and without sufficient means," can continue to receive child support beyond the age of 18. Because these orders are not made on the basis of the child's minority, the age of majority will not be a terminating event.

Family Code 3587 offers an exception where parents enter into a mutual agreement between themselves for the support of their adult children. Section 3587 allows the court to approve a stipulated agreement for the support of any adult child or for the continuation of child support after that child has obtained majority, and to enter a support award accordingly. Liability for the order will simply be determined as per the terms of the parents' agreement and will be enforceable in the same manner as any other child support order.

A question that often arises in this context is whether or not child support arrearages[14] will be enforced beyond the age of majority. The answer is yes. The right to enforce support arrearages is not lost when the child attains the age of majority. In fact, Family Code section 4503 (discussed below) provides that an action for the recovery of child support arrearages may be maintained "at any time within the period otherwise specified for the enforcement of such a judgment, notwithstanding the fact that the child has attained the age of 18 years." The period of time that is "otherwise allowed" for the enforcement of child, family or spousal support order is established by Family Code section 291, which provides that such orders may be enforced "until paid in full," no matter how long that may take. Care must be taken, however, not to "sit on one's rights." If a support recipient waits too long to seek to enforce a support order, he may find himself subject to a defense of laches.[15]

2. Emancipation of Minors Law

Another event that triggers the termination of child support is the emancipation of the minor child. For purposes of child support liability, an *emancipated minor* is a person who is considered to be over the age of majority, regardless of his or her actual chronological age. The emancipation statutes are set out at Family Code sections 7000 through 7143 ("Emancipation of Minors Law") and generally provide that any child under the age of 18 who comes within the following description will be recognized, upon appropriate application to the court, as an emancipated minor. Section 7002 declares a person under 18 to be an emancipated minor if *any* of the following conditions are met:

> (a) The person has entered into a valid marriage, whether or not the marriage has been dissolved.
> (b) The person is on active duty with the armed forces of the United States.
> (c) The person has received a declaration of emancipation pursuant to Section 7122.

Family Code section 7050 provides that an emancipated minor will be considered an adult for the following purposes:

> (a) The minor's rights to support by the minor's parents(b) The right of the minor's parents to the minor's earnings and to control the minor.
> (c) The application of Sections 300 and 601 of the Welfare and Institutions Code.

(d) Ending all vicarious or imputed liability of the minor's parents or guardian for the minor's torts. Nothing in this section affects any liability of a parent, guardian, spouse, or employer imposed by the Vehicle Code, or any vicarious liability that arises from an agency relationship.

(e) The minor's capacity to do any of the following:

(1) Consent to medical, dental, or psychiatric care, without parental consent, knowledge, or liability.

(2) Enter into a binding contract or give a delegation of power.

(3) Buy, sell, lease, encumber, exchange, or transfer an interest in real or personal property, including, but not limited to, shares of stock in a domestic or foreign corporation or a membership in a nonprofit corporation.

(4) Sue or be sued in the minor's own name.

(5) Compromise, settle, arbitrate, or otherwise adjust a claim, action, or proceeding by or against the minor.

(6) Make or revoke a will.

(7) Make a gift, outright or in trust.

(8) Convey or release contingent or expectant interests in property, including marital property rights and any right of survivorship incident to joint tenancy, and consent to a transfer, encumbrance, or gift of marital property.

(9) Exercise or release the minor's powers ad donee of a power of appointment unless the creating instrument otherwise provides.

(10) Create for the minor's own benefit or for the benefit of others a revocable or irrevocable trust.

(11) Revoke a revocable trust.

(12) Elect to take under or against a will.

(13) Renounce or disclaim any interest acquired by testate or intestate succession or by inter vivos transfer, including exercise of the right to surrender the right to revoke a revocable trust.

(14) Make an election referred to in Section 13502 of, or an election and agreement referred to in Section 13503 of, the Probate Code.

(15) Establish the minor's own residence.

(16) Apply for a work permit pursuant to Section 49110 of the Education Code without the request of the minor's parents.

(17) Enroll in a school or college.

To petition the court for emancipation, the child must be at least 14 years of age. The petition must also establish (under penalty of perjury) that the child is willingly living separate and apart from his or her parents with their consent or acquiescence. The child must also establish to the court's satisfaction that he is managing his own financial affairs, and in that regard he must supply the court with his own income and expense declaration pursuant to Judicial Council form FL-150. The minor must also prove that the source of income is not derived from any activity declared to be a crime by the laws of the State of California or the United States.

Notice of the minor's petition for emancipation is given to the child's parents or guardian or any other person entitled to custody of the child. The district attorney is also automatically notified of a petition for emancipation by the court clerk. At the hearing, the court is directed by Family Code section 7122 to sustain the petition "if it finds that the minor is a person described by Section 7120 and that emancipation would not be contrary to the minor's best interest."

Family Code sections 7130 to 7135 provide authority for the declaration of emancipation to be rescinded or voided upon proper application. A declaration of emancipation may be voided if the court finds that it was obtained by fraud or by withholding of material information. A petition to void a declaration of emancipation may be brought by "any person or by any public or private agency." This is in contrast to the parties who can request *rescission* of a declaration of emancipation. The petition to rescind the declaration will generally be granted if the court finds that the minor child is indigent and has no means of support, or if the court finds that the minor's only source of support or income is from public assistance benefits. Once an order of emancipation is so rescinded, then the natural parents, the adoptive parents, or the guardian (as appropriate) are once again responsible for the payment of child support. However, pursuant to Family Code section 7135, any contractual obligations that arose during the period the declaration was in effect are not altered by the order of rescission or voiding.

In contrast to the emancipation of a minor, other circumstances do not operate to terminate child support. For example, child support obligations are not dischargeable in bankruptcy. In addition, child support obligations are generally not dischargeable upon the death of a supporting parent; this makes sense because a child's need for support does not decrease upon the supporting parent's death, unless the support obligation has otherwise expired either by its own terms or by some other operation of law (as referenced above). A child support obligation may terminate upon a parent's death if such parent's obligation was memorialized in a court order or marital settlement agreement. Under those circumstances, the deceased parent's estate is not liable for the support of the child. However, Probate Code sections 6540 through 6545 provide a system by which an award of a "family allowance" from the estate of a deceased parent can be made. Assuming that the support obligation is presented in a court order or marital settlement agreement, however, that order is enforceable directly against the estate of the deceased parent by filing a creditor's claim in the probate action.

In the event that the supporting parent's assets are not probated and pass directly to a surviving second husband or wife, an action for support or insurance proceeds may be maintained directly against that second spouse. This can come as a tremendous shock to a second spouse who, after losing a husband or wife, must support the child alone. This non-parent liability is limited, however. The surviving second spouse is only personally liable if she elects to avoid probate administration of the community property estate.[16]

Summary

Both parents, we have seen, have a reciprocal duty to support and maintain their minor children. In certain circumstances this duty extends beyond the child's attainment of "adult" status. In fact, under certain circumstances, children can be called upon to provide support for their parents. The payment of child support is typically made on a monthly basis and is usually (although not always) paid by the noncustodial parent to the custodial parent. The payments are generally designed to ensure that the minor child enjoys a standard of living comparable to that enjoyed by both parents and, of course, to ensure that the child's basic needs and expenses are met.

The calculation of child support in California was historically a hit-or-miss proposition, a function of the nearly unfettered discretion of the trial court. It was not uncommon, in fact, for two different judges to render completely different child support under nearly identical facts. Further, many child support awards simply did not keep pace with the costs of raising children and certainly were not in line with the amounts of money being paid under the welfare system.

To remedy this situation, in 1984 California "officially" sanctioned a statutorily imposed guideline for the calculation of monthly child support. That system has been refined over the years. Today's version constitutes little more than a straight algebraic calculation utilizing easily ascertainable numbers (gross and net income, for example). By so doing, the legislature has assured that most child support orders will be predictable and easily determined. In that regard, several computer programs have been developed for the purpose of making these calculations.

In addition to ordering the payment of a set dollar amount each month for child support, the court has the power to allocate other orders it makes as "additional child support." These include requiring the parties to maintain health insurance for the children as well as the deferred sale of home order where, under certain circumstances, the custodial parent will be given the exclusive use of the family home until such time as the children turn 18.

Key Terms

The following is a list of key terms and phrases that you should be able to define and use in context. Only then will you have demonstrated a command of the material in this chapter.

- child support
- family support
- minor child
- stepchild
- paternity
- Agnos Act
- gross vs. net income
- guideline child support
- *Duke* order
- home equity
- Deferred Sale of Family House Order
- wage assignment
- stay of service (of wage assignment)
- Child Support Security Act
- laches
- emancipation

Questions for Discussion

1. Under what circumstances will a court make a *Duke* order (a deferred sale of home award)?
2. When will a stepparent be liable for child support of a stepchild?
3. What constitutes a "change in circumstances" sufficient to justify the modification of a child support order? Is your answer any different if the order sought to be modified is one for spousal support?
4. Discuss the historical underpinnings of the calculation of child support in California and the way in which the current system has changed the manner in which child support is calculated.
5. What is the significance of the term "earning capacity" vs. "actual earnings" in the context of a support analysis?

ENDNOTES

1. Note the distinction in this Code section between support provided by "the other parent or a relative or . . . a stranger." The section specifically excludes support provided by any state, county, or other governmental entity. It would seem, therefore, that a welfare agency that provides support for a minor child is entitled to reimbursement by the parent regardless of whether the child has abandoned that parent or not.

2. As a practical matter, however, there is also ample authority in the Family Code commencing at section 270 for the award of attorney's fees as between litigants to a Family Code proceeding under the appropriate circumstances. This issue will be discussed in a later chapter.

3. As a precondition to receive welfare payments in the form of Aid to Families with Dependent Children, the intended recipient must sign over the right to receive child support payments from the noncustodial parent to the county in an amount up to the amounts being received by them. The theory behind this is as follows: By making these welfare payments on behalf of the noncustodial parent, the county essentially steps in and fulfills the caretaker role statutorily reserved to (and imposed upon) the noncustodial parent. Under these circumstances, a right to reimbursement arises on behalf of the third party (in this case the county) to recover these sums from the noncustodial parent (at least such sums as would normally be the responsibility of the noncustodial parent). In order to ensure that the child support awards made by the courts (which up to that time had been entirely discretionary) were at *least* as much as the amounts for which reimbursement was being sought by the county, the Agnos Act and its formula for the structure of support was enacted.

4. Thus far, this book has used the abbreviation CRC to designate judicial council forms. The convention employed throughout this book to refer to the identifying number of the court form is, in fact, making reference to the specific *rule* of court (hence the designation "CRC [California Rules of Court]") identified by that number. In this particular instance, California Rules of Court number 1274 contained the text of the state's interim child support guidelines, which were designed to repeal and replace the Agnos Act. CRC 1274 was repealed in 1994.

5. As strange as it may seem, it became evident to the California legislature that California was actually one of the states with an unusually low average child support award. One of the basic amendments to Civil Code §4721, which delayed its effective date until July 1, 1992, was a change in the formula that resulted in making the child support awards in California roughly 15 percent to 25 percent higher, on the average, than before the change, thus (in the eyes of the legislature at least) bringing California more in line with the rest of the country as to the *amount* of child support being ordered in the average case.

6. If the gross amount of $3,444.48 was simply reduced by 25 percent when the oldest child reached majority, the total child support would drop from $3,444.48 to $2,583.36. However, if the support was calculated using only the three remaining children (all other factors being equal), the guideline amount would be $1,497.60 × 2, or $2,995.20. It is to prevent this disparity that the amounts are allocated unevenly between the children.

7. The statutory authority for these concepts is found in Family Code §§4058-4060.

8. In so doing, the parties must also be able to agree that the stipulated amount is in the child's best interests, it will adequately meet the child's needs, there has been no assignment of support rights, each party is informed of his rights under Civil Code §§4700 et seq., and the agreement is not a result of coercion or duress.

9. Most notable in this area are the programs provided by Thomson West legal publishers: "DissoMaster" and "Supportax." Both computer programs perform essentially the same functions.

10. "Equity" refers to the difference between what a home (or any piece of property) is worth and how much is owed on it. For example, if a home is worth $100,000 (i.e., it sells for that amount) and has $20,000 owing on it, then there is $80,000 in equity. This represents the "profit" that will be paid to the owner when it is sold.

11. The sale of an asset as large as a home can, and does, carry with it significant tax consequences. One such consequence has to do with the ability to defer the payment of tax on the capital gains recognized when a house is sold if the proceeds of sale are rolled over into (or used for the purchase of) a *new* home. This deferral of taxes is provided by Internal Revenue Code §1034. However, the rollover must occur within 24 months of the sale and is only available to an individual who is selling her *residence*. If she no longer *lives* in the house, then she may lose that status and be prevented from taking advantage of the IRC §1034 rollover, which could cost her quite a lot of money. This is a factor (among many others) that the court can and will consider when contemplating making a deferred sale of home order.

12. The reader should note, however, that for purposes of contempt of court, which will be discussed later, a finding of contempt for failure to pay support cannot be based on the citee's capacity to earn. Rather, it must be based on the citee's ability to *pay*, which is based on his or her actual earnings.

13. The change in circumstances rule for modification of child support does not apply to support orders that were enacted before the effective date of the statewide permanent child support guidelines. The new statutory scheme for uniformity in child support awards specifically provides that its mere enactment constitutes a sufficient change in circumstances to support a request to modify an existing child support award.

14. The term *child support arrearages* refers to support that was ordered, but not paid, during the child's minority. The question presented here is: to what extent can a support order be enforced *after* the child becomes an adult and after the order in question has terminated?

15. Laches is an equitable concept designed to limit the recovery of an individual who waits an unnecessarily long time before seeking to enforce his rights. This defense will generally not be successful unless the person who is asserting the defense can establish that he has somehow been prejudiced by the unusually long delay in enforcement. Note, however, that a defense of laches can only be asserted against an action for enforcement brought by the state. See Family Code §291.

16. When a married individual dies, the community property she owns passes directly to the surviving spouse, who can elect not to probate this community portion of the estate. An election of this kind might be made to save administrative or executor's fees, which are typically based upon the total value of the gross estate of the deceased individual. By making such an election, however, the surviving second spouse runs the risk of exposure to a surviving child of the deceased individual for a portion of those community proceeds that are being kept out of the probate estate. As such, to avoid the personal liability to the surviving child, the second spouse need only submit the entirety of the community proceeds to the probate court for administration. By so doing, the probate court has the basis upon which to satisfy the child's creditor's claim against the deceased parent's portion of the community property.

CHAPTER 6

Spousal Support

A. Spousal Support
B. Modification; Termination of Spousal Support

CHAPTER OVERVIEW

Over the years the concept of spousal support has been heavily debated. Very few spouses pay spousal support without feeling that the system is operating at the height of injustice when they are compelled to provide support to a person who is no longer their spouse; similarly, few are the recipients of spousal support who do not believe that this support is in fact monies they are not only deserving of receiving, but monies that they have in fact *earned*. Either way you look at it, in California at least, the concept of spousal support is here to stay.

Most spousal support analyses focus on the duty to provide support, the factors under which support is appropriate (or inappropriate), and the manner in which the actual support award will be structured.

A. Spousal Support

1. Preliminary Considerations

Family Code section 4300 provides the reciprocal obligation of spouses to support each other. In what can only be called a model of brevity, it provides (in pertinent part): "Subject to this division, a person shall support the person's spouse." The obligation of support is reciprocal as between spouses, it is easy to understand, and it leaves little room for doubt with regard to its intended meaning. The Family Code requires a person to support his or her spouse while they are living together; further, that person must maintain that support out of his or her separate property if there is no community property or quasi community property available to serve that purpose. Of course, by virtue of this language, the opposite would also be true: To the extent that separate property is used while community property is available, the owner of the separate property is entitled to reimbursement to the extent that the separate property was used to pay for family expenses notwithstanding the availability of the community property. This right of reimbursement does not, of course, exist once the community property has been exhausted.

Pursuant to Family Code section 4303, the obligee spouse (or the county on his or her behalf if the county is providing support to the spouse) may bring a direct civil action against the obligor spouse to enforce this duty of support. Civil actions to enforce support obligations and the like are generally believed to be the part and parcel of the spousal support that is awarded pursuant to a dissolution of marriage or legal separation proceeding. This is not necessarily the case, although it is the Family Code section 4300 duty that in no small way gives rise to the spousal support obligations encountered in marital termination proceedings. Rather, these code sections provide ample avenues for one spouse to secure support for family expenses and for the general necessities of life as those needs are not being met by the other spouse. Perhaps more likely is an action brought by the county to obtain reimbursement for monies spent on behalf of a person who is not being supported by her spouse. This is similar to the actions made available through Family Code section 4002, regarding the county's enforcement of the duty to support a child, and section 4403, which gives the county the opportunity to secure enforcement of the duty to support the parents.

Family Code section 4320 sets forth a very thorough list of factors and circumstances to be considered in awarding spousal support:

> In ordering spousal support under this part, the court shall consider all of the following circumstances:
>
> (a) The extent to which the earning capacity of each party is sufficient to maintain the standard of living established during the marriage, taking into account all of the following:
>
> (1) The marketable skills of the supported party; the job market for those skills; the time and expenses required for the supported party to acquire the appropriate education or training to develop those skills; and the possible need for retraining or education to acquire other, more marketable skills or employment.
>
> (2) The extent to which the supported party's present or future earning capacity is impaired by periods of unemployment that were incurred during the marriage to permit the supported party to devote time to domestic duties.

(b) The extent to which the supported party contributed to the attainment of an education, training, a career position, or a license by the supporting party.

(c) The ability of the supporting party to pay spousal support, taking into account the supporting party's earning capacity, earned and unearned income, assets, and standard of living.

(d) The needs of each party based on the standard of living established during the marriage.

(e) The obligations and assets, including the separate property, of each party.

(f) The duration of the marriage.

(g) The ability of the supported party to engage in gainful employment without unduly interfering with the interests of dependent children in the custody of the party.

(h) The age and health of the parties.

(i) Documented evidence of any history of domestic violence, as defined in Section 6211, between the parties, including, but not limited to, consideration of emotional distress resulting from domestic violence perpetrated against the supported party by the supporting party, and consideration of any history of violence against the supporting party by the supported party.

(j) The immediate and specific tax consequences to each party.

(k) The balance of the hardships to each party.

(l) The goal that the supported party shall be self-supporting within a reasonable period of time. Except in the case of a marriage of long duration as described in Section 4336, a "reasonable period of time" for purposes of this section generally shall be one-half the length of the marriage. However, nothing in this section is intended to limit the court's discretion to order support for a greater or lesser length of time, based on any of the other factors listed in this section, Section 4336, and the circumstances of the parties.

(m) The criminal conviction of an abusive spouse shall be considered in making a reduction or elimination of a spousal support award in accordance with Section 4325.

(n) Any other factors the court determines are just and equitable.

Despite these factors, there are circumstances under which the court may deny support. Specifically, Family Code sections 4321 and 4322 provide that in a judgment of dissolution or legal separation, the court may deny support to a party out of the separate property of the other party when the proposed supported party has her own separate property or earns a livelihood sufficient to give her proper support. Section 4321 also permits the court to deny spousal support if custody is awarded to the proposed supporting party, who is supporting the children. The reader should note, however, that this Code section is discretionary. Similarly, Family Code section 4322 provides that when there are no children, but the proposed supported party either owns or acquires a separate property estate that includes income from employment sufficient to maintain her own support, then no support will be ordered. Note that this Code section is *not* discretionary.

Finally, in spousal support proceedings, there is a direct correlation between a proposed order and the supported or supporting party cohabiting with a person of the opposite sex. (This is not true in child support proceedings.) Family Code section 4323 provides that unless the parties have agreed to the contrary in writing, there is a rebuttable presumption affecting the burden of proof of a decreased need for spousal support if the supported party is cohabiting with a person of the opposite sex. Yet, section 4323(b) provides that the income of the *supporting* spouse's subsequent spouse or nonmarital partner will *not* be considered in determining or modifying spousal support. Accordingly, the penalty for cohabiting with a person of the opposite sex is primarily directed toward the supported spouse. One must question the logic of this distinction. A supported spouse presumably decreases his need for support by cohabiting with someone (who is presumably sharing their expenses); accordingly, a supporting spouse presumably decreases her expenses by cohabiting with someone—and thus can provide more funds to the supported spouse. The term "cohabitation" does indeed entail more than simply living together and sharing expenses. It requires a romantic relationship as well. Simply holding one's self out to be husband or wife does not necessarily create a circumstance of cohabitation.

The operative Code section when considering spousal support upon dissolution or legal separation is section 4330, which reads as follows:

> (a) In a judgment of dissolution of marriage or legal separation of the parties, the court may order a party to pay for the support of the other party an amount, for a period of time, that the court determines is just and reasonable, based on the standard of living established during the marriage, taking into consideration the circumstances as provided in Chapter 2 (commencing with Section 4320).
>
> (b) When making an order for spousal support, the court may advise the recipient of support that he or she should make reasonable efforts to assist in providing for his or her support needs, taking into account the particular circumstances considered by the court pursuant to Section 4320, unless, in the case of a marriage of long duration as provided for in Section 4336, the court decides this warning is inadvisable.

It is easy to see that spousal support in marital termination proceedings is available and based in large measure on the factors enumerated in Family Code section 4320. There are, however, some additional considerations germane to the termination of spousal support.

Specifically, Family Code section 4331 authorizes the court, under certain circumstances, to order a potential supported spouse to undergo a vocational examination. (This subject will be discussed at greater length later in this section.) Further, section 4332 mandates that the court make specific factual findings with regard to the standard of living enjoyed by the parties during the marriage, as well as any other appropriate factual determinations with regard to the other circumstances enumerated in Family Code section 4320.

The court is granted a great deal of discretion with regard to spousal support awards, including the amount, duration, and jurisdiction to modify. The court must, however, consider and give due weight to the factors discussed above. The court is also empowered to require that the supporting spouse post some form of security for the protection of the supported spouse in the event there is any interruption in payments. Further, the court can make an order of spousal support retroactive in effect not only to the date of the filing of the noticed motion or the order to show cause, which raised the issue of spousal support, but even to the date of filing the petition itself. This rule of law was first espoused in no uncertain terms in Marriage of Dick, 15 Cal. App. 4th 144 (1993).

With regard to the retention of jurisdiction mentioned briefly above, section 4336 of the Family Code instructs the court that in the absence of a written agreement of the parties to the contrary or a court order terminating spousal support, the court must retain jurisdiction indefinitely in a proceeding for dissolution of marriage or legal separation over the issue of spousal support where the marriage has been one of long duration. This instruction has been defined statutorily as follows:

> For the purpose of retaining jurisdiction, there is a presumption affecting the burden of producing evidence that a marriage of ten years or more, from the date of marriage to the date of separation, is a marriage of long duration, however, the court may consider periods of separation during the marriage in determining whether the marriage is in fact of long duration. Nothing in this subdivision precludes a court from determining that a marriage of less than ten years is a marriage of long duration.

A court-ordered spousal support award, unless specified to the contrary in a written agreement by the parties, will terminate on the death of either party or the remarriage of the supported party. With regard to the death of either party, however, the court does have the power to require, under certain circumstances, that the supporting spouse maintain insurance for the benefit of the supported spouse to ensure that support will continue after the supporting spouse's death. Family Code section 4360 provides instruction in this area:

(a) For the purpose of Section 4320, where it is just and reasonable in view of the circumstances of the parties, the court, in determining the needs of a supported spouse, may include an amount sufficient to purchase an annuity for the supported spouse or to maintain insurance for the benefit of the supported spouse on the life of the spouse required to make the payment of support, or may require the spouse required to make the payment of support to establish a trust to provide for the support of the supported spouse, so that the supported spouse will not be left without means of support in the event that the spousal support is terminated by the death of the party required to make the payment of support.

The provisions of section 4320 are somewhat inconsistent with the directive of section 4337, which requires that upon the death of either party support terminates. Nevertheless, this is the manner in which the Code has been structured.

When fashioning an award of spousal support, the court has several options available. Essentially, the court contemplates an initial award of support that is subject to a date certain for termination; an award of support that is "open-ended," remaining in effect until the death of either party or the remarriage of the supported spouse; or some combination of a jurisdictional stepdown or a substantive stepdown (terms to be fully explained below).

The most fundamental requirement of a spousal support award is the existence of a valid marriage. Indeed, there can be no "spousal" support unless there is a "spouse."[1] Additionally, the existence or nonexistence of "fault" on the part of one or both parties has no effect on an award of spousal support. Spousal support cannot be ordered or withheld to reward or punish either party, and the court is prohibited from conducting any examination into the "bad faith" or "good faith" of either party in making its award of spousal support (with the obvious exception of proceedings involving "putative" support, where the designation as a "putative spouse" is dependent upon a finding of fault).

The subject matter jurisdiction for the contemplation of an award of spousal support is, pursuant to Family Code section 2010, appropriately with the superior court. And, as with child support awards, before the court can order a party to pay spousal support, the court must have personal jurisdiction over that individual. This would, of course, involve a determination of that person's "minimum contacts" with the state of California.

2. Factors Considered in the Award of Spousal Support

It is difficult to determine the proper amount of spousal support. Although the Code provides the factors that must be considered,[2] little else exists to provide guideposts or points of reference when determining the amount of a spousal support award once all of these factors have been considered. For practical purposes, in order to avoid reversal on appeal, the court must simply consider the enumerated factors, state that they have been considered (and make appropriate findings), and enter an award in whatever amount it deems warranted. It is for this reason that the marital standard of living becomes the legislatively directed initial "point of reference" when establishing a spousal support award. It is this author's opinion that, notwithstanding the foregoing sentences, if it appears after consideration of a spousal support award that the court, after considering the appropriate factors, simply did "whatever it wanted" on the issue of spousal support, such an award is subject to reversal. However, to the extent that some rational relationship to the marital standard of living can be shown, that award will most likely stand.

Section 4320 emphasizes that the court should try to maintain the marital standard of living in light of the earning capacities of the parties. This requires consideration of the marketable skills of the supported spouse, the job market for those skills, any education or training of the supported spouse required to develop those skills (or improve upon them), and the effect that the existence of the marriage has had on the marketability of those skills. The reader must note that in the context of spousal support, it is not the intention of the legislature to simply provide a "free ride" to a supported spouse. That individual is required (and encouraged) to, in essence, "pick up where he or she left off," develop marketable skills, and become self-sufficient and self-supporting at a particular date in the future. For this reason the court undertakes an extensive review of the supported spouse's ability to reenter the job market with an eye toward providing support for that person only until he or she can "come up to speed" and effectively compete in the job market.

The court requires the supported spouse to fulfill his or her obligation to enhance and utilize marketable skills; in fact, the court can even deny (or terminate at an earlier date than might otherwise be contemplated) spousal support if the recipient is unwilling to take steps to develop skills and become self-supporting. Of course, the court is not authorized to allow a support award that contemplates simply assisting an already self-supporting spouse in making a career change that would not otherwise place her in a better economic position. For example, a supported spouse who is an attorney and capable of earning a self-supporting income will not be awarded spousal support if the only reason for the spousal support is to allow the supported spouse to quit her job as an attorney and go to medical school.

In this context, the court has wide latitude to order the supported spouse (as well as the supporting spouse) to attend vocational rehabilitation counseling. A vocational rehabilitation counselor is typically an individual who has significant experience in job analysis and job placement.

This person can interview the individual in question and evaluate his marketable skills, ability to earn, and likelihood of successful entry into the job market. These counselors will then testify either orally or by written report to assist the court in understanding the marketability of the spouse's skills and the income generating potential thereof. A request for a vocational rehabilitation examination must be the subject of a noticed motion wherein one spouse asks the court to compel the other spouse to submit to such an examination.

Family Code section 4331 establishes the statutory authority for this examination as well as the minimum qualifications that a vocational training counselor must meet to be accepted by the court. The minimum qualifications, as listed in the Code, are as follows:

(1) A master's degree in the behavioral sciences
(2) [Qualification] to administer and interpret inventories for assessing career potential
(3) Demonstrated ability in interviewing clients and assessing marketable skills with understanding of age constraints, physical and mental health, previous education and experience, and time and geographic mobility constraints
(4) Knowledge of current employment conditions, job market, and wages in the indicated geographic area
(5) Knowledge of education and training programs in the area with costs and time plans for these programs

Further, section 4331(a) establishes the legislative intent on this subject. It states:

> (a) In a proceeding for dissolution of marriage or for legal separation of the parties, the court may order a party to submit to an examination by a vocational training counselor. The examination shall include an assessment of the party's ability to obtain employment based upon the party's age, health, education, marketable skills, employment history, and the current availability of employment opportunities. The focus of the examination shall be on an assessment of the party's ability to obtain employment that would allow the party to maintain herself or himself at the marital standard of living.

As a practical matter, most family law attorneys can recognize the circumstances under which a vocational training counseling referral is warranted. When a vocational examination is warranted, attorneys should consider signing a stipulation rather than vigorously opposing the examination with a noticed motion.[3] The vocational counselor's report can serve as a tool of settlement and can help the parties avoid a time-consuming and expensive trial.

The second of the factors enumerated in Family Code section 4320 recognizes that, to the extent a supported spouse has been out of the job market for an extended period of time so as to devote time to domestic duties, thus (arguably) freeing up the other spouse to further his career, the payment and continuation of spousal support may be in order. This codifies existing case law and establishes the general proposition that the longer the supported spouse is out of the job market devoting time to domestic duties, the longer it may take for that spouse to develop marketable skills to reenter the job market.

Family Code section 4320(b) requires the court to consider the extent to which the supported spouse contributed to the enhancement or development of the supporting spouse's marketable skills. In other words, to what extent did the supported spouse further the education and career of the supporting spouse? Section 4320 does not replace or duplicate section 2641 (dealing with reimbursement rights to the community for monies paid toward the education of one party); yet, it does allow the court to consider those kinds of circumstances in determining the needs and abilities of the respective parties. Section 4320 could thus be used by a supported spouse to request support while she completes educational development as a trade-off for the years she devoted to domestic duties during the marriage that enabled the other spouse to further his career.

The next factor set forth in section 4320 requires the court to consider the supporting spouse's ability to pay a spousal support award, taking into account the supporting spouse's earning capacity, income from all sources, assets, and standard of living. Thus the court looks beyond what the supporting spouse actually earns to determine his full "earning capacity." If the court determines that he is not earning at full capacity, it will most likely grant a spousal support award that is in excess of an award based on his "actual earnings." Such a ruling would presumably motivate the supporting spouse to maximize his earning capacity..

In light of this statutory scheme, some spouses choose to retire early rather than work until their company's standard retirement age (typically 65). In this context, at least one court has found that, to the extent the supporting spouse opted for an early retirement date at 62 (rather than 65) for the sole purpose of avoiding support obligations, his request to terminate the support obligation was denied. Marriage of Sinks, 204 Cal. App. 3d 586 (1988). This is not to say that an individual who is eligible for retirement must continue to work simply to finance his support obligations; rather, the *Sinks* case demonstrates that when one chooses early retirement solely to avoid support obligations, the court may deny a request for termination or modification of spousal support. To rule otherwise would essentially reward the supporting spouse's bad faith behavior.

The fourth factor contained in section 4320 is the specific instruction for the court to consider "the needs of each party based on the standard of living established during the marriage." This does not mean simply the absolute necessities of life. It has long been established in California by case law that a spouse's need in this context is judged not only in terms of the necessities of life but also in terms of their "station in life," both during marriage and post separation. This is not to say that a spousal support award must be sufficient to match the marital standard of living in all circumstances. In some cases (indeed, in most cases) it would be difficult if not impossible for the parties to separately maintain the standard of living that they were able to enjoy together. It is much more costly to maintain two households than one, and the standard of living of both parties is bound to suffer under those circumstances.

Both "need" and "standard of living" are typically established through evidence of the personal expenses incurred by the parties during marriage. For example, how often did they go out to eat, how often did they go on vacation, and when vacations were taken, what kinds of accommodations were enjoyed? As stated above, the amount of temporary (*pendente lite*) spousal support is irrelevant when establishing the amount of long-term support. The ability of the supporting spouse to maintain the temporary orders, however, does evidence his ability to pay a long-term order in that amount. The general guideline for the courts to employ in this context, however, no matter how complicated the inquiry may be, is rather simple: the supported spouse should not receive an amount of spousal support that provides her a "disproportionately lower standard of living than that of the supporting spouse." This analysis is also performed on a case-by-case basis and constitutes a factual determination by the court. There is much latitude, then, for the court to exercise discretion in making these awards.

Section 4320(e) makes the parties' respective assets and obligations, including their separate property, a proper subject of inquiry when establishing the amount of spousal support. In fact, in some circumstances the amount of the supported spouse's separate property estate after dissolution may provide the court sufficient authority to withhold an award of spousal support.[5] This particular factor makes virtually all aspects of both the supported and the supporting spouse's financial picture open for inquiry and discussion by the parties and the court.[6]

The sixth factor for consideration under section 4320 establishes the length of the marriage as an appropriate benchmark by which spousal support can be measured. Indeed, it has long been established that the length of a marriage will have a bearing both on the amount and duration of spousal support inasmuch as this factor is demonstrative of the mutual expectations of the parties as to support and the appropriate application of some of the other factors discussed above.

In theory a marriage is analogous to a business partnership. In a general business partnership, the partners develop certain expectations regarding the manner in which each will be treated by the other partner and as regards each partner's ability to participate in the future good fortune of the partnership. In a marriage the concept of partnership is no less prevalent than in general civil law. The individuals who are entering into the marital union are in essence allowing mutual expectations to be built up within each of them for, among other things, continuing support "for richer or poorer, for better or worse, in sickness and in health, 'til death do [they] part."

Obviously, marital dissolution (or legal separation) proceedings destroy those expectations. However, the concept of spousal support is designed to, in part at least, fulfill the reasonable expectations of the spouses relative to each other in this context. In longer marriages, the spouses have developed—and relied—upon these expectations. Further, the longer the marriage, the more reasonable this reliance becomes, and the more dependent upon the fulfillment of these expectations a low earner (or no earner) spouse may become.

As such, the length of a marriage can significantly affect the amount and, most importantly, the duration of spousal support. In fact, the law has developed to a point where the distinction between *lengthy marriages* and marriages of short duration falls at the ten-year mark. When a marriage is categorized as one of long duration, the court may extend the duration of spousal support. (This concept is discussed below in the section on long-term spousal support.)

Section 4320(g) codifies public policy concerns regarding the welfare of minor children. Subsection (h) makes the age and health of the parties a relevant factor pertinent both to the initial award and to an extension of or withholding of support. Subsection (i) mandates the court to review any history of domestic violence between the parties in this context. Subsection (j) allows the court to consider the "immediate and specific" tax consequences to each party of an award of spousal support, a concept discussed in greater detail below. Subsection (k) seeks to "balance the hardships" between the parties when setting spousal support. Subsection (l) sets forth the Legislature's expectation that a supported spouse will become "self supporting within a 'reasonable' period of time," which is defined as equal to one-half the length of a "short-term" marriage (as defined in section 4336—less than ten years in length). Subsection (m) requires the court to consider any criminal conviction of an abusive spouse. Finally, subsection (n) is a catchall provision, which basically codifies the court's authority to consider virtually any circumstance it so chooses that, in the court's opinion and discretion, has a bearing on the nature, scope, amount, and duration of the award of spousal support.

3.   Structure of the Award

There are essentially two phases of spousal support: temporary and permanent. They serve different functions, and different guidelines and factors are pertinent to the consideration of each. A *temporary* award of spousal support contemplates payment of support during that period of time between the filing of the petition and the time of trial. A *permanent* award of spousal support is contemplated to cover the period of time post trial.

4.   Temporary Support

As stated above, temporary support is ordered during that period of time between the filing of the petition and the trial of the matter before the court. Its purpose is to provide funds with which to allow both parties to maintain the standard of living they enjoyed during the marriage pending final determination of the action (to the extent that is financially possible). It is typically requested in the form of an order to show cause brought at the outset of a marital termination proceeding.

Athough the temporary support award lasts only until the time of trial (or until a further order of court), its importance cannot be overstated. Just as it is essential to establish the status quo in a child custody determination early in the proceedings, the same is true with an award of spousal support. The court is required to reexamine the issue of spousal support from a fresh perspective at trial (without regard to the temporary, *pendente lite* award). Yet, as a practical matter, the court relies heavily on the amount of support that has been paid pursuant to a temporary support order for, if nothing else, evidence of the supporting spouse's ability to make payments in at least that amount. As such, great care must be taken in the presentation of temporary support issues at the order to show cause.

Family Code section 3600 contains the statutory authority for an award of temporary spousal support. That section specifically vests the superior court with the power to order the husband or wife to pay "any amount" necessary for the "support of the wife or husband." As a general rule, the court tries to set temporary spousal support at a level where both parties continue to enjoy the marital standard of living as reasonably (and financially) practical, based upon the requesting party's need and the supporting party's ability to pay. This determination is primarily made by a review of the income and expense declarations filed by the parties and by a review of related documents pertinent to the earnings and expenses of the spouses.

The reader should note that the discussion pertinent to a deliberate and willful suppression of income in the section above dealing with child support has equal application to spousal support. Further, while some courts have developed guidelines with respect to an award of spousal support on a temporary basis related to each party's net income, such a system for calculating support can only be used for purposes of awarding temporary spousal support. The guidelines cannot be used in determining an award of permanent spousal support. The rationale behind this rule is related to the legislatively imposed guidelines of section 4320 and the court's recognition of the value of these guidelines and the concomitant need to give close and careful consideration to each factor prior to making an award of permanent support.

This rationale is in keeping with the two different purposes served by temporary and permanent spousal support. The temporary support award is simply designed to maintain the status quo until the issue is ultimately tried (or resolved by settlement). A permanent award is designed to provide continuing and ongoing financial assistance to the supported spouse after consideration of the Family Code section 4320 standards. Merely resorting to some formula involving a comparison of net income for a determination of permanent support would serve no other purpose than to frustrate the legislative mandate contained in section 4320.[7]

Unlike a permanent award of spousal or child support, no change in circumstances is required to modify an award of temporary spousal support. As a general rule, however, most courts require some form of new information to be present prior to modifying a temporary spousal support.

5. Permanent Support

A *permanent* or *long-term* award of spousal support is composed of four parts: (1) amount of the award; (2) substantive stepdown; (3) jurisdictional stepdown; and (4) reservation of jurisdiction.

a) Amount

As stated above, Family Code section 4320 establishes ten factors that must be considered by the court in setting an award of long-term spousal support.[8] Pursuant to section 4320, the court's fundamental inquiry is the parties' marital standard of living. Indeed, in the preface to the list of factors the Legislature states that "the amount of spousal support shall be based on the standard of living established during the marriage" and then refers the reader to consider the factors and circumstances set forth therein, ostensibly to provide guidance in the determination as to the marital standard of living.[9]

b) Substantive Stepdown

The concept of *substantive stepdown* is actually quite descriptive. Such an award contemplates that the substance of the award (that is, the amount being paid every month) will be reduced at periodic intervals down to (usually) zero with an ultimate retention of jurisdiction component (explained below). For example, an initial spousal support award could contemplate the payment of $1,000 per month for the first year, $800 per month for the second year, $500 per month for the third year, and so on. The support award could either terminate indefinitely, or it could simply drop down to a payment of zero with the understanding that the court would retain jurisdiction over any subsequent requests for modification or termination.

This kind of award is only appropriate if the court can make specific factual findings that at the time of the initial award there are facts and evidence in the record that support the prediction that the requirements for support of the supported spouse will justify a periodic lowering of the amount as contemplated in the order. Obviously, this is a determination made on a case-by-case basis and could be envisioned, for example, when the supported spouse is being retrained for reentry into the job market, which contemplates a period of little or no income followed by entry level income with periodic increases along a rather predictable timetable.

c) Jurisdictional Stepdown

A jurisdictional stepdown is fundamentally the same as a substantive stepdown. However, in this context the court is limiting its *jurisdiction* (or power) to award support above a certain level. Some explanation is in order.

The concept of the court's jurisdiction to award spousal support is not unlike that of an open door. When the door is open as wide as it can be, the court is free to make whatever award it deems appropriate after consideration of the various factors discussed above. If the door is closed, however, the court is denied the opportunity to reenter the arena of spousal support. The door can be closed in three ways: (1) The court takes it upon itself to close the door either completely or partially, (2) the parties themselves close the door, or (3) the door closes upon the occurrence of an event that operates to terminate spousal support. Either way, the result is the same: To the extent that the door has been closed, the court is limited in its ability to make orders pertinent to spousal support.

As long as the door is open at all, the court is free to entertain the subject of spousal support and generally make whatever orders it deems appropriate. If, however, the closure of the door has been tied to a limitation on the amount of spousal support that can be paid, then that limitation will be respected. For example, if a "wide open" door justifies an award of $1,000 per month, one can envision how a door that is only open halfway would only justify an award of $500 per month. With this in mind, the reader should be able to envision a court limiting its jurisdiction to award an amount of spousal support in excess of $500 per month after a particular period of time, notwithstanding its original order of $1,000 per month. For example, a court can award payment of $500 per month for five years and then limit its jurisdiction to award any more than $500 per month in the future.

This type of order is only appropriate in cases in which the court is able to make a specific factual finding that evidence exists to support the proposition that, over time, the supported spouse's needs for spousal support will in fact decrease to the level contemplated at each stepdown date.

d) *Reservation of Jurisdiction*

The fourth component of a long-term award of spousal support is known as a *reservation of jurisdiction*. This contemplates payment of spousal support for a period of time with a specific termination date as to the amount paid, but no termination date as to the jurisdiction to modify spousal support should circumstances develop in the future. In other words, the court will require that payments be made for a particular period of time and then cease; however, the court will reserve jurisdiction and keep the door open if the circumstances are appropriate. An example of such an order would be a payment of $1,000 per month for five years, at which time the amount would drop to zero, yet jurisdiction would be specifically reserved and no termination date over the issue of spousal support would be entered.

This type of an award contemplates that there is a specific date in the future at which time the supported spouse will no longer need spousal support. This has the effect of shifting the burden on the issue of continued spousal support away from the supporting spouse (who would be requesting that the court terminate the payments) and onto the supported spouse, who will then be in the position of convincing the court that spousal support payments should be continued. Essentially, the supported spouse must convince the court that its earlier decisions on the issue of support and the employability and "marketability" of the supported spouse were in error; it is only under those circumstances that the court will extend the payments and continue the spousal support.

This is not to say that such circumstances never occur. A drastic change in the economy, a supported spouse's emotional problems, and situations of that nature can indeed provide the basis for a reactivation of a spousal support award under which payments have terminated. Perhaps the case most often cited in this context is Marriage of Richmond, 105 Cal. App. 3d 352 (1980), whose name has been given to the concept being discussed herein, to wit: the so-called *Richmond* order.

A *Richmond order* is an award of spousal support that contemplates termination on a specific date unless the supported spouse successfully brings a motion to continue support *before the termination date.*[10]

This deadline contemplated in the *Richmond* order context has been somewhat softened by a line of cases beginning with Marriage of Maxfield, 142 Cal. App. 3d 755 (1983), and including Marriage of Vomacka, 36 Cal. 3d 459 (1984), and Marriage of Benson, 171 Cal. App. 3d 907 (1985). These cases generally provided that, unless appropriate language was included either in the order or in the marital settlement agreement, the court, notwithstanding the existence of a *Richmond* order, maintains the jurisdiction and the discretion to extend and modify the spousal support award. Accordingly, it is extremely important for spouses who bargain for a specific spousal support termination date to include specific language in their marital settlement agreements (and to request similar language in a court judgment) that specifies exactly what the parties intend and exactly what the parties are bargaining (and paying) for with regard to a marital settlement agreement.

Set forth below is language used by the author in marital settlement agreements in an attempt to lock in the absolute termination date on the issue of spousal support:

> Neither the amount nor the duration of spousal support is modifiable under any circumstances. No court will have jurisdiction to modify the amount of support or to extend the duration of support beyond the termination date specified above. The court will have no jurisdiction of any kind to modify or extend its jurisdiction beyond the period of time referenced in this agreement. As regards to modification of spousal support, the parties waive their rights under Marriage of Vomacka, 36 Cal. 3d 459, 204 Cal. Rptr. 568 (1984), Marriage of Benson, 171 Cal. App. 3d 907, 217 Cal. Rptr. 589 (1985), and Marriage of Jones, 222 Cal. App. 3d 505, 271 Cal. Rptr. 761 (1990).
>
> Husband and wife have carefully bargained in this agreement concerning all issues relating to their support obligations, including the amount of spousal support, its duration, and whether or not it should be extendible. The termination date concerning spousal support specified in this agreement is absolute. As of [date of termination established by the agreement] this agreement cuts off forever the right of either party to ask for support payments, the power of the court to order support payments, and the right of the other party to receive support payments. No court has jurisdiction to extend or order any payments (except arrearages) beyond that date. Counsel have advised the parties that this clause may work great and unexpected hardship on one or both of the parties, and

the parties have considered that possibility in electing to fix a specific date after which there will remain no spousal support obligation.

In this context, the adage "less is more" does not apply. When dealing with the potential for virtually unlimited exposure to spousal support (subject to the natural termination of spousal support discussed below), one cannot do enough to ensure that an unexpected spousal support obligation will not resurface when it is least desired. Naturally, one representing the supported party will be less anxious to include language of this type. From this attorney's perspective, the more vague and ambiguous the parties' agreement to a specific termination date for spousal support, the better. However, an attorney representing the payor spouse should definitely employ the foregoing language (or language significantly similar). Although there is no guarantee that this will produce the desired result, the foregoing language is designed to come as close as possible.

e) The Lengthy Marriage

Notwithstanding the discussion under jurisdictional stepdown and reservation of jurisdiction, there are certain aspects to a blanket reservation of jurisdiction by the court in this area of spousal support that bear comment. Family Code section 4335 reads as follows: "An order for spousal support terminates at the end of the period provided in the order and shall not be extended unless the court retains jurisdiction in the order or under Section 4336."

Section 4336(b) provides in part: "For the purpose of retaining jurisdiction, there is a presumption affecting the burden of producing evidence that a marriage of 10 years or more, from the date of marriage to the date of separation, is a marriage of long duration."

Section 4335 thus begins with language that seems to make the reservation of jurisdiction over spousal support potentially inappropriate. The next section, however, indicates that the court's refusal to reserve jurisdiction in a lengthy marriage is itself inappropriate. This language essentially codifies the law as stated by the court in Morrison v. Morrison, 20 Cal. 3d 437, 453 (1978). That court stated: "A trial court should not terminate jurisdiction to extend a future support order after a lengthy marriage, unless the record clearly indicates that the supported spouse will be able to adequately meet his or her financial needs at the time of selection of jurisdiction." This case has been followed and cited extensively since 1978 and has essentially been codified in Family Code section 4336.

This ten-year "cut-off" date is not absolute. Indeed, some cases have found marriages shorter than ten years to be of long duration, while other cases have found marriages longer than ten years to be of short duration.

Section 4336 is significant for its instruction that the court must maintain jurisdiction "indefinitely" for a marriage of long duration. Practically speaking, marriages of ten years in length or more are simply presumed to be of long duration, thus warranting the court's retention of jurisdiction over the award of spousal support indefinitely. Indefinitely translates to "until the death of either party, or the remarriage of the supported spouse." This can be a very, very long time.[11]

Note that Family Code section 4336 does not compel a finding that a marriage of ten years or more is lengthy; it simply establishes a rebuttable presumption. However, from a practical standpoint, it is difficult to rebut this presumption. The ultimate determination and finding on the issue of whether or not a marriage is of "long duration" rests within the sound discretion of the trial court and is fundamentally a factual determination. The reader should note, however, that for purposes of calculating the length of marriage, the period of time that the parties may have cohabited on a nonmarital basis is not included. Accordingly, parties can live together (cohabit) for a period of ten years, get married, and then separate after five years, and still not be able to take advantage of the presumption set forth in section 4336.

6. Selected Issues Regarding Spousal Support

In the context of a spousal support award, certain issues tend to bear greater importance than others and also tend to occur with greater frequency. Indeed, the concept of spousal support contemplates more than simply the payment of money for a specific period of time. Spousal support (in theory at least) is designed to provide an equitable balance between the parties and some sort of equanimity in their reasonable expectations. This can, and very often does, extend beyond the mere payment of a specific amount per month. Spousal support issues include the establishment of health insurance protection for the supported spouse, the availability of security for the payment of spousal support, and the effect of a nonmarital "live-in" partner, to name but a few examples.

a) Cohabitation

Family Code section 4323 establishes a rebuttable presumption of decreased need on the part of the supported spouse if that person is cohabiting with a person of the opposite sex. This section further provides that it is not necessary for the supported spouse and the "nonmarital cohabitant" to hold themselves out as husband and wife for purposes of determining cohabitation. This section requires the supported spouse to demonstrate to the court that her needs have not in fact decreased by virtue of the non-marital relationship. If the supported spouse succeeds, she ostensibly can provide an effective defense to a supporting spouse's request to reduce spousal support.

The term *cohabitation* is not defined with any specificity. It does, however, contemplate more than simply living together. One case, Marriage of Leib, 80 Cal. App. 3d 629 (1978), found cohabitation where the parties had enjoyed joint vacations, exchanged expensive gifts, and basically treated each other as mutual homemakers, housekeepers, and companions. Once again, a finding of "cohabitation" is just one of a series of factual determinations that the court must make on a case-by-case basis. What is important for the reader to remember, however, is that under the appropriate circumstances, invocation of Family Code section 4323 can operate to greatly affect the outcome in a spousal support proceeding.

b) Health Insurance

In this day and age, the issue of health insurance is one that must be approached in each and every case with the utmost of care. As a practical matter, most health insurance is provided to a family by virtue of one or both spouses. This is known as *employer-provided* group health insurance, and its availability is keyed to the continuing employment of the covered employee. Unfortunately, in many situations involving divorce, the supported spouse is also the nonemployee spouse, which makes that person's health insurance dependent upon the continued marital relationship with the employee spouse. Obviously, once the divorce occurs, the nonemployee spouse will no longer be eligible for coverage under the employee spouse's health insurance. If for some reason the nonemployee spouse is uninsurable (for example, has suffered some form of serious and significant health problem), the loss of health coverage to this person will be disastrous.

As a result, various sections of California law provide that all group disability insurance and health insurance offered in California must give the insured the right to convert his or her policy from a group policy to an individual policy without requiring further evidence of insurability. These insurance companies are free to charge whatever they deem appropriate under the circumstances for such insurance (which can be almost as financially disastrous as the lack of insurance itself); however, at least the availability of insurance is protected under California law.

Additionally, the Consolidated Omnibus Reconciliation Act of 1985 (COBRA) allows a nonemployee to continue to participate in the employer's group health insurance plan for a period of up to three years following a change in status from employee to nonemployee or from a termination of status as the employee's dependent (that is, following dissolution). This is a rather technical law, and great care must be taken *before* the insured spouse's status changes to ensure that coverage will continue post dissolution.

c) Security for the Payment of Spousal Support

Another subarea in the context of spousal support, which is of great concern to recipient spouses, concerns security for the payment of spousal support obligations. Unless otherwise agreed by the parties, a spousal support order will typically terminate at the death of *either* party. The support obligation will not continue after the payor's death, notwithstanding the fact that the supported spouse's need for the support can, and most often does, continue beyond this event.

Family Code section 4360 is designed to address this situation. That section provides, in pertinent part:

> . . . the court, in determining the needs of a supported spouse, may include an amount sufficient to purchase an annuity for the supported spouse or to maintain insurance for the benefit of the supported spouse on the life of the spouse required to make the payment of support, or may require the spouse required to make the payment of support to establish a trust to provide for the support of the supported spouse, so that the supported spouse will not be left without means of support in the event that the spousal support is terminated by the death of the party required to make the payment of support.

Note, section 4360 does not indicate that such a device will be in lieu of support, nor will it be used merely as security to compel the *payment* of a support order; rather, section 4360 addresses this concept as an element *in addition to* the initial award of spousal support. This Code section is discretionary, which means that the court will review all of the facts and circumstances of each particular case prior to entering an order under section 4360. Such an order most likely will be granted, however, in situations where age, infirmity, and employability of the supported spouse make it highly likely that he will never become fully self-supporting following dissolution and will therefore need support long after the supporting spouse's death. Additionally, section 4339 gives the court authority to require the supporting spouse to provide *security* for the payments of spousal support contemplated in that section. Section 4339 states: "The court may order the supporting party to give reasonable security for payment of spousal support." Typical security devices include a lien on the supporting spouse's property, a bond, the appointment of a receiver, or even a wage assignment.

Just as with child support, California law provides for a *mandatory* issuance of a wage assignment to secure spousal support orders. (These concepts are discussed at length in this book's chapter "Enforcement of Orders.")

B. Modification of Spousal Support

As with child support, the party requesting modification of spousal support must demonstrate to the court's satisfaction that some change of circumstances occurred after the order was entered. A change of circumstances could be demonstrated by the supported spouse's failure to become self-supporting, the unexpected failure of the court's expectations with regard to its earlier orders, or a significant change in the financial situation of either spouse. The reader should note, however, that if the only change in circumstance is the supporting spouse's increased ability to pay (based on a pay raise or some other form of financial good fortune), this will be insufficient to constitute a change in circumstances allowing for a modification of support. The supported spouse must demonstrate not only the supporting spouse's increased ability to pay, but also that the supported spouse's needs are not being satisfied by the existing spousal support award. This is directly contrary to the manner in which these concepts are applied in the context of increasing child support awards.

Changed circumstances in the context of spousal support modifications are discussed in the *Hoffmeister* cases at length: Marriage of Hoffmeister (*Hoffmeister I*), 161 Cal. App. 3d 1163 (1984), and Marriage of Hoffmeister (*Hoffmeister II*), 191 Cal. App. 3d 351 (1987). The *Hoffmeister II* court made it clear that although changed circumstances can be found when an increased ability to pay exists on the part of the supporting spouse, the spouse receiving spousal support must also demonstrate that his needs at the time of the date of separation were not met. The inability of the supported spouse to meet his *present* needs is not sufficient to warrant a modification in spousal support, notwithstanding the fact that the paying spouse otherwise has the financial ability to increase the amount being paid. The appropriate time of determination on this issue is the date of separation. In other words, the court asks: "To what extent were the supported spouse's needs met as of the date of separation?"

As a result of the reasoning set forth in the *Hoffmeister* cases, a supporting spouse should ensure that the original spousal support order is based on a specific finding that the recipient spouse's needs are being met. On the other hand, a recipient spouse should attempt to have the court characterize the basis for its award on the payor's ability to pay, rather than the recipient spouse's needs. By so doing, if the payor's ability to pay increases after the passage of time, the recipient spouse will be in a much better position to argue that her needs were never being met and now that the paying spouse is doing better financially, there is a much better opportunity to have her "date of separation needs" adequately satisfied.

The reader should also note that the mere passage of time will not justify modification of support, although there is authority for the proposition that the effect of the passage of time on the value of money (as reflected in, for example, the Consumer Price Index) may provide the basis for a modification of spousal support to counteract the effects of inflation. This concept is discussed briefly in Edwards v. Edwards, 52 Cal. App. 3d 12 (1975).

It should be obvious after reading the foregoing sections that spousal support typically terminates at a date fixed at the time the original court order is entered or upon the occurrence of a particular condition (for example, the death or remarriage of the supported spouse). Further, the court has discretion to reserve jurisdiction to extend a payment obligation as the circumstances warrant. Finally, unless the parties agree to the contrary, the court retains jurisdiction over the issue of spousal support indefinitely where the marriage was of "long duration."

The most typical terminating conditions for an award of spousal support (in the absence of a specific termination date) are the death of either party and the remarriage of a supported spouse. This is, of course, in the absence of an agreement of the parties to the contrary. As indicated above, the parties are indeed free to make whatever spousal support agreement they choose. If the parties wish to waive spousal support indefinitely, or if the parties wish to establish spousal support for a specific period of time and under specific circumstances, the court will not upset that agreement. In fact, the parties are free to make whatever agreement with regard to spousal support they so desire without fear of judicial interference. The only inquiry that the court must make with respect to a spousal support agreement is whether the agreement is entered into freely and with full, informed consent. No magic language is required, although it is advisable to include specific provisions that make the parties' agreement perfectly clear.

The concept of remarriage as a terminating event is based on the idea that once a supported spouse remarries, his or her expectations for continued support ("til death do us part") shift from the original spouse to the new spouse. However, under certain circumstances, a supported spouse will simply cohabit with another individual rather than marry so as to preserve the ability to receive continued support from the initial spouse. As should be apparent, this runs somewhat contrary to the "expectation" concepts discussed herein. Nevertheless, nonmarital cohabitation is not the equivalent of remarriage for purposes of automatic spousal support termination. It is not, therefore, a terminating event unless the parties' agreement or the court order specifies it as such. However, the nonmarital cohabitation of a supported spouse will most certainly give rise to a modification of spousal support based on, among other things, decreased need.

The concepts discussed above find additional authority in Chapter 6 of Part 1, Division 9, titled "Modification or Termination of Support" commencing at Family Code sections 3650 et seq. Family Code section 3650 statutorily defines a *support order* as "a child, family, or spousal support order." Section 3651 grants the court authority to modify or terminate such support orders "at any time as the court determines to be necessary." (This unfettered discretion to modify or terminate is, of course, subject to the provisions of sections 3587 and 4004 of the Family Code, generally related to support orders entered pursuant to the agreement of the parties or in situations in which a child is receiving public assistance.) Notwithstanding this authority, section 3651(c)(1) prohibits, under most circumstances, the court from modifying or terminating a support order as to any amount that accrued before the date of the filing of the notice of motion or the order to show cause requesting such modification or termination. Additionally, an order for spousal support cannot be modified or terminated to the extent that an agreement, either written or oral (entered into in open court between the parties), specifically provides that the spousal support order is not subject to modification or termination. Section 3652 of Chapter 6 also provides that an order modifying or terminating a child support order may include an award of attorney's fees and court costs to the prevailing party.

1. Selected Procedural Aspects of Support Modification

Sections 3660 and 3680 contain simplified procedures to obtain discovery and to modify support orders.

Section 3660—Purpose of Article
The purpose of this article [Discovery Before Commencing Modification or Termination Proceeding] is to permit inexpensive discovery of facts before the commencement of a proceeding for modification or termination of an order for child, family, or spousal support.

Section 3680—Purpose of Article
(a) The Legislature finds and declares the following:
(1) There is currently no simple method available to parents to quickly modify their support orders when circumstances warrant a change in the amount of support.
(2) The lack of a simple method for parents to use to modify support orders has led to orders in which the amount of support ordered is inappropriate based on the parents' financial circumstances.
(3) Parents should not have to incur significant costs or experience significant delays in obtaining an appropriate support order.
(b) Therefore, it is the intent of the Legislature that the Judicial Council adopt rules of court and forms for a simplified method to modify support orders. This simplified method should be designed to be used by parents who are not represented by counsel.

In essence, the Legislature intended to limit the use of these discovery tools to cases in which they are truly relevant to the situation at hand.[12]

The discovery contemplated under this particular statutory scheme is to be used only when a request for the modification of support is not, in fact, pending. In other words, an individual utilizing this discovery would be doing so to determine if it was appropriate to file such a request. In order to prevent abuses, however, Article 2 limits the use of this discovery. For example, section 3663 provides that the use of the discovery contemplated by this instant article may not be used more than once every 12 months. Additionally, sections 3664 and 3665 establish that the *only* vehicles of discovery that may be utilized in this circumstance are requests for the production of a completed current Income and Expense Declaration (on judicial council forms) and a Request for Production of the other party's federal and state income tax returns. Finally, in order to ensure that the responding party provide complete responses, Family Code section 3667 provides as follows:

> Upon the subsequent filing of a motion for modification or termination of the support order by the requesting party, if the court finds that the income and expense declaration submitted by the responding party pursuant to this article was incomplete, inaccurate, or missing the prior year's federal and state personal income tax returns, or that the declaration was not submitted in good faith, the court may order sanctions against the responding party in the form of payment of all costs of the motion, including the filing fee and the costs of the depositions and subpoenas necessary to be utilized in order to obtain complete and accurate information. This section is applicable regardless of whether a party has utilized subdivision (b) of Section 3664.

After all, if the responding party did not take his or her obligation to provide complete and accurate responses to this discovery seriously, it would undermine the purpose of these code sections entirely.

As indicated above, Article 3 of Chapter 6 provides a simplified procedure for requesting the modification of a support order. Unfortunately, an individual may choose not to seek a support modification because he simply cannot afford to hire an attorney. In turn, a recipient may not receive the appropriate amount of support under the Code, or a payor may not be able to meet his support obligations. In these situations, the payor typically stops paying, thus subjecting himself to all manner of difficulties, including civil contempt. Accordingly, this simplified procedure was enacted in hopes that more people would find the judicial system accessible and be empowered to seek modifications without the aid of an attorney.

Requests for modification under Article 6 must be made using the forms promulgated by the Judicial Council (see generally Form FL-390).

Summary

There are two basic types of spousal support: temporary and permanent (or long-term). Each of these serves a unique purpose: temporary support is designed to maintain the status quo, while permanent support is designed to both satisfy expectations (within reason) and provide the basis for rehabilitation of the supported spouse so that he or she may become self-supporting.

The actual calculation of spousal support is not nearly as rigid as that employed for child support. In fact, the amount is left almost entirely up to the trial court's discretion, subject only to its consideration of the many factors set out in the Family Code.

Finally, we have seen that orders for spousal support are generally modifiable upon a showing of changed circumstances surrounding the order or the parties.

Key Terms

The following is a list of key terms and phrases that you should be able to define and use in context. Only then will you have demonstrated a command of the material in this chapter.

- spousal support
- gross v. net income
- wage assignment
- stay of service (of wage assignment)
- putative spouse
- temporary spousal support
- permanent spousal support
- substantive stepdown
- jurisdictional stepdown
- reservation of jurisdiction
- *Richmond* order
- COBRA
- nonmarital cohabitation

Questions for Discussion

1. Define a "lengthy marriage." What is the significance of this term in the context of spousal support, and how is the concept used in the family law context?
2. How does the marital standard of living figure in a support calculation?

223

3. What constitutes a "change in circumstances" sufficient to justify the modification of a spousal support order? Is your answer any different if the order sought to be modified is one for child support?

4. Explain the concept of a reservation of jurisdiction in the context of an award of spousal support.

5. What is the significance of the term "earning capacity" vs. "actual earnings" in the context of a support analysis?

ENDNOTES

1. Under certain circumstances relating to actions for nullity involving a void or voidable marriage, the existence of a "putative" spouse may give rise to spousal support to the extent provided by law, notwithstanding the absence of a valid marriage.

2. In fact, it has been deemed to be an abuse of discretion for a court to fail to consider all these factors when making a spousal support award.

3. The noticed motion procedure simply increases dissolution costs. Further, if the court grants the motion and determines that the opposition was not in good faith or was not calculated to arrive at an equitable resolution of the spousal support issue, the court may allocate the costs of the motion to the losing party.

4. The reader should note that what was community property during marriage and is ultimately distributed to the spouses upon judgment of dissolution or legal separation changes from community property to post dissolution separate property. This is a rather loose application of these terms, but hopefully the concept is clear.

5. A very detailed analysis of this aspect of section 4320 is found in Marriage of Terry, 80 Cal. App. 4th 921 (2000).

6. That said, many courts nevertheless utilize a simple mathematical formula to calculate temporary spousal support. One variation of that formula is as follows: [(HEN × .40) minus (LEN × .50) = SS], where HEN = High Earner's Net, LEN = Low Earner's Net, and SS = Spousal Support. For example, if the high earner's net is $10,000 per month and the low earner's net is $4,000 per month, the amount of spousal support would be calculated as follows:

$$[\$\,10{,}000 \times .40) - (\$\,4{,}000 \times .50)] = SS$$
$$\$\,4{,}000 - \$\,2{,}000 = \$\,2{,}000.$$

7. The guideline amount of temporary support under these circumstances would thus require a payment by the high earner to the low earner of $2,000 per month.

8. The reader should note that the term long-term support is used interchangeably with *permanent support* and sometimes *rehabilitative support*.

9. The establishment of the marital standard of living is one of the functions of the "expense portion" of the form 1285.50 income and expense declaration packet. It is typically in this context of support when the expenses of the parties are considered, not so much as to establish the amount of support by direct reference to the expenses; rather, the listing of the expenses will provide some indication of the marital standard of living.

10. This emphasized language is extremely important. If the supported spouse desires to be successful in a request to continue or extend spousal support payments, this request must be brought to the court's attention.

11. Individuals who marry right out of high school can find themselves faced, at the ripe old age of 29 or 30 years, with a spousal support award that can theoretically continue

until the death or remarriage of this 30-year-old supported spouse. This conceivably could last 50 years or more.

12. As the reader will learn in subsequent chapters, discovery (the process through which parties investigate their case and seek information from the opposition) can be very time-consuming and expensive. The procedures detailed in this chapter are designed to avoid such expense.

CHAPTER 7

Property Rights and Obligations

CHAPTER OVERVIEW

The division of community property is second only, perhaps, to custody and visitation litigation, the issue that generates the most confrontation, manipulation, and, sometimes, deception. Here the practitioner must be part advocate, part research expert, part CPA, and part detective. This area of family law is inundated with rules, regulations, statutes, presumptions, and formulas. However, once the basic concepts are mastered, they all come together in a manner that leaves the practitioner wondering what all the fuss was about.

Perhaps because there *are* so many rules and presumptions, and the issues are not as exciting as, for example, heated custody disputes, this area is not everybody's favorite. However, parties to divorce litigation can be very creative when it comes to keeping a spouse from getting as much property as possible. After all, this *is* litigation, and it is only human nature to want to *win*. That is why the practitioner must be ready to delve well below the surface to uncover the true nature of the transaction and the resultant property issues.

This chapter will concentrate on identifying the various property issues involved in a marital dissolution proceeding. Once the issues have been determined, the inquiry turns to the characterization of the property involved as either separate, community, or some combination of the two. We will learn how various presumptions relating to the manner in which property is held can significantly impact upon the character of an asset. We will discuss specific types of property, and any special rules pertinent to those properties; the liability of various properties involved in marital dissolution proceedings; and issues relating to the management and control of property. Finally, we will review special issues related to tracing, commingling, and apportionment.

A.   Introduction

Perhaps no other term is as commonly used and equally misunderstood as "community property."[1] This term, along with the related concepts of determination and division of assets acquired during marriage, is the defining concept of divorce, second only to custody litigation.

The California community property system traces its roots back to Mexico and Spain and their community property law, which was first adopted by the State of California in 1848. The California Constitution (adopted in 1849) recognized and guaranteed the separate property rights of individuals, and instructed the legislature to devise a statutory scheme that defined these rights and responsibilities. Interestingly, these initial laws focused on the protection of married women's property rights, specifically the property that they brought with them to the marriage. Statutes passed by the legislature expressly exempted the separate property of a wife from liability for her husband's debts.[2] Nevertheless, the husband was still given exclusive management and control of his wife's separate property. The law offered very limited protection against the husband's mismanagement (or outright theft): it merely provided that the wife's separate property could be neither sold nor encumbered without her consent and her voluntary participation in the transaction. The husband also had exclusive management and control over the couple's "community property."[3]

Over the years, these property laws were expanded upon, usually with an eye towards allowing a woman to have somewhat greater control over the destiny of her separate property. She was still, nonetheless, subject to the absolute domination by her husband over the community property. Not long after these statutes were initially enacted, the court examined some of the finer points of the property system as it was applied between spouses. The original community property statutes provided that the income derived from separate property (for example, interest earned during the marriage on separate property money that was placed in a savings account) would be classified as "community property." The logic of this classification is obvious: The term *community property* as used then (and, for the most part, now) generally referred to property acquired by the parties during marriage. Clearly, interest earned on money in a bank account (or in some similar fashion) is indeed "property acquired during marriage." As such, because the community property was reachable by the husband's creditors to satisfy his debts, the interest and other passive income flowing from the wife's separate property could also be reached by the husband's creditors (to the extent that it was deemed to be community property).

In an attempt to protect and preserve the separate property of the wife, the California Supreme Court, in the case of George v. Ransom, 15 Cal. 322 (1860), created the rule currently known as the "source rule." The source rule gave birth to the concepts of "tracing" and "apportionment." In essence, the *Ransom* court concluded that passive income (rents, interest) flowing from a wife's separate property remains the wife's separate property; thus, it is shielded from the reach of her husband's creditors. The concept of defining a property—as well as its passive income—with the same character has endured and is currently codified in Family Code section 770. The source rule is applied by an examination not only of the property as it was originally acquired, but also the source of the funds used to acquire that property. The classification of property acquired during marriage is one of the most heavily litigated aspects of the community property system in California. It consumes enormous amounts of the parties' time and money.

In California the fundamental legal premise of a marital relationship, even dating back to the mid-1800s, was the recognition and preservation of the equality of the spouses in regard to their relationship. This equality was not in fact recognized by the California legislature until 1975 when various sections of the (then) Family Law Act were amended to provide complete equality, joint management, and control over the community property. Prior to that time, dating back to 1850, the rights of the wife were limited to power and control over her own separate property. Subsequent amendments established protections to prevent her husband from disposing of the community estate over her objection, followed by a gradual recognition of the wife's control over the disposition of her own separate property, her right to engage in certain limited business enterprises on her own, and the right to pass her property by will over the objection of her husband.

In the early 1950s, wives finally won the right to manage and control their earnings during marriage, and in 1975 they won the right to manage and control the community property as equals of their husbands. The fundamental principle underlying the 1975 legislation was that each spouse is entitled to exercise complete management and control over all the community property regardless of which spouse was responsible for acquiring that community property. These concepts have been further refined over the years. And today, there is an expanded fiduciary[4] duty between husbands and wives, which is designed to protect each spouse from the irresponsible or malicious acts of the other.

These concepts of equal management and control over marital property are found in sections 1100 et seq. of the Family Code under the heading, "Management and Control of Marital Property." The definitive section,1100, provides in part:

> (a) Except as provided in subdivisions (b), (c), and (d) and Sections 761 and 1103, either spouse has the management and control of the community personal property, whether acquired prior to or on or after January 1, 1975, with like absolute power of disposition, other than testamentary, as the spouse has of the separate estate of the spouse.

A discussion of California's community property system, with application of *all* its various rules and regulations, greatly exceeds the scope of this text. This chapter limits the discussion to the fundamental underpinnings of the community property system and its current application. We will cover jurisdictional questions regarding the division of community property, characterization of property (as either separate, community, or a hybrid), and various presumptions recognized within the California and their effect on such characterization. We will also address issues related to the management and control of community property, with particular reference to recent fiduciary relationship rules. Next, we will explore the role of community obligations in the division of property. In conclusion, we will tackle subjects frequently raised in the context of marital termination proceedings, including tracing, commingling, apportionment, and reimbursement.

B. General Concepts

As might be expected, the superior court has exclusive jurisdiction over the division of property in the context of Family Code proceedings. Family Code section 2550 provides as follows:

> Except upon the written agreement of the parties, or on oral stipulation of the parties in open court, or as otherwise provided in this division, in a proceeding for dissolution of marriage or for legal separation of the parties, the court shall, either in its judgment of dissolution of the marriage, in its judgment of legal separation of the parties, or at a later time if it expressly reserves jurisdiction to make such a property division, divide the community estate of the parties equally.

Obviously, because the superior court has exclusive jurisdiction over the "dissolution of the marriage" and the "decreeing [of] legal separation of the parties" by virtue of other Family Code provisions, the enabling provisions of section 2550 apply directly to the superior court. As the reader might note from a review of Family Code section 2550, this section does not commence with a definition of the term, "community property." Indeed, over the years, the court has grappled long and hard with its definition. Over the years, parties to dissolution and legal separation proceedings have presented the court with theories of community property that run from the mundane to the bizarre, no doubt in an attempt to secure a favorable property division. Further, Family Code section 2010(e) specifically allows the court to "inquire into and render any judgment and make such orders as are appropriate concerning . . . the settlement of the property rights of the parties."

The California Constitution provides rights to both husbands and wives to property acquired during marriage. For purposes of making this determination, the property need not necessarily be located within California. It has been determined that for purposes of marital property division, the parties' domicile is the controlling jurisdiction. This is a deviation from the generally accepted concept that the law of the jurisdiction in which the property (real property) is located will generally provide the basis for determinations made pertinent to disputes surrounding it.

Because only certain kinds of property are subject to the court's jurisdiction, one of the most important aspects to the determination and resolution of marital property disputes concerns the appropriate classification of that property. Interestingly, prior to 1986, the court lacked jurisdiction to divide separate property, as well as jointly held property (joint tenancies or tenancies in common). As might be imagined, this was a source of great consternation because most family residences are held in joint form, and they are usually the parties' most significant asset. This anomaly in the law was remedied in 1986 when Civil Code section 4800.4 (currently Family Code section 2650) became operative. That code section generally provides that jointly held separate property can be the subject of a division of property pursuant to a legal separation or dissolution action at the request of either party. Since enactment of that code section, virtually all of the property held by the parties, even separate property (provided it was held jointly with the other party), can become the subject of division by the superior court.

There are four basic categories of property over which the court has jurisdiction in this context: community property, separate property, quasi-community property, and quasi-marital property. The statutory scheme laid out at Family Code sections 760 et seq. generally defines community and separate property as follows:

Section 760 Community Property:
Except as otherwise provided by statute, all property, real or personal, wherever situated, acquired by a married person during the marriage while domiciled in this state is community property.

Section 770 Separate Property:
   (a) Separate property of a married person includes all of the following:
      (1) All property owned by the person before marriage.
      (2) All property acquired by the person after marriage by gift, bequest, devise, or descent.
      (3) The rents, issues, and profits of the property described in this section.
   (b) A married person may, without the consent of the person's spouse, convey the person's separate property.

It is clear, then, that all property acquired during the marriage by the parties while domiciled in this state that is not separate property is, by process of elimination, community property. Similarly, property acquired before the marriage (together with all "rents, issues and profits"[5]) is separate property. In addition, certain other items are deemed by statute to be separate property by their very nature (gifts and inheritances for example, together with certain categories of personal injury damages).

The term *quasi-community property* is used to describe property that would have been community property had it been acquired by the parties while they were married and domiciled in this state. Inasmuch as this is a very mobile society, many people will live in one state for some period of time during their marriage, acquire property there, relocate to California, and then ultimately seek a divorce. If one reads Family Code section 760 carefully, it is apparent that contained within the definition of community property is the requirement that the parties be domiciled within this state at the time the property is acquired. The manner in which the legislature has decided to treat property that is not exactly community property (because the parties were not domiciled in California when it was acquired), but in all other respects falls under the definition of community property, is simply to give it a new name (quasi-community property). Quasi-community property is treated for all practical purposes like true community property. As with everything else, of course, there are significant exceptions to this rule, which will be discussed later in the text.

Quasi-marital property refers to property acquired by the parties during a putative marriage, which would have been community or quasi-community property had the marriage in fact been valid. This property is divided upon dissolution as if it were community property, a concept that generally works to the benefit of the putative spouse.[6]

One troubling aspect of community property law is that many assets are hybrids of the categories referenced above. For example, a particular asset could not only have separate property characteristics, but community property characteristics as well. A house purchased prior to marriage and paid for with premarital funds will, following the marriage (assuming payments are made on the house with community funds during the marriage), acquire community property characteristics. Further, following separation, payments made on the house will generally be characterized as the separate property of the payor spouse. Thus, it is necessary to trace the source of funds used to acquire the house both before and during marriage, as well as the manner in which title to the house is held.

In order to navigate the stormy waters of a community property analysis, it helps to begin with a firm understanding of some general concepts and how they apply in day-to-day cases. Once the reader understands the difference between community and separate property, and accepts the fact that sometimes a piece of property (be it a car, house, parcel of land, etc.) can possess aspects of both separate and community property at the same time, the rest of the analysis becomes basically an exercise in accounting. The examination of a community property issue is typically a seven-step process:

1. Is it "property" of the kind that can be divided in a Family Law Act proceeding?[7]
2. What is the character of the property (separate, community, hybrid)?
3. Do any special rules apply to this property (for example, statutory presumptions, tracing, apportionment)?
4. Are there debts associated with this property that must be considered?
5. Determine the valuation of the assets (unless they are to be divided "in-kind").
6. Distribute the property equally, unless some special rule applies (for example, the rule that personal injury damages must be distributed to the injured spouse).
7. Determine the tax impact of what has been done (to ensure an equal division).

Once these questions are answered (for each piece of property), the division of property becomes simple: The separate property is confirmed to the owner spouse, and the community property is divided equally between the spouses.[8]

C. Property in General

A few words on the concept of *property* are appropriate here. When this term is used, most people think of land or homes, and they are correct: Both of these items are appropriately classified as property. This term includes, however, much more than simply these two examples. A good rule of thumb is that if it is capable of being owned, then it is usually considered property.

In general, the term property can be further divided into two subcategories: (1) personal property and real property or (2) real estate. *Personal property* is defined by Black's Law Dictionary as "[g]enerally all property other than real estate" and "everything that is the subject of ownership, not coming under the denomination of real estate." *Real estate* is defined as "[l]and anything permanently affixed [attached] to the land, such as buildings, fences, and those things attached to the buildings, such as light fixtures, plumbing and heating fixtures, or other such items which would be personal property if not attached."[9] Black's Law Dictionary further recognizes that the term real estate is synonymous with real property.

As can be seen, the term personal property is defined somewhat in the negative: If it is not real property, then it must be personal property. All property (real or personal) is subject to division by the court in a Family Law Act proceeding.

The reader must note, however, that these concepts are very broad. The general definition of property includes the language: "everything which is capable of being owned." *Everything.* Real or personal, tangible or intangible, visible or invisible—all of this falls within the context of property and can thus be recognized, valued, and divided by the superior court. Most people do not have difficulty grasping this concept. Their difficulty comes from their need to expand the scope of their inquiry and to learn to recognize the many different shapes, or more accurately forms, that property can take. For example, at one time or another all of the following "things" have been recognized as property and have been valued and divided:

- land
- houses and other buildings
- cars, boats, and airplanes
- furniture, furnishings, and appliances
- bank accounts
- money
- jewelry and precious metals (gold, etc.)
- promissory notes
- earnings
- insurance
- retirement benefits (pensions, etc.)
- stock options
- businesses
- copyrights, patents, royalties, and trademarks

This list is far from conclusive. It demonstrates, however, the far range of "things," or property, that can become the subject of a Family Code proceeding. Of course, this book cannot cover all items of property. What it will do, however, is show the manner in which property is divided; demonstrate how certain statutory presumptions can impact characterization; and explain some common rules for "special" items of property (for example, the family residence, retirement benefits, and business goodwill).

D. Characterization of Marital Property

As indicated above, property involved in a Family Code proceeding generally falls into one of two categories: community or separate. Community property constitutes all property acquired by married persons while domiciled in this state except as is otherwise provided by statute (that is, except separate property). Separate property is property owned before marriage, acquired after separation (Family Code section 771), or acquired by a specific statutory exception to the community property rules (for example, by inheritance or gift). Two additional statutory exceptions to the community property presumption include: (1) property *transmuted* to separate property by the actions of one or both of the parties, and (2) certain personal injury damages. (Both of these concepts are discussed below.)

Sections 770, 771 and 772 provide the statutory bases for the definition of separate property. Essentially, separate property includes all property owned before marriage (tracing plays a big role here); property acquired after the date of separation; property acquired during marriage by a statutory provision that establishes an item as separate property by definition (for example, property acquired by inheritance, gift or bequest); and interspousal gifts (although it is harder to make a gift to a spouse than a stranger due to the anti-*Lucas* rules, discussed later in this chapter).

Section 771 establishes that property acquired during the period of separation is separate property. However, the tricky part is in determining the date of separation. That is not always as simple or as obvious as it appears at first blush, because the concept of "living separate and apart" is more easily stated than demonstrated. This is an extremely important section of the law, because it involves a particularly volatile time. The property at this point is, in essence, becoming "uncommunity" since the earnings and accumulations post-separation are the separate property of the separatizer.[10]

Many cases have grappled with this concept, with varying results. Actually living "separate and apart" is a fundamental requirement for a finding of post-separation earnings and accumulations. This issue becomes much more complicated because we can never really know exactly when the parties separated.

The date of separation is a discretionary, factual determination to be made by the trier of fact (i.e., the judge). In practice, courts tend to be suspect of people who do not objectively assert their separation (that is, they fail to file a petition, move out of the house, or take some other overt action demonstrative of actually "separating" from their spouse), and those who fail to subjectively show it (i.e., they neither appear nor behave as people who are "separated" from their spouse). The determination of the date of separation is purely a function of case law.

When is the date of separation? That question is not easily resolved. The case of Makeig v. United Sec. Bank & Trust Co. 112 Cal.App. 138 (1931) determined that living separate and apart for essentially all of a 14-year marriage was NOT enough to demonstrate a "separation" as that term is contemplated by (now) Family Code section 771. In *Makeig*, the court stated:

> Living separate and apart, however, as contemplated by said section 169, [the precursor to Family Code section 771] does not apply to a case where a man and wife are residing temporarily in different places due to economic or social reasons, but applies to a condition where the spouses have come to a parting of the ways and have no present intention of resuming the marital relations and taking up life together under the same roof. Under modern conditions there is many a man living and working in one place and his wife living and working in another, seeing one another only on week ends, sometimes not for months at a time, yet they are not living separate and apart within the meaning of the section, for there has been no marital rupture, and there is a present intention to live together as man and wife, and their status is only temporary, although it may happen that the condition might exist for some years.

The *Makeig* court instructed that we look for a "complete and final break" to indicate actual "separation."

The (relatively) more recent case *In re* Marriage of Baragry (1977) 73 Cal.App.3d 444 further defined these concepts. In *Baragry*, the husband moved out of the house to live with his girlfriend. Nevertheless, he continued to maintain close contact with his wife; for example, he frequently ate at home, went on vacation with her, went out socially with her, attended sporting events with her, sent her gifts and cards, and brought his laundry home. They did not have sex during this period. Mrs. Baragry knew that her husband was living with another woman, but she hoped that he would ultimately return home to her. This went on for over four years.

The court found that he was not separated during this period of time even though he had moved out of the house, because he continued to maintain the trappings of marriage: social interaction with his wife, who continued to perform some (albeit not all) of the duties she had previously provided when the parties were living together. The court asked "whether the parties' conduct evidences a complete and final break in the marital relationship." In *Baragry*, the court was not convinced.

In the *Marsden* case (discussed at length elsewhere in this book), even the filing of a petition for dissolution did not trigger a finding of separation. In that case the husband moved out of the house after the dissolution petition had been filed, and went on a two-year speaking tour in the Middle East. Upon his return, the court found that he had *intended* to return and, therefore, this did not constitute a final separation.

In *In re* Marriage of Peters (1997) 52 Cal.App.4th 1487, the husband left the family residence. *Nine years later* his wife filed for dissolution. While the husband was gone from the home he and his wife occasionally had social and business contact and filed joint income tax returns. Husband argued that the standard of evidence to determine the date of separation is "preponderance of the evidence." Wife, on the other hand, argued that the standard is "clear and convincing evidence." The trial court agreed with the husband, and the appellate court affirmed that ruling, finding that the standard of proof to be used in determining the date of separation is the lower "preponderance of the evidence" test. The important point here is that this ruling made it easier for a party to claim either an act of separation or not. In other words, the court will simply listen to both parties and make a ruling as to which story is more convincing, all other things being equal.

The case of *In re Marriage* of Von der Nuell (1994) 23 Cal.App.4th 730, presented the dissolution of a 28-year marriage. In 1987 Wife asked Husband to move out. He did, never to return. In June 1988 Husband (who had been living with his girlfriend) left Wife and moved into a separate house. In July of 1989, Husband filed for dissolution but did not serve Wife with the papers. Further, Husband contributed to Wife's expenses for a period of time. Wife believed that the marriage was salvageable and sought counseling, but Husband refused to participate.

Husband claimed a 1987 date of separation. Wife disputed this. She based her argument on the facts that during this supposed period of separation, she and Husband continued to maintain joint checking and credit accounts; they filed joint tax returns; they socialized together; they took vacations together; they maintained a sexual relationship; and they bought a car together and titled it in both of their names. The appellate court found no separation because the conduct of the parties did not show a "complete and final break" as was required under the law. The husband and wife's ongoing economic, emotional, sexual, and social ties, and attempts at reconciliation, demonstrated to the court that no separation had taken place.

The courts have stated the test for a date of separation to include the following basic factors:

1. One party does not intend to resume the marriage; and,
2. His or her actions bespeak finality.

3. The ultimate test is the parties' subjective intent, coupled with some objective manifestation of that intent.
4. Bottom line: If there is any doubt about it there will generally *not* be a separation.

In this context, the person claiming a particular date of separation must meet two tests:

1. Subjective: intention, clearly shown by the evidence.
2. Objective: appearances and actions and statements evidencing a complete and final break must be present.

In re Marriage of Norviel (2002) 102 Cal.App.4th 1152, presented a 15-year marriage wherein the parties essentially lived as roommates. One night Husband told Wife that the marriage was over; he then told his son and coworkers. Husband and Wife agreed that Husband would move out of the house once the parties' rental property was vacated by the tenants. While waiting for the tenants to move out (a three-month period) Husband's stock options increased significantly in value and Wife sought to have the date of separation established at the later date. The appellate court reversed the trial court's finding of an early date of separation and established the following test:

1. There must be substantial evidence of the actual separation.
2. The intent to separate and the representative conduct must be simultaneous.
3. A party must physically move out of the house to trigger separation.[11] Otherwise, "the evidence would need to demonstrate unambiguous, objectively ascertainable conduct amounting to a physical separation under the same roof." The *Norviel* decision has led to the so-called "sheet rock rule," wherein parties who choose to be "separated" while living in the same house are well advised to literally erect drywall boundaries within the house. A move must take place into another room or there must be an otherwise very strong showing of a physical separation within the house to support a claim for date of separation.

The dissent in *Norviel* felt that the "simultaneous rule of intent and conduct" was inconsistent with the emotional realities of a couple who is going through a period of separation (which, in this author's opinion, is correct). Nevertheless, that is not the rule of this case.

The bottom line in date of separation cases is that courts favor later dates of separation. Some basic rules to follow in advising clients on what to do to ensure a date of separation can thus be summed up as follows.

The party leaving must:

1. Clearly communicate the intention to separate to the other spouse and third parties (friends and family);
2. Move out of or physically partition the house;
3. Divide all formerly joint bank and credit accounts;
4. Decline counseling;
5. Cancel any prepaid vacation plans, etc.;
6. Refrain from socializing or allowing the estranged spouse from performing "spouse-like" duties (cooking, cleaning, doing the laundry, etc).
7. Stop being intimate with the estranged spouse;
8. Stop receiving mail at the home of the estranged spouse;
9. File for dissolution; and (only slightly tongue in cheek)
10. Expect to lose anyway!

The statutory definitions set out in sections 760 and 770 are just that: definitions. They fail to demonstrate how the various statutory and case law *presumptions* apply to marital assets. As the reader will recall, the concept of a presumption is primarily one of evidence: To what extent does a party have the *burden* to produce evidence sufficient to convince the trier of fact of the accuracy of the position he is advocating, such as the manner of acquisition or the characterization of the asset? A presumption, to the extent it operates in favor of the party seeking to establish a fact governed by that presumption, will make the determination quite simple. This is because a presumption shifts the burden of proof on a given subject to the other side.

For example, the presumption regarding marital property set out in Family Code section 760 is that property acquired during marriage is community. The effect of this presumption is that once it is shown that an asset was acquired during the marriage (and that no statutory exception applies), the court will treat that asset as community in nature; the community character of the asset is *presumed*. Thus it is the other party, the one who contends that the asset is in reality not a community asset, who must produce evidence to that effect.

The reader must also be aware that presumptions are divided into two categories: conclusive and rebuttable. A *conclusive presumption* is one that cannot be rebutted, regardless of what the actual facts are. A conclusive presumption thus has the effect of establishing the facts surrounding that presumption by operation of law. A *rebuttable presumption*, on the other hand, simply shifts the burden of proof to the party contesting the presumption. Providing the party can establish a sufficient basis for rebutting the presumption, however, it will be rebutted. Most presumptions are rebuttable rather than conclusive due in no small part to the draconian nature of a conclusive presumption.

1. Presumptions Concerning Characterization

Family Code section 760 provides the general presumption with respect to property acquired during marriage. That section states, in pertinent part, that all property acquired by the parties during the marriage is presumed to be community property. Of course, this can be rebutted with an affirmative showing that the property was not intended by the parties to be community in nature. The burden of carrying this proof is, of course, on the party who contends that the property is not, in fact, community. In contrast to the presumption created by Family Code section 2581 (discussed below), Family Code section 760 is not a "title presumption." As such, virtually any admissible evidence can be used to rebut the presumption, including tracing the source of the acquisition of the asset back to separate property funds, or an agreement between the parties (oral or written).

Family Code section 803 provides an additional statutory presumption generally known as the *married woman's presumption*. This section states that any acquisition of property by a married woman in her own name by a written instrument prior to January 1, 1975, is presumed to be her sole and separate property. The reader will recall that January 1, 1975, was the operative date for the amendments to the Family Law Act, which provided for equal management and control over all property by both the husband and wife. Prior to that time, the husband was presumed to have sole management and control over all items of community property. Thus, to the extent that the wife was able to acquire property in her own name prior to that date, the statute presumed that such property was her separate property inasmuch as the husband would arguably not have allowed his wife to have acquired property in her own name if he in fact had an ownership interest in that property.

Section 803 further provides that if a married woman acquired property prior to January 1, 1975, with any other person, her share will be presumed to be held by her as a tenant in common (thus giving her the ability to transfer her interest without the consent of her co-tenant in common), unless the writing by which she acquired ownership states a different intention. Finally, section 803 states that property acquired by a married woman with her husband prior to January 1, 1975, as "husband and wife" creates the presumption that such property is in fact their community property, unless the writing by which they acquired the property states a different intention.

The presumptions are conclusive as between a married woman and a bona fide third-party stranger to the marriage who purchases the property for valuable consideration. What this means, for example, is that if a bona fide third-party purchaser buys property that was acquired by a married woman by a written instrument in her name only prior to January 1, 1975, her husband will not be able to set aside that sale on the grounds that he maintains some ownership interest in the property; the fact that the property is the wife's separate property is conclusively established by operation of this statute, and no amount of evidence introduced by the husband to refute it will be sufficient, no matter how "correct" it might otherwise be. The conclusiveness of this presumption only applies as to these bona fide third-party purchasers for value, however. As between husband and wife, the presumption is rebuttable. The reader must also remember, however, that these presumptions only apply to property "acquired before January 1, 1975, by a married woman, by an instrument in writing. . . . "

2. Presumptions Concerning Property Held in Joint Form

As stated above, once an asset (or obligation) has been identified as something that must be divided and distributed, the next step is to determine its character, or status, as community, separate, or some combination of the two. The status of an asset generally depends on the time and manner of its acquisition. However, there are other statutory presumptions that can affect its character.

One of the more significant presumptions with regard to the status of property acquired during a marriage has to do with the manner in which title to that property is held. The term *title* to property generally refers to the documents of ownership. For example, a grant deed is the title document by which the owners to property can establish that they *are* in fact the owners of that property. A grant deed generally recites something along the lines of "John Doe hereby grants to John Roe and Mary Roe, as joint tenants, the following described property." In this example, the manner in which title is held by John and Mary Roe is reflected in the words, "as joint tenants." The Family Code provides that when title is held in this fashion (and in other ways as will be discussed below), certain ramifications as to that property's character will follow.

Under common law, the form of a property's title gives rise to a rebuttable presumption as to its status. As such, unless the parties introduce contrary evidence, the manner in which the "record title" reflects ownership will in fact determine its status in a dissolution of marriage proceeding. For example, if John and Mary Roe acquire title to a piece of property in Mary's name alone as her "sole and separate property," a rebuttable presumption has been created that the property is in fact Mary's "sole and separate property" regardless of the fact that community funds may have been used for its purchase.

The same is true if the parties, subsequent to the property's acquisition, convey the property back and forth between each other pursuant to quitclaim deeds. For example, if John and Mary Roe acquired a piece of property during their marriage using community funds and took title as follows: "John and Mary Roe, husband and wife, as community property," the common law presumption would provide a rebuttable presumption that the property is community in nature. However, if subsequent to its acquisition, John quitclaimed the property to Mary (that is, signed a quit-claim deed transferring his interest to her) so that its title read, "Mary Roe, a married woman, as her sole and separate property," the rebuttable presumption would provide that the property is Mary's separate property. Accordingly, spouses must take great care when they initially acquire property and when they transfer it into some other form of ownership.

Perhaps the most significant of the so-called "title presumptions" is found at section 2581. That section, in its entirety, states as follows:

> For the purpose of division of property on dissolution of marriage or legal separation of the parties, property acquired by the parties during marriage in joint form, including property held in tenancy in common, joint tenancy, or tenancy by the entirety, or as community property, is presumed to be community property. This presumption is a presumption affecting the burden of proof and may be rebutted by either of the following:
>
> (a) A clear statement in the deed or other documentary evidence of title by which the property is acquired that the property is separate property and not community property.
>
> (b) Proof that the parties have made a written agreement that the property is separate property.

Please note that although the statute quoted above provides examples of ways in which "jointly held" property can be described on a title document, these are merely examples. The focus of Family Code section 2581 is to clearly establish that whenever married persons take title to a piece of property such that both their names are jointly set forth thereon, there is a statutory presumption that this property is community in nature and, upon termination of the marriage, should be divided equally between the spouses. The statute indicates that this presumption may only be rebutted by "a clear statement in the deed or other documentary evidence of title by which the property is acquired that the property is separate property and not community property," or by "proof that the parties have made a written agreement that the property is separate property." Such proof must take the form of a written agreement.[12] In other words, unless it is written down somewhere (even on the title document itself) that this "jointly held" property is not community property, the statutory presumption will control, and the property will be deemed community. (Note: this subsequent writing must be signed by the party who stands to lose if the property is characterized as separate property.)

A companion statute to Family Code section 2581 is Family Code section 2640, which provides as follows:

(a) "Contributions to the acquisition of the property," as used in this section, include downpayments, payments for improvements, and payments that reduce the principal of a loan used to finance the purchase or improvement of the property but do not include payments of interest on the loan or payments made for maintenance, insurance, or taxation of the property.

(b) In the division of the community estate under this division, unless a party has made a written waiver of the right to reimbursement or has signed a writing that has the effect of a waiver, the party shall be reimbursed for the party's contributions to the acquisition of property of the community property estate to the extent the party traces the contributions to a separate property source. The amount reimbursed shall be without interest or adjustment for change in monetary values and may not exceed the net value of the property at the time of the division.

(c) A party shall be reimbursed for the party's separate property contributions to the acquisition of property of the other spouse's separate property estate during the marriage, unless there has been a transmutation in writing pursuant to Chapter 5 (commencing with Section 850) of Part 2 of Division 4, or a written waiver of the right to reimbursement. The amount reimbursed shall be without interest or adjustment for change in monetary values and may not exceed the net value of the property at the time of the division.

Accordingly, even when jointly held property is deemed "community," a spouse may be entitled to a credit to the extent that he invested his separate property into this asset (e.g., through down payments). Of course, a spouse who seeks such a credit must be able to trace his separate property contributions, which is not always easy.

Section 2640, is limited in application, however. The "separate property contributor" cannot receive interest on his contributions; he cannot receive an adjustment for a change in monetary values since the initial investment was made; and he cannot receive reimbursement, even if it is traceable, to the extent that such reimbursement would exceed the net value of the property at the time of the division.

Some history on the subject of sections 2640 and 2581 is enlightening. Historically, under common law, there was a rebuttable presumption that the title to a property controlled its characterization. Thus, under common law, even when community property was used to acquire an asset, if title to that asset stated that one of the parties owned it "as her sole and separate property," there was a presumption as to the correctness of that statement. Of course, that presumption could be rebutted. The case of *Marriage of Lucas*, 27 Cal. 3d 808 (1980) discussed these concepts at some length and ultimately established the standard for rebutting the presumption. According to this standard, merely tracing the acquisition funds to a source (community or separate) different from that reflected in the title document was not sufficient to overcome the presumption; tracing was insufficient because the court simply presumed that the contributing party intended to make a *gift* of her separate property to the community. Instead, the court required evidence of an *agreement* between the spouses that reflected by "clear and convincing evidence" that the parties intended the status of the asset to be other than as shown on the title document. And, while the standard of evidence ("clear and convincing") was high, the agreement did not need to be in writing. Evidence of an oral agreement sufficed, so long as the standard of "clear and convincing" was met.

As might be imagined, the courts and legislature worried whether it was prudent to allow proof of an oral agreement to disturb the manner in which record title to assets was held. So, to provide uniformity in the manner in which these assets were treated by the various courts, in 1984 the legislature enacted Civil Code section 4800.1. That section was substantially similar to the current Family Code section 2581, with the exception that it applied only to property held in *joint tenancy*. No other forms of jointly held property were included in its provisions. In 1987, however, Civil Code section 4800.1 was amended to include all forms of jointly held property. A companion section, substantially similar to the above-quoted Family Code section 2640, was enacted as well in Civil Code section 4800.2. Their Family Code counterparts have long since replaced these sections.

The aspect of this legislation that caused so much concern was not the presumption as to the form of title but the more stringent application of the rebuttal provisions. Recall that, per *Lucas*, the common law presumption could be rebutted by an oral agreement to the contrary so long as it was deemed to be "clear and convincing evidence" on that point. Civil Code section 4800.1, however, elevated the rebuttal standard to encompass only *written* evidence.[13] The problem became the application of these "new" rules: Should they apply in all cases, even those commenced before the operative date of the statute, and thus be applied *retroactively* (a concept not automatically looked upon with favor by the courts); or, should the new rules apply only to cases commenced *after* the legislation took effect?

This question was the subject of significant litigation. Opponents to retroactive application (there was no compelling argument in favor of it) argued that it would destroy vested property rights, a notion generally not allowed by the U.S. or State Constitution. For example, a person could contribute separate property to the acquisition of an asset, yet take title in joint tenancy for estate planning reasons,[14] all the while intending that the property remain her separate property. Under the *Lucas* rule, this intent could be demonstrated and the separate property interest could be protected. Under Civil Code section 4800.1 (and Family Code section 2581), however, that vested property right would vanish upon application of the statute. This controversy was ultimately decided against retroactivity.

The state supreme court addressed this question in Marriage of Buol, 39 Cal. 3d 751 (1985). In *Buol*, the wife used separate property funds to purchase a house, title to which was taken in joint tenancy with her husband. At trial, the house had substantially increased in value, but Mrs. Buol was able to satisfy the *Lucas* standards for proving an oral agreement between her and her husband that the property would remain her separate property. While the case was on appeal, Civil Code section 4800.1 became operative. Mr. Buol then argued that because the house was held by them in joint tenancy, it should be characterized as community property unless his wife could produce a written agreement to the contrary (which she obviously could not). The court found that Mrs. Buol's interest in the property characterization under a *Lucas* analysis had vested. Thus, absent a "compelling state interest," retroactive application of the writing requirement of section 4800.1 was unconstitutional because it would destroy Mrs. Buol's vested property right. In summary, *Buol* holds that Civil Code section 4800.1 and Family Code 2581 do not apply to cases commenced before January 1, 1984 (the effective date of section 4800.1). Because the *Buol* court was unable to discern a "compelling interest" in retroactive application of the section, it chose not to do so. In light of extensive litigation on this subject, the legislature attempted to create the requisite "compelling interest" in Family Code section 2580(c), which states in no uncertain terms:

> [A] compelling state interest exists to provide for uniform treatment of property. Thus, former Sections 4800.1 and 4800.2 of the Civil Code, as operative on January 1, 1987, and as continued in Sections 2581 and 2640 of this code, apply to all property held in joint title regardless of the date of acquisition of the property. . . . However, those sections do not apply to property settlement agreements executed before January 1, 1987, or proceedings in which judgments were rendered before January 1, 1987, regardless of whether those judgments have become final.

Note that this anti-*Lucas* legislation applies not only to property that is *acquired* jointly, but also to property that is *converted* into joint ownership subsequent to its original date of acquisition. These statutes are also not confined to real property but have application to *any* property, real or personal, by which title is held pursuant to a written document. Finally, these statutes only have application in situations involving the division of property upon *dissolution or legal separation*.

Property transfers incidental to death are governed by the *Lucas* rules. For example, when a joint tenant dies, the property passes to the other joint tenant by right of survivorship. This means that the surviving joint tenant receives 100 percent of the property. If that same property is divided upon dissolution or legal separation, however, each joint tenant only receives 50 percent (because the property must be divided equally). With this in mind, what happens if a person who holds property as a joint tenant with her spouse (a very common situation) *dies* while a dissolution is pending? This question becomes important because if she had lived, she could have passed to her heirs by will her 50 percent post-dissolution "share" in the property (which she arguably would have received out of the dissolution). Because she did not live, however, the property automatically passed to the surviving tenant; must he share the property with his wife's heirs?

The answer to these questions depends upon the timing of the death. As explained earlier in this book, death will terminate a marriage. Accordingly, if a death occurs while a marital dissolution proceeding is pending, but before a judgment of dissolution has been entered, the question of marital status is moot, and the jurisdictional basis for the court's involvement ends.[15] There is simply nothing left for the court to do. As such, the dissolution proceeding is dismissed, which for all practical purposes is the same as if it had never started. However, what if a death occurs *after* a judgment terminating the marital status has been entered, but *before* the property issues have been resolved? Here, the court would have specifically reserved jurisdiction over those issues (as would be the situation in the case of a bifurcated judgment of marital status). Therefore, the court would address the property issues in accordance with the appropriate provisions of the Family Code (in this case, section 2581). Care must be taken, then, in situations involving the potential application of these various statutory presumptions.

Consider the following example: After marriage, the husband uses $20,000 of his separate property to buy a boat, title to which is taken by him and his wife as "joint tenants." It is undisputed, however, that putting the boat in joint tenancy was simply for estate planning purposes. The husband can satisfy the "clear and convincing" standards set out in *Lucas*; and he can establish that there was an actual agreement between him and his wife whereby they intended the boat to remain his separate property. We know from the above discussion, however, that this property is presumed by section 2581 to be community in nature. Assuming that the boat increases in value from $20,000 to $80,000 during the marriage; upon dissolution, how much can the husband expect to receive? The answer is $50,000: Pursuant to section 2640 he will receive his traceable $20,000, and he will share equally in the remaining $60,000 community value.[16] Had the community property presumption of section 2581 not been in effect, however, he (arguably) could have demonstrated that the entire asset was his separate property and thus receive the entire $80,000. Obviously, then, these presumptions can have significant financial impact on the parties to a dissolution or legal separation proceeding.

In 2000, the legislature added a new form of title, "Community Property with Right of Survivorship." Civil Code section 682.1, effective July 1, 2001, provides as follows:

(a) Community property of a husband and wife, when expressly declared in the transfer document to be community property with right of survivorship, and which may be accepted in writing on the face of the document by a statement signed or initialed by the grantees, shall, upon the death of one of the spouses, pass to the survivor, without administration, pursuant to the terms of the instrument, subject to the same procedures, as property held in joint tenancy. Prior to the death of either spouse, the right of survivorship may be terminated pursuant to the same procedures by which a joint tenancy may be severed. Part I (commencing with Section 5000) of Division 5 of the Probate Code and Chapter 2 (commencing with Section 13540), Chapter 3 (commencing with Section 13550) and Chapter 3.5 (commencing with Section 13560) of Part 2 of Division 8 of the Probate Code apply to this property.

(b) This section does not apply to a joint account in a financial institution to which Part 2 (commencing with Section 5100) of Division 5 of the Probate Code applies.

(c) This section shall become operative on July 1, 2001, and shall apply to instruments created on or after that date.

The general purpose of this legislation is unrelated to family law concepts. Rather, it is primarily designed to ensure a step-up in basis of the property upon the death of the joint tenant (a tax-related concept). The general community property presumption discussed above applies to *any* property held in joint form, and this new form of title falls within the category of "joint form." Thus, the reader should be aware of its existence and should note that Family Code section 2581 will include property held in this new form of title as well.

3. Tracing

The concept of tracing, both in general and in the context of section 2640, requires some further explanation. In general, *tracing* allows the tracing party to rebut the general presumption of section 760 (that property acquired during marriage is community in nature). Tracing is accomplished by tracing the source of the funds used to acquire the property to a separate property source.[17] If successful, the proponent of the tracing will be in a position to demonstrate to the court that the asset in question is not, in fact, appropriately characterized as "community." Rather, it may be entirely separate, or some hybrid asset, with both separate and community aspects. In this context, the court must determine the appropriate ratio of the asset's separate to community value and allocate the value of the asset, including appreciation, accordingly.

The concept of general tracing has less application with titled assets for, as we have seen, these are controlled by section 2581. If section 2581 operates to presume that an asset is community in nature, unless that presumption is rebutted in accordance with the provision of that section, general tracing becomes irrelevant. The only way tracing becomes an issue is under section 2640, which will allow limited reimbursement of a separate property contribution to the asset.

When successful, general tracing can establish ownership in a "piece" of the asset in question, not simply the cash equivalent of the original investment. Through *general tracing*, one determines the source of funds used to acquire an asset, examines the separate or community character of the "source funds," and thus establishes a separate, community, or blended interest in the subsequently acquired assets. This is possible because a change in the form of a piece of property does not change its status as community or separate. For example, an individual owns an automobile outright before he is married, subsequently marries, sells the automobile, and invests the proceeds of that sale in a diamond (buying it outright); even though the diamond was in fact "acquired" during the marriage, the separate property merely changed *form* (from an automobile to a diamond). Accordingly, to the extent that a spouse can trace the source funds of an asset acquired during marriage to separate property, that spouse can successfully argue that all that has happened is that the separate property source funds have simply been invested in the post-maritally acquired asset, thus vesting in that asset separate property characteristics.

This is the basic difference between general tracing and the more specific concept set out in section 2640. Under section 2640, the question of the character of the asset is no longer in dispute. For section 2640 to apply, the asset's character must already have been determined to be community. Under those circumstances, then, the best that a party can hope to recover is her original separate property contribution—without interest and without regard to the appreciation, if any, of the asset.

In this context (assuming the asset is not otherwise presumed to be community in nature), if a spouse can trace the source of all or a portion of an asset acquired after marriage to his separate property funds (for example, a 10 percent share of the asset), he can make a credible argument that he is entitled to 10 percent of the appreciation of that asset, which may very well greatly exceed the actual dollar amount of the separate property contribution. For example, if $1,000 of separate property funds was used to purchase $10,000 of stocks after marriage, the spouse who owned the separate property could claim a 10 percent ownership interest in the stock portfolio. If the stock portfolio increased in value to $100,000, the spouse who owned the separate property could claim a $10,000 separate property interest in the stock portfolio. However, if the asset was found to be community in nature, according to section 2640, the spouse would, at best, be entitled to a reimbursement of his $1,000 separate property contribution. This distinction between application of section 2640 and standard concepts of general tracing can be significant and very costly.[18]

4. Transmutations

In addition to the various presumptions found in the common law or created by statute with respect to the status of property, sometimes the parties themselves can take certain actions that will have an impact on the characterization of marital property. The most commonly discussed situation involves the concept of *transmutation*. This term generally describes an agreement between the spouses to change the status of an asset from either separate to community or community to separate. It has long been recognized that spouses are free to agree between each other to change the status of either a single asset or all of their assets in bulk. There are, however, some rules that apply in these situations.

Family Code section 850 provides as follows:

> Subject to sections 851 to 853, inclusive, married persons may by agreement or transfer, with or without consideration, do any of the following:
>   (a) Transmute community property to separate property of either spouse.
>   (b) Transmute separate property of either spouse to community property.
>   (c) Transmute separate property of one spouse to separate property of the other spouse.

Family Code section 852 provides in pertinent part: "(a) A transmutation of real or personal property is not valid unless made in writing by an express declaration that is made, joined in, consented to, or accepted by the spouse whose interest in the property is adversely affected."

Accordingly, oral transmutations of property are simply no longer allowed. The term "no longer" is used because before sections 850-853 were enacted, such oral transmutations were authorized, and, as might be expected, allegations of such oral transmutation found their way into virtually every dissolution action wherein there were significant assets at stake. The courts had to struggle with these circumstances long and hard and had to listen to significant testimony on the issues with respect to whether an oral transmutation had in fact taken place. This could be both time-consuming and costly and rarely yielded results that were acceptable to the parties. Thus the legislature enacted sections 850-853 to put to rest once and for all the concept of an "oral transmutation." The law in this area is quite clear: If a spouse claims that a certain asset was given to him by the other spouse pertinent to a transmutation, he must produce a writing, signed by the other spouse, that acknowledges the existence of this transmutation.

The reader must now be wondering to what extent the foregoing rule applies to the normal everyday gifts so often exchanged between spouses.

Fortunately, Family Code section 852 provides instruction in this regard. That Code section states, in pertinent part, as follows:

> (c) This section does not apply to a gift between the spouses of clothing, wearing apparel, jewelry, or other tangible articles of a personal nature that is used solely or principally by the spouse to whom the gift is made and that is not substantial in value taking into account the circumstances of the marriage.

Under these circumstances, everyday gifts between spouses are in fact allowed. The reader should note with care, however, the last clause of this section, which provides that the gift must not be "substantial in value taking into account the circumstances of the marriage." A married couple whose combined annual income is $60,000 will have no trouble convincing the court that a gift valued at $300 is not "substantial in value." Yet, one of those spouses could not contend that a $30,000 automobile was simply "given" to him by the other spouse without producing a writing signed by the spouse who supposedly made this very generous gift, which by its terms recognizes that a gift was in fact intended. A different outcome could very well be warranted, however, if the spouses' annual income was closer to $1 million.

Now that the reader has been exposed to the basic concepts concerning the characterization of assets acquired before and during marriage, as well as post-separation, an examination of some of the more common circumstances in which these issues arise is appropriate. Accordingly, we will now discuss the specific circumstances arising out of and pertaining to earnings and employment benefits, gifts and inheritances, personal injury awards, rents, income and profits, professional education, business interests, and retirement benefits.

5. Personal Injury Awards

During marriage, one or both spouses may be involved in an incident that gives rise to a cause of action for personal injury against some third-party tortfeasor. Under these circumstances, a significant period of time (upwards of five years in some cases) can elapse between the time of the injury and the time that recovery for those damages is achieved by the injured spouse. During the intervening period, of course, marital difficulties can arise that lead to termination of the marriage, resulting in the necessity to characterize the personal injury award that is ultimately received by the injured spouse.

Family Code sections 780 and 781 address this situation and provide that if the cause of action giving rise to the personal injury claim arose during the marriage, the recovery is community property. If, however, the cause of action arose after either a judgment of dissolution or legal separation or while the parties were living "separate and apart," the recovery is the injured spouse's separate property. Section 781 also provides, however, that if the community advanced expenses as a result of the injury, but the recovery turns out to be separate property, the community is entitled to reimbursement.

Family Code section 2603 also addresses the division of personal injury awards:

> (a) "Community estate personal injury damages" as used in this section means all money or other property received or to be received by a person in satisfaction of a judgment for damages for the person's personal injuries or pursuant to an agreement for the settlement or compromise of a claim for the damages, if the cause of action for the damages arose during the marriage but is not separate property as described in Section 781, unless the money or other property has been commingled with other assets of the community estate.
>
> (b) Community estate personal injury damages shall be assigned to the party who suffered the injuries unless the court, after taking into account the economic condition and needs of each party, the time that has elapsed since the recovery of the damages or the accrual of the cause of action, and all other facts of the case, determines that the interests of justice require another disposition. In such a case, the community estate personal injury damages shall be assigned to the respective parties in such proportions as the court determines to be just, except that at least one-half of the damages shall be assigned to the party who suffered the injuries.

In determining the character of a personal injury award, it is important to pinpoint the date on which the cause of action gave rise to the plaintiff's damages. A cause of action *accrues* at the time the event giving rise to the right to recover took place. For example, a cause of action for injuries resulting from an automobile accident accrues on the date the accident happened. A cause of action for breach of contract accrues on the date that the contract was in fact breached.

It sometimes appears that community personal injury damages are treated as separate property by virtue of the language of section 2603, which mandates that these damage awards be assigned to the party who suffered the injury. Section 2603 does not, however, actually make these damages separate property. They are simply accorded special treatment by statute. In fact, pursuant to Family Code section 781, the damages will only be treated as separate property if the cause of action arose after a judgment of dissolution or decree of legal separation; if the cause of action arose (or accrued) while the injured person was living separate and apart from the other spouse; or, if the cause of action arose during the marriage but on behalf of one spouse as against the other (which is a special circumstance statutorily deemed to constitute a separate property matter as set out in Family Code section 782).

Thus, although the statute recognizes the community nature of these funds, the court has broad discretion to ignore the general rule of dividing community property 50/50. In fact, the court may award personal injury damages 100 percent to the injured spouse (and in no event less than 50 percent to the injured spouse) even if it means an inequitable division of community property will result.

The appellate court in Marriage of Morris, 139 Cal. App. 3d 823 (1983) used its discretion to deny Husband's request for an offsetting amount of community property assets to compensate for the $43,000 award (100 percent) of wife's personal injury damage award obtained during the marriage. The court held that the operative statute (former Civil Code section 4800, now Family Code section 2603) is unambiguous: it permits the trial court to grant 100 percent of a personal injury award to the injured spouse without offsetting the award to the other spouse. "The statute is designed to assure that other than in exceptional circumstances, community property **personal injury** damages, or the bulk thereof, will be awarded to the injured spouse and that under no circumstances will the injured spouse receive less than one-half of such damages."

From this author's perspective, it makes little sense to continue to rely on these statutes for the characterization of personal injury damages as "community but treated as separate." Rather, it makes more sense to simply carve out an exception to the community property rule and just characterize these damages as separate property.

6. Earnings; Employment Benefits

There should be little doubt in the reader's mind that earnings such as wages and bonuses fall within the general category of property. It should be equally without question that to the extent that these are earned during the marriage by one of the spouses, they constitute community property. What the reader may not be aware of, however, is that the concept of "earnings" is much broader than simply a wage earner's paycheck. Black's Law Dictionary defines this term in a somewhat circular fashion by stating that *earnings* are equivalent to income or that which is earned. In all fairness, this definition continues and states that earnings are "the fruit or reward of labor; the fruits of the proper skill, experience and industry; the gains of a person derived from his services or labor without the aid of capital. . . . " The long and short of it is that if someone performs services and is given compensation for those services, and those services are performed during the marriage and before separation, then that compensation will be deemed to be property, and community property at that, regardless of the form of the compensation.

The many different forms that such compensation can take include: stock options, deferred compensation (401K plans, pension plans), vacation pay, bonuses, fringe benefits, and any other similar "reward" or compensation for the labor and services of the employee spouse. The easiest way to approach the question of whether an asset constitutes earnings is to ask yourself the following: "Would this asset (be it cash, vacation pay, bonuses) have been transferred to the employee spouse had that person not performed some form of service or otherwise expended labor for the benefit of the individual (or entity) transferring the asset?"[19] If the answer to that question is "yes," then further inquiry is needed to determine the purpose of the transfer. If, however, the answer to the question is "no," then the transferred asset constitutes "earnings and accumulations" as those terms are used in this context.

Similarly, the profits realized by an individual who is in business for him or herself constitutes earnings to the extent that these profits are reflective of income generated by labor or skill. If that income is not the product of the sole proprietor's (or partner's) labor or skill, then it will not be considered earnings; rather, it will be construed to be either a return on capital, or passive income[20] flowing from some other asset.

Where a spouse is the primary shareholder or the sole shareholder of a corporation, the earnings of that corporation will generally not be considered earnings and accumulations of the shareholder spouse. In the corporate context, the shareholder spouse is also generally a salaried employee of the corporation. Therefore, that spouse's salary or paycheck would fall in the context of earnings, but dividends or an increase in the value of the shares of stock he owns would not necessarily be construed as earnings and accumulations as that term is being used herein.

Retirement benefits, pensions, and deferred compensation packages also fall within the context of earnings and accumulations because they constitute income that is earned currently but paid later. These concepts will be discussed in greater detail in the section dealing with pension plans below.

A final note: For purposes of the division of community property, "income" as a divisible community asset obtains its character as either separate or community not necessarily when the income is paid but rather when the income is earned. For example, an individual may receive an employment bonus at the end of the year in satisfaction and recognition of work he performed during the year. However, some companies choose not to pay these bonuses until a couple of months into the next year. Accordingly, a bonus that was paid in March of 2009 in recognition of work performed during 2008 would be classified as community property even if the parties separated in February of 2009 if they were living together at the time the bonus was earned. Accounts receivable would also constitute community property generated by individuals who are in business for themselves,[21] to the extent that these accounts represent monies owed for work performed (and therefore compensation earned) during the marriage and before separation.

Similarly, income earned post-separation constitutes the sole and separate property of the employee spouse. In recognition of this fact, Family Code section 771 clearly states that "the earnings and accumulations of a spouse . . . while living separate and apart from the other spouse, are the separate property of the spouse."

7. Gifts and Inheritances

As mentioned above, certain assets, simply by operation of law, are specifically classified as separate property. Two such examples are gifts and inheritances. Family Code section 770 specifically mandates that property received by "gift," "bequest," "devise," or "descent" constitutes separate property. A *gift*, simply put, constitutes some item of value that is transferred by one person to another gratuitously and without receiving anything in return for the transfer. An *inheritance* is somewhat similar to a gift, except that it takes place after the death of the donor. A gift is made while the donor is living.[22]

This discussion, of course, would seem to imply that we are talking about gifts between spouses, and indeed these rules do apply to that situation. They also apply, however, to gifts made by third parties to one or both of the spouses. Technically speaking, if the husband and wife receive a gift that is made to both of them, they each hold a separate property interest in one-half of the item. Under these circumstances, great care must be taken to ascertain the donor's intent at the time he made the gift to determine if he intended the gift for one or both of the spouses. This situation typically involves wedding gifts. Generally, the wife will argue that gifts by her friends were intended solely for her while the husband will argue that gifts made by his friends were intended solely for him. As a practical matter, unless we are talking about gifts of significant value, this is a dispute whose resolution is best left directly to the parties themselves.

Care must also be taken to examine gifts made by an employer to an employee spouse. A problem exists under these circumstances when the so-called "gift" is actually some form of reward or bonus for a job well done. To the extent that it does constitute such a reward or bonus, that item would become the community property of both spouses. It is community property when it is characterized as earnings and accumulations of the recipient spouse earned during the marriage (before separation).

8. Rents, Income, and Profits

All forms of income produced by an asset maintain the character of the asset from which they flow. Accordingly, if $10,000 of separate property cash is placed into an interest-bearing deposit account on the day before marriage, all the interest accumulating on this $10,000 during the marriage will maintain the separate property character of the initial fund from which it flowed. As was the case with acquisitions by gift, bequest, devise, or descent, Family Code section 770 mandates that the "rents, issues and profits [of property]" constitute separate property as well, when those rents, issues, and profits flow from the separate property of the spouses. The operation of this rule, together with the recognition of the fact that many assets acquired during a marriage contain both separate and community property elements, has given rise to the need to apportion those profits as between their separate property source and their community property source. These concepts will be discussed in greater detail below in the section dealing with apportionment.

The point to bear in mind in this immediate discussion is that care must be taken to examine not only the nature of the assets involved in the marital dissolution proceeding, but also the source underlying those assets. It is only then that the parties will obtain a true picture of the exact nature and extent of all of the community property. For example, copyrights, royalties, and other income from an artistic work (for example, a book, a recording, or a work of art) will share the same character as the work of art itself. If the artistic work constitutes community property (for example, because it was created during the marriage while the parties were living together), then the royalties and earnings from the sale of that artistic work will also be community property.

Similarly, gambling winnings will share the same status as the source money used to generate those winnings. For example, if an individual uses community property to buy a lottery ticket and in fact wins the lottery, the entirety of the winnings will be community property. On the other hand, if that same individual purchases the same winning lottery ticket with separate property money, the entirety of those earnings will be characterized as separate property.

9. Community Contributions for Education and Training

A professional license and a degree of higher education have long been recognized in California as valuable property rights. They are valuable, however, to whom? There is no doubt that the ability to practice a profession has value to the person who received the education or professional license. Yet, that education or license is uniquely valuable to the individual who earned it. In other words, most licenses in California cannot be freely transferred by the recipient and thus, arguably, have no value outside of the hands of the recipient. Nor is an education that "substantially enhances a person's earning capacity" freely transferable. Courts across the country have grappled with the problem of whether to award the non-licensed spouse an amount of money equal to his or her share of the "value" of the education or license.

Perhaps the most famous case in California to address this situation is Marriage of Sullivan, 37 Cal. 3d 762, (1984). Janet and Mark Sullivan were married in 1967, immediately after which Mark entered medical school. From 1968 through 1971, Mark attended medical school while Janet, for all practical purposes, supported him. Shortly after Mark completed his residency in 1978, he and Janet separated. Janet subsequently asked the court to value Mark's medical license and award her an equitable portion.

While this case was pending before the California Supreme Court, the California Legislature enacted Civil Code section 4800.3 (current Family Code section 2641). Section 2641 basically denies the community the right to claim an interest in the enhanced education and subsequent license of a spouse following dissolution. It does, however, create a right of reimbursement for community contributions made to education or training that "substantially enhances the earning capacity" of the professional spouse. These reimbursement rights are not, however, absolute. In fact, section 2641 specifically provides that a reimbursement award may be reduced or modified to the extent that the community has, as of the date of separation, "substantially benefited" from the education and training obtained by the professional spouse. If the education or training received by the professional spouse is offset by similar education or training received by the other spouse for which community contributions were made, there is no reimbursement; and, if the education or training of the professional spouse allows the other spouse to engage in gainful employment that "substantially reduces the need of the [educated] party for support that would otherwise be required," the court may modify the community's right to reimbursement.

The theoretical bases for these rules trace back to the expectations of the spouses. Generally, when one spouse sacrifices his own education or training or simply expends the additional effort to put the other spouse through specialized education and training, he does so with the expectation that, inasmuch as he is married to this person, he will then benefit from the higher earnings of the student spouse once the education and training has been completed. These expectations are not met, however, and the community in fact does not benefit from this education and training if the spouses divorce before the student spouse completes her education or training.

Under these circumstances, Family Code section 2641 provides that the community shall be for all contributions to the education and training of the party that have substantially enhanced that party's earning capacity. These contributions are very broadly perceived and include virtually all education-related expenses. Contributions do not, however, include ordinary living expenses, which would have been incurred whether the spouse was in school or not. The question of whether the education or training has "substantially enhanced" the student spouse's earning capacity is a fact for the judge to decide. As might be imagined, the judge has a wide amount of discretion in making this determination.

Family Code section 2641 limits this reimbursement right by providing that such reimbursement will only be appropriate if the community has not already "substantially benefited" from the education or training. In that regard, the statute further establishes a rebuttable presumption that the community has not substantially benefited from the community contributions to this education or training if they were made less than ten years before the proceeding commenced. Similarly, there is also a presumption that the community *has* substantially benefited from its contributions to the education or training to the extent that they were made more than ten years before the proceeding commenced. The rationale behind this presumption should be clear: if the community enjoyed a higher standard of living for over ten years due to the education and training of the student spouse, the community is not entitled to reimbursement for funds it contributed toward this education and training.[23]

Finally, Family Code section 2641(b)(2) states that any student loans "incurred during marriage for the education or training of a party shall not be included among the liabilities of the community for the purpose of division pursuant to this division but shall be assigned for payment by the party." This section essentially provides that student loans are, for all practical purposes, treated as the separate property of the spouse who incurred the debt.

10. Business Interests

A review of the foregoing discussion on community property in general should make it clear that the interests of a spouse (or both spouses) in an ongoing business are indeed "property" as that term is used in the context of the division of marital assets; accordingly, those business interests are also capable of being valued for purposes of division. With respect to the valuation of a business, however, an additional element must be explored: the value of the business' "goodwill." Business goodwill is an intangible but nonetheless valuable property right, and it is an asset that must be accounted for in the division of marital property.

257

a) Valuation of the Business

How is a business' goodwill valued? Valuation has always been an important aspect of the division of marital property. However, the manner in which assets are valued has been the subject of continuing debate as. Valuation must be as accurate as possible, which is difficult to achieve when one is evaluating an intangible asset such as goodwill.

The term *goodwill* refers to the portion of a business that represents the likelihood that it will have repeat business. For example, an individual who practices as an attorney over some period of time will build up a reputation in the community and will develop a client base of (hopefully) satisfied clients. These satisfied clients will recommend the attorney to their friends and family. Over time, the attorney will have a business that is valued by virtue of the assets that it holds (the photocopier, the computers, the books) together with the accounts receivable (money currently owed to the lawyer for work already performed); plus, it will have an additional component: goodwill. Simply stated, goodwill is the component of an ongoing business that represents the likelihood of future patronage. Most businesses have a positive goodwill. These businesses can expect that in the future people will continue to purchase their goods and services. It is of course also possible, however, for a business to have negative goodwill. Indeed, if the lawyer in the above example were found liable for malpractice, and word got out that he is an incompetent attorney, the likelihood of future patronage would be greatly reduced, thus generating negative goodwill.

As a general rule, the concept of goodwill finds application in the context of sole proprietorships or business ventures in which the spouse who owns the goodwill owns a significant share of the business. This is because the concept of goodwill as a valuable community asset is based on the fact that its existence is in no small part tied to the energy, efforts, and labor of the owner-spouse; and as we have seen above, the owner-spouse's energy, efforts, and labor are community assets. If the owner-spouse has a very small ownership interest in the company, it would be difficult, if not impossible, to determine his exact contribution to the overall goodwill of the company (as compared to the other owner-participants). The trial court may refuse to consider a goodwill factor when the owner-spouse has only a very small interest in the business enterprise. Similarly, not every business has a valuable goodwill. However, those determinations are best left to the discretion of the trial court. As a practical matter, if there is a market for the business' services, some level of goodwill should be considered in the valuation of the business as a whole.

It is important to note that the method of valuing business goodwill must be keyed to the expected earnings—rather than the actual earnings—of the business. Business appraisers use various methods to determine the value of goodwill. An appraiser's choice of method depends on the facts and circumstances of the case, the particulars of the business involved, and the expertise of the appraiser himself. Such methods of valuation can include book value, liquidation value, replacement value, fair market value, and literally any other method that is supportable under the facts and circumstances of the case.[24]

This discussion of goodwill is not intended to ignore the other aspects of business valuation. These include the value of the inventory on hand, the physical assets of the business enterprise (machinery, desks, copiers, computers), the accounts receivable, and the work in progress (for example, contingency fee lawsuits for a lawyer's practice or an ongoing construction contract under which periodic "progress payments" are being made to a construction company). These assets are no less important than the goodwill aspect of an ongoing business and in fact are usually much simpler to value. They will be included in the overall business evaluation undertaken by the appraiser.

b) Valuation Methods

In the context of actually valuing the business, several factors, definitions and key points must be explored. The law in this area is complex and contradictory, and presents a moving target, because typically nothing is really being sold. Indeed, generally speaking, there is typically no willing seller for the business in question, which clearly and objectively affects its value. Nevertheless, the business must be valued in order for it to be divided or awarded in the context of a dissolution, and there are a variety of methods. The law instructs us to use the simplest valuation method available. They include (going from most simple to most complex):

a. **Sales proceeds method**. If a business is in the process of being sold, there is case law that instructs us to delay the family law case until after the sale.
b. **Comparables.** These, while not our specific asset, are nonetheless actual sales, and will provide very persuasive guidance in setting the value.
c. **Liquidation value.** Cut the business into pieces and sell it separately. This does not include a component for goodwill. This process is more complicated but it avoids the difficulty of trying to value a going concern. This is really only appropriate for valuation if it is legitimately believed that the business will in fact be liquidated.
d. **Book value.** What do the financial books and records of the business say about its retained value? This is usually too simple a process to be practical in a divorce context. Also, the books may be "cooked"

and/or adjusted or subject to tax write-offs that are inappropriate and that will impact on the valuation. Indeed, certain tax write-offs and deductions, while otherwise legal, may not be appropriate in the context of a divorce involving a business valuation, so careful attention and review of the Schedule C attached to the income tax returns must be undertaken. Just because something is appropriate to the IRS for tax purposes will not make it necessarily acceptable for business valuation purposes.[25]

e. **Adjusted book value.** This requires a forensic analysis.[26] Typically, these analyses are performed on a cash basis. In this context we must analyze the accounts receivable plus the other business records to arrive at a value for the business.

f. **Going concern value.** This means the whole business is worth the sum of its parts, or even more than its individual parts. A variety of external factors also apply.

g. **Capitalized earnings.** Capitalize the excess earnings: this is the most common method employed by trial courts. It is not, however, mandated by law.[27]

c) *Date of Valuation*

Once the parties value the business, they must consider the date on which the business should be valued. As a general rule, marital assets are valued as of the date on which the dissolution action is tried. There are, however, circumstances under which it is appropriate to value an asset at a different point in time. There is no bright line test here, but in general it should be valued as near as practical to the date of trial. There are some informal rules of thumb, however: It is generally considered appropriate to value a small business, typically owned and operated by one person (one of the spouses), such as a professional practice (doctor, lawyer, etc.) or other small business, by using a date close to the date of separation as the valuation date. This is considered appropriate because it is believed that a small business of this type is more susceptible to the influences of the estranged spouse; further, it is believed that once a divorce proceeding is filed there is greater motivation of the spouse who runs the business to suppress its value. By valuing the business at the date of separation it is believed that this effect can be minimized if not avoided altogether.

One of the earlier examples of this process is found in the case of *In re* Marriage of Green (1989) 213 Cal.App.3d 14. This case involved a solo law practice that declined in value post-separation. The husband's lawyer argued that, notwithstanding the decrease in value, it was error not to value the business at the time of trial. The appellate court rejected that argument and held that the date of separation was the appropriate valuation date in small law practices such as Mr. Green's; additionally, the court indicated that only in situations where the actions of the business owner had "minimal impact" on the operation of the firm would it be appropriate to consider any other valuation date. It should be noted that this rule is not designed to operate as a punishment, nor does it mean that the court believes that the operating spouse will deliberately "trash" the business. Rather, it is simply a rule conceived out of a practical realization of who is in fact running the business.

Although the *Green* decision was limited to law firms, that limitation was wiped away by the case of *In re* Marriage of Stevenson (1993) 20 Cal. App.4th 250. In *Stevenson*, the husband owned a small contracting business as well as a Christmas tree lot. The wife argued that her husband deliberately trashed his contracting business after separation, and if the court did not value that business as of the date of separation she would be denied her share of its real value. The appellate court agreed with the wife, and specifically held that, although prior cases had focused on small professional practices (e.g., *Green*), there is no distinction between those practices and any small business that relies on the skill and reputation of the spouse who operates the business. As such, the better approach is to value the business at the date of separation.

d) Elements of Business Valuation

A business valuation must include all of the business's components, the aggregate of which constitutes the final valuation figure. These items include the following:

1. **Real property.** Usually this can be valued simply by obtaining comparable sale values and the like through a real estate appraiser.
2. **Personal property.** Like real property, this category is subject to similar valuations. The actual items involved are verified, inventoried and appraised.
3. **Work in process.** This simply involves an analysis of the business's ongoing work and, more importantly, how much money that work is expected to generate.
4. **Accounts receivable.** The primary question is: are these actually worth anything? They need to be aged in order to be appropriately valued. Generally speaking, if they are more than 90 days old, they are most likely worth very little, if anything.
5. **Goodwill.** This is the "going concern" value. After all of the above factors have been determined, the analysis of going concerns/ goodwill is applied to determine the business's ultimate value. This is the most difficult element to value and it is discussed above.[28]

11. Retirement Benefits

a) *Types of Plans*

The concepts of deferred compensation and retirement benefit plans both refer to compensation that is earned by the employee currently but paid at some later date. Most retirement plans fall into one of two categories: (1) defined contribution plans or (2) defined benefit plans. The distinction between these has to do with the manner in which they are funded. With a *defined contribution plan*, the ultimate amount of the benefits to be provided at retirement is not known until the date of such retirement—because the ultimate amount depends on the future investment performance of the fund. The benefits are simply defined by a formula for contribution.

With the *defined benefit plan*, the known variable is the amount of the benefit to be received at retirement, and the required contribution over time is adjusted to meet that goal. Under either plan, the employee spouse typically has the option to contribute his own funds to the plan in addition to those funds contributed by the employer. Additional forms of retirement benefit plans are available, but, for all practical purposes, these two are the most common.

b) *Division of Retirement Benefits*

Historically, courts have had trouble valuing and dividing retirement benefits in the context of marital dissolution proceedings. Retirement benefit plans are sometimes known as deferred compensation plans, pension plans, or 401(k) plans. According to any of these plans, an employee has the right to receive either periodic payments or a lump-sum payment upon retirement from his employer. These retirement benefits are usually provided as a source of additional compensation, which is deferred until a later date when the employee spouse moves into a lower tax bracket. Additionally, these plans are offered as incentives for employees to remain with the company over a long period of time. In this context, the concept of vesting becomes important.

An individual can possess a right to obtain property in the future. A *vested* right is secure: it survives even if the employee is terminated or leaves voluntarily. In contrast, a *non-vested* right is subject to revocation by the employer. Usually, rights vest after an employee works for his employer for a minimum period of time. In a *vested* situation, this right is one that will survive the discharge or the voluntary termination of the employee such that the employee can continue to participate in the fund even after leaving the employ of the company. In contrast, a *non-vested* right is one in which the employer maintains the right to revoke the employee's ownership interest in the fund until such time as the employee has satisfied the vesting requirements. These vesting requirements usually require that the employee work for the employer for a minimum period of time prior to the benefits vesting. Employers use this system to help ensure the employers can anticipate their employees' uninterrupted performance (at least to the extent that the employee views the non-vested rights as valuable and wishes to secure vesting in that fund).

Problems in this area arose when parties argued that to the extent these plans were non-vested, the rights to such were mere expectancies. As such, the argument went, it was impossible to value a mere expectancy because if the circumstances giving rise to the vesting did not occur, the employee would never receive a valuable asset the plan.[29]

This was exactly the argument addressed by the court in Marriage of Brown, 15 Cal. 3d 838 (1976). The *Brown* court considered the non-vested pension rights of the husband, Mr. Robert Brown, who was an employee of General Telephone Company. Under the General Telephone plan, an employee would forfeit all his rights if he were discharged before accumulating sufficient points to provide vesting in the plan. Conversely, an employee who had accumulated sufficient points was guaranteed to receive the pension plan. As of the date of separation, Mr. Brown had not accumulated the requisite number of points to entitle him to a vested interest in the pension plan. He thus argued that, because his interest was not vested, it constituted nothing more than a "mere expectancy"; therefore, it should not be valued or divided. Mr. Brown's argument was based on a long line of cases in California, including French v. French, 17 Cal. 2d 775 (1941), which held that non-vested pension rights are not property but mere expectancies, and thus not a community asset subject to division upon dissolution of marriage.

The state supreme court in *Brown* overruled the *French* case and stated, in pertinent part:

> We have concluded, however, that the *French* court's characterization of non-vested pension rights as expectancies errs. The term 'expectancy' describes the interests of a person who merely foresees that he might receive a future beneficence, such as the interest of an heir apparent [citations omitted], or of a beneficiary designated by a living insured who has the right to change the beneficiary [citations omitted]. As these examples demonstrate, the defining characteristic of an expectancy is that its holder has no enforceable right to his beneficence.
>
> Although some jurisdictions classify retirement pensions as gratuities, it has long been settled that under California law such benefits 'do not derive from the beneficence of the employer, but are properly part of the consideration earned by the employee.' (*In re* Marriage of Fithian, supra, 10 Cal. 3d 592, 596.) Since pension benefits represent a form of deferred compensation for services rendered [citations omitted], the employee's

right to such benefits is a contractual right, derived from the terms of the employment contract. Since a contractual right is not an expectancy but a chose in action, a form of property [citations omitted], we held in Dryden v. Board of Pension Commrs., supra, 6 Cal. 2d 575, 579, that an employee acquires a property right to pension benefits when he enters upon the performance of his employment contract. . . .

Although, as we have pointed out, supra, courts have previously refused to allocate this right in a non-vested pension between the spouses as community property on the grounds that such pension is contingent upon continued employment, we reject this theory. In other situations when community funds or efforts are expended to acquire conditional rights to future income, the courts do not hesitate to treat that right as a community asset. For example, in Waters v. Waters (1946) 75 Cal. App. 2d 265 [170 P.2d 494], the attorney husband had a contingent interest in a suit pending on appeal at the time of the divorce; the court held that his fee, when and if collected, would be a community asset. Indeed, in the several recent pension cases, the courts have asserted that vested but immature pensions are community assets although such pensions are commonly subject to the condition that the employee survive until retirement [citations omitted]. . . .

A division of community property which awards one spouse the entire value of this asset, without any offsetting award to the other spouse, does not represent that equal division of community property contemplated by Civil Code section 4800. . . .

In dividing non-vested pension rights as community property, the court must take account of the possibility that death or termination of employment may destroy those rights before they mature. In some cases the trial court may be able to evaluate this risk in determining the present value of those rights [citations omitted]. But if the court concludes that because of uncertainties affecting the vesting or maturation of the pension that it should not attempt to divide the present value of pension rights, it can instead award each spouse an appropriate portion of each pension payment as it is paid. This method of dividing the community interest in the pension renders it unnecessary for the court to compute the present value of the pension rights, and divide equally the risk that the pension will fail to vest. . . .

In sum, we submit that whatever abstract terminology we impose, the joint effort that composes the community and the respective contributions of the spouses that make up its assets, are the meaningful criteria. The wife's contribution to the community is not one whit less if we declare the husband's pension rights not a contingent asset but a mere 'expectancy.' Fortunately, we can appropriately reflect the realistic situation by recognizing that the husband's pension rights, a contingent interest, whether vested or not vested, comprise a property interest of the community and that the wife may properly share in it.

The *Brown* opinion allowed courts to value both vested and non-vested rights in employer-granted pension plans. Moreover, the *Brown* court indicated that to the extent that these rights are not vested—and thus not capable of valuation with certainty—the trial court is free to fashion a formula by which each spouse will participate in the benefits of the fund when (and most importantly if) those benefits are received by the employee spouse. *Brown* has given way to a significant body of law focusing not only on the valuation of pension plans, but on their division as well.

c) Special Issues Regarding Retirement Benefits

1) Disability Pay

One popular area of retirement benefit litigation concerns the disability pay received by an employee. Disability pay is not in fact a retirement benefit. Rather, it is compensation for income. More specifically, it is compensation for income that an employee can no longer earn because he is disabled or incapacitated in some way. When valuing disability pay, the court asks: When did the employee become disabled? For what are the disability payments designed to compensate?

In general, disability benefits received after separation are the separate property of the recipient. This approach makes sense inasmuch as disability payments are designed to compensate the recipient for the loss of his income stream. Since post-separation income is separate property, money paid to the disabled employee for a post-separation loss of income should also be characterized as separate property. The question becomes somewhat less clear when the employee-spouse receives disability benefits for injuries he suffered during the marriage. Additionally, the court has the ability to classify those payments as personal injury awards, which, as we have seen above, will be awarded to the injured employee.

2) Joinder

In this context, the reader may confront the concept of joinder.[30] It must be remembered that a pension plan cannot be a "party" to a dissolution or legal separation action. As such, the court cannot exercise power over the pension plan. What happens, then, if the pension plan simply ignores the agreement of the parties and pays benefits to the employee spouse without regard to the interests of the nonemployee spouse? Under those circumstances, there is little the nonemployee spouse can do to protect his or her interests. It is this situation that a joinder proceeding is designed to prevent.

A joinder proceeding is designed to prevent this situation. Under the concept of *joinder*, one of the parties to the litigation (typically the nonemployee spouse) prepares and files a one-page judicial council form, entitled "Request for Joinder" (Judicial Council form FL-372). After the party files the Request for Joinder, the clerk enters an Order of Joinder. Next, the party requesting joinder files a pleading in which she sets forth her claim against the plan and specifies the relief she desires. All of these documents are served on the pension plan itself, together with a summons, thus bringing the pension plan into the dissolution action as a party litigant. Once that happens, the pension plan becomes subject to the powers of the superior court. If the pension plan chooses to ignore the orders of the superior court with respect to the manner in which it is to be divided, then various penalties and remedies will follow on behalf of the nonemployee spouse whose interests are being adversely affected.

3) Qualified Domestic Relations Order

Along related lines is the Qualified Domestic Relations Order (QDRO). QDROs operate pursuant to the provisions of federal statutes, specifically the Retirement Equity Act (REA) and the federal Employees Retirement Income and Security Act of 1974 (ERISA). QDROs were created to resolve jurisdictional conflicts that arose when state courts made orders that affected pension and retirement plans established under federal law. QDROs provide state courts an appropriate vehicle by which to make orders that affect retirement plans that would otherwise be governed by federal law.

The specific guidelines with respect to the drafting of QDROs have been the subject of significant material in many treatises and a further examination of those requirements is best left to one of those sources. Volumes have been written on retirement benefits litigation in the context of marital dissolution. The foregoing text is designed to provide an overview of the many issues involved and to provide minimal guidance on the basic rules.

E. Liability of Marital Property

Just as important as division of community assets is the equally troubling allocation of community liabilities. This text will explain what property (community or separate) may be available to the parties' creditors. Much depends on the nature of the debt, the nature of the property being sought by the creditor, and the availability of other property to satisfy the debtor spouse's obligations.

Family Code sections 900 et seq. provide the basic rules with respect to the liability of marital property for the debts of the parties. It also provides rules regarding rights of reimbursement that either party may have against the other for using community property to pay community and separate debts. Section 910 provides as follows:

> (a) Except as otherwise expressly provided by statute, the community estate is liable for a debt incurred by either spouse before or during marriage, regardless of which spouse has the management and control of the property and regardless of whether one or both spouses are parties to the debt or to a judgment for the debt.
>
> (b) "During marriage" for purposes of this section does not include the period during which the spouses are living separate and apart before a judgment of dissolution of marriage or legal separation of the parties.

This section, therefore, makes it clear that community property is liable to satisfy a debt that either spouse incurred before or during the marriage. The reader may be somewhat surprised to learn that even premarital debts can be satisfied through community assets. This is not, however, as drastic as it first appears. As will be discussed below, the Family Code also provides a right to reimbursement in certain circumstances under which community property has been used to satisfy a premarital debt.

1. Liability of Community Estate

As a general rule, the community estate is liable for any debt incurred by either spouse before or during marriage and prior to separation, regardless of who has the management and control over the community property.[31] As seen above, this is clearly provided for in Family Code section 910. As such, even debts that are incurred by either spouse before marriage can be satisfied by the current community property. As an example of this unhappy circumstance, an individual who has a spousal support obligation from his first marriage may find the community property of his second marriage liable for the satisfaction of that obligation. This is true even though wife number two is not a party to that original debt.[32]

Family Code section 911 protects the earnings of a spouse that are earned "during marriage" from liability for debts incurred by the other spouse before the current marriage. However, in order to take advantage of this protection, the spouse who is earning the money must, in essence, place it out of the reach of the current spouse; she must not commingle (or "mix") her earnings with other community assets. This Family Code section makes it clear that these earnings will maintain their protection from premarital debts so long as they are held "in a deposit account in which the person's spouse has no right of withdrawal and are uncommingled with other property in the community estate, except property insignificant in amount." As such, spouses would be well advised to segregate their assets (to the extent this is reasonably practical), especially if one spouse has reason to suspect that her earnings may fall prey to the other's premarital obligations.

As mentioned above, these premarital obligations can even extend to child and spousal support. In this regard, Family Code section 915 was enacted.

> (a) For the purpose of this part, a child or spousal support obligation of a married person that does not arise out of the marriage shall be treated as a debt incurred before marriage, regardless of whether a court order for support is made or modified before or during marriage and regardless of whether any installment payment on the obligation accrues before or during marriage.

Section 915 also provides a system of reimbursement in circumstances where community assets of the second marriage are used to satisfy the premarital debt of one spouse. Family Code section 915(b) states:

> (b) If property in the community estate is applied to the satisfaction of a child or spousal support obligation of a married person that does not arise out of the marriage, at a time when nonexempt separate income of the person is available but is not applied to the satisfaction of the obligation, the community estate is entitled to reimbursement from the person in the amount of the separate income, not exceeding the property in the community estate so applied.

In other words, if a preexisting support obligation is satisfied from community property of the second marriage, and the obligor spouse owned nonexempt separate property that could have been used to satisfy that debt, the community should be reimbursed for all amounts that it paid up to the amount of nonexempt separate property that was available. Section 915 encourages the obligor spouse to use his separate property (to the extent it is available) to satisfy his premarital obligations. The reader should note, however, that the community cannot get reimbursement unless nonexempt separate property was available at the time the debt was paid. Family Code section 915 does not shelter community funds from satisfaction of this premarital obligation; it merely provides the community with the right to be reimbursed if community funds are used instead of the obligor spouse's separate property. Assuming there is no such separate property, however, the community funds will be reachable by this premarital creditor and there will be no right to reimbursement, even if the obligor spouse later acquires separate property (for example, by inheritance) that, had they owned it at the time the debt was satisfied, could have been used to pay the debt.

2. Liability of Separate Property

Family Code section 913 details the liability of separate property for debts incurred before or during marriage. That section provides as follows:

> (a) The separate property of a married person is liable for a debt incurred by the person before or during marriage.
> (b) Except as otherwise provided by statute:
> > (1) The separate property of a married person is not liable for a debt incurred by the person's spouse before or during marriage.
> > (2) The joinder or consent of a married person to an encumbrance of community estate property to secure payment of a debt incurred by the person's spouse does not subject the person's separate property to liability for the debt unless the person also incurred the debt.

As a general rule a spouse's separate property is liable only for his own debts that he incurred before and during marriage. That separate property is also immune from liability for debts incurred by the other spouse either before or during the marriage.

There are exceptions to the general rule, however. Family Code section 914 provides that, notwithstanding the provisions of section 913, a nondebtor spouse's separate property can, under certain circumstances, become liable for *some* of the debtor spouse's debts.

> (a) . . . a married person is personally liable for the following debts incurred by the person's spouse during marriage:
> > (1) A debt incurred for necessaries of life of the person's spouse while the spouses are living together.
> > (2) Except as provided in section 4302 [spousal support], a debt incurred for common necessaries of life of the person's spouse while the persons are living separately.
> (b) The separate property of a married person may be applied to the satisfaction of a debt for which the person is personally liable pursuant to this section. If separate property is so applied at a time when non-exempt property in the community estate or separate property of the person's spouse is available but is not applied to the satisfaction of the debt, the married person is entitled to reimbursement to the extent such property was available.

The term "necessaries of life" as used in this section generally means food, clothing, shelter, necessary medical expenses, and things of that nature. Note, this section provides that a spouse's separate property is liable for necessaries of life while the parties are living together—and while they are living separately and apart; this is true unless, as is provided in Family Code section 4302, the parties are operating under some form of agreement that specifies the nondebtor spouse will not make support payments. Recall that section 915 provides for a reimbursement right to the community in the event that community assets were used to satisfy a premarital child or spousal support obligation. Section 914(b) provides a similar right to reimbursement in the event that the "nonobligor" spouse's separate property was used at a time when nonexempt community property or separate property of the obligor spouse was available to pay for these "necessaries of life" but was simply not used.

3. Debt Liability Following Division of Property

Generally, once a dissolution or legal separation matter concludes, the property that was subject to the proceeding must be distributed to the spouses according to the terms of a settlement agreement or judicial decree. In making this division, the court must effect an equal division of the net community estate. In other words, not only will the court distribute the assets equitably to the parties, but it will also allocate an equitable share of the community debt to them as well.

Before 1985, courts could not make orders that directly affected creditors because creditors are not parties to dissolution or legal separation proceedings. This was true regardless of which spouse was assigned a particular debt. Accordingly, a creditor in those circumstances could attempt to collect the debt by utilizing any property that would have been liable for the debt before the court divided the property (so-called *former community property*). The law changed in 1985, however, with the enactment of (current) Family Code section 916, which provides as follows:

> (a) Notwithstanding any other provision of this chapter, after division of community and quasi community property pursuant to Division 7 (commencing with Section 2500):
>
> (1) The separate property owned by a married person at the time of the division and the property received by the person in the division is liable for a debt incurred by the person before or during marriage and the person is personally liable for the debt, whether or not the debt was assigned for payment by the person's spouse in the division.
>
> (2) The separate property owned by a married person at the time of the division and the property received by the person in the division is not liable for a debt incurred by the person's spouse before or during marriage, and the person is not personally liable for the debt, unless the debt was assigned for payment by the person in the division of the property. . . .
>
> (3) The separate property owned by a married person at the time of the division and the property received by the person in the division is liable for a debt incurred by that person's spouse before or during marriage, and the person is personally liable for the debt, if the debt

was assigned for payment by the person in the division of property. If a money judgment for the debt is entered after the division, the property is not subject to enforcement of the judgment and the judgment may not be enforced against the married person, unless the person is made a party to the judgment for the purposes of this paragraph.

(b) If property of a married person is applied to the satisfaction of a money judgment pursuant to subdivision (a) for a debt incurred by a person that is assigned for payment by the person's spouse, the person has a right of reimbursement from the person's spouse to the extent of the property applied, with interest at the legal rate, and may recover reasonable attorney's fees incurred in enforcing the right of reimbursement.

The best way to approach this rather complicated section is to divide the spouses into two separate categories: the debtor spouse and the nondebtor spouse. The *debtor spouse* is the individual who personally incurred the debt; the *nondebtor spouse* is the individual who is married to the debtor spouse. Pursuant to section 916, a creditor can always pursue the property of the debtor spouse, both separate property and former community property, regardless of whether the court assigned the debt to the nondebtor spouse. The debtor spouse will always remain personally liable, whether he incurred the debt before or during marriage, and a creditor who has not been paid may utilize any property of the debtor spouse. Of course, Family Code section 916(b) does provide that if this debt was assigned to the nondebtor spouse as part of the property division but instead the debtor spouse paid, the debtor spouse has a right of reimbursement against the nondebtor spouse; accordingly, the debtor spouse can collect, in addition to the monies he paid to the creditor, interest at the legal rate and attorney's fees that he incurred in an effort to claim his reimbursement from the nondebtor spouse.

In contrast to the liability of the debtor spouse, the nondebtor spouse is only liable if she was assigned the debt as part of the property division. If she was not assigned the debt, then she is not personally liable following dissolution for the other spouse's debts, regardless of when they were incurred. As such, the nondebtor spouse's separate property as well as the "former community property" received by the nondebtor spouse is shielded from liability against creditors—unless the nondebtor spouse was assigned that debt as part of the property division.

4. Tort Liability

The discussion above centered upon debts created by contract: credit card charges, long-term purchase agreements (for items such as cars or homes), etc. As we have seen, the structure of the liability provisions pertinent to such contractual debts was generally a question of management and control by the spouses over the community property. In contrast to these contract debts, however, are debts created by tort (for example, the commission of a "family wrong" by one of the spouses against a third party).[33] When evaluating the liability of the community for claims that arose out of the commission of a tort, the question is: to what extent was this debt incurred for the "benefit of the community"?

Family Code section 1000 establishes the statutory ground rules. Basically, if the spouse committed the tort while he was engaged in an activity that was "for the benefit of the community," community funds are firstly liable; only if the community funds are exhausted does the tortfeasor spouse's separate property become liable. Family Code section 1000 is worth quoting in its entirety:

> (a) A married person is not liable for any injury or damage caused by the other spouse except in cases where the married person would be liable therefor if the marriage did not exist.
> (b) The liability of a married person for death or injury to a person or property shall be satisfied as follows:
> (1) If the liability of the married person is based upon an act or omission which occurred while the married person was performing an activity for the benefit of the community, the liability shall first be satisfied from the community estate and second from the separate property of the married person.
> (2) If the liability of the married person is not based upon an act or omission which occurred while the married person was performing an activity for benefit of the community, the liability shall first be satisfied from the separate property of the married person and second from the community estate.
> (c) This section does not apply to the extent the liability is satisfied out of proceeds of insurance for the liability, whether the proceeds are from property in the community estate or separate property. Notwithstanding Section 920, no right of reimbursement under this section shall be exercised more than seven years after the spouse in whose favor the right arises has actual knowledge of the application of the property to the satisfaction of the debt.

As might be expected, the latter portion of Family Code section 1000 established a right of reimbursement in the "nontortfeasor" spouse as per the provisions of section 920. This right of reimbursement is specifically limited, however; it expires seven years after the spouse in whose favor that right arose had actual knowledge that community property was "inappropriately" applied. Accordingly, and as we have seen, it is not wise to "sit on one's rights."

Family Code section 1000 provides that neither spouse is liable for the injuries or debts of the other spouse; further, the innocent spouse's separate property cannot be used to satisfy a damages award incurred by the tortfeasor or debtor spouse. Yet, section 1000(b) provides a rather large exception: an innocent spouse's separate property is not exempt from a tort creditor if the tortfeasor spouse committed the tort "for the benefit of the community."

If the liability is based upon an act or omission that occurs while the spouse is performing an activity that benefits the community, first community property will be used to satisfy that debt and then, to the extent there is an insufficient amount of community property available, the separate property of the tortfeasor spouse will be used; and

Further, if the liability did not occur during the course of an activity for the benefit of the community, then the preference is reversed: This debt must first be satisfied from the tortfeasor's separate property and then, to the extent there is an insufficient amount of such separate property, the debt will be satisfied from the community property.

Section 1000(b) also establishes the order of preference to satisfy a third-party tort claim:

(1)   If the liability of the married person is based upon an act or omission which occurred while the married person was performing an activity for the benefit of the community, the liability shall first be satisfied from the community estate and second from the separate property of the married person.

(2)   If the liability of the married person is not based upon an act or omission which occurred while the married person was performing an activity for the benefit of the community, the liability shall first be satisfied from the separate property of the married person and second from the community estate.

The term "for the benefit of the community" has been the subject of much debate. Unfortunately, this term has not been specifically defined by the legislature or the judiciary. Instead, it is a question of fact for the trier of fact (that is, the judge) to determine based on the facts and circumstances and evidence as presented at the time of trial. This factual inquiry tends to focus on whether the community derived benefit from the conduct. For example, an intentional tort of assault and battery would not seem to benefit the community because the result of this activity is criminal punishment. However, the intentional tort of embezzlement might very well benefit the community to the extent that the tortfeasor spouse provided "income" to the community by diverting money improperly into a community bank account. Under these circumstances, it could be argued that the community directly benefited from the commission of the tort and therefore Family Code section 1000(b)(1) should be employed.

In addition to debts created by contract and tort, a third category requires brief examination: debts created by one spouse by virtue of the commission of a tort against the other spouse. Fortunately, the law in this area is rather clear. Family Code section 781(c) provides that personal injury damages suffered by one spouse at the hands of the other spouse should be paid with the tortfeasor's separate property. Those damages also become the innocent spouse's separate property.

F. Management and Control of Marital Property

Family Code sections 1100 through 1103 provide the statutory framework for defining the rights and obligations of spouses to each other with regard to the management and control of marital property. Most significant in this grouping of statutes are Family Code sections 1100 and 1101, which provide for obligations of a spouse operating a community business as well as claims by one spouse against the other for breaches of fiduciary duties and items of that nature.

Family Code section 1100 (in what would seem to be a monument to complicated and strained wording of statutes) provides that each spouse is given equal management and control over the community personal property regardless of whether that property was acquired prior to or after January 1, 1975.[34] This Code section also provides that each party has absolute power of disposition (other than by will) over the community estate as if that spouse was disposing of his own separate property. Further, section 1100 provides that neither spouse may make a gift of community personal property or dispose of community property for less than its fair and reasonable value without the written consent of the other spouse. The statute excepts gifts that are mutually given by both spouses to third parties and gifts that are given by one spouse to the other. Similarly, pursuant to this code section, a spouse may not "sell, convey, or encumber community personal property used in the family dwelling, or the furniture, furnishing, or fittings of the home, or the clothing or the wearing apparel of the other spouse or minor children which is community personal property, without the written consent of the other spouse."

These rules follow what this author believes to be a common sense approach. Family Code section 1100(d) provides that a spouse who operates or manages a business (or an interest in a business) that is substantially all community property has "primary management and control" over that business interest. The term "primary management and control" means that the managing spouse is entitled to act alone in all transactions but "shall give prior written notice to the other spouse of any sale, lease, exchange, encumbrance, or other disposition of all or substantially all of the personal property used in the operation of the business."

One of the more significant aspects of section 1100 is its recognition of the strict duties that each spouse owes to the other with regard to transactions involving the community property. Subsection (e) of Family Code section 1100 provides as follows:

> (e) Each spouse shall act with respect to the other spouse in the management and control of the community assets and liabilities in accordance with the general rules governing fiduciary relationships which control the actions of persons having relationships of personal confidence as specified in section 721, until such time as the assets and liabilities have been divided by the parties or by a court. This duty includes the obligation to make full disclosure to the other spouse of all material facts and information regarding the existence, characterization, and valuation of all assets in which the community has or may have an interest and debts for which the community is or may be liable and to provide equal access to all information, records and books that pertain to the value and character of those assets and debts upon request.[35]

The thrust of this Code section is to prevent one spouse from taking advantage of her position as the owner or operator of a business (or as the individual who exercises primary control over one or all of the community's assets), and in so doing mislead the other spouse with regard to the exact nature, scope, and extent of those assets. Former law stated simply that husbands and wives had to treat each other in "good faith" with regard to these issues. The legislature, however, found that this was not sufficient to adequately protect the spouse who is less than actively involved in the management and control over the community property. As such, the Family Code was amended to include the term "fiduciary."

Family Code section 1101 expands upon the concept of fiduciary duty and provides a statutorily mandated system of remedies, which are available to the spouse who has a claim against the other spouse for violation of these duties. Subsection (a) establishes the existence of a claim by one spouse against the other spouse for breach of the fiduciary duties defined in sections 1100 and 1102. The balance of section 1101 grants the court authority to: (1) order an accounting of all property and obligations of the parties to the marriage, (2) determine the rights of the parties in the ownership and beneficial enjoyment of some or all of the community property, and (3) order that the name of a spouse be added to a community asset held in the other spouse's name to protect the interests of the "innocent" spouse. Section 1101(e) is perhaps most significant. It states that the court is empowered, in any transaction affecting community property in which the consent of both spouses is required, to "upon the motion of a spouse, dispense with the requirement of the other spouse's consent if both of the following requirements are met: (1) the proposed transaction is in the best interest of the community [and] (2) consent has been arbitrarily refused or cannot be obtained due to the physical incapacity, mental incapacity, or prolonged absence of the non-consenting spouse."

Thus, upon motion of one spouse the court can simply go forward with the transaction so long as it finds that the transaction is in the best interest of the community and the consent of the other spouse was arbitrarily refused or (for the reasons set forth in the statute) cannot be obtained. The enactment of this particular subsection has created some concern because it empowers the court to substitute its own judgment for that of the "nonconsenting spouse" with respect to what is or is not in the best interest of the community regarding property issues. Some argue that the court's power improperly interferes with spouses' constitutionally protected property rights. Nevertheless, the statute exists and its stated intent is clear.

Apparently not content to rest upon the protections provided by Family Code section 1100, the legislature enacted section 2100 in 1993. Section 2100 established very strict and specific requirements for disclosure between spouses of the exact nature, scope, and extent of the community and quasi-community assets and liabilities.

The Legislature finds and declares the following:

> (a) It is the policy of the State of California (1) to marshal, preserve, and protect community and quasi community assets and liabilities that exist at the date of separation so as to avoid dissipation of the community estate prior to distribution; (2) to ensure fair and sufficient child and spousal support awards, and (3) to achieve a division of community and quasi community assets and liabilities on the dissolution of marriage or nullity of marriage or legal separation of the parties as provided under California law.
>
> (b) Sound public policy further favors the reduction of the adversarial nature of marital dissolution and the attendant costs by fostering full disclosure and cooperative discovery.
>
> (c) In order to promote this public policy, a full and accurate disclosure of all assets and liabilities in which one or both parties have or may have an interest must be made in the early stages of a proceeding for dissolution of marriage or legal separation of the parties, regardless of the characterization as community or separate, together with a disclosure of all income and expenses of the parties. Moreover, each party has a continuing duty to update and augment that disclosure to the extent there have been any material changes so that at the time the parties enter into an agreement for the resolution of any of these issues, or at the time of trial on these issues, each party will have as full and complete knowledge of the relevant underlying facts.

The Code sections that follow provide a very detailed description of the exact nature, scope, and extent of the disclosure that must follow between spouses in the context of a termination of marriage proceeding. There can be little doubt, then, of the seriousness with which the legislature approaches the fiduciary duties between spouses. Indeed, a thorough reading of these Family Code sections demonstrates not only a strong desire to protect the interests of both spouses through the use of full disclosure, it also demonstrates what would appear to be a strong sense of cynicism and skepticism on the part of the legislature when it comes to evaluating the motivations and actions of individuals going through a divorce. What the legislature is basically trying to achieve through the enactment of this code section is strict adherence to the tenets of Family Code sections 1100 et seq. by simply forcing the parties to be open, complete, and accurate in their dealings with each other. As might be imagined, the judicial council of the State of California has promulgated forms for use with respect to meeting these disclosure requirements.

G.   The Division of Marital Property

1.   Dividing the Community Estate

Even though the court has a theoretically limitless range of possibilities with respect to structuring a division of community property, the mechanics of virtually all community property division can be broken down into one of five categories.

Perhaps the easiest and most preferable method of division awards certain assets to one spouse and certain other assets to the other spouse, and in so doing tries to ensure that each spouse ends up with assets totaling the same amount of value. To the extent that one spouse ends up with a little more than the other spouse, the court will order that spouse to make an "equalizing payment" to the other spouse. This payment can (and usually does) take the form of an interest-bearing promissory note made by the spouse who received the excess amount of assets in favor of the other spouse.

The court also can award assets *in kind* to the extent that they lend themselves to such a division. Such assets as money, shares of stock, and things of this nature can usually be divided in kind, with half to one spouse and half to the other spouse.

Somewhat related to an in-kind division is the conversion of title to a property from whatever its status during marriage was to tenancy in common. The concept of "tenancy in common" contemplates that each spouse continues to own an undivided one-half interest in the asset post-dissolution; and in so doing, the spouses remain tenants in common with each other. This is not, however, true joint tenancy, which contemplates that each joint tenant owns an undivided interest in the entire property. The adherence to the concept of tenants in common ensures that upon the death of a tenant in common, his undivided one-half interest in the property will not inure to the benefit of the other tenant. In other words, when he dies, his property can be passed by will rather than simply disappearing in favor of the ownership interest of the other owner. If the court does order that the former spouse should continue to hold title to the property as a tenant in common, it must also reserve jurisdiction on the ultimate disposition of this asset; the court must reserve jurisdiction in order to give the parties an opportunity to partition the interests, sell the property, and divide the proceeds if they cannot agree to do that between themselves.

The fourth method in which the court can divide community property involves simply selling the properties and dividing the money equally. This concept goes hand in hand with an in-kind division inasmuch as all it really does is turn the "troublesome" asset into property that can be easily divided in kind.

Finally, the fifth method typically employed by the courts simply contemplates a reservation of jurisdiction over the issue until such time as the asset can be valued and divided. This method is usually applied in situations where the actual division of the assets is somewhat premature at the time of trial. One example of this situation existed in the case of Marriage of Kilbourne, 232 Cal. App. 3d 1518 (1991). In that case, Mr. Kilbourne was an attorney who at the time of trial in his dissolution action still had several contingency fee cases open and unresolved.[36] Under that circumstance, the trial court deemed it appropriate to reserve jurisdiction over these contingency fee cases and divide the money as and when it was received.

The Family Code does not state a preference for application of the above-referenced methods of division of community property. However, one noted treatise has recognized that the in-kind division is generally preferred by judges because of its greater probability to achieve a precise equality of division as well as the fact that its use generally prevents the various problems that arise with respect to valuing particular assets.[37]

The statutory mandate to the court regarding the division of the community estate ensures an equal and equitable division of the community property. The manner in which this result is achieved, of course, is less important than the achievement of the result itself. In a sense, therefore, in this context, the "ends" really do justify the "means." The trial court is thus granted a broad amount of discretion in determining the manner in which the community estate will be divided.

The court generally prefers to allow parties to a dissolution to work out the division of their property between them, and in fact, the court will usually not interfere with such an agreement entered into outside of court even if it does not constitute an equal division. If the parties cannot agree on a division of their property, however, the court will do it for them. And, while the statutory mandate is to divide the community property equally, this does not mean that each separate asset must actually be split in half. In fact, the court will take great pains to prevent the sale of an asset followed by an equal division of the proceeds if at all possible. The way the court achieves this result is by dividing assets in kind.

With in-kind divisions of assets, the court offsets assets of equal value against each other rather than selling them all and dividing the cash. For example, assume a community estate as follows:

	Asset	Value
1.	House	$100,000
2.	Car #1	10,000
3.	Car #2	15,000
4.	Wife's business	95,000
	Total	$220,000

<u>divided by 2 = $110,000 to husband and $110,000 to wife</u>

The court could order that the house, cars, and business be sold (assuming there is a market for these assets) and the money divided equally. Or the court could award (divide) these assets in kind and award the business ($95,000) and car #2 ($15,000) to wife (since the business was "hers").[38] Thus, wife would receive community assets totaling $110,000. Accordingly, the court would award car #1 ($10,000) and the house ($100,000) to husband, giving him assets totaling $110,000 as well. As the reader can see, in this example the community was divided equally and the specific assets remained intact. The court has a wide amount of discretion in making such an in-kind division of assets of comparable value, and its determination in this regard is rarely reversed on appeal.

Sometimes assets will have to be divided unequally in order to prevent impairing their value. Assume, for example, the same facts as in the above example, but the only assets the parties have are car #2 and the wife's law business. In that case, the law practice cannot easily be sold without substantially impairing its value. It makes sense, then, to award it to the wife since she is the only one licensed to practice law (and is also the one with whom the clients have developed a working relationship). After awarding the car to husband ($15,000), he is still $40,000 short:

Assets	FMV	To Husband	To Wife
Wife's business	$95,000		$95,000
Car #2	15,000	$15,000	
TOTALS:		$15,000	$95,000
Husband is short by:		40,000	(40,000)
		$55,000	$55,000

In order to equalize this division of property, wife must pay husband $40,000. This payment can either be in cash or pursuant to a promissory note on which wife will make periodic payments. Either option accomplishes the same result: Each party receives one half of the community estate. In cases such as the second example above where the large asset in question is not something unique to one spouse (such as a business) but instead is more "spouse-neutral" (such as a house), the court will typically order that it be sold, and the proceeds of sale (that is, the cash) divided equally.[39]

In addition to the present, equal division of community property, the court also has the power to postpone the use (or sale) of a particular asset pending the occurrence of some other event (for example, the deferred sale of home award of Family Code sections 3800 et seq.). The court can even adjust spousal support to effect an equal division of property, but only upon the agreement of both parties. The court can also divide out-of-state property under the authority of Family Code section 2660. Of course, the court cannot actually affect the title to such property since it does not have jurisdiction over out-of-state property; but it can, however, adjudicate the rights to such property of the parties over whom it does have jurisdiction, and in so doing render a judgment pertinent to those rights that can then be enforced in the other state.

Family Code sections 2500 to 2660 govern the actual division of the community estate. These sections codify the concepts discussed above. They compel an equal division of the community estate; they mandate that all assets and liabilities be characterized as either community or separate; and they make provision for arbitration of disputes between the parties as to the character, value, or division of the community estate where the total value of the estate does not exceed $50,000.

When attempting to value community assets for purposes of division, care must be taken to ensure that these assets are valued at the appropriate time. As explained in earlier chapters, a significant period of time can elapse between the date of separation and the date of trial in a marital termination proceeding. During that time, certain assets can significantly decrease in value. Many spouses try to take advantage of this situation. Indeed, spouses have been known to allow (or even facilitate) the diminution in value of certain community assets so they will not be forced to provide their soon-to-be ex-spouse with any more money than is absolutely necessary. This is especially troublesome in situations in which a community asset business that is operated by one of the spouses is most likely to be awarded to that spouse.[40] Under these circumstances, the spouse who knows that he will be awarded the ongoing business enterprise as an asset after dissolution has a significant incentive to decrease the value of that asset so that he can obtain an even greater share of the other community property.

Thus, if one spouse suspects that the other allowed a community asset to diminish in value since the date of separation, he or she can present evidence to the court that the asset decreased in value due to the other spouse's action (or inaction). Based on this evidence, the court can issue an order stating that the asset will be valued at the date of separation instead of at the time of trial. In so doing, the court prevents the errant spouse from profiting from what is mismanagement at best and deliberate spoliation (waste of an asset) at worst.

The *alternate valuation date* provided by Family Code section 2552 also has application to businesses that are primarily dependent for their operation (and value) on the owner spouse's energy, labor, and efforts. As discussed above, the energy, efforts, and labor of a spouse are community assets only during the marriage. Post-separation, these same efforts and labors become that spouse's separate property. To the extent that a business owned and operated by a spouse increases in value post-separation as a result of that spouse's separate property energy, efforts, and labor, that increase is appropriately characterized as separate rather than community property. A spouse in such a position would thus request that the business be valued as of the date of separation rather than the date of trial. This request would find significant support in case law, particularly Marriage of Imperato, 45 Cal. App. 3d 432 (1975), which recognizes the requirement of this section to value the assets and liabilities of the parties as close to the date of trial as practical; plus Marriage of Green, 213 Cal. App. 3d 14 (1989) and Marriage of Kilbourne, 232 Cal. App. 3d 1518 (1991), which recognize that the date of separation is the appropriate valuation date to determine the value of professional practices and personal service businesses.

2. Division of Retirement Plan Benefits

It is incumbent upon the trial court to determine the value of only the community interest in retirement plans. As such, plan increases and contributions resulting from pre-marital and post-separation efforts of the employee spouse should not be included in the calculation of the community value. Additionally, because most plans usually provide an income stream over time, commencing at some date far in the future (typically when the employee turns 65), the actuarial "present day" value of that income stream must be determined and evidence must be presented on that amount. As complicated as this may sound, there are individuals and businesses that specialize in performing these accounting functions. These individuals are available to testify as expert witnesses on the subject of pension evaluation and have, for the most part, taken the mystery out of these calculations. Once the present value of the income stream is determined, the court may further reduce that amount due to the likelihood that the pension holder may die before he reaches the specified retirement age.

Once these values have been determined, it then becomes necessary for the court to actually divide the present value of the community interest so determined. Such division can take two distinct forms. In the first scenario, the employee spouse cashes out the nonemployee's interest in the plan pursuant to one lump sum payment of money (or by virtue of an offsetting division of other community assets "in kind"). In the second scenario, the employee and nonemployee spouse continue to participate in the plan until such time as the employee spouse is first eligible for retirement; at this time, the monthly proceeds of the plan are divided between the parties pursuant to the ratio derived at the time of trial.

This latter method contemplates ascertaining the respective interests of the parties using a formula approach, sometimes called the *time rule.* Under the time rule, the community interest in the pension is ascertained by determining the ratio of the length of employment between the date of marriage and the date of separation to the total length of employment. Once this has been determined, it is a simple matter of arithmetic to divide that amount in half and then allocate the same percentage (ratio) to the retirement benefits themselves once they are being paid out by the employer.

Situations involving a cash buyout of the nonemployee spouse's interest in the pension plan by the employee spouse are, of course, the cleanest and most favorable. In many cases, however, the pension plan is the largest single asset of the marital estate (sometimes well in excess of three to four hundred thousand dollars in value); in these cases, such a cash-out is sometimes difficult to come by. The other method of dividing interests in pension plans contemplates a payout of the pension benefits over time, as and when received by the employee spouse.

There are several other alternatives to the disposition of the community interest in this asset, the exact nature and extent of which exceed the scope of this chapter. The reader should merely note that there are as many methods of distributing this asset as there are imaginative practitioners in this field. As a practical matter, if the reader is presented with a situation involving retirement benefits, the inquiry must be fully researched before any action is undertaken. Indeed, this is an area of the law that is fraught with malpractice even on the part of the most experienced family law practitioners. There are questions relating to joinder of the pension plan or non-joinder, technical application with both federal and state laws, adherence to tax codes and regulations pertinent to this division, dividing the separate property aspects from the community property aspects of this community asset, and items of this nature. For anyone other than the skilled, experienced practitioner in retirement benefit marital dissolution litigation, the experience will prove lengthy and difficult at best and a nightmare in malpractice at worst.

3. Dividing Debts and Liabilities

As seen above, the court may divide community assets according to many different methods. When dividing (or, more accurately, allocating) community *debts*, however, there is a statutory system for preference. Family Code sections 2620 to 2627 establish this system in some detail, as follows:

Section 2620—Confirmation or Division of Community Estate Debts

The debts for which the community estate is liable which are unpaid at the time of trial, or for which the community estate becomes liable after trial, shall be confirmed or divided as provided in this part.

Section 2621—Premarital debts; confirmation

Debts incurred by either spouse before the date of marriage shall be confirmed without offset to the spouse who incurred the debt.

Section 2622—Debts incurred after marriage but before separation

(a) . . . Debts incurred by either spouse after the date of marriage but before the date of separation shall be divided as set forth in Sections 2550 to 2552, inclusive, and Sections 2601 to 2604, inclusive [the general division of community liabilities laws discussed above].

(b) To the extent that community debts exceed total community and quasi community assets, the excess of debt shall be assigned as the Court deems just and equitable, taking into account factors such as the parties' relative ability to pay.

Section 2623—Marital debts incurred after the date of separation; confirmation

Debts incurred by either spouse after the date of separation but before entry of a judgment of dissolution or a legal separation shall be confirmed as follows:

(a) Debts incurred by either spouse for the common necessaries of life of either spouse or the necessaries of life of the children of the marriage for whom support may be ordered, in the absence of a court order or a written agreement for support or for the payment of these debts, shall be confirmed to either spouse according to the parties' respective needs and abilities to pay at the time the debt was incurred.

(b) Debts incurred by either spouse for non necessaries of that spouse or children of the marriage for whom support may be ordered shall be confirmed without offset to the spouse who incurred the debt.

Section 2624—Marital debts incurred after entry of judgment of dissolution or after entry of judgment of legal separation; confirmation

Debts incurred by either spouse after entry of a judgment of dissolution of marriage but before termination of the parties' marital status or after entry of a judgment of legal separation of the parties shall be confirmed without offset to the spouse who incurred the debt.

Section 2625—Separate debts incurred before date of separation; confirmation

Notwithstanding sections 2620 to 2624, inclusive, all separate debts, including those debts incurred by a spouse during marriage and before the date of separation that were not incurred for the benefit of the community, shall be confirmed without offset to the spouse who incurred the debt.

These various Code sections are very straightforward and should be quite understandable.

Section 2601 contains a noteworthy provision that grants the court authority to deviate from the standard "equal division" rule of section 2550 (division of the community estate); the court may deviate under appropriate "economic circumstances" so as to effect a "substantially equal division of the community estate" or to reimburse a so-called "innocent spouse" for amounts that "have been deliberately misappropriated [by the other party] to the exclusion of the interest of the [innocent spouse] in the community estate" (section 2602). The trial court has wide discretion to decide when to invoke these provisions, and its decision will generally not be disturbed on appeal, assuming there was a "basically equal" division of the community estate.

Thus, debts incurred by a spouse prior to the date of marriage or following the date of separation are confirmed to that spouse without right of offset. Similarly, debts incurred by a spouse during the marriage (prior to the date of separation) are simply divided equally. Remember, however, that community debt—and all other community property—are subject to the "economic circumstances" and "deliberate misappropriation" provisions mentioned immediately above.

Family Code section 2621 mandates that separate property debts be confirmed without offset to the spouse who incurred the debt—except if such debts were incurred for the benefit of the community. As such, once the court determines that the debt is one spouse's separate property, it no longer figures in the offset process when it comes to dividing up the community estate.

In some cases (in fact, in many cases), the community does not have a *positive* balance or value. In situations where the community liabilities exceed its assets, the community has a *negative estate value*. Family Code section 2622(b) provides that "to the extent that community debts exceed total community and quasi community assets, the excess of debts shall be assigned as the Court deems just and equitable, taking into account factors such as the parties' relative ability to pay." Thus, the court has power to make an unequal distribution of excess debt; it does not need to allocate the debt equally between the two spouses. Utilizing the "ability to pay" standard, the court will most likely allocate the excess debt to the spouse who has income or assets sufficient to pay it. Therefore, the high income earning spouse may find him or herself in the unenviable position of shouldering more than 50 percent of the community debt.

H. Special Issues Regarding Marital Property

In the context of the allocation, valuation, and distribution of marital assets and liabilities, several circumstances arise with regularity. These include tracing and commingling, apportionment, acquisitions on credit, special issues relating to the family residence, claims to reimbursement, and issues regarding quasi-marital property and the putative spouse.

1. Tracing and Commingling

The concepts of tracing (discussed at some length above) and commingling find most of their application when requests for reimbursement are made. Accordingly, these concepts should be read in conjunction with those pertinent to reimbursement mentioned below. The term *commingling* is simply a fancy way to describe what happens when separate property and community property become so mixed together that it is impossible to tell them apart. Questions then arise such as "which character does this (new) form of property take? Community property or separate property? This is where the concept of tracing comes in. The term *tracing* simply describes the procedure employed to determine the source of these funds that have been so commingled. Certain provisions of the Family Code (for example, Family Code 2640) provide authority for tracing. If a party can demonstrate a separate or community property source for funds that have been commingled, he may obtain reimbursement for that contribution.

Property that is commingled does not necessarily lose its character simply by virtue of commingling. If the respective amounts of each component (separate or community) can be ascertained, these source components will be confirmed back to the contributor. Note, the contributor may be an individual spouse who contributed his separate property, or the community that contributed community property. Of course, if funds have been so commingled that it is impossible to trace them back to their source, then the entire fund will be presumed to be community. It is for this reason that, to the extent a spouse is interested in maintaining the separate property character of his or her property, that spouse must be very careful to keep detailed records whenever this separate property money is transferred in and out of community accounts. Of course, the spouse who claims to have the separate property ownership interest in a piece of commingled property has the burden of proving that such property can be traced back to a separate property source, hence the need for accurate bookkeeping.

The court uses two basic methods to trace assets that have been commingled: (1) direct tracing and (2) the family expense method (also sometimes called the recapitulation method).

The concept of *direct tracing* is exactly as it seems: to the extent that the spouse claiming a separate property interest in a commingled asset can directly trace its acquisition (or a portion thereof) to a separate property source, that spouse is entitled to recover that separate property share from the community. To succeed, the spouse claiming a separate property interest must demonstrate that when the disputed assets were acquired, there were sufficient funds available from his separate property source to make the purchase; further, the spouse making the purchase intended to and did in fact use his separate property to acquire the asset. It is not enough, therefore, for the spouse who is claiming the separate property interest to simply demonstrate that there were sufficient separate property funds on hand at the time the asset was acquired. The spouse must also show that the parties intended to use those separate property funds for that purchase. This will very often require a chronological itemization of monies that are deposited or withdrawn from the parties' bank accounts so as to demonstrate the fact that the separate funds were on hand as of the date of acquisition.

In other words, it is not enough for a party claiming a $5,000 separate interest in certain community assets to demonstrate to the court that over the course of the marriage, $5,000 of his separate property funds was depleted. Rather, he must show (1) the separate property source was available at the time the disputed asset was acquired, *and* (2) the parties intended to use the separate property to acquire the asset. These are all questions of fact for the court to determine. In addition to the accurate (and detailed) record keeping required by this procedure, the court must also be persuaded as to the credibility of the witnesses involved in these issues. From a practical standpoint, any spouse who is concerned about preserving his or her separate property interest in assets acquired with commingled funds should obtain written statements from the other spouse acknowledging the intent to use the separate property funds for the acquisition of the particular assets. (Query how likely it is that such a statement could be obtained in the context of most marriages.)

The second common approach to tracing is called the *family expense* or *recapitulation* method. This approach operates under the presumption that all family living expenses are paid for out of community funds; as such, to the extent that an asset was acquired at a time when the community expenses exceeded the community income, separate property must have been used to pay for the balance of the asset. This is an indirect method of tracing and tends to provide a back door avenue of establishing the separate property character of a portion of a commingled asset. However, just as was the case with direct tracing, the spouse who claims the separate property interest must also demonstrate that (1) separate property funds were available at the time the asset was acquired, and (2) the community income was depleted to zero (or below) at the time the asset was acquired. By demonstrating these two facts, the spouse prevents the court and/or other spouse from undertaking a "total recapitulation." According to a total recapitulation method, one would simply add up all of the community income over the life of the marriage and subtract out all of the community expenses over the life of the marriage, then argue that everything left over must be separate.

The discussion above presupposes, of course, that a commingling of funds and assets has occurred. Obviously, the easiest (and most secure) method of ensuring the recovery of any separate property expenditures occurring during the marriage is to not commingle the separate and community property in the first place. Further, the spouse who is being called on by the community to contribute separate property funds should obtain a document signed by the other spouse acknowledging the existence of the separate property so used, the intent of the parties to use the separate property for the acquisition, and the right to reimbursement discussed herein. However, one must wonder what the likelihood of getting a spouse to sign such a document truly is.

2. Apportionment

The term "apportionment" refers to the sorting out the separate and community aspects of any given asset. A business, a home, a car, or any asset owned by the community or as the separate property of one of the spouses, but that has maintained both separate and community property characteristics, is subject to having its separate and community characteristics "apportioned" for subsequent confirmation and division by the court. As such, the concept of apportionment is simply an extension of the concept of commingling discussed above. In a sense, apportionment can be described as the end result of source-tracing with commingled assets.

Apportionment occurs most often in current family law practice in two specific situations.[41] The first involves a diversion of community assets for the improvement or management of a separate property asset (for example, a business). The second situation arises out of mixed interests in real property, typically the family home.

a) *Pereira and Van Camp*

In the first apportionment scenario, community property assets are used to improve a separate property asset. As was discussed earlier in this chapter, each spouse's energy, efforts, and labors constitute a very valuable community asset. And when this valuable community asset is diverted (or devoted) to that spouse's separate property asset, it becomes necessary to determine to what extent, if any, the community obtains an interest in that separate property asset. For example, Husband brings to the marriage a stock portfolio worth $10,000, which is his sole and separate property. But, during the marriage, he devotes some measure of his time, energy, efforts, skill, and labor to enhance the stock portfolio's value. At the date of separation, the portfolio is worth $100,000 (an increase in value of $90,000 during the marriage). To what extent may the community share in this increase in value? Remember, the rents, issues, and profits of separate property maintain the same separate property character as the source of these rents, issues, and profits; yet, a spouse's energy, efforts, and labors are a community asset.

The courts have developed two basic approaches to solve this problem, both of which were named for and defined by case law: the *Pereira* method and the *Van Camp* method. These cases defined two separate approaches to determine the predominant source of an increase in value of separate property assets. The increase in value may be primarily the result of the labors and efforts of the spouse, in which case the *Pereira* method is employed; or, the increase in value may be a result of the natural tendency of the asset to increase in value by virtue of circumstances outside of the control of the owner spouse, in which case the *Van Camp* method is employed. Each method provides distinct results.

In *Pereira v. Pereira*, 156 Cal. 1 (1909), the court found that the principal source of gains was the skill and labor of the spouse. Following the *Pereira* approach, the court allocates a "fair rate of return" on the separate property investment and calls that "separate property." Any excess in value over this amount belongs to the community by process of elimination. The excess in value represents the increase in value that was due to the owner spouse's labor and efforts. For example, assume Husband, at the date of marriage, owns a stock portfolio valued at $10,000. Over the course of his three-year marriage, his stock portfolio increases in value to $100,000. During marriage, Husband devotes some portion of his time, energy, and efforts into the management of the portfolio. Utilizing a *Pereira* approach, the court first ascertains a "fair rate of return," which could have been realized by Husband had he invested the property in a long-term, well-secured investment. For purposes of this example, let us assume that the court makes a finding that such "fair rate of return" constitutes 8.5 percent per annum.[42]

Once the court determines a fair rate of return, it allocates that amount to the separate property. The balance of the increase must (by process of elimination) be the result of the spouse's community property efforts and will thus be allocated to the community. Applying these concepts to the numbers herein, assuming an 8.5 percent per annum "fair rate of return" on $10,000 over three years, the amount of the $90,000 increase in value, which constitutes a fair rate of return on the underlying $10,000 investment, is $2,550. Accordingly, of the $90,000 increase in value, $2,250 would be classified as separate property while $87,450 would be characterized as community property.

The other approach to apportioning mixed separate and community interests is defined by the case of Van Camp v. Van Camp, 53 Cal. App. 17 (1921). Under the *Van Camp* approach, the court determines how much the owner spouse's effort and labor was worth and assigns that figure to the community property. The balance of the increase in value is characterized as separate property by process of elimination. Thus, assuming the same example referenced above, if the court makes a finding that the energy, efforts, and labor of the owner spouse were worth approximately $10,000 per year, the court will allocate $30,000 as the value of the community portion, leaving $60,000 characterized as separate property.[43]

The reader must be wondering when to use the *Van Camp* approach and when to use the *Pereira* approach; indeed, there are no clear-cut guidelines for making that determination. As a practical matter, however, most courts favor the *Pereira* method in cases where the business is particularly labor-intensive and the owner spouse invested a significant amount of time in its operation. Similarly, the court generally prefers to use the *Van Camp* method if the business is not particularly labor-intensive and the overall economic circumstances of the increase in value indicate that the increase was primarily the result of economic factors (for example, inflation). Many courts have grappled with this question, and there is a significant body of law from which to make arguments both for and against each method. As a practical matter, many family law attorneys simply apply both formulas to their particular situation, and argue the one most favorable to their position. Few courts (if any), however, will be so easily persuaded. The facts and circumstances surrounding the nature, scope, and extent of the services provided by the owner spouse, the conditions of the economy, and a wide range of other factors will ultimately form the basis for the court's decision.

In deciding whether to apply the *Pereira* or *Van Camp* formula, the court also asks whether the owner spouse received an adequate salary for his efforts devoted to the separate property business. To the extent that he did, the *Pereira* approach may be inappropriate because the community was already compensated for the owner spouse's effort. In those situations, therefore, many courts favor the *Van Camp* approach.

b) *Moore/Marsden*

The second area in which apportionment is commonly used concerns acquisitions of both separate and community property, most often with respect to purchases involving the family residence and assets purchased before the marriage. Fundamental to this particular discussion are general concepts related to acquisitions of assets on credit. When most people buy a car or a house, they do not necessarily purchase 100 percent of this asset at the time of acquisition. Indeed, most people make a down payment on the asset and then make monthly payments over time. By so doing, they essentially purchase the asset a little piece at a time, month by month, until the entire purchase contract is complete. For example, if Wife purchases a $20,000 automobile by placing $5,000 down and financing the remaining $15,000 over five years, before the first month's payment is made she only owns a 25 percent interest in the $20,000 car (by virtue of the down payment). Thereafter, every month as she makes payments, Wife acquires a slightly greater interest in the car until the entire purchase contract is paid off at the end of five years; at that time, she owns 100 percent of the car.

The same is true of acquiring a home, only the numbers are bigger. Somebody who purchases a $100,000 home will typically put $20,000 down and will finance the remaining $80,000 with the bank. Before the first monthly payment is made, this person owns a 20 percent interest in the home by virtue of the down payment. As each subsequent monthly payment on the note is made over the life of the loan (typically 30 years), the owner acquires a larger and larger interest in the house until the purchase contract is complete. At that time, the person owns 100 percent of the property.

The issue of apportionment in this context arises when somebody purchases an asset before marriage and finances that purchase. As he makes payments on the asset before marriage, he acquires a larger interest in it. After getting married, the person continues to make monthly payments, but now he uses community property funds (for example, salary) rather than his separate property funds. In these circumstances, it is necessary to apportion the interests between separate and community so as to preserve the reimbursement rights of the respective parties.[44]

For a thorough understanding of apportionment, it is important to understand the manner in which acquisitions on credit are paid off over time. As illustrated above, when someone purchases an asset of significant value, he typically makes a down payment, followed by regular monthly payments for the life of the purchase contract. By financing a purchase, a buyer usually pays more for the asset than if he simply pays the entire purchase price at the time of sale. He usually pays more because by financing a purchase, he must usually pay interest charges. For example, if a buyer purchases a $20,000 automobile by placing $5,000 down and financing the remaining $15,000 over a three-year period at 15 percent interest, he will pay $23,720 rather than $20,000 for the car. He pays an extra $3,720 because he must make monthly payments of approximately $520 for 36 months (the number of months called for in the contract) plus the down payment of $5,000, or $23,720. This difference in price becomes even more dramatic when considering the purchase of a home. Assume, for example, the purchase of a $200,000 home coupled with a $40,000 down payment, with the balance being paid out over a 30-year period at 8.15 percent per annum interest (on these facts the amount borrowed is $160,000). Using these facts, the note would require a monthly payment of $1,190.80. When this amount is multiplied by 360 months (the total life of the purchase contract) and the amount of the down payment ($40,000) is added to that sum, it can be seen that the purchaser has actually paid $468,688 for his $200,000 home.

The rather extreme differences between the price of the asset as purchased and the price of the asset as paid for has to do with the fact that the purchaser acquires the property on credit and pays interest over time. This difference ($3,720 in the car example) is representative of the amount of interest payments made to the lender. In the context of apportionment, the community does not acquire a right to be reimbursed for payments made on *interest*. It is only entitled to credit for the amounts of *principal* paid with respect to the acquisition of the asset. Accordingly, every month it must be determined how much of the monthly payment is going toward *interest* and how much of the monthly payment is going toward *principal*. In the above example of the home purchase, of the approximately $1,200 per month payment, only $150 is going toward principal. Put more simply, even though $1,200 of community funds were spent, only $150 worth of asset was purchased.

The particular analysis applied in the context of the *Moore/Marsden* formula is affected by the timing of the acquisition of the asset. In the case of Marriage of Marsden, 130 Cal. App. 3d 426 (1982), Mr. Marsden purchased a home for $38,300 while he was single, paying $8,300 down and signing a promissory note for $30,000 for the balance of the loan. He took title to the property in his name only. On the date of his marriage, he had paid down the principal amount of the loan by $7,000, and the property had increased in value by $26,700 (its fair market value was thus $65,000). During the marriage and before separation the community paid down the principal amount of the loan by $9,200. During this time, the property had appreciated in value by an additional $117,500, bringing its value as of the date of trial to $182,500. Finally, Mr. Marsden paid down the loan principal by $655 post-separation such that as of the date of trial the balance owing on the loan was $13,145.

Under these facts, the *Marsden* court found that Mr. Marsden held a 75.98 percent separate property interest in the house. The court came to this conclusion by adding the down payment ($8,300) plus the principal payments ($20,800), then dividing that total ($29,100) by the purchase price ($38,300).

Down payment:	$8,300
Principal pay down:	$20,800

$29,100 ÷ $38,300 = .7598 => 75.98%

The court found that the community had a 24.02 percent interest in the home. It could have arrived at this conclusion in two ways. The court could have simply subtracted the separate property interest (75.98 percent) from 100 percent. Or, the court could have divided the community interest ($9,200 of payments made during marriage) by the total purchase price ($39,300). Loan (principal) pay down: $9,200 \div $38,300 = .2402 => 24.02%

The foregoing clearly establishes the relationship of separate to community property with respect to the *original purchase price* of the home. What then of the increase in value that occurred over time? This simply becomes a matter of applying the percentages derived above to the total amount of appreciation. We know that at the time of trial the house was worth $182,500, and it had appreciated over the term of the marriage by $117,500. Applying the figures referenced above, the respective separate and community interests in this appreciation are as follows:

$$\$117,500 \times 75.98\% = \$89,276.50 = \text{Separate property}$$
$$\$117,500 \times 24.02\% = \$28,223.50 = \text{Community property}$$

Finally, to determine the husband and wife's respective equity interests, we must add the various components as follows:

Husband's Separate Property Share:

Down payment:	$8,300.00
Loan pay down (pre-marriage):	$7,000.00
Loan pay down (post-separation):	$655.00
Premarital appreciation:	$26,700.00
75.98% of marital appreciation:	<u>$89,276.50</u>
	$131,931.50

Community Share:

Loan pay down during marriage:	$9,200.00
24.02% of marital appreciation:	<u>$28,223.50</u>
	$37,423.50

Based on the foregoing calculations, it is apparent that the court awarded Mr. Marsden a $150,643.25 separate property interest in the house. (His separate property interest ($131,931.50) plus half of the community interest ($37,423.50).) The court awarded Mrs. Marsden $18,711.75, which represents one half of the community portion as calculated above.

The *Moore* court made clear that in apportioning spousal property rights, payments for interest, taxes, and insurance on monthly acquisition payments should be disregarded. And the *Marsden* court provided an articulate explanation of the principles announced in *Moore*. Overwhelming citation to these cases resulted in what is now known as the *Moore/Marsden* calculation.

Of course, an owner spouse who acquired an asset before marriage, then transferred title to both spouses' names after marriage would need to overcome the presumptions of Family Code section 2581 before the court would apply a *Moore/Marsden* calculation. Recall that to overcome a section 2581 presumption, the owner spouse must produce a writing that showed he was supposed to maintain his separate property interest. Even if the owner spouse could not rebut the presumption, he would still have a claim for reimbursement for all traceable separate property contributions to the purchase of the asset according to Family code section 2640.

3. Reimbursement Claims

As the reader has probably surmised, the Family Code provides for rights of reimbursement under a myriad of circumstances. These include the reimbursement rights provided by Family Code sections 910 et seq. (when the non-obligor spouse's separate property or the community property is used to satisfy the obligor spouse's separate property debt). There is also a reimbursement right when debts were incurred to pay for the "necessaries of life." Family Code section 2641 provides reimbursement for community contributions to a spouse's education or training. And Family Code section 2640 provides reimbursement rights for "contributions to the acquisition of property."

Reimbursement claims also arise when separate property is used to acquire, improve, or maintain a community asset. As a general rule, during the marriage while the parties are living together, if a spouse chooses to use his separate property for a community purpose, the court presumes that the spouse made a gift to the community. As such, the spouse who made a separate property contribution is not entitled to reimbursement unless he can produce evidence of an agreement to the contrary that is signed by the other spouse. Usually these issues arise when a spouse uses separate property to maintain or acquire community assets post-separation.[45] In these circumstances, one well-known case clearly provides for a right of reimbursement to the extent these payments can be traced to their separate property source. That case is Marriage of Epstein, 24 Cal. 3d 76 (1979), and it has gained such notoriety in the family law field that the concepts it describes (that is, the right to be reimbursed for post-separation payments made to improve or maintain community assets) have become known as *Epstein credits*.

The *Epstein* court found that it would be appropriate to reimburse a spouse who made post-separation contributions, unless: (1) the spouses agreed that the payments would not be reimbursed (because they were intended as a gift or a discharge of one spouse's support obligations), or (2) the contributing spouse's use of the asset constituted a "trade-off" for the amounts he paid to acquire or maintain the asset.

The second example is the most common situation in which the courts consider *Epstein* credits. An example of these circumstances follows. Post-separation, one spouse remains in the community property home and makes payments thereon. At the time of trial, this spouse might, under *Epstein*, request reimbursement for these payments; she would need to offer evidence that she did not intend the payments to constitute a gift or support. The court could deny her request, however, under the theory that even though she made payments to maintain or acquire the home, she also enjoyed exclusive use of the home; thus, she denied the "out spouse" his share of the home's reasonable rental value. Under these circumstances, the court would deny her request for *Epstein* credits to the extent that the reasonable rental value offset the payments she made to acquire the home.[46]

A concept related to *Epstein* credits was established in Marriage of Watts, 171 Cal. App. 3d 366 (1985). Pursuant to the *Watts* case, if one spouse has exclusive use of a community property asset post-separation, the community may be entitled to a reimbursement on the value of that exclusive use between the date of separation and the date of trial. *Watts* charges are essentially the flip side to *Epstein* "credits." *Watts* credits constitute "usage charges" to the spouse who exercises exclusive control over the asset. For example, the court may find *Watts* charges in the following scenario: A spouse has exclusive use of the family home post-separation. The court determines that the family home has a rental value of $10,000 per month (thus theoretically entitling the out spouse to $5,000 per month). Yet, the "in spouse" is only making mortgage payments of $4,000 per month. Thus, the in spouse is realizing a $6,000 per month use value excess. Under these circumstances, the out spouse could argue that he is entitled to $3,000 per month in *Watts* charges.

4. Quasi-Community and Marital Property

Under certain circumstances, spouses can acquire property that falls into two additional categories beyond those already discussed: "quasi-community" property and "quasi-marital" property. Both are essentially property which, but for the occurrence of some particular circumstances, would otherwise be treated as community property. And, for most practical purposes, "quasi-property" is treated the same as community property.

Family Code section 125 defines quasi-community property as follows:

> "Quasi-community property" means all real or personal property, wherever situated, acquired before or after the operative date of this code in any of the following ways:

(a) By either spouse while domiciled elsewhere which would have been community property if the spouse who acquired the property had been domiciled in this state at the time of its acquisition.

(b) In exchange for real or personal property, wherever situated, which would have been community property if the spouse who acquired the property so exchanged had been domiciled in this state at the time of its acquisition.

The reader will recall that community property is that which the parties acquired while they were domiciled in California. Quasi-community property is property that the spouses acquired while they were domiciled *outside* of California. For all practical purposes, quasi-community property is treated community property. However, in order to be true to the statutory definition of community property, the term quasi-community property came into being to describe property that falls within the strict language of Family Code section 125.

Family Code section 2660 governs the division of property that is located outside California (which by definition includes *quasi-community property*).

(a) Except as provided in subdivision (b), if the property subject to division includes real property situated in another state, the Court shall, if possible, divide the community property and quasi community property as provided for in this division ["Division of Property"—Sections 2500-2660] in such a manner that it is not necessary to change the nature of the interests held in the real property situated in the other state.

(b) If it is not possible to divide the property in the manner provided for in subdivision (a), the Court may do any of the following in order effect a division of the property as provided for in this division:

(1) Require the parties to execute conveyances or take other actions with respect to the real property situated in the other state as are necessary.

(2) Award to the party who would have been benefited by the conveyances or other actions the money value of the interest in the property that the party would have received if the conveyances had been executed or other actions taken.

According to this statutory preference, when dividing marital property, California courts try not to disturb the title to community real property that is located outside California (including quasi-community property). In order to avoid disturbing title, the California court may, pursuant to Family Code section 2660(b), order the parties to reconvey the property so that title is ultimately held by both parties as tenants in common. The reconveyance helps to ensure each spouse's separate property interests in the property. The reader should note that the California courts, of course, do not have direct jurisdiction over property that is not located within their boundaries. They do, however, have jurisdiction over the parties to the dissolution action; as such, the courts may order the parties to take steps necessary to comply with the court's orders with respect to division of property.

Like quasi-community property, *quasi-marital property* is property that, but for some extenuating circumstance, would be community property. With respect to quasi-marital property, the extenuating circumstance is that the marriage was invalid. As the reader will recall, a putative spouse is a party who in good faith believed that his marriage was valid before he learned the marriage was in fact a nullity. "Quasi-marital property" refers to the property that the "innocent spouse" acquired during the time when he thought he was party to a valid marriage.

In all essential respects, a putative spouse enjoys the same property rights as a legal spouse. Further, the property acquired during the "marriage," which would have been community or quasi-community property had the marriage been valid, is termed quasi-marital property. The court divides quasi-marital property exactly the same way that it divides community and quasi-community property. Family Code section 2251 addresses this circumstance:

> (a) If a determination is made that a marriage is void or voidable and the Court finds that either party or both parties believed in good faith that the marriage was valid, the court shall
> (1) Declare the party or parties to have the status of a putative spouse.
> (2) If the division of property is in issue, divide, in accordance with Division 7 (commencing with section 2550), that property acquired during the union which would have been community property or quasi-community property if the union had not been void or voidable. The property is known as "quasi-marital property."

Further, section 2252 provides that this property, once divided, is liable for the debts of the parties to the same extent as if the property had been community property or quasi-community property.

Similarly, Family Code sections 2254 and 2255 provide that a putative spouse is entitled to spousal support and an award of attorney's fees and costs as would a legal spouse. In order to establish the status of a putative spouse, it is of paramount importance that this person convince the court that she believed in *good faith* that the marriage was valid. This is a question of fact for the court to determine based on all the facts and circumstances. As a practical matter, however, because the putative spouse's own good faith belief in the marriage's validity is the central issue, it would seem that the putative spouse's credible testimony would be sufficient.

Summary

In this chapter we learned that virtually any item of any nature whatsoever can constitute an item of property subject to division or confirmation by the court in a family law proceeding. The key factor in that regard is that the asset must be capable of being valued, although even if it cannot be evaluated, under certain circumstances the court will still "divide" it.

We learned that the term "community property" refers to all property acquired by the parties while they lived together as husband and wife that is not "separate property." Property that the spouses acquired while they lived outside of California is called quasi-community property. The term separate property refers to property acquired either before marriage or after separation, or by way of inheritance, gift, devise, or bequest. The parties are free to agree between themselves how the various items of property will be characterized, and by their own actions can significantly impact on the ultimate determination of these issues (for example, transmutation). The characterization of property is extremely important because community property is divided equally between the parties, while separate property is confirmed directly to the owner thereof.

We have also learned that not only the community estate but the separate estate as well can be liable for debts incurred both before and during marriage and after separation. Generally, the debtor spouse and his property will remain liable for the debts he incurs. The nondebtor's liability for debts is generally a function of the court's orders regarding distribution of those debts or by virtue of the operation of law (for example, the necessaries of life).

Additionally, we have seen that both parties have equal management and control over the community estate, and in fact owe to each other the highest of duties: that of a fiduciary. Along with this duty comes all manner of voluntary reporting and disclosure designed to both streamline this area of litigation as well as to "keep the parties honest." Finally, we explored the areas of tracing, commingling, and apportionment and learned that under certain circumstances the parties will be entitled to reimbursement for property contributed to the separate property of the other, provided that they are capable of tracing the source of the funds used to either community or separate property. There are special rules and procedures employed in this area, including the *Moore/Marsden* rule and the *Pereira/Van Camp* formulas.

Key Terms

The following is a list of key terms and phrases that you should be able to define and use in context. Only then will you have demonstrated a command of the material in this chapter.

- property
- real v. personal property
- community v. separate property
- source rule
- tracing
- apportionment
- commingling
- reimbursement
- quasi-community property
- quasi-marital property
- presumptions
- title documents
- quitclaim deed
- transmutation
- passive income
- gift
- devise
- bequest
- inheritance
- goodwill
- alternate valuation date
- pensions (retirement plans and benefits)
- vested v. non-vested
- the "Time Rule"
- joinder
- Qualified Domestic Relations Order (QDRO)
- debtor spouse v. nondebtor spouse
- tortfeasor v. nontortfeasor spouse
- fiduciary duty
- *Pereira/VanCamp*
- *Moore/Marsden*
- *Epstein* and *Watts* reimbursement credits

Questions for Discussion

1. Describe and discuss the seven-step method to solve a community property question.
2. List at least three different *categories* of property and list at least two *specific items* of property for each category.
3. What is the difference between *community* and *separate* property? Be specific, and give examples of each.
4. What is meant by the phrase "transmutation of property" and how is it used in a family law context?

5. In a dissolution action, the most important dates are the date of marriage, the date of separation, and the date of trial. Why?

6. List at least five different examples of things that could constitute "earnings."

7. Is the community ever entitled to reimbursement for contributions made by it to one of the spouse's education? If so, does that right expire? What is the rationale behind these rules?

8. In the context of the value of a business, what is meant by the term "goodwill" and how is that term used in family law matters?

9. Under what circumstances is it appropriate to request an alternate valuation date?

10. How are debts divided in a marital termination proceeding? Under what circumstance will the separate property of the nondebtor spouse be liable for debts incurred by the debtor spouse?

11. Discuss the statutory preference of the allocation of debts between spouses upon termination of the marriage.

12. Explain the *Pereira* and *Van Camp* rules. What are they and how are they used?

13. What is meant by the terms "tracing," "commingling," and "apportionment"? How are they used in a family law context?

14. Compare and contrast the concepts of reimbursement set out in the *Epstein* and *Watts* cases.

15. Compare and contrast the terms "quasi-community property" and "quasi-marital property."

ENDNOTES

1. In this context the term "community" refers generally to the marital estate.

2. The term "separate property" in this context includes property that the wife brought to the marriage and acquired during the marriage by way of gift or inheritance.

3. The term "community property," as used in this context, generally means property acquired by the parties *during* the marriage.

4. The concept of a *fiduciary* is defined by Black's Law Dictionary as "a person having duty, created by his undertaking, to act primarily for another's benefit in matters connected with such undertaking." In a practical sense, to be a fiduciary means that you owe somebody a special duty to treat him fairly.

5. An example of this is interest received from the bank on money deposited there or other passive income from investments.

6. The concepts of the putative spouse and quasi-marital property are briefly touched upon elsewhere in the text in the chapters dealing with support.

7. Almost always, the answer to this question is yes.

8. Interestingly, California is the only state that absolutely mandates an exact (50/50) split of community property.

9. For example, a new water heater is personal property when purchased. Only when the heater is installed (in a home or other building, for example) does it become part of the real property.

10. This is "lawyer speak" for the person who claims that an asset is separate. Similarly, "communitizer" refers to the person who claims that an asset is community property. An interesting and somewhat light-hearted trend has developed in California over the years directly due, in this author's opinion [and this is meant in a complimentary manner], to the good humor and wit of one California's leading experts in the area of family law, Stephen Adams. Mr. Adams has been providing entertaining and informative educational seminars in this area of law for well over 20 years, leading to the "convention" of taking a concept's root word, such as "separate," and converting it into a descriptive noun simply by adding "izer" to its end. We all seem to know what he means, however, so it must be having an effect!

11. Not all appellate courts require this, so it is advisable to review all decisions in this area and argue the better reasoned ones that support your particular position.

12. The reader should note the significant difference between the presumption created by §760 and that created by Family Code §2581. The section 760 presumption is broad: all property acquired during the marriage while the couple is domiciled in California is presumed to be community. In contrast, the section 2581 presumption is much narrower: it only applies to the manner in which title to the property is held. Because §2581 specifically applies to the manner in which "record title" to the property

is held, and further because of the specific language of that Code section, any rebuttal evidence is limited to the written evidence required by §2581.

13. It is for this reason that this legislation came to be known (and still is known) as the anti-*Lucas* legislation.

14. Property held in joint tenancy automatically passes to a surviving joint tenant upon the death of the other, without the need to probate it. This can constitute a significant advantage and thus is generally desirable from an estate planning standpoint.

15. Recall that Family Code §2010 gives the court jurisdiction to enter orders relative to the parties' property only incident to "a proceeding for dissolution of marriage. . . . "

16. The mathematics of this calculation are as follows: First the separate property interest traceable pursuant to §2640 is deducted "off the top," then the balance is divided as the community's share.

17. For purposes of this discussion, this concept will be referred to as general tracing so as to distinguish it from the concepts of tracing as described in §2640.

18. Please note that the application of Family Code §§2581 and 2640 to the division of marital property is extremely complex. Issues including retroactivity, tracing, and commingling, arise, which greatly exceed the scope of this text. This chapter references these sections to allow the reader to become conversant with these concepts. For a thorough understanding of these concepts, however, the reader is advised to consult any of the excellent treatises on the subject, including the Rutter Group's treatise, *Family Law*, written by Judge William Hogoboom and Justice Donald King, which is part of its *California Practice Guide* series. Similarly, California Family Law Report, Inc., publishes an excellent treatise entitled *California Family Law Practice*, written by Stephen Adams.

19. Sometimes writing a technical text such as this requires the use of very strained sentence structure. The thrust of this sentence is: "Would the recipient have been given the compensation had he not earned it?"

20. An example of passive income is interest on money deposited in the bank.

21. That is, they perform services and send out bills on a monthly basis that are not necessarily paid in full at the time the bills are sent out. As such, the clients or customers of the business owe money to the business, which is classified as an "account receivable."

22. The terms "devise" and "bequest," for the purposes of this discussion, can be equated with "inheritance."

23. The reader should note that the community does not actually have to enjoy a "higher standard of living." The presumption of Family Code §2641(c)(1) is not keyed to an actual realization of a "higher standard of living." It is simply a presumption based upon the passage of time.

24. Any attempt to explain these various methods would not only exceed the scope of this chapter, but exceed the qualifications of this author. As such, an explanation will not

be offered here. The reader is referred to the many excellent treatises on the subject of business valuation for additional information .

25. Do not be concerned if you're not sure what this means. These are tax and accounting concepts that are presented for purposes of completeness of the analysis. No intention is meant to provide anything other than the most fleeting of brushes with these concepts, essentially for the purpose of allowing the reader to recognize having seen them here when they are confronted with them in the "real world."

26. Typically undertaken by a forensic accountant, that is, an accountant whose business specialty is the performance of accounting functions in the context of litigation; a co-called "expert witness."

27. Capitalization of earnings is essentially taking gross earnings for a one year period and then applying a "capitalization rate," (essentially a multiplier) to that figure to arrive at a value. For example, an industry with a typical capitalization rate of 2.75 of gross earnings would produce a value of $275,000 for a company with gross earnings of $100,000. The reader should note that this is an incredibly simplistic description of an incredibly complex concept. My best advice is this: if you need or want to place a value on an on-going business, hire a forensic accountant and let them do it; that's what they're trained to do.

28. As indicated elsewhere in this chapter, these concepts cannot be explained in any detail in this text. These are best left to the accounting professionals who make a business of valuing businesses. It will be sufficient, then, if the reader takes from this chapter an awareness of the necessity to value a business as a going concern before it can be divided in a divorce case, and a basic understanding of some of the components involved in this type of work.

29. The parties' rationale for making this argument is hopefully clear: If they can convince the court that it has no value, they will receive the fund without having to give up another community asset of corresponding value.

30. The mechanics of joinder are discussed at some length in the chapter entitled "Selected Topics."

31. Prior to 1975, the concept of management and control over community property was particularly noteworthy because during that time period, for all practical purposes, the husband had the exclusive right to manage and control all community property. Effective in 1975, that law was changed to expand the wife's role in this management system to provide her with equal management and control over all of the community property. The basic premise regarding asset liability for debts in this family law context is that the liability for a debt went hand in hand with the right to management and control over the property. As such (and as continues to this date), a creditor could use all property that was subject to the management and control of the spouse incurring the obligation to satisfy his debt. Presently, inasmuch as both the husband and wife have equal management and control over all of the community property, this leaves *all* of the community property available to satisfy the obligation of *either* spouse.

32. She would, of course, have a right to be reimbursed for her portion of the community property that is used to satisfy this premarital debt under certain circumstances.

33. There is also another category of debt allocation that concerns torts committed by one spouse against the other.

34. This was the operative date that the law was changed to provide both spouses equal management and control of community property.

35. This disclosure is similar to that discussed in the chapter entitled "Selected Topics" under the heading *Disclosure of Assets and Liabilities*.

36. A contingency fee lawsuit is generally one in which no money is paid to the lawyer until (and unless) the lawyer wins the case or in some other way obtains settlement monies on behalf of his client. At that time, the lawyer generally takes a percentage (typically one-third) of the client's recovery. Lawyers commonly work on a contingency basis in personal injury cases, but they cannot work on a contingency basis in dissolution of marriage cases.

37. Reference is made to the Rutter Group treatise *Family Law* written by Judge William Hogoboom and Justice Donald King, part of the Rutter Group's *California Practice Guide* series.

38. For example, if the wife is an attorney and the husband is not, it is not only unwise but impossible to award the law business to him.

39. Although it does not arise often, there are circumstances in which the court may make an *unequal* division of community property: For example, Family Code §2602 provides for an unequal division (in the discretion of the court) in favor of the "innocent" spouse and against a spouse who has concealed or misappropriated community property.

40. In these situations the law is clear that in most cases if both of the parties have been active in the operation of the business during the marriage, the court will award the ongoing business to the spouse who is most capable of continuing its operation. In situations where only one spouse has been active in the operation of a marital business, the court will under most all circumstances award the operation of that business to that spouse.

41. Apportionment is in no way limited to these two situations.

42. This is in no way meant to indicate that 8.5 percent is any kind of "magic number." It is not. The determination of what constitutes a fair rate of return will be made by the court on a case-by-case basis.

43. A simple method of understanding the *Van Camp* approach involves simply asking the question: "How much would it have cost to hire somebody to do what the owner spouse did with regard to the separate property asset?" The answer to that question constitutes the community property portion of the increase in value.

44. The reader should bear in mind that certain statutory presumptions as to title have a significant impact on this analysis. Most notable are the statutory presumptions contained in Family Code §§2580, 2581, and 2640 discussed elsewhere in this chapter.

45. The concept of "acquisition" of a community asset post-separation does not contemplate going out and buying a new smaller asset (such as a television or couch) post-separation. Rather, the term "acquisition" refers to a situation in which one or both parties made a down payment on a large asset (such as a house or car) while they were married and living together; then, one party continued to make regular monthly payments on that asset while the parties were living separate and apart.

46. Interestingly, in this situation a spouse who made the post-separation payments on the preexisting community debt is not limited in his reimbursement to the amount by which he paid down the principal of the loan. He is instead entitled to receive full reimbursement of all monies paid, unless the court deems those amounts paid to be in lieu of support or offset by the use value of the asset.

CHAPTER 8

The Litigation Process

CHAPTER OVERVIEW

This chapter explores the procedural aspects of dissolution, legal separation, and nullity actions. We cover the initial client interview through default, uncontested, and contested proceedings. Our primary focus is the preparation of judicial council forms used in this area of the law.

By working through the various forms in this chapter, you will have truly mastered their preparation and be ready to work with them in daily practice. Of course, along with a discussion of the preparation of these forms, you will be exposed to the underlying law related to the actual *procedure* of family law.

A. Overview of the Litigation Process

The Family Code is used to dissolve marriages and other personal relationships between two people (i.e. domestic partnerships). The Family

Code also addresses post-trial (post-termination) modifications. Finally, the Family Code provides assistance in a non-marital context (for example, the Domestic Violence Prevention Act found in Family Code sections 6200 et seq.).

Navigation through these procedural waters can, however, be quite confusing. Much of the paralegal's time will be devoted to assistance at virtually every phase of the litigation process, from the initial commencement of the proceedings, obtaining relief pending trial, obtaining judgment, and finally any post-judgment modifications that may be necessary. A thorough understanding of the process involved is thus absolutely essential.

Litigation is not, in concept at least, an overwhelmingly complicated process. In fact, it is a process experienced on a daily basis by literally everyone who has ever debated a position with a friend, spouse, or business colleague. This process is merely the act of marshaling the facts in support of your position and against those offered by your opponent and presenting them in a clear and convincing manner to the trier of fact, in this context, the judge.[1] While most courts differ as to time parameters and local procedures, the basic structure of a lawsuit is for the most part the same in all locales.

Some form of initial presentation of a party's position is required to get the ball rolling. This is typically called the *Complaint* in most civil matters, the *Indictment* or *Information* in criminal matters, and the *Petition* in family law cases.[2] As will be shown in greater detail below, the Petition is basically a position paper setting forth the *petitioner's* (the person commencing the litigation) position on the various issues to be addressed in the case. The Petition is then *served* upon the other party to the proceeding, thus giving him *notice* of what it is the petitioner desires by virtue of this action.

Because all parties to litigation are allowed an opportunity to be heard (that is, a chance to tell their side of the story), the next step in the litigation process is typically taken by the opposing party by filing his own position paper. In family law, this document is known as the *Response*. In most other civil matters it is called an *Answer* because its function is to answer the allegations made in the Complaint.[3]

Once the Petition (Complaint) and the Response (Answer) have been filed, the matter is ready to be scheduled for trial. That is not to say that the trial is the next thing to happen, however; quite the contrary. There next ensues a sometimes significant waiting period during which time discovery is conducted, pretrial orders are requested and often made, and general preparations for trial are undertaken by all sides to the litigation.

Once the matter is called for trial, assuming all parties are ready (and sometimes whether they are ready or not), the parties are usually required to present themselves to a judicial officer who conducts a *mandatory settlement conference*[4] in an attempt to achieve an amicable resolution of the issues without the necessity of trial. On the day of trial, the trial judge may refer the parties to *mediation* in yet another attempt at settlement, and a trip to the *conciliation court* is also required if there are issues of child custody or visitation involved.

When trial starts, the issues are presented in an orderly manner with the petitioner going first, and the respondent responding to the petitioner's claims, raising issues of his or her own as the circumstances may require. Following the trial, the judicial officer weighs all the evidence, makes various *findings* (factual and legal conclusions based on the evidence presented), and renders a decision on all issues in controversy. In the family law context, this decision will typically divide all community property and obligations, determine custody of the children, determine issues of support, and determine all other matters relevant and necessary to an orderly termination of the relationship. Like most other court orders, the orders made at trial are subject to review by the appellate court. Many orders made at trial in a family law matter are also subject to post-trial modification as the circumstances may require.

B. The Initial Client Interview

Nothing can substitute for thorough preparation, and it is never too early to start. Many attorneys include their paralegal in the initial intake interview, and so familiarity with this process is a must. The paralegal's role in this process may rise to the level of collecting much of the information him or herself or may simply consist of observing the dialogue between the client and the attorney, taking notes of the meeting as the context requires, depending upon the particular attorney and client involved and the degree of experience of the paralegal. However, because the paralegal provides a cost-effective liaison between the client and the attorney, and because a thorough understanding of all issues and facts involved in a litigated matter is essential in virtually every aspect of the litigation, it is this author's opinion that except in rare cases it is never too early to have the paralegal become involved in the case.

During the initial contact between the client and the attorney (generally the meeting or meetings that resulted in the client's decision to retain the attorney) the attorney will have already ascertained many of the basic facts and will have begun to identify the issues of the case and formulate strategy. Subsequent to the client retaining the attorney, however, a great deal more detailed information will be required. Documents will have to be gathered and reviewed and, of course, paperwork will have to be prepared. In that regard, many of the forms used in family law practice have become the subject of various computer programs that can utilize information compiled in a database specific to a particular client, automatically incorporate that information into the specific form to be used, and then print out a completed form ready for filing, all in a matter of minutes. Many attorneys have streamlined the preparation of these documents in such a fashion as to allow their basic preparation utilizing information culled during the initial interview updated and modified as the case progresses. It is in this context that the client information sheet becomes invaluable.

The *client information sheet* is simply a list of information collected from the client in order to create a "database" about that client.[5] It can be called a checklist, a questionnaire, or any other name that is descriptive and familiar to the user. There is no particular form, and there are few rules regarding its preparation except these two: (1) it must be maintained; and (2) it must be thorough. It will suffice if it can be easily understood and contains information about the client. Of course, you do not want this document to be so long and cumbersome that its use becomes more trouble than it is worth. Unless it is so required for any particular purpose, the list should be relatively short and succinct and easily browsed to facilitate locating a particular piece of information.

No doubt you will ultimately develop your own list or use and adapt a list already in use by the attorney with whom you are working. Sometimes clients are sent home with this list and asked to complete it themselves; sometimes it is completed in the office. There are pros and cons to each approach. On the one hand, completion in the office can be very time-consuming and expensive; however, it gives the client the confidence that the attorney is giving personal attention to his matter. It also gives the client a sense of the breadth of the issues involved and the realization that the work done in an attorney's office does not just "happen." This can help to educate the client to the realities of the work and in so doing help him to understand and appreciate that for which he is paying. On the other hand, of course, many clients have neither the time nor the money to complete this task in the attorney's office, at least not while the meter is running. In those circumstances, it is sometimes helpful to have the client complete this form in the reception area while waiting to see the attorney. By so doing, the client does not feel that this time is wasted, and because the attorney (or paralegal) will be reviewing it immediately after its preparation, any problems or questions encountered in its completion can be addressed right away.

Whether done in the office with the attorney, in the reception area, or at home, the important point is that it should be *done*. Figure 8-1 on pages 309-311 is an example of a client information sheet used by the author.

C. Choice of Actions

Obviously, when two people decide to terminate their relationship, decisions must be made regarding how this will be accomplished: put

Figure 8-1
CLIENT INFORMATION SHEET

1. PERSONAL FACTS

   (a) Name: _____

        Address: _____

        Telephone: Home: (_____)

                     Work: (_____)

        Date of Birth: _____

        Driver's License: _____

        Social Security Number: _____

   (b) Spouse's Name: _____

        Address: _____

        Telephone: Home: (_____)

                     Work: (_____)

        Date of Birth: _____

        Driver's License: _____

        Social Security Number: _____

   (c) Have you been a resident of California for the last six months and a resident of Los Angeles County for the last three months? yes__ no__

   (d) Child(ren)'s Name(s), Birthdate(s) and Birthplace(s):

_____   _____

_____   _____

_____   _____

   (e) Date/Place of Marriage: _____

2. PROPERTY

   (a) Family Residence

   1. Address: _____

_____

   2. How is title held: _____

   3. Date of purchase: _____

   4. Purchase price: _____

   5. Amount borrowed at time of purchase: _____

   6. Loan balance currently: _____

   7. Current approximate fair market value: _____

   (b) Other Real Property:

   1. Address: _____

_____

   2. How is title held: _____

   3. Date of purchase: _____

Figure 8-1 (continued)

4. Purchase price: _____

5. Amount borrowed at time of purchase: _____

6. Loan balance currently: _____

7. Current approximate fair market value: _____

(c) Other Property:

1. Automobiles:

    a. make:_____ model: _____ year: _____ driven by: _____

    b. make:_____ model: _____ year: _____ driven by: _____

    c. make:_____ model: _____ year: _____ driven by: _____

    d. make:_____ model: _____ year: _____ driven by: _____

Are any of these leased? _____; If yes, which one(s): _____

(d) Bank Accounts:

Bank: _____ Branch: _____ Type: _____ Acct. No._____

Bank: _____ Branch: _____ Type: _____ Acct. No._____

Bank: _____ Branch: _____ Type: _____ Acct. No._____

Bank: _____ Branch: _____ Type: _____ Acct. No._____

Bank: _____ Branch: _____ Type: _____ Acct. No._____

Bank: _____ Branch: _____ Type: _____ Acct. No._____

Bank: _____ Branch: _____ Type: _____ Acct. No._____

(e) Stocks and Bonds:

Company name (or symbol): _____ No. of Shares:_____ Broker: _____

Company name (or symbol): _____ No. of Shares:_____ Broker: _____

(f) Pension Plans:

You: _____

Your Spouse: _____

(g) Other Assets:

_____

_____

_____

Figure 8-1 (continued)

(h) Separate Property:

_____

_____

_____

_____

3. OBLIGATIONS

Creditor: _____ Acct. No.: _____ Amt. Owed (DOS): _____
Creditor: _____ Acct. No.: _____ Amt. Owed (DOS): _____
Creditor: _____ Acct. No.: _____ Amt. Owed (DOS): _____
Creditor: _____ Acct. No.: _____ Amt. Owed (DOS): _____

4. INCOME

(a) Your Employer: _____
    Occupation: _____
    Gross Monthly Income: _____
(b) Your Spouse's Employer: _____
    Occupation: _____
    Gross Monthly Income: _____

5. LIQUID ASSETS

(a) Liquid Assets under your control: _____
    _____

(b) Liquid Assets under your spouse's control: _____
    _____

6. MONTHLY EXPENSES

Mortgage/Rent: _____   Child Care: _____
Maintenance: _____   Education: _____
Food/eating out: _____   Entertainment/Vacations: _____
Utilities: _____ Transportation and auto expense: ____
Clothing: _____   Incidentals: _____
Medical: _____   Credit Cards: _____
Insurance: _____   Food at home/household supplies: ___

succinctly, what *type* of action will be filed. Fortunately, the choices are simple. Indeed, some are only available under certain, somewhat unique circumstances.

There are three types of actions available when commencing litigation in this area: *dissolution, legal separation,* and *nullity.* Family Code section 310 instructs that a marriage can only be terminated by death, a judgment of dissolution of marriage, or a judgment of nullity of marriage. A judgment of legal separation, while available, will not terminate a marriage. Thus if termination of the marriage is the goal, only two options are available: dissolution or nullity.

1. Nullity

An action for nullity is actually somewhat of a rarity due to the very specific and unique grounds under which it is available. While an action for dissolution presupposes a valid marriage, an action for *nullity* does just the opposite. It presumes (or at least argues) that the marriage was not in fact valid, and as such must not be recognized. Because a decree of dissolution is so readily available[6] one may wonder why anyone would go through the trouble of seeking a nullity. As will become clear in the sections below, certain orders such as spousal support are dependent upon the existence of a valid marriage. Thus, if one can prove the basis for a decree of nullity, the existence of the marriage is denied and along with it the availability of many incidents to the marriage (for example, spousal support). The marriage is declared void, and the parties are returned to the status of unmarried persons as if the marriage had never taken place.

Several other factors might prove attractive in selecting an action for nullity over one for dissolution. For example, the six-month waiting period before a judgment of dissolution becomes final does not apply.

The six-month residence requirement is also inapplicable to nullity proceedings. Further, in an action for dissolution, the grounds for the action are immaterial. California is a "no-fault" state, which means that if a party wants to dissolve her marriage, she need only ask. Nullity, on the other hand, can be directly concerned with fault, especially when it comes to assessing attorney's fees and costs against one of the parties.

An action for nullity can also adversely affect the "innocent" spouse's property rights following the termination of the marriage. As will be discussed in greater detail in the section dealing with property rights, certain rights are generally only available incident to a valid marriage. Similarly, certain other rights that may have been terminated by operation of the questionable marriage can be restored once that marriage is annulled. Because an action for nullity presupposes that one of the parties to the marriage did something "wrong" (thus providing the basis of the nullity action), it follows that in those situations the other spouse (the spouse who was "wronged") is called the *innocent* spouse.

In order to provide some relief for innocent parties to an invalid marriage when dealing with the property of that "marriage," the law has created a separate category applicable to such persons. They are called *putative spouses*. This is an equitable concept designed to provide an innocent spouse (one who in good faith believed the marriage was valid and acted accordingly) with a fair realization of the expectations formed during the marriage.[7] Such spouses will generally be granted certain rights usually reserved for parties to a valid marriage regardless of the fact that the marriage was in fact not valid.

Another interesting distinction between a nullity action and one for dissolution has to do with the *parties* to the litigation. While in a dissolution (or legal separation) action, the party commencing the proceeding must be one of the parties to the marriage, such is not necessarily the case in an action for nullity. Other interested persons such as parents and other relatives can commence a nullity action on behalf of one of the parties to the "marriage."

Because the grounds for nullity are not always easily proven, if termination of the marriage, one way or another, is the client's ultimate goal, then the action should be pled in the alternative: nullity or, if unavailable, then dissolution. In this way the client's goals will be met without the need for the additional time and expense involved in a second action for dissolution if the request for a decree of nullity is denied.

a) Void versus Voidable Marriages

In the context of an action for nullity, a distinction is made between a *void* marriage and one that is merely *voidable*. In the latter case, the marriage is actually valid until such time as whatever defect rendering it subject to attack in the nullity action is proven, at which point the marriage will then be deemed *void*. Some "marriages" however are never *valid*, and never carry with them the benefits of a valid marriage, not even for a short time. This distinction becomes important when assessing the availability of certain temporary, pretrial orders (such as temporary spousal support) and when determining issues related to community property.[8]

The grounds upon which a nullity action can be brought are specific and are provided by statute. They are:

Void: (1)   Incestuous marriage: *Family Code §2200*
                (2)   Bigamous; polygamous marriages: *Family Code §2201*
Voidable: (1)   Petitioner's age at the time of the marriage: *Family Code §2210(a)*

(2) Prior existing marriage: *Family Code §2210(b)*
(3) Unsound mind: *Family Code §2210(c)*
(4) Fraud: *Family Code §2210(d)*
(5) Force: *Family Code §2210(e)*
(6) Physical incapacity: *Family Code §2210(f)*

b) *Nullity Based on Void Marriages*

Statutorily speaking, there are only two grounds upon which a marriage will be declared a nullity as *void* or never of any force and effect. These are *incestuous* and *bigamous* and *polygamous* marriages. Family Code section 2200 describes as incestuous any marriage between parents and children, brothers and sisters (half brothers and sisters also), uncles and nieces, aunts and nephews, and ancestors and descendants of every degree.[9]

Family Code section 2201 describes a bigamous marriage as one created when a person, after having married one person subsequently marries another person without having terminated the first marriage (by dissolution or a decree of nullity). In other words, the classic description of a bigamist, someone with two spouses (a polygamist is someone with *more* than two spouses).

This statute reads in pertinent part as follows:

> (a) A subsequent marriage contracted by a person during the life of a former husband or wife of the person, with a person other than the former husband or wife, is illegal and void from the beginning, unless:
>> (1) the former marriage has been dissolved or adjudged a nullity before the date of the subsequent marriage.
>> (2) the former husband or wife (i) is absent, and not known to the person to be living for the period of five successive years immediately preceding the subsequent marriage, or (ii) is generally reputed or believed by the person to be dead at the time the subsequent marriage was contracted.

Not every bigamist, however, fits the classic description of what our society has declared to be a bad or morally misguided individual. While it is true that some people deliberately mislead others and try to maintain multiple marriages concurrently, usually bigamous circumstances arise through inadvertence or oversight. Accordingly, Family Code section 2201(a)(2) provides an exception to the rule of an automatically void marriage. The generally mandated terms of section 2201 do not apply if the former spouse is absent (missing), and has been absent for at least five successive years immediately preceding the subsequent marriage; the mandatory terms of section 2201 also do not apply if the former spouse was generally presumed to be dead at the time of the subsequent marriage (which took place before five years elapsed since the spouse went missing).

In this case the marriage is considered valid until its nullity is declared. For example, if a spouse were declared missing (for example, in combat), five years later that person's spouse could freely remarry without the new marriage being considered void from the outset. A shorter period would be acceptable if facts were present giving rise to a general (and reasonable) presumption of death on the part of the first spouse.

What if the former spouse is *not* dead though, and he returns? The answer is found below in the discussion of *voidable* marriages.

c) Nullity Based on Voidable Marriages

Not all defective marriages are void from the start. (In fact, as seen above, only two are void from the start.) Several marriages may start out valid on their face and later end up being declared null and of no force or effect. These marriages are said to be *voidable*. It is important to note that these marriages are completely valid for all purposes until they are declared a nullity. However, it is not the occurrence of some later event (after the marriage) that renders it voidable and subject to being set aside. The legal defect must exist *at the time of the marriage*. If the marriage is valid at its inception (that is, there are no legal defects then in existence), it cannot be set aside later and declared a nullity. It can only be terminated by dissolution.

The basic distinction between voidable and void marriages primarily has to do with the *availability* of the nullity action. For all practical purposes, in a void marriage no rights or incidents of the marriage can attach to the relationship. A void marriage *is never valid*. A voidable marriage, on the other hand, *is* valid on its face (that is, for all appearances it is valid) until someone attempts to have it set aside. If no one takes action to set it aside, it simply continues until it is terminated in some other way.[10]

The grounds for terminating a voidable marriage are set out in Family Code section 2210:

- **Section 2210(a)** provides that a marriage can be annulled if the petitioner in the nullity proceeding was not old enough to legally consent to the marriage. *Legal* consent and *actual* consent are distinguishable: Someone who is 16 years of age may want to consent and may in fact actually agree to the marriage. This does not, however, make him legally capable of consenting. He cannot consent until he reaches 18 years of age (in California, the age of consent is 18. Family Code section 301. In other states it could be higher or lower).

> Once the underage party comes of age, however, if he continues to cohabit with his spouse as husband and wife, this avenue of nullity will no longer be available.

- **Section 2210(b)** provides the answer to the missing/presumed dead spouse question presented above. If Husband One were declared missing in 2000, Wife could legally remarry five years later, in 2005. If Husband One returned in 2006, Wife's marriage to Husband Two would be *voidable*. Recall that Wife could marry Husband Two before five years had elapsed since Husband One's disappearance if there were facts giving rise to a general (and reasonable) presumption that Husband One was dead.

- **Section 2210(c)** makes a marriage voidable if either party was of unsound mind at the time of the marriage. This is similar to the provisions of 2210(a) inasmuch as it goes to the party's legal ability to consent to (or enter) a contract. Just as when age is a factor, if, when the party comes to reason, he continues to freely cohabit with the other spouse, then the marriage will no longer be voidable. This section is probably the most frequently used ground for declaring a marriage void. It is typically used when one party is too intoxicated to realize what is going on when he marries. Then, when he "sobers up" (comes to reason), he may seek to have the marriage annulled.

- **Section 2210(d)** makes marriages voidable when the consent of either party was the product of fraud. For example, one party lies to the other just to convince her to marry. Once the fraud is discovered, the marriage can be set aside.

- **Section 2210(e)** is similar to (d) above, only it speaks to consent through the use of force.

- **Section 2210(f)** renders a marriage voidable if, at the time of the marriage, either party was "physically incapable of entering into the marriage state, and the incapacity continues and appears to be incurable."

While actions for dissolution and legal separation are not restricted by statutes of limitations,[11] actions for nullity based on a voidable marriage are. Family Code section 2211 specifies the limitation period and proper petitioning party in these actions. Actions brought under 2210(a) are limited to those brought within four years after reaching the age of consent. If a parent or guardian wishes to bring the action, he or she must do so *before* the underage married person comes of age. As can be seen, then, if one does not take action to protect his rights, he will lose them. Once a party turns 18, he has four years to seek to have the marriage declared a nullity due to the fact of his minority at the time of the marriage. Note, however, the specific language of Family Code section 2210: ". . . a marriage is voidable . . . if . . . *the party who commences the action* . . . was without the capability of consenting to the marriage [that is, was underage] . . . [emphasis added]." The highlighted language indicates that only the spouse who was underage at the time of the marriage (or a party acting on his behalf, a concept explained below) may bring the action. As such, if a 17-year-old boy marries an 18-year-old woman, as between the two of them, only the husband has the right to have this marriage declared a nullity on these grounds; the wife does not. And, as stated above, the husband must bring such an action within four years of his turning 18 or lose the right to do so forever.

A much more interesting aspect of the provisions of this statute is found in the language identifying the underage spouse as either the petitioning party or the party "on whose behalf the proceeding is commenced" (Family Code section 2210). Family Code section 2211 answers the question of just who this other person who commences the action on behalf of the underage spouse is: that spouse's parent(s) or legal guardian. Accordingly, the minor's parents or legal guardian can act to foil the plans of the minor child simply by filing an action on the child's behalf to have the marriage declared a nullity. So when parents tell children that they cannot marry without their consent, they mean it. The limitation period on the parents' action is very short, however. According to Family Code section 2211(a)(2), they must bring their action *before* their child becomes an adult.

Finally, although extremely rare, one circumstance does exist that might otherwise defeat a minor's claim for nullity based on his status as a minor. Section 302 of the Family Code gives a minor the ability to consent to a marriage when accompanied by a consent from his parents and "a court order granting permission to marry, obtained on the showing the court requires."

A marriage voidable by reason of the missing/presumed dead section (Family Code section 2210(b)) can be brought by either party to the marriage at any time during the marriage. The "former" (missing or presumed dead) spouse can also bring this action as the petitioning party.

Because this section is often a source of confusion due to the provisions of Family Code section 2201 (bigamous marriages), a few words of explanation on its operation are necessary. Many students ask why Family Code section 2210(b) even exists given that section 2201 declares these marriages *void*. "What is the purpose of a similar section declaring these marriages voidable?" they ask. The answer is simple. Family Code section 2201 does not declare marriages that fall into the "presumed dead/missing" category to be void. In fact, section 2201 specifically recites that such marriages are *not* void. A bigamous (or polygamous) marriage is only void if the subsequent marriage is entered into "during the *life* of the former husband or wife of the person." If the spouse is *not* alive (or at least presumed not to be alive), then the marriage is not declared void. Unfortunately, section 2201 does not indicate what *does* happen to the second marriage if the former spouse is missing or presumed dead. It merely eliminates a declaration of nullity as one of the options.

The result is explained, however, in 2201(b). When a party enters into a subsequent marriage under circumstances where the former spouse is missing or presumed dead, the *subsequent* marriage is *voidable*, not void, upon the timely request of either of the "new" spouses as well as the previously believed to be dead or missing spouse.

Section 2211(c) limits section 2210(c) actions to the injured party (or a relative or conservator of a person of unsound mind). There is no time limit for bringing this action. It can be brought at any time before the death of either party.

For marriages voidable by reason of fraud, the injured party must bring the action within four years of first discovering the facts constituting the fraud. When force is the issue, the action must be brought within four years of the marriage. This is also the case when dealing with issues of physical incapacity.

d) *The Putative Spouse*

Earlier in this book you learned basic concepts regarding the division of property and the determination of child and spousal support, child custody and visitation, and similar issues involved in terminating a marriage. For the most part, legal claims related to property and support are dependent upon the existence of a valid marriage and are lost following a decree of nullity.[12] As stated above, however, some provision is made to resolve these issues in the context of a void or voidable marriage as well. The concept at work is the desire not to "punish" an innocent party to one of these marriages who entered into the union in good faith and with the reasonable expectation that the marriage was valid.

Family Code section 2251 speaks to this issue and provides that, in the context of a void or voidable marriage, whenever one or both of the parties believed in good faith that the marriage was valid, the court shall decree such person(s) to have the status of *putative spouse* and as such be eligible to receive the benefits of the provisions of Family Code sections 2500 et seq. regarding property acquired during the "marriage" that would have been community or quasi-community[13] property had the marriage not been void or voidable.

Section 2254 of the Family Code provides that a putative spouse is also entitled to the benefits of an award of spousal support in the same manner as if the marriage had not been void or voidable. Section 2255 makes an award of attorney's fees and costs available to putative spouses, and section 2080 gives the court the power to restore the wife's former name to her following entry of a judgment of nullity. Of course, for the innocent spouse to qualify for putative status, he must in fact be "innocent" and unaware of the invalidity of the marriage. Without a good-faith belief in the validity of the marriage, such a spouse will not be allowed the benefits of putative status. In fact, on the other side of this coin is the "bad" spouse, who ostensibly knew about the defect and went forward with the marriage anyway. Under these circumstances not only will that spouse be denied putative status (for obvious reasons), he may also be denied the right to later raise the de facto invalidity of the marriage as a bar to a request for spousal support or other incidents of a putative marriage.

2. Dissolution and Legal Separation

In California the most common method of terminating a marital union is through the procedure of *dissolution*. California also offers an action that results in a decree of *legal separation*.[14] It is important to note, however, that an action for legal separation will *not* terminate the marriage. Procedurally these two actions are virtually identical; and, with the exception of the rather major distinction of the continuing marital union, the results available in a legal separation action are exactly the same as those obtained through dissolution. Issues of child custody and visitation, child and spousal support, attorney's fees and costs, property division, restraining orders, and other injunctive relief are all equally available whether through dissolution or legal separation. The same procedure is applied and the same forms are used in the prosecution of the action for legal separation and dissolution. The fundamental differences between these two procedures are noted below:

- A decree of legal separation does not end the marriage.
- There is no residency requirement to obtain a judgment of legal separation, whereas in dissolution actions, one of the parties must have been a resident of California for at least six months preceding the date on which the action was filed.
- There is no six-month "waiting period" before entry of a "final judgment" of legal separation, whereas Family Code section 2339 provides for such a waiting period in dissolution actions.
- A judgment of legal separation can only be obtained if *both* parties consent to it (absent entry of default against the respondent), whereas a decree of dissolution of marriage is available even over one party's objection.
- By proceeding with a legal separation instead of dissolution of marriage, certain "marriage dependent" benefits will continue to be available. For example, many policies of health insurance provided by employers provide coverage for a non-employee spouse.

By proceeding with a legal separation instead of dissolution, the non-employee continues to be treated as the spouse of the covered employee and may still be entitled to health care. Following a judgment of dissolution, such is not the case.

- A dissolution can restore the wife's maiden name. Legal separation cannot.
- A "legally separated" spouse retains the benefits of being a surviving spouse contained in the Probate Code. A decree of dissolution terminates these rights.
- An action for legal separation may be much more tolerable for certain persons for religious or moral reasons than one for dissolution.

The grounds for obtaining a dissolution and legal separation are the same and are found in Family Code section 2310: irreconcilable differences and incurable insanity. These concepts are the result of the enactment of the Family Law Act (FLA) in 1970 and the introduction of the concept of no-fault divorce.[15]

Incurable insanity, while available, is virtually never used as grounds for a dissolution action. This is because the existence of irreconcilable differences is extremely easy to prove and also because the existence of incurable insanity on the part of one of the spouses would most certainly also equate with irreconcilable differences. Also, to prove incurable insanity requires introduction of medical expert opinion testimony attesting to the party's incurable insanity at the time the Petition is filed and its continuance through the hearing on the dissolution. Sections 2312 and 2313 address incurable insanity as a ground for dissolving the marriage in greater detail. The reader is invited to review those sections for further details.

While it is not difficult to establish the existence of "irreconcilable differences," it is harder to define this term. Family Code section 2311 defines this term as follows: "Irreconcilable differences are those grounds which are determined by the court to be substantial reasons for not continuing the marriage and which make it appear that the marriage should be dissolved." Does that clear it up for you? If you answered "no," you are not alone. As nonspecific as section 2311 appears to be on its face, in practice all that is necessary is a judicial determination that there are "substantial reasons" to end the marriage. These are usually found when one party testifies that the marriage is, in her opinion and belief, over and not capable of being saved. Usually the court simply accepts this statement and does not inquire further into the reasons for this belief. Simply put, for all practical purposes the marriage is over when one of the parties says it is over.

3. Summary Dissolution

Under certain limited and strict circumstances, parties to a marriage may be able to avail themselves of the statutory procedure known as *summary dissolution.* This process is quick and inexpensive and is designed to be obtained easily and without participation by attorneys. The clerk's office provides a rather lengthy booklet that contains all of the necessary forms along with detailed instructions for their preparation and subsequent filing. A summary dissolution procedure does not require a court hearing or appearance and is set out in detail in Family Code sections 2400 et seq.

Summary dissolution is only available if *all* of the following conditions are met:

- At least one party has been a resident of California for six months and the county in which the action is commenced for at least three months before the action is filed.
- Irreconcilable differences have caused an "irremedial breakdown" of the marriage, and the marriage should be dissolved.
- There are no children of the relationship.[16]
- The wife is not pregnant.
- The parties were married to each other for no more than five years before the petition for summary dissolution was filed.
- Neither party owns any interest in any real property except a *lease* of the residence in which they live, so long as the lease does not contain an option to purchase the property.[17] Further, such a lease must terminate by its own terms within one year of filing the petition.
- There were no debts incurred during the marriage by either of the spouses greater than $4,000[18] with the exception of a car loan.
- The total fair market value of all assets acquired during the marriage (that is, community assets) does not exceed $25,000 (with the exception of automobiles), and neither party has separate property assets (except automobiles) that exceed $25,000[19] in value.
- The parties have signed an agreement dividing all their assets and debts and have also signed all other documents necessary to transfer title of assets to give effect to the terms of the agreement.
- Both parties waived all rights to spousal support, and to request an appeal or new trial.
- The parties indicated to the court that they read and understood the brochure contemplated in Family Code section 2406, and they wish to dissolve the marriage.

Although there are several hurdles to clear before obtaining a summary dissolution, in the right circumstances it can be a quick and inexpensive way for parties to dissolve their marriage. While the Family code contains provisions to revoke a petition for summary dissolution or to challenge a judgment made pertinent to its provisions,[20] such action is rare. Inasmuch as this area of family law is one in which the paralegal may spend a great deal of time, it is strongly suggested that the reader become thoroughly familiar with the provisions of Family Code sections 2400 to 2406 as well as the brochure supplied by the court and described in Family Code section 2406.

D. The Summons

One of the documents that must be prepared and accompany the Petition when taken to the clerk's office for filing is the *Summons*. This document is *issued* by the court clerk and acts as an officially issued document that gives notice to the respondent that legal proceedings have been instituted against him and advises him to retain counsel. The *original* Summons as issued by the clerk is *not* given to the respondent. A copy of that document is served on the respondent along with the Petition, and the original is kept by the petitioner (or her attorney). It is important for the petitioner to keep the original Summons because if the respondent fails to timely respond, the petitioner must produce it to obtain a judgment of default. This requirement of service is discussed in Family Code section 2331.

If after 30 days following service, the petitioner does not receive a response (or other acceptable responsive document), the petitioner should file a Request to Enter Default (form FL-165) with the court clerk; the petitioner must also include the original summons (to prove that it was issued) and the original proof of service (to prove that the papers were served). Once the clerk has received form FL-165, the original summons, and the original proof of service, he or she will file the original summons. This is the procedure used to obtain entry of petitioner's default, a procedure discussed in greater detail later in this chapter.

Assuming all the other papers are in order and it is otherwise appropriate, the clerk will also enter the respondent's default. This will not happen, however, if the original summons is not available. If the original summons is lost or destroyed, there are procedures for obtaining a replacement; these tend to be somewhat complicated and time-consuming, however. These procedures are discussed at Code of Civil Procedure section 417.30.

Proper service is extremely important in the context of a legal proceeding because it is necessary to satisfy due process considerations, namely notice and the opportunity to be heard. Improper service can, absent a general appearance entered by the respondent, result in a *void* judgment. As discussed above, a void judgment completely lacks power over the respondent. It need not be obeyed and can be attacked and set aside at any time.

We will not discuss the proper methods for service of process. For complete information on this subject, please review Code of Civil Procedure sections 413.10 et seq. and the California Rules of Court. Note, however, that a party subpoenas, writs, and orders to show cause for contempt. As a general rule, all other pleadings, motions, and papers may be served by mail.[21]

Once the petitioner serves the Petition and Summons, the person who actually physically served the documents (the attorney's courier, for example) must complete a separate document known as a "proof of service." The attorney maintains the proof of service until it files it with the court.

When reviewing the Family Law Summons, it is important to examine the back side. The Code of Civil Procedure requires that Automatic Temporary Restraining Orders be included as part of the commencement of a Family Code proceeding. Family Code sections 213, et. seq. provide for the *automatic* issuance of temporary restraining orders against both the petitioner (effective when the summons is issued by the clerk) *and* the respondent (effective once the respondent has been personally served with the summons and petition). These orders are self-explanatory and are printed on the back side of the family law summons. They are primarily designed to maintain the status quo between the parties during that time after filing the petition and before a court hearing. Figure 8-2 is a reproduction of these orders as they appear on the summons (form FL-110).

Because the court may find a party in contempt of court for violating these orders,[22] the attorney should explain them in detail to the petitioner before the summons is issued and to the respondent at the very first opportunity following service of these documents. These orders are also found in Family Code section 2040 and are covered somewhat extensively in Part 3 of Division 2 of the Family Code, specifically sections 231 to 235. These sections statutorily mandate the inclusion of these orders on the summons and provide some insight into their operation. Section 233 discusses the enforcement of these orders and the manner in which they become effective (on the petitioner when the Summons is issued, on the respondent when it is served); and section 235 authorizes modifications of these orders by the court upon a showing of good cause.

Figure 8-2

Form FL-110—Standard Family Law Restraining Orders

FL-110

SUMMONS (Family Law)	CITACIÓN (Derecho familiar)

NOTICE TO RESPONDENT *(Name):*

AVISO AL DEMANDADO (Nombre):

You are being sued. *Lo están demandando.*	**FOR COURT USE ONLY** *(SÓLO PARA USO DE LA CORTE)*

Petitioner's name is:

Nombre del demandante:

CASE NUMBER *(NÚMERO DE CASO):*

You have **30 calendar days** after this *Summons* and *Petition* are served on you to file a *Response* (form FL-120 or FL-123) at the court and have a copy served on the petitioner. A letter or phone call will not protect you.	*Tiene 30 días corridos después de haber recibido la entrega legal de esta Citación y Petición para presentar una Respuesta (formulario FL-120 ó FL-123) ante la corte y efectuar la entrega legal de una copia al demandante. Una carta o llamada telefónica no basta para protegerlo.*
If you do not file your *Response* on time, the court may make orders affecting your marriage or domestic partnership, your property, and custody of your children. You may be ordered to pay support and attorney fees and costs. If you cannot pay the filing fee, ask the clerk for a fee waiver form.	*Si no presenta su Respuesta a tiempo, la corte puede dar órdenes que afecten su matrimonio o pareja de hecho, sus bienes y la custodia de sus hijos. La corte también le puede ordenar que pague manutención, y honorarios y costos legales. Si no puede pagar la cuota de presentación, pida al secretario un formulario de exención de cuotas.*
If you want legal advice, contact a lawyer immediately. You can get information about finding lawyers at the California Courts Online Self-Help Center *(www.courtinfo.ca.gov/selfhelp),* at the California Legal Services Web site *(www.lawhelpcalifornia.org),* or by contacting your local county bar association.	*Si desea obtener asesoramiento legal, póngase en contacto de inmediato con un abogado. Puede obtener información para encontrar a un abogado en el Centro de Ayuda de las Cortes de California (www.sucorte.ca.gov), en el sitio Web de los Servicios Legales de California (www.lawhelpcalifornia.org) o poniéndose en contacto con el colegio de abogados de su condado.*

NOTICE: The restraining orders on page 2 are effective against both spouses or domestic partners until the petition is dismissed, a judgment is entered, or the court makes further orders. These orders are enforceable anywhere in California by any law enforcement officer who has received or seen a copy of them.

AVISO: *Las órdenes de restricción que figuran en la página 2 valen para ambos cónyuges o pareja de hecho hasta que se despida la petición, se emita un fallo o la corte dé otras órdenes. Cualquier autoridad de la ley que haya recibido o visto una copia de estas órdenes puede hacerlas acatar en cualquier lugar de California.*

NOTE: If a judgment or support order is entered, the court may order you to pay all or part of the fees and costs that the court waived for yourself or for the other party. If this happens, the party ordered to pay fees shall be given notice and an opportunity to request a hearing to set aside the order to pay waived court fees.

AVISO: *Si se emite un fallo u orden de manutención, la corte puede ordenar que usted pague parte de, o todas las cuotas y costos de la corte previamente exentas a petición de usted o de la otra parte. Si esto ocurre, la parte ordenada a pagar estas cuotas debe recibir aviso y la oportunidad de solicitar una audiencia para anular la orden de pagar las cuotas exentas.*

1. The name and address of the court are *(El nombre y dirección de la corte son):*

2. The name, address, and telephone number of the petitioner's attorney, or the petitioner without an attorney, are:
   (El nombre, dirección y número de teléfono del abogado del demandante, o del demandante si no tiene abogado, son):

Date *(Fecha):* _____ Clerk, by *(Secretario, por)*_____, Deputy *(Asistente)*

[SEAL]	**NOTICE TO THE PERSON SERVED:** You are served
	AVISO A LA PERSONA QUE RECIBIÓ LA ENTREGA: Esta entrega se realiza

a. ☐ as an individual. *(a usted como individuo.)*

b. ☐ on behalf of respondent who is a *(en nombre de un demandado que es):*

(1) ☐ minor *(menor de edad)*

(2) ☐ ward or conservatee *(dependiente de la corte o pupilo)*

(3) ☐ other *(specify) (otro – especifique):*

(Read the reverse for important information.) *(Lea importante información al dorso.)* Page 1 of 2

Form Adopted for Mandatory Use Judicial Council of California FL-110 [Rev. July 1, 2009]	**SUMMONS** **(Family Law)**	Family Code §§ 232, 233, 2040,7700; Code of Civil Procedure, §§ 412.20, 416.60—416.90 Government Code, § 68637 www.courtinfo.ca.gov

Figure 8-2 (continued)

WARNING—IMPORTANT INFORMATION

WARNING: California law provides that, for purposes of division of property upon dissolution of a marriage or domestic partnership or upon legal separation, property acquired by the parties during marriage or domestic partnership in joint form is presumed to be community property. If either party to this action should die before the jointly held community property is divided, the language in the deed that characterizes how title is held (i.e., joint tenancy, tenants in common, or community property) will be controlling, and not the community property presumption. You should consult your attorney if you want the community property presumption to be written into the recorded title to the property.

STANDARD FAMILY LAW RESTRAINING ORDERS

Starting immediately, you and your spouse or domestic partner are restrained from

1. Removing the minor child or children of the parties, if any, from the state without the prior written consent of the other party or an order of the court;

2. Cashing, borrowing against, canceling, transferring, disposing of, or changing the beneficiaries of any insurance or other coverage, including life, health, automobile, and disability, held for the benefit of the parties and their minor child or children;

3. Transferring, encumbering, hypothecating, concealing, or in any way disposing of any property, real or personal, whether community, quasi-community, or separate, without the written consent of the other party or an order of the court, except in the usual course of business or for the necessities of life; and

4. Creating a nonprobate transfer or modifying a nonprobate transfer in a manner that affects the disposition of property subject to the transfer, without the written consent of the other party or an order of the court. Before revocation of a nonprobate transfer can take effect or a right of survivorship to property can be eliminated, notice of the change must be filed and served on the other party.

You must notify each other of any proposed extraordinary expenditures at least five business days prior to incurring these extraordinary expenditures and account to the court for all extraordinary expenditures made after these restraining orders are effective. However, you may use community property, quasi-community property, or your own separate property to pay an attorney to help you or to pay court costs.

ADVERTENCIA – INFORMACIÓN IMPORTANTE

ADVERTENCIA: De acuerdo a la ley de California, las propiedades adquiridas por las partes durante su matrimonio o pareja de hecho en forma conjunta se consideran propiedad comunitaria para los fines de la división de bienes que ocurre cuando se produce una disolución o separación legal del matrimonio o pareja de hecho. Si cualquiera de las partes de este caso llega a fallecer antes de que se divida la propiedad comunitaria de tenencia conjunta, el destino de la misma quedará determinado por las cláusulas de la escritura correspondiente que describen su tenencia (por ej., tenencia conjunta, tenencia en común o propiedad comunitaria) y no por la presunción de propiedad comunitaria. Si quiere que la presunción comunitaria quede registrada en la escritura de la propiedad, debería consultar con un abogado.

ÓRDENES DE RESTRICCIÓN NORMALES DE DERECHO FAMILIAR

En forma inmediata, usted y su cónyuge o pareja de hecho tienen prohibido:

1. *Llevarse del estado de California a los hijos menores de las partes, si los hubiera, sin el consentimiento previo por escrito de la otra parte o una orden de la corte;*

2. *Cobrar, pedir prestado, cancelar, transferir, deshacerse o cambiar el nombre de los beneficiarios de cualquier seguro u otro tipo de cobertura, tal como de vida, salud, vehículo y discapacidad, que tenga como beneficiario(s) a las partes y su(s) hijo(s) menor(es);*

3. *Transferir, gravar, hipotecar, ocultar o deshacerse de cualquier manera de cualquier propiedad, inmueble o personal, ya sea comunitaria, cuasicomunitaria o separada, sin el consentimiento escrito de la otra parte o una orden de la corte, con excepción las operaciones realizadas en el curso normal de actividades o para satisfacer las necesidades de la vida; y*

4. *Crear o modificar una transferencia no testamentaria de manera que afecte el destino de una propiedad sujeta a transferencia, sin el consentimiento por escrito de la otra parte o una orden de la corte. Antes de que se pueda eliminar la revocación de una transferencia no testamentaria, se debe presentar ante la corte un aviso del cambio y hacer una entrega legal de dicho aviso a la otra parte.*

Cada parte tiene que notificar a la otra sobre cualquier gasto extraordinario propuesto, por lo menos cinco días laborales antes de realizarlo, y rendir cuenta a la corte de todos los gastos extraordinarios realizados después de que estas órdenes de restricción hayan entrado en vigencia. No obstante, puede usar propiedad comunitaria, cuasicomunitaria o suya separada para pagar a un abogado o para ayudarle a pagar los costos de la corte.

FL-110 [Rev. July 1, 2009]

SUMMONS
(Family Law)

Page 2 of 2

E. The Initial Filing

Once the attorney completes the initial client interview, he may officially commence the proceedings. If he represents the petitioner, the attorney typically must prepare the initial papers needed to petition the court for relief (in the family law context), including the Summons and Petition at the very least. With the exception of the summons, which is not prepared by the responding party, the respondent must complete documents that are substantially similar to the petitioner's, at least at the outset.

These initial papers (and, in fact, almost all of the papers used in a family law proceeding), are actually preprinted forms, which are filled out and modified as needed. These forms are, for the most part, designed and promulgated by the California Judicial Council. They are available at the court clerk's office in virtually every county courthouse.

Most of the forms available for use in family law proceedings are mandatory and *must* be used. Others are simply optional, although whenever a form is available it is advisable to use it rather than try to custom-make your own document. The easiest way to tell the difference is by looking in the lower left corner of the form. This space indicates whether a form has been *adopted* for use (mandatory) or merely *approved* for use (optional).

It is important to take several precautions when using these forms. Most notably, check and recheck them for accuracy before submitting them to be filed. Mistakes are usually made due to their ease of use. As can be seen from a review of the petition set forth in Figure 8-3 on pages 327 and 328, preparation of this form consists primarily of checking boxes. Checking the wrong box or missing one altogether can have severe consequences. These are, after all, court documents. They are taken quite literally and at face value by the court so there is little (if any) margin for error.

These forms can be modified as needed, and extra pages can be attached to provide information that does not otherwise fit into the space provided. Of course, care must be taken to ensure that the most current form is used. They are amended regularly, and use of an old form could result in its rejection by the court clerk, which could prove embarrassing at the least and damaging at the worst.

1. The Petition and Response Forms

We will discuss the Petition and the Response together because they are virtually identical, except for a few relatively minor differences. The two documents are the rough equivalent to the complaint and answer in a non-family law proceeding and can generally be described as "position papers." Essentially, the parties set forth the nature of their request

Figure 8-3
Form FL-100—Petition

FL-100

ATTORNEY OR PARTY WITHOUT ATTORNEY *(Name, State Bar number, and address):*	FOR COURT USE ONLY

TELEPHONE NO.:   FAX NO. *(Optional):*

E-MAIL ADDRESS *(Optional):*

ATTORNEY FOR *(Name):*

SUPERIOR COURT OF CALIFORNIA, COUNTY OF

STREET ADDRESS:

MAILING ADDRESS:

CITY AND ZIP CODE:

BRANCH NAME:

MARRIAGE OF

PETITIONER:

RESPONDENT:

PETITION FOR	CASE NUMBER:
☐ **Dissolution of Marriage**	
☐ **Legal Separation**	
☐ **Nullity of Marriage** ☐ **AMENDED**	

1. RESIDENCE (Dissolution only) ☐ Petitioner ☐ Respondent has been a resident of this state for at least six months and of this county for at least three months immediately preceding the filing of this *Petition for Dissolution of Marriage.*

2. STATISTICAL FACTS
   a. Date of marriage: c. Time from date of marriage to date of separation *(specify):*
   b. Date of separation: Years: Months:

3. DECLARATION REGARDING MINOR CHILDREN *(include children of this relationship born prior to or during the marriage or adopted during the marriage):*
   a. ☐ There are no minor children.
   b. ☐ The minor children are:

Child's name	Birthdate	Age	Sex

    ☐ Continued on Attachment 3b.
   c. If there are minor children of the Petitioner and Respondent, a completed *Declaration Under Uniform Child Custody Jurisdiction and Enforcement Act (UCCJEA)* (form FL-105) must be attached.
   d. ☐ A completed voluntary declaration of paternity regarding minor children born to the Petitioner and Respondent prior to the marriage is attached.

4. SEPARATE PROPERTY
   Petitioner requests that the assets and debts listed ☐ in *Property Declaration* (form FL-160) ☐ in Attachment 4
   ☐ below be confirmed as separate property.
   Item   Confirm to

NOTICE: You may redact (black out) social security numbers from any written material filed with the court in this case other than a form used to collect child or spousal support.

Page 1 of 2

Form Adopted for Mandatory Use Judicial Council of California FL-100 [Rev. January 1, 2005]	**PETITION—MARRIAGE** **(Family Law)**	Family Code, §§ 2330, 3409; www.courtinfo.ca.gov

Figure 8-3 (continued)

MARRIAGE OF *(last name, first name of parties):*	CASE NUMBER:

5. DECLARATION REGARDING COMMUNITY AND QUASI-COMMUNITY ASSETS AND DEBTS AS CURRENTLY KNOWN
   a. ☐ There are no such assets or debts subject to disposition by the court in this proceeding.
   b. ☐ All such assets and debts are listed ☐ in *Property Declaration* (form FL-160) ☐ in Attachment 5b.
   ☐ below *(specify):*

6. **Petitioner requests**
   a. ☐ dissolution of the marriage based on
      (1) ☐ irreconcilable differences. (Fam. Code, § 2310(a).)
      (2) ☐ incurable insanity. (Fam. Code, § 2310(b).)
   b. ☐ legal separation of the parties based on
      (1) ☐ irreconcilable differences. (Fam. Code, § 2310(a).)
      (2) ☐ incurable insanity. (Fam. Code, § 2310(b).)
   c. ☐ nullity of void marriage based on
      (1) ☐ incestuous marriage. (Fam. Code, § 2200.)
      (2) ☐ bigamous marriage. (Fam. Code, § 2201.)

   d. ☐ nullity of voidable marriage based on
      (1) ☐ petitioner's age at time of marriage. (Fam. Code, § 2210(a).)
      (2) ☐ prior existing marriage. (Fam. Code, § 2210(b).)
      (3) ☐ unsound mind. (Fam. Code, § 2210(c).)
      (4) ☐ fraud. (Fam. Code, § 2210(d).)
      (5) ☐ force. (Fam. Code, § 2210(e).)
      (6) ☐ physical incapacity. (Fam. Code, § 2210(f).)

7. **Petitioner requests** that the court grant the above relief and make injunctive (including restraining) and other orders as follows:

	Petitioner	Respondent	Joint	Other
a. Legal custody of children to	☐	☐	☐	☐
b. Physical custody of children to	☐	☐	☐	☐
c. Child visitation be granted to	☐	☐	☐	☐

   As requested in form: ☐ FL-311 ☐ FL-312 ☐ FL-341(C) ☐ FL-341(D) ☐ FL-341(E) ☐ Attachment 7c.
   d. ☐ Determination of parentage of any children born to the Petitioner and Respondent prior to the marriage.
   e. Attorney fees and costs payable by .... ☐ ☐
   f. Spousal support payable to (earnings assignment will be issued) .... ☐ ☐
   g. ☐ Terminate the court's jurisdiction (ability) to award spousal support to Respondent.
   h. ☐ Property rights be determined.
   i. ☐ Petitioner's former name be restored to *(specify):*
   j. ☐ Other *(specify):*

   ☐ Continued on Attachment 7j.

8. **Child support**–If there are minor children born to or adopted by the Petitioner and Respondent before or during this marriage, the court will make orders for the support of the children upon request and submission of financial forms by the requesting party. An earnings assignment may be issued without further notice. Any party required to pay support must pay interest on overdue amounts at the "legal" rate, which is currently 10 percent.

9. **I HAVE READ THE RESTRAINING ORDERS ON THE BACK OF THE SUMMONS, AND I UNDERSTAND THAT THEY APPLY TO ME WHEN THIS PETITION IS FILED.**

I declare under penalty of perjury under the laws of the State of California that the foregoing is true and correct.

Date:

▶

_____
(TYPE OR PRINT NAME)

(SIGNATURE OF PETITIONER)

Date:

▶

_____
(TYPE OR PRINT NAME)

(SIGNATURE OF ATTORNEY FOR PETITIONER)

NOTICE: Dissolution or legal separation may automatically cancel the rights of a spouse under the other spouse's will, trust, retirement plan, power of attorney, pay on death bank account, survivorship rights to any property owned in joint tenancy, and any other similar thing. It does not automatically cancel the right of a spouse as beneficiary of the other spouse's life insurance policy. You should review these matters, as well as any credit cards, other credit accounts, insurance polices, retirement plans, and credit reports to determine whether they should be changed or whether you should take any other actions. However, some changes may require the agreement of your spouse or a court order (see Family Code sections 231–235).

FL-100 [Rev. January 1, 2005]	**PETITION—MARRIAGE** **(Family Law)**	Page 2 of 2

(dissolution of marriage, legal separation, or nullity); the contentions as to basic statistical information (date of marriage and date of separation); the property rights (both separate and community); and the various requests pertinent to issues of custody and visitation of children, support (spousal and child), and attorney's fees and costs. Both of these forms are *adopted* by the judicial council, which means that their use is *mandatory*.

The Petition (form FL-100) is the form used whenever a party seeks to change his marital status whether by dissolution, legal separation, or nullity. Once this document is properly completed and filed, the proceeding has started. With the exception of a summary dissolution proceeding (which uses a different form of petition), the Petition is the only document that can be used to alter one's marital state.

The Petition and the Response (form FL-120) are substantially identical both in structure and substance. In fact, nearly all of the judicial council forms are laid out in a similar manner. The first section of these forms contains basic information regarding the parties, the attorney representing the party filing the form, the case number (if it has been assigned), and the location of the court. Figure 8-4 illustrates this basic format. For instructional purposes, this book labels each separate area of the section with a letter. (They are not so labeled in actually use.)

Section A is sometimes called the "card."[23] In this area the author of the document inserts his or her name, address, and telephone number. This person is usually the attorney, and that relationship is set out following the words, "ATTORNEY FOR (Name)," for example, "ATTORNEY FOR (Name): *Petitioner, John Doe*." Yet, because a party is not required to use an attorney, if she chooses to represent herself, she can simply insert the words, "In Pro Per"[24] in this space.

The next section, labeled B, contains information about the location of the superior court in which the matter is set for hearing. Recall that an action can generally be filed either in the county seat or in the *branch* court in which the petitioner resides. Further, the proper county for trial of a dissolution action is that in which the petitioner has been residing for at least three months immediately preceding commencement of the action.[25] The street, mailing address, and branch name can be obtained either from a court directory (these are readily available) or directly from the court.

Section C concerns itself with the title of the action and identifies the parties involved in the litigation. The petitioner is the person who commences the action, while the respondent is the person who must respond.[26] The full legal names of the spouses should be placed here along with any aliases they may use.

Section D contains the choices pertinent to the relief requested. Check whichever one is appropriate. One of the choices simply advises the court that a declaration under the Uniform Child Custody Jurisdiction Act has

Figure 8-4
Informational Portion of the Petition

ATTORNEY OR PARTY WITHOUT ATTORNEY *(Name, State Bar number, and address):*	FOR COURT USE ONLY
TELEPHONE NO.: FAX NO. *(Optional):* E-MAIL ADDRESS *(Optional):* ATTORNEY FOR *(Name):*	
SUPERIOR COURT OF CALIFORNIA, COUNTY OF STREET ADDRESS: MAILING ADDRESS: CITY AND ZIP CODE: BRANCH NAME:	
MARRIAGE OF PETITIONER: RESPONDENT:	
PETITION FOR ☐ **Dissolution of Marriage** ☐ **Legal Separation** ☐ **Nullity of Marriage** ☐ **AMENDED**	CASE NUMBER:

been attached to the Petition. (The propriety of attaching this form is addressed below in Step 3 of the Petition.)

Section E is the area in which the case number is placed. If filing a Petition, there will be no case number until the clerk of the court assigns one to the case. Once the clerk assigns a case number, that number appears in this area on all subsequent filings.

Section F is for use by the court *only*. The litigants or their attorneys do not insert anything in this space. Only the court clerk uses this space, usually to place filing stamps and items of primary interest to the court.

As can be seen from Figure 8-5, this portion of the Response (form FL-120) is virtually identical to the Petition.

Note that in area D of the Response the respondent need not request the same relief as was sought in the Petition. In fact, the respondent need not request any relief at all, and may simply proceed according to petitioner's request. However, if the petitioner requests a legal separation, the respondent can respond with a request for dissolution of marriage and thus deny the petitioner that avenue of relief (you will recall that a legal separation can only be obtained if both parties consent to it).

The balance of the Petition is identified by numbered items on the form itself. These numbered items on the Response form (for the most part) correspond to the numbers used in the Petition. Figure 8-6 on page 332 reflects the balance of the first (front) page of the Petition.

These sections will be discussed in numerical order:

1. Simply check the appropriate box. This establishes a jurisdictional component to the filing.
2. This section contains information required by Family Code section 2330. Its importance becomes evident during the discussion of community property earlier in this book.

Figure 8-5
Informational Portion of the Response

		FL-120
ATTORNEY OR PARTY WITHOUT ATTORNEY *(Name, State Bar number, and address)*:		FOR COURT USE ONLY
TELEPHONE NO.: FAX NO. *(Optional)*: E-MAIL ADDRESS *(Optional)*: ATTORNEY FOR *(Name)*:		
SUPERIOR COURT OF CALIFORNIA, COUNTY OF STREET ADDRESS: MAILING ADDRESS: CITY AND ZIP CODE: BRANCH NAME:		
MARRIAGE OF PETITIONER: RESPONDENT:		
RESPONSE ☐ and REQUEST FOR ☐ Dissolution of Marriage ☐ Legal Separation ☐ Nullity of Marriage ☐ AMENDED		CASE NUMBER:

3. This rather self-explanatory item seeks information relative to the minor child(ren) of the marriage. If there are minor children of the marriage, then item 3 instructs that a separate form must be completed and attached. This is form FL-105 and is entitled "Declaration Under Uniform Child Custody Jurisdiction and Enforcement Act (UCCJEA)."

The UCCJEA declaration breaks down the five-year period preceding the filing and requests the residence address and guardian information for each child during this time span. It also requests information relating to other actions involving these children that may be pending in other jurisdictions. The purpose of this form is to allow the court to make a determination as to the propriety of asserting jurisdiction over the children of this union. The UCCJEA is discussed at length elsewhere in this book.

4. This area requests information related to which property is claimed by the petitioner (or the respondent on the Response form) to be *separate* property (as opposed to community property). An additional sheet may be added, labeled "Attachment 4," if there is not enough space on the form itself to list all the items claimed to be separate property. Of course, the determination of exactly what items fall into this category will be much clearer once the reader has studied this book's sections on property characterization.

Some attorneys do not list the separate property, but instead use rather vague language in an effort to avoid restrictions. An example of such language is as follows: "The [petitioner or respondent] is unaware of the exact nature, scope and extent of the separate property and will seek leave to amend this [Petition or Response] when same has been ascertained."

Figure 8-6
Items 1 to 4 of the Petition

1. RESIDENCE (Dissolution only) ☐ Petitioner ☐ Respondent has been a resident of this state for at least six months and of this county for at least three months immediately preceding the filing of this *Petition for Dissolution of Marriage*.

2. STATISTICAL FACTS
   a. Date of marriage:
   b. Date of separation:

   c. Time from date of marriage to date of separation *(specify)*:
   Years: Months:

3. DECLARATION REGARDING MINOR CHILDREN *(include children of this relationship born prior to or during the marriage or adopted during the marriage)*:
   a. ☐ There are no minor children.
   b. ☐ The minor children are:

Child's name	Birthdate	Age	Sex

   ☐ Continued on Attachment 3b.
   c. If there are minor children of the Petitioner and Respondent, a completed *Declaration Under Uniform Child Custody Jurisdiction and Enforcement Act (UCCJEA)* (form FL-105) must be attached.
   d. ☐ A completed voluntary declaration of paternity regarding minor children born to the Petitioner and Respondent prior to the marriage is attached.

4. SEPARATE PROPERTY
   Petitioner requests that the assets and debts listed ☐ in *Property Declaration* (form FL-160) ☐ in Attachment 4
   ☐ below be confirmed as separate property.
   Item   Confirm to

NOTICE: You may redact (black out) social security numbers from any written material filed with the court in this case other than a form used to collect child or spousal support.

Page 1 of 2

Form Adopted for Mandatory Use
Judicial Council of California
FL-100 [Rev. January 1, 2005]

PETITION—MARRIAGE
(Family Law)

Family Code, §§ 2330, 3409;
www.courtinfo.ca.gov

American LegalNet, Inc.
www.USCourtForms.com

As a practical matter, this language is much simpler to use and certainly less time-consuming than taking the trouble to list and categorize the various items of property owned by the parties. Use of this language can have its drawbacks, however. In the event of a default (that is, the respondent chooses not to appear), the court is not empowered to enter any orders on matters not pleaded in the Petition with sufficient specificity to allow the respondent to have been deemed by the court to be "on notice" of the petitioner's intention to litigate that issue.

If language such as this is used and if at the default prove-up hearing (that is, default trial) the petitioner seeks to have specific items confirmed to him or her as separate property, the court will deny that request on the grounds that the general language used was not sufficient to put the respondent "on notice" that those requests would be made. Since the court will only proceed on issues for which sufficient and adequate notice was given, the petitioner is now faced with amending the Petition, finding and serving the respondent, and then waiting an additional 30 days to see if the respondent will default once again or file his Response and participate in the litigation.

All of this is time-consuming and expensive and can prove damaging to the petitioner's case. As such, this general language should only be used when the petitioner is absolutely certain that the respondent will *not* default and *will* participate in the action. Simply put, when in doubt, itemize these items at the beginning. The Petition can almost always be amended later if need be.

The back side of the Petition is set forth in Figure 8-7 on page 334. It follows the same form and order as that commenced on the front side (page 1). The separate items are discussed below:

5. This section is very similar to item 4, and the discussion immediately above applies here too. There are two choices:
   e. To be checked *only* if there are no assets or obligations at issue in the proceeding;
   f. If the parties have assets subject to division through a separate form (FL-160), an attachment, or the Petition itself.

The person who prepares this form must be *very careful* when entering this information. If the wrong box is checked, it can have devastating consequences to the client, not the least of which could be the loss of all rights to his or her share of the marital property.

Items 6 and 7 contain the various requests for relief made by the petitioner. Item 6 sets out the means by which the petitioner seeks to alter the marital status and the grounds supporting that request. Item 7 contains a laundry list of requests covering child custody, visitation, spousal support, and attorney's fees. Also included is a request for an award of costs.

The court's determination of property rights is also a specific item to be requested (or not) by checking box 7h. This box is only checked if item 5 was also checked.

In the area marked "other" (item 7j), such things as injunctive relief and restraining orders can be requested. Item 7i is self-explanatory (and not available in legal separation proceedings). (See Family Code section 2080.)

Note that there is no box next to item 8. In essence, this is a request that is *always* before the court whenever there are minor children of the marriage. In those cases, support for those children is always at issue, and the responding party is always on notice of this fact because it is not an option to be checked (or inadvertently missed) by the petitioning party.

The importance of carefully selecting (or not selecting) the various choices set out on the petition cannot be overstated, primarily because of concerns over due process. Whatever is checked (or not checked) puts the respondent on notice of what specific relief is being sought in the Petition. Any failure to specifically request certain relief will result in an automatic denial of a default judgment for that relief. The only exception to this rule concerns item 7i, restoration of the wife's former name. This is always available if desired by the wife's motion.[27]

Figure 8-7
Form FL-100—Petition Items 5 to 9

MARRIAGE OF *(last name, first name of parties):*	CASE NUMBER:

5. DECLARATION REGARDING COMMUNITY AND QUASI-COMMUNITY ASSETS AND DEBTS AS CURRENTLY KNOWN

   a. ☐ There are no such assets or debts subject to disposition by the court in this proceeding.

   b. ☐ All such assets and debts are listed ☐ in *Property Declaration* (form FL-160) ☐ in Attachment 5b.

       ☐ below *(specify):*

6. **Petitioner requests**

   a. ☐ dissolution of the marriage based on   d. ☐ nullity of voidable marriage based on

      (1) ☐ irreconcilable differences. (Fam. Code, § 2310(a).)   (1) ☐ petitioner's age at time of marriage.

      (2) ☐ incurable insanity. (Fam. Code, § 2310(b).)   (Fam. Code, § 2210(a).)

   b. ☐ legal separation of the parties based on   (2) ☐ prior existing marriage.

      (1) ☐ irreconcilable differences. (Fam. Code, § 2310(a).)   (Fam. Code, § 2210(b).)

      (2) ☐ incurable insanity. (Fam. Code, § 2310(b).)   (3) ☐ unsound mind. (Fam. Code, § 2210(c).)

   c. ☐ nullity of void marriage based on   (4) ☐ fraud. (Fam. Code, § 2210(d).)

      (1) ☐ incestuous marriage. (Fam. Code, § 2200.)   (5) ☐ force. (Fam. Code, § 2210(e).)

      (2) ☐ bigamous marriage. (Fam. Code, § 2201.)   (6) ☐ physical incapacity. (Fam. Code, § 2210(f).)

7. **Petitioner requests** that the court grant the above relief and make injunctive (including restraining) and other orders as follows:

	Petitioner	Respondent	Joint	Other
a. Legal custody of children to	☐	☐	☐	☐
b. Physical custody of children to	☐	☐	☐	☐
c. Child visitation be granted to	☐	☐		☐

     As requested in form: ☐ FL-311 ☐ FL-312 ☐ FL-341(C) ☐ FL-341(D) ☐ FL-341(E) ☐ Attachment 7c.

   d. ☐ Determination of parentage of any children born to the Petitioner and Respondent prior to the marriage.

   e. Attorney fees and costs payable by .... ☐ ☐

   f. Spousal support payable to (earnings assignment will be issued) .... ☐

   g. ☐ Terminate the court's jurisdiction (ability) to award spousal support to Respondent.

   h. ☐ Property rights be determined.

   i. ☐ Petitioner's former name be restored to *(specify):*

   j. ☐ Other *(specify):*

       ☐ Continued on Attachment 7j.

8. **Child support**—If there are minor children born to or adopted by the Petitioner and Respondent before or during this marriage, the court will make orders for the support of the children upon request and submission of financial forms by the requesting party. An earnings assignment may be issued without further notice. Any party required to pay support must pay interest on overdue amounts at the "legal" rate, which is currently 10 percent.

9. **I HAVE READ THE RESTRAINING ORDERS ON THE BACK OF THE SUMMONS, AND I UNDERSTAND THAT THEY APPLY TO ME WHEN THIS PETITION IS FILED.**

I declare under penalty of perjury under the laws of the State of California that the foregoing is true and correct.

Date: _____

▶

_____   _____
     (TYPE OR PRINT NAME)   (SIGNATURE OF PETITIONER)

Date: _____

▶

_____   _____
     (TYPE OR PRINT NAME)   (SIGNATURE OF ATTORNEY FOR PETITIONER)

NOTICE: Dissolution or legal separation may automatically cancel the rights of a spouse under the other spouse's will, trust, retirement plan, power of attorney, pay on death bank account, survivorship rights to any property owned in joint tenancy, and any other similar thing. It does not automatically cancel the right of a spouse as beneficiary of the other spouse's life insurance policy. You should review these matters, as well as any credit cards, other credit accounts, insurance polices, retirement plans, and credit reports to determine whether they should be changed or whether you should take any other actions. However, some changes may require the agreement of your spouse or a court order (see Family Code sections 231–235).

FL-100 [Rev. January 1, 2005]	**PETITION—MARRIAGE**	Page 2 of 2
	(Family Law)	

Item 9 contains an acknowledgment by the petitioner that the automatic temporary restraining orders set out on the back side of the Summons (discussed above) have been read and understood. Remember, the Petition is signed by the petitioner under penalty of perjury and thus has the same force and effect as testimony in court before a judge. Once signed, the petitioner concedes notice of these automatic temporary restraining orders, thus making them enforceable against the petitioner by contempt.

The signature portion of the form is self-explanatory. Note that the petitioner and his or her attorney must *personally* sign this section.

Figure 8-8, on pages 336 and 337, represents the first and second pages of the Response (form FL-120). This form is nearly identical to the Petition. The numbering, however, is different to provide the respondent an opportunity to contend that there was never a valid marriage or to deny the grounds set forth in the Petition.

2. Additional Options Available to the Respondent

The petitioner must file the Petition when he commences the proceedings. The respondent, however, does not necessarily have to file a Response.

Once served, the respondent must decide whether to submit to the court's jurisdiction or challenge the court's exercise of power over him. This decision is usually based on a contention by the respondent that the court does not have personal jurisdiction over him. Care must be taken, however, not to submit to such jurisdiction by the very act used to challenge it.[28] Family Code section 2012 does, however, make provision for appearances to contest certain orders while a motion to quash is pending without inadvertently submitting to the court's jurisdiction. To challenge jurisdiction, the respondent must make a *special appearance* and contest jurisdiction by filing a *motion to quash the service of summons*. This will have the effect, if successful, of denying the petitioner's attempt to seek relief against the respondent in that state.

Another motion available to the respondent is called a *motion to quash the proceeding*. The grounds for such a motion are specific and address themselves to the legal ability of the petitioner to institute the proceedings. The basis for such a motion is set out in detail in CRC 5.121 and includes challenges based on allegations that the petitioner lacks the capacity to file a lawsuit; the residence requirements have not been met; or, there is another action already pending between these parties on the same issues.

CRC 3.1326 gives the respondent the opportunity to request, by motion, that the venue (location) of the proceedings be changed. This is called a *motion to change venue.* The rules relating to venue and the grounds for changing venue can be found in C.C.P. sections 396 et. seq. Finally, CRC

**Figure 8-8
Form FL-120—Response**

FL-120

ATTORNEY OR PARTY WITHOUT ATTORNEY *(Name, State Bar number, and address)*:	FOR COURT USE ONLY
TELEPHONE NO.: FAX NO. *(Optional)*:	
E-MAIL ADDRESS *(Optional)*:	
ATTORNEY FOR *(Name)*:	

SUPERIOR COURT OF CALIFORNIA, COUNTY OF
STREET ADDRESS:
MAILING ADDRESS:
CITY AND ZIP CODE:
BRANCH NAME:

MARRIAGE OF
PETITIONER:
RESPONDENT:

RESPONSE ☐ and **REQUEST FOR**	CASE NUMBER:
☐ **Dissolution of Marriage**	
☐ **Legal Separation**	
☐ **Nullity of Marriage** ☐ AMENDED	

1. RESIDENCE (Dissolution only) ☐ Petitioner ☐ Respondent has been a resident of this state for at least six months and of this county for at least three months immediately preceding the filing of the *Petition for Dissolution of Marriage.*

2. STATISTICAL FACTS
   a. Date of marriage: c. Time from date of marriage to date of separation *(specify):*
   b. Date of separation: Years: Months:

3. DECLARATION REGARDING MINOR CHILDREN *(include children of this relationship born prior to or during the marriage or adopted during the marriage):*
   a. ☐ There are no minor children.
   b. ☐ The minor children are:

Child's name	Birthdate	Age	Sex

   ☐ Continued on Attachment 3b.
   c. If there are minor children of the Petitioner and Respondent, a completed *Declaration Under Uniform Child Custody Jurisdiction and Enforcement Act (UCCJEA)* (form FL-105) must be attached.
   d. ☐ A completed voluntary declaration of paternity regarding minor children born to the Petitioner and Respondent prior to the marriage is attached.

4. SEPARATE PROPERTY
   Respondent requests that the assets and debts listed ☐ in *Property Declaration* (form FL-160) ☐ in Attachment 4
   ☐ below be confirmed as separate property.

Item	Confirm to

NOTICE: You may redact (black out) social security numbers from any written material filed with the court in this case other than a form used to collect child or spousal support.

Form Adopted for Mandatory Use
Judicial Council of California
FL-120 [Rev. January 1, 2005]

RESPONSE—MARRIAGE
(Family Law)

Family Code, § 2020
www.courtinfo.ca.gov.

Figure 8-8 (continued)

MARRIAGE OF *(last name, first name of parties)*:	CASE NUMBER:

5. DECLARATION REGARDING COMMUNITY AND QUASI-COMMUNITY ASSETS AND DEBTS AS CURRENTLY KNOWN
   a. ☐ There are no such assets or debts subject to disposition by the court in this proceeding.
   b. ☐ All such assets and debts are listed ☐ in *Property Declaration* (form FL-160) ☐ in Attachment 5b.
        ☐ below *(specify):*

6. ☐ **Respondent contends** that the parties were never legally married.
7. ☐ **Respondent denies** the grounds set forth in item 6 of the petition.
8. **Respondent requests**
   a. ☐ dissolution of the marriage based on
       (1) ☐ irreconcilable differences. (Fam. Code, § 2310(a).)
       (2) ☐ incurable insanity. (Fam. Code, § 2310(b).)
   b. ☐ legal separation of the parties based on
       (1) ☐ irreconcilable differences. (Fam. Code, § 2310(a).)
       (2) ☐ incurable insanity. (Fam. Code, § 2310(b).)
   c. ☐ nullity of void marriage based on
       (1) ☐ incestuous marriage. (Fam. Code, § 2200.)
       (2) ☐ bigamous marriage. (Fam. Code, § 2201.)
   d. ☐ nullity of voidable marriage based on
       (1) ☐ respondent's age at time of marriage. (Fam. Code, § 2210(a).)
       (2) ☐ prior existing marriage. (Fam. Code, § 2210(b).)
       (3) ☐ unsound mind. (Fam. Code, § 2210(c).)
       (4) ☐ fraud. (Fam. Code, § 2210(d).)
       (5) ☐ force. (Fam. Code, § 2210(e).)
       (6) ☐ physical incapacity. (Fam. Code, § 2210(f).)

9. **Respondent requests** that the court grant the above relief and make injunctive (including restraining) and other orders as follows:

	Petitioner	Respondent	Joint	Other
a. Legal custody of children to	☐	☐	☐	☐
b. Physical custody of children to	☐	☐	☐	☐
c. Child visitation be granted to	☐	☐	☐	☐

       As requested in form: ☐ FL-311 ☐ FL-312 ☐ FL-341(C) ☐ FL-341(D) ☐ FL-341(E) ☐ Attachment 9c.
   d. ☐ Determination of parentage of any children born to the Petitioner and Respondent prior to the marriage.
   e. Attorney fees and costs payable by.................................... ☐ ☐
   f. Spousal support payable to (wage assignment will be issued) .... ☐ ☐
   g. ☐ Terminate the court's jurisdiction (ability) to award spousal support to Petitioner.
   h. ☐ Property rights be determined.
   i. ☐ Respondent's former name be restored to *(specify):*
   j. ☐ Other *(specify):*

        ☐ Continued on Attachment 9j.

10. **Child support–** If there are minor children born to or adopted by the Petitioner and Respondent before or during this marriage, the court will make orders for the support of the children upon request and submission of financial forms by the requesting party. An earnings assignment may be issued without further notice. Any party required to pay support must pay interest on overdue amounts at the "legal" rate, which is currently 10 percent.

I declare under penalty of perjury under the laws of the State of California that the foregoing is true and correct.

Date:

▶

_____   _____
(TYPE OR PRINT NAME)   (SIGNATURE OF RESPONDENT)

Date:

▶

_____   _____
(TYPE OR PRINT NAME)   (SIGNATURE OF ATTORNEY FOR RESPONDENT)

The original response must be filed in the court with proof of service of a copy on Petitioner.

FL-120 [Rev. January 1, 2005]   **RESPONSE—MARRIAGE**   Page 2 of 2
                         (Family Law)

3.1322 makes provision for filing a motion to strike (remove) certain items contained in the Petition not specifically required by FL-100. A similar motion can be made by the petitioner regarding improper items contained in the Response.

In addition to the preparation and filing of the Petition, the petitioner must also prepare a Summons (form FL-110).

3. Filing and Service Requirement

Once the various papers have been prepared, they must be *filed* with the appropriate office of the superior court clerk and then *served* on the responding party. The act of filing involves nothing particularly mystifying. Original and sufficient copies of the papers are delivered to the clerk of the superior court. The clerk files them (keeping the originals) and stamps the copies (to show that the originals were filed); the clerk then returns the copies to the person who filed the documents. A fee is involved for an initial filing (Petition and Response). This fee is currently about $320 for the Petition and roughly $320 for the Response. Indigent litigants can have this fee waived. It is always a good idea to call the clerk before making the trip to the courthouse to ensure that all local rules have been followed and that the proper fee is provided.

As indicated above, Family Code section 2331 mandates service of the Summons and the Petition on the respondent, while section 2020 addresses service of the Response on the petitioner.

F. Default and Uncontested Hearings

It is not uncommon for family law matters to resolve through default or uncontested proceedings. From a procedural standpoint (and as evident from the Summons), once the petitioner serves the Petition, the respondent has 30 days to either file and serve a Response or some other appropriate paper. If the respondent fails to file responsive papers within 30 days, the petitioner can ask the clerk to enter a default ruling against the respondent. If the clerk enters a default against the respondent, the respondent cannot participate in any aspect of the proceedings until and unless the default is set aside.[29]

A *default* arises when the respondent ignores the warnings printed on the Summons advising that he has a mere 30 days in which to respond to the Petition. Assuming that the respondent allows this 30-day period to come and go without filing a response, a motion to quash, or some other appropriate motion, the petitioner is free to request that the default of the respondent be entered by the court clerk. This is accomplished by preparing a document entitled "Request to Enter Default" on form FL-165, shown in Figure 8-9, which is then filed with the court clerk. The court clerk will examine the file, verify that service has been properly made upon the respondent,[30] and if it appears that 30 days has indeed elapsed since service of process and the respondent has failed to file a Response or some other appropriate motion, then the clerk will enter the respondent's default. A default severs the respondent's right to participate in the proceedings until the default is set aside.

As mentioned in earlier chapters of this book, great care must be taken with respect to proceeding on the default because the relief that can be obtained from the court pursuant to a default is limited to the relief requested in the Petition. To the extent that something is desired but not specifically requested in the Petition, it will not be allowed upon a default proceeding.

Once the Request to Enter Default is properly completed and filed with the court, the court clerk will enter the default of the respondent. The default reads as follows:

> The respondent cannot appear at the hearing on the uncontested matter, cannot file any papers, cannot make any objections to any of the requests made by the petitioner, is no longer entitled to further notice of the status of the proceedings, and for all practical purposes is "invisible" in the eyes of the court until such time as the default is set aside.[31]

At this time the matter can be set for hearing on the default "prove-up." At a typical prove–up, the petitioner makes a court appearance. He provides the court with paperwork and testimony to support the relief he requests. In some larger counties, the petitioner does not need to personally appear. He may simply file documentation and an evidentiary declaration with the court, along with a proposed judgment to be signed and entered by the court. As a general rule, barring some procedural deficiency, the court will sign the judgment and grant the relief as requested.

Obtaining entry of the respondent's default is only the first part of the process, however. Once that step is completed, there are several other papers that must be completed by the petitioner and submitted to the court. They include:

1. Declaration for Default or Uncontested Dissolution (form FL-170)
2. Income and Expense Declaration (form FL-150)[32]
3. Declaration of Disclosure (form FL-140)
4. Judgment (form FL-180)
5. Notice of Entry of Judgment (form FL-190) along with two *stamped* envelopes, one addressed to the petitioner and one addressed to the respondent

Figure 8-9
Form FL-165—Request to Enter Default

FL-165

ATTORNEY OR PARTY WITHOUT ATTORNEY *(Name, State Bar number, and address)*:	FOR COURT USE ONLY
TELEPHONE NO.: FAX NO. *(Optional)*: E-MAIL ADDRESS *(Optional)*: ATTORNEY FOR *(Name)*:	

SUPERIOR COURT OF CALIFORNIA, COUNTY OF

STREET ADDRESS:

MAILING ADDRESS:

CITY AND ZIP CODE:

BRANCH NAME:

PETITIONER:

RESPONDENT:

REQUEST TO ENTER DEFAULT	CASE NUMBER:

1. **To the clerk:** Please enter the default of the respondent who has failed to respond to the petition.

2. A completed *Income and Expense Declaration* (form FL-150) or *Financial Statement (Simplified)* (form FL-155)
   ☐ is attached ☐ is not attached.
   A completed *Property Declaration* (form FL-160) ☐ is attached ☐ is not attached
   because *(check at least one of the following)*:
   (a) ☐ there have been no changes since the previous filing.
   (b) ☐ the issues subject to disposition by the court in this proceeding are the subject of a written agreement.
   (c) ☐ there are no issues of child, spousal, or partner support or attorney fees and costs subject to determination by the court.
   (d) ☐ the petition does not request money, property, costs, or attorney fees. (Fam. Code, § 2330.5.)
   (e) ☐ there are no issues of division of community property.
   (f) ☐ this is an action to establish parental relationship.

Date:

_____ ▶ _____
(TYPE OR PRINT NAME)   (SIGNATURE OF [ATTORNEY FOR] PETITIONER)

3. **Declaration**
   a. ☐ No mailing is required because service was by publication or posting and the address of the respondent remains unknown.
   b. ☐ A copy of this *Request to Enter Default*, including any attachments and an envelope with sufficient postage, was provided to the court clerk, with the envelope addressed as follows *(address of the respondent's attorney or, if none, the respondent's last known address)*:

I declare under penalty of perjury under the laws of the State of California that the foregoing is true and correct.

Date:

_____ ▶ _____
(TYPE OR PRINT NAME)   (SIGNATURE OF DECLARANT)

FOR COURT USE ONLY
☐ *Request to Enter Default* mailed to the respondent or the respondent's attorney on *(date)*:   ☐ Default entered as requested on *(date)*:   ☐ Default **not** entered. Reason: Clerk, by _____ , Deputy

Page 1 of 2

Form Adopted for Mandatory Use Judicial Council of California FL-165 [Rev. January 1, 2005]	**REQUEST TO ENTER DEFAULT** **(Family Law—Uniform Parentage)**	Code of Civil Procedure, §§ 585, 587; Family Code, § 2335.5 *www.courtinfo.ca.gov*

Figure 8-9 (continued)

CASE NAME *(Last name, first name of each party):*	CASE NUMBER:

4. **Memorandum of costs**

    a. ☐ Costs and disbursements are waived.

    b. Costs and disbursements are listed as follows:

        (1) ☐ Clerk's fees .... $..............................

        (2) ☐ Process server's fees .... $..............................

        (3) ☐ Other *(specify):* .... $..............................

        .... $..............................

        .... $..............................

        .... $ _____

    TOTAL .... $..............................

    c. I am the attorney, agent, or party who claims these costs. To the best of my knowledge and belief, the foregoing items of cost are correct and have been necessarily incurred in this cause or proceeding.

I declare under penalty of perjury under the laws of the State of California that the foregoing is true and correct.

Date:

_____   ▶   _____
      (TYPE OR PRINT NAME)   (SIGNATURE OF DECLARANT)

5. **Declaration of nonmilitary status.** The respondent is not in the military service of the United States as defined in section 511 et seq. of the Servicemembers Civil Relief Act (50 U.S.C. Appen. § 501 et seq.), and is not entitled to the benefits of such act.

I declare under penalty of perjury under the laws of the State of California that the foregoing is true and correct.

Date:

_____   ▶   _____
      (TYPE OR PRINT NAME)   (SIGNATURE OF DECLARANT)

Additionally, each individual county may require the use of some local forms in this context. It is recommended that the reader check with the clerk of the specific county before filing this documentation.

The first form mentioned above is entitled "Declaration for Default or Uncontested Dissolution or Legal Separation." Its use is mandated by operation of Family Code section 2336, which generally establishes that only the court is empowered to make the findings called for in the context of granting a default dissolution or legal separation. That section also provides a list of circumstances in which such a default dissolution or legal separation will *not* be granted.

By authorizing the parties to proceed in a default context by affidavit and by enumerating the circumstances under which a default will not be granted, section 2336 sets the stage for the content of the appropriate form of affidavit to be used: the above-referenced Declaration for Default or Uncontested Dissolution or Legal Separation is set out in Figure 8-10 in its entirety on pages 343 and 344.

Like most judicial council forms, FL-170's format is straightforward.[33] The petitioner completes the questions listed in the form, thus advising the court of the issues involved.

Item 4 tells the court whether this is a default or an uncontested matter, the chief difference being that in the latter case the respondent participates in the process. If the parties have stipulated that this matter will proceed as an uncontested matter, an additional form (discussed below) is provided.

Item 5 tells the court whether or not the parties have reached an agreement (an uncontested dissolution) regarding the issues in this marital termination action. If the parties have not reached an agreement (a default dissolution), the petitioner must answer additional questions. Item 6 advises the court of the status of the disclosure of information made by the parties.

Item 9 requests financial orders and is accompanied by an Income and Expense Declaration (discussed below). Items 11 and 12 educate the court as to the welfare status of the parties, and items 7 and 8 are used to request orders in the area of child custody and visitation. Note that items 7, 8, 9, 10, 12, 14, and 15 refer to a document entitled "Judgment (Family Law)." This document is not entirely a judicial council form (although its face sheet is). Generally speaking, it is a document prepared by the party who requested the default (both parties in an uncontested case) for the judge's signature; it contains the basic language that the parties wish the court to enter. In the interest of simplicity, the form specifies that the court should enter the order contained in the proposed judgment rather than restate the order in a separate declaration.

Item 17 establishes the grounds for the proceeding, and items 19 through 21 (used in dissolution matters only) provide the statutory and jurisdictional bases for a grant of dissolution of marriage. Item 22, applicable to

Figure 8-10
Form FL-170—Declaration for Default et al.

FL-170

ATTORNEY OR PARTY WITHOUT ATTORNEY *(Name, State Bar number, and address):*	FOR COURT USE ONLY
TELEPHONE NO.: FAX NO. *(Optional):* E-MAIL ADDRESS *(Optional):* ATTORNEY FOR *(Name):*	

SUPERIOR COURT OF CALIFORNIA, COUNTY OF

STREET ADDRESS:

MAILING ADDRESS:

CITY AND ZIP CODE:

BRANCH NAME:

PETITIONER:

RESPONDENT:

DECLARATION FOR DEFAULT OR UNCONTESTED ☐ DISSOLUTION ☐ LEGAL SEPARATION	CASE NUMBER:

(NOTE: Items 1 through 16 apply to both dissolution and legal separation proceedings.)

1. I declare that if I appeared in court and were sworn, I would testify to the truth of the facts in this declaration.

2. I agree that my case will be proven by this declaration and that I will not appear before the court unless I am ordered by the court to do so.

3. All the information in the ☐ *Petition* ☐ *Response* is true and correct.

4. **Default or uncontested** *(Check a or b.)*
   a. ☐ The default of the respondent was entered or is being requested, and I am not seeking any relief not requested in the petition. **OR**
   b. ☐ The parties have agreed that the matter may proceed as an uncontested matter without notice, and the agreement is attached or is incorporated in the attached settlement agreement or stipulated judgment.

5. **Settlement agreement** *(Check a or b.)*
   a. ☐ The parties have entered into ☐ **an agreement** ☐ **a stipulated judgment** regarding their property their marriage or domestic partnership rights, including support, the original of which is or has been submitted to the court. I request that the court approve the agreement. **OR**
   b. ☐ **There is no agreement or stipulated judgment,** and the following statements are true *(check at least one, including item (2) if a community estate exists):*
      (1) ☐ There are no community or quasi-community assets or community debts to be disposed of by the court.
      (2) ☐ The community and quasi-community assets and debts are listed on the attached **completed** current *Property Declaration* (form FL-160), which includes an estimate of the value of the assets and debts that I propose to be distributed to each party. The division in the proposed *Judgment (Family Law)* (form FL-180) is a fair and equal division of the property and debts, or if there is a negative estate, the debts are assigned fairly and equitably.

6. **Declaration of disclosure** *(Check a, b, or c.)*
   a. ☐ Both the petitioner and respondent have filed, or are filing concurrently, a *Declaration Regarding Service of Declaration of Disclosure* (form FL-141) and an *Income and Expense Declaration* (form FL-150).
   b. ☐ This matter is proceeding by default. I am the petitioner in this action and have filed a proof of service of the preliminary *Declaration of Disclosure* (form FL-140) with the court. I hereby waive receipt of the final *Declaration of Disclosure* (form FL-140) from the respondent.
   c. ☐ This matter is proceeding as an uncontested action. Service of the final *Declaration of Disclosure* (form FL-140) is mutually waived by both parties. A waiver provision executed by both parties under penalty of perjury is contained in the settlement agreement or proposed judgment or another, separate stipulation.

7. ☐ **Child custody** should be ordered as set forth in the proposed *Judgment (Family Law)* (form FL-180).

8. ☐ **Child visitation** should be ordered as set forth in the proposed *Judgment (Family Law)* (form FL-180).

9. **Spousal, partner, and family support** *(If a support order or attorney fees are requested, submit a completed* Income and Expense Declaration *(form FL-150) unless a current form is on file. Include your best estimate of the other party's income. Check at least one of the following.)*
   a. ☐ I knowingly give up forever any right to receive spousal or partner support.
   b. ☐ I ask the court to reserve jurisdiction to award spousal or partner support in the future to *(name):*
   c. ☐ Spousal support should be ordered as set forth in the proposed *Judgment (Family Law)* (form FL-180).
   d. ☐ Family support should be ordered as set forth in the proposed *Judgment (Family Law)* (form FL-180).

Form Adopted for Mandatory Use
Judicial Council of California
FL-170 [Rev. January 1, 2007]

DECLARATION FOR DEFAULT OR UNCONTESTED
DISSOLUTION or LEGAL SEPARATION
(Family Law)

Page 1 of 2
Family Code, § 2336
www.courtinfo.ca.gov

Figure 8-10 (continued)

FL-170

PETITIONER:	CASE NUMBER:
RESPONDENT:	

10. ☐ **Child support** should be ordered as set forth in the proposed *Judgment (Family Law)* (form FL-180).

11. a. I ☐ am receiving ☐ am not receiving ☐ intend to apply for   public assistance for the child or children listed in the proposed order.

    b. To the best of my knowledge, the other party ☐ is ☐ is not   receiving public assistance.

12. ☐ The petitioner ☐ respondent   is presently receiving public assistance, and all support should be made payable to the local child support agency at the address set forth in the proposed judgment. A representative of the local child support agency has signed the proposed judgment.

13. If there are minor children, check and complete item a and item b or c:

    a. My gross (before taxes) monthly income is *(specify)*: $

    b. ☐ The estimated gross monthly income of the other party is *(specify)*: $

    c. ☐ I have no knowledge of the estimated monthly income of the other party for the following reasons *(specify)*:

    d. ☐ I request that this order be based on the ☐ petitioner's ☐ respondent's   earning ability. The facts in support of my estimate of earning ability are *(specify)*:

        ☐ Continued on Attachment 13d.

14. ☐ **Parentage** of the children of the petitioner and respondent born prior to their marriage or domestic partnership should be ordered as set forth in the proposed *Judgment (Family Law)* (form FL-180). A declaration regarding parentage is attached.

15. ☐ **Attorney fees** should be ordered as set forth in the proposed *Judgment (Family Law)* (form FL-180).

16. ☐ The petitioner ☐ respondent   requests restoration of his or her former name as set forth in the proposed *Judgment (Family Law)* (form FL-180).

17. There are irreconcilable differences that have led to the irremediable breakdown of the marriage or domestic partnership, and there is no possibility of saving the marriage or domestic partnership through counseling or other means.

18. This declaration may be reviewed by a commissioner sitting as a temporary judge, who may determine whether to grant this request or require my appearance under Family Code section 2336.

STATEMENTS IN THIS BOX APPLY ONLY TO DISSOLUTIONS—Items 19 through 21

19. If this is a dissolution of marriage or of a domestic partnership created in another state, the petitioner and/or the respondent has been a resident of this county for at least three months and of the state of California for at least six months continuously and immediately preceding the date of the filing of the petition for dissolution of marriage or domestic partnership.

20. I ask that the court grant the request for a judgment for dissolution of marriage or domestic partnership based upon irreconcilable differences and that the court make the orders set forth in the proposed *Judgment (Family Law)* (form FL-180) submitted with this declaration.

21. ☐ This declaration is for the termination of **marital or domestic partner status only.** I ask the court to reserve jurisdiction over all issues whose determination is not requested in this declaration.

THIS STATEMENT APPLIES ONLY TO LEGAL SEPARATIONS

22. I ask that the court grant the request for a judgment for legal separation based upon irreconcilable differences and that the court make the orders set forth in the proposed *Judgment (Family Law)* (form FL-180) submitted with this declaration.

I understand that a judgment of legal separation does not terminate a marriage or domestic partnership and that I am still married or a partner in a domestic partnership.

---

23. ☐ Other *(specify)*:

I declare under penalty of perjury under the laws of the State of California that the foregoing is true and correct.

Date:

▶

_____   _____
(TYPE OR PRINT NAME)   (SIGNATURE OF DECLARANT)

FL-170 [Rev. January 1, 2007]	**DECLARATION FOR DEFAULT OR UNCONTESTED DISSOLUTION or LEGAL SEPARATION** (Family Law)	Page 2 of 2

legal separations only, simply recites that the declarant is aware that he is still married.

The next form in the above list, the Income and Expense Declaration, is discussed in detail in Chapter 9. The reader is invited to review that section for an explanation of the preparation of this form.

The third item on the list is the Declaration of Disclosure. This form finds its genesis in Chapter 9 of Division 6 of the Family Code, sections 2100 to 2113. These sections became operative January 1, 1993. The legislative intent of these sections (which is set out in detail in section 2100) can be generalized as follows: To avoid dissipation of the community and quasi-community estate (the assets and liabilities) and to promote full disclosure and cooperation between parties to a marital termination proceeding, these statutes require the parties to engage in a systematic and complete exchange of information so as to put each of them in the best position possible to gather information and evidence about the issues in the case. In theory at least, it is hoped that this will diffuse some of the hostilities inherent in these proceedings and thus foster settlement. In the context of a default proceeding, compliance with these disclosure requirements is not all that burdensome, although these requirements become more stringent in contested matters (or those that proceed through trial).

Family Code section 2110 limits the disclosure required in default cases to the Declaration of Disclosure form (form FL-140). This form is reproduced in Figure 8-11 on page 346 in its entirety.

This form is basically a face sheet, incorporating by reference the various forms that are to be attached. Although it appears that the person preparing this declaration has several choices regarding the forms to be attached, as a practical matter the only optional form is the Income and Expense Declaration, and then only if there is "no demand for money, costs, or attorney's fees contained in the petition and the judgment of dissolution of marriage is entered by default. . . ." (See generally Family Code section 2330.5.)

The next form on the list is the proposed Judgment. Judicial Council form FL-180 is printed in its entirety in Figure 8-12 on pages 347 and 348. This form, like the preliminary disclosure declaration, is basically a face sheet. In some instances (usually those involving virtually no issues other than the dissolution of the marital union itself), it is all that is required to complete the judgment. Usually, however, several additional sheets are attached, which establish the specifics of the orders entered by the court.

Like virtually all judicial council forms, FL-180 is set out to request basic information about the attorneys, parties, and the case (caption, and so on) up front. The form then moves on in item 2 to recite the manner in which the case led up to the entry of the judgment. For example, item 2 indicates if the parties appeared in court and the matter was heard as an uncontested or "default prove-up," or if the paperwork was simply provided for the

Figure 8-11
Form FL-140—Declaration of Disclosure

FL-140

ATTORNEY OR PARTY WITHOUT ATTORNEY *(Name and Address)*:	TELEPHONE NO.:

ATTORNEY FOR *(Name)*:

SUPERIOR COURT OF CALIFORNIA, COUNTY OF
STREET ADDRESS:
MAILING ADDRESS:
CITY AND ZIP CODE:
BRANCH NAME:

PETITIONER:

RESPONDENT:

DECLARATION OF DISCLOSURE

☐ Petitioner's   ☐ Preliminary
☐ Respondent's   ☐ Final

CASE NUMBER:

DO NOT FILE WITH THE COURT

Both the preliminary and the final declaration of disclosure must be served on the other party with certain exceptions. Neither disclosure is filed with the court. A declaration stating service was made of the final declaration of disclosure must be filed with the court (see form FL-141).

A preliminary declaration of disclosure but not a final declaration of disclosure is required in the case of a summary dissolution (see Family Code section 2109) or in a default judgment (see Family Code section 2110) provided the default is not a stipulated judgment or a judgment based upon a marriage settlement agreement.

A declaration of disclosure is required in a nullity or legal separation action as well as in a dissolution action.

Attached are the following:

1. ☐ A completed *Schedule of Assets and Debts* (form FL-142).

2. ☐ A completed *Income and Expense Declaration* (form FL-150 (as applicable)).

3. ☐ A statement of all material facts and information regarding valuation of all assets that are community property or in which the community has an interest *(not a form)*.

4. ☐ A statement of all material facts and information regarding obligations for which the community is liable *(not a form)*.

5. ☐ An accurate and complete written disclosure of any investment opportunity, business opportunity, or other income-producing opportunity presented since the date of separation that results from any investment, significant business, or other income-producing opportunity from the date of marriage to the date of separation *(not a form)*.

I declare under penalty of perjury under the laws of the State of California that the foregoing is true and correct.

Date:

▶

_____
(TYPE OR PRINT NAME)

_____
(SIGNATURE)

Page 1 of 1

Form Adopted for Mandatory Use Judicial Council of California FL-140 [Rev. January 1, 2003]	**DECLARATION OF DISCLOSURE** **(Family Law)**	Family Code, §§ 2102, 2104, 2105, 2106, 2112 www.courtinfo.ca.gov

Figure 8-12
Form FL-180—Judgment

FL-180

ATTORNEY OR PARTY WITHOUT ATTORNEY *(Name, State Bar number, and address)* :	FOR COURT USE ONLY

TELEPHONE NO.:   FAX NO. *(Optional)*:

E-MAIL ADDRESS *(Optional)*:

ATTORNEY FOR *(Name)*:

SUPERIOR COURT OF CALIFORNIA, COUNTY OF

STREET ADDRESS:

MAILING ADDRESS:

CITY AND ZIP CODE:

BRANCH NAME:

MARRIAGE OF

PETITIONER:

RESPONDENT:

JUDGMENT	CASE NUMBER:

☐ **DISSOLUTION**   ☐ **LEGAL SEPARATION**   ☐ **NULLITY**

    ☐ **Status only**

    ☐ **Reserving jurisdiction over termination of marital or domestic partnership status**

    ☐ **Judgment on reserved issues**

Date marital or domestic partnership status ends:

1. ☐ This judgment ☐ contains personal conduct restraining orders ☐ modifies existing restraining orders. The restraining orders are contained on page(s)   of the attachment. They expire on *(date)*:

2. This proceeding was heard as follows: ☐ Default or uncontested ☐ By declaration under Family Code section 2336
   ☐ Contested
   a. Date: Dept.:   Room:
   b. Judicial officer *(name)*:   ☐ Temporary judge
   c. ☐ Petitioner present in court   ☐ Attorney present in court *(name)*:
   d. ☐ Respondent present in court   ☐ Attorney present in court *(name)*:
   e. ☐ Claimant present in court *(name)*:   ☐ Attorney present in court *(name)*:
   f. ☐ Other *(specify name)*:

3. The court acquired jurisdiction of the respondent on *(date)*:
   a. ☐ The respondent was served with process.
   b. ☐ The respondent appeared.

THE COURT ORDERS, GOOD CAUSE APPEARING

4. a. ☐ Judgment of dissolution is entered. Marital or domestic partnership status is terminated and the parties are restored to the status of single persons
      (1) ☐ on *(specify date)*:
      (2) ☐ on a date to be determined on noticed motion of either party or on stipulation.
   b. ☐ Judgment of legal separation is entered.
   c. ☐ Judgment of nullity is entered. The parties are declared to be single persons on the ground of *(specify)*:

   d. ☐ This judgment will be entered nunc pro tunc as of *(date)*:
   e. ☐ Judgment on reserved issues.
   f. The ☐ petitioner's ☐ respondent's former name is restored to *(specify)*:
   g. ☐ Jurisdiction is reserved over all other issues, and all present orders remain in effect except as provided below.
   h. ☐ This judgment contains provisions for child support or family support. Each party must complete and file with the court a *Child Support Case Registry Form* (form FL-191) within 10 days of the date of this judgment. The parents must notify the court of any change in the information submitted within 10 days of the change, by filing an updated form. The *Notice of Rights and Responsibilities—Health Care Costs and Reimbursement Procedures and Information Sheet on Changing a Child Support Order* (form FL-192) is attached.

Page 1 of 2

Form Adopted for Mandatory Use
Judicial Council of California
FL-180 [Rev. January 1, 2007]

JUDGMENT
(Family Law)

Family Code, §§ 2024, 2340, 2343, 2346
www.courtinfo.ca.gov

Figure 8-12 (continued)

FL-180

CASE NAME *(Last name, first name of each party):*	CASE NUMBER:

4. *(Cont'd.)*

i. ☐ A settlement agreement between the parties is attached.

j. ☐ A written stipulation for judgment between the parties is attached.

k. ☐ The children of this marriage or domestic partnership.

    (1) ☐ The children of this marriage or domestic partnership are:

       Name   Birthdate

    (2) ☐ Parentage is established for children of this relationship born prior to the marriage or domestic partnership.

l. ☐ Child custody and visitation are ordered as set forth in the attached

    (1) ☐ settlement agreement, stipulation for judgment, or other written agreement.

    (2) ☐ *Child Custody and Visitation Order Attachment* (form FL-341).

    (3) ☐ *Stipulation and Order for Custody and/or Visitation of Children* (form FL-355).

    (4) ☐ other *(specify):*

m. ☐ Child support is ordered as set forth in the attached

    (1) ☐ settlement agreement, stipulation for judgment, or other written agreement.

    (2) ☐ *Child Support Information and Order Attachment* (form FL-342).

    (3) ☐ *Stipulation to Establish or Modify Child Support and Order* (form FL-350).

    (4) ☐ other *(specify):*

n. ☐ Spousal or partner support is ordered as set forth in the attached

    (1) ☐ settlement agreement, stipulation for judgment, or other written agreement.

    (2) ☐ *Spousal, Partner, or Family Support Order Attachment* (form FL-343).

    (3) ☐ other *(specify):*

    NOTICE: It is the goal of this state that each party will make reasonable good faith efforts to become self-supporting as provided for in Family Code section 4320. The failure to make reasonable good faith efforts may be one of the factors considered by the court as a basis for modifying or terminating spousal or partner support.

o. ☐ Property division is ordered as set forth in the attached

    (1) ☐ settlement agreement, stipulation for judgment, or other written agreement.

    (2) ☐ *Property Order Attachment to Judgment* (form FL-345).

    (3) ☐ other *(specify):*

p. ☐ Other *(specify):*

Each attachment to this judgment is incorporated into this judgment, and the parties are ordered to comply with each attachment's provisions.

Jurisdiction is reserved to make other orders necessary to carry out this judgment.

Date:

                            JUDICIAL OFFICER

5. Number of pages attached: _____   ☐ SIGNATURE FOLLOWS LAST ATTACHMENT

NOTICE

Dissolution or legal separation may automatically cancel the rights of a spouse or domestic partner under the other spouse's or domestic partner's will, trust, retirement plan, power of attorney, pay-on-death bank account, transfer-on-death vehicle registration, survivorship rights to any property owned in joint tenancy, and any other similar thing. It does not automatically cancel the rights of a spouse or domestic partner as beneficiary of the other spouse's or domestic partner's life insurance policy. You should review these matters, as well as any credit cards, other credit accounts, insurance policies, retirement plans, and credit reports, to determine whether they should be changed or whether you should take any other actions.

A debt or obligation may be assigned to one party as part of the dissolution of property and debts, but if that party does not pay the debt or obligation, the creditor may be able to collect from the other party.

An earnings assignment may be issued without additional proof if child, family, partner, or spousal support is ordered.

Any party required to pay support must pay interest on overdue amounts at the "legal rate," which is currently 10 percent.

FL-180 [Rev. January 1, 2007]   **JUDGMENT**   Page 2 of 2
                                (Family Law)

court to review and sign. The reader should note that it is no longer necessary for the parties to actually appear before the judge in order to obtain a default or uncontested dissolution (or legal separation). In either case, the party (or parties) simply fills out the paperwork and delivers it to the court where it is reviewed by a court clerk (sometimes referred to as the default clerk). If it has been properly prepared, the clerk gives it to the judge for final review and signature. The parties are notified by mail that their marriage has been terminated (or judgment of legal separation granted).

Item 3 on the judgment form requests statistical information that advises the court of the jurisdictional bases for proceeding with the default or uncontested matter. As can be seen, the respondent must have either appeared or been served. This, of course, is required for jurisdictional reasons and also establishes the commencement of the six-month waiting period mandated by Family Code section 2339.

The court's orders in the case begin in item 4 of the judgment form. The choices are self-explanatory; however, item 4g bears further examination. That item refers to the court *reserving jurisdiction* "over all other issues." This language makes reference to a procedure provided for by Code, which is known as *bifurcation*. Family Code section 2337, authorizes the court, upon the request of one (or both) of the parties, to sever out from the "normal" progression of the case the issue of the status of the marriage and resolve that issue first. Sometimes the court determines this issue right away, leaving all the other issues (custody, support, property division) to be tried later in what would be considered the "usual" course of events for a litigated dissolution. In other words, because it can sometimes take a very long time to bring a case to trial, in order to accommodate those people who "just have to get divorced *now*," this procedure known as bifurcation was devised. The reasons for getting divorced "right away" vary, but the usual reasons are to allow one of the parties (usually the one requesting the bifurcation) to remarry (to someone new) or simply to allow the parties to close the door on that aspect of the relationship, establishing a sense of finality to the union.

Bifurcation proceedings are handled very carefully to ensure that the party who did *not* request the bifurcation does not suffer any hardship as a result. Accordingly, Family Code section 2337 sets forth the conditions under which bifurcation may be granted. The conditions are designed to protect the "non-requesting party" in the event that something happens between the time the bifurcation is granted and the time the matter is finally called for trial in the usual course of events. These protections typically attempt to ensure that if the requesting party dies before the "normal" trial date, the non-requesting party may nonetheless claim the benefits and protections typically afforded to the *spouse* of the decedent, notwithstanding the fact that, by virtue of the bifurcation proceeding, his or her status as *spouse* was prematurely terminated.

Another example of these protections at work is found in the area of health insurance. As the reader is no doubt aware, most health insurance plans cover the spouse of the insured as well as the insured himself. Of course, once the marital status is terminated, that coverage is threatened. A bifurcation accelerates the date of marital termination and thus accelerates the date on which the non-requesting spouse loses his or her health insurance. Therefore, the Code provides that a party requesting bifurcation must maintain the non-requesting party's health insurance.

Item 4p on form FL-180, simply labeled "Other," references by far the most significant portion of the court's orders. For obvious reasons, the party preparing this form is not able to list each and every order made by the court unless that order is limited to termination of the marriage. Item 4p, therefore, exists to provide the basis for incorporating by reference all other orders made by the court in the case, which are set out on attached pages. Perhaps the easiest way to explain how this works is to review an example of a judgment prepared in a default or uncontested setting:

1. The Court finds that the parties have executed an Appearance, Stipulation and Waivers (Form FL-130), permitting this matter to be tried as an uncontested matter; and, the parties have waived their rights to notice of trial, findings of fact and conclusions of law, motion for a new trial and the right to appeal.

2. The Court finds that each party has waived his or her respective present right to spousal support from the other party. Thus, the Court makes no award of spousal support at this time. The foregoing terms and conditions relative to spousal support are not modifiable by this or any Court of competent jurisdiction, such that the rights of the parties to spousal support shall, upon the effective date of termination as set forth in this Judgment, forever cease and terminate.

3. The Petitioner is awarded sole legal and primary physical custody of the minor child of the parties, to wit: Baby Doe, born June 23, 2006.

4. Subject to further agreement of the parties, and/or further order of this or any court of competent jurisdiction, the minor child, to wit: Baby Doe, born June 23, 2008, shall reside with Petitioner; this order is valid, however, only if Respondent is granted rights of reasonable visitation as follows:

   a. From 9:00 a.m. Saturday to 5:00 p.m. the following Monday, commencing October 2, 2011, and continuing for the next two consecutive weekends, for a total of three weekends per month (the first three);
   b. Holiday visitation shall be as follows:

Holiday/ Special Day	Odd Numbered Year	Even Numbered Year
Easter Sunday	Father	Mother
July 4th	Mother	Father
Thanksgiving Day	Father	Mother
Christmas Day	Mother	Father
Child's Birthday (6/23)	Mother	Father
Mother's Day	Mother	Mother
Father's Day	Father	Father
Mother's Birthday	Mother	Mother
Father's Birthday	Father	Father

c. Visitation on these holidays shall be from 9:00 a.m. to 5:00 p.m.

d. The parties shall alternate responsibility for pick-up of the minor child when the exchange is to take place on a non-school day. For example, on one Saturday, Respondent shall pick up the minor child from Petitioner, and on the next Saturday Petitioner shall drop off the minor child to Respondent.

e. The parties shall ensure that the minor child is dropped off at school on time, which term is defined herein as before the start of his first class. After school, the parent with the responsibility of picking up the child after school shall ensure that the minor child is picked up "on time," which for purposes of this order is defined as before the end of the regularly scheduled after school care (currently 6:30 p.m.).

f. The parties shall exert every reasonable effort to maintain access between each of them and the minor child and to foster a feeling of affection between each of them and the minor child. Neither shall do anything to hamper the natural development of the love and respect of said minor child for the other party (parent).

g. The Court orders that there will be no use of nonprescription drugs of any kind in the presence of the minor child. Further, as to prescription drugs, there shall be allowed no consumption of such drugs in the presence of the minor except by the person(s) in whose name the prescription is written. It is further ordered that the minor shall not be exposed to second-hand smoke from cigarette, cigar or pipe tobacco. Finally, neither parent shall expose the minor child to drunk and disorderly behavior. In this regard, therefore, not only shall the parties refrain from taking the minor child into a situation where such behavior is occurring, but shall also leave the premises with the minor child whenever such behavior is taking place.

h. The Court orders that neither party will allow friends to sleep over at their house and share the same bed with them during their custodial time with the minor child.

i. The Court finds that the child's bed-time currently is 9:00 p.m. The parties are ordered to respect and adhere to this bed-time at all times.

j. Neither party shall relocate the residence of the minor child, Baby Doe, born June 23, 2006, more than thirty (30) miles from the San Fernando Valley area without first obtaining the written consent of the other, or further order of Court.

k. Neither parent shall employ corporal punishment of the minor child, Baby Doe, born June 23, 2006.

l. As long as the minor child is enrolled in private school, and as long as Petitioner maintains a minimum of 70% physical custody time share of the minor child, Baby Doe, born June 23, 2006, Petitioner shall pay the tuition associated with such private school.

m. The parties shall jointly confer on all issues related to the minor child's well-being and upbringing.

5.a. Having given extensive consideration to the parties' needs and abilities, coupled with the contemplated residence of the minor child and the payment by Petitioner of the minor child's private school tuition, the court makes no award of child support at this time.

5.b. Petitioner and Respondent shall equally divide all extraordinary medical, dental and orthodontic expenses incurred for the benefit of the minor child, and not otherwise covered by medical (i.e., health) insurance provided to Petitioner, Respondent and/or the minor child.

5.c. The parties are ordered to cooperate with each other in tendering medical bills or other insurance claims reasonably necessary to provide payment for the above-referenced insurance benefits covering the minor child.

6. The following community property and/or community obligations of the parties are awarded to Petitioner, as his sole and separate property or separate obligation:

Property:

a. Personal belongings, clothing and jewelry of Husband.

b. An equitable portion of the household furniture, furnishings and appliances, as already divided between the parties.

c. A portion of the bank accounts as already divided between the parties.

d. Community portion of Husband's 401K retirement plan through his employment, approximate value at date of separation: $600.

Debts:

a. Community Visa card debt in the amount of $600.

7. The following community property and/or community obligations of the parties are awarded to Respondent, as her sole and separate property or separate obligation:

Property:

    a.   Personal belongings, clothing and jewelry of Wife.

    b.   An equitable portion of the household furniture, furnishings and appliances, as already divided between the parties.

    c.   A portion of the bank accounts as already divided between the parties.

Debts:
NONE

8.   Petitioner is ordered to indemnify and save harmless the Respondent from any and all liabilities and/or obligations so assumed by Petitioner.

9.   Respondent is ordered to indemnify and save harmless the Petitioner from any and all liabilities and/or obligations so assumed by Respondent.

10.   If it is hereafter determined that either the Petitioner or Respondent has an interest in any community property of any kind or description whatsoever, other than specifically listed in this Order and/or the Marital Settlement Agreement, or that a party has made, without the knowledge and consent of the other party, any gift or transfer of any community property, not set forth or otherwise disclosed to the other party, the warrantor is ordered to pay the other party, at the other party's election, either the market value of the warrantee's interest in said property, as of the date of this Order, on the date the warrantor's ownership is discovered by the warrantee or on the date said gift was made. This Order will not impair the availability of any other remedy to the warrantee party.

11.   If any party brings any action or proceeding, relating to or arising out of the subject matter of this Order the Court in that action has the power against either party to make whatever order it deems proper under all circumstances, then present, for attorney's fees and other reasonably necessary costs.

12.   Each party is hereby restrained from incurring any further obligations involving the credit of the other party or upon any joint credit cards, and each party is hereby restrained hereafter from using any credit cards issued in their joint names. Each party is responsible hereafter for the charges he or she may have incurred on any credit and/or charge accounts.

13.   If any claim, action or proceeding is hereafter brought seeking to hold Petitioner liable on account of any debt, liability, act or omission of the Respondent, the Respondent is ordered, at her sole expense, to defend the Petitioner against any such claim or

demand (whether or not well founded) and to hold him free and harmless therefrom.

14. If any claim, action or proceeding is hereafter brought seeking to hold Respondent liable on account of any debt, liability, act or omission of the Petitioner, the Petitioner is ordered, at his sole expense, to defend the Respondent against any such claim or demand (whether or not well founded) and to hold her free and harmless therefrom.

15. Both parties are mutually restrained from annoying, harassing, or disturbing the peace of the other party, in any manner, and from interfering with the other party's employment or business activities or the use, ownership or disposition of any property now owned or hereafter acquired by the other party.

16. Each party is ordered to execute any and all instruments necessary and convenient to carry out this Order. Failure to do so within 10 days after oral request of same by the other party shall entitle the requesting party to apply ex parte for an order directing the Clerk of the Court to execute such documents as are reasonably requested on behalf of the refusing party.

17. By their signatures below, the parties to this action represent as follows:

   h. We are fully informed of our rights concerning child support;
   i. The child support awarded is agreed to without coercion or duress;
   j. The agreement is in the best interest of the child(ren) involved;
   k. The needs of the children will be adequately met by said award; and
   l. Neither party has applied for or is receiving public assistance.

18. This Order may be signed by a Commissioner sitting as a Judge Pro Tempore.

_____   _____
[Name of Petitioner]   [Name of Respondent]
Dated: _____   Dated: _____

Order

The clerk of the court is directed to enter the foregoing as the order of this court.

DATED: _____   _____
                              Judge/Commissioner of the Superior Court

This sample judgment is an example of one that was agreed to by both of the parties, which explains the fact that they both signed it. The act of signing the judgment in this context tells the court that the parties agree to the proposed orders contained in this document. Had this been a default situation, the petitioner would most likely not have signed the judgment (she would have prepared it, however). In the context of these types of proceedings, all documents, including the proposed judgment, are prepared in advance by the party submitting the paperwork to the court. By so doing, these documents are proposed. Once the judge signs the judgment, of course, it is no longer proposed; it is an order of the court.

The next document required to be prepared and submitted to the court in the context of a default (or uncontested) dissolution or legal separation is entitled "Notice of Entry of Judgment" (form FL-190). Included with this document must be two stamped envelopes, one addressed to each party. Preparing this form is simply a matter of checking the appropriate boxes and filling in the correct addresses. The purpose of this form is exactly as presented in its title: to give each party a written record of the official notification that a judgment has been entered in their case. This form is set out in Figure 8-13 on page 356.

Once these documents are prepared and ready for filing, the attorney (or party in pro per) has two choices: (1) personally bring the papers to the courthouse and process them himself, or (2) mail the papers to the courthouse for the clerk to process.[34] There are advantages to a personal walk-through. First, it is much quicker than proceeding by mail. Second, because the attorney is present when the clerk reviews the papers, the attorney can correct errors on the spot. Very often only attorneys are allowed to utilize the walk-through procedure, and it is not available in every county.

When a default is processed by mail, the procedure takes approximately six weeks to complete. If the court determines that the petitioner must make a personal appearance, the clerk will notify the petitioner and obtain (or simply set) a date for the hearing. Such an appearance will generally not be required unless the court determines that the proposed judgment is not supported by adequate facts in the declaration.

Once the court enters a default judgment, it is good practice to *personally* serve the respondent with a copy of the judgment (assuming that is possible). Knowledge of the order(s) is one of the elements for contempt, a procedure that is sometimes used to enforce these orders; and there is no better way to prove actual knowledge than by proof that the order was hand-delivered. Of course, if personal service is not possible, at the very least the orders should be mailed to the respondent's last known address.

A close relative to the default procedure is an uncontested matter. The reader might be surprised to learn that the vast majority of family law cases are disposed of without a contested trial. Not every litigant takes his case "to the mat." Many individuals wish to avoid the inconvenience

Figure 8-13
Form FL-190—Notice of Entry of Judgment

FL-190

ATTORNEY OR PARTY WITHOUT ATTORNEY *(Name, State Bar number, and address):*	FOR COURT USE ONLY
TELEPHONE NO.: FAX NO. *(Optional):* E-MAIL ADDRESS *(Optional):* ATTORNEY FOR *(Name):*	

SUPERIOR COURT OF CALIFORNIA, COUNTY OF
STREET ADDRESS:
MAILING ADDRESS:
CITY AND ZIP CODE:
BRANCH NAME:

PETITIONER:

RESPONDENT:

NOTICE OF ENTRY OF JUDGMENT	CASE NUMBER:

You are notified that the following judgment was entered on *(date):*

1. ☐ Dissolution
2. ☐ Dissolution—status only
3. ☐ Dissolution—reserving jurisdiction over termination of marital status or domestic partnership
4. ☐ Legal separation
5. ☐ Nullity
6. ☐ Parent-child relationship
7. ☐ Judgment on reserved issues
8. ☐ Other *(specify):*

Date:

Clerk, by _____, Deputy

—NOTICE TO ATTORNEY OF RECORD OR PARTY WITHOUT ATTORNEY—

Under the provisions of Code of Civil Procedure section 1952, if no appeal is filed the court may order the exhibits destroyed or otherwise disposed of after 60 days from the expiration of the appeal time.

STATEMENT IN THIS BOX APPLIES ONLY TO JUDGMENT OF DISSOLUTION
Effective date of termination of marital or domestic partnership status *(specify):*
WARNING: Neither party may remarry or enter into a new domestic partnership until the effective date of the termination of marital or domestic partnership status, as shown in this box.

CLERK'S CERTIFICATE OF MAILING

I certify that I am not a party to this cause and that a true copy of the *Notice of Entry of Judgment* was mailed first class, postage fully prepaid, in a sealed envelope addressed as shown below, and that the notice was mailed

at *(place):* _____, California, on *(date):* _____

Date:

Clerk, by _____, Deputy

Name and address of petitioner or petitioner's attorney	Name and address of respondent or respondent's attorney

Page 1 of 1

Form Adopted for Mandatory Use Judicial Council of California FL-190 [Rev. January 1, 2005]	**NOTICE OF ENTRY OF JUDGMENT** (Family Law—Uniform Parentage—Custody and Support)	Family Code, §§ 2338, 7636, 7637 www.courtinfo.ca.gov

and expense associated with a protracted trial in a family law matter. As such, they are free to (and quite often do) agree between each other on all issues. Once this agreement has been achieved, the divorce must only be processed through the system to "make everything official." Default proceedings are distinguishable in that the defaulting spouse simply does not care to participate in the divorce process at all; he is content, for whatever reason, to allow the other spouse to proceed alone.

The process for uncontested dissolutions is basically the same as the process for default matters. The only fundamental difference is that uncontested dissolutions are based on a judgment to which both parties stipulate, while default matters are based on the respondent's failure to participate. In an uncontested dissolution, the petitioner and respondent must both sign a *stipulated judgment* to demonstrate that they agree to the proposed orders contained in the judgment.[35] In addition, the parties must pay the respondent's first appearance fee (if it has not already been paid), and they must sign form FL-130, "Appearance, Stipulation and Waivers." This form (set out in Figure 8-14 on page 358) is self-explanatory. It establishes that the respondent is making (or has already made) a general appearance to satisfy jurisdictional requirements; the parties agree to resolve the litigation as an uncontested matter; and, the parties both waive various other rights (to a new trial, to appeal).

Assuming the matter proceeds as uncontested rather than by default, the respondent *will* participate in the proceedings by virtue of filing the appearance, stipulation, and waivers and also by signing off on the proposed judgment.

On a final note, in both default and uncontested dissolutions,[36] the effective date of the dissolution of marriage is: (1) the date which is six months from the date the respondent was served with the summons and complaint, (2) the date on which the respondent entered a general appearance in the action, or (3) the date on which the judgment was entered (signed by the judge and entered in the court's minutes by the clerk), whichever is *later*. The parties are free to remarry after the date of dissolution.

G. Contested Trials

Unless acting a a pro per litigant, a paralegals will not appear in court on behalf of a client. That function is currently reserved to active members of the State Bar. However, we will cover the general nature of contested trials in the family law context to establish a framework for understanding the various procedural rules as well as the rules related to discovery and trial preparation.

As indicated throughout this text, most family law trials are conducted in much the same manner as other civil trials. In both types of trials, the

Figure 8-14
Form FL-130—Appearance, Stipulation and Waivers

FL-130

ATTORNEY OR PARTY WITHOUT ATTORNEY *(Name, State Bar number, and address):*	FOR COURT USE ONLY
TELEPHONE NO.: FAX NO. *(Optional):* E-MAIL ADDRESS *(Optional):* ATTORNEY FOR *(Name):*	

SUPERIOR COURT OF CALIFORNIA, COUNTY OF
STREET ADDRESS:
MAILING ADDRESS:
CITY AND ZIP CODE:
BRANCH NAME:

PETITIONER:

RESPONDENT:

APPEARANCE, STIPULATIONS, AND WAIVERS	CASE NUMBER:

1. **Appearance by respondent** *(you must choose one):*

    a. ☐ By filing this form, I make a general appearance.

    b. ☐ I have previously made a general appearance.

    c. ☐ I am a member of the military services of the United States of America. I have completed and attached to this form *Declaration and Conditional Waiver of Rights Under the Servicemembers Civil Relief Act of 2003* (form FL-130(A)).

2. **Agreements, stipulations, and waivers** *(choose all that apply):*

    a. ☐ The parties agree that this cause may be decided as an uncontested matter.

    b. ☐ The parties waive their rights to notice of trial, a statement of decision, a motion for new trial, and the right to appeal.

    c. ☐ This matter may be decided by a commissioner sitting as a temporary judge.

    d. ☐ The parties have a written agreement that will be submitted to the court, or a stipulation for judgment will be submitted to the court and attached to *Judgment (Family Law)* (form FL-180).

    e. ☐ None of these agreements or waivers will apply unless the court approves the stipulation for judgment or incorporates the written settlement agreement into the judgment.

    f. ☐ This is a parentage case, and both parties have signed an *Advisement and Waiver of Rights Re: Establishment of Parental Relationship* (form FL-235) or its equivalent.

3. **Other** *(specify):*

Date: _____

_____
(TYPE OR PRINT NAME)

▶ _____
(SIGNATURE OF PETITIONER)

Date: _____

_____
(TYPE OR PRINT NAME)

▶ _____
(SIGNATURE OF RESPONDENT)

Date: _____

_____
(TYPE OR PRINT NAME)

▶ _____
(SIGNATURE OF ATTORNEY FOR PETITIONER)

Date: _____

_____
(TYPE OR PRINT NAME)

▶ _____
(SIGNATURE OF ATTORNEY FOR RESPONDENT)

Page 1 of 1

Form Approved for Optional Use Judicial Council of California FL-130 [Rev. January 1, 2011]	**APPEARANCE, STIPULATIONS, AND WAIVERS** **(Family Law—Uniform Parentage—Custody and Support)**	Government Code, § 70673 www.courtinfo.ca.gov

parties may participate in formal discovery and law and motion procedure, pretrial conferences, and mandatory settlement conferences. In the past, one judge might hear an order to show cause, another judge might hear a law and motion matter, another judge might hear a pretrial conference or a discovery motion, and a fourth judge (or fifth or sixth) would hear the trial itself. Currently, in many counties (including Los Angeles), the courts use a *direct assignment* system, where one judge is responsible for all facets of a case from start to finish. The same judge hears law and motion, discovery disputes, pretrial conferences, orders to show cause, mandatory settlement conferences, and ultimately the trial. This system parallels that used in federal court, and it is, in this author's opinion, a vast improvement over the old "catch as catch can" system.

Once a trial date approaches, it is necessary to organize the evidence acquired during the discovery process and distill that information into a cohesive body of facts that can be presented to the trial judge in an organized manner. The paralegal is most often intimately associated with this process, which tends to be quite labor intensive and time-consuming. A paralegal's tasks often include summarizing depositions, organizing documentary evidence both by subject matter and by the identity of the witnesses, and helping to prepare the trial briefs and documents to be used at trial. Additionally, the paralegal will often interview potential witnesses and prepare them to testify, and help prepare pretrial motions, trial briefs, mandatory settlement conference statements, and items of this nature.

Once a lengthy or complex case is within 60 to 90 days of the date of trial and has an estimated trial date in excess of one or two days, the trial judge will generally call both counsel into chambers for a "pretrial conference." During this conference, the judge and counsel informally discuss certain aspects of the trial in hopes that it can be streamlined. The judge and counsel will attempt to cover certain objections, obtain stipulations to the admissibility of certain evidence, pre-mark exhibits, and exchange and identify lists of exhibits and witnesses. As a general rule, it is a good practice for the parties to stipulate to issues about which there are no genuine disputes. Additionally, counsel should be prepared to discuss evidentiary matters with the judge and the opposing counsel; and counsel should be prepared to stipulate to the admissibility of certain evidence in those situations in which the evidentiary objection will serve no legitimate purpose in the litigation except to harass the opposing side. The lawyers and the judge will also discuss the order in which the various issues will be tried. For example, it may be important to these litigants to try the issues of child support and custody prior to the issues of spousal support and property. This is generally a judgment call on the part of the parties and the judge involved, and the ultimate decision will be left to the sound discretion of the trial judge. The pre-trial conference can also (and very often does) lead to settlement discussions. Judges are always anxious to resolve matters amicably by way of settlement for two basic reasons. First, the parties are more capable of living with a decision of which they are the fundamental architects; and, second, judges are happy to clear their calendar because they truly have more cases than they can possibly handle at any given time.

Following the informal pretrial conference, the judge will typically schedule a mandatory settlement conference. This is a conference in which the attorneys and the parties appear in court and participate in a discussion, using the offices of the judge as a mediator, in an attempt to resolve the contested issues. Basically the judge tells each side how bad their case is and gives them each reasons as to why they should settle. Of course, this is a highly oversimplified version of what transpires at a mandatory settlement conference; however, as a general rule, the description is not all that far off.

Once the parties have completed the informal pretrial conference and the mandatory settlement conference, it is time to start the trial. At trial, the petitioner typically presents her case first, by presenting witnesses and documents to support her position and requests.

After the petitioner has completed her presentation, the respondent presents witnesses and documents in support of his position. These presentations will, of course, include testimony by expert witnesses (accountants, child custody evaluators, actuaries).

Once all the evidence has been presented to the court, the lawyers are entitled to give a closing or *final* argument to the judge. At this time, the attorney for each side attempts to summarize the facts and the evidence introduced at trial, apply those facts to the law, and argue why that combination adds up to the relief requested. Once both sides have given their closing arguments, the judge may make a decision on all of the contested issues right then from the bench. Alternatively, the judge may take the matter under submission, preferring to give additional thought to the evidence that has been presented and formulate an opinion accordingly.

After the court enters judgment, one or both parties may appeal—under the appropriate circumstances. As a general rule, the appellate court will not interpose its judgment on factual issues in favor of that of the trial judge. Rather, the basic function of the appellate court is to simply determine whether the trial judge applied the law properly and whether the facts presented at trial support the ruling. Assuming the answer to these questions is yes, the appellate court will usually leave the decision unchanged, and it will ultimately become the "final order" of the court.

H. Conciliation Proceedings

The foregoing discussion has focused on judicially supervised proceedings that were designed (at their most fundamental level) to terminate the marital relationship, whether by dissolution, legal separation, or nullity. The Family Code does, however, make provision for the superior court to intervene on an informal basis and work with the parties to save their marriage. These are conducted under the auspices of the Family Conciliation Court, established by the Family Conciliation Court Law, contained in Division 5 of the Family Code, sections 1800 to 1852.

Not all counties are required to establish and maintain a conciliation court, although most larger counties do The establishment of this court is basically left up to the superior court judges on a county by county basis. Each county must decide whether "the social conditions in the county and the number of domestic relations cases in the courts render the procedures provided in [the Family Conciliation Court Law] necessary to the full and proper consideration of those cases and the effectuation of the purposes of [the Family Conciliation Court Law]" (Family Code section 1802).

Family Code section 1830 establishes the jurisdiction of the Family Conciliation Court as follows:

> (a) When a controversy exists between spouses, or when a controversy relating to child custody or visitation exists between parents regardless of their marital status, and the controversy may, unless a reconciliation is achieved, result in dissolution of the marriage, nullity of the marriage, or legal separation of the parties, or in the disruption of the household, and there is a minor child of the spouses or parents or of either of them whose welfare might be affected thereby, the family conciliation court has jurisdiction as provided in this part over the controversy and over the parties to the controversy and over all persons having any relation to the controversy.
>
> (b) The family conciliation court also has jurisdiction over the controversy, whether or not there is a minor child of the parties or either of them, where the controversy involves domestic violence.

Therefore, the Family Conciliation Court has jurisdiction to resolve disputes between parents when: (1) it is believed that without such resolution a disruption of the household will occur (whether by dissolution or some other form of marital termination proceeding or simply the break-up of two unmarried parents), and (2) the welfare of minor children in that household might be affected by such a disruption. In general, then, the Family Conciliation Court only handles situations involving children.

Of course, there is an exception to this "children only" rule: In cases involving domestic violence, the Family Conciliation Court has the power to intervene and attempt to reconcile the parties or, at the very least, deal with the violence and (hopefully) prevent further violence.

The statutorily decreed purpose of the Family Conciliation Court Law is set out in Family Code section 1801:

> The purposes of this part are to protect the rights of children and to promote the public welfare by preserving, promoting, and protecting family life and the institution of matrimony, and to provide means for the reconciliation of spouses and the amicable settlement of domestic and family controversies.

The parties do not need to work together to invoke Family Conciliation Court jurisdiction. Either parent (or spouse) or both may file a petition for conciliation. This petition for conciliation is very straightforward and is designed to frame the issues in dispute. It is intended that this petition will be filed *before* any litigation is commenced. In fact, once the petition for conciliation has been filed and the jurisdiction of the Family Conciliation Court has been invoked, the parties are statutorily prevented from filing a petition for dissolution, legal separation, nullity, or a proceeding to determine custody or visitation of the minor children by the provisions of Family Code section 1840. The stay of proceeding provided by this code section will last for a period of 30 days following the hearing on the petition for conciliation.

The contents of the petition for conciliation are quite straightforward and are set out in detail in Family Code section 1833.

> The petition shall:
> (a) Allege that a controversy exists between the spouses or parents and request the aid of the court to effect a reconciliation or an amicable settlement of the controversy.
> (b) State the name and age of each minor child whose welfare may be affected by the controversy.
> (c) State the name and address of the petitioner or the names and addresses of the petitioners.
> (d) If the petition is presented by one spouse or parent only, the name of the other spouse or parent as a respondent, and state the address of that spouse or parent.
> (e) Name as a respondent any other person who has any relation to the controversy, and state the address of the person if known to the petitioner.
> (f) If the petition arises out of an instance of domestic violence, so state generally and without specific allegations as to the incident.
> (g) State any other information the court by rule requires.

The format of the petition is also provided for by statute (a judicial council form has not yet been developed for this purpose). Section 1832 of the Family Code requires use of the following caption, however:

In the Superior Court of the State of California
In and for the County of _____

Upon the Petition of   )

)

_____,   )   **Petition for Conciliation**

(Petitioner)   )   **(under the Family**

)   **Conciliation Court Law)**

and concerning   )

)

_____, and   )

_____   )

(Respondents)   )

)

_____   )

To the Family Conciliation Court: . . .

Therefore the petitioning party would follow the salutation with a description of the controversy and a request for intervention by the Family Conciliation Court in accordance with the guidelines established in Family Code section 1833.

In contrast to other legal proceedings wherein court personnel are specifically prevented from rendering legal assistance to litigants, Family Code section 1834 statutorily authorizes certain court personnel (probation officers) to provide assistance in the preparation of any forms required under this chapter of the Family Code. Additionally, no fee is required to file this petition.

Once the petition has been filed, the court sets a time and place for the hearing and will give notice of this hearing to all interested parties. If this is not a joint petition (that is, one where both parents or spouses request Family Conciliation Court intervention), the court will issue a citation *requiring* the respondent to appear. The court also has the power to compel the attendance of witnesses at the hearing, just as in any other civil case. This hearing can be held just about anywhere the conciliator chooses; however, if one of the parties objects to the location of the hearing, then it must be held at the same time and location as that used for the trial of civil action. In other words, if the conciliator chooses to hold the hearing at 6:00 p.m. at her or his office, either party may object and thus compel the hearing to be held at the local courthouse during normal business hours (typically 8:30 a.m. to 4:30 p.m.).

The hearings themselves are informal and are conducted not as trials but as conferences, much like traditional marriage counseling. The Code requires that the presiding judge of the superior court designate at least one judge to hear all conciliation court cases. The Code provides further, however, that the superior court may also appoint a supervising counselor and associate counselor to assist the judge in carrying out the duties required by this statutory scheme. The duties of these persons are defined by section 1814 of the Family Code.

The qualifications of these counselors are strictly construed by statute in sections 1815 of the Family Code.

Section 1815:

(a) A person employed as a supervising counselor of conciliation or as an associate counselor of conciliation shall have all of the following minimum qualifications:

(1) A master's degree in psychology, social work, marriage, family and child counseling, or other behavioral science substantially related to marriage and family interpersonal relationships.

(2) At least two years of experience in counseling or psychotherapy, or both, preferably in a setting related to the areas of responsibility of the family conciliation court and with the ethnic population to be served.

(3) Knowledge of the court system of California and the procedures used in family law cases.

(4) Knowledge of other resources in the community to which clients can be referred for assistance.

(5) Knowledge of adult psychopathology and the psychology of families.

(6) Knowledge of child development, child abuse, clinical issues relating to children, the effects of divorce on children, the effects of domestic violence on children, and child custody research sufficient to enable a counselor to assess the mental health needs of children.

(7) Training in domestic violence issues as described in Section 1816.

(b) The family conciliation court may substitute additional experience for a portion of the education, or additional education for a portion of the experience, required under subdivision (a).

(c) This section does not apply to any supervising counselor of conciliation who was in office on March 27, 1980.

In essence, then, the supervising and associate counselors take the laboring oar in conducting these hearings, and making recommendations to the judge as appropriate. Remember, the goal of the Family Conciliation Court is to provide *reconciliation* services, not to generate court *orders*; after all, no judge can order parties to stay together. The judge *is* allowed, however, to make orders with respect to the conduct of the spouses or parents; further, the judge can make orders with respect to any subject matter of the controversy that the court deems necessary to preserve the marriage or to implement the reconciliation of the spouses (Family Code section 1839). These orders are only good for 30 days, however, unless the parties mutually agree to extend them.

By making these orders, the court can "force" the parties to modify their behavior in a way that, in the opinion of the court, will help them overcome their differences and hopefully salvage their relationship. While this approach to regulating the parties' behavior may seem harsh, it is grounded on the theory that some people who would not otherwise voluntarily modify their behavior will, once they are compelled to do so, "see the light" and adopt the court-ordered behavior as their own.

The court is also empowered by Family Code section 1839 to make support orders pending the completion of conciliation proceedings. These financial orders are modifiable and will not operate to prejudice any similar orders made in subsequent proceedings. The conciliation court proceedings are confidential once the files are closed, meaning that the public cannot review these files, unlike most other court files. These proceedings, while not always successful, reflect the legislature's commitment to preserve the institution of marriage and protect the welfare of minor children. Everything about the proceedings of the conciliation court is designed to allow the parties easy access to the court free of charge and the opportunity to present their differences to counselors trained in the fields of psychology, social work, marriage and family counseling, child development, child abuse, and many other related areas. Thus, although some believe California encourages divorce through its no-fault system, it is clear that the State Legislature is committed to preserving marriage through its conciliation court.

I. Mediation Proceedings

A concept closely related to conciliation is *mediation*, a process in which the parties are encouraged to amicably resolve their differences. Mediation is not identical to conciliation, however and is mandated by a completely different set of Family Code statutes.

The statutory scheme that establishes and regulates the mediation process is found in Part 2 ("Right to Custody of Minor Child") of Division 8

("Custody of Children") of the Family Code. It is entitled "Mediation of Custody and Visitation Issues" and is found in sections 3160 to 3186. Just as with conciliation, the superior court is charged with providing the services of a mediator but is not required to establish a conciliation court just to provide mediation services. The first major distinction between conciliation and mediation, then, is found in its implementation: although establishing a conciliation court is basically voluntary and up to each individual county, there is no such latitude with mediation. The Code specifically states that "[e]ach Superior Court *shall* make a mediator available. . . . [emphasis added]" (Family Code section 3160).

The primary distinction between conciliation and mediation is that conciliation seeks (and in fact can compel) to *avoid* litigation. Mediation presupposes that litigation has already commenced. The purpose of mediation is to reduce acrimony and help the parties come to an agreement regarding custody and visitation issues. Contrast this with one of the goals of conciliation: to assist the parties in resolving their difficulties and reconciling (that is, saving the marriage). The avoidance of litigation is also borne out by Family Code section 3162, which recognizes that the standards of practice for mediation shall include, among other things, adoption of a plan that will facilitate the best interests of the children in the context of the family transition anticipated in marital termination (or legal separation) proceedings.

These standards of practice are worth reciting in their entirety since careful review of this code section will provide significant insight into the mediation process:

> (a) Mediation of cases involving custody and visitation concerning children shall be governed by uniform standards of practice adopted by the Judicial Council.
>
> (b) The standards of practice shall include, but not be limited to, all of the following:
>
>> (1) Provision for the best interest of the child and the safeguarding of the rights of the child to frequent and continuing contact with both parents, consistent with Sections 3011 and 3020.
>>
>> (2) Facilitation of the transition of the family by detailing factors to be considered in decisions concerning the child's future.
>>
>> (3) The conducting of negotiations in such a way as to equalize power relationships between the parties.
>
> (c) In adopting the standards of practice, the Judicial Council shall consider standards developed by recognized associations of mediators and attorneys and other relevant standards governing mediation of proceedings for the dissolution of marriage.
>
> (d) The Judicial Council shall offer training with respect to the standards to mediators.

The qualifications of mediators are similar to those imposed upon conciliation court counselors. Family Code section 3164 provides that the mediator can be a member of the professional staff of a family conciliation court (recall the stringent qualifications set out in Family Code sections 1815 and 1816) or can be "any other person . . . designated by the court" so long as they meet the minimum requirements of section 1815. These minimum requirements bear comment. Section 1815, while detailing significant educational and experience-related requirements, also provides as follows: "(b) The Family Conciliation court may substitute additional experience for a portion of the education, or additional education for a portion of the experience, required under subdivision (a)."

To the extent this language gives the Family Conciliation Court considerable leeway to assess the qualifications of its counselors, it can also be read to provide similar leeway to the superior court to select its mediators. In practice, many courts select experienced family law attorneys to act as mediators on a temporary basis.

Article 2 of this chapter on mediation makes the mediation process available in virtually every instance in which custody or visitation of children is at issue. For example, mediation is available in all contested custody or visitation proceedings (section 3170, where paternity is at issue (section 3172), or when the dispute relates to an existing order (section 3173), for example, when the parties cannot agree how to implement an existing order.

The mediation proceeding itself must be set so that it will take place either before or on the same date as the custody or visitation hearing. As with conciliation, the interested parties are given notice of the hearing, which is usually held in an informal setting and is confidential. The goal of the mediation process is to help the parties reach an agreement on the disputed issues, which is prepared by the mediator and presented to the court for signature, thus converting the agreement to an enforceable court order. The mediator's goal is not simply to effect an agreement of the parties. The mediator is duly bound to assess the needs and interests of the children involved and to fashion an agreement that is consistent with those factors. The mediator is even allowed, if appropriate, to interview the child and exclude the lawyers from the mediation process. Further, the mediator must meet with parties separately in situations involving a history of domestic violence.

Of course, not all mediation sessions produce agreement between the parties, and in those instances the mediator usually refers the parties back to the court for resolution of the dispute. The mediator is empowered, however (despite the confidential nature of the proceedings), to make recommendations to the judge on the issues of custody and visitation; moreover, the mediator can recommend to the court that independent counsel be appointed for the child.

J. Parental Counseling

Also related to the conciliation and mediation proceedings are the provisions of Chapter 12 of Division 8 ("Custody of Children") entitled "Counseling of Parents and Child," found in Family Code sections 3190 to 3192. In order to facilitate communication between parents regarding their children's best interest (as this is related to custody and visitation) and to improve the parenting skills of both parents, the court is empowered to *require* parents who are involved in a custody or visitation dispute (and the children if old enough) to participate in "outpatient counseling with a licensed mental health professional, or through other community programs and services that provide appropriate counseling . . . for not more than one year."

Before it can make such an order, the court must make *two* separate findings both set out in section 3190 of the Family Code: "(a) (1) The dispute between the parents, between the parent or parents and the child, between the parent or parents and another party seeking custody or visitation rights with the child, or between a party seeking custody or visitation rights and the child, poses a substantial danger to the best interest of the child"; and "(a) (2) The counseling is in the best interest of the child."

Each party typically pays for his or her own counseling under these provisions. Additionally, the parties share the costs of the counseling for the child in a proportion deemed appropriate by the court.

Family Code sections 3190-3192 give the court the opportunity to evaluate the situation existing between the parties. Rather than simply imposing its orders on the parties, the court refers them to counseling in hopes that the facts and circumstances at the heart of the problem can be addressed and remedied. The reader should note that the parties do not return to court at the completion of counseling; instead, they must file a new order to show cause should either so desire.

Summary

In this chapter, we reviewed how to interview a client and, using that information, how to prepare the various pleadings and forms needed to process a dissolution, legal separation, or nullity action through the court system. We learned that the petition and response are nearly identical in format and, for the most part, represent the "position papers" of the parties. We also discussed the various options available to a party who wishes to terminate a marital relationship, from mediation and conciliation through the selection of an appropriate "cause of action" (that is, dissolution, legal separation, or nullity). Further, we learned which procedures are used to obtain an uncontested dissolution or legal separation, or one that resolves by way of the respondent's default. Finally, we explored the process of mediation and conciliation as viable alternatives to contested litigation

Key Terms

The following is a list of key terms and phrases that you should be able to define and use in context. Only then will you have demonstrated a command of the material in this chapter.

- Complaint; Petition
- Answer; Response
- Service of Process
- mediation; conciliation court
- findings
- dissolution
- legal separation
- nullity
- void v. voidable
- incestuous
- bigamist
- legal consent v. actual consent
- Statute of Limitations
- putative spouse
- Summons
- Proof of Service
- Automatic Temporary Restraining Orders
- adopted v. approved (concerning judicial council forms)
- in propria persona
- attorney service
- Marital Settlement Agreement

Questions for Discussion

1. Briefly describe the structure of a lawsuit in general, and compare that structure to a family law lawsuit (for example, dissolution).
2. List at least five items that should be included in a client information sheet, and explain the significance of their inclusion.
3. Should the paralegal participate in the initial client interview? Explain why or why not.
4. Describe the difference between a *void* marriage and one that is *voidable*.
5. How does someone become a putative spouse?
6. Compare and contrast dissolution and legal separation.
7. Discuss fully at least two responsive options available to a respondent after being served with a petition, *not including* the response itself.

ENDNOTES

1. The facts may also be presented before a commissioner or judge pro tempore, as the case may be.

2. Not all states refer to the initial papers in family law matters as the Petition. That is the practice in California, however, and is the convention used in this book.

3. These are not the only responses available to a responding party in a lawsuit. Other possibilities will be discussed in greater detail below in the section on the Response.

4. In many counties this is only required when the parties estimate that their matter will require more than one day to try.

5. The reader should note, however, that the client information sheet is of equal value to the attorney or paralegal who does *not* use a computer database.

6. It is readily available because of the no-fault "irreconcilable differences" grounds for dissolution.

7. These concepts are discussed in greater detail earlier in this book, primarily in the section covering property rights.

8. In a void marriage, no "community" is ever created, and thus no community *property* is generated. This is not exactly the case with a voidable marriage.

9. This last category basically eliminates everyone in the same lineal path from marrying each other. For example, grandparents and grandchildren, and great grandparents and great grandchildren cannot marry.

10. A marriage will be legally terminated in California *only* upon the death of either party, a decree of dissolution, or a decree of nullity. Family Code §310.

11. A "statute of limitation" is a statutorily determined time period during which a lawsuit must be brought. If a party waits beyond this time period he will not be allowed to bring the lawsuit without obtaining a judicially declared exception to the statute's operation. Different types of lawsuits have different limitation periods, all of which are spelled out (generally) in the Code of Civil Procedure. A lawsuit for personal injury, for example, must be brought within one year of the date of the injury. An action for breach of a written contract must be brought within four years of the alleged breach.

12. Issues relating to child custody, visitation, and support are not dependent upon the existence of a valid marriage (or any marriage) for their determination.

13. These terms are explained further in this book's discussion of property.

14. A judgment (or decree) of legal separation must not be confused with the concept of "separation" as in "date of separation" or used in the context "My wife and I recently 'separated.'" This does not mean that this husband and wife have obtained a judgment

of legal separation. It simply means that the intent to terminate the marital union has been given existence by some act of one or both of the parties, such as when one party moves out of the family home. At that moment, the parties are said to be "separated." This is a factual question that has at its core a determination of the parties' state of mind and intent. This concept of "separation" is of primary importance when discussing issues relating to community property and is discussed further in that section of this book.

15. Preceding enactment of the FLA, in order to obtain a divorce, a party had to prove one of several "reasons" for the divorce: adultery, extreme cruelty, willful desertion, willful neglect, habitual intemperance, or conviction of a felony. As can be seen, current dissolution practice is much simpler (and a lot less colorful) when it comes to obtaining a divorce.

16. This includes children born to these two people *before* their marriage or children adopted by these parties.

17. The term "real property" typically means vacant land and homes.

18. This amount is subject to adjustment by the legislature every odd-numbered year to reflect changes in inflation, and so on.

19. This amount is also subject to adjustment.

20. The grounds for such a challenge are typically fraud, duress, mistake, or some other equitable ground.

21. Note that if papers are served by mail, C.C.P. §1013 provides an automatic extension of five days for the recipient to complete any task called for in those papers (longer if served by mail outside of the state).

22. Violation is potentially punishable by a jail sentence or a significant fine, or both.

23. Actually, this designation is rather old and somewhat outdated, especially when speaking of these forms. However, on all non-form pleadings and documents filed with the court, the upper left corner has traditionally been reserved for purposes of identifying the author of the document and that person's relationship to the litigants. Because it consists primarily of the author's name, address, and telephone number, much like a business card, the area came to be known as the "card."

24. This is an abbreviated form of the Latin *in propria persona*, which loosely translated means "appearing in person."

25. In nullity or legal separation proceedings, the proper place of trial is in the county of the *respondent's* residence.

26. For all practical purposes there is no distinction between these two labels. It makes little difference who is the petitioner and who is the respondent.

27. A "motion" is a procedure whereby a party requests, either formally or informally, that a court grant a particular request.

28. This is of concern because, as a general rule, *any* filing by the respondent, even a request to quash service of summons, can constitute a general appearance if not handled properly. Once such a general appearance has been made, the attack on jurisdiction is no longer valid. The remedy to this problem is to advise the court that the respondent is making a *special appearance* to quash service of the summons. By using these words, a general appearance will be avoided.

29. The procedure for setting aside a default will be discussed in detail later in this section.

30. Verification is done by reviewing the original *proof of service*, which is prepared and signed by the person who served the petition on the respondent.

31. The most common method to set aside a default that has been entered against a respondent is for the respondent to bring a motion under Code of Civil Procedure §473, which allows for relief from default to be granted by the court upon a showing of "inadvertence, mistake or excusable neglect" on the part of the responding party. Assuming that the responding party can demonstrate these factors, the court will most likely relieve the respondent of the default and allow him to file a response.

32. This is only necessary if the court is asked to grant financial orders (that is, child or spousal support, attorney's fees or costs). See Family Code §2330.5.

33. Because this form is used in both default *and* uncontested proceedings (discussed later in this chapter), the declarant need not always be the petitioner. In the context of a default proceeding the declarant *will* always be the petitioner.

34. In practice, the attorney typically submits it through an attorney service rather than the mail. An attorney service is a business that makes regular (usually daily) trips to various courthouses in the county for its attorney clients. The attorney service is not unlike a well-informed messenger service that specializes in the delivery and processing of legal documents. It is also typically a registered process server.

35. Sometimes these parties will sign a separate contract usually called a *Marital Settlement Agreement*, the executory provisions of which are then incorporated into the judgment. Whether by MSA or stipulated judgment, the agreement of the parties, and thus the uncontested nature of the proceedings, is evident from the existence of both parties' signatures.

36. This also applies to contested dissolutions.

CHAPTER 9

Resolving Issues before Trial

A. Preliminary Considerations
B. The Order to Show Cause
C. The Noticed Motion
D. Responding to the OSC; Motion
E. Temporary and Ex Parte Orders
F. Domestic Violence Prevention Act

CHAPTER OVERVIEW

This chapter, like the last one, explores the procedural aspects of working one's way through the court system in an attempt to process a dissolution, legal separation, or nullity action. However, this chapter concentrates on the procedures used by the parties to obtain temporary relief while awaiting the trial.

There is often a gap of several months between the time a dissolution or legal separation action is commenced and the date of trial. During this interim period, emotions between the spouses are typically at an all-time high, and the atmosphere is volatile to say the least. Many questions must be confronted by the parties, even those who do not desire to seek "revenge" against a spouse: Who will live in the house? Who will have custody of the children, and who will visit? How much should child or spousal support be? Who will pay the bills? How can I keep my spouse from harassing me?

These questions must be resolved in a manner that is enforceable and that establishes the ground rules for the parties to follow during this difficult time. Fortunately, there are procedures for doing just that. Most notable is the Order to Show Cause. While other methods are also available in one form or another, they typically are centered around either the order to show cause or a noticed motion.

A. Preliminary Considerations

Before learning the nuts and bolts of "law and motion" and "order to show cause" practice, some initial concepts must be identified, discussed, and explained, including temporary orders, ex parte relief, injunctions, and stipulations.

Temporary orders are just that: orders made at the request of either party (assuming sufficient factual and legal bases exist) during the time period between the filing of the Petition and the trial. These orders are sometimes called *pendente lite*, which is Latin for "pending trial." Included in this term are virtually all orders made pretrial, including restraining orders, injunctive orders, and orders regarding child custody, support, and other financial matters. In fact, the most commonly requested temporary orders are those that determine preliminary custody, visitation, support, and attorney's fees, along with injunctive orders designed to restrain behavior.

Ex parte is a term used to describe the process undertaken when the requesting party does not (or cannot) give the responding party[1] the usually required notice of the request. For example, as a general rule the party responding to (or opposing) the requested temporary orders must be given notice of the request 16 court days before the hearing date (the date on which the court will address the matter and rule upon it). This time period is extended an additional five days by Code of Civil Procedure section 1013 if the request is served by mail.[2]

Sometimes certain orders must be made immediately. For example, orders restraining a spouse from taking the children out of state would be moot (of no effect) if, by the time the request came before the judge, that spouse had already taken the children and left. Accordingly, the ex parte procedure was created to provide relief on an expedited basis. In ex parte proceedings, the respondent receives notice of a matter mere hours before it is set to be heard by the court, and the usual three-week waiting period between notice and hearing is shortened to days. We will discuss ex partes at greater length later in this section.

An *injunction* can be either *preliminary* or *permanent*. Code of Civil Procedure sections 525 et seq. discuss these terms in detail. By definition, an injunction is an order of court that either prohibits someone from doing an act (a *prohibitory* injunction) or one that requires, or compels, a person to perform some act (a *mandatory* injunction). Prohibitory injunctions are much more common, although in family law both types are regularly issued. Stay away, non-harassment, and non-molestation orders are examples of prohibitive injunctions. A move-away order (requiring a party to move out of the family residence) is an example of a mandatory injunction.

A *temporary restraining order*, or TRO, is typically issued ex parte. It is of brief duration (usually no more than 21 days) and expires at the time of the hearing on the preliminary injunction. Its purpose is to maintain the status quo (or provide immediate relief) during the waiting period for the hearing on the subject of the TRO.[3]

The *preliminary injunction* is an order of court made only after a noticed hearing. As we will see in our review of various judicial council forms below, a preliminary injunction is what the requesting party, through the order to show cause, is actually seeking (from the perspective of injunctive relief). The purpose of this order is to maintain the status quo pending trial. TROs that were issued before the preliminary injunction (if requested and obtained) eventually become the preliminary injunctive orders. The preliminary injunctive orders continue until further order of court or trial (which for all practical purposes is the same as "further order of court").

A *permanent injunction* is an injunctive order that continues to exist after the trial. A permanent injunction is issued (if requested and supported by sufficient evidence) following the trial and, as its name implies, continues until further order of the court.

A *stipulation* simply refers to an agreement between the parties to litigation. A stipulation can be the result of rational discussion between opposing parties and a desire to save legal fees, or it can represent the unenthusiastic capitulation of one side to the requests of the other. The motivation for this type of agreement varies. However the agreement is reached, it is essential that its provisions be written down as soon as possible and that the agreement be turned into an order accordingly. In this fashion it will become enforceable. Further, no matter how well the parties are getting along, an oral agreement is only as good as the paper on which it is written.

B. The Order to Show Cause

As stated above, the usual manner in which requests for orders pending trial are brought to the court is through use of an Order to Show Cause (OSC) or a motion. Ex parte temporary restraining orders are equally available in both procedures, although TROs are typically sought in the context of a preliminary injunction, which is raised through an OSC.

To obtain an OSC, the requesting party makes ex parte application to the court.[4] The requesting party serves the OSC on the responding party, making certain to provide for the minimum amount of notice required by statute: 16 court days (plus 5 days for mailing). The Order to Show Cause is in actuality an order to appear, directed to the responding party to appear at the hearing date referenced thereon and *show cause* why the relief requested in the attached application should not be granted. If the responding party ignores the order and does not attend the hearing, the court will hold the hearing without his input and make orders accordingly.

The following section explains how to use the judicial council forms to obtain an OSC.

1. The Face Sheet

To prepare an OSC, one must prepare several documents. The first such document is form FL-300, which is in essence a cover sheet. Figure 9-1 on page 377 is a reproduction of this form.

As seen in Figure 9-1, the top third of FL-300 is reserved for information relating to the attorney's identity and relationship to the party submitting the form; the title of the case; the location of the court; the case number; and a laundry list of subjects to be addressed by the court at the hearing (depending on what is requested in the OSC). This section presents a fair checklist of the areas of relief most commonly requested by participants to a marital termination action. Usually, if the form is submitted as the initial OSC (the first time orders are requested from the court), every box will be checked (if there are children of the union) so as to resolve as many of these issues pretrial as possible.

To complete item 1, insert the name of the party who is expected to respond to this order—typically the petitioner or respondent.

Item 2 explains the nature of the order and the requirement to appear at the hearing. Note the lower portion of the form (the box just below the judge's signature). This box contains additional warnings, which should not be ignored. Item 2 also sets forth the location, date, and time for the hearing in order to provide the responding party with proper notice.

The item in the center of the page above item 3 contains instructions pertinent to issues regarding children (specifically custody and visitation—not support). These instructions direct the litigants to participate in mediation *before* their hearing date.[5]

For purposes of this discussion, the important point to bear in mind is that if custody or visitation is at issue in the OSC, then an appointment for the parties must be made (and kept) with the mediator *before* the hearing. The court will not entertain a hearing on these issues until and unless the parties have been to mediation. The mediation process typically does not require extensive participation by the attorneys. Thus, if the parties wait to attend mediation until the day of the hearing (when their attorneys are present) they may find themselves paying their attorneys to sit around and wait for them during the mediation process. It is not unusual for this process to take several *hours* (usually after a wait of at least one to two hours if the parties simply "walk in" on the day of the hearing without an appointment). This can add up to several hundred, if not *thousands*, of dollars of wasted client funds.

Item 3 of the OSC form FL-130 lists additional items that the judge can (and typically will) order in this context. Item 3(1) reflects the inclusion of an Income and Expense Declaration (discussed below). This form is almost always required with Orders to Show Cause. Item 3(a)(3) is usually not required, or even desirable in this author's opinion. The forms referenced

Figure 9-1
Form FL-300—Order to Show Cause

FL-300

ATTORNEY OR PARTY WITHOUT ATTORNEY *(Name, State Bar number, and address):*	*FOR COURT USE ONLY*

TELEPHONE NO.:   FAX NO. *(Optional):*
E-MAIL ADDRESS *(Optional):*
ATTORNEY FOR *(Name):*

SUPERIOR COURT OF CALIFORNIA, COUNTY OF

STREET ADDRESS:
MAILING ADDRESS:
CITY AND ZIP CODE:
BRANCH NAME:

PETITIONER/PLAINTIFF:
RESPONDENT/DEFENDANT:

ORDER TO SHOW CAUSE **MODIFICATION**	CASE NUMBER:
☐ Child Custody ☐ Visitation ☐ Injunctive Order ☐ Child Support ☐ Spousal Support ☐ Other *(specify):* ☐ Attorney Fees and Costs	

1. TO *(name):*

2. YOU ARE ORDERED TO APPEAR IN THIS COURT AS FOLLOWS TO GIVE ANY LEGAL REASON WHY THE RELIEF SOUGHT IN THE ATTACHED APPLICATION SHOULD NOT BE GRANTED. **If child custody or visitation is an issue in this proceeding, Family Code section 3170 requires mediation before or concurrently with the hearing listed below.**

   a. Date: Time: ☐ Dept.:   ☐ Room:

   b. The address of the court is ☐ same as noted above ☐ other *(specify):*

   c. ☐ The parties are ordered to attend custody mediation services as follows:

3. THE COURT FURTHER ORDERS that a completed *Application for Order and Supporting Declaration* (form FL-310), a **blank** *Responsive Declaration* (form FL-320), and the following documents be served with this order:

   a. (1) ☐ Completed *Income and Expense Declaration* (form FL-150) and a **blank** *Income and Expense Declaration*
      (2) ☐ Completed *Financial Statement (Simplified)* (form FL-155) and a **blank** *Financial Statement (Simplified)*
      (3) ☐ Completed *Property Declaration* (form FL-160) and a **blank** *Property Declaration*
      (4) ☐ Points and authorities
      (5) ☐ Other *(specify):*

   b. ☐ Time for ☐ service ☐ hearing   is shortened. Service must be on or before *(date):*
      Any responsive declaration must be served on or before *(date):*
   c. ☐ You are ordered to comply with the temporary orders attached.
   d. ☐ Other *(specify):*

Date: _____

JUDICIAL OFFICER

NOTICE: If you have children from this relationship, the court is required to order payment of child support based on the incomes of both parents. The amount of child support can be large. It normally continues until the child is 18. You should supply the court with information about your finances. Otherwise, the child support order will be based on the information supplied by the other parent.

You do not have to pay any fee to file declarations in response to this order to show cause (including a completed Income and Expense Declaration (form FL-150) or Financial Statement *(Simplified)* (form FL-155) that will show your finances). In the absence of an order shortening time, the original of the responsive declaration must be filed with the court and a copy served on the other party at least nine court days before the hearing date. Add five calendar days if you serve by mail within California. (See Code of Civil Procedure 1005 for other situations.) To determine court and calendar days, go to *www.courtinfo.ca.gov/selfhelp/courtcalendars/.*

Requests for Accommodations
Assistive listening systems, computer-assisted real-time captioning, or sign language interpreter services are available if you ask at least five days before the proceeding. Contact the clerk's office or go to *www.courtinfo.ca.gov/forms* for *Request for Accommodations by Persons With Disabilities and Response* (Form MC-410). (Civil Code, § 54.8.)

Page 1 of 1

Form Adopted for Mandatory Use Judicial Council of California FL-300 [Rev. January 1, 2007]	**ORDER TO SHOW CAUSE**	Family Code, §§ 215, 270 et seq., 3000 et seq., 3500 et seq., 4300 *www.courtinfo.ca.gov*

in this item (Property Declaration) are typically used in preparation for trial or whenever the division and distribution of assets is in issue. At the initial OSC stage (or at any time pretrial) these issues are rare.

Item 3(4) refers to a filed document that contains legal authority in the form of a discussion of cases and statutes as they apply to the specific requests made in the OSC. Unless the OSC presents unusual or untested legal arguments, points and authorities are usually not required. If such a document is included with the OSC packet, this box must be checked because these papers must be served in their entirety on the responding party. A good rule of thumb is that if a party serves papers on the judge, that party must file copies of those papers on the other party too. Finally, item 3(4) is the place to include any other documents that will be served with the OSC that were not otherwise listed in item 3.

Item 3.b is used when the requesting party seeks an order to shorten time to set the hearing. One of the more commonly requested ex parte orders is for an order shortening time. The reader will recall that an ex parte request is typically used to obtain temporary restraining orders on very short notice (usually only a few hours). In situations where immediate relief is not required, yet a delay of time equal to the typical 16- to 21-day notice period is unacceptable (for good cause, not simply because the requesting party does not want to wait that long), a request can be made to the court to shorten this notice period. The courts generally do not like to do this because it can (and usually does) work a hardship both on the responding party and on the court, which has to rearrange its schedule to accommodate a case set outside of the usual timetable. However, if the requesting party shows good cause for shortening time, the court will allow the hearing to be set on less than 16 days' notice.

Item 3.c should be checked if temporary orders have been requested (and obtained). To obtain a temporary order, one must prepare all the papers necessary for an OSC and include with them a separate form (FL-305 or sometimes, in the event of allegations of domestic violence, DV-110. et. al.), which sets forth the orders requested and obtained. As such, if form FL-305 (discussed below) has been completed and signed by the judge, this box is checked.

Item 3.d. contains orders not otherwise provided for by the options immediately above. If there is something else that either the requesting party or judge believes should be ordered, it should be itemized here. A separate sheet, labeled "Attachment 3.d." may be used if there is not enough room on the form. An example of such an order would be one that requires the responding party to bring to the hearing financial or other records (if financial issues are to be determined), or similar items of interest or necessity to the requesting party at the time of the hearing.

Assuming all is in order, the clerk will set the date and time, the judge will sign the form, and the OSC may be served on the responding party.

2. The Application for Order and Supporting Declaration

Figure 9-2 is the front side (page 1) of form FL-310, "Application for Order and Supporting Declaration." This document accompanies the OSC face sheet when an order to show cause is filed[6] and is self-explanatory. The form is divided into 9 different pre-printed requests, each covering a different subject matter.

Items 1 through 3 concern issues regarding children. In item 1, if custody is an issue to be decided at the hearing, the appropriate box pertinent to "Petitioner" or "Respondent" is checked to identify the requesting party. The box immediately next to item 1, "child custody," is checked and then the information in items 1a, 1b, and 1c is filled out. If there is more than one child, then the name and age for each child should be listed under item 1a; further, the *name* of the party requesting custody (not their legal status [that is, "Petitioner" or "Respondent"]) should be inserted.

As with all other forms, if there is insufficient space to list all of the children of the union, then a page labeled "Attachment 1—Child Custody" can be attached.

The box next to "modify" is checked if the court already entered orders on this subject in this case and the requesting party seeks to have those orders modified. The requesting party must advise the court of previously issued orders, when they were entered, and their content. Note that item 1 is simply a generic child custody request, which includes both legal and physical custody (concepts discussed earlier in the section on child custody).

Item 2 concerns child visitation and requests that the court enter visitation orders as specifically requested on the form. Just as with item 1, the applicant should check the appropriate boxes and attach a labeled document that sets forth his proposed visitation plan.

Item 3 contains a request for an award of child support. As a practical matter, whenever the court hears a custody issue, it also considers the issue of child support. Recall that the OSC face sheet (form FL-300) contains the following warning pertinent to child support: "*Notice: if you have children from this relationship, the court is required to order payment of child support based on the incomes of both parents.*" This language puts the recipient of the Order to Show Cause on notice that the issue of child support, even if not checked by the requesting party, can become an appropriate issue for determination by the court. Of course, it is always good practice to put the responding party on notice that this subject will be discussed at the time of the hearing. It is also good practice to indicate, as to each child, the amount of support requested on a monthly basis.[7] As with the previous two sections, item 3.c. references modification requests.

The requesting party uses item 4 if he seeks an award of spousal support. When requesting spousal support, the requesting party should insert

Figure 9-2
Form FL-310—Application for Order and
Supporting Declaration (front)

FL-310

| PETITIONER/PLAINTIFF: | CASE NUMBER: |
| RESPONDENT/DEFENDANT: | |

APPLICATION FOR ORDER AND SUPPORTING DECLARATION
—THIS IS NOT AN ORDER—

☐ Petitioner   ☐ Respondent   ☐ Claimant   requests the following orders:

1. ☐ CHILD CUSTODY   ☐ To be ordered pending the hearing
   a. Child's name and age   b. Legal custody to (name of person who   c. Physical custody to (name of
                                      makes decisions about health, education, etc.)   person with whom child will live.)

   d. ☐ Modify existing order
       (1) filed on *(date):*
       (2) ordering *(specify):*

   e. ☐ As requested in form   ☐ FL-311   ☐ FL-312   ☐ FL-341(C)   ☐ FL-341(D)   ☐ FL-341(E)

2. ☐ CHILD VISITATION   ☐ To be ordered pending the hearing
   a. As requested in: (1) ☐ Attachment 2a   (2) ☐ Form FL-311   (3) ☐ Other *(specify):*

   b. ☐ Modify existing order
       (1) filed on *(date):*
       (2) ordering *(specify):*

   c. ☐ One or more domestic violence restraining/protective orders are now in effect. *(Attach a copy of the orders if you*
       have one.) The orders are from the following court or courts *(specify county and state):*

       (1) ☐ Criminal: County/state: (3) ☐ Juvenile: County/state:
           Case No. *(if known).*   Case No. *(if known):*
       (2) ☐ Family: County/state: (4) ☐ Other: County/state:
           Case No. *(if known):*   Case No. *(if known):*

3. ☐ CHILD SUPPORT *(An earnings assignment order may be issued.)*
   a. Child's name and age   b. Monthly amount requested (if not by guideline)
                                         $

   c. ☐ Modify existing order
       (1) filed on *(date):*
       (2) ordering *(specify):*

4. ☐ SPOUSAL OR PARTNER SUPPORT *(An earnings assignment order may be issued.)*
   a. ☐ Amount requested *(monthly):* $ c. ☐ Modify existing order
   b. ☐ Terminate existing order   (1) filed on *(date):*
       (1) filed on *(date):*   (2) ordering *(specify):*
       (2) ordering *(specify):*

NOTE: To obtain domestic violence restraining orders, you must use the forms *Request for Order*
(Domestic Violence Prevention) (form DV-100), Temporary Restraining Order (Domestic Violence
Prevention) (form DV-110), and Notice of Court Hearing (Domestic Violence Prevention) (form DV-109).

Page 1 of 2

Form Adopted for Mandatory Use
Judicial Council of California
FL-310 [Rev. July 1, 2011]

APPLICATION FOR ORDER AND SUPPORTING DECLARATION

Family Code, §§ 2045, 2107, 6224,
6226, 6320–6326, 6380–6383
www.courtinfo.ca.gov

the specific amount that he requests; this figure provides the court with guidance and provides the responding party with notice that the request for a specific amount will be made.[8] The notice is very important in the event that the responding party ignores the OSC and does not appear at the hearing. The court can only enter orders against a responding party to the extent that the responding party was given notice of the relief to be sought. Arguably, if the requesting party checks the box and asks for $100 per month in spousal support, then asks for $500 per month *after* the hearing, the court cannot make such a large award. The court cannot make the $500 per month award because the responding party did not receive notice of the fact that an award in excess of $100 would be sought.

Item 4.c. contains a request to modify an existing order of spousal support. Item 4.b. contains a request to terminate an existing spousal support order. In both instances, the court requires information regarding the date and other specifics of those prior orders.

Item 5 requests an award of attorney's fees and costs. In many instances one party to a family law action may be entitled to receive a contribution from the other party to his attorney's fees and costs incurred in the prosecution of (or in responding to) that action. For the party to avail himself of this opportunity, the payment must be specifically requested in item 5. Because the actual amount of fees is unknown until the proceedings conclude, when requesting fees it is best to insert the word "reasonable" following the dollar sign in item 5.a; when requesting a contribution to costs, notice is deemed sufficient if the word "actual" is inserted alongside the dollar sign in item 5.b. As a practical matter, the requesting party will not get an award of attorney's fees unless his attorney submits a detailed declaration supporting that request. The attorney typically submits his declaration in a "complete" fashion at the conclusion of the proceedings, when the actual amounts involved are known.

Items 6 and 7, on page 2, contain general requests for injunctive relief, both prohibitive and mandatory. Item 6 is a request for certain property restraints. Item 7 is entitled "Property Control" and seeks exclusive use of particular assets.

Figure 9-3 is the back side (page 2) of form FL-310. This side is arranged similarly to side 1 and contains requests pertinent to property restraints and control and related matters. It also provides for a discussion of the propriety of the issuance of these orders by the requesting party, which is set forth in that party's declaration.

Item 6 contains language very similar to the property-related automatic temporary restraining orders found on the back side of the summons (form FL-110). It is often considered a good practice for the requesting party to voluntarily check all the boxes in item 6 so as to make these orders mutual. It is always easier for the court to justify restraining one party from exercising this type of control over property if the requesting party is also willing

Figure 9-3
Form FL-310—Application for Order and
Supporting Declaration (back)

FL-310

PETITIONER/PLAINTIFF:	CASE NUMBER:
RESPONDENT/DEFENDANT:	

5. ☐ ATTORNEY FEES AND COSTS   a. ☐ Fees: $ b. ☐ Costs: $

6. ☐ PROPERTY RESTRAINT   ☐ **To be ordered pending the hearing**
   a. The ☐ petitioner ☐ respondent ☐ claimant   is restrained from transferring, encumbering, hypothecating, concealing, or in any way disposing of any property, real or personal, whether community, quasi-community, or separate, except in the usual course of business or for the necessities of life.
       ☐ The applicant will be notified at least five business days before any proposed extraordinary expenditures, and an accounting of such will be made to the court.
   b. ☐ Both parties are restrained and enjoined from cashing, borrowing against, canceling, transferring, disposing of, or changing the beneficiaries of any insurance or other coverage, including life, health, automobile, and disability, held for the benefit of the parties or their minor children.
   c. ☐ Neither party may incur any debts or liabilities for which the other may be held responsible, other than in the ordinary course of business or for the necessities of life.

7. ☐ PROPERTY CONTROL   ☐ **To be ordered pending the hearing**
   a. ☐ The petitioner ☐ respondent   is given the exclusive temporary use, possession, and control of the following property that we own or are buying *(specify):*

   b. ☐ The petitioner ☐ respondent   is ordered to make the following payments on liens and encumbrances coming due while the order is in effect:

Debt	Amount of payment	Pay to

8. ☐ OTHER RELIEF *(specify):*

9. ☐ **I request** that time for service of the *Order to Show Cause* and accompanying papers be shortened so that these documents may be served no less than *(specify number):*   days before the time set for the hearing. I need to have the order shortening time because of the facts specified in item 10 or the attached declaration.

10. ☐ FACTS IN SUPPORT of relief requested and change of circumstances for any modification are *(specify):*
   ☐ Contained in the attached declaration. (You may use *Attached Declaration* (form MC-031) for this purpose).

I declare under penalty of perjury under the laws of the State of California that the foregoing is true and correct.
Date:

▶

_____   _____
(TYPE OR PRINT NAME)   (SIGNATURE OF APPLICANT)

to submit to the same restrictions. Setting the request up in this fashion also typically makes the request much more palatable from the responding party's standpoint. Usually, if any of the requests in item 6 are made, all of the boxes should be checked with the exception of the box referencing "claimant."

In item 7, the applicant requests that she be given exclusive use, possession, and control of certain property pending the hearing or trial. For example, the requesting party may seek exclusive use of the couple's car. The applicant would also use this portion of the form to request exclusive use of the family home.[9] If there is insufficient space to list the various assets over which the requesting party seeks exclusive use and control, then a document labeled "Attachment 7.a." can be attached.

Item 7.b. contains requests by the applicant that certain ongoing community debts be paid by the responding party as they come due.[10] Depending on the parties' financial situation, the court certainly has the power to make these kinds of orders. Item 7.b. of the application is an often ignored portion of the application, and foolishly so because this request is very powerful and can be a life saver for an applicant with little or no income.

Item 8 contains the request to shorten time for service of the Order to Show Cause, which was discussed above. The applicant should specify the number of days that she believes the court should accept as "sufficient notice" of the hearing. As a practical matter, however, the court will not entertain requests that it believes to be excessive or impermissible. The court will generally not shorten time for service of papers to a point that contemplates less than three court days between the date of service and the date of hearing.

Item 9 contains an area for the applicant to insert any requests that have not been covered by the standard form set forth in the preceding sections of the application. An example of such a request might include the return of a specific asset, the delivery of certain documents, or the exchange of financial information. An additional sheet may be attached if needed.

Item 10 is perhaps the most important part of the application for order. Here the applicant provides the court with the factual bases for making the orders requested. These orders are not granted in a vacuum. All orders requested of the court must be supported by admissible evidence that gives rise to the necessity and propriety of granting these requests. Such evidence takes the form of *facts* given to the court to evaluate and consider prior to issuing these orders. It is thus absolutely crucial to give the court all the facts that support the applicant's particular request. *Exactly* what happened between the parties that justifies this relief? *When* did this take place? The applicant cannot simply state her fears, speculations, and conclusions as to ultimate facts; instead, she must provide the court with all of the specific facts that support her request.

The preparation of an adequate declaration is a process of trial and error. There are no magic words to be used nor is there any specific form.[11] It is good practice to structure the applicant's declaration along the same lines as the form FL-310 application and structure: a paragraph-by-paragraph analysis of the request and recitation of facts in support of each request, which follows (or tracks) the application itself. This will make the declaration much more readable from the court's perspective and will also provide a structure for the applicant to follow when formulating her thoughts with regard to the declaration. With respect to each request, it is usually good practice for the applicant to "tell his story" (which is, after all, the factual basis for the requested relief) on a chronological basis. Once again, this is usually the most logical structure for a factual discussion of these various subject areas and also serves as a good structure for the applicant to follow in preparing the declaration.

Of significant importance in this context is a revision to the California Rules of Court limiting the length of declarations provided in the context of an Order to Show Cause or noticed Motion to a maximum of ten (10) pages, unless the court grants an exception to that rule based upon a finding of good cause following a request of the party seeking to submit a longer declaration. This page limitation does not apply to declarations of expert witnesses.

An example of a declaration in support of an application for temporary orders as contained in an Order to Show Cause is set forth below:

DECLARATION OF JANE DOE

1. I am the Respondent in the above-entitled action. This declaration is made in support of an Order to Show Cause Re: Determination of Arrearages and Penalties.
2. I have personal knowledge of all of the following facts set forth herein and if called to testify as a witness, I am competent to testify thereon.
3. On December 11, 2007, the court ordered that Petitioner pay to me as and for child support the sum of $400.00 per month, payable one-half on the 1st and one-half on the 15th of each month commencing on January 1, 2008, and continuing until the occurrence of standard termination conditions relative to child support, none of which has occurred to date.
4. As is set forth in more detail on the schedule attached to this Order to Show Cause, Petitioner made some sporadic payments through October 2009. These payments were never timely made, nor were they made in the court ordered amount. From and since November

1, 2009, I have not received any child support payments. The total amount of arrearages now due, with interest thereon (as of this writing), is $5,722.30.

5. Petitioner's failure to make his child support payments has created an extreme financial hardship on me and has hindered my ability to provide for our children, John Doe and Jake Doe. I am informed and believe that Petitioner is gainfully employed and has been, throughout the duration of this order, financially capable of making these child support payments. I have at no time agreed, either explicitly or by implication, to waive any of these payments. I therefore request that this Court determine the amount of child support and accrued interest to be in the amount requested herein.

I declare under the penalty of perjury under the laws of the State of California that the foregoing is true and correct.

Executed on _____, at Los Angeles, California.

_____

Jane Doe

It has been this author's practice to prepare declarations by dictation with the applicant present. In such fashion, the client is able to express her thoughts to the lawyer who can then accurately and concisely dictate them in an organized manner. The advantage of having the client present is that the client can stop the dictation and make corrections as the declaration is being prepared. This tends to be much quicker and also provides for direct input from the client, which is essential in the preparation of the declaration. The client also feels a part of the process rather than a mere observer. This is very important because most clients have never been to a lawyer before and are particularly vulnerable due to the nature of what they are going through. By working with the attorney instead of just watching (or learning about the work after the fact), the client is able to develop a sense of control over her life, which is very important at this time.

Successful preparation of these declarations is a trial-and-error process that is directly related to the amount of experience one has in their preparation. Over time the reader will develop his or her own style and become comfortable with preparing these declarations based on the facts provided by the client.

There is almost never enough space on the application form to accommodate a declaration sufficient to justify a request contained in the form FL-310. As such, both boxes at item 10 are usually checked and the multipage declaration discussed above is attached at the end of this document.

The reader should note that the application form itself is a declaration that is signed under penalty of perjury by the client. This means that the information contained in this document constitutes admissions that can later be used against the client. The client's information as set forth in these documents also carries with it the same force and effect as if the client was testifying in court before a judge. As such, great care must be taken in every aspect of preparing these documents and the supporting declaration.

It is appropriate to make one final note about the importance of the declaration[12] accompanying the Application for Order (as well as the declaration(s) accompanying the responding papers, discussed below). As the reader might imagine, the court reviews and hears dozens of similar requests each day. Yet there are a finite number of judges, commissioners, and judges pro tempore available to hear these OSCs.[13] In larger counties such as Los Angeles and San Francisco, it is not uncommon for one judge to have 15 to 20 of these Orders to Show Cause on calendar for hearing on any given day. It may very well take one-half of a court day to put the petitioner and respondent on the stand to testify to certain facts germane to the issues framed by the OSC. As such, the court can only resolve approximately two matters at best on any given day. The court must then move the other matters to other days. But what of the 15 or 20 matters scheduled for *that* day? They too have to be moved to accommodate the transferred items. It is easy to see how a judge would find it virtually impossible to hear family law matters in a timely fashion. Something had to be done—and something was. The judges were given discretion to clear their heavily congested calendars and resolve these cases. To that end, most local rules made it clear that taking oral testimony at an OSC was the exception and not the rule. Most judges thus expected all issues to be *fully* and *completely* discussed in the supporting and opposing declarations. These local rules were sanctioned by the appellate courts even when the trial courts based their rulings on the papers filed and *nothing else*. This was known as the *Reifler* or *Stevenot* rule, named after two cases that considered this very issue: Reifler v. Superior Court, 39 Cal. App. 3d 479 (1974), and Marriage of Stevenot, 154 Cal. App. 3d 1051 (1984). The *Stevenot* case tempered *Reifler's* blanket approval of the "declarations only" approach by allowing, in addition to the declarations, the cross-examination of some of the declarants and direct questioning by the judge on issues deemed to be important to the inquiry.

The "declarations only" approach was turned on its head, however, when the California Supreme Court decided Jeffrey Elkins v. Superior Court, 41 Cal. 4th 1337 (2007). In *Elkins*, the court ruled that the Contra Costa County Superior Court's local rules violated litigants' due process rights to present all relevant, competent evidence on material issues; the rules prevented judges from fully assessing a witness' demeanor and credibility through live testimony. Specifically, the court found that the local rules could not: (1) limit parties to marital dissolution actions from introducing evidence in written declaration form that had to be submitted before trial, and (2) prohibit one party from cross-examining the other about the contents of the declarations, except in "unusual circumstances."

The *Elkins* court found that although the Contra Costa County local rules served the interest of judicial economy, that interest does not trump litigants' due process rights, particularly those who are self-represented:

> We are aware that superior courts face a heavy volume of marital dissolution matters, and the case load is made all the more difficult because a substantial majority of cases are litigated by parties who are not represented by counsel. [Reference omitted] . . .
>
> In light of the volume of cases faced by trial courts, we understand their efforts to streamline family law procedures. But family law litigants should not be subjected to second-class status or deprived of access to justice. Litigants with other civil claims are entitled to resolve their disputes in the usual adversary trail proceeding governed by the rules of evidence established by statute. It is at least as important that courts employ fair proceedings when the stakes involve a judgment providing for custody in the best interest of a child and governing a parent's future involvement in his or her child's life, dividing all of a family's assets, or determining levels of spousal and child support. The same judicial resources and safeguards should be committed to a family law trial as are committed to other civil proceedings. Trial courts certainly require resources adequate to enable them to perform their function. If sufficient resources are lacking in the superior court or have not been allocated to the family courts, courts should not obscure the source of their difficulties by adopting programs that exalt efficiency over fairness, but instead should devote their efforts to allocating or securing the necessary resources.

Elkins also prompted the State Supreme Court to recommend that the California Judicial Council create a task force (the Elkins Task Force) "to study and propose measures to assist trial courts in achieving efficiency and fairness in marital proceedings and to ensure access to justice for litigants, many of whom are self-represented." The Elkins Task force issued its recommendations in October of 2009, and the first changes are set to take effect on January 1, 2011. One of the most notable changes is codified in Family Code section 217, which states:

> (a) At a hearing on any order to show cause or notice of motion brought pursuant to this code, absent a stipulation of the parties or a finding of good cause pursuant to subdivision (b), the court shall receive any live, competent testimony that is relevant and within the scope of the hearing and the court may ask questions of the parties.
>
> (b) In appropriate cases, a court may make a finding of good cause to refuse to receive live testimony and shall state its reasons for the finding on the record or in writing. The Judicial Council shall, by January 1, 2012, adopt a statewide rule of court regarding the factors a court shall consider in making a finding of good cause.
>
> (c) A party seeking to present live testimony from witnesses other than the parties shall, prior to the hearing, file and serve a witness list

with a brief description of the anticipated testimony. If the witness list is not served prior to the hearing, the court may, on request, grant a brief continuance and may make appropriate temporary orders pending the continued hearing.

Many believe that Family Code section 217 will seriously affect family law court proceedings in California. As court calendars begin to overflow, new procedures will need to be developed that both serve the interests of judicial economy and protect litigants' due process rights.

Either way, the consequences of weak (or missing) declarations in support of or in opposition to the requested relief can be disastrous. Remember, the parties are real people with real problems that must be addressed immediately. If time were not of the essence in these matters, they would simply wait until the trial. They cannot afford to go into court unprepared.

3. The Income and Expense Declaration

Whenever financial relief is sought (most commonly spousal and child support or attorney's fees), the court requires both parties to submit a form document that details their income and expenses. This form is a four-page document adopted for use by the Judicial Council, thus making its use mandatory. Not unlike a tax return, this form is often met with anxiety by clients, not for the information it seeks, but because most people shy away from numbers-oriented forms fearing they will be too difficult to fill out. This form is quite self-explanatory, however, and if the directions printed on it are followed carefully, it is actually quite simple.

The first page of this form summarizes general information, plus additional information provided in subsequent pages, relative to the person filling it out. The income and expense declaration seeks general information regarding age, employment, and education, along with tax information and an estimate of the other party's income. Item 4 requests information about the other party's income. This is a very important item and should not be overlooked or ignored simply because exact information is not available. If the matter turns out to be uncontested (that is, only the party seeking relief appears in court and the other party ignores the proceeding), the court must have some information about the defaulting person's income; without such information, the court cannot enter any financial orders. Therefore, each party should complete item 4, even if he or she has to make a wild guess as to the other party's income based on past experience. Figure 9-11 presents a sample of page 1 to the income and expense declaration.

Page 2 of FL-150 seeks information about the income of the person who is completing the form. Its main section (items 5, 6, 7, 8, and 9) requests information related to income received during the 12-month period preceding completion of the form from salary, wages, and bonuses, and so on, along with the same numbers for the immediately preceding month. Income from all sources (for example, rental income, stock dividends, interest, royalties) is also requested. The income portion of this form essentially seeks all pertinent information relative to the income of the party filling it out, in a manner that is (in this author's opinion) clear and easy to understand.

Figure 9-4 contains a sample of the income portion of form FL-150. Note that the form seeks information about income received during the "last 12 months," not the "last year." This is an important distinction. It is not uncommon for parties to "monkey around" with their income once they learn that their financial situation will be strictly scrutinized. (They tend to think: "the less I make, the less I have to pay/the more I can get.") To prevent this, the court seeks the parties' *historical* income. The court averages income received over the preceding 12 months, believing (correctly so in this author's opinion) that this will create a much more realistic income picture for the people involved. Form FL-150 also instructs each party to include pay stubs from the previous two months. Do not ignore this instruction.[14]

Figure 9-4
Form FL-150—Income Section

Attach copies of your pay stubs for the last two months and proof of any other income. Take a copy of your latest federal tax return to the court hearing. *(Black out your social security number on the pay stub and tax return.)*

5. **Income** *(For average monthly, add up all the income you received in each category in the last 12 months and divide the total by 12.)*   Last month   Average monthly

    a. Salary or wages (gross, before taxes) . . . . $_____ _____

    b. Overtime (gross, before taxes) . . . . $_____ _____

    c. Commissions or bonuses. . . . . $_____ _____

    d. Public assistance (for example: TANF, SSI, GA/GR) ☐ currently receiving . . . . $_____ _____

    e. Spousal support ☐ from this marriage ☐ from a different marriage . . . . $_____ _____

    f. Partner support ☐ from this domestic partnership ☐ from a different domestic partnership $_____ _____

    g. Pension/retirement fund payments. . . . . $_____ _____

    h. Social security retirement (not SSI) . . . . $_____ _____

    i. Disability: ☐ Social security (not SSI) ☐ State disability (SDI) ☐ Private insurance . $_____ _____

    j. Unemployment compensation . . . . $_____ _____

    k. Workers' compensation . . . . $_____ _____

    l. Other (military BAQ, royalty payments, etc.) *(specify):* . . . . $_____ _____

6. **Investment Income** *(Attach a schedule showing gross receipts less cash expenses for each piece of property.)*

    a. Dividends/interest. . . . . $_____ _____

    b. Rental property income . . . . $_____ _____

    c. Trust income. . . . . $_____ _____

    d. Other *(specify):* . . . . $_____ _____

7. **Income from self-employment, after business expenses for all businesses.** . . . . $_____ _____

    I am the ☐ owner/sole proprietor ☐ business partner ☐ other *(specify):*

    Number of years in this business *(specify):*

    Name of business *(specify):*

    Type of business *(specify):*

    Attach a profit and loss statement for the last two years or a Schedule C from your last federal tax return. Black out your social security number. If you have more than one business, provide the information above for each of your businesses.

8. ☐ **Additional income.** I received one-time money (lottery winnings, inheritance, etc.) in the last 12 months *(specify source and amount):*

9. ☐ **Change in income.** My financial situation has changed significantly over the last 12 months because *(specify):*

In the older version of this form, the second, or middle, portion contained items that took the preparer from gross to net income.[15] The current form FL-150 does not require the preparer to provide this information. To date, virtually every family court in California utilizes some form of computer software to calculate support; and such software contains all the requisite tax tables to allow the user to see how tax laws can impact the calculation of his or her income. The court is of course interested in learning the amount of gross income (as opposed to just net income) because sometimes people over-withhold from their pay checks, deferring the over-withheld income until it is returned to them in a tax refund. Indeed, in the example from footnote 15, the individual grossed $3,000 per month and would normally be expected to net $2,400 per month (which would become the basis of his "ability to pay" or "need for payment"). Suppose, however, that this person had his employer withhold based not on four withholding allowances, but on zero.[16] In this situation, the person's "take home" (or net) pay would drop to approximately $2,250 per month. Theoretically, because he would no doubt take all four deductions when filing his tax return, this over-withheld $150 per month would come back to him as a $1,800 dollar tax refund. The refund would need to be added back in to his monthly take home pay, however, to provide a realistic picture of his true financial situation.[17] Accordingly, the software discussed in this paragraph seeks to avoid games that taxpayers play by demonstrating an accurate picture of the gross to net calculation.

The newer version of this form does not concentrate on a tax calculation or analysis. Rather (in item 10) it simply requests a listing of the deductions that are claimed by the person completing the form. The court or opposing attorney can then explore the deductions in greater detail. Item 10 is set out in Figure 9-5.

Figure 9-6 illustrates the third section of this form, item 11. Item 11 seeks general information regarding the size and content of the party's estate (cash on hand, liquid assets, and general net worth). Generally, the court uses this information to better understand "where the parties are coming from" in the context of their requests for financial orders.

Figure 9-5
Form FL-150—Deductions Section

10. **Deductions**   Last month
    a. Required union dues . . . . $ _____
    b. Required retirement payments (not social security, FICA, 401(k), or IRA). . . . . $ _____
    c. Medical, hospital, dental, and other health insurance premiums *(total monthly amount)*. . . . . $ _____
    d. Child support that I pay for children from other relationships. . . . . $ _____
    e. Spousal support that I pay by court order from a different marriage. . . . . $ _____
    f. Partner support that I pay by court order from a different domestic partnership . . . . $ _____
    g. Necessary job-related expenses not reimbursed by my employer *(attach explanation labeled "Question 10g")* . . . . . $ _____

Figure 9-6
Form FL-150— "Assets" Section

11. **Assets**   Total
  a. Cash and checking accounts, savings, credit union, money market, and other deposit accounts . . . . $ _____
  b. Stocks, bonds, and other assets I could easily sell . . . . $ _____
  c. All other property, ☐ real and ☐ personal *(estimate fair market value minus the debts you owe)* . . . . $ _____

Page 3 of form FL-150 is the expense portion of the Income and Expense Declaration. It is divided into five sections.

Item 12, shown in Figure 9-7, requests the name, age, relationship, and *gross* monthly income of all persons living in the preparer's home. Item 12 also requests information as to the contributions made, if any, by the various people living in the household.

Items 13 and 14 require the user to indicate his average monthly expenses in various common categories. Many people try to exaggerate these numbers. They believe that by claiming high personal expenses, they will be saved from paying what might otherwise be a reasonable amount of support or attorney's fees; or, they believe that by claiming high personal expenses, they will establish a much greater "need" for support than is actually the case. These are foolish assumptions. The attorneys, or the court, can inquire into these expenses and request verification (for example, receipts and monthly bills). Because these papers are filled out and signed under *penalty of perjury*, if the numbers cannot be backed up, there will be some serious explaining to do with potentially grave consequences if one is caught lying. Estimates made in the absence of receipts are allowed so long as they are reasonable and can be demonstrated through testimony or other evidence. These sections are shown in Figure 9-8.

Item 15 of FL-150 covers information pertaining to attorney's fees—the fees owed, the amounts paid, and the attorney's billing arrangement. The court needs information on attorney's fees so it can, in conjunction with

Figure 9-7
Form FL-150—General Information Section

12. **The following people live with me:**

Name	Age	How the person is related to me? *(ex: son)*	That person's gross monthly income	Pays some of the household expenses?
a.				☐ Yes ☐ No
b.				☐ Yes ☐ No
c.				☐ Yes ☐ No
d.				☐ Yes ☐ No
e.				☐ Yes ☐ No

Figure 9-8
Form FL-150—Monthly Expenses Section

13. **Average monthly expenses** ☐ Estimated expenses ☐ Actual expenses ☐ Proposed needs

a. Home:

(1) ☐ Rent or ☐ mortgage... $ _____

If mortgage:

(a) average principal: $ _____
(b) average interest: $ _____

(2) Real property taxes .... , $ _____

(3) Homeowner's or renter's insurance
(if not included above) .... $ _____

(4) Maintenance and repair .... $ _____

b. Health-care costs not paid by insurance...$ _____

c. Child care .... $ _____

d. Groceries and household supplies....... $ _____

e. Eating out........................ $ _____

f. Utilities (gas, electric, water, trash) ..... $ _____

g. Telephone, cell phone, and e-mail ......$ _____

h. Laundry and cleaning .... $ _____

i. Clothes .... $ _____

j. Education .... $ _____

k. Entertainment, gifts, and vacation. ...... $ _____

l. Auto expenses and transportation
(insurance, gas, repairs, bus, etc.) ...... $ _____

m. Insurance (life, accident, etc.; do not
include auto, home, or health insurance)... $ _____

n. Savings and investments............. $ _____

o. Charitable contributions............... $ _____

p. Monthly payments listed in item 14
(itemize below in 14 and insert total here). . $ _____

q. Other *(specify)*: .... $ _____

r. **TOTAL EXPENSES** (a–q) *(do not add in
the amounts in a(1)(a) and (b))* $ _____

s. **Amount of expenses paid by others** $ _____

14. **Installment payments and debts not listed above**

Paid to	For	Amount	Balance	Date of last payment
		$	$	
		$	$	
		$	$	
		$	$	
		$	$	
		$	$	

the other parts of this form, determine an equitable allocation of attorney's fees between the parties. Item 15 is shown in Figure 9-9.

Page 4 of form FL-150 (shown in Figure 9-10 on page 393) is only required in cases where child support is at issue. The chapter on child support explains page 4 in greater detail. For now, the reader should simply become familiar with its format.

The Income and Expense Declaration (all four pages) is generally stapled together to form one document, separate from the other forms in the OSC packet. It is filed at the same time as the OSC, however, because it is

Figure 9-9
Form FL-150—Attorney's Fees

15. **Attorney fees** *(This is required if either party is requesting attorney fees.)*:

a. To date, I have paid my attorney this amount for fees and costs *(specify)*: $

b. The source of this money was *(specify)*:

c. I still owe the following fees and costs to my attorney *(specify total owed)*: $

d. My attorney's hourly rate is *(specify)*: $

I confirm this fee arrangement.

Date:

▶

_____
(TYPE OR PRINT NAME OF ATTORNEY)

_____
(SIGNATURE OF ATTORNEY)

FL-150 [Rev. January 1, 2007]   **INCOME AND EXPENSE DECLARATION**   Page 3 of 4

Figure 9-10
Form FL-150—Child Support Information

FL-150

PETITIONER/PLAINTIFF:	CASE NUMBER:
RESPONDENT/DEFENDANT:	
OTHER PARENT/CLAIMANT:	

CHILD SUPPORT INFORMATION
(NOTE: Fill out this page only if your case involves child support.)

16. **Number of children**
    a. I have *(specify number):* _____ children under the age of 18 with the other parent in this case.
    b. The children spend _____ percent of their time with me and _____ percent of their time with the other parent.
       (If you're not sure about percentage or it has not been agreed on, please describe your parenting schedule here.)

17. **Children's health-care expenses**
    a. ☐ I do ☐ I do not have health insurance available to me for the children through my job.
    b. Name of insurance company:
    c. Address of insurance company:

    d. The monthly cost for the **children's** health insurance is or would be *(specify):* $ _____
       (Do not include the amount your employer pays.)

18. **Additional expenses for the children in this case**   Amount per month
    a. Child care so I can work or get job training . . . . $ _____
    b. Children's health care not covered by insurance . . . . $ _____
    c. Travel expenses for visitation . . . . $ _____
    d. Children's educational or other special needs *(specify below):* . . . . $ _____

19. **Special hardships.** I ask the court to consider the following special financial circumstances
    (attach documentation of any item listed here, including court orders):   Amount per month   For how many months?
    a. Extraordinary health expenses not included in 18b . . . . $ _____   _____
    b. Major losses not covered by insurance (examples: fire, theft, other
       insured loss) . . . . $ _____   _____
    c. (1) Expenses for my minor children who are from other relationships and
          are living with me . . . . $ _____   _____
       (2) Names and ages of those children *(specify):*

       (3) Child support I receive for those children . . . . $ _____

    The expenses listed in a, b, and c create an extreme financial hardship because *(explain):*

20. **Other information I want the court to know concerning support in my case** *(specify):*

FL-150 [Rev. January 1, 2007]   **INCOME AND EXPENSE DECLARATION**   Page 4 of 4

Figure 9-11
Form FL-150—Income and Expense Declaration

FL-150

ATTORNEY OR PARTY WITHOUT ATTORNEY *(Name, State Bar number, and address):*	FOR COURT USE ONLY
TELEPHONE NO.: E-MAIL ADDRESS *(Optional):* ATTORNEY FOR *(Name):*	

SUPERIOR COURT OF CALIFORNIA, COUNTY OF

STREET ADDRESS:

MAILING ADDRESS:

CITY AND ZIP CODE:

BRANCH NAME:

PETITIONER/PLAINTIFF:

RESPONDENT/DEFENDANT:

OTHER PARENT/CLAIMANT:

INCOME AND EXPENSE DECLARATION	CASE NUMBER:

1. **Employment** *(Give information on your current job or, if you're unemployed, your most recent job.)*

> **Attach copies of your pay stubs for last two months (black out social security numbers).**

   a. Employer:

   b. Employer's address:

   c. Employer's phone number:

   d. Occupation:

   e. Date job started:

   f. If unemployed, date job ended:

   g. I work about _____ hours per week.

   h. I get paid $ _____ gross (before taxes) ☐ per month ☐ per week ☐ per hour.

(If you have more than one job, attach an 8½-by-11-inch sheet of paper and list the same information as above for your other jobs. Write "Question 1—Other Jobs" at the top.)

2. **Age and education**

   a. My age is *(specify):*

   b. I have completed high school or the equivalent: ☐ Yes ☐ No   If no, highest grade completed *(specify):*

   c. Number of years of college completed *(specify):* ☐ Degree(s) obtained *(specify):*

   d. Number of years of graduate school completed *(specify):* ☐ Degree(s) obtained *(specify):*

   e. I have: ☐ professional/occupational license(s) *(specify):*

       ☐ vocational training *(specify):*

3. **Tax information**

   a. ☐ I last filed taxes for tax year *(specify year):*

   b. My tax filing status is ☐ single ☐ head of household ☐ married, filing separately

       ☐ married, filing jointly with *(specify name):*

   c. I file state tax returns in ☐ California ☐ other *(specify state):*

   d. I claim the following number of exemptions (including myself) on my taxes *(specify):*

4. **Other party's income.** I estimate the gross monthly income (before taxes) of the other party in this case at *(specify):* $ _____
This estimate is based on *(explain):*

(If you need more space to answer any questions on this form, attach an 8½-by-11-inch sheet of paper and write the question number before your answer.) Number of pages attached: _____

I declare under penalty of perjury under the laws of the State of California that the information contained on all pages of this form and any attachments is true and correct.

Date:

▶

_____   _____
(TYPE OR PRINT NAME)   (SIGNATURE OF DECLARANT)

Page 1 of 4

Form Adopted for Mandatory Use
Judicial Council of California
FL-150 [Rev. January 1, 2007]

INCOME AND EXPENSE DECLARATION

Family Code, §§ 2030–2032,
2100–2113, 3552, 3620–3634,
4050–4076, 4300–4339
www.courtinfo.ca.gov

essential to a review of any financial issues at the hearing on the order to show cause where financial relief is being sought.

4. Temporary Orders

Temporary Orders are available in an OSC proceeding and are typically used to maintain the status quo between the time a party files the OSC papers and the hearing date; in other words, temporary orders provide immediate relief on very short notice.[18] This text's section on temporary orders discusses the subject in greater detail. To request a temporary order, parties must use Judicial Council form FL-305 (shown in Figure 9-12 on page 396).

Form FL-305 constitutes an official court order once the judge signs it. Form FL-310, however, is merely an application signed by the requesting party. (Hence, FL-310 bears the title "Application for Order and Supporting Declaration.")

The format of FL-305 is rather similar to that of FL-310. This explains the notation at the top of form FL-310 (the Application for Order) that *"This Is Not an Order,"* which helps to reduce any confusion created in the mind of the recipient of these forms.

Form FL-305 sets forth options (much like FL-310) in the areas most commonly subject to temporary orders. Generally, these orders restrict or restrain conduct related to property (items 1 and 2) or children (item 3). These orders, when signed by the judge, are effective immediately[19] and are enforceable by all law enforcement personnel as well as by a judge in a civil contempt matter.

The structure of the form is essentially similar to the Application for Order (form FL-310), and it is completed in the same manner. The reader should note that once the form is signed by a judge, whatever is contained in the form constitutes a court order. It is filled out by the applicant, however. As such, care must be taken in its preparation,[20] and the applicant should not be surprised if the judge modifies the form to convert it from a list of what the applicant *wants* to a list of what the court is willing to *give*. To accomplish this, the judge will simply cross out entire sections or portions of sections that she feels should not be made part of the order. Most judges also have a stamp that they place next to other items that they will not order ex parte but will consider ordering after a hearing.

While not essential from a jurisdictional perspective, many court clerks and judges require that these various forms that make up the entire OSC/ Temporary Order[21] packet (forms FL-300, FL-305, FL-310, FL-150 and the supporting declaration) be placed in a particular order when stapled together to form the document commonly described as the "OSC." That order is as follows:

Figure 9-12
Form FL-305—Temporary Orders

FL-305

PETITIONER/PLAINTIFF:	CASE NUMBER:
RESPONDENT/DEFENDANT:	

TEMPORARY ORDERS
Attachment to Order to Show Cause (FL-300)

1. ☐ PROPERTY RESTRAINT
   - a. ☐ Petitioner ☐ Respondent is restrained from transferring, encumbering, hypothecating, concealing, or in any way disposing of any property, real or personal, whether community, quasi-community, or separate, except in the usual course of business or for the necessities of life.
     - ☐ The other party is to be notified of any proposed extraordinary expenditures and an accounting of such is to be made to the court.
   - b. ☐ Both parties are restrained and enjoined from cashing, borrowing against, canceling, transferring, disposing of, or changing the beneficiaries of any insurance or other coverage including life, health, automobile, and disability held for the benefit of the parties or their minor child or children.
   - c. ☐ Neither party may incur any debts or liabilities for which the other may be held responsible, other than in the ordinary course of business or for the necessities of life.

2. ☐ PROPERTY CONTROL
   - a. ☐ Petitioner ☐ Respondent is given the exclusive temporary use, possession, and control of the following property the parties own or are buying (specify):

   - b. ☐ Petitioner ☐ Respondent is ordered to make the following payments on liens and encumbrances coming due while the order is in effect:

Debt	Amount of payment	Pay to

3. ☐ MINOR CHILDREN
   - a. ☐ Petitioner ☐ Respondent will have the temporary physical custody, care, and control of the minor children of the parties, ☐ subject to the other party's rights of visitation as follows:

   - b. ☐ Petitioner ☐ Respondent must not remove the minor child or children of the parties
     - (1) ☐ from the State of California.
     - (2) ☐ from the following counties (specify):
     - (3) ☐ other (specify):
   - c. ☐ Child abduction prevention orders are attached (see form FL-341(B)).
   - d. (1) Jurisdiction: This court has jurisdiction to make child custody orders in this case under the Uniform Child Custody Jurisdiction and Enforcement Act (part 3 of the California Family Code, commencing with § 3400).
     - (2) Notice and opportunity to be heard: The responding party was given notice and an opportunity to be heard as provided by the laws of the State of California.
     - (3) Country of habitual residence: The country of habitual residence of the child or children is ☐ the United States of America ☐ other (specify):
     - **(4) Penalties for violating this order: If you violate this order you may be subject to civil or criminal penalties, or both.**

4. ☐ OTHER ORDERS (specify):

Date: _____   _____
                                      JUDGE OF THE SUPERIOR COURT

5. **The date of the court hearing is** (insert date when known):

CLERK'S CERTIFICATE

[SEAL]   I certify that the foregoing is a true and correct copy of the original on file in my office.

Date: _____   Clerk, by _____, Deputy

Page 1 of 1

Form Adopted for Mandatory Use
Judicial Council of California
FL-305 [Rev. July 1, 2003]

TEMPORARY ORDERS

Family Code, §§ 2045, 6224, 6226, 6302
6320–6326, 6380–6383
www.courtinfo.ca.gov

1. The face sheet (form FL-300) plus any attachments
2. Temporary Orders (form FL-305) and any attachments
3. Application for Order and Supporting Declaration (form FL-310)
4. The Income and Expense Declaration (form FL-150), filed as a separate document at the same time as the above if financial relief is sought.

This filing (the request) includes not only the attachment pages used but also the multi-page declaration of the applicant in support of the requested relief and any other declarations and documents the applicant would like the court to consider.

C. The Noticed Motion

A *motion*, much like an order to show cause, is a written request for relief that is filed with the court. It is called a *noticed motion* because the opposing party must be given *notice* of the request at least 21 days before the court hearing. At this hearing the court will listen to the arguments of both sides and decide whether to grant the *moving party* the relief that he requested.[22] It is very similar to the order to show cause procedure and the forms used are nearly identical.

Shown on page 398 in Figure 9-13 is the face sheet for a noticed motion. The reader will note its similarity to the face sheet used for Orders to Show Cause (form FL-310). There are, however, some significant differences between a noticed motion and an Order to Show Cause. For example, a noticed motion cannot be used until and unless the other party has appeared in the action, and it can never be used to obtain ex parte temporary restraining orders or orders pertaining to child custody. An Order to Show Cause can be used in these circumstances. Further, a noticed motion does not require the attendance of the other party at the hearing and is typically accompanied by a Memorandum of Points and Authorities (a legal brief addressing the facts of the case and the law supporting the relief requested); an Order to Show Cause *does* require the attendance of the parties and is almost never accompanied by a Memorandum of Points and Authorities. Further, and perhaps most importantly, with certain limitations, at the hearing on an Order to Show Cause the court will hear testimony from witnesses (somewhat like a mini-trial),[23] whereas such testimony is almost never allowed in a hearing on a *motion*.

A noticed motion is simply an application to a court for an *order* to obtain relief or instructions pre-trial. (An order is an instruction issued by the court that is not contained in a judgment.) The procedure for noticed motions is discussed generally at sections 1005 et seq. of the Code of Civil Procedure.

Figure 9-13
Form FL-301—Notice of Motion

FL-301

ATTORNEY OR PARTY WITHOUT ATTORNEY *(Name, State Bar number, and address):*	FOR COURT USE ONLY

TELEPHONE NO.:   FAX NO. *(Optional):*

E-MAIL ADDRESS *(Optional):*

ATTORNEY FOR *(Name):*

SUPERIOR COURT OF CALIFORNIA, COUNTY OF

  STREET ADDRESS:

  MAILING ADDRESS:

  CITY AND ZIP CODE:

  BRANCH NAME:

PETITIONER/PLAINTIFF:

RESPONDENT/DEFENDANT:

NOTICE OF MOTION
- ☐ **Child Custody**
- ☐ **Child Support**
- ☐ **Attorney Fees and Costs**

MODIFICATION
- ☐ **Visitation**
- ☐ **Spousal Support**

- ☐ **Injunctive Order**
- ☐ **Other** *(specify):*

CASE NUMBER:

1. TO *(name):*

2. A hearing on this motion for the relief requested in the attached application will be held as follows:

  a. Date: Time: ☐ Dept.:   ☐ Rm.:

  b. Address of court   ☐ same as noted above   ☐ other *(specify):*

3. Supporting attachments:

  a. Completed *Application for Order and Supporting Declaration* (form FL-310) and a **blank** *Responsive Declaration* (form FL-320)

  b. ☐ Completed *Income and Expense Declaration* (form FL-150) and a **blank** *Income and Expense Declaration*

  c. ☐ Completed *Financial Statement (Simplified)* (form FL-155) and a **blank** *Financial Statement (Simplified)*

  d. ☐ Completed *Property Declaration* (form FL-160) and a **blank** *Property Declaration*

  e. ☐ Points and authorities

  f. ☐ Other *(specify):*

Date: _____ ▶ _____

(TYPE OR PRINT NAME)   (SIGNATURE)

ORDER

4. ☐ Time for ☐ service ☐ hearing   is shortened. Service must be on or before *(date):*

5. Any responsive declaration must be served on or before *(date):*

6. If child custody or visitation is an issue in this proceeding, *Family Code* section 3170 requires mediation before or concurrently with the hearing listed above. The parties are ordered to attend orientation and mandatory custody services as follows:

Date: _____

JUDICIAL OFFICER

NOTICE: If you have children from this relationship, the court is required to order payment of child support based on the incomes of both parents. The amount of child support can be large. It normally continues until the child is 18. You should supply the court with information about your finances. Otherwise, the child support order will be based on the information supplied by the other parent.

You do not have to pay any fee to file declarations in response to this *Notice of Motion* (including a completed Income and Expense Declaration (form FL-150) or Financial Statement *(Simplified)* (form FL-155) that will show your finances). In the absence of an order shortening time, the original of the responsive declaration must be filed with the court and a copy served on the other party at least nine court days before the hearing date. Add five calendar days if you serve by mail within California. (See Code of Civil Procedure 1005 for other situations.) To determine court and calendar days, go to *www.courtinfo.ca.gov/selfhelp/courtcalendars/*.

Form Adopted for Mandatory Use Judicial Council of California FL-301 [Rev. January 1, 2007]	**NOTICE OF MOTION**	Page 1 of 2 Government Code, § 26826 *www.courtinfo.ca.gov*

Figure 9-13 (continued)

FL-301

PETITIONER/PLAINTIFF:	CASE NUMBER:
RESPONDENT/DEFENDANT:	

7. PROOF OF SERVICE BY MAIL

    a. I am at least age 18, **not a party to this action,** and am a resident or employed in the county where the mailing took place. My residence or business address is:

    b. I served copies of the following documents by enclosing them in a sealed envelope with postage fully prepaid, depositing them in the United States mail as follows:

      (1) Papers served:

        (a) *Notice of Motion* and a completed *Application for Order and Supporting Declaration* (form FL-310) **and** a blank *Responsive Declaration* (form FL-320)

        (b) ☐ Completed *Income and Expense Declaration* (form FL-150) **and** a blank *Income and Expense Declaration*

        (c) ☐ Completed *Financial Statement (Simplified)* (form FL-155) **and** a blank *Financial Statement (Simplified)*

        (d) ☐ Completed *Property Declaration* (form FL-160) **and** a blank *Property Declaration*

        (e) ☐ Points and authorities

        (f) Other *(specify):*

      (2) Manner of service:

        (a) Date of deposit:

        (b) Place of deposit *(city and state):*

        (c) Addressed as follows:

    c. I declare under penalty of perjury under the laws of the State of California that the foregoing is true and correct.

Date:

▶

(TYPE OR PRINT NAME)	(SIGNATURE OF DECLARANT)

Requests for Accommodations
Assistive listening systems, computer-assisted real-time captioning, or sign language interpreter services are available if you ask at least five days before the proceeding. Contact the clerk's office or go to *www.courtinfo.ca.gov/forms* for *Request for Accommodations by Persons With Disabilities and Response* (Form MC-410). (Civil Code, § 54.8.)

FL-301 [Rev. January 1, 2007]	**NOTICE OF MOTION**	Page 2 of 2

Noticed motions are rarely used in family law matters because they are very similar to OSCs but are subject to additional limitations.

1. The Face Sheet

Judicial Council form FL-301(adopted for use) shown in Figure 9-13 is the form to use when requesting relief from the court by way of a noticed motion. The reader will note its similarity to FL-300, used with Orders to Show Cause. As might be expected, it is completed in essentially the same manner.

Note, however, that FL-301 simply conveys *notice* to the other party that on the referenced day and time the relief described in the motion will be requested. The responding party can either respond or not.[24]

As discussed above, in various court proceedings, the requesting party must provide notice to the opposing party. A noticed motion is no exception. The notice required is set out in C.C.P. section 1005(b) and is generally 21 days from the date of service. If service is by mail, an extra five days are automatically added.

FL-301 contains a section entitled "Order," located near the bottom of the form. Where waiting the usual time period required for notice is seen to be detrimental to a party's request, the party can ask the court to shorten this time period to allow the hearing to go forward on less than the statutorily mandated time. Such a request is made in this section. The factual and legal bases for the request are set out in the Application for Order and Supporting Declaration (form FL-310), which should be attached to FL-301.

2. The Application for Order and Supporting Declaration

Whenever a request is made to the court by noticed motion (or by OSC), it must be accompanied by an Application for Order and Supporting Declaration, form FL-310. This form was discussed at length in this text's section on Orders to Show Cause. The comments made there have equal application here, and the reader is referred to that discussion for more information regarding this form.

3. The Income and Expense Declaration

If any financial issues are to be addressed by the court pursuant to the noticed motion, even only attorney's fees and costs, form FL-150) must be completed and submitted to the court. This text discusses FL-150 more fully in its section on Orders to Show Cause. The reader is referred to that discussion for more information on this subject.

4. Points and Authorities

A noticed motion typically addresses questions of *law* rather than questions of *fact* (which are typically addressed using the Order to Show Cause procedure); thus, when submitting a noticed motion, it is generally a good idea to submit a memorandum of points and authorities too—even though the court does not always require both. This book will not discuss in detail the structure and content of a memorandum of points and authorities. That is better left to a class or treatise on legal writing. Some general points are worthwhile, however.

A Memorandum of Points and Authorities (sometimes called "P's & A's") requires no particular format except that required by common sense and good writing skills. It can either be a separately captioned (and filed) document or merely stapled to the Notice of Motion face sheet and the Application for Order and Supporting Declaration.[25] The P's and A's should generally begin with an introduction that alerts the court to the nature of the case and the relief requested. It is also a good idea to describe the procedural posture of the case. For example, when was the case filed? What motions have been heard? And is a trial date approaching? This is also the first opportunity to state why the court should grant the relief requested.

Next, the moving party should insert a heading that summarizes the relief requested. For example:

Good Cause Exists to Continue Trial Because Respondent Frustrated Petitioner's Attempts to Obtain Responses to Discovery

This alerts the court to the nature of your point and acts as a preview of the discussion that follows.

The main body of this section contains the argument, factual and legal, annotated by supporting citations to the law (cases and codes). This main body of text is generally thought of as the "authority" for the point (hence the term *points and authorities*). The process of a point followed by a discussion of the supporting authorities continues in this fashion for as many points as are desired to be made. Obviously, the points are selected on the basis of their likelihood to support the overall position framed by the request. For example, as used above, the overall request was to continue the trial.

Finally, a concluding section (usually labeled "Conclusion") summarizes and reiterates the nature of the request, and argues for the court to grant the request. The conclusion should be concise, typically no more than two or three paragraphs, for two reasons. First, brevity is treasured by the court. Remember, your case is but one among hundreds that the judge must review and rule upon, and the time available for reading it is limited. Second, most jurisdictions have page limitations on the length of points and authorities, which, if not adhered to, can cause the court to reject your filing. The rule here is "less is more." Follow it.

C. The Noticed Motion

Below is an example of points and authorities, which, if written properly, should be self-explanatory as to the nature of the request and the reasons for granting the motion. These P's and A's have been captioned as a separate document. This is not always necessary, however. It is equally acceptable to attach the P's and A's to the motion papers themselves (forms FL-301 and FL-310) with a heading across the top (in place of the caption): "Memorandum of Points and Authorities." The captioned document would appear as follows:

SUPERIOR COURT OF THE STATE OF CALIFORNIA
FOR THE COUNTY OF LOS ANGELES

In Re the Marriage of:	)	CASE NO. BD 123 456
	)	
Petitioner: Jane Doe,	)	**MEMORANDUM OF POINTS**
	)	**AND AUTHORITIES IN**
	)	**SUPPORT OF MOTION TO**
and	)	**BIFURCATE DISSOLUTION**
	)	**OF MARRIAGE**
Respondent: John Doe	)	
	)	
_____	)	

1. **The Court Has Discretion to Bifurcate Trial and to Enter a Separate Interlocutory Judgment on the Dissolution Issue.** California Practice Guide, Family Law, Section 8:203 et seq. (The Rutter Group, 2008).
2. **The Court Has Authority to Order Separate Hearings on Issues Pursuant to Family Code Section 2337.** California Family Code Section 2337 specifically provides that upon noticed motion the Court may "sever and grant an early and separate trial on the issue of the dissolution of the status of the marriage apart from other issues." Fam. Code §2337(a).

Section 2337(c) further provides that the court may impose certain conditions on a party when granting a severance of the dissolution issue. For example, the order for dissolution may be made conditionally upon certain indemnification and other protections afforded to parties pending final judgment. The moving party has no objection to entry of any such reasonable precautions.

In establishing "irreconcilable differences" as the sole ground for dissolution (except in cases of incurable insanity), the Legislature made possible a prompt and economical determination of the issue of the parties' marital status. At the same time the minimum waiting period for a final decree was changed from one year after the interlocutory (former Civ. Code, Section 132) to six months after service of process (Family Code Section 2339). All of this reflects the legislative policy of permitting the prompt severance of a marriage relationship that has proved unworkable. The California Supreme Court expressed the same philosophy long before the State Legislature. (126 Cal. Rptr. at page 630).

Section 1048(b) of the California Code of Civil Procedure also provides general authority for bifurcation of trials. See McLellan v. McLellan (1972) 23 Cal. App. 3d 343, 353-354. Section 1048(b)) provides in pertinent part:

> The court, in furtherance of convenience or to avoid prejudice, or when separate trials will be conducive to expedition and economy, may order a separate trial of any cause of action, including a cause of action asserted in a cross-complaint, or of any separate issue or of any number of causes of action or issues, preserving the right of trial by jury required by the Constitution or a statute of this state or of the United States. Such bifurcation is even recognized in the context of putative spouses and "quasi-marital property." (See Section 2251 of the Family Code.)

3. Bifurcations Are Clearly Recognized in General Civil Actions.

California Code of Civil Procedure, Section 598.

By application of California Rule of Court 5.21, Section 598 of the California Code of Civil Procedure is authority itself for bifurcation in family law matters. Rule 5.21 provides:

> Except as otherwise provided in these rules, all provisions of law applicable to civil actions generally apply to a proceeding under the Family Code if they would otherwise apply to such proceeding without reference to this rule. To the extent that these rules conflict with provisions in other statutes or rules, these rules prevail.

4. The Court Has Authority to Try the Issue of Dissolution Before Collateral Issues, Including Division of Marital Property, Custody of Minor Children, Spousal Support, and Child Support.

In re Marriage of Van Sickle, 68 Cal. App. 3d 728, 137 (1977).

In light of the above codification and legal precepts, Petitioner has authority to seek and secure a bifurcation so as to litigate and dispense with the issue of marriage first.

The law and codification are clear that bifurcations are called for as a matter of justice and equity. They clearly assist in the economical and expeditious flow of litigation.

Dated: Feinberg & Waller

                                              by:___*Marshall W. Waller*___

                                              Marshall W. Waller

                                              Attorney for Petitioner

D. Responding to the OSC; Motion

When faced with an OSC or a Noticed Motion, a party has two choices: (1) simply agree with the relief sought or some similarly acceptable compromise (thus obviating the OSC or motion proceedings), or (2) oppose the request. Assuming the latter decision is made, various forms must be prepared and filed with the court for consideration prior to the hearing.[27] Considerations as to affirmative relief are also appropriate at this stage. Pursuant to Family Code section 213, a party responding to an OSC (or noticed motion) may object to the relief sought; further, he may propose affirmative relief of his own so long as the affirmative relief is on the same issue(s) raised by the applicant party. The uniqueness of this ability becomes worth comment when consideration is given to the due process notice requirement.

As stated above, an applicant (in either an Order to Show Cause or motion proceeding) must give notice to the opposing party of at least 16 court days. The responding party need only file her opposition (at the same time giving the other party notice) a mere nine court days[28] before the hearing. Because the applicant has placed a particular issue before the court (for example, child support or custody), he cannot complain if the responding party makes a different suggestion *on the same issues* on only five days' notice. This distinction is illustrated in the following example. Assume a party files an Order to Show Cause for $500 per month in spousal support. He has his OSC issued and then has it served on his wife. He has given at least 16 court days' notice of this request, so his wife cannot complain about not having been given enough time to prepare a response. The husband in this scenario has prepared for two ways in which his wife might respond: (1) she agrees with the request ($500) or (2) she opposes the request and the court decides how much he should get. What he may not be counting on, however, is that his wife has a third alternative: She can, as part of her responding position, ask the court to order her husband to pay *her* spousal support. And, because he raised the issue in his OSC, she does not have to file her own OSC; she is allowed by Family Code section 213 to ask for her own affirmative relief on only ten days' notice. While this might not seem to be enough notice to satisfy due process requirements, because he raised the issue himself, he is deemed to be already "on notice" of the possibility that *any* aspect of relief related to that issue might be raised. If the responding party wishes to have orders made on issues *not* framed by the applicant's papers, she will have to file her own OSC or noticed motion. But as long as the moving party has raised an issue, it becomes fair game for the court to make any order related to that issue.

The responding party must use the "Responsive Declaration" adopted by form FL-320 (Figure 9-14) to object or request affirmative relief. For the most part, its structure mirrors that of the Application for Order and Supporting Declaration (form FL-310), and it is prepared in much the same way.

FL-320 can be used when responding to an Order to Show Cause *or* a Noticed Motion. The choices available are simple and correspond to the orders requested in the application: (a) consent to the order requested, (b) consent to an order proposed by the party responding to the OSC or motion (that is, a request for affirmative relief), or (c) state a flat opposition to the requested relief.

Also noteworthy is the fact that the party responding to an Order to Show Cause or Noticed Motion may attach a declaration of her own (or as many additional declarations as she deems necessary) to her responding papers. This opportunity must not be overlooked. The earlier discussion relative to the applicant's supporting declaration should be reviewed at this time as its comments have equal application here.

The Income and Expense Declaration (form FL-150) must also accompany the responsive declaration if financial issues are to be determined at the hearing. A Memorandum of Points and Authorities is also advised, especially if the applicant has presented them.

E. Temporary and Ex Parte Orders

Earlier in this chapter we touched on the subject of temporary orders. We focused on how to prepare the forms associated with temporary orders. We will now review the various (and more common) statutory bases for requesting these orders.

The Family Code is replete with statutes that authorize a request for a temporary order. These orders are requested on an ex parte basis and are

Figure 9-14
Form FL-320—Responsive Declaration to Order to Show Cause or Notice of Motion

FL-320

ATTORNEY OR PARTY WITHOUT ATTORNEY (Name, State Bar number, and address):	FOR COURT USE ONLY

TELEPHONE NO.:   FAX NO. (Optional):

E-MAIL ADDRESS (Optional):

ATTORNEY FOR (Name):

SUPERIOR COURT OF CALIFORNIA, COUNTY OF

STREET ADDRESS:

MAILING ADDRESS:

CITY AND ZIP CODE:

BRANCH NAME:

PETITIONER/PLAINTIFF:

RESPONDENT/DEFENDANT:

OTHER PARENT:

RESPONSIVE DECLARATION TO ORDER TO SHOW CAUSE OR NOTICE OF MOTION	CASE NUMBER:
HEARING DATE: TIME: DEPARTMENT OR ROOM:	

1. ☐ CHILD CUSTODY
   a. ☐ I consent to the order requested.
   b. ☐ I do not consent to the order requested, but I consent to the following order:

2. ☐ CHILD VISITATION
   a. ☐ I consent to the order requested.
   b. ☐ I do not consent to the order requested, but I consent to the following order:

3. ☐ CHILD SUPPORT
   a. ☐ I consent to the order requested.
   b. ☐ I consent to guideline support.
   c. ☐ I do not consent to the order requested, but I consent to the following order:
      (1) ☐ Guideline
      (2) ☐ Other (specify):

4. ☐ SPOUSAL OR PARTNER SUPPORT
   a. ☐ I consent to the order requested.
   b. ☐ I do not consent to the order requested.
   c. ☐ I consent to the following order:

5. ☐ ATTORNEY FEES AND COSTS
   a. ☐ I consent to the order requested.
   b. ☐ I do not consent to the order requested.
   c. ☐ I consent to the following order:

Page 1 of 2

Form Adopted for Mandatory Use
Judicial Council of California
FL-320 [Rev. July 1, 2011]

RESPONSIVE DECLARATION TO ORDER TO SHOW CAUSE OR NOTICE OF MOTION

www.courts.ca.gov

Figure 9-14 (continued)

FL-320

PETITIONER/PLAINTIFF:	CASE NUMBER:
RESPONDENT/DEFENDANT:	
OTHER PARENT:	

6. ☐ PROPERTY RESTRAINT
    a. ☐ I consent to the order requested.
    b. ☐ I do not consent to the order requested.
    c. ☐ I consent to the following order:

7. ☐ PROPERTY CONTROL
    a. ☐ I consent to the order requested.
    b. ☐ I do not consent to the order requested.
    c. ☐ I consent to the following order:

8. ☐ OTHER RELIEF
    a. ☐ I consent to the order requested.
    b. ☐ I do not consent to the order requested.
    c. ☐ I consent to the following order:

9. ☐ SUPPORTING INFORMATION
    ☐ Contained in the attached declaration. (You may use *Attached Declaration* (form MC-031) for this purpose).

NOTE: To respond to domestic violence restraining orders requested in the *Request for Order (Domestic Violence Prevention)* (form DV-100), you must use the *Answer to Temporary Restraining Order (Domestic Violence Prevention)* (form DV-120).

I declare under penalty of perjury under the laws of the State of California that the foregoing is true and correct.

Date:

▶

_____
(TYPE OR PRINT NAME)

_____
(SIGNATURE OF DECLARANT)

| FL-320 [Rev. July 1, 2011] | **RESPONSIVE DECLARATION TO ORDER TO SHOW CAUSE OR NOTICE OF MOTION** | Page 2 of 2 |

designed to provide immediate relief during the period between the time that the request is filed and the time that the court conducts its hearing. A pure temporary order (although not generally thought of as such) also includes orders granted at an OSC or motion hearing following normal notice; a pure temporary order is designed to last until the time of trial (that is, orders *pendente lite*). It is important to note that there is no difference between "temporary" and "normal" orders. Nor is there any such distinction with ex parte orders. They are all *orders*: fully enforceable, modifiable, and subject to the same bases for review. The only difference lies in the amount of *time* given for notice. The ex parte order requires very short (if any) notice, but it is in every other respect the same as an order granted after notice, or even after trial.

The court cannot grant temporary restraining orders to parties to a marital dissolution, legal separation, nullity action, or action under the Uniform Parentage Act until it issues the family law summons. (The summons is discussed thoroughly in Chapter 8.) Temporary restraining orders (TROs) are authorized by Family Code sections 231 to 235 and described in section 2040. TROs are automatic and become effective against the petitioner once the summons is issued, and effective against the respondent when served. These orders are fully enforceable and modifiable, just as orders obtained after a hearing.

The next kind of temporary order available on shortened notice is described in Family Code sections 240 et seq. This section of the Code is entitled "Ex Parte Temporary Restraining Orders." Its title is quite informative. This statute authorizes the issuance of TROs without *any* notice whatsoever. Of course, the circumstances under which the normal requirements of due process will be waived are strictly construed and very limited. In fact, section 241 actually establishes that TROs will *not* be issued without notice "unless it appears from facts shown by the affidavit [declaration] in support of the application for the order, or in the application for the order, that *great or irreparable injury would result to the applicant before the matter can be heard on notice*" [emphasis added].

The highlighted portion of this statute describes the circumstances under which a request for TROs without giving notice to the responding party will be tested. As can be seen, this is not a black and white inquiry. These requests will be decided on a case-by-case basis by the judge hearing the matter. Assuming the case is pleaded convincingly and the facts exist to justify this request, it stands a good chance of being granted, but it is a difficult hurdle to overcome.

Assuming the request is granted, the court is obligated to set the matter over for a full hearing "on the earliest day that the business of the court will permit, but not later than 20 days or, if good cause appears to the court, 25 days from the date of the order." (Family Code section 242.) In other words, the court must set the hearing as soon as possible. Once the matter is heard, it will take precedence over all other matters on the calendar except others like it and those entitled by law to an even higher priority.

We have thus far reviewed examples of temporary orders issued under circumstances of normal notice, shortened notice, and, in extreme cases, no notice whatsoever. The substantive context in which these orders are requested and granted is also very diverse. The automatic restraining orders contained in the Summons cover many of the instances in which this type of relief typically will be requested: preventing the parties from removing the children from the state or disposing of their property and things of this nature. The Family Code has established general and specific statutory provisions for the grant of this type of relief as well.

Family Code sections 3060 to 3064 establish a statutory scheme for the request for temporary custody orders during the pendency of the litigation, and sections 3600 to 3604 provide for pendente lite support orders. Sections 3620 to 3634 establish a means of obtaining expedited child support while an action is pending. Section 4620 allows the court to, on an ex parte basis, restrain a party from disposing of his assets during the pendency of a request for the establishment of a deposit of assets to secure payment of future child support.[29]

F. Domestic Violence Prevention Act

Discussed above are some of the statutory circumstances under which an applicant may, during the pendency of the overall litigation (for example, dissolution of marriage) obtain temporary orders. In special circumstances, however, one may obtain a court order even if she is not involved in underling litigation. Division 10 of the Family Code, entitled "Prevention of Domestic Violence," found at sections 6200 et seq., describes such a circumstance.

The Domestic Violence Prevention Act (DVPA), as this set of statutes is known, was established "to prevent the recurrence of acts of violence and sexual abuse and to provide for separation of the persons involved in the domestic violence for a period sufficient to enable these persons to seek a resolution of the causes of the violence." (Family Code section 6220.) The California Legislature deemed the prevention of domestic violence so important that it devoted an entire *Division* of the Family Code to the subject. The Act is designed to make temporary orders easily obtainable by persons free of charge without the necessity of hiring attorneys. Of course, the parties are free to use lawyers if they can afford to do so but the forms are designed to be easily understood and used by laypersons.

Orders may be obtained in the context of the Domestic Violence Prevention Act in basically two ways. First, a party may file an application and declaration under the DVPA in which he seeks to have a hearing on the application set, and he requests, if appropriate, temporary orders ex parte. Second, a law enforcement officer may request orders under the DVPA. These orders are known as *Emergency Protective Orders* and are prepared and applied for by law enforcement personnel. These actions are provided for in Part 3 of Division 10 and are found in Family Code sections 6240 to 6275.

These emergency protective orders are basically prepared "in the field" under circumstances in which a law enforcement officer[30] appears on the scene of an incident of domestic violence (usually at someone's specific request). The officer must, after assessing the situation, determine that reasonable grounds exist to believe any (or all) of the following statutory bases (Family Code section 6250) exist:

(a) That a person is in immediate and present danger of domestic violence, based on the person's allegation of a recent incident of abuse or threat of abuse by the person against whom the order is sought.

(b) That a child is in immediate and present danger of abuse by a family or household member, based on an allegation of a recent incident of abuse or threat of abuse by the family or household member.

(c) That a child is in immediate and present danger of being abducted by a parent or relative, based on a reasonable belief that a person has an intent to abduct the child or flee with the child from the jurisdiction or based on an allegation of a recent threat to abduct the child or flee with the child from the jurisdiction.

(d) That an elder or dependent adult is in immediate and present danger of abuse as defined in Section 15610.07 of the Welfare and Institutions Code, based on an allegation of a recent incident of abuse or threat of abuse by the person against whom the order is sought, except that no emergency protective order shall be issued based solely on an allegation of financial abuse.

The law enforcement officer will, once he has satisfied himself as to the existence of one of the following conditions, then transmit (by telephone) his beliefs to a judicial officer[31] who is empowered to issue protective and restraining orders over the telephone. By statute (Family Code section 6251), prior to being able to issue these orders, the judicial officer must make *both* of the following factual findings:

(a) That reasonable grounds have been asserted to believe that an immediate and present danger of domestic violence exists, that a child is in immediate and present danger of abuse or abduction, or that an elder or dependent adult is in immediate and present danger of abuse as defined in Section 15610.07 of the Welfare and Institutions Code.

(b) That an emergency protective order is necessary to prevent the occurrence or recurrence of domestic violence, child abuse, child abduction, or abuse of an elder or dependent adult.

Assuming the requisite findings are made, the judicial officer can issue protective orders, orders delegating temporary care and control of the parties' minor children, and orders placing those children in the care of the non-restrained party (the party who is not causing the trouble). These orders will only last for five business days or seven calendar days after their issuance, during which time the non-restrained party is expected to make application for more permanent orders.

Once the law enforcement officer has received the orders from the judicial officer, he must: (1) reduce the orders to writing and sign them, (2) serve the restrained person with a copy and give a copy to the *protected person* (the non-restrained party), (3) keep a copy, and (4) file a copy with the court as soon as possible. He is also required to carry a copy of the order with him while on duty. As might be expected, the judicial council has adopted a form for this purpose. It is set forth in its entirety (both front and back pages thereof) in Figure 9-15 on pages 412 and 413. The specific contents of this form are described by Family Code section 6253.

Once prepared, signed, and served, this order carries with it during its short life the effect of a "regular" court order. In other words, it is as subject to enforcement by appropriate personnel as any other court order.

The endangered person herself may also invoke the DVPA. Sections 6300 et seq. of the Family Code discuss this avenue of relief in detail. These sections allow for the issuance of DVPA orders with or without notice, and the orders are available to victims of domestic violence, as that term is defined in Family Code section 6211:

> "Domestic violence" is abuse perpetrated against any of the following persons:
>
> (a) A spouse or former spouse.
>
> (b) A cohabitant or former cohabitant, as defined in Section 6209.
>
> (c) A person with whom the respondent is having or has had a dating or engagement relationship.
>
> (d) A person with whom the respondent has had a child, where the presumption applies that the male parent is the father of the child of the female parent under the Uniform Parentage Act (Part 3 (commencing with Section 7600) of Division 12).
>
> (e) A child of a party or a child who is the subject of an action under the Uniform Parentage Act, where the presumption applies that the male parent is the father of the child to be protected.
>
> (f) Any other person related by consanguinity or affinity within the second degree.

The term "abuse," used in the above definition, is itself defined by statute. Family Code section 6203 provides as follows:

Figure 9-15
Form EPO-001—Emergency Protective Order (CLETS)

APPLICATION FOR EMERGENCY PROTECTIVE ORDER (CLETS)   **EPO-001**

(Name): _____ has provided the information in items 1-5.   LAW ENFORCEMENT CASE NUMBER:

1. **PERSONS TO BE PROTECTED** *(insert names of all persons to be protected by this order):*
_____

2. **PERSON TO BE RESTRAINED** *(name):* _____

Sex: ☐ M ☐ F   Ht.: ____ Wt.: ____ Hair color: ____ Eye color: ____ Race: ____ Age: ____ Date of birth: ____

3. The events that cause the protected person to fear immediate and present danger of domestic violence, child abuse, child abduction, elder or dependent adult abuse (other than **solely** financial abuse), or stalking are *(give facts and dates; specify weapons):* _____

4. ☐ The person to be protected lives with the person to be restrained and requests an order that the restrained person move out immediately from the address in item 9.

5. a. ☐ The person to be protected has minor children in common with the person to be restrained, and a temporary custody order is requested because of the facts alleged in item 3. A custody order ☐ does ☐ does not exist.
   b. ☐ The person to be protected is a minor child in immediate danger of being abducted by the person to be restrained because of the facts alleged in item 3.

6. ☐ A child welfare worker or probation officer has advised the undersigned that a juvenile court petition
   ☐ has already been filed. ☐ will be filed. ☐ will NOT be filed.

7. ☐ Adult Protective Services has been notified.

8. Judicial officer *(name):* _____ was contacted on *(date):* ____ at *(time):* ____
   ☐ The judicial officer granted the **Emergency Protective Order** that follows.

By: _____ ▶ _____
   (PRINT NAME OF LAW ENFORCEMENT OFFICER)   (SIGNATURE OF LAW ENFORCEMENT OFFICER)

Agency: _____ Telephone No.: _____ Badge No.: _____

EMERGENCY PROTECTIVE ORDER *(See reverse for important notices.)*

9. **To restrained person** *(name):* _____
   a. ☐ You must not contact, molest, harass, attack, strike, threaten, sexually assault, batter, telephone, send any messages to, follow, stalk, destroy any personal property of, disturb the peace of, or take any action to obtain the address or location of each person named in item 1.
   b. ☐ You must ☐ stay away at least ____ yards from each person named in item 1.
      ☐ stay away at least ____ yards from ☐ move out immediately from
      (address): _____

10. ☐ *(Name):* _____ is given temporary care and control of the following
    minor children of the parties *(names and ages):* _____

11. Reasonable grounds for the issuance of this order exist and an emergency protective order is necessary to prevent the occurrence or recurrence of domestic violence, child abuse, child abduction, elder or dependent adult abuse, or stalking.

12. **THIS EMERGENCY PROTECTIVE ORDER WILL EXPIRE AT 5:00 P.M. ON:** _____

13. **To protected person:** If you need protection for a longer period of time, you must request restraining orders at *(court name and address):* _____
    INSERT DATE OF FIFTH COURT DAY OR SEVENTH CALENDAR DAY, WHICHEVER IS EARLIER; DO NOT COUNT DAY THE ORDER IS GRANTED

PROOF OF SERVICE

14. Person served *(name):* _____

15. I personally delivered copies to the person served as follows: Date: ____ Time: ____
    Address: _____

16. At the time of service I was at least 18 years of age and not a party to this cause. ☐ I am a California sheriff or marshal.

17. My name, address, and telephone number are *(this does not have to be server's home telephone number or address):* _____

I declare under penalty of perjury under the laws of the State of California that the foregoing is true and correct.

Date: _____ ▶ _____
   (TYPE OR PRINT NAME OF SERVER)   (SIGNATURE OF SERVER)   Page 1 of 2

Form Adopted for Mandatory Use
Judicial Council of California
EPO-001 [Rev. January 1, 2007]
Approved by DOJ

EMERGENCY PROTECTIVE ORDER (CLETS–EPO)
(Domestic Violence, Child Abuse, Elder or Dependent Adult Abuse, or Stalking)
ONE copy to court, ONE copy to restrained person, ONE copy to protected person, ONE copy to issuing agency

Family Code, § 6200 et seq.
Penal Code, § 646.91
www.courtinfo.ca.gov

Figure 9-15 (continued)

EMERGENCY PROTECTIVE ORDER | EPO-001
WARNINGS AND INFORMATION

VIOLATION OF THIS ORDER IS A MISDEMEANOR PUNISHABLE BY A $1,000 FINE, ONE YEAR IN JAIL, OR BOTH, OR MAY BE PUNISHABLE AS A FELONY. PERSONS SUBJECT TO A RESTRAINING ORDER ARE PROHIBITED FROM OWNING, POSSESSING, PURCHASING, RECEIVING, OR ATTEMPTING TO PURCHASE OR RECEIVE A FIREARM (PENAL CODE SECTION 12021(g)). SUCH CONDUCT IS SUBJECT TO A $1,000 FINE AND IMPRISONMENT OR BOTH. THIS ORDER SHALL BE ENFORCED BY ALL LAW ENFORCEMENT OFFICERS IN THE STATE OF CALIFORNIA WHO ARE AWARE OF OR SHOWN A COPY OF THE ORDER. UNDER PENAL CODE SECTION 13710(b), "THE TERMS AND CONDITIONS OF THE PROTECTION ORDER REMAIN ENFORCEABLE, NOTWITHSTANDING THE ACTS OF THE PARTIES, AND MAY BE CHANGED ONLY BY ORDER OF THE COURT."

To the restrained person: This order will last until the date and time in item 12 on the reverse. The protected person may, however, obtain a more permanent restraining order from the court. You may seek the advice of an attorney as to any matter connected with this order. The attorney should be consulted promptly so that the attorney may assist you in responding to the order.

A la persona bajo restricción judicial: Esta orden durará hasta la fecha y hora indicadas en el punto 12 al dorso. La persona protegida puede, sin embargo, obtener una orden de entredicho (restricción judicial) más permanente de la corte. Usted puede consultar a un abogado en conexión con cualquier asunto relacionado con esta orden. Debe consultar al abogado sin pérdida de tiempo para que él o ella le pueda ayudar a responder a la orden.

To the protected person: This order will last only until the date and time noted in item 12 on the reverse. If you wish to seek continuing protection, you will have to apply for an order from the court at the address in item 13, or you should apply to the court in the county where you live if it is a different county and the violence is likely to occur there. You may apply for a protective order free of charge. In the case of an endangered child, you may also apply for a more permanent order at the address in item 13, or if there is a juvenile dependency action pending you may apply for a more permanent order under section 213.5 of the Welfare and Institutions Code. In the case of a child being abducted, you may apply for a *Child Custody Order* from the court at the address in item 13. You may seek the advice of an attorney as to any matter connected with your application for any future court orders. The attorney should be consulted promptly so that the attorney may assist you in making your application. You do not have to have an attorney to get the protective order.

A la persona protegida: Esta orden durará sólo hasta la fecha y hora indicadas en el punto 12 al dorso. Si usted desea que la protección continúe, tendrá que solicitar una orden de la corte en la dirección indicada en el artículo 13, o tendrá que hacer la solicitud ante la corte del condado donde usted vive, si se trata de un condado diferente y es probable que la violencia ocurra allí. La solicitud de la orden de protección es gratis. En el caso de que un niño o una niña se encuentre en peligro, puede solicitar una orden más permanente en la dirección indicada en el artículo 13 o, si hay una acción legal pendiente de tutela juvenil, puede solicitar una orden más permanente conforme a la sección 213.5 del código titulado en inglés **Welfare and Institutions Code.** En el caso del secuestro de un niño o una niña, usted puede solicitar de la corte una orden para la guarda del niño o de la niña *(Child Custody Order)*, en la dirección indicada en el artículo 13 de este formulario. Puede consultar a un abogado en conexión con cualquier asunto relacionado con las solicitudes de órdenes de la corte que usted presente en el futuro. Debe consultar un abogado sin perdida de tiempo para que él o ella le pueda ayudar a presentar su solicitud. Para obtener la orden de protección no es necesario que un abogado le represente.

To law enforcement: Penal Code section 13710(c) provides that, upon request, law enforcement shall serve the party to be restrained at the scene of a domestic violence incident or at any time the restrained party is in custody. The officer who requested the emergency protective order, while on duty, shall carry copies of the order. The emergency protective order shall be served upon the restrained party by the officer, if the restrained party can reasonably be located, and a copy shall be given to the protected party. A copy also shall be filed with the court as soon as practicable after issuance. The availability of an emergency protective order shall not be affected by the fact that the endangered person has vacated the household to avoid abuse. A law enforcement officer shall use every reasonable means to enforce an emergency protective order issued pursuant to this subdivision. A law enforcement officer acting pursuant to this subdivision shall not be held civilly or criminally liable if he or she has acted in good faith with regard thereto.

If a child is in danger of being abducted: This order will last only until the date and time noted in item 12 on the reverse. You may apply for a child custody order from the court.

En el caso de peligro de secuestro de un niño o de una niña: Esta orden será válida sólo hasta la hora y fecha indicadas en el punto 12 al dorso. Usted puede solicitar de la corte una orden para la guarda del niño o de la niña *(Child Custody Order)*.

This emergency protective order is effective when made. This order shall expire on the date and time specified in item 12 on the reverse. The provisions of this emergency protective order take precedence in enforcement over provisions of other existing protective orders between the same protected and restrained persons to the extent the provisions of this order are more restrictive. In other words, the provisions in this emergency protective order take precedence over the provisions in any other protective order, including a criminal protective order, if (1) the person to be protected is already protected by the other protective order, (2) the person to be restrained is subject to that other order, and (3) the provisions in this emergency order are more restrictive than the provisions in that other order. The provisions in another existing protective order remain in effect and take precedence if they are more restrictive than the provisions in this emergency protective order.

EPO-001 [Rev. January 1, 2007] | **EMERGENCY PROTECTIVE ORDER (CLETS–EPO)** | Page 2 of 2
(Domestic Violence, Child Abuse, Elder or Dependent Adult Abuse, or Stalking)
ONE copy to court, ONE copy to restrained person, ONE copy to protected person, ONE copy to issuing agency

For purposes of this act, "abuse" means any of the following:

(a) Intentionally or recklessly to cause or attempt to cause bodily injury.

(b) Sexual assault.

(c) To place a person in reasonable apprehension of imminent serious bodily injury to that person or to another.

(d) To engage in any behavior that has been or could be enjoined pursuant to Section 6320.

The orders available on an ex parte basis to the applicant include exclusion of the restrained person from the family home, a determination of temporary custody and visitation, a restraint on the use or disposal of community and separate property, and orders for exclusive use of certain assets and property (for example, a car) as well as the payment of certain debts. After a hearing the court can also award payment of child support, payment of restitution to the protected party for out-of-pocket expenses caused by the incident leading up to the application, and attorney's fees and costs; the court can even include an order that the restrained party (or both if the court so decides) participate in counseling.

These orders will last, if issued ex parte, until the date of the hearing on the application (usually about three weeks). After notice and hearing, these orders will generally last three years unless otherwise specified by the court. They are subject to full enforcement as are any other court orders, the violation of which is punishable as a crime under Penal Code section 273.6.

There are, of course, judicial council forms for this process. The application form itself, reflected by form DV-100, is four pages long and is set out in Figure 9-16. This form is self-explanatory. Its preparation should pose no problem to the applicant or the paralegal assisting him.

One interesting note before leaving this area is appropriate. In virtually all civil and criminal matters, a party is allowed to either represent himself or have an attorney represent him in court. Other than this person (with certain limited exceptions, for example, an interpreter), no one else can accompany the party to the counsel table. Recognizing the highly volatile and emotional nature of an abusive situation, however, Family Code section 6303 specifically authorizes a "support person" to attend the DVPA hearing with the applicant and to be present with him at counsel table. The support person may, in fact, accompany the applicant to any proceeding called for, even confidential mediation proceedings. She cannot, of course, give legal advice, and the court is always free to remove her from the proceedings in its discretion. This provision is, however, a big step in giving access and emotional support to litigants in a judicial proceeding.

Part and parcel of this statutory scheme are provisions related to the enforcement of these laws both here and across state lines. This has been the general purview of Family Code sections 6380 et seq., which generally

Figure 9-16
Form DV-100—Application and Declaration for Order

DV-100	**Request for Order**	Clerk stamps date here when form is filed.

(1) Your name (person asking for protection):
_____

Your address *(skip this if you have a lawyer):* *(If you want your address to be private, give a mailing address instead):*
_____

City: _____ State: _____ Zip: _____

Your telephone number *(optional):* _____

Your lawyer *(if you have one): (Name, address, telephone number, and State Bar number):*
_____
_____
_____

Fill in court name and street address:

Superior Court of California, County of

(2) Name of person you want protection from:
_____

Description of that person: Sex: ☐ M ☐ F Height: _____
Weight: _____ Race: _____ Hair Color: _____
Eye Color: _____ Age: _____ Date of Birth: _____

Clerk fills in case number when form is filed.

Case Number:

(3) Besides you, who needs protection? *(Family or household members):*

Full Name	Age	Lives with you?	How are they related to you?
_____	_____	☐ Yes ☐ No	_____
_____	_____	☐ Yes ☐ No	_____
_____	_____	☐ Yes ☐ No	_____
_____	_____	☐ Yes ☐ No	_____

☐ *Check here if you need more space. Attach Form MC-020 and write "DV-100, Item 3—Protected People" by your statement. NOTE: In any item that asks for Form MC-020, you can use an 8 1/2 x 11-inch sheet of paper instead.*

(4) What is your relationship to the person in **②**? *(Check all that apply):*

a. ☐ We are now married or registered domestic partners.
b. ☐ We used to be married or registered domestic partners.
c. ☐ We live together.
d. ☐ We used to live together.
e. ☐ We are relatives, in-laws, or related by adoption *(specify relationship):* _____
f. ☐ We are dating or used to date.
g. ☐ We are engaged to be married or were engaged to be married.
h. ☐ We are the parents together of a child or children under 18:
    Child's Name: _____ Date of Birth: _____
    Child's Name: _____ Date of Birth: _____
    Child's Name: _____ Date of Birth: _____
    ☐ *Check here if you need more space. Attach Form MC-020 and write "DV-100, Item 4h" by your statement.*
i. ☐ We have signed a Voluntary Declaration of Paternity for our child or children. *(Attach a copy if you have one.)*

This is not a Court Order.

Judicial Council of California, www.courtinfo.ca.gov
Revised July 1, 2009, Mandatory Form
Family Code, § 6200 et seq.

Request for Order
(Domestic Violence Prevention)

DV-100, Page 1 of 4 →

Figure 9-16 (continued)

Case Number:

Your name: _____

(5) Other Court Cases

   a. Have you and the person in ② been involved in another court case? ☐ No ☐ Yes
      If yes, where? County: _____ State: _____
      What are the case numbers? *(If you know):* _____
      What kind of case? *(Check all that apply):*
      ☐ Registered Domestic Partnership ☐ Divorce/Dissolution ☐ Parentage/Paternity ☐ Legal Separation
      ☐ Domestic Violence ☐ Criminal ☐ Juvenile ☐ Child Support ☐ Nullity ☐ Civil Harassment
      ☐ Other *(specify):* _____

   b. Are there any domestic violence restraining/protective orders now (criminal, juvenile, family)?
      ☐ No ☐ Yes *If yes, attach a copy if you have one.*

What orders do you want? Check the boxes that apply to your case. ☑

(6) ☐ **Personal Conduct Orders**

   I ask the court to order the person in ② not to do the following things to me or any of the people listed in ③:

   a. ☐ Harass, attack, strike, threaten, assault (sexually or otherwise), hit, follow, stalk, molest, destroy
      personal property, disturb the peace, keep under surveillance, or block movements
   b. ☐ Contact (either directly or indirectly), or telephone, or send messages or mail or e-mail
   *The person in ② will be ordered not to take any action to get the addresses or locations of any protected
   person, their family members, caretakers, or guardians unless the court finds good cause not to make the order.*

(7) ☐ **Stay-Away Order**

   I ask the court to order the person in ② to stay at least _____ yards away from *(check all that apply):*

   a. ☐ Me   e. ☐ The children's school or child care
   b. ☐ The people listed in ③   f. ☐ My vehicle
   c. ☐ My home   g. ☐ Other *(specify):* _____
   d. ☐ My job or workplace   _____

   If the person listed in ② is ordered to stay away from all the places listed above, will he or she still be able
   to get to his or her home, school, job, or place of worship? ☐ Yes ☐ No *(If no, explain):* _____
   _____

(8) ☐ **Move-Out Order**

   I ask the court to order the person in ② to move out from and not return to *(address):*
   _____

   I have the right to live at the above address because *(explain):* _____
   _____

(9) ☐ **Child Custody, Visitation, and Child Support**

   I ask the court to order child custody, visitation, and/or child support. *You must fill out and attach
   Form DV-105.*

(10) ☐ **Spousal Support**

   *You can make this request only if you are married to, or are a registered domestic partner of, the person in ②
   and no spousal support order exists. To ask for spousal support, you must fill out, file, and serve Form FL-150
   before your hearing.*

This is not a Court Order.

Figure 9-16 (continued)

Your name: _____

Case Number: _____

(11) ☐ **Record Unlawful Communications**
I ask for the right to record communications made to me by the person in ② that violate the judge's orders.

(12) ☐ **Property Control**
I ask the court to give *only* me temporary use, possession, and control of the property listed here:
_____

(13) ☐ **Animals: Possession and Stay-Away Order**
I ask for the sole possession, care, and control of the animals listed below. I ask the court to order the person in ② to stay at least _____ yards away from and not take, sell, transfer, encumber, conceal, molest, attack, strike, threaten, harm, or otherwise dispose of the following animals: _____

I ask for the animals to be with me because: _____

(14) ☐ **Debt Payment**
I ask the court to order the person in ②to make these payments while the order is in effect:
☐ *Check here if you need more space. Attach Form MC-020 and write "DV-100, Item 14—Debt Payment" by your statement.*
Pay to: _____ For: _____ Amount: $ _____ Due date: _____
Pay to: _____ For: _____ Amount: $ _____ Due date: _____

(15) ☐ **Property Restraint**
I am married to or have a registered domestic partnership with the person in ②. I ask the judge to order that the person in ② not borrow against, sell, hide, or get rid of or destroy any possessions or property, except in the usual course of business or for necessities of life. I also ask the judge to order the person in ② to notify me of any new or big expenses and to explain them to the court.

(16) ☐ **Attorney Fees and Costs**
I ask that the person in ② pay some or all of my attorney fees and costs.
You must complete and file Form FL-150, Income and Expense Declaration.

(17) ☐ **Payments for Costs and Services**
I ask that the person in ② pay the following:
You can ask for lost earnings or your costs for services caused directly by the person in ② (damaged property, medical care, counseling, temporary housing, etc.). You must bring proof of these expenses to your hearing.
Pay to: _____ For: _____ Amount: $ _____
Pay to: _____ For: _____ Amount: $ _____

(18) ☐ **Batterer Intervention Program**
I ask the court to order the person listed in ② to go to a 52-week batterer intervention program and show proof of completion to the court.

(19) **No Fee to Serve (Notify) Restrained Person**
If you want the sheriff or marshal to serve (notify) the restrained person about the orders for free, ask the court clerk what you need to do.

This is not a Court Order.

Revised July 1, 2009   **Request for Order**
(Domestic Violence Prevention)   DV-100, Page 3 of 4 →

Figure 9-16 (continued)

	Case Number:

Your name: _____

(20) ☐ **More Time for Notice**

I need extra time to notify the person in ② about these papers. Because of the facts explained on this form, I want the papers served up to _____ days before the date of the hearing. *For help, read Form DV-210-INFO.*

If necessary, add additional facts: _____

_____

(21) ☐ **Other Orders**

What other orders are you asking for? _____

_____

☐ *Check here if you need more space. Attach Form MC-020 and write "DV-100, Item 21—Other Orders" by your statement.*

(22) **Guns or Other Firearms**

I believe the person in ② owns or possesses guns or firearms. ☐ Yes ☐ No ☐ I don't know

If the judge approves the order, the person in ② will be required to sell to a gun dealer or turn in to police any guns or firearms that he or she owns or possesses.

(23) Describe the most recent abuse.

a. Date of most recent abuse: _____

b. Who was there? _____

c. What did the person in ② do or say that made you afraid?

_____
_____
_____
_____
_____
_____

d. Describe any use or threatened use of guns or other weapons: _____

_____

e. Describe any injuries: _____

_____

f. Did the police come? ☐ No ☐ Yes

If yes, did they give you an Emergency Protective Order? ☐ Yes ☐ No ☐ I don't know

Attach a copy if you have one.

☐ *Check here if you need more space. Use Form MC-020 and write "DV-100, Item 23—Recent Abuse" by your statement.*

☐ *Check here if the person in ② has abused you (or your children) other times. Use Form DV-101 or Form MC-020 to describe any previous abuse.*

I declare under penalty of perjury under the laws of the State of California that the information above is true and correct.

Date: _____

_____   ▶   _____
Type or print your name   *Sign your name*

This is not a Court Order.

418

provide that a protective or restraining order related to domestic or family violence and issued by a court of another state, a tribe, or a military tribunal shall be deemed valid if the issuing court had jurisdiction over the parties and the matter. These sections also provide a system for electronic sharing of this information across political and geographical borders. It is known as CLETS, which stands for California Law Enforcement Telecommunications System.

Summary

We have seen in this chapter how to prepare for, and prepare, the initial and subsequent Order to Show Cause. This is the basic vehicle used in the family law context to obtain temporary relief pending trial, including, without limitation, child and spousal support, custody and visitation, restraining orders, and certain property orders. In addition to the Order to Show Cause procedure, the parties are free to proceed by way of noticed motion. Each procedure has its pluses and minuses. We have also explored the various responses available to a party served with either an Order to Show Cause or a Noticed Motion. Finally, we have seen that the Family Code includes a very powerful statutory scheme designed for use in the area of domestic violence, the Domestic Violence Prevention Act.

Key Terms

The following is a list of key terms and phrases that you should be able to define and use in context. Only then will you have demonstrated a command of the material in this chapter.

- Order to Show Cause
- Temporary Orders
- ex parte relief
- pendente lite
- injunctions
- stipulations
- permanent v. preliminary injunction
- licensed clinical social worker (LCSW)
- Application for Order and Supporting Declaration
- declaration
- *Reifler* and *Stevenot* rule
- income and expense declaration
- gross v. net income
- Noticed Motion

- Memorandum of Points and Authorities
- statutory v. common law

Questions for Discussion

1. Define and describe statutory law and common law. Contrast these two concepts.
2. Compare and contrast preliminary and permanent injunctions.
3. Discuss the processes involved in applying for and obtaining temporary restraining orders. Include in your discussion reference to the various forms used.
4. What is the *Reifler* and *Stevenot* rule, and how is it used?
5. What is the difference between gross and net income, and what is the significance of this distinction in the context of an Order to Show Cause?
6. What is a Memorandum of Points and Authorities, and how and when is it used?
7. Describe the circumstances under which Temporary Orders would be requested and issued.

ENDNOTES

1. In this context, the responding party could be either the petitioner or respondent, whichever one is *responding* to the immediate request before the court.

2. The reader will recall that not all documents must be served in person. Service by mail is, in fact, the most common method.

3. A request for initial orders pending trial is typically made upon 16 court days' notice to the responding party, 21 if served by mail. Often these requests include an application for issuance of a preliminary injunction, which will only be granted following the noticed hearing and, just as the preliminary injunction serves to preserve the status quo pending trial, the TRO serves to preserve the status quo pending the hearing on the application for a preliminary injunction. This is very useful since it is not uncommon for the waiting period to be well in excess of the 16-plus-day notice period due to congestion of the court's calendar. Most courts are setting these hearings within 30 to 45 days of the filing of the request. One way to compel the court to set your request for hearing in no more than 21 to 25 days from the date of filing is to request a TRO. Once granted, the hearing on the preliminary injunction that is the subject of a TRO must be held within 21 to 25 days of issuance of the TRO.

4. The use of the term *ex parte* in this context is quite literal and not used in the sense it has become to be understood in general practice. When one speaks of an ex parte hearing or application, reference is usually being made to an emergency situation requiring speed of issuance as the ultimate and immediate goal. In that context the responding party is typically given approximately 24 hours' notice (depending upon the local rules of the issuing court) and is given the opportunity to oppose the issuance of the orders so requested. In the context referenced above regarding issuance of the OSC, the term simply refers to the fact that the Order to Show Cause itself (which is actually nothing more than an order to appear) is issued without first notifying the responding party. In a practical sense, it is issued automatically by the clerk acting on behalf of the judge at the time it is sent down for filing. A date for hearing is assigned and the OSC is then served upon the responding party, being certain to provide them with (at least) the required 16 to 21 days' notice.

5. The concept of mediation is described in Family Code §§1800-1842. Family Code §§3160-3190 further describe this process and mandate the parties' participation. Mediation is discussed in detail in Chapter 10.

6. This form also accompanies the filing of a motion.

7. As is discussed in greater detail in the section dealing with child support, there are several computer programs and preprinted guidelines available that help the attorneys and the parties determine the probable amount of child support. The calculation of child support is in no small way the function of a comparison of the respective after-tax incomes of the two parties and, as such, these computer programs and preprinted guidelines have become prevalent in current family law practice because these calculations can become very complicated.

8. The same computer programs and preprinted guidelines discussed above regarding child support are also used to calculate *temporary* spousal support.

9. Of course, such a request would usually go hand-in-hand with a request made in item 6 for the exclusion from the residence of the responding party.

10 It is not unusual in a marital termination proceeding that one of the parties enjoys significant financial leverage over the other party. For example, if the applicant is unemployed and has been staying at home taking care of the children and thus has no means of income, he or she could formulate a request for child custody, exclusive use of the family residence and the car that he or she had been driving. He or she would also, in addition to requesting child support, request that the responding party be responsible for payment of the mortgage (or rent) on the house and for payment of the car loan, so as not to jeopardize the applicant's use of these assets pending the hearing.

11. Most declarations take the form of numbered paragraphs that set forth the bases for the orders requested in an organized (usually chronological) manner.

12. The applicant is not confined to offering only his *own* declaration. As many as are needed to fully (albeit briefly and concisely) explain the factual basis for the requested orders to the judge are allowed.

13. The hearing on an OSC is not unlike a "mini-trial": sometimes (but not always) evidence is offered and testimony received by witnesses testifying in court on the day of the hearing.

14. In fact, in Los Angeles county (and others), local rules require the parties to bring their tax returns to court with them on the day of the hearing.

15. Gross income is the total amount received before any deductions are taken from the income for taxes, social security, and similar items. For example, an individual who earns $36,000 per year does not actually "take home"$3,000 each month to spend. Assuming this wage earner is married with three dependents, the "net income" (that is, "take-home pay") received from a salary of $36,000 per year ($3,000 per month) is approximately $2,400 per month. The balance ($600) has been withheld by the employer as a pre-payment on income taxes, social security, and the like.

16. This is possible, albeit not recommended.

17. These concepts are discussed in much greater detail in the section of this book dealing with support.

18. Although it is rare, in cases of actual physical violence and articulable threats of such violence against the applicant, the court will sometimes waive the usual notice requirement for an ex parte hearing (typically 24 hours) and allow the applicant to proceed without *any* notice at all on a request for TROs seeking to impose a restraint on physical conduct and other stay away orders. Good cause for such a request typically depends upon facts and allegations of past physical violence against the applicant by the responding party and actual threats of continued harm if legal action is commenced.

19. They are not, however, enforceable against the responding party until personal service of the orders is effected on him.

20. This is always a good idea in any event.

21. Temporary orders are not always requested.

22. The court will have already read and considered before the hearing the moving (that is, "asking") and opposition papers filed by the parties' attorneys (or the parties themselves if they have no attorney).

23. The *Reifler* and *Stevenot* cases (discussed above) impact this practice, however.

24. Note, however, that if the responding party chooses not to appear, the relief requested is not simply given automatically by the court. The applicant must still establish the legal propriety of his request. Such lack of opposition does, however, generally make the courts somewhat more inclined to grant the requested relief.

25. The "caption" of the case is that section of the document containing the names of the parties, the title of the document, and the case number. All papers filed with the court must have this information on their face sheet, or they must be *attached* to a page (that is, face sheet) containing this information. Thus, if the memorandum of points and authorities is going to be filed separately from the motion papers, care must be taken to ensure that they carry the case caption on their front page.

26. The concept of a "hearing" of an OSC or a noticed motion has been referenced, but not fully explored, in this book. Because the focus of this book is a general discussion of basic concepts of family law, a detailed discussion of the "ins and outs" of the court hearing is not germane. Generally, however, the OSC and motion papers are filed with the court and a hearing on the request is scheduled. These hearings are usually heard by judges, although commissioners and judges pro tempore are also used for this purpose. The hearing on the OSC is not unlike a "mini-trial." Evidence is received and testimony by "live" witnesses is often taken (subject to certain limitations discussed earlier in this section). The hearing on the noticed motion typically consists of the lawyers (or the parties in pro per) arguing the facts and the law of their case to the judge in hopes of persuading a favorable outcome.

27. The discussion above in the section dealing with the Order to Show Cause found at page 377 should be reviewed at this time.

28. These various enabling sections will be discussed later in this book in the areas thereof devoted to their substantive context.

29. The term "law enforcement officer" is defined by statute (Family Code section 6240) to include the following 12 categories of enforcement personnel:

    (b) "Law enforcement officer" means one of the following officers who requests or enforces an emergency protective order under this part:

    (1) A police officer.

    (2) A sheriff's officer.

    (3) A peace officer of the Department of the California Highway Patrol.

    (4) A peace officer of the University of California Police Department.

(5) A peace officer of the California State University and College Police Departments.

(6) A peace officer of the Department of Parks and Recreation, as defined in subdivision (f) of Section 830.2 of the Penal Code.

(7) A peace officer of the Department of General Services of the City of Los Angeles, as defined in subdivision (c) of Section 830.31 of the Penal Code.

(8) A housing authority patrol officer, as defined in subdivision (d) of Section 830.31 of the Penal Code.

(9) A peace officer for a district attorney, as defined in Section 830.1 or 830.35 of the Penal Code.

(10) A parole officer, probation officer, or deputy probation officer, as defined in Section 830.5 of the Penal Code.

(11) A peace officer of a California Community College police department, as defined in subdivision (a) of Section 830.32.

(12) A peace officer employed by a police department of a school district, as defined in subdivision (b) of Section 830.32.

30. The presiding judge of each county's superior court is directed by statute to designate at least one judge, commissioner, or referee to be "reasonably available" on a 24-hour basis to issue these orders orally or by telephone.

CHAPTER 10

Enforcement

CHAPTER OVERVIEW

Obtaining the orders in a litigated matter is only half of the battle. The other half is securing enforcement of those orders from the opposing side. After all, a piece of paper entitling a party to support will not, in and of itself, put food on the table. This chapter explores the various methods available to enforce court orders, with particular reference, of course, to family law orders. This includes, but is not limited to, general civil debt collection methods and civil ("quasi-criminal") contempt.

A. Introduction

This chapter focuses on events that transpire when a party refuses to follow a court order. The court can issue an order after conducting a trial or after hearing an Order to Show Cause or other motion. One of the interesting aspects of our legal system is that it only operates at maximum efficiency when all parties involved in the process submit to the court's jurisdiction and follow its orders. Obviously, in every piece of contested litigation there is one side who is satisfied with the outcome and another side who is not so satisfied. In a perfect world both sides would adhere to the judge's decisions and ruling and govern their actions accordingly. Of course, this is not a perfect world, and very often it becomes necessary to compel the parties to follow court orders.

At the conclusion of a trial (or a similar proceeding at which certain orders are requested) the so-called "winner" generally comes away with a piece of paper signed by the judge that instructs the opposing side to perform, or refrain from performing, certain acts. The judge can issue a number of orders, including restraining orders (one party must stay away from the other party, or not call or harass the other party) and money orders (one party must pay the other party money, including spousal support, child support, or an equalizing payment). These examples are, of course, found in a family law context; however, these concepts also arise in virtually every other court action. Every action has its "winners" and "losers" and as such generally entails some sort of judicial decree or commandment that must be followed. When it is not followed, be it the payment of money or the modification of an individual's behavior, the need arises to extract compliance with the order or punishment for disobeying the order, usually over the other side's objection.

In general, parties use two proceedings to enforce court orders: (1) contempt actions and (2) property transfer orders. Through an action for contempt, a party aims to punish the transgressor for failing to adhere to the court's order. Through a property transfer order, a party secures the transfer of property (usually money) from the opposing party (usually the "loser").

Court orders may be enforced through a variety of statutory schemes, so many, in fact, that parties usually comply with court orders voluntarily. In the family law context many Family Code sections provide the trial court wide discretion to enforce its judgments, orders, and decrees. Section 290, the first enforcement section in the Code, provides (in pertinent part) that: "A judgment or order made or entered pursuant to this code may be enforced by the court by execution, the appointment of a receiver, or contempt, or by such other order as the court in its discretion determines from time to time to be necessary."

The last clause of this Code section proposes that virtually any enforcement procedure authorized by law is "fair game" when it comes to enforcing a judgment, order, or decree obtained in a family law proceeding.

B. Contempt

Family Code section 290 makes it clear that any judgment or order made or entered in a family law proceeding is enforceable through the use of a contempt proceeding. Additionally, orders for child and spousal support, the payment of attorney's fees, orders relating to custody and visitation, and even orders requiring the division of community property are enforceable by contempt. Contempt is very possibly one of the most potent weapons in the court's arsenal against the recalcitrant party because a contempt proceeding is what is called "quasi-criminal" in nature. The penalty for contempt includes the potential for a jail sentence. As such, an action for contempt is subject to much stricter guidelines and protections than many other civil remedies.

When a person blatantly disobeys a court order, he can be held in contempt of court. If the fabric of our judicial system is to be kept from unraveling in its entirety, the court must be able to impose significant penalties for the outright refusal to obey its orders. Thus, the court may hold a person in contempt if he has knowledge of and the ability to comply with a court order, yet refuses to obey the order. The concept of contempt is more simply put in terms explained to this author by his father when he was a young child: "I can't *make* you do anything. I can, however, make you very sorry you didn't."[1] That is basically at the heart of a contempt proceeding: make the transgressing party "very sorry" he did not obey the court order (in hopes, of course, of ensuring future compliance).

In the context of contempt litigation, there is both a civil component and a criminal component, which are concurrent and cumulative remedies. The civil contempt aspect of a general contempt proceeding is that the person charged with the contempt is sentenced with imprisonment (or assessed a fine) only until he or she does that which is called for in the court order. Conversely, a contempt is criminal in nature if the fundamental purpose is to punish.

A contempt proceeding is primarily "civil" in nature when it is used to compel compliance with the court's order. In other words, the *citee* (the word used to describe the individual charged with the contempt) can "purge" himself of the contempt simply by doing that which is expected of him. On the other hand, if the contempt proceeding is designed to punish the citee rather than to extract some sort of performance, it is criminal in nature, and the citee cannot purge himself of the contempt.

As stated by the Appellate Court in Albrecht v. Superior Court (Laird), 132 Cal. App. 3d 612 (1982):

> Although the order to show cause in re contempt arises out of the main civil action, the contempt proceeding itself is separate and distinct. It is a quasi-criminal proceeding, and may result in a fine or jail sentence, or both. [Citations.][¶] Thus, a contempt proceeding in the context of a domestic relations action is uniquely situated. It has attributes of a new, criminal matter, yet is also a principal means of enforcing the court's orders as the court exercises its continuing jurisdiction over the parties and subject matter.

Even though a contempt action involves issues "between the judge and the citee," the court leaves it up to the other parties to the litigation to file, on judicial council forms, citations for contempt against the offending party. This system works rather well because as a practical matter the court will not bother itself with individuals who disobey its orders until and unless the disobedience is brought to its attention. Who better to bring to the court's attention the refusal of a party to obey a court order than the person who is supposed to benefit from that court order: the other party in the litigation. As such, when filing an action for contempt (which action is initiated pursuant to the Order to Show Cause procedure[2]) the other party to the litigation must plead and prove the existence of four elements to establish a prima facie case against the citee. These four elements are:

1. the existence of a lawful order
2. the citee had knowledge of the order
3. the citee had the ability to comply with the order, and
4. the citee willfully disobeyed the order

Because of the quasi-criminal nature of the contempt charge, the citee is entitled to several of the due process rights accorded to other criminal defendants, including: (1) a formal hearing on the existence of the contempt, (2) a lawyer appointed free of charge to represent him in the contempt action if he cannot afford one, (3) formal notice of the charge, and (4) the right to remain silent. Additionally, the party who brings the contempt proceeding must prove the contempt beyond a reasonable doubt (rather than the lesser preponderance of the evidence standard).[3] Finally, there is some question as to whether a contempt citee is entitled to a jury trial. As a general rule, there is no right to a trial by jury in California on a civil contempt. There is some authority that allows a jury trial in situations involving potential penalties of six months or more jail time, however, and there is a strong argument that the right to a jury trial should be enforced in a "criminal" civil contempt proceeding.

One of the most fundamental rights that this text has emphasized is the litigant's right to notice and opportunity to be heard. This right is no less fundamental in contempt proceedings. In fact, the Order to Show Cause for Contempt (the "citation"), which establishes the charge of contempt, must be personally served on the citee for the court to acquire jurisdiction. Service must be effected in the manner authorized for the service of summons. For all practical purposes, this means that the charging papers (that is, the Order to Show Cause for Contempt) must be personally served on the citee. Once jurisdiction has been properly invoked, the inquiry moves on to the establishment of the four elements listed above.

In an action for contempt, the claimant must first show that the court order was in fact valid at the time of its issuance. The order must have been clear, unambiguous, and capable of being understood by the citee. Any ambiguities in the order will be resolved in favor of a finding that the citee is not in contempt. As a general rule, in order to establish this element, the claimant merely needs to ask the court to take judicial notice of the order that it previously entered in the action. In the family law context an Order to Show Cause for Contempt is brought in the family law court and is typically heard by the same judge who issued the order in the first instance. However, to the extent that the order as entered does not constitute a valid order, the citee is not guilty of contempt. Indeed, one cannot be found in contempt of an order that is invalid on its face.

Second, the claimant must establish that the citee had knowledge of the contents of the order. This does not mean to say that the citee must have been personally served with a copy of the order. All that is required is that the citee actually have notice or knowledge of the order, however such knowledge or notice is achieved. This is typically established by requesting the court to take judicial notice that the citee was present when the order was made. If the citee was not present in court when the order was made but had an attorney who was present on his or her behalf, then a rebuttable presumption arises that the citee had knowledge of the court order, which will be enough to satisfy this element of a successful contempt action. The burden would then shift to the citee client to prove that the attorney never communicated the order to the citee client, who thus did not have actual knowledge of the court's order.[4]

The third element for contempt is that the citee had the ability to comply with the court's orders. This is perhaps the most difficult element to establish because it must be done without the benefit of any input from the citee. The reader will recall that the citee has the right to remain silent. This means that no testimony can be elicited from the citee on the subject of his contempt. He cannot be called to the stand to testify against himself nor can any statements previously made by the citee be used (for example, in a deposition or in discovery responses) to establish the prima facie case of contempt.[5] The party bringing the contempt must establish what is sometimes a subjective element without the benefit of input from the one person who is capable of providing the best evidence on this subject. How then is this accomplished?

In contempt actions for failure to pay support, perhaps the best way to establish the ability to comply is to subpoena payroll records from the citee's employer or subpoena checking or savings account records from the citee's bank or other financial institution. This is perfectly appropriate and does not violate the citee's right to remain silent; further, such evidence can be used to establish a current income flow that demonstrates the citee's ability to comply with the financial order.

Additionally, certain presumptions are present in the family law context that can help establish the ability to comply. There is authority in

California that if an order for the payment of money is violated within a short period of time after its issuance, the court is free to presume (rebuttably) that the trial court would not have made the order in the first place if it had not already made a specific finding of the citee's ability to pay. However, if any significant period of time has lapsed since the issuance of the order and the alleged noncompliance, there is no basis for this presumption. Furthermore, simply demonstrating that a citee currently has the capability to pay a financial order is not the same as establishing that the citee—at the time of his alleged non-compliance—had the ability to pay. For example, assume that at a dissolution action, the obligor spouse earns $100,000 per year as an attorney. Based on his income (approximately $8,300 per month), the court orders him to pay approximately $4,000 per month in support. Approximately six months later, the obligor spouse quits his job as an attorney and takes a job as a gas station attendant. His income drops from $8,300 per month to $1,800 per month. In the subsequent contempt action brought by the recipient spouse for nonpayment of support, she must establish that over the past six months the obligor spouse actually had the ability to pay $4,000 per month in support. Assuming only the facts set forth above, the obligor spouse does not have the present ability to pay $4,000 per month because he only makes $1,800 per month. Accordingly, establishment of this third element of contempt would be incomplete. Of course, if the obligor spouse returned to work as an attorney, he would have a demonstrated earning capacity of $4,000 per month. This is not, however, the same as the ability to pay.

One of the exceptions to the establishment of the third element in a contempt action concerns nonpayment of a child support order. California Code of Civil Procedure section 1209.5 provides that in a contempt proceeding for failure to pay a child support order, a prima facie case will be established on evidence that the order was made, the citee had knowledge of the order, and the citee failed to comply with the order. The third element (ability to pay) is not part of the prima facie case for contempt. In essence, it is presumed to have been met; thus, the citee has the burden to establish his inability to pay. This is an extremely powerful tool in the fight against parents who refuse to pay child support. This Code section has withstood constitutional attack and continues to be good law in California.

Code of Civil Procedure section 1209.5 does not apply in cases of spousal support; however, as mentioned above, the court will assume that the issuing court made an order for spousal support in an amount that is within the citee's ability to pay. As such, for all practical purposes, in a contempt action arising out of the nonpayment of spousal support, the citee must raise his inability to pay as a defense to the citation. The reader should also note that even when a citee is in fact unable to fully comply with the court's order, to the extent that he *is* capable of complying at all he must make such payment. In other words, the citee must pay the portion of the ordered amount that is within his ability to pay. It is therefore improper for someone who cannot afford to pay $4,000 per month—but *can* pay $3,000 per month—to simply pay nothing. The citee cannot assume that if he cannot make the entire payment then he should not make any payment at all. Such an assumption is foolhardy and may very well result in a finding of contempt.

The fourth element of contempt is that the citee's disobedience of the court order was willful or, for all practical purposes, inexcusable. This element is almost always established in the prima facie case, and when it is, the citee must establish a defense (or an excuse for noncompliance). In other words, the citee must establish that his refusal to obey was not "willful." The reader should note that a citee cannot claim that he was simply following his attorney's advice as a defense. In fact, an attorney herself may be held in contempt for advising a client to disobey a court order.

Once the moving party makes a prima facie case for contempt, the citee must establish any defense he may have for his disobedience. In his defense, the citee could attempt to demonstrate that: (1) the order, as made, is either invalid or ambiguous, (2) he did not have the ability to comply with the order, (3) the moving party by virtue of her conduct waived substantial compliance with the court's orders or is estopped from raising contempt as a defense to noncompliance,[6] or (4) the contempt action violates the statute of limitations.

With respect to contempt proceedings in a family law context, the court will employ the statute of limitations set out in Code of Civil Procedure section 1218.5(b): "If the contempt alleged is the failure to pay child, family, or spousal support, the period of limitations for commencing a contempt action is three years from the date that the payment was due. If the action before the court is enforcement of another order under the Family Code, the period of limitations for commencing a contempt action is two years from the time that the alleged contempt occurred." Accordingly, if a citee has not paid child support for 48 months, the citation for contempt can only seek redress for nonpayment of the support order for the 36 months immediately preceding the filing of the contempt. An interesting problem in the context of family law contempt concerns children who are unwilling to visit the noncustodial parent. Under these circumstances, the noncustodial parent will, in many instances, file an Order to Show Cause for Contempt against the custodial parent, seeking to have that parent held in contempt of court for willfully disobeying the court's orders with respect to visitation. The court has considered an interesting defense to this citation with respect to parents who do not have sufficient control over the conduct of their children to "make" them visit. In this context, it has been held that a custodial parent can only be held in contempt of a visitation order if he possesses sufficient control over the child to actually have the ability to make the child available for visitation. As the child gets older, however, it may become more and more difficult for the parent to exercise control over the child. Indeed, if a teenage child refuses to visit with the noncustodial parent, through no fault of the custodial parent, query whether this custodial parent possesses the ability to comply with the court's order. The chances are very good he does not.

The appellate court confronted this situation in Coursey v. Superior Court, 194 Cal. App. 3d 147 (1987). In *Coursey*, the court found that the mother was unable to compel her 14-year-old child to visit with her father. The *Coursey* court stated:

> To be held in contempt, the accused must have the ability to render compliance with the order. . . . We have been cited to no rule of law holding that a 14-year-old child is under the absolute control of his or her parent, nor are we aware of any. Common experience tells us we may not merely assume without proof that a mother can reasonably compel a teenage daughter to visit against the daughter's strong wishes. Here, the question whether the mother could reasonably compel her daughter to visit depended on proof of the circumstances surrounding the contemplated visit, including the relationships between the parties and their attitudes vis-à-vis the visit.

Under these circumstances, however, the court might very well be inclined to shift custody from the custodial parent to the noncustodial parent, thus presenting the recalcitrant child with the option of either visiting with the noncustodial parent or living with him.

The penalties for contempt in the context of a family law matter include five days in jail, a fine of $1,000, or both, for each count of contempt. This last clause is worth noting. Formerly, if an individual was ordered to pay one-half spousal support on the first and one-half on the fifteenth of each month, but he refused to pay that support for 12 months, he could be found guilty of 24 counts of contempt, which could result in imprisonment in the county jail for 120 days and a fine of $24,000. This rule has since been changed, such that an order to pay monthly support, even if the monthly payment was allowed to be split up during the month, will now only be treated as one count of contempt.

The Order to Show Cause for Contempt is initiated through the use of judicial council forms. Figure 10-1 includes the form and its information sheet.

C. Enforcement of Support Orders

Needless to say, obtaining an award for support is only half the battle when the obligor party refuses to make the ordered payments. Notwithstanding the fact that court orders for support are enforceable

Figure 10-1
Form FL-410—Order to Show Cause and
Affidavit for Contempt

FL-410

ATTORNEY OR PARTY WITHOUT ATTORNEY *(Name, state bar number, and address):*	FOR COURT USE ONLY

TELEPHONE NO.:   FAX NO.:

ATTORNEY FOR *(Name)*:

SUPERIOR COURT OF CALIFORNIA, COUNTY OF

STREET ADDRESS:

MAILING ADDRESS:

CITY AND ZIP CODE:

BRANCH NAME:

PETITIONER/PLAINTIFF:

RESPONDENT/DEFENDANT:

OTHER PARENT:

ORDER TO SHOW CAUSE AND AFFIDAVIT FOR CONTEMPT	CASE NUMBER:

NOTICE!	**¡AVISO!**
A contempt proceeding is criminal in nature. If the court finds you in contempt, the possible penalties include jail sentence, community service, and fine.	Un proceso judicial por desacato es de índole criminal. Si la corte le declara a usted en desacato, las sanciones posibles incluyen penas de prisión y de servicio a la comunidad, y multas.
You are entitled to the services of an attorney, who should be consulted promptly in order to assist you. If you cannot afford an attorney, the court may appoint an attorney to represent you.	Usted tiene derecho a los servicios de un abogado, a quien debe consultar sin demora para obtener ayuda. Si no puede pagar a un abogado, la corte podrá nombrar a un abogado para que le represente.

1. TO CITEE *(name of person you allege has violated the orders):*

2. YOU ARE ORDERED TO APPEAR IN THIS COURT AS FOLLOWS, TO GIVE ANY LEGAL REASON WHY THIS COURT SHOULD NOT FIND YOU GUILTY OF CONTEMPT, PUNISH YOU FOR WILLFULLY DISOBEYING ITS ORDERS AS SET FORTH IN THE AFFIDAVIT BELOW AND ANY ATTACHED *AFFIDAVIT OF FACTS CONSTITUTING CONTEMPT*; AND REQUIRE YOU TO PAY, FOR THE BENEFIT OF THE MOVING PARTY, THE ATTORNEY FEES AND COSTS OF THIS PROCEEDING.

   a. Date: Time: Dept.:   Rm.:

   b. Address of court: ☐ same as noted above   ☐ other *(specify):*

Date:

_____
JUDICIAL OFFICER

AFFIDAVIT SUPPORTING ORDER TO SHOW CAUSE FOR CONTEMPT

3. ☐ An *Affidavit of Facts Constituting Contempt* (form FL-411 or FL-412) is attached.

4. Citee has willfully disobeyed certain orders of this court as set forth in this affidavit and any attached affidavits.

5. a. Citee had knowledge of the order in that
    (1) ☐ citee was present in court at the time the order was made.
    (2) ☐ citee was served with a copy of the order.
    (3) ☐ citee signed a stipulation upon which the order was based.
    (4) ☐ other *(specify):*

        ☐ Continued on Attachment 5a(4).
   b. Citee was able to comply with each order when it was disobeyed.

6. Based on the instances of disobedience described in this affidavit
   a. ☐ I have not previously filed a request with the court that the citee be held in contempt.
   b. ☐ I have previously filed a request with the court that the citee be held in contempt *(specify date filed and results):*

    ☐ Continued on Attachment 6b.

Page 1 of 4

Form Adopted for Mandatory Use
Judicial Council of California
FL-410 [Rev. January 1, 2003]

ORDER TO SHOW CAUSE AND AFFIDAVIT FOR CONTEMPT

Family Code, § 292;
Code of Civil Procedure, §§ 1211.5, 2015.5
www.courtinfo.ca.gov

Figure 10-1 (continued)

PETITIONER/PLAINTIFF:	CASE NUMBER:
RESPONDENT/DEFENDANT:	
OTHER PARENT:	

7. ☐ Citee has previously been found in contempt of a court order *(specify case, court, date):*

☐ Continued on Attachment 7.

8. ☐ Each order disobeyed and each instance of disobedience is described as follows:

    a. ☐ Orders for child support, spousal support, family support, attorney fees, and court or other litigation costs (see attached *Affidavit of Facts Constituting Contempt* (form FL-411))

    b. ☐ Domestic violence restraining orders and child custody and visitation orders (see attached *Affidavit of Facts Constituting Contempt* (form FL-412))

    c. ☐ Injunctive or other order *(specify which order was violated, how the order was violated, and when the order was violated):*

☐ Continued on Attachment 8c.

    d. ☐ Other material facts, including facts indicating that the violation of the orders was without justification or excuse *(specify):*

☐ Continued on Attachment 8d.

    e. ☐ I am requesting that attorney fees and costs be awarded to me for the costs of pursuing this contempt action. (A copy of my *Income and Expense Declaration* (form FL-150) is attached.)

WARNING: IF YOU PURSUE THIS CONTEMPT ACTION, IT MAY AFFECT THE ABILITY OF THE DISTRICT ATTORNEY TO PROSECUTE THE CITEE CRIMINALLY FOR THE SAME VIOLATIONS.

I declare under penalty of perjury under the laws of the State of California that the foregoing is true and correct.

Date:

▶

_____
(TYPE OR PRINT NAME)

_____
(SIGNATURE)

FL-410 [Rev. January 1, 2003]

ORDER TO SHOW CAUSE AND AFFIDAVIT FOR CONTEMPT

Page 2 of 4

Figure 10-1 (continued)

**INFORMATION SHEET FOR ORDER TO SHOW CAUSE
AND AFFIDAVIT OF FACTS CONSTITUTING CONTEMPT**

(Do NOT deliver this Information Sheet to the court clerk.)

Please follow these instructions to complete the *Order to Show Cause and Affidavit for Contempt* (form FL-410) if you do not have an attorney to represent you. Your attorney, if you have one, should complete this form, as well as the *Affidavit of Facts Constituting Contempt* (form FL-411 or form FL-412). You may wish to consult an attorney for assistance. Contempt actions are very difficult to prove. An attorney may be appointed for the citee.

INSTRUCTIONS FOR COMPLETING THE ORDER TO SHOW CAUSE AND AFFIDAVIT OF FACTS CONSTITUTING CONTEMPT (TYPE OR PRINT FORM IN INK):

If the top section of the form has already been filled out, skip down to number 1 below. If the top section of the form is blank, you must provide this information.

Front page, first box, top of form, left side: Print your name, address, telephone number, and fax number, if any, in this box. If you have a restraining order and wish to keep your address confidential, you may use any address where you can receive mail. **You can be legally served court papers at this address.**

Front page, second box, left side: Print the name of the county where the court is located and insert the address and any branch name of the court building where you are seeking to obtain a contempt order. You may get this information from the court clerk. This should be the same court in which the original order was issued.

Front page, third box, left side: Print the names of the Petitioner, Respondent, and Other Parent (if any) in this box. Use the same names as appear on the most recent court order disobeyed.

Front page, first box, top of form, right side: Leave this box blank for the court's use.

Front page, second box, right side: Print the court case number in this box. This number is also shown on the most recent court order disobeyed.

Item 1: Insert the name of the party who disobeyed the order ("the citee").

Item 2: The court clerk will provide the hearing date and location.

Item 3: Either check the box in item 3 and attach an *Affidavit of Facts Constituting Contempt* (form FL-411 for financial orders or form FL-412 for domestic violence, or custody and visitation orders), or leave the box in item 3 blank but check and complete item 8.

Item 5: Check the box that describes how the citee knew about the order that has been disobeyed.

Item 6: a. Check this box if you have not previously applied for a contempt order.

b. Check this box if you have previously applied for a contempt order and briefly explain when you requested the order and results of your request. If you need more space, check the box that says "continued on Attachment 6b" and attach a separate sheet to this order to show cause.

Item 7: Check this box if the citee has previously been found in contempt by a court of law. Briefly explain when the citee was found in contempt and for what. If there is not enough space to write all the facts, check the box that says "continued on Attachment 7" and attach a separate sheet to this order to show cause.

Item 8: a. Check this box if the citee has disobeyed orders for child support, custody, visitation, spousal support, family support, attorney fees, and court or litigation costs. Refer to item 1a on *Affidavit of Facts Constituting Contempt* (form FL-411).

b. Check this box if the citee has disobeyed domestic violence orders or child custody and visitation orders. Refer to *Affidavit of Facts Constituting Contempt* (form FL-412).

FL-410 [Rev. January 1, 2003]   **ORDER TO SHOW CAUSE AND AFFIDAVIT FOR CONTEMPT**   Page 3 of 4

Figure 10-1 (continued)

Information Sheet *(continued)*

<u>Item 8</u>: c. If you are completing this item, use facts personally known to you or known to the best of your knowledge. State the facts in detail. if there is not enough space to write all the facts, check the box that says "continued on Attachment 8c" and attach a separate sheet to this order to show cause, including facts indicating that the violation of the orders was without justification or excuse.

    d. Use this item to write other facts that are important to this order. If you are completing this item, insert facts personally known to you, or known to the best of your knowledge. State facts in detail. If there is not enough space to write all the facts, check the box that says "Continued on Attachment 8d" and attach a separate sheet to the order to show cause.

    e. If you request attorney fees and/or costs for pursuing this contempt action, check this box. Attach a copy of your *Income and Expense Declaration* (form FL-150).

Type or print and sign your name at the bottom of page 2.

If you checked the boxes in item 3 and item 8a or 8b, complete the appropriate *Affidavit of Facts Constituting Contempt* (form FL-411), following the instructions for the affidavit above.

Make at least three copies of the *Order to Show Cause and Affidavit for Contempt* (form FL-410) and any supporting *Affidavit of Facts Constituting Contempt* (form FL-411 or FL-412) and the *Income and Expense Declaration* (form FL-150) for the court clerk, the citee, and yourself. If the district attorney or local child support agency is involved in your case, you must provide a copy to the district attorney or local child support agency.

Take the completed form(s) to the court clerk's office. The clerk will provide hearing date and location in item 2, obtain the judicial officer's signature, file the originals, and return the copies to you.

Have someone who is at least 18 years of age, who is not a party, serve the order and any attached papers on the disobedient party. For example, a process server or someone you know may serve the papers. **You may not serve the papers yourself. Service must be personal; service by mail is insufficient.** The papers must be served at least 21 calendar days before the court hearing. The person serving papers must complete a *Proof of Personal Service* (form FL-330) and give the original to you. Keep a copy for yourself and file the original *Proof of Personal Service* (form FL-330) with the court.

If you need assistance with these forms, contact an attorney or the Family Law Facilitator in your county.

under general civil enforcement procedures, as well as specialized statutory schemes designed for that purpose (discussed in a subsequent chapter), the legislature recognized that implementing those various procedures can be both costly and time-consuming for the recipient party. Accordingly, the statutory scheme unique to enforcement of support orders under the Family Code was established in Part 5 of Division 9 of the Family Code, commencing at section 4500. Section 4500 provides: "An order for child, family, or spousal support that is made, entered, or enforceable in this state is enforceable under this Code, whether or not the order was made and entered pursuant to this Code."

Further, a "family support" order is enforceable in the same manner and to the same extent as one for child support. As the reader will recall, an order for family support contemplates a combination of spousal support and child support so as to take advantage of the deductibility of spousal support provisions of the Internal Revenue Code. Because the method and manner in which spousal support is enforced is somewhat different than the manner in which child support is enforced (and somewhat less stringent), the legislature felt it best to enforce family support as if it were child support in order to provide the most protection for supported children in a family support setting.

1. Earnings Withholding Order Support

A wage assignment or garnishment is a procedure by which a portion of a judgment debtor's paycheck is withheld by the employer and paid directly to the judgment creditor in satisfaction of a money judgment. In the context of spousal and child support, two such procedures fall into this general description of orders. One is the *Earnings Withholding Order for Support* contemplated by Code of Civil Procedure sections 706.030 et seq. The other is known as an *Earnings Assignment Order for Support*, which is provided for by Family Code sections 5200 et seq. The provisions of these sections were essentially enacted pursuant to a federally imposed mandate that all support orders, unless stayed by the court for good cause, be subject to an immediate wage assignment. This mandate thus shifted the mechanics for the payment of child and spousal support away from the judgment debtor and on to the judgment debtor's employer. The benefit of this shift is hopefully clear: Where the individual obligated to make the child or spousal support payment might be perceived to have an incentive *not* to pay the award, the employer has the incentive *to* pay the award. If the employer improperly violates a Wage Assignment for Support award, the employer will find himself in the unhappy position of making the obligor parent or spouse's support payment.

The Withholding Orders for Support provided by Code of Civil Procedure sections 706.030 et seq. is distinguishable from the Family Code section 5208 Earnings Assignment for Support because the Withholding Order for Support can only be used to collect amounts of support that are delinquent (that is, in arrears). A Family Code section 5208 Earnings Assignment can reach earnings to satisfy both arrearages and future installment obligations. While a Withholding Order for Support can be used to satisfy *all* money judgments, the wage assignment provided for in Family Code section 5208 is exclusive to the enforcement of court-ordered support. Imposition of this Earnings Assignment order is automatically incorporated into *every* support order. Family Code section 5230 clarifies the issuance of this mandatory wage assignment as follows:

> (a) When the court orders a party to pay an amount for support or orders a modification of the amount of support to be paid, the court shall include in its order an earnings assignment order for support that orders the employer of the obligor to pay to the obligee that portion of the obligor's earnings due or to become due in the future as will be sufficient to pay an amount to cover both of the following:
> (1) The amount ordered by the court for support.
> (2) An amount which shall be ordered by the court to be paid toward the liquidation of any arrearage.
> (b) An earnings assignment order for support shall be issued, and shall be effective and enforceable pursuant to Section 5231, notwithstanding the absence of the name, address, or other identifying information regarding the obligor's employer.

The genesis of the mandatory wage assignment law is interesting. An order for child support (and spousal support) is basically the same as any other "typical" civil court order. An order for child or spousal support can be enforced in the specific manner described by the Family Code (and related sections); it can *also* be enforced in the manner described by any other general civil judgment or order. In that regard, a general civil judgment for money may be enforced (that is, collected) by issuing a wage assignment to the debtor's employer. The wage assignment is a court-issued directive that requires the debtor's employer to withhold an amount of money from the debtor's paycheck each month (or each paycheck) as will be sufficient to satisfy the court order. A wage assignment for child support typically withholds the entire amount payable as child support on a monthly basis per paycheck.

The wage assignment order is a very effective tool for the enforcement and collection of spousal and child support, but only (obviously) in situations where the obligor parent or spouse is in fact employed. Unfortunately, an employee debtor often suffers when the court issues a wage assignment on his or her employer. Unless the employer is already equipped to handle such matters, it must perform a significant amount of extra work to process the assignment. Moreover, the employer typically considers the wage assignment to be a negative mark in the employee's personnel file for a variety of reasons. For example, it can indicate that the employee does not service his debts in a timely manner, the employee costs the employer additional monies in process fees, and the employee has other "poor character" traits.

To help eliminate this stigma, the 1990 amendment to the (then) Family Law Act made the issuance of a wage assignment mandatory, and thus not subject to anyone's discretion. The employee was then free to explain to the employer that service of the wage assignment was beyond the employee's control.[7]

While the court has no discretion when it comes to issuing a wage assignment (it must, in other words, issue the wage assignment in all cases), the court may order that service of the wage assignment be stayed upon a finding of "good cause." Family Code section 5260 defines good cause as follows:

> (a) The court may order that service of the assignment order be stayed only if the court makes a finding of good cause or if an alternative arrangement exists for payment in accordance with paragraph (2) of subdivision (b). Notwithstanding any other provision of law, service of wage assignments issued for foreign orders for support, and service of foreign orders for the assignment of wages registered pursuant to Article 6 (commencing with Section 4950) of Chapter 6 shall not be stayed pursuant to this subdivision.
>
> (b) For purposes of this section, good cause or an alternative arrangement for staying an assignment order is as follows:
>
> (1) Good cause for staying a wage assignment exists only when all of the following conditions exist:
>
> (A) The court provides a written explanation of why the stay of the wage assignment would be in the best interests of the child.
>
> (B) The obligor has a history of uninterrupted, full, and timely payment, other than through a wage assignment or other mandatory process of previously ordered support, during the previous 12 months.
>
> (C) The obligor does not owe an arrearage for prior support.
>
> (D) The obligor proves, and the court finds, by clear and convincing evidence that service of the wage assignment would cause extraordinary hardship upon the obligor. Whenever possible, the court shall specify a date that any stay ordered under this section will automatically terminate.
>
> (2) An alternative arrangement for staying a wage assignment order requires a written agreement between the parties that provides for payment of the support obligation as ordered other than through

the immediate service of a wage assignment. Any agreement between the parties which includes the staying of a service of a wage assignment shall include the concurrence of the local child support agency in any case in which support is ordered to be paid through a county officer designated for that purpose. The execution of an agreement pursuant to this paragraph shall not preclude a party from thereafter seeking a wage assignment in accordance with the procedures specified in Section 5261 upon violation of the agreement.

Similarly, section 5261(a) provides that the stay of wage assignment issued pursuant to section 5260 will terminate "upon the obligor's failure to make timely support payments or earlier by court order if requested by the local child support agency or by the obligor." The process for terminating a stay of the service of the wage assignment order is very straightforward. The obligee simply files a declaration signed under penalty of perjury to the effect that the obligor is in arrears in payment of any portion of the support. Upon so filing, this stay automatically terminates by operation of law without the requirement of notice to the obligor.

The reader should note that special statutory provisions exist with regard to support orders issued or modified before July 1, 1990 (the effective date of the mandatory inclusion of an automatic earnings assignment order with all support orders). Family Code sections 5250 to 5253 allow a support claimant to apply for an earnings withholding order with regard to a pre-July 1990 support order inasmuch as the earnings assignment order was not automatically put in place at the time that the original order was issued. The process is very straightforward. The oblige must sign, under penalty of perjury, an application stating that the obligor is in default on support payments of at least one month. Once it receives the application, the court must issue, without notice to the obligor, the requested earnings assignment order.

Once obtained, the earnings assignment order is not served on the obligor; rather, it is served on the obligor's *employer*. Immediately thereafter, the employer must withhold enough money from the employee's paycheck to cover the amounts set forth in the assignment order; further, the employer must forward this amount it to the obligee within ten days of the obligor's pay date. It is the employer's obligation to deliver a copy of the assignment order, as well as a copy of the employee's rights to move to quash the assignment order, on the employee.

Sections 5250-5253 impose severe penalties on employers who fail to comply with an assignment order. Section 5241 provides that any employer who willfully fails to withhold and forward support pursuant to a valid assignment order entered and served upon the employer is liable to the obligee for the amount of support not withheld. In other words, if the employer does not withhold the amount of support required by the assignment order and pay it over to the obligee on behalf of the employee, then the employer itself must pay the employee's support obligations.

Of course, under appropriate circumstances, the Code provides for stay of service of the assignment order plus the procedural vehicle for an obligor to move to quash the assignment order. Such circumstances include: (1) the amount of current or overdue support reflected on the assignment order is incorrect, (2) the obligor is not the appropriate obligor under the support order in question, or (3) the amount sought to be withheld exceeds that allowable under federal law. The obligor files the motion to quash under procedures similar to any other motion before the family court.

Finally, to further avoid the stigma discussed above, Family Code section 5290 provides that "no employer shall use any assignment authorized by this chapter as grounds for refusing to hire a person or for discharging, taking disciplinary action against, denying a promotion to, or for taking any other action adversely affecting the terms and conditions of employment of an employee. An employer who engages in the conduct prohibited by this section may be assessed a civil penalty of a maximum of Five Hundred dollars ($500.00)." It would seem then that not only is the stigma of a wage assignment in this context gone, but any attempt by an employer to bring it back carries with it serious consequences.

The wage assignment need not be served on the employer personally. It can be served by first-class mail pursuant to Family Code section 5232. The Family Code contains additional provisions that govern the mechanics of the issuance and enforcement of wage assignments. For example, the Code requires an obligor to follow certain procedures when attempting to quash the wage assignment, and the Code requires an obligor to forward his current employer's identity to the oblige in the event that the obligor changes employers. The Earnings Withholding Order for Support is also the subject of a judicial council form, specifically WG-004. It is shown in its entirety in Figure 10-2.

2. Abstract of Judgment

Division 9, Part 5 of the Code is divided into several chapters, each of which describes a unique facet of enforcement in the area of support orders. Chapter 1, titled "General Provisions," identifies the awards that are susceptible to enforcement under this Part. Section 4502 of this chapter (through its reference to Family Code section 291) provides that support orders are not subject to the Code of Civil Procedure's general requirement that a judgment or order be renewed every ten years. The chapter further makes general provisions for other aspects of enforcement; the most explicit of these is found in Family Code section 4506, which defines the appropriate contents for an Abstract of Judgment of a support order.

Figure 10-2
FormWG-004—Earnings Withholding Order
for Support

WG-004

ATTORNEY OR PARTY WITHOUT ATTORNEY *(Name, State Bar number, and address):*	TELEPHONE NO.:	LEVYING OFFICER *(Name and Address):*

ATTORNEY FOR *(Name):*

NAME OF COURT, JUDICIAL DISTRICT, OR BRANCH COURT, IF ANY:

PLAINTIFF:

DEFENDANT:

EARNINGS WITHHOLDING ORDER FOR SUPPORT (Wage Garnishment)	LEVYING OFFICER FILE NO.:	COURT CASE NO.:

EMPLOYEE: *KEEP YOUR COPY OF THIS LEGAL PAPER.*   ***EMPLEADO:*** *GUARDE ESTE PAPEL OFICIAL.*

EMPLOYER: Enter the following date to assist your record keeping.

Date this order was received by employer (specify the date of personal delivery by levying officer or registered process server or the date mail receipt was signed):

TO THE EMPLOYER REGARDING YOUR EMPLOYEE:

Name and address of employer   Name and address of employee

Social Security Number (if known):

1. A judgment creditor has obtained this order to collect a court judgment against your employee. You are directed to withhold part of the earnings of the employee *(see instructions on reverse of this form).* Pay the withheld sums to the **levying officer** *(name and address above).*

    If the employee works for you now, you must **give the employee a copy of this order and the Employee Instructions** within 10 days after receiving this order.

    Complete both copies of the form Employer's Return and mail them to the levying officer within 15 days after receiving this order, whether or not the employee works for you.

2. The total amount due is $

    Count 10 calendar days from the date when you received this order. If your employee's pay period ends before the tenth day, **do not** withhold earnings payable for that pay period. **Do** withhold from earnings that are payable for any pay period ending on or after that tenth day.

    Continue withholding until
    (1) the total amount due has been withheld; or
    (2) you receive a court order or an order from the levying officer telling you to stop the withholding earlier.

3. The judgment was entered in the court shown above. The judgment creditor is *(name):*

4. The EMPLOYER'S INSTRUCTIONS on the reverse tell you how much of the employee's earnings to withhold each payday. Follow those instructions unless you receive a court order or order from the levying officer giving you other instructions.

Date:

....
 (TYPE OR PRINT NAME)

▶ _____
 (SIGNATURE)

☐ LEVYING OFFICER   ☐ REGISTERED PROCESS SERVER

*The **EMPLOYER'S INSTRUCTIONS** on the reverse contain special rules that apply to Earnings Withholding Order For Support. Read the instructions carefully.*

(Employer's Instructions on reverse)   Page 1 of 2

Form Adopted by the
Judicial Council of California
WG-004 [Rev. January 1, 2007]

EARNINGS WITHHOLDING ORDER FOR SUPPORT
(Wage Garnishment)

Code of Civil Procedure, §§ 706.030,
706.108, 706.052
www.courtinfo.ca.gov

Figure 10-2 (continued)

EMPLOYER'S INSTRUCTIONS WG-004
(EARNINGS WITHHOLDING ORDERS FOR SUPPORT)

These instructions apply *only* to Earnings Withholding Orders for Support. Applicable instructions appear on the reverse of the other types of Earnings Withholding Orders.

The instructions in paragraph 1 on the reverse of this form describe your early duties to provide information to your employee and the levying officer.

Your other duties are TO WITHHOLD THE CORRECT AMOUNT OF EARNINGS (if any) and PAY IT TO THE LEVYING OFFICER during the *withholding period*.

The usual *withholding period* begins ten (10) calendar days after you receive the Earnings Withholding Order. In the case of an Earnings Withholding Order for Support (this Order) the *withholding period continues* until one of two things happens: (1) the total amount specified in the Order, plus any amounts listed in a notice from the levying officer, has been withheld, or (2) you receive a court order or notice signed by the levying officer specifying a termination date.

You are entitled to rely on and should obey all written notices signed by the levying officer.

The form Employer's Return describes several situations that could affect the withholding period for this order. If you receive more than one Earnings Withholding Order during a withholding period, review that form (Employer's Return) for instructions.

Your duty to withhold does not end merely because the employee no longer works for you. Withholding for an Earnings Withholding Order for Support does not automatically terminate until one year after the employment of the employee by the employer ends.

WHAT TO DO WITH THE MONEY

The amounts withheld during the withholding period must be paid to the levying officer by the 15th of the next month after each payday. If you wish to pay more frequently than monthly, each payment must be made within ten (10) days after the close of the pay period.

Be sure to mark each check with the case number, the levying officer's file number, if different, and the employee's name so the money will be applied to the correct account

WHAT IF YOU STILL HAVE QUESTIONS?

The garnishment law is contained in the Code of Civil Procedure beginning with section 706.010. Sections 706.022, 706.025, and 706.104 explain the employer's duties.

The Federal Wage Garnishment Law and federal rules provide the basic protections on which the California law is based.

Inquiries about the federal law will be answered by mail, telephone or personal interview at any office of the Wage and Hour Division of the U.S. Department of Labor. Offices are listed in the telephone directory under the U.S. Department of Labor in the U.S. Government listing.

COMPUTATION INSTRUCTIONS

State and federal law limits the amount of earnings that can be withheld. The limitations are based on the employee's disposable earnings, which are different from gross pay or take-home pay.

To determine the CORRECT AMOUNT OF EARNINGS TO BE WITHHELD (if any), compute the employee's *disposable earnings*.

(A) Earnings include any money, (whether called wages, salary, commissions, bonuses or anything else) that is paid by an employer to an employee for personal services. Vacation or sick pay is subject to withholding as it is received by the employee. Tips are generally not included as earning since they are not paid by the employer.

(B) *Disposable earnings* are the earnings left after subtracting the part of the earnings a state or federal law requires an employer to withhold. Generally these required deductions are (1) federal income tax, (2) federal social security, (3) state income tax, (4) state disability insurance, and (5) payments to public employees' retirement systems. Disposable earnings will change when the required deductions change.

After the employee's disposable earnings are known, WITHHOLD FIFTY (50) PERCENT of the *disposable earnings* for the Withholding Order for Support. For example, if the employee has monthly disposable earnings of $1,432, the sum of $716 would be withheld to pay to the levying officer on account of this order.

Occasionally, the employee's earnings will also be subject to a Wage and Earnings Assignment Order, an order available for child support or spousal support. The amount required to be withheld for that order should be deducted from the amount to be withheld for this order. For example, if the employee is subject to a Wage and Earnings Assignment Order and the employer is required to withhold $300 per month to pay on that order, when the employer receives this Earnings Withholding Order for Support, the employer should deduct the $300 for the Wage and Earnings Assignment Order from the $716 and pay the balance to the levying officer each month for this order.

— IMPORTANT WARNINGS —

1. IT IS AGAINST THE LAW TO FIRE THE EMPLOYEE BECAUSE OF EARNINGS WITHHOLDING ORDERS FOR THE PAYMENT OF ONLY ONE INDEBTEDNESS. No matter how many orders you receive, so long as they all relate to judgment (no matter how many debts are represented in that judgment) the employee may not be fired.

2. IT IS ILLEGAL TO AVOID AN EARNINGS WITHHOLDING ORDER BY POSTPONING OR ADVANCING THE PAYMENT OF EARNINGS. The employee's pay period must not be changed to prevent the order from taking effect.

3. IT IS ILLEGAL NOT TO PAY AMOUNTS WITHHELD FOR THE EARNINGS WITHHOLDING ORDER TO THE LEVYING OFFICER. Your duty is to pay the money to the levying officer who will pay the money in accordance with the laws that apply to this case.

IF YOU VIOLATE ANY OF THESE LAWS, YOU MAY BE HELD LIABLE TO PAY CIVIL DAMAGES AND YOU MAY BE SUBJECT TO CRIMINAL PROSECUTION!

An Abstract of Judgment is simply a piece of paper (usually a court form) that certifies the general contents of a particular court judgment. This document is recorded with the county recorder of every county in which the obligor is believed to own property. Once recorded, it constitutes an automatic lien on any such property existing in the county at that time; it also operates as an automatic lien on any property that the obligor acquires and records at a later date. An Abstract of Judgment generally serves to notify any party interested in the obligor's property that this prior judgment exists.

Under current law, when an individual acquires a parcel of property, he acquires that property subject to any and all existing liens thereon. When an Abstract of Judgment is recorded, it creates a lien on all of the obligor's property. Therefore, a buyer or lender should undertake a search of the records of the county in which the seller's property is located to determine if any liens on the property exist. If the buyer or lender learns of an Abstract of Judgment, he can seek a release of that abstract from the judgment creditor (the party to whom the money was supposed to be paid) before concluding the transaction. Obviously, the obligee party will not give that release until and unless it is brought current in all respects. The obligee will notify the buyer or lender of any existing arrearages and the buyer or lender will then contact the obligor to say that the transaction will not go forward until and unless the lien is cleared (that is, the judgment is satisfied or brought current). In this fashion, the obligor has significant incentive to clear this judgment off the record and bring all his support payments current.

With this background in mind, Family Code section 4506 outlines the items that must be contained in any abstract of judgment for spousal, child, or family support prior to certification by the court clerk. These items are as follows:

(1) The title of the court where the judgment is entered and the cause and number of the proceeding.

(2) The date of entry of the judgment and of any renewal of the judgment.

(3) Where the judgment and any renewals are entered in the records of the court.

(4) The name and last known address of the party ordered to pay support.

(5) The name and address of the party to whom support payments are ordered to be paid.

(6) The social security number, birth date, and driver's license number of the party to whom support payments are to be paid. If any of those numbers are not known to the party to whom support payments are to be paid, that fact shall be indicated on the abstract of the court judgment.

(7) Whether a stay of enforcement has been ordered by the court and, if so, the date the stay ends.

(8) The date of issuance of the Abstract.

(9) Any other information deemed reasonable and appropriate by the Judicial Council.

3. Child Support Security Deposit

Chapter 2 of Part 5 describes the manner in which a deposit of money to secure payment of future child support will be allowed. Family Code sections 4550 to 4573 generally provide that every order or judgment to pay child support may also require the supporting parent to pay a deposit of up to one year's worth of child support. This deposit is known as a *child support security deposit*. These monies are to be deposited by the supporting parent in an interest-bearing account with a state or federally chartered commercial bank, trust company, savings and loan, or credit union doing business in California and maintaining a trust department. The funds are subject to withdrawal only upon court authorization and shall be used "exclusively to guarantee the monthly payment of child support" (Family Code section 4561).

Upon the application of the recipient parent verifying under penalty of perjury that a support payment is ten or more days late, the court will immediately order disbursement of sufficient funds from this child support security deposit account to bring the child support in arrears current. The funds must be used exclusively for the support, maintenance, and education of the children who are subject to the child support order. The court may also order that the account be replenished from time to time by the child support obligor in the same amounts as are expended from the account to keep the total amount in the account equal to at least one year's worth of child support (Family Code section 4570).

The legislative history to these statutes (former Civil Code sections 4710 et seq.) is instructive on the genesis of the trust account. Further, the legislature's comment demonstrates its concern with evasive obligors and the lack of remedies for obligees.

The Legislature hereby finds and declares as follows:

(a) That the current ways and means of public and private enforcement of these support obligations are often frustrated by the sheer number of delinquent obligors and the insufficiency of available techniques to enforce child support when the legally obligated parent is self employed, employed in the private sector, or changes jobs frequently.

(b) That even when existing public and private child support enforcement mechanisms are used, child support delinquencies nonetheless can endure for one year or more, potentially causing the obligee parent to be deprived of his or her own savings to pay for legal and household expenses, and in other cases, causing the obligee parent to be forced into receiving welfare assistance thereby causing the state to incur additional expenses. During the child support delinquency, the obligee parent may be unable to pay for food, clothing or shelter for the dependent child or children, a situation which cannot be remedied in a timely manner by existing procedures available under Section 4701.1 of the Civil Code [Family Code section 4610, generally providing for an order for deposit of assets, a subject discussed in greater detail later in this chapter] and other provisions of existing law. In addition, if the loss of child support extends beyond a brief period without access to immediate funds, the obligee parent is more likely to be coerced into unwise or unfair legal settlements or other decisions adversely affecting his or her legal rights.

(c) That the means of public and private enforcement of child support needs to be strengthened to a point of providing a quicker, less expensive, more certain means of collecting child support arrearages and maintaining the custodial family's standard of living while these arrearages are recovered using child support enforcement procedures provided in Section 4701.1 of the Civil Code and other provisions of existing law.

It is clear that the California Legislature believes that problems regarding collection and enforcement of child support awards are of the utmost importance.

Additionally, it is noteworthy that the legislature made the child support security deposit discretionary: ". . . every order or judgment to pay child support *may* also require the payment by the child support obligor of up to one year's child support . . . This amount shall be known as the "child support security deposit." (California Family Code 4560(a), emphasis added.) As such, the court still has wide discretion in examining the pertinent facts and circumstances relative to any particular case before making an order for establishment of a child support security deposit account.

Pursuant to Family Code section 4560(b) the court may decline to make an order establishing the fund if the recipient waives the right to have one established or if the court finds some other reason not to establish the account. For example, if the payor already established a trust account for child support, the court may find that it is unnecessary to establish a second trust account. The court may also decline to make an order based on "undue financial hardship." In these cases, the court examines how an account might affect the paying parent and, if the circumstances warrant, hold off on establishing such an account. To claim undue financial hardship, the obligor must make an application to reduce or eliminate his child support security deposit and provide reasonable notice to the obligee. The obligee may of course oppose the application and attend a hearing on the subject (Family Code section 4565).

4. Order for Deposit of Assets

While the court has discretion over whether to establish a trust account for child support, under specific circumstances, it *must* establish an order for desposit of assets. Family Code section 4610(a) *requires* the court to order any child support payor who is 60 days in arrears to deposit security for child support upon receipt of a recipient's (or county officer's) petition for same after notice and opportunity for hearing on the issue. This scheme is set forth in Article 2 of Chapter 3, entitled "Order for Deposit of Assets," commencing at Family Code section 4610. The amount of this security is established by Family Code section 4614 as being assets or cash equal in value to one year's support payments or $6,000, whichever is less. The only way the payor can avoid paying this security deposit is to rebut the statutory presumption created by section 4611, which presumes that the non-payment was "willful, without good faith" and "the obligor had the ability to pay the support." Indeed, according to section 4613, the trial court must make a security order if the obligor parent is 60 days in arrears and at least one of the following conditions exist:

> (a) The obligor-parent is not receiving salary or wages subject to an assignment pursuant to Chapter 8 (commencing with Section 5200) and there is reason to believe that the obligor-parent has earned income from some source of employment.
> (b) An assignment of a portion of salary or wages pursuant to Chapter 8 (commencing with Section 5200) would not be sufficient to meet the amount of the support obligation, for reasons other than a change of circumstances which would qualify for a reduction in the amount of child support ordered.
> (c) The job history of the obligor-parent shows that an assignment of a portion of salary or wages pursuant to Chapter 8 (commencing with Section 5200), would be difficult to enforce or would not be a practical means for securing the payment of the support obligation, due to circumstances including, but not limited to, multiple concurrent or consecutive employers.

Thus, this statute allows the court to require the child support security as referenced in Family Code section 4610 upon a finding that use of the more traditional methods of collection of child support (for example, wage assignment) is either impossible or impractical. The Family Code further provides that in lieu of depositing cash or other assets, the obligor parent may, with the court's approval, provide a performance bond secured by real property or other assets equal in value to one year's payments. In that case, or in the case of a deposit of real property (authorized by section 4617), after the hearing the court may order the sale of that asset so as to convert same to cash per use in accordance with the provisions of this article.

Article 3 of this chapter makes provision for application, ex parte, by either party for orders restraining the transfer, concealment, or any other disposition of any property during the pendency of proceedings designed to establish the order for deposit of assets described at sections 4610 et seq. The logic of this Code section should be obvious: Without such power, the court would have to stand idly by during the notice period while the obligor parent transferred his or her assets or, in some other way, rendered them valueless for purposes of these proceedings. Inasmuch as this would completely undermine the legislative purpose in enacting these code sections, the ex parte application for restraining orders was established.

Article 4 contains the Code sections pertinent to actual use of these deposited assets to satisfy support payments. Section 4630 provides that, following an obligor parent's failure to make reasonable efforts to cure the default in child support payments or to comply with a court-approved payment plan, the court, after written notice is served on the obligor parent, may order that the deposit of assets be sold and the money used for an amount sufficient to pay the arrearage on child support. Of course, the obligor parent may bring a motion or an order to show cause to prevent this sale or use of the money; that issue, however, will simply present both sides of the controversy to the court for ultimate determination as to the reasonableness of ordering the sale. The specifics with regard to making a motion to stop the sale or the use of the assets are set forth in sections 4631 and 4632.

Finally, Article 5 of this chapter makes provision for returning the assets so deposited to the obligor on the occurrence of both of the following events:

> (1) One year has elapsed since the court issued the order described in Article 2 (commencing with Section 4610).
> (2) The obligor-parent has made all support payments on time during that one year period.

If these two conditions are met, the deposited assets, whether real or personal property, shall be released back to the obligor parent.

5. Notice of Delinquency

One of the more remarkable enforcement mechanisms is based on a monetary penalty. Chapter 5 of Division 9, The Civil Penalty for Child Support Delinquency, imposes a hefty penalty on overdue child support arrearages. In fact, obligors can be forced to pay up to a 72 percent interest charge on child support arrearages that are more than 30 days overdue.

(a) Any person with a court order for child support, the payments on which are more than 30 days in arrears, may file and then serve a notice of delinquency, as described in this chapter.

(b) Except as provided in Section 4726, and subject to Section 4727, any amount of child support specified in a notice of delinquency that remains unpaid for more than 30 days after the notice of delinquency has been filed and served shall incur a penalty of 6 percent of the delinquent payment for each month that it remains unpaid, up to a maximum of 72 percent of the unpaid balance due.

The Notice of Delinquency is prepared on a judicial council form and must state all of the following: (1) the amount of child support that is in arrears, (2) the installments of support due that have been paid, and (3) any unpaid installment of child support will incur the penalty referenced in section 4722. The Notice of Delinquency is served on the obligor parent who has 30 days within which to either pay the noticed delinquency, or file a motion to determine arrearages and to show cause why the penalties referenced in section 4722 should not be imposed. In that regard, the court will not impose a penalty if it finds that the support obligor has proved: (1) the child support payments were not 30 days in arrears as of the date of service and they are not in arrears as of the date of hearing, or (2) the support obligor suffered a serious illness, disability, or unemployment that "substantially impaired the ability of the support obligor to comply fully with the support order and the support obligor has made every possible effort to comply with the support order," or (3) the support obligor is a public employee and "for reasons relating to fiscal difficulties of the employing entity the obligor has not received a paycheck for more than thirty days," or (4) it would not be in the interests of justice to impose the penalty.

This provision gives the trial court a great amount of discretion with regard to fixing these penalties. As a general rule (especially upon an initial application) if the obligor parent offers a credible reason for not paying support, the court will most likely not impose the section 4722 penalties. The obligor parent will, of course, have to pay the support arrearages, which will be determined at the penalty hearing; however, the penalties generally will not be imposed unless the obligor parent makes no showing to justify the nonpayment or the obligor parent simply defaults. The penalties due under this chapter are generally enforceable in the same manner that any other money judgment is enforced: pursuant to the issuance of a Writ of Execution, and so forth.

D. Uniform Interstate Family Support Act

It is not uncommon for parties to divorce or otherwise obtain orders for support in one state prior to relocating to California (or vice versa), and in so doing leave the obligor spouse behind in the issuing state. Similarly, it is not uncommon for a parent or spouse who is obligated to pay child or spousal support to relocate outside of the jurisdiction of the issuing state. When this happens, there are special provisions for the enforcement of support obligations across state lines. One such statutory scheme is known as the Uniform Interstate Family Support Act (UIFSA), found at Family Code sections 4900 et seq. The UIFSA basically provides for a uniform system of enforcing out-of-state support orders. The remedies provided by the UIFSA are *in addition* to any other enforcement remedies that may be available; thus, a support oblige may pursue recovery through the Act as well as general civil methods discussed above. The UIFSA is applicable in all 50 states as well as the possessions of the United States (U.S. Virgin Islands, Puerto Rico, and so on).

Pursuant to the U.S. Constitution, a judgment of any of the 50 states (and, by implication, the possessions of the United States) is entitled to "full faith and credit" in all the other states. Thus, a court order made in California is entitled to be enforced in any other state of the United States provided it is a lawful order. This means, generally, that the issuing state must have had subject-matter jurisdiction over the subject of the judgment and personal jurisdiction over the judgment debtor. The Uniform Interstate Family Support Act provides a specific procedure, which is common to all 50 states, for the perfection of this right. The reader should note, however, that the only orders that can be enforced by this Act are orders for *support*.

The general provisions of the Uniform Interstate Family Support Act closely follow the provisions of its predecessor statutory scheme, the Uniform Reciprocal Enforcement of Support Act. The URESA's purpose was to "improve and extend by reciprocal legislation the enforcement of duties of support and to make uniform the law with respect thereto." The term *reciprocal legislation* means that each state that enacted this legislation must reciprocate in its enforcement. For example, California must enforce Ohio's support orders provided Ohio *reciprocates* and agrees to enforce California's orders. The Uniform Reciprocal Enforcement of Support Act simplified the enforcement process by making the law uniform across all 50 states.

A few of the definitions provided in Family Code section 4901 are worthy of special note. *Duty of support* is defined to mean any duty of support whether imposed by law or by order, decree, or judgment of any court, regardless of whether the order has become a final judgment. Additionally, the duty of support as used in the uniform reciprocal portion of the Support Act includes orders incidental to dissolution of marriage proceedings, nullity of marriage proceedings, and similar actions throughout the state.

The term "obligee" as used in this chapter is defined to mean a person(including a state or political subdivision) to whom a duty of support is owed, or a person (including a state or political subdivision) that has commenced a proceeding for enforcement of an alleged duty of support. It is immaterial if the person to whom a duty of support is owed is a recipient of public assistance. The term *obligor* is defined to mean a person owing a duty of support or against whom a proceeding for the enforcement of a duty of support is commenced.[8]

The term "state" is defined by statute to include "a state of the United States, the District of Columbia, Puerto Rico, the United States Virgin Islands, or any territory or insular possession subject to the jurisdiction of the United States." The term *support order* is defined to include judgments, decrees, or orders of support in favor of an obligee whether temporary or final, or subject to modification, revocation or remission, regardless of the kind of action or proceeding in which it is entered.

The remedies available under the Uniform Interstate Family Support Act are in addition to any other remedies that might be available for the enforcement of support.

The duties of support arising under California law, when applicable under a Uniform Interstate Family Support Act proceeding, will bind the obligor who is present in the State of California, regardless of the presence or residence of the obligee. This makes sense, inasmuch as most UIFSA proceedings in this state involve obligees who are located outside of the State of California.

Article 6 of Chapter 6 (Enforcement and Modification of Support Order After Registration) establishes the basic statutory system of civil enforcement under the Act. This article includes a recitation that the particular duties of support that are applicable under the UIFSA are those that have been imposed on the obligor under the laws of any state where the obligor was present for the period during which the support is being sought. For example, assume that Harold and Wanda were married and living in Ohio when they decided to terminate their marriage in January of 2005. Assume also that at that time the Ohio court ordered Harold to pay Wanda $500 per month in child support. If Harold stopped paying support on January 1, 2006, and Wanda subsequently moved to California at the end of 2006, she could utilize the provisions of the UIFSA to enforce her Ohio order for support. The duty of support that is enforceable pursuant to the UIFSA would be the Ohio court order discussed above, compelling Harold to pay Wanda $500 per month during the period of nonpayment; this is true regardless of the fact that neither party was in California during that initial period.

A UIFSA proceeding is commenced when the support order and related information (letter of transmittal, sworn statement(s), etc.) are registered in California. Additional information must also be registered in California, including the obligor's name and address, the obligee's name and address, plus whatever information the initiating jurisdiction deems necessary. Once a support order has been properly registered, it is filed in the appropriate court of the state in which the obligee resides. The court in that state must accept the order and must agree to act on it, assuming that it is substantially in compliance with the UIFSA. The court may not reject an order merely because it should have been filed in some other court or it should have been filed in a jurisdiction where a proceeding for dissolution of marriage or legal separation between the parties is pending. In addition, the court may not reject an order based on the fact that another court already issued a support order and retained jurisdiction for its enforcement. This makes eminent sense, of course, because many courts retain jurisdiction to enforce support orders that they make. The entire purpose of the UIFSA would be frustrated if the initiating court could simply refuse to accept a complaint under the UIFSA for enforcement on the ground that the out-of-state court retained jurisdiction to enforce that order.

In the next step of a UIFSA proceeding, the non-registering party is notified that the order has been registered; he is also notified of his right to contest the proceeding within a limited time frame. If the non-registering party fails to contest, the order is confirmed as valid and becomes fully enforceable as if it were an original order of this jurisdiction.

If the non-registering party appropriately files for review, the court in the responding state will then hold a hearing on the prosecuting attorney's order to show cause to determine to what extent the court should confirm the order or, if appropriate, modify it.

Once the order is ultimately confirmed, it can be enforced by local authorities. The legislature enacted this statutory scheme in an effort to streamline the otherwise awkward process of enforcing support orders across state lines. It is presented in a rather uncomplicated, simplified manner in this text. For a more comprehensive understanding of this statutory scheme, the reader should read the Act in its entirety.

As can be seen from the above discussion, California can either act as an initiating state or as a responding state depending on the particular facts and circumstances. For example, if Wanda left Ohio without first obtaining an order for child support, subsequent to her relocation to California, she would be free to petition the California court for a child support order and then seek enforcement of that order under the UIFSA with California acting as the "initiating state." However, if Harold (rather than Wanda) relocated to California and then stopped making his child support payments, Wanda could start her UIFSA proceeding in Ohio, with Ohio acting as the initiating court and California acting as the responding court. The basic concept behind the UIFSA is quite simple: together with the Federal Full Faith and Credit for Child Support Orders Act (FFCCSOA, 28 U.S.C. section 1738B), the UIFSA is designed to ensure that only one state will have jurisdiction over support at any given point in time. To accomplish this, UIFSA sets exclusive jurisdiction for support adjudication and requires sister states to recognize and enforce support orders rendered by a court of competent jurisdiction. Orders contemplated to be the subject of the Act are judgments, decrees or orders, whether temporary, final, or subject to modification, for the benefit of a child, spouse, or former spouse, that provide for monetary support, health care, arrearages, or reimbursement, and "may include related costs and fees, interest, income withholding, attorney's fees, or other relief."

E. Registration of Intercounty Support Orders

The UIFSA applies only to the registration and enforcement of out-of-state support orders; it does not govern the enforcement of support orders between California counties (as where either party to a California support order moves to another county after entry of the initial order). Instead, Family Code sections 5600 et seq. establish separate procedures for intercounty registration of support orders within California. These statutory provisions are fundamentally the same as those mandated by the UIFSA. Section 5600 states:

> (a) A local child support agency or obligee may register an order for support or earnings withholding, or both, obtained in another county of the state.
> (b) An obligee may register a support order in the court of another county of this state in the manner, with the effect, and for the purposes provided in this part. The orders may be registered in any county in which the obligor, the obligee, or the child who is the subject of the order resides, or in any county in which the obligor has income, assets, or any other property.

A local child support enforcement agency may also register these orders. Family Code section 5601 provides instruction as follows:

> (a) When the local child support agency is responsible for the enforcement of a support order pursuant to Section 17400, the local child support agency may register a support order made in another county by utilizing the procedures set forth in Section 5602 or by filing all of the following in the superior court of his or her county:
> (1) An endorsed file copy of the most recent support order or a copy thereof.
> (2) A statement of arrearages, including an accounting of amounts ordered and paid each month, together with any added costs, fees, and interest.
> (3) A statement prepared by the local child support agency showing the post office address of the local child support agency, the last known place of residence or post office address of the obligor; the

most recent address of the obligor set forth in the licensing records of the Department of Motor Vehicles, if known; and a list of other states and counties in California that are known to the local child support agency in which the original order of support and any modifications are registered.

(b) The filing of the documents described in subdivision (a) constitutes registration under this chapter.

(c) Promptly upon registration, the local child support agency shall, in compliance with the requirements of Section 1013 of the Code of Civil Procedure, or in any other manner as provided by law, serve the obligor with copies of the documents described in subdivision (a).

(d) If a motion to vacate registration is filed under Section 5603, any party may introduce into evidence copies of any pleadings, documents, or orders that have been filed in the original court or other courts where the support order has been registered or modified. Certified copies of the documents shall not be required unless a party objects to the authenticity or accuracy of the document in which case it shall be the responsibility of the party who is asserting the authenticity of the document to obtain a certified copy of the questioned document.

(e) Upon registration, the clerk of the court shall forward a notice of registration to the courts in other counties and states in which the original order for support and any modifications were issued or registered. No further proceedings regarding the obligor's support obligations shall be filed in other counties.

(f) The procedure prescribed by this section may also be used to register support or wage and earnings assignment orders of other California jurisdictions that previously have been registered for purposes of enforcement only pursuant to the Uniform Interstate Family Support Act (Chapter 6 (commencing with Section 4900)) in another California county. The local child support agency may register such an order by filing an endorsed file copy of the registered California order plus any subsequent orders, including procedural amendments.

(g) The Judicial Council shall develop the forms necessary to effectuate this section. These forms shall be available no later than July 1, 1998.

The procedure for registering these support orders by the individual obligee is relatively straightforward and is set out in Family Code section 5602:

(a) An obligee other than the local child support agency may register an order issued in this state using the same procedures specified in subdivision (a) of Section 5601, except that the obligee shall prepare and file the statement of registration. The statement shall be verified and signed by the obligee showing the mailing address of the obligee, the last known place of residence or mailing address of the obligor, and a list of other states and counties in California in which, to the obligee's knowledge, the original order of support and any modifications are registered.

(b) Upon receipt of the documents described in subdivision (a) of Section 5601, the clerk of the court shall file them without payment of a filing fee or other cost to the obligee. The filing constitutes registration under this chapter.

(c) Promptly upon registration, the clerk of the court shall send, by any form of mail requiring a return receipt from the addressee only, to the obligor at the address given a notice of the registration with a copy of the registered support order and the post office address of the obligee. Proof shall be made to the satisfaction of the court that the obligor personally received the notice of registration by mail or other method of service. A return receipt signed by the obligor shall be satisfactory evidence of personal receipt.

Once the obligor receives the above documents, he may vacate or modify the order as provided by the UIFSA. Once the obligor receives notice from the court clerk that the support order has been registered in that court, the obligor has 20 days to file a notice of motion requesting the court to vacate the registration. The circumstances under which registration will be vacated are somewhat limited. The defenses to the registration are limited strictly to the identity of the obligor, the validity of the underlying foreign support order, or the accuracy of the obligee's statements with regard to the amount of support remaining unpaid. Once filed, the obligor serves this motion on the obligee and the court schedules a hearing on the subject of the motion.

At the hearing, the obligor is only allowed to present the court with matters that would be available to the obligor as defenses in an action to enforce a support judgment. In other words, the obligor cannot seek to re-litigate de novo the *amount* of child support.

Once the foreign support order has been registered and the obligor has litigated any defenses or claims, the foreign order (assuming the court did not vacate the order) is treated for all purposes as a local order. In sum, the foreign order will be enforced as a local order would be enforced.

F.   General Civil Debt Collection Methods

In addition to the Order to Show Cause for Contempt, there is a virtual cornucopia of collection procedures that can be invoked to secure compliance with orders issued by a family law court. For practical purposes, these other civil collection procedures are designed for the collection of money or to enforce the transfer of property and items of this nature. This is not, of course, a text on civil debt collection procedures, and as such these methods of enforcement will only briefly be touched upon here with special emphasis given to any aspects of these procedures that are peculiar to a family law context.

1. Writ of Execution

The most common procedure for collecting a money judgment is known as *execution*. In this procedure, the court clerk issues a document (on a judicial council form) known as a Writ of Execution. This document is in essence an instruction from the court to the *levying officer* (typically a sheriff or marshal) to enforce the judgment by seizing property belonging to the *judgment debtor* (the person who owes the money). For example, in the family law context, if the wife was ordered to make a $100,000 equalizing payment to the husband but refused to do so, the husband could obtain a Writ of Execution from the court instructing the levying officer to seize enough of the wife's property to satisfy the $100,000 debt. The levying officer could take this Writ of Execution to the wife's bank and seize the money held in her account; or, the officer could take the Writ of Execution to a third party who owes the wife money and divert that payment to the husband. Additionally, the levying officer could seize real property, cars, stocks, bonds, and virtually any other tangible asset of ascertainable value, sell it at auction, and apply the proceeds of that sale to the underlying debt. Provision is also made in the Family Code for enforcement of child, family, or spousal support at sections 5100 to 5104.

Execution is a highly technical area of the law, and several statutory exemptions make certain property immune from execution. Any detailed inquiry into the civil debt collection arena greatly exceeds the scope of this book. The reader is instead requested to review the provisions of the California Code of Civil Procedure dealing with civil debt collection, notably Code of Civil Procedure sections 699.510 et seq.

2. Abstract of Judgment (Civil)

The *judgment creditor* can also use an *Abstract of Judgment* to recover a debt. The judgment creditor must fill out a judicial council form, which will then be issued by the court. The form must state the basic provisions of the judgment and will be recorded in the office of the county recorder in any county where the judgment debtor is suspected to own property. Once recorded, this judgment will automatically attach as a lien to all property held by the judgment debtor in the county that is subject to recordation (for example, real estate).

3. Appointment of Receiver

Alternatively, a judgment creditor may request the court to appoint a receiver. Receivership is a very drastic and expensive measure. Essentially, the judgment debtor asks the receiver to take responsibility for the management and control of a piece of property. The receiver acts to protect the property's value and to extract sufficient funds to assure satisfaction (payment) of the judgment.

4. Writ of Possession

Yet another commonly used method for collecting a money judgment involves the issuance of a *Writ of Possession or Sale*. When the subject of the order is the possession of real or personal property, and the judgment debtor refuses to turn over this real or personal property, a Writ of Possession or Sale can be requested. If the court issues a writ of possession or sale, the levying officer may search for the property and take it from the judgment debtor (or third party) just as under a Writ of Execution. Additionally, the levying officer may (after complying with many technical requirements) seize certain property and sell it at auction. (The proceeds are used to satisfy the judgment.)

5. Installation of a "Keeper"

Still another method for enforcing a money judgment involves installing a keeper in the judgment debtor's place of business. A *keeper* is an individual (typically a sheriff or marshal) who enters the debtor's place of business and intercepts, for the benefit of the creditors, all cash, mail, checks, or similar items of value as and when they are received. For example, if the judgment debtor owns and operates a hardware store, once a keeper is "installed," that person will actually stand next to the cash register and, as the product is sold, take money and apply it toward the judgment debtor's debt. A keeper performs a similar function to a receiver. Once the Writ of Execution is obtained, the levying officer goes to the judgment debtor's place of business, sits at the cash register, and collects money from the patrons as they buy items. In the absence of a cash register, the keeper will open the mail as it arrives, take checks and other forms of payment, and apply them to the debt. This is an expensive method of enforcement; however, the costs of having the keeper in place will be added to the amount of the judgment. So, if there are funds sufficient to satisfy the judgment, presumably there will also be sufficient funds to satisfy the keeper's fees.

6. Debtor's Examination

The so-called *Debtor's Examination* is a very effective method of debt collection. A debtor's examination is a relatively informal question and answer period whereby the debtor answers questions, under oath and in court, propounded by the creditor in hopes of eliciting the location and identity of assets that could be used to satisfy the debt. Before he may examine the debtor, however, the creditor must prepare his request on a judicial council form, wait for the court to issue an Order for Debtor's Examination (which is a court order to appear), and serve the order on the debtor.

7. Wage Assignment (Civil)

A *wage assignment* or *garnishment* is also available to satisfy a money judgment or an ongoing order for the payment of support. To use a garnishment, the creditor must serve a Writ of Execution or, in this context, a wage garnishment, on the judgment debtor's employer, who must withhold from the judgment debtor's paycheck an amount sufficient to satisfy the money judgment. Along the same lines, and with specific reference in a family law context, is the wage assignment for support provided by Family Code sections 5200 et seq., which is discussed above.

The various remedies touched on here are best left to a detailed textbook or course on civil debt collection. Volumes have been written on this subject, which is highly technical in nature. If all the requirements are not followed exactly as required by Code, the effort will be futile. Accordingly, before undertaking any action in this area, the reader is encouraged to seek out an individual who specializes in debt collection procedures or a very detailed treatise on the subject.

G. Sister State Money-Judgments Act

The *Sister State Money-Judgments Act* (SSMJA), found at Code of Civil Procedure sections 1710.10 et seq., provides another avenue for enforcing out-of-state money judgments. The primary distinction between the Sister State Money-Judgments Act and the Uniform Interstate Family Support Act is that the SSMJA can be used to enforce orders that are not necessarily for the payment of support. From a conceptual standpoint, the SSMJA is substantially the same as the UIFSA. Another fundamental distinction is the fact that by statute, foreign *support orders* are not enforceable under the SSMJA. They must be enforced under the UIFSA. However, the SSMJA can be used to the extent that some other aspect of a family law judgment results in a judgment or order stating that the obligor must pay funds to the obligee.

The procedure to obtain an order under the Sister State Money-Judgments Act is simple. First, apply for entry of judgment in California based on the out-of-state order, taking care to comply with the various statutory requirements.[9] Next, file the application with the appropriate court. The clerk of that court must then enter the judgment on the sister state decree, thus making it a California judgment. As soon as the California court enters the judgment, the creditor should notify the debtor pursuant to service of process (that is, service must be accomplished in the same manner required for service of Summons). Finally, the judgment creditor will be free to enforce the (now) California judgment in exactly the same fashion as if California were the initiating jurisdiction.

The basic procedures for using the SSMJA are set out in Code of Civil Procedure section 1710.15:

(a) A judgment creditor may apply for the entry of a judgment based on a sister state judgment by filing an application pursuant to Section 1710.20.

(b) The application shall be executed under oath and shall include all of the following:

(1) A statement that an action in this state on the sister state judgment is not barred by the applicable statute of limitations.

(2) A statement, based on the applicant's information and belief, that no stay of enforcement of the sister state judgment is currently in effect in the sister state.

(3) A statement of the amount remaining unpaid under the sister state judgment and, if accrued interest on the sister state judgment is to be included in the California judgment, a statement of the amount of interest accrued on the sister state judgment (computed at the rate of interest applicable to the judgment under the law of the sister state), a statement of the rate of interest applicable to the judgment under the law of the sister state, and a citation to the law of the sister state establishing the rate of interest.

(4) A statement that no action based on the sister state judgment is currently pending in any court in this state and that no judgment based on the sister state judgment has previously been entered in any proceeding in this state.

(5) Where the judgment debtor is an individual, a statement setting forth the name and last known residence address of the judgment debtor. Where the judgment debtor is a corporation, a statement of the corporation's name, place of incorporation, and whether the corporation, if foreign, has qualified to do business in this state under the provisions of Chapter 21 (commencing with Section 2100) of Division 1 of Title 1 of the Corporations Code. Where the judgment debtor is a partnership, a statement of the name of the partnership, whether it is a foreign partnership, and, if it is a foreign partnership, whether it has filed a statement pursuant to Section 15800 of the Corporations Code designating an agent for service of process. Except for facts which are matters of public record in this state, the statements required by this paragraph may be made on the basis of the judgment creditor's information and belief.

(6) A statement setting forth the name and address of the judgment creditor.

(c) A properly authenticated copy of the sister state judgment shall be attached to the application.

Once the California court enters the judgment, it will be enforced just as if it had been originally entered in California.

Summary

There are many ways to secure compliance with a court's orders. Perhaps the most effective (albeit the most difficult to prove) is the civil contempt procedure. This method of enforcement is effective because the potential penalties for noncompliance include jail time. It is the most difficult to secure for the same reason: the courts in this country cannot imprison people without strong evidence. Further, the accused has strong due process rights. An accused person cannot be called to the stand to testify and she is entitled to many of the same protections afforded to "regular" criminal defendants. In the area of child support enforcement, however, this burden of proof is not quite so great.

In addition, all of the other, general civil methods of debt collection are available to the family law judgment creditor. These include abstracts of judgment, debtor's examinations, and writs of execution. Finally, several statutory schemes exist for the enforcement of orders, including the Sister State Money-Judgments Act, the Uniform Reciprocal Enforcement of Support Act, and the procedures for obtaining a Wage Assignment for Support.

Key Terms

The following is a list of key terms and phrases that you should be able to define and use in context. Only then will you have demonstrated a command of the material in this chapter.

- contempt
- lawful order
- citee
- quasi-criminal
- reasonable doubt
- preponderance of evidence
- Citation of Contempt
- Statute of Limitation

- Writ of Execution
- levying officer
- Abstract of Judgment
- receiver
- Writ of Possession or Sale
- keeper
- Debtor's Examination
- wage assignment/garnishment
- Wage Assignment for Support; Support Withholding Order
- Uniform Interstate Family Support Act (UIFSA)
- full faith and credit
- Sister States Money-Judgments Act (SSMJA)

Questions for Discussion

1. What are the elements of a prima facie action for contempt?
2. A citee in a contempt action is entitled to several protections normally reserved for defendants in criminal proceedings. Discuss two such protections.
3. Can a citee in a contempt action be called to the stand to testify by the adverse party? Explain.
4. List at least two general debt collection procedures and give examples of their use.
5. Compare and contrast a writ of execution and an abstract of judgment.
6. What is the purpose and function of a "keeper"?
7. Under what circumstances will the court grant a stay of the service of a wage assignment for support?
8. Compare and contrast the Uniform Interstate Family Support Act (UIFSA) and the Sister State Money-Judgments Act (SSMJA).

ENDNOTES

1. Now that I am a father, I must say that this phrase has become much more meaningful to me!

2. Elsewhere in this book the Order to Show Cause procedure is discussed at length. An Order to Show Cause for Contempt is handled essentially the same way and is prepared on judicial council forms. While these forms are unique to the contempt procedure, they are basically similar in form and content to the forms discussed in the chapter covering Orders to Show Cause.

3. Proof "beyond a reasonable doubt" is primarily confined to criminal matters. Literally *volumes* have been written about this standard, and rarely is a criminal matter tried where this term is explained and defined by the attorneys in those cases in understandable terms. Ask ten lawyers to define it, and you will get ten different answers.
    Put most simply, proof by a "preponderance" of the evidence means 51 percent versus 49 percent—evidence (or proof) that finds acceptance 51 percent of the time. This, of course, is not much. It just means that there is a 51 percent chance of the result being accurate. There is also a 49 percent chance, however, that it is *wrong*. This is similar to a weatherman warning that there is a 20 percent chance of rain. Watch how people react to this news: they start carrying umbrellas even though it is just as accurate for the weatherman to say there is an *80 percent* chance of sunshine.
    To prove something *beyond a reasonable doubt*, however, is very different indeed. Although not expressed as a percentage, it literally means proof that rises to the level of a near *certainty:* 95 percent? 99 percent? Perhaps. It is very high, to be sure, and very difficult to prove.

4. An attorney breaches his ethical obligation if he fails to report to his client the contents of a court order that affects the client. It seems likely that the only credible way in which a citee could establish this defense would be to have his attorney appear and testify in court under oath that, notwithstanding the fact that he was present in court when the court's orders were issued, he neglected to so inform his client of the contents of those orders; in essence, the attorney would need to admit under penalty of perjury what is tantamount to a breach of his ethical obligation. It seems unlikely that this would happen.

5. In fact, he cannot be called to the stand *at all*.

6. For example, a recipient advises the citee that he will accept $100 per month for child support rather than the court-ordered $300 per month. Then, the recipient turns around and tries to have the citee held in contempt of court for not paying the $300 per month award. Under these circumstances, the court could find that the recipient spouse waived her right to pursue contempt as a remedy for nonpayment of these sums.

7. The mandatory issuance of a wage assignment for support also finds support in the federal system, which requires "immediate wage withholding" for all child support orders issued on or after January 1, 1994. This is found in the Family Support Act of 1988.

8. All of the definitions discussed herein can be found at Family Code §4901.

9. The reader should note that the SSMJA is not a "uniform act" and hence does not necessarily exist in substantially identical form in all 50 states. As a practical matter, however, most other jurisdictions in the United States have statutes that are substantially similar to the SSMJA.

CHAPTER 11

Selected Issues

CHAPTER OVERVIEW

In this chapter, we will examine a potpourri of issues, which by themselves are either too extensive or not extensive enough to cover in one chapter. Either way, because these issues come up with regularity in the area of family law, we must at least touch on them. Consider this chapter a warm-up for a more thorough review of these various subjects.

The topics include attorney's fees, domestic violence, injunctive relief, Family Code disclosure requirements, discovery, joinder, employment benefits, bankruptcy, taxation, marital agreements, collaborative law, and same-sex marriage. This is a chapter that can, and most likely will, expand over time to address the many varied issues that compose the study of family law.

A. Attorney's Fees and Costs

Interestingly, in family law, it is widely believed that all parties to the litigation should be given the opportunity to retain capable counsel—regardless of their economic position. In other words, if Husband cannot afford a lawyer, Wife may need to pay her own attorney *and* Husband's attorney.

Family Code section 2030 authorizes the court in a family law proceeding to order "any party . . . except a governmental entity, to pay the amount reasonably necessary for attorney's fees and for the cost of maintaining or defending the proceeding." [1] The full text of this statute provides as follows:

(a)(1) In a proceeding for dissolution of marriage, nullity of marriage, or legal separation of the parties, and in any proceeding subsequent to entry of a related judgment, the court shall ensure that each party has access to legal representation, including access early in the proceedings, to preserve each party's rights by ordering, if necessary based on the income and needs assessments, one party, except a governmental entity, to pay to the other party, or to the other party's attorney, whatever amount is reasonably necessary for attorney's fees and for the cost of maintaining or defending the proceeding during the pendency of the proceeding.

(2) When a request for attorney's fees and costs is made, the court shall make findings on whether an attorney's fees and costs under this section is appropriate, whether there is a disparity in access to funds to retain counsel, and whether one party is able to pay for legal representation of both parties. If the findings demonstrate disparity in access and ability to pay, the court shall make an order awarding attorney's fees and costs. A party who lacks the financial ability to hire an attorney may request, as an in pro per litigant, that the court order the other party, if that other party has the financial ability, to pay a reasonable amount to allow the unrepresented party to retain an attorney in a timely manner before proceedings in the matter go forward.

(b) Attorney's fees and costs within this section may be awarded for legal services rendered or costs incurred before or after the commencement of the proceeding.

(c) The court shall augment or modify the original award for attorney's fees and costs as may be reasonably necessary for the prosecution or defense of the proceeding, or any proceeding related thereto, including after any appeal has been concluded.

(d) Any order requiring a party who is not the spouse of another party to the proceeding to pay attorney's fees or costs shall be limited to an amount reasonably necessary to maintain or defend the action on the issues relating to that party.

(e) The Judicial Council shall, by January 1, 2012, adopt a statewide rule of court to implement this section and develop a form for the information that shall be submitted to the court to obtain an award of attorney's fees under this section.

The basic criteria for determining the necessity and the amount of attorney's fees and costs is based on "whether there is a disparity in access to funds to retain counsel, and whether one party is able to pay for legal representation of both parties." (Family Code section 2030(a)(2).)[2] Section 2031 ensures that a request for attorney's fees in this context can be made at any time during the pendency of the proceedings and in some circumstances even on oral motion without notice.

This criterion is further described by Family Code section 2032, which provides, in pertinent part

(a) The court may make an award of attorney's fees and costs under section 2030 or 2031 where the making of the award, and the amount of the award, are just and reasonable under the relative circumstances of the respective parties.

(b) In determining what is just and reasonable under the relative circumstances, the court shall take into consideration the need for the award to enable each party, to the extent practical, to have sufficient financial resources to present the party's case adequately, taking into consideration, to the extent relevant, the circumstances of the respective parties described in Section 4320. The fact that the party requesting an award of attorney's fees and costs has resources from which the party could pay the party's own attorney's fees and costs is not itself a bar to an order that the other party pay part or all of the fees and costs requested. Financial resources are only one factor for the court to consider in determining how to apportion the overall cost of the litigation equitably between the parties under their relative circumstances.

(c) The court may order payment of an award of attorney's fees and costs from any type of property, whether community or separate, principal or income.

(d) Either party may, at any time before the hearing of the cause on the merits, on noticed motion, request the court to make a finding that the case involves complex or substantial issues of fact or law related to property rights, visitation, custody, or support. Upon that finding, the court may in its discretion determine the appropriate equitable allocation of attorney's fees, court costs, expert fees, and consultant fees between the parties. The court may provide for the allocation of separate or community assets, security against these assets, and for payments from income or anticipated income of either party for the purpose described in this subdivision and for the benefit of one or both parties. Payments shall be authorized only on agreement of the parties or, in the absence thereof, by court order. The court may order that a referee be appointment pursuant to Section 639 of the Code of Civil Procedure to oversee the allocation of fees and costs.

The court considers a number of factors when determining fees, including: the assets of the supported and supporting spouse, the difficulties encountered during discovery, the parties' comparative wealth, the parties' conduct throughout the litigation, the results obtained, and the reasonable value of the attorney or other professional's services.

Sections 2450-2452 set forth the case management plan (also called a family centered case resolution), which is designed for the parties' benefit. Such a plan helps speed processing of the case, reduce litigation expenses, and facilitate early settlement. Section 2451(j) states that a court-ordered case management plan, as stipulated by the parties, may include a case management plan pursuant to section 2032(d). Additionally, the court can appoint a referee to oversee the implementation of this plan. All of this is done to keep the fees from unnecessarily escalating in a complex case and also to prevent one spouse (typically the one with control over the money) from taking financial advantage of the other spouse.

The request for fees can be made either pending the trial, after the trial, or even after judgment has been entered, by the spouse who desires the award. The award can also be modified as the circumstances may require as the case progresses, and even after an appeal has concluded (2030(c).) All awards are primarily left to the discretion of the court, which means that they will usually not be reversed on appeal.

Finally, section 2030 provides authority for an award of attorney's fees "in a proceeding for dissolution of marriage, nullity of marriage, or legal separation of the parties, and in any proceeding subsequent to entry of a related judgment." What is a "related judgment?" This language is vague, and its application to a particular case will depend on the advocacy of the party requesting the fee award and his or her ability to convince the court that the judgment in question is "related." Of course, the fundamental basis for demonstrating such a relation is the extent to which that judgment furthers or serves the purposes of the Family Code proceeding. The concept of an action that is related to a family law judgment may be quite liberally applied. Remember, the general object of the attorney's fee statute is to provide the parties with "equal litigating power" and to prevent one party from taking financial advantage of the other.

The issue of attorney's fees in a related judgment was litigated at some length in *In re* Marriage of Green, 6 Cal. App. 4th 584 (1992). In *Green* the trial court awarded the wife over $100,000 in attorney's fees after finding that the husband (who was acting as his own attorney) had filed six different pleadings that were "related" to the dissolution judgment. The court also made a specific factual finding that the husband's actions in filing these various lawsuits were a direct attempt to gain an unfair advantage over his wife in the family law action. On appeal from the court's ruling, the husband argued that the other actions were not in fact related to the family law judgment, and therefore the court exceeded its authority in granting attorney's fees. The court of appeal found that as a general rule the determination as to whether or not a case is related to a family law judgment is best left to the trial court's discretion as a finding of fact. One of the related actions that the husband filed included a malicious prosecution action against the wife's attorney. In that case, the husband tried to argue that attorney's fees were inappropriate because his wife was not a party to that lawsuit. Nevertheless, the court of appeal was strongly persuaded by the husband's apparent motivation as determined at the trial level. In its opinion, the court of appeal stated that these unrelated lawsuits "might fall within the purview of the statute because of their effect on the FLA action. Thus, [former Civil Code section 4370] enables a trial court to prevent the spouse with greater financial resources from harassing or coercing the less advantaged spouse into submission in the [family law] case by forcing him or her to defend other lawsuits; such independent suits are 'related' within the meaning of §4370 because they are intended to produce some results in [a family law] case. "The entire concept of an attorney's fees and costs award from one spouse (usually the high earner) to the other (low earner) spouse is met with quite a bit of resistance and confusion by those parties who are placed in the position of actually paying the award. Questions such as "Do you mean I not only have to pay my husband spousal support, but I have to pay his *attorney as well*?" abound in this context. "Yes," these people are often told, "even if it turns out that you 'won.'" This last clause should not be read as some kind of "rule." It simply reflects the reality that a party need not be the *prevailing party* to obtain a fee award. The criterion is instead whether the party requesting the award "needs" that award to allow him to protect and preserve his interests in the litigation under circumstances that are "just and reasonable" and in keeping with the other party's "ability to pay."

Only *parties* to the litigation are entitled to attorney's fees awards. Further, a party acting in pro per (acting as his own attorney) is eligible for an attorney's fee award. As a practical matter, however, pro per litigants rarely receive an award of attorney's fees. (They more commonly, however, receive an award of costs).

The section 2030 attorney's fees award is designed to provide *both* parties with adequate resources to litigate the action and to prevent a disparity in representation. Thus, the attorney's fees awards contemplated by this section are keyed to the concepts of *need* and *ability to pay*; both of these concepts are viewed within the framework of the overall premise that the fee award must be "just and reasonable under the relative circumstances of the respective parties" (California Family Code 2032(a)). This last clause simply means that just because a spouse has the money to pay for her own attorney does not necessarily mean that she does not *need* the other spouse to contribute to her attorney's fees.

In determining *need* and *ability to pay*, it is necessary to examine the spouses' relative incomes. This involves a review of the parties' Income and Expense Declarations, as well as their moving and responsive declarations that were filed in support of their requests for attorney's fees. Furthermore, although the court has the ability to investigate the historical income of both spouses, as a general rule, an attorney's fees award will be based upon the parties' *current* financial position.

Unfortunately, there are no specific guidelines as to when a fee award will be allowed and when it will not. Family Code section 2032, by direct reference to section 4320, grants the court wide authority to examine the income available to the parties from all sources, whether it be community property, separate property, or both. This section even allows the court to consider the existence of assets that are not *liquid* (that is, readily convertible into cash, such as land and homes). In other words, the court may deny a party an award of attorney's fees if he has an estate of significant value—even if that estate is entirely *non-liquid* (for example, composed entirely of real estate holdings that are not readily convertible to cash). Of course, the parties are free to agree between each other as to who will pay the attorney's fees. The court will not upset this agreement and will usually accept the parties' representations in this regard.

The court may consider other factors in addition to need and ability to pay. For example, the court may consider the nature and difficulty of the litigation, the length and complexity of the litigation, the skill required by counsel in preparing for and conducting the litigation, the success of the attorney, as well as the attorney's level of experience.

A request for attorney's fees must be made by noticed motion. The court will hold a hearing with respect to this request; at that time, it will (ostensibly) consider the relevant factors and criteria discussed above and entertain an award that it feels, in its discretion, is appropriate under the circumstances. Unfortunately, there are no "rules of thumb" that can give quick guidance in this area. Indeed, it is one of the more frustrating aspects of family law practice to have to explain to a client when he asks, "Will I have to pay attorney's fees?" that the best answer is "Maybe." There certainly is authority for the court to order a discretionary award of attorney's fees if it feels that such an award is appropriate. As might be imagined, however, this leaves the client feeling less than adequately informed on this subject. Unfortunately, until the legislature or case law delineates a more specific formula with respect to an award of attorney's fees, this answer will have to do.

In addition to an award of attorney's fees, the referenced Code sections also provide for the recovery of costs. Costs awards are also based on the relative circumstances of the parties and are awarded to provide the parties with an equal ability to maintain the litigation. Costs awards go beyond the usual costs for filing a petition and response. A cost award might also include an order that one spouse pay for the accountants, business appraisers, and actuaries employed by the other spouse in order to give that spouse the opportunity to fully present her position to the court.[3] As a general rule, the attorney will provide a declaration in support of the request for attorney's fees. In this declaration, the attorney will detail the procedures he anticipates using, along with an estimate of associated fees. The client will also provide a declaration. In this declaration, the client will set forth his present financial ability to pay litigation costs. Finally, if a party requests fees for an accountant's or other expert's services, it is advisable to supply a declaration of this expert An expert's declaration should detail the exact nature, scope, and extent of the services contemplated and should provide a breakdown of the fees and costs associated with those services.

In addition to the section 2030 attorney's fee award, section 271 gives the court rather broad authority to assess attorney's fees and costs against a party to a family law matter as a *sanction*. Under section 271, the court may find that a party to the family law action: (1) engaged in tactics that frustrate, rather than further, the policy of the law to promote settlement, or (2) implemented some other tactic designed to discourage settlement and simply run up fees. Section 271 fee awards operate as a sanction or *punishment* against such litigants as well as their attorneys and aim to discourage detrimental litigation tactics. Family Code section 271 provides as follows:

> (a) Notwithstanding any other provision of this code, the court may base an award of attorney's fees and costs on the extent to which the conduct of each party or attorney furthers or frustrates the policy of the law to promote settlement of litigation and, where possible, to reduce the cost of litigation by encouraging cooperation between the parties and attorneys. An award of attorney's fees and costs pursuant to this section is in the nature of a sanction. In making an award pursuant to this section, the court shall take into consideration all evidence concerning the parties' incomes, assets, and liabilities. The court shall not impose a sanction pursuant to this section that imposes an unreasonable financial burden on the party against whom the sanction is imposed. In order to obtain an award under this section, the party requesting an award of attorney's fees and costs is not required to demonstrate any financial need for the award.
>
> (b) An award of attorney's fees and costs as a sanction pursuant to this section shall be imposed only after notice to the party against whom the sanction is proposed to be imposed and opportunity for that party to be heard.
>
> (c) An award of attorney's fees and costs as a sanction pursuant to this section is payable only from the property or income of the party against whom the sanction is imposed, except that the award may be against the sanctioned party's share of the community property.

It is noteworthy that in the context of the section 271 sanctions the concept of *need* is irrelevant. This is consistent with the underlying policy of section 271 to make the party whose conduct or tactics are creating the undue expense bear the burden of that expense. By so doing, the legislature is no doubt hopeful that parties and their attorneys will think twice before undertaking a "scorched earth" policy of running up fees. For example, one party may file numerous motions or Orders to Show Cause, or file unnecessary extensive discovery to financially pressure the other party. To the extent that the court makes a finding that these tactics are unnecessary and not calculated to promote settlement, it can simply shift the costs of responding to the propounding party. The reader can no doubt see how the 271 sanction is an effective tool to discourage parties and their attorneys from engaging in unsavory behavior.

Code of Civil Procedure section 128.5 provides an additional avenue under which the court can award monetary sanctions against parties and attorneys who engage in *bad faith* or *frivolous* actions or tactics. Interestingly, although this Code section is very possibly one of the most cited in current litigation practice, it is not that easy to obtain an award pursuant to its provisions. For example, before the court can make a finding under Code of Civil Procedure section 128.5 on the basis that the action was *frivolous*, it must make a finding that the action was "totally and completely without merit" and was for the "sole purpose of harassing an opposing party." As might be imagined, this is not an easy burden to meet.

Perhaps the only consistency about the cases that have interpreted Family Code section 271 is that they confirm that the court has tremendous discretion in making these awards. In cases involving possible 271 sanctions, a "common sense" approach may be best: If, after reviewing the facts of a particular scenario, the reader believes that sanctions *should* be awarded, there is a strong likelihood that they *will* be awarded. There is certainly ample authority to argue either way. Further, provided the trial court has carefully reviewed and considered all of the facts pertinent to the behaviors in the particular case, the ultimate determination will typically not be disturbed on appeal.

An award of attorney's fees and costs may also be enforced through use of the contempt procedures discussed in this text's chapter on enforcement of orders. The concept of contempt flies squarely in the face of the general guarantee against imprisonment for debt. However, it has been established law since 1970 that when an individual fails to pay attorney's fees as ordered, that person is showing contempt not against the spouse or attorney, but against the court, which can order that person to make these payments. And, as the reader is aware, one of the penalties available is imprisonment.

However, an award of attorney's fees is dischargeable in bankruptcy. If an individual is ordered to contribute to a person's attorney's fees in the context of a family law proceeding, that individual can have the debt discharged through bankruptcy proceedings, which will wipe that debt clean. This is not to say that bankruptcy proceedings are easily undertaken; they are not. If somebody filed for bankruptcy simply to avoid paying an attorney's fee award, it would probably be a foolish thing indeed (unless, of course, the award of attorney's fees was very high in relationship to the available assets). Filing for bankruptcy would be foolish because the general concept of bankruptcy is to gather all of the individual's assets and, for all practical purposes, sell them off, using the funds generated to pay off that individual's debt; such debt would include any attorney's fees award. Recognizing that attorney's fees awards are dischargeable in bankruptcy, many courts have taken to characterizing its award of attorney's fees as being in the manner of "additional support" for the party to whom the award is given. This is because an award for support is *not* dischargeable in bankruptcy. Accordingly, to the extent an award of attorney's fees is designated by the court as being in the manner of support, the bankruptcy court will not discharge that award.

B. Prevention of Domestic Violence

Family Code sections 6200 et seq. provide the statutory structure of the Domestic Violence Prevention Act. The purposes of this Act is just as its title implies: "to prevent the recurrence of acts of violence and sexual abuse and to provide for a separation of the persons involved in the domestic violence for a period sufficient to seek a resolution of the causes of the violence" (section 6220). Sections 6203 through 6218 provide basic definitions that control the construction and application of this Act (sometimes referred to as the DVPA). Those definitions are as follows (Family Code sections 6203 through 6218 respectively):

> "Abuse" means intentionally or recklessly to cause or attempt to cause bodily injury, or sexual assault, or to place a person in reasonable apprehension of imminent serious bodily injury to that person or to another, or to engage in any other behavior that could be enjoined pursuant to Family Code section 6320.

> "Affinity," when applied to the marriage relation, signifies the connection existing in consequence of marriage between each of the married persons and the blood relatives of the other.

> "Co-habitant" means a person who regularly resides in the household. "Former co-habitant" means a person who formerly regularly resided in the household.

> "Dating relationship" means frequent, intimate associations primarily characterized by the expectation of affection or sexual involvement independent of financial considerations.

"Domestic Violence" is abuse perpetrated against any of the following persons:

(a) a spouse or former spouse.

(b) a co-habitant or former co-habitant as defined in §6209.

(c) a person with whom the respondent is having or has had a dating or engagement relationship.

(d) a person with whom the respondent has had a child, where the presumption applies that the male parent is the father of the child of the female parent under the Uniform Parentage Act (Part 3 (commencing with section 7600) of Division 12).

(e) a child of a party or a child who is the subject of an action under the Uniform Parentage Act, where the presumption applies that the male parent is the father of the child to be protected.

(f) any other person related by consanguinity or affinity within the second degree.

"Emergency Protective Order" means an order issued under Part 3 (commencing with Section 6240), and essentially including an order described in section 6250 and 6252 enjoining the specific acts of abuse.

There are no fees for filing a petition, a response, or a modification of the protective order in a DVPA proceeding. Additionally, the judicial council has developed forms for use in proceedings under this Act so as to allow easy access to its protections. The remedies established in the DVPA are not exclusive. They are in addition to any other remedies that may be available throughout the body of law in the State of California on this subject.

The DVPA divides its provisions into two basic categories: those pertaining to emergency protective orders, and those pertaining to "regular" protective orders and other violence prevention orders. The specific procedures employed when seeking and obtaining orders under the Domestic Violence Prevention Act are discussed earlier in this book in the context of obtaining temporary relief and orders pending trial.

C. Injunctions Prohibiting Harassment

The Family Code is not the only source for laws that regulate an individual's conduct under inappropriate or dangerous circumstances. One example of such a provision is found at section 527.6 of the Code of Civil Procedure. Section 527.6 defines harassment as "unlawful violence, a credible threat of violence, or a knowing and willful course of conduct directed at a specific person that seriously alarms, annoys, or harasses the person, and that serves no legitimate purpose. The course of conduct must be such as would cause a reasonable person to suffer substantial emotional distress, and must actually cause substantial emotional distress to the plaintiff."

Having defined "harassment," this Code section then goes on to provide that an individual who is the victim of such harassment may file a petition under this section seeking injunctive relief by way of a temporary restraining order. Such relief can be granted either with or without notice to the other side, depending on the circumstances. To obtain such an order without notice, however, the court must find that harm would result to the applicant if notice is given to the other side. Within 15 days of filing the petition and receiving the temporary restraining order, a hearing is held by the court on the petition for the injunction. At this hearing, the defendant may respond and explain, excuse, justify, or deny the alleged harassment. At the time of the hearing, the judge will receive testimony from the relevant witnesses and is also free to make any independent investigation the court deems necessary. If the judge finds by "clear and convincing evidence" that unlawful harassment exists, the judge will order an injunction prohibiting the harassment. An injunction issued pursuant to this section will stay in effect for no more than three years; however, at any time within the three-month period immediately preceding the expiration of the injunction, the plaintiff may apply for a renewal of the injunction by filing a new petition and by demonstrating good cause for such renewal.

Both parties are free to retain counsel in these proceedings or to represent themselves (in pro per). As a general rule, only parties and their counsel may partake in litigation proceedings. In cases involving allegations of domestic violence, however, an additional person may join the proceedings: a "support person." A support person may accompany the petitioner in court and even sit with her at counsel's table to provide "moral and emotional support." The Code does not contemplate that the support person will give legal advice; rather, the support person should assure the petitioner that she is safe during the proceedings. Code of Civil Procedure 527.6 also provides for the recovery of attorney's fees and costs to the prevailing party. Additionally, section 527.6 instructs the judicial council to create forms and instructions for their use so to provide easy access to the court. The injunction provided by this section should be cross-referenced with the Domestic Violence Prevention Act, discussed above, and set out at Family Code sections 6200 et seq.

D. Disclosure of Assets and Liabilities

Family Code section 2100 declares the legislative intent in its enactment of Chapter 9 of Division 6, "Disclosure of Assets and Liabilities," as follows:

> (a) It is the policy of the State of California (1) to marshal, preserve, and protect community and quasi-community assets and liabilities that

exist at the date of separation so as to avoid dissipation of the community estate before distribution, (2) to ensure fair and sufficient child and spousal support awards, and (3) to achieve a division of community and quasi-community assets and liabilities on the dissolution or nullity of marriage or legal separation of the parties as provided under California law.

(b) Sound public policy further favors the reduction of the adversarial nature of marital dissolution and the attendant costs by fostering full disclosure and cooperative discovery.

(c) In order to promote this public policy, a full and accurate disclosure of all assets and liabilities in which one or both parties have or may have an interest must be made in the early stages of a proceeding for dissolution of marriage or legal separation of the parties, regardless of the characterization as community or separate, together with a disclosure of all income and expenses of the parties. Moreover, each party has a continuing duty to immediately, fully, and accurately update and augment that disclosure to the extent there have been any material changes so that at the time the parties enter into an agreement for the resolution of any of these issues, or at the time of trial on these issues, each party will have a full and complete knowledge of the relevant underlying facts as is reasonably possible under the circumstances of the case.

Next, Family Code section 2102, through its cross-reference to section 721, establishes and recognizes the existence of a fiduciary relationship between the husband and wife from the date of separation (or earlier) to the date when the community assets and/or liabilities are distributed. Thus, each party must: (1) accurately and completely disclose the exact nature, scope, and extent of all assets and liabilities in which that party has or may have an interest, (2) accurately and completely disclose to the other party the existence of any investment opportunity that presents itself after the date of separation but that results from any investment of either spouse from the date of marriage to the date of separation, and (3) further provide complete and accurate disclosure with regard to his or her present income.

This statutory scheme requires each party to prepare a preliminary and final disclosure declaration, plus an income and expense declaration, and serve them on the opposing party. The preliminary disclosure declaration is described at section 2104 of the Family Code and mandates that within 60 days of service of the petition of dissolution or nullity of marriage or legal separation, each party shall serve on the other party a preliminary declaration of disclosure, executed under penalty of perjury on judicial council forms. The preliminary disclosure is not filed with the court and the declaration must set forth with sufficient particularity, in a plain and understandable manner, the following:

(1) . . . The identity of all assets in which the declarant has or may have an interest and all liabilities for which the declarant is or may be liable,

regardless of the characterization of the asset or liability as community, quasi-community, or separate.

(2) The declarant's percentage of ownership in each asset and percentage of obligation for each liability where property is not solely owned by one or both of the parties. The preliminary declaration may also set forth the declarant's characterization of each asset or liability [as separate or community].

When preparing the preliminary disclosure declaration, a party is free to amend the declaration without permission of the court—provided, of course, that he serves the amended declaration on the other party in a reasonably timely manner. Finally, along with the preliminary disclosure declaration, each party must serve a current income and expense declaration (unless one has already been provided and is current, and the information contained thereon continues to be accurate). The term "current" is not defined by the statute. It is generally thought, however, to encompass a period preceding the period in question by no more than six months.

The provision for the final disclosure declaration is set forth at section 2105 of the Code. Section 2105 mandates that each party must serve on the other a final declaration of disclosure and current income and expense declaration before entering into an agreement for resolution of property or support issues (other than temporary support); if the case goes to trial, each party must serve a final declaration of disclosure and current income and expense declaration not later than 45 days before the first assigned trial date. The contents of the final disclosure declaration are substantially similar to the contents of the preliminary disclosure declaration: both must provide all material facts and information regarding how each asset is characterized and valued. Finally, each spouse must provide the other with similar information with regard to obligations that are at issue in the proceeding.

Family Code section 2106 provides that no judgment will be entered with regard to the party's property rights until and unless each party has prepared and served a copy of the final declaration of disclosure, together with a current income and expense declaration, on the other. Although the parties do not need to file the actual disclosure document with the court, they are required to file with the court a declaration signed under penalty of perjury to the effect that they have served the final declaration of disclosure and current income and expense declaration on the other party.

If one party fails to comply with these requirements, and the other party does comply, the complying party may, within a reasonable time, formally request the non-complying party to prepare the appropriate declaration of disclosure. If at that time the non-complying party still fails to produce the documents, the complying party may file a motion to compel or file a motion for an order to prevent the non-complying party from presenting evidence on issues that should have been covered in the declaration of disclosure. This latter option is an extremely significant sanction for failure to comply with these requirements. Imagine the result if a party who refused to provide a preliminary or final disclosure of assets was not allowed to introduce any evidence whatsoever at the trial on the subject of those assets. For all practical purposes, that aspect of the case would be handled in much the same way as a default judgment to the default proceeding: The matter would be decided based solely on the evidence supplied by the complying party.

Non-complying parties who have suffered this type of sanction do have statutory means of relief; they may seek relief from the court for default and failure to appropriately comply. Some of these statutes include Code of Civil Procedure section 473 (request to vacate entry of default) and Family Code sections 2120 through 2129. The fundamental distinction between the latter and former statutory provisions for relief of default lies in the fact that motions made under C.C.P. section 473 have an absolute cut-off date of six months from the date of entry of the "offensive judgment." A Family Code section 2121 request is not so limited.

It is imperative for parties to fully comply with Family Code section 2106 disclosure requirements. The penalties for violating these fiduciary duties can be dramatic and far-reaching. Since the somewhat recent publication of *In re Marriage of Feldman* (153 Cal. App. 4th 1470), seminars and entire treatises have been presented on this sole subject. The point to take away is this: Read the *Feldman* case, learn its theories and reasoning, and comply with its instructions as completely as possible. It is a long opinion, but it provides an easy-to-understand, timely discussion of the issue.

In re The Marriage of Elena and Aaron Feldman, 153 Cal. App. 4th 1470

APPEAL from an order of the Superior Court of San Diego County, Randa Trapp, Judge. Affirmed.

In this marital dissolution proceeding, Aaron Feldman appeals from the trial court's order requiring him to pay sanctions and attorney fees based on his nondisclosure of financial information to respondent Elena Feldman. As we will explain, we conclude that the appeal lacks merit, and accordingly we affirm.

I.   FACTUAL AND PROCEDURAL BACKGROUND

Aaron and Elena[1] were married in 1969 and separated after 34 years of marriage. Elena filed a petition for dissolution of marriage in August 2003.

---

1. For purposes of clarity, we refer to the parties by their first names and intend no disrespect.

During the marriage Aaron created a large number of privately held companies referred to as Sunroad Enterprises (the Sunroad entities). The Sunroad entities are devoted to, among other things, investing in and developing real estate and owning auto dealerships. According to Aaron, his assets are worth in excess of $50 million. The characterization of the Sunroad entities as either separate or community property is an issue in the dissolution proceeding.

As the litigation proceeded, Elena served interrogatories and a request for production of documents on Aaron and conducted depositions of Aaron and employees of the Sunroad entities. Aaron provided responses to interrogatories and a schedule of assets and debts (the Schedule) on November 24, 2003. He subsequently provided updates to the Schedule at the request of Elena's attorney. Aaron also produced a significant number of documents in response to the request for production.

On September 2, 2004, Elena filed an application for an order (1) imposing monetary sanctions against Aaron for a violation of his fiduciary duty to make financial disclosures to her during the dissolution proceedings, and (2) requiring Aaron to pay her attorney fees (the sanctions motion). The sanctions motion was based on Family Code section 1101, subdivision (g),[2] section 2107, subdivision (c), and section 271, subdivision (a), which collectively give the trial court authority to order sanctions and the payment of attorney fees for breach of a party's fiduciary duty of disclosure and for conduct which frustrates the policy of promoting settlement.

Elena's declaration in support of the sanctions motion alleged that Aaron had failed to disclose several different financial transactions, including the purchase of a personal residence through one of his companies, the purchase of a $1 million bond, the existence of a 401(k) account, and the existence of several of the Sunroad entities.

The sanctions motion was taken off calendar while the parties pursued mediation. When the mediation was unsuccessful, Elena renoticed the sanctions motion and submitted a supplemental declaration, which described additional instances of nondisclosure.

Following full briefing and a hearing, the trial court ruled that Aaron breached his fiduciary duty to disclose financial information to Elena, and it ordered Aaron to pay sanctions in the amount of $250,000 and attorney fees of $140,000.[3] As part of its ruling, the trial court found that Aaron intentionally had sought to circumvent the disclosure process and that his

---

2.   Unless otherwise indicated, all further statutory references are to the Family Code.

3.   Elena requested that Aaron be sanctioned in the amount of $250,000, and that the trial court impose an additional conditional sanction of $750,000, which would be stayed on the condition that Aaron read the statutory provisions concerning his duty of disclosure and that he immediately, fully and accurately comply with his duty of disclosure. The trial court did not order conditional sanctions.

conduct had frustrated the policy of promoting settlement. Aaron appeals from the trial court's order.

II. DISCUSSION

Our analysis of Aaron's appeal requires us (1) to review the duty of disclosure that applies to spouses involved in dissolution proceedings and (2) to apply those principles to the several instances of nondisclosure alleged by Elena and cited by the trial court in support of its sanctions order.

A. Applicable Statutory Provisions

We first examine the fiduciary obligations of disclosure that govern the relationship between spouses involved in a dissolution proceeding and the sanctions available for the breach of such obligations.

The fiduciary obligations of spouses to each other are set forth in section 721,[4] and are made specifically applicable during dissolution proceedings by section 1100, subdivision (e). "Each spouse shall act with respect to the other spouse in the management and control of the community assets and liabilities in accordance with the general rules governing fiduciary relationships which control the actions of persons having relationships of personal confidence as specified in Section 721, until such time as the assets and liabilities have been divided by the parties or by a court. This duty includes the obligation to make full disclosure to the other spouse of all material facts and information regarding the existence, characterization, and valuation of all assets in which the community has or may have an interest and debts for which the community is or may be liable, and to provide equal access to all information, records, and books that pertain to the value and character of those assets and debts, upon request." (§1100, subd. (e).)

Consistent with these fiduciary obligations, section 2100, subdivision (c) provides that "a full and accurate disclosure of all assets and liabilities in which one or both parties have or may have an interest must be made in the early stages of a proceeding for dissolution of marriage or legal separation of the parties, regardless of the characterization as community or separate, together with a disclosure of all income and expenses of the parties." This disclosure duty is ongoing, as section 2100 provides that "*each party*

---

4. Section 721, subdivision (b) provides that generally "in transactions between themselves, a husband and wife are subject to the general rules governing fiduciary relationships which control the actions of persons occupying confidential relations with each other. This confidential relationship imposes a duty of the highest good faith and fair dealing on each spouse, and neither shall take any unfair advantage of the other. This confidential relationship is a fiduciary relationship subject to the same rights and duties of nonmarital business partners. . . . "

has a continuing duty to immediately, fully, and accurately update and augment that disclosure to the extent there have been any material changes so that at the time the parties enter into an agreement for the resolution of any of these issues, or at the time of trial on these issues, each party will have a full and complete knowledge of the relevant underlying facts." (§2100, subd. (c), italics added.)[5]

To implement the disclosure obligation, the Family Code requires the service of a preliminary and final declaration of disclosure "[i]n order to provide full and accurate disclosure of all assets and liabilities in which one or both parties may have an interest. . . ." (§2103.) Specifically, "the preliminary declaration of disclosure shall set forth with sufficient particularity," to the extent that "a person of reasonable and ordinary intelligence can ascertain [them]," "[t]he identity of all assets in which the declarant has or may have an interest and all liabilities for which the declarant is or may be liable, regardless of the characterization of the asset or liability as community, quasi-community, or separate." (§2104, subd. (c)(1).) It also shall include "[t]he declarant's percentage of ownership in each asset and percentage of obligation for each liability where property is not solely owned by one or both of the parties." (§2104, subd. (c)(2).)

Section 2107, subdivision (c) requires the trial court to impose monetary sanctions and award reasonable attorney fees if a party fails to comply with any portion of the chapter of the Family Code that deals with spouse's fiduciary duty of disclosure during dissolution proceedings, i.e., sections 2100 to 2113. The statute provides, "If a party fails to comply with any provision of this chapter, the court shall, in addition to any other remedy provided by law, impose money sanctions against the noncomplying party. Sanctions shall be in an amount sufficient to deter repetition of the conduct or comparable conduct, and shall include reasonable attorney's fees, costs incurred, or both, unless the court finds that the noncomplying party acted with substantial justification or that other circumstances make the imposition of the sanction unjust." (§2107, subd. (c).)

Similarly, section 271, subdivision (a) provides the trial court with authority to order the opposing party to pay attorney fees and costs in the nature of a sanction when "the conduct of each party or attorney . . . frustrates the policy of the law to promote settlement of litigation." Specifically the statute provides: "Notwithstanding any other provision of this code,

---

5. Similarly, section 2102, subdivision (a) states: "From the date of separation to the date of the distribution of the community or quasi-community asset or liability in question, each party is subject to the standards provided in Section 721, as to all activities that affect the assets and liabilities of the other party, including, but not limited to. . . . [¶] (1) The accurate and complete disclosure of all assets and liabilities in which the party has or may have an interest or obligation and all current earnings, accumulations, and expenses, *including an immediate, full, and accurate update or augmentation* to the extent there have been any material changes." (Italics added.)

the court may base an award of attorney's fees and costs on the extent to which the conduct of each party or attorney furthers or frustrates the policy of the law to promote settlement of litigation and, where possible, to reduce the cost of litigation by encouraging cooperation between the parties and attorneys. An award of attorney's fees and costs pursuant to this section is in the nature of a sanction. In making an award pursuant to this section, the court shall take into consideration all evidence concerning the parties' incomes, assets, and liabilities. The court shall not impose a sanction pursuant to this section that imposes an unreasonable financial burden on the party against whom the sanction is imposed. In order to obtain an award under this section, the party requesting an award of attorney's fees and costs is not required to demonstrate any financial need for the award." (§271, subd. (a).) Section 271 "advances the policy of the law 'to promote settlement and to encourage cooperation which will reduce the cost of litigation.' " (*In re Marriage of Petropoulos* (2001) 91 Cal.App.4th 161, 177 (*Petropoulos*).)[6]

B. *Standard of Review*

"A sanction order under . . . section 271 is reviewed under the abuse of discretion standard. ' "[T]he trial court's order will be overturned only if, considering all the evidence viewed most favorably in support of its order, no judge could reasonably make the order." ' " (*In re Marriage of Burgard* (1999) 72 Cal.App.4th 74, 82.) "In reviewing such an award, we must indulge all reasonable inferences to uphold the court's order." (*In re Marriage of Abrams* (2003) 105 Cal.App.4th 979, 991.) Although no case law discusses which standard of review we should apply to an order awarding sanctions under section 2107, subdivision (c), because the sanction is similar to that imposed under section 271 as well as similar to a sanction for civil discovery abuses (which are reviewed for abuse of discretion), we will apply an abuse of discretion standard to an order for sanctions under section 2107, subdivision (c). (*See American Home Assurance Co. v. Société*

---

6. Setting forth additional remedies available when a spouse breaches a fiduciary duty of disclosure, section 1101, subdivision (g) provides that "[r]emedies for breach of the fiduciary duty by one spouse, including those set out in Sections 721 and 1100, shall include, but not be limited to, an award to the other spouse of 50 percent, or an amount equal to 50 percent, of any asset undisclosed or transferred in breach of the fiduciary duty *plus attorney's fees and court costs*." (Italics added.) In its written order, the trial court cited this provision, along with others, as support for the sanctions award, but cited only section 1101, subdivision (g) as the basis for the attorney fee award. Because we determine that the sanctions award (including the payment of attorney fees) is well-supported by the authority provided in section 2107, subdivision (c) and section 271, subdivision (a), we need not, and do not, discuss whether the award of attorney fees might also properly be premised ̄ection 1101, subdivision (g). We may affirm the order on any ground supported by the (See *In re Marriage of Mathews* (2005) 133 Cal.App.4th 624, 632.)

Commerciale Toutélectric (2002) 104 Cal.App.4th 406, 435 ["The court's discretion to impose discovery sanctions is broad, subject to reversal only for manifest abuse exceeding the bounds of reason"].)[7]

To the extent that we are called upon to interpret the statutes relied on by the trial court to impose sanctions, we apply a de novo standard of review. (See *In re Marriage of Hokinson* (1998) 68 Cal.App.4th 987, 992.) We review any findings of fact that formed the basis for the award of sanctions under a substantial evidence standard of review. (*In re Marriage of Rossi* (2001) 90 Cal. App. 4th 34, 40.) "In reviewing the evidence on . . . appeal all conflicts must be resolved in favor of the [prevailing party], and all legitimate and reasonable inferences indulged in [order] to uphold the [finding] if possible." (*Ibid.*)

C. *Aaron's Argument Concerning Statutory Interpretation Issues*

Before discussing the particular instances of nondisclosure at issue in this case, we pause to address some of Aaron's arguments concerning the applicable statutory standards.

1. *No Injury to the Other Party Is Required for the Trial Court to Impose Sanctions*

Aaron argues that sanctions may not be imposed on a spouse who breaches his fiduciary duty of disclosure if the other party fails to establish any *harm* resulting from the breach. We disagree.

According to Aaron, "[t]hematic to the . . . statutes is the presence of some injury to the complaining party as a prerequisite to the remedy." However, we conclude that this argument finds no support in the language of the relevant statutes that authorize the imposition of sanctions here, i.e., sections 2107, subdivision (c) and 271, subdivision (a). Neither statute sets

---

7. Aaron argues that the imposition of sanctions should be reviewed under the standards applicable to the award of punitive damages, including the undertaking of a de novo review, because punitive damages, like sanctions, are intended to deter and punish. Aaron has cited no authority for this novel argument, and we are aware of no case law that would support it. We accordingly reject Aaron's argument and apply the well-settled abuse of discretion standard of review. Indeed, Aaron concedes in his reply brief that the abuse of discretion standard of review is applicable. To the extent Aaron is arguing that we should borrow from the United Supreme Court's case law to determine whether the trial court selected an appropriate dollar amount for the sanctions award, we reject this argument. We rely instead on the text of the relevant statutes to determine whether sanctions were warranted and whether the trial court was within its discretion in setting the amount of the sanction. Specifically, we apply the standard set forth in section 2107, subdivision (c), which requires sanctions when a party fails to comply with disclosure obligations, unless the imposition of sanctions would be unjust, and states that the "[s]anctions shall be in an amount sufficient to deter repetition of the conduct or comparable conduct. . . ."

forth any requirement of separate injury to the complaining spouse as a precondition to the imposition of sanctions.

Section 2107, subdivision (c) indicates that sanctions are to be imposed to effectuate *compliance with the laws* that require spouses to make disclosure to each other. (See §2107, subd. (c) [referring to sanctions imposed to "deter repetition" of conduct that "fails to comply" with the disclosure requirements].) The statute is not aimed at redressing an actual injury. Section 271, subdivision (a) authorizes sanctions to advance the *policy* of promoting settlement of litigation and encouraging cooperation of the litigants. This statute, too, does not require any actual injury.

Indeed, as expressed in section 2100, subdivision (b), the Legislature has indicated that "[s]ound public policy . . . favors the reduction of the adversarial nature of marital dissolution and the attendant costs by fostering full disclosure and cooperative discovery." In light of this legislatively expressed intention, the authority to impose sanctions for nondisclosure is plainly aimed at effectuating the goal of reducing the adversarial nature of marital dissolution rather than at redressing any *actual harm* inflicted on the complaining spouse.

In addition to relying on the purported "thematic" approach of the applicable statutes, Aaron attempts to rely on case law for his argument that *harm* is a prerequisite to the imposition of sanctions. However, the cases that Aaron cites are not applicable here because they address a different issue—whether a party must show prejudice *when seeking to vacate a judgment of dissolution* on the ground that the other party did not comply with disclosure obligations. (See *In re Marriage of Jones* (1998) 60 Cal. App.4th 685, 695 [denying relief to party who sought to have a dissolution judgment vacated for failure of the opposing party to formally comply with certain disclosure requirements because "[s]he failed to show how she was prejudiced"]; *In re Marriage of Brewer & Federici* (2001) 93 Cal.App.4th 1334, 1345 (*Brewer & Federici*) [in a case where one party sought to vacate the judgment because the other party did not comply with disclosure obligations, the court cited the principle, established by §2121, subd. (b), that a party seeking relief from a judgment of dissolution must show that " 'the facts alleged as the grounds for relief materially affected the original outcome' "].) Elena did not seek to vacate a judgment of dissolution; she sought to impose sanctions aimed at deterring future misconduct in the *ongoing* dissolution proceedings. Thus neither the case law that Aaron cites, nor the statutory authority relied on by those cases, apply here.

Because there is no requirement that Elena show harm as a prerequisite to an award of sanctions, we need not and do not analyze whether Elena was harmed by Aaron's failure to disclose.

2. The Imposition of Sanctions Does Not Require Additional Procedural Prerequisites

Aaron argues that sanctions may not be imposed under section 2107, subdivision (c) unless the complaining party first makes a request for the information that has not been disclosed and then brings either (1) a motion to compel further response or (2) a motion to preclude evidence on the nondisclosed issue. His argument is based on a misreading of section 2107, and we reject it.

The initial portion of section 2107 provides as follows:

> "(a) If one party fails to serve on the other party a preliminary declaration of disclosure under Section 2104 or a final declaration of disclosure under Section 2105, or fails to provide the information required in the respective declarations with sufficient particularity, and if the other party has served the respective declaration of disclosure on the noncomplying party, the complying party may, within a reasonable time, request preparation of the appropriate declaration of disclosure or further particularity.
>
> (b) If the noncomplying party fails to comply with a request under subdivision (a), the complying party may do either or both of the following:
>
> (1) File a motion to compel a further response.
>
> (2) File a motion for an order preventing the noncomplying party from presenting evidence on issues that should have been covered in the declaration of disclosure."

Independent of these remedies, section 2107, subdivision (c) states that "[i]f a party fails to comply with any provision of this chapter [i.e., sections 2100 to 2113], the court shall, in addition to any other remedy provided by law, impose money sanctions against the noncomplying party." The terms of the statute simply do not require that before seeking sanctions for nondisclosure a party (1) seek further disclosure and (2) bring a motion to either compel further responses or preclude evidence.[8]

Thus, sanctions were available here despite the fact that Elena did not avail herself of the remedies set forth in subdivisions (a) and (b) of section 2107.

D. Aaron's Nondisclosures

We next review the nondisclosures that Elena alleged as the basis for the sanctions motion and that the trial court relied on in ordering sanctions.

---

8. According to Aaron, *Elden v. Superior Court* (1997) 53 Cal.App.4th 1497, 1510 "suggests that the remedies [in section 2107] are available to the complying party in the order presented in the statute." The availability of sanctions was not at issue in *Elden*, and we do not perceive *Elden* as advancing any such interpretation of section 2107. Moreover, as we have explained, such an interpretation would, in any event, find no support in the statutory language.

D. Disclosure of Assets and Liabilities

1. The Israeli Bond

On November 24, 2003, Aaron served the Schedule. It is undisputed that the Schedule failed to list a $1 million bond that Aaron personally had purchased from the Israeli government in October 2003 (the Israeli bond).

Aaron signed the agreement to acquire the Israeli bond on July 10, 2003, the bond was issued on October 8, 2003, and Aaron was notified of that fact by a letter dated October 27, 2003. Thus Aaron clearly knew about the Israeli bond when he served the Schedule, but he did not list it as one of his assets.

Further, the bond was purchased with borrowed funds. According to Aaron, he "borrowed $1,000,000 from Bank Leumi, USA; purchased an Israeli bond with the proceeds; and, in turn, assigned to Bank Leumi USA as collateral for the loan." Aaron also did not disclose the loan from Bank Leumi on the Schedule as one of his debts.

Not only did Aaron fail to disclose the Israeli bond and the Bank Leumi loan on the Schedule, he also did not timely produce *documents* about the transaction. Although Elena served Aaron with a request for production asking for all bond certificates and any documents evidencing loans, Aaron produced no documents concerning the Israeli bond or the corresponding loan from Bank Leumi either in his initial October 2003 production or in his supplemental production in January 2004. In addition, during his January 28, 2004 deposition, in response to a direct question on the subject, Aaron stated that he had no personal loans from Bank Leumi.

Elena's attorney sent a letter to Aaron's attorney on February 20, 2004, requesting that Aaron update the Schedule. Aaron replied on February 27, 2004, with a notice of correction to the Schedule. Among other things, the corrections identified the Israeli bond, which Aaron claimed was acquired in December 2003,[9] and the $1 million loan payable to Bank Leumi. On March 1, 2004, Aaron produced documents relating to the Israeli bond and the Bank Leumi loan.

In her sanctions motion Elena argued that Aaron's failure to disclose the Israeli bond and the Bank Leumi loan in the Schedule, his failure to produce corresponding documents, and his failure to disclose the Bank Leumi loan during his deposition was a breach of his duty under section 2102, subdivision (a)(1), which requires "[t]he accurate and complete disclosure of all assets and liabilities in which the party has or may have an interest or obligation and all current earnings, accumulations, and expenses,

---

9. Contrary to Aaron's representation in his notice of corrections to the Schedule, subsequently produced documents show that the Israeli bond was acquired in October 2003, not December 2003, which was *before* Aaron served the Schedule on November 24, 2003. The trial court might reasonably infer that Aaron's claim that he acquired the bond in December 2003 was a deliberate misstatement calculated to hide the fact that in November 2003 he ~~ identified the Israeli bond on the Schedule. This conduct would further support sanctions.

including an immediate, full, and accurate update or augmentation to the extent there have been any material changes." The trial court agreed, concluding that the nondisclosure of the Israeli bond was part of a "clear pattern that [Aaron] has no intentions of complying with the policy . . . that this information is to be shared from the very beginning." The trial court also found that Aaron's conduct was intentional, that he was "trying to circumvent the process, hide the ball," and it stated that "[g]o fish, you figure it out, is not acceptable."

On appeal Aaron argues that "[a]s the bond was purchased with Bank Leumi *loan* proceeds and as the loan was to be paid off with the *bond* proceeds, the bond and loan were a self-contained, symbiotic package with *zero* effect on Aaron's net worth." He argues that "[g]iven the off-setting relationship[, he] forgot to list either the bond or the debt on his November 24, 2003 Schedule of Assets and Debts." Aaron also claims that he "misspoke" when he stated at his deposition that he had no personal debt to Bank Leumi.

To the extent that Aaron is attempting, through these statements, to excuse his nondisclosure, we conclude that Aaron's position lacks merit. The statutory policy in favor of disclosure contains no exception for debts and assets that offset each other, and Aaron has cited no authority to support such an exception. Instead, Aaron was required to provide a "complete disclosure of all assets and liabilities." (§2102, subd. (a)(1).)[10] Further, the trial court explained that in light of the other nondisclosures detailed in the sanctions motion, it was rejecting Aaron's explanation that the failure to disclose the Israeli bond and the Bank Leumi loan was a mere oversight. The trial court's inference is reasonable, and in light of the standard of review we will not disturb it.

2. *The Calumet Avenue Property*

The next nondisclosed item identified in the sanctions motion was Aaron's acquisition in early 2004, through a newly created business entity, of a multi-million dollar home that became his personal residence.

The factual background to this issue begins with a letter sent by Elena's attorney to Aaron's attorney on March 1, 2004, specifically asking "whether [Aaron] has acquired, or is in the process of acquiring, any interest in any assets or incurred any obligations. . . ." This letter followed up on a February 20, 2004 letter, which asked "if there have been any financial changes with regard to [Aaron], including the acquisition of any new interests in properties, either personal or business in nature. . . ."

---

10. As is required of any litigant, Aaron was also required to respond in good faith to Elena's request for production of documents by producing all relevant documents and to refrain from giving false answers in his deposition testimony, which he failed to do with respect to the Israeli bond and the Bank Leumi loan.

On April 1, 2004, Aaron's attorney sent a letter stating that "[Aaron], along with his son Dan, recently moved to a residence on Calumet Street [*sic*] in the Birdrock area of La Jolla. [Aaron] is leasing the residence for $15,000 a month. Otherwise, we are not aware of any substantial changes that warrant an update of [Aaron's] Income and Expense Declaration or further corrections to his Schedule of Assets and Debts."

However, the next day, April 2, 2004, in response to questions asked during the deposition of Frederick Tronboll, a senior vice president for Sunroad Holding, Inc. (Sunroad Holding), Elena learned that an entity created by Sunroad Holding—Calumet Real Estate Holdings, LLC—had purchased a residence on Calumet Avenue in La Jolla in a cash transaction for $5,797,500.[11]

The contract to purchase was signed on February 3, 2004, and the transaction closed on March 12, 2004. Calumet Real Estate Holdings, LLC is 100 percent owned by Sunroad Holding, which in turn is 100 percent owned by Aaron. The funds for the purchase were originally provided by Sunroad Auto Holding, which is 100 percent owned by Sunroad Holding, and thus ultimately 100 percent owned by Aaron. Aaron pays a monthly lease of $15,000 to Calumet Real Estate Holdings, LLC, which transfers the funds to Sunroad Holding, which in turn repays Aaron's company Sunroad Auto Holding for the funds used to purchase the property. In his September 2004 income and expense declaration, Aaron disclosed for the first time that he *personally* pays the property taxes, insurance and maintenance on the Calumet Avenue property.

In short, Aaron caused one of the Sunroad entities to buy the Calumet Avenue property, he made the property into his personal residence, and he funded the purchase with funds that because they came from one of the Sunroad entities, could possibly be characterized as community property. However, Aaron told Elena in the April 1, 2004 letter only that he was leasing a residence for $15,000 per month.

Elena argued that Aaron's selective disclosure of the nature of the transaction involving the Calumet Avenue property was inconsistent with Aaron's fiduciary obligation toward her. The trial court agreed, citing the transaction involving the Calumet Avenue property as one example of Aaron's pattern of nondisclosure.

Aaron argues that he complied with his fiduciary obligation because he "disclosed the acquisition of the Calumet Avenue property within one month of the close of escrow." We disagree. Significantly, Aaron did *not* disclose the transaction; instead Elena stumbled upon the fact of the transaction while deposing Tronboll. Indeed, Elena may never have found out about the transaction had her attorney not asked the appropriate question

---

11. According to Aaron's briefing, almost three months later, on June 28, 2004, Aaron produced documents about the transaction.

of Tronboll. Based on the content of the April 1, 2004 letter, the trial court could reasonably conclude that contrary to his fiduciary duty of disclosure, Aaron was attempting to *hide* or *delay* Elena's discovery of the fact that he had used possible community property assets to buy a house in which he was residing. Indeed, the trial court could reasonably assume that absent Elena's discovery of the true facts, Aaron intended to maintain that he was merely leasing his residence from an unrelated third party. Aaron's conduct was inconsistent with his duty under section 1100, subdivision (e), which gave him an obligation "to make full disclosure to the other spouse of all material facts and information regarding the existence, characterization, and valuation of all assets in which the community has or may have an interest."

In at least two separate respects, the transaction involving the Calumet Avenue property was a "material fact," giving Aaron a duty to disclose it under section 1100, subdivision (e).

First, Elena is claiming that the Sunroad entities are community assets. In order for Elena to trace those community assets, she needs to obtain information about whether, postseparation, Aaron used any of those alleged community assets to capitalize new companies. Thus, the fact that Aaron took approximately $6 million from one of the other Sunroad entities and used it to capitalize Calumet Real Estate Holdings, LLC (and to purchase a personal residence in the name of that company) is a material fact concerning the community assets. Aaron accordingly had a duty of candor regarding that transaction.

Second, in the division of community property, Elena may attempt to claim reimbursement for any postseparation benefit that Aaron obtained from the use of community property. (See *In re Marriage of Watts* (1985) 171 Cal.App.3d 366, 374.) The knowledge that Aaron is living in a house that was bought with alleged community assets would be material information to Elena because it would allow her to evaluate whether, postseparation, Aaron has used community property for his personal benefit under circumstances that would give rise to an obligation to reimburse the community.[12]

---

12. Aaron argues that he did not have to disclose the transaction involving the Calumet Avenue property because the purchase of real estate is the type of transaction that the Sunroad entities carry out in the ordinary course of business, and that, in fact, during the marriage, he had purchased the family's personal residences through the Sunroad entities. We reject Aaron's argument. As we have explained, the transaction involving the Calumet Avenue property is material to this litigation because (1) Elena must know about it to be able to trace alleged community assets and (2) Elena must know about it to determine if the community is entitled to reimbursement. On these two grounds, the transaction involving the Calumet Avenue property is distinguishable from a transaction in the ordinary course of business of the Sunroad entities, and Aaron breached his duty to disclose by attempting to hide its existence in the April 1, 2004 letter.

In light of the facts in the record, we conclude that the trial court did not abuse its discretion in concluding that Aaron's lack of candor about the transaction involving the Calumet Avenue property was part of a pattern of nondisclosure that warranted the imposition of sanctions.[13]

3. 401(k) Account

In the Schedule, Aaron stated that he did not have any retirement or pension assets. In response to Elena's request for production of documents relating to Aaron's pension plans and retirement and investment programs, Aaron produced no responsive documents, either in his initial production or in his January 2004 supplemental production. Similarly, in response to form interrogatories propounded by Elena, Aaron stated in November 2003 that he had no interest in any retirement plan.

However, during a July 23, 2004 deposition, when Aaron was asked why, according to his disclosures, he did *not* participate in the Sunroad entities' 401(k) plan, Aaron stated that he probably *did* participate. At Elena's request, Aaron subsequently produced information about his 401(k) account, showing that he had an account in the amount of $8,679.20.

In the sanctions motion, Elena argued that Aaron's failure to disclose his 401(k) account was a breach of his fiduciary duty to disclose his assets. Aaron conceded that he had not disclosed the 401(k) account and that he did indeed receive statements for the account, but he explained that he did not review the statements and that no contribution had been made to the account for 12 years. The trial court agreed with Elena that the failure to disclose the 401(k) account was another instance of Aaron's breach of his duty of disclosure, and it cited the omission of the 401(k) account as part of Aaron's pattern of misconduct.

---

13. Relying on the fact that section 2102, subdivision (a)(1) and section 2104, subdivision (c)(1) call upon a spouse to disclose only "assets in which [the spouse] has or may have an interest," Aaron argues at length that he was not obligated to disclose the transaction involving the Calumet Avenue property because that property was an asset of the Sunroad entities, and was thus not one of his personal assets. Further, he argues that the trial court and Elena have confused Aaron as an *individual* with Aaron as a *shareholder* of the Sunroad entities. We acknowledge the distinction between a shareholder and a corporation, and we recognize that a listing of the *corporation's* assets need not be provided when section 2102, subdivision (a)(1) and section 2104, subdivision (c) call for a party to disclose "assets in which [the party] has or may have an interest." However, different statutory provisions obligate a spouse to disclose information concerning all *community* assets, not just assets directly held by the spouse as an individual. Specifically, under section 1100, subdivision (e), Aaron had an obligation "to make full disclosure to the other spouse of all material facts and information regarding the existence, characterization, and valuation of all assets in which the community has or may have an interest." The transaction involving the Calumet Avenue property is clearly relevant to understand "the existence, characterization, and valuation of all assets in which the community has or may have an interest." (*Ibid.*)

On appeal Aaron argues that he did not breach his fiduciary duty to Elena by not disclosing the 401(k) account, because Elena had been secretly copying financial documents during their marriage and as a result she had copies of certain account statements from 1998 through 2000 for the 401(k) account, which she produced to Aaron on April 29, 2004.

We do not view this fact as in any way exonerative of Aaron's failure to disclose the information about the 401(k) account on the Schedule or to produce documents concerning the account in response to Elena's request for production. The 401(k) account is clearly one of Aaron's assets and may be community property. He was thus required to disclose it in the Schedule and to disclose it upon request from Elena. (See §§2102, subd. (a)(1), 2104, subd. (c)(1), 1100, subd. (e), 721, subd. (b)(2).) "[A] spouse who is in a superior position to obtain records or information from which an asset can be valued and can reasonably do so must acquire and disclose such information to the other spouse" and should not expect the spouse who is not in a superior position to search for the information. (*Brewer & Federici, supra,* 93 Cal.App.4th at p. 1348.) If Elena had not, without Aaron's knowledge, obtained statements from the 401(k) account, Elena may *never* have found out about the account, and her attorney may not have known to ask Aaron about this asset during the deposition.

We note that in November 2003 when Aaron omitted the 401(k) account from the Schedule, and in January 2004 when he omitted the account statements from his supplemental document production, Aaron likely did *not* know that Elena had any account statements. In contrast, at the time of his deposition in July 2004 when he admitted to the 401(k) account, Aaron *did* know that Elena had the documents, as she had produced them in April 2004. The trial court might reasonably have inferred that Elena's demonstrated knowledge of the 401(k) account was what prompted Aaron to finally admit to the existence of the asset and that Aaron's conduct was not consistent with his fiduciary duty of disclosure.[14]

In sum, Aaron had a fiduciary duty to disclose the existence of the 401(k) account on the Schedule in the first place without prodding from Elena and to produce relevant documents upon Elena's request. The trial court reasonably concluded that Aaron breached that duty by not disclosing the existence of the 401(k) account until July 2004 in response to an inquiry during his deposition.

---

14. Aaron also appears to believe that in light of his wealth, the $8,679.20 in the 401(k) account was immaterial and thus he did not breach a duty to Elena by not disclosing it. We reject this argument. As the trial court pointed out, the nondisclosure of the 401(k) account was part of a *pattern* of nondisclosure. Although the amount of the account may not be significant standing alone, the trial court was within its discretion to conclude that taken together with Aaron's other nondisclosures, Aaron's nondisclosure of the 401(k) account demonstrated a pattern of misconduct that justified the imposition of sanctions.

4. *The Addition of New Companies*

As another basis for its conclusion that Aaron had engaged in a pattern of nondisclosure, the trial court cited "the addition of new companies." Although the trial court could have been more clear about the transactions to which it was referring, our review of the record reveals several instances of documented nondisclosure of new Sunroad entities that the trial court reasonably could have relied upon to support its decision to order sanctions.

a. *Inmobiliaria Camino del Sol*

Two of the Sunroad entities owned by Aaron created the Mexican subsidiary Inmobiliaria Camino del Sol, S de R.L. de C.V. (Inmobiliaria) at some point in 2003.[15] Inmobiliaria was formed to own land for an auto dealership in Mexico City. Sunroad Auto Holding Corporation loaned $2.52 million to Inmobiliaria, evidenced by an October 23, 2003 promissory note signed by Aaron.

In October 2003 and January 2004, Aaron responded to Elena's request for production which sought, among other things, (1) articles of incorporation and similar documents for the Sunroad entities and (2) evidence of any loans to the Sunroad entities. Aaron did not produce any documents concerning Inmobiliaria.

In February 2004, Elena's attorney asked "if there have been any financial changes with regard to [Aaron], including the acquisition of any new interests in properties, either personal or business in nature." In June 2004, Elena's attorney asked if there had been "any changes to [Aaron's] income or assets, whether personally or through Sunroad Holding Corporation or any other subsidiary corporation" and whether "[Aaron] has created any new corporations or subsidiary corporations." Despite these requests, Aaron did not disclose the existence of Inmobiliaria or the loan to it.

Further, until he produced a copy of the promissory note in August 2004, Aaron did not produce documents concerning Inmobiliaria or evidencing the $2.52 million loan to it. The existence of Inmobiliaria was also not disclosed on the organizational chart of the Sunroad entities that

---

15. Aaron makes conflicting statements about the date on which Inmobiliaria was formed. Aaron's appellate briefing states that the company was formed in October 2003, but a letter in the record written by Aaron's attorney states that the company was incorporated on January 22, 2003.

Aaron produced in December 2003, even though it clearly existed at that time.[16]

Thus, the trial court could reasonably conclude that by failing to disclose the information about Inmobiliaria when specifically requested to do so by Elena, Aaron breached his duty under section 1100, subdivision (e) "to make full disclosure to the other spouse of all material facts and information regarding the existence, characterization, and valuation of all assets in which the community has or may have an interest." As we have explained, Elena had an interest in ascertaining and valuing all of the Sunroad entities, and in tracing any transfer of capital from the Sunroad entities to newly created entities. Because Aaron failed to disclose the existence of Inmobiliaria and the $2.52 million loan made to it by another Sunroad entity, Aaron did not comply with his duty of disclosure.

b. *Entities Appearing on Later Organizational Charts*

In Elena's July 2005 supplemental declaration in support of the sanctions motion, she described several new Sunroad entities that she had learned of in January 2005, although they were formed several months earlier.

On January 25, 2005, Aaron produced corporate organizational charts for the Sunroad entities dated December 31, 2004. Despite the fact that Aaron has admitted that new organizational charts are created on a quarterly basis, this was Aaron's first production of organizational charts since December 2003 when he produced organizational charts dated September 30, 2003.

Upon reviewing the new charts, Elena noticed that nine new entities were listed. Several rounds of correspondence between Elena's and Aaron's attorneys followed between January 28, 2005, and May 16, 2005, as Elena attempted to obtain detailed information about the new entities. Like Inmobiliaria, several of the companies were associated with automobile dealerships in Mexico. Another two of the new entities owned real property in Chula Vista, and still another owned land in San Diego. Six of the companies were incorporated in June or July 2004, one was incorporated

---

16. Aaron points out that in response to questions during his May 2004 deposition, he stated that he had formed an entity to invest in Mexican real estate for an auto dealership. In our view, this fact does not establish that Aaron complied with his fiduciary duty of disclosure. The information was offered only upon exact questioning by Elena's attorney, and even then, Aaron was not able to provide many of the relevant details, including the name of the entity. Moreover, as we have explained, the information about Inmobiliaria was available months before the May 2004 deposition.

in August 2004, one was incorporated in January 2005, and one was still in the process of being incorporated as of February 2005.

Thus, several of these new entities had been in existence for several months before Aaron disclosed their existence by producing updated organizational charts in January 2005.

As we have explained, Aaron was under a duty, among other things, to give "an immediate, full, and accurate update or augmentation to the extent there have been any material changes" as to his assets and liabilities (§2102, subd. (a)(1)). Under section 1100, subdivision (e), Aaron had an obligation "to make full disclosure to the other spouse of all material facts and information regarding the existence, characterization, and valuation of all assets in which the community has or may have an interest." (See also §721, subd. (b)(2) [requiring a spouse to provide upon request "true and full information affecting any transaction which concerns the community property"].) Further, based on the inquiry of Elena's attorneys in June 2004 as to whether "[Aaron] has created any new corporations or subsidiary corporations," Aaron knew that Elena was interested in receiving updates concerning the creation of any new Sunroad entities.

On these facts, the trial court was within its discretion to conclude that Aaron's tardy disclosure of the new entities was another instance of Aaron's pattern of noncompliance with the statutory policy of disclosure.

Aaron argues that he was not required to disclose the existence of Inmobiliaria, the $2.52 million loan, or the creation of the new entities, because they were "standard business transaction[s]." Specifically, Aaron disputes that "every transaction" of a business must be reported under section 2102, "even when the transactions are within the 'ordinary course of business' of the reported asset."

Aaron relies on section 2102 for his argument. That section provides:

> "(a) From the date of separation to the date of the distribution of the community or quasi-community asset or liability in question, each party is subject to the standards provided in Section 721, as to all activities that affect the assets and liabilities of the other party, including, but not limited to, the following activities:
>
> (1) The accurate and complete disclosure of all assets and liabilities in which the party has or may have an interest or obligation and all current earnings, accumulations, and expenses, including an immediate, full, and accurate update or augmentation to the extent there have been any material changes.
>
> (2) The accurate and complete written disclosure of any investment opportunity, business opportunity, or other income-producing opportunity that presents itself after the date of separation, but that results from any investment, significant business activity outside the ordinary course of business, or other income-producing opportunity of either spouse from the date of marriage to the date of separation,

inclusive. The written disclosure shall be made in sufficient time for the other spouse to make an informed decision as to whether he or she desires to participate in the investment opportunity, business, or other potential income-producing opportunity, and for the court to resolve any dispute regarding the right of the other spouse to participate in the opportunity. In the event of nondisclosure of an investment opportunity, the division of any gain resulting from that opportunity is governed by the standard provided in Section 2556.

(3) The operation or management of a business or an interest in a business in which the community may have an interest.

(b) From the date that a valid, enforceable, and binding resolution of the disposition of the asset or liability in question is reached, until the asset or liability has actually been distributed, each party is subject to the standards provided in Section 721 as to all activities that affect the assets or liabilities of the other party. Once a particular asset or liability has been distributed, the duties and standards set forth in Section 721 shall end as to that asset or liability."

Despite Aaron's argument to the contrary, this statute does not contain an exception that exempts a spouse from having to disclose transactions "in the ordinary course of business." Aaron points out that section 2102, subdivision (a)(2) refers to disclosures that must be made only when "outside the ordinary course of business." However, that provision describes the circumstances in which one spouse must disclose a postseparation business opportunity to the other spouse *prior* to the transaction so that the spouse may decide whether to participate in the opportunity. Under the statute, a spouse is required to give *prior* written disclosure with respect to a "significant business activity *outside the ordinary course of business.*" (*Ibid.*, italics added.)

The issue here is not whether Aaron was required to disclose the various activities of Sunroad Holdings *before* they occurred. Elena's motion for sanctions is not based on Aaron's failure to disclose business opportunities *before* the Sunroad entities took advantage of them. Instead, the request for sanctions was warranted because he failed, even when Elena made it clear that she desired the information, "to make full disclosure to the other spouse of all material facts and information regarding the existence, characterization, and valuation of all assets in which the community has or may have an interest." (§1100, subd. (e).)[17] As the spouse involved in

---

17. Citing *Gale v. Superior Court* (2004) 122 Cal.App.4th 1388, 1393, Aaron argues that he was not required to disclose the business dealings of the Sunroad entities that he made in "the ordinary course of business." *Gale* is not on point. It addresses whether an automatic restraining order prevents a spouse, who runs a family owned real estate investment business, from selling one of the properties in the " 'usual course of business.' " (*Ibid.*) Here, the issue is not whether Aaron was authorized to conduct ordinary business on behalf of the Sunroad entities, it was whether Aaron was required to *disclose* such business transactions, immediately, fully and accurately, to the extent they impacted his assets and liabilities.

running the Sunroad entities, Aaron was in a superior position to obtain information about those entities and was thus obligated to disclose material information regarding them to Elena.[18]

We agree with Aaron that as a matter of common sense, a spouse who runs a business is not under a duty to sua sponte update every *insignificant* occurrence in the operation of a business. We note as well that the statutes refer to the immediate disclosure of "material changes" and "material facts and information." (§§2100, subd. (c), 2102, subd. (a), 1100, subd. (e).) However, as we will explain, the facts here clearly justify the trial court's exercise of its discretion to conclude that the existence of Inmobiliaria, the $2.52 million loan, and the creation of the entities shown on the December 31, 2005 organizational chart were items that Aaron had a duty to promptly disclose.[19]

Significantly, with respect to the creation of the new entities, because Elena specifically asked about the creation of any new corporations or subsidiary corporations in June 2004, Aaron was on notice that the creation of the entities reflected on the December 31, 2004 organizational charts was a significant event that he should promptly disclose. Further, any spouse seeking to ascertain the value of a community business and to trace community assets would reasonably need to know of the existence of all of the business entities existing at the time of separation and the creation of any new postseparation entities. With respect to Inmobiliaria, Elena served a request for production seeking documents that encompassed evidence of the creation of new Sunroad entities and any loans

---

18. It is significant that the Sunroad entities are privately held corporations. Because of their privately held status, information regarding them is not available to Elena, but it is available to Aaron as a shareholder and manager of the company, giving him a duty to obtain that information in carrying out his duty to provide disclosure about community assets. (See *Brewer & Federici, supra*, 93 Cal.App.4th at p. 1348 [the spouse in a superior position to obtain information has a duty to do so]; *In re Marriage of Heggie* (2002) 99 Cal.App.4th 28, 34 [because the value of the stock of a public company was publicly available information, spouse did not breach duty by failing to disclose the value].)

19. Aaron argues that because he personally did not own any of the Sunroad Holding assets, including its numerous subsidiary entities, he did not have a duty to disclose their existence. Although acknowledging that he was 100 percent owner of Sunroad Holding and the other Sunroad entities, Aaron argues that because section 1100, subdivision (d) "allows the spouse who is managing and controlling the asset to act alone in all transaction[s] except those which would result in a liquidation of the business[,] Aaron's conduct [in not disclosing some of Sunroad's assets] was consistent with his fiduciary duties." We reject this argument. The issue of which assets must be *disclosed* under section 2102 is a distinct issue from whether one spouse is permitted exclusive *management and control* of the assets of a business owned by the community. Section 2102, subdivision (a)(1) requires "[t]he accurate and complete disclosure of all assets and liabilities in which the party has or may have an interest or obligation" and imposes a duty to immediately, fully and accurately update the disclosure upon a material change. Aaron breached that duty of disclosure when, despite Elena's request for the information, he failed to disclose documents concerning Inmobiliaria and the formation of new Sunroad entities.

made by those entities. These requests put Aaron on notice that he had a duty to disclose the information.[20]

5.   *Other Instances of Nondisclosure Not Cited by the Trial Court*

In support of the sanctions motion, Elena cited several other alleged instances of nondisclosure.[21] On appeal the parties have briefed whether those alleged nondisclosures warranted the imposition of sanctions. However, because the trial court did not cite those items as the basis on which it was exercising its discretion to impose sanctions, we do not analyze whether they support the trial court's ruling. Instead, we have limited our analysis to whether, under the applicable standard of review, the instances of nondisclosure cited by the trial court support its order requiring Aaron to pay sanctions and attorney fees.

E.   *Attorney Fees*

We next discuss Aaron's challenges to the trial court's attorney fee award.

1.   *The Award of Fees Under Section 271 Prior to the Conclusion of the Litigation*

As we have explained, attorney fees are statutorily authorized in this case either under (1) section 2107, subdivision (c) in connection with the imposition of sanctions for violation of disclosure obligations; or (2) section 271, subdivision (a), based on the trial court's finding that Aaron's acts of nondisclosure frustrated the statutory policy to promote settlement.

---

20.   Aaron argues that he has complied with his disclosure obligations because he has produced extensive documentation, and that the parties have hired a joint appraiser regarding the value of Sunroad businesses and a joint financial expert to determine monies available for support. These facts do not persuade us that the trial court abused its discretion in imposing sanctions. First, the trial court reasonably concluded that the documentation Aaron provided did not sufficiently fulfill his fiduciary duty of disclosure because the undisclosed items noted by the trial court were not contained in that production, namely, information about the Calumet Avenue property, information about the Israeli bond, information about the 401(k) account, and information about Inmobiliaria. Second, the parties retained the appraiser and financial expert *after* most of the conduct by Aaron that gave rise to the sanctions, and *after* Elena filed the application for sanctions. Thus, Aaron's agreement to the appraiser and financial expert is not relevant to whether his conduct during the relevant time frame warranted the imposition of sanctions.

21.   For example, Elena complained that Aaron did not disclose the subsidiaries of Sunroad Holding on the Schedule, that he did not disclose several other business transactions of the Sunroad entities, that he did not disclose that he converted the Sunroad entities from C corporations to S corporations, and that he did not produce a draft appraisal report concerning the value of the Sunroad entities.

Aaron contends that to the extent the award of attorney fees was premised on section 271, subdivision (a), that award was improper because attorney fees may not be ordered under section 271, subdivision (a) until the end of the lawsuit.

In support of his argument, Aaron cites *In re Marriage of Freeman* (2005) 132 Cal.App.4th 1, 6, and *In re Marriage of Quay* (1993) 18 Cal.App.4th 961, 970. *Quay* concerned the predecessor statute to section 271 (former Civ. Code, §4370.6). In the context of rejecting an argument that the attorney fee sanction was improper because "the only attorney's fees before the court were incurred after [the party's] wrongful conduct," *Quay* stated that "[t]he statute, we think, contemplates assessing a sanction at the end of the lawsuit, when the extent and severity of the party's bad conduct can be judged." (*Quay*, at p. 970.) In the course of deciding that a trial court could require the payment of attorney fees incurred on appeal under section 271, *Freeman* quoted this language from *Quay*. (*Freeman*, at p. 6.)

Thus, neither *Quay* nor *Freeman* dealt with the issue that we consider here, i.e., whether a trial court must wait until the end of the lawsuit to assess attorney fees as sanctions under section 271. We accordingly do not rely on those authorities in assessing Aaron's argument. Instead, in conducting our analysis we rely on the language of the statute.

The text of section 271 contains no requirement that the trial court impose the sanction at the end of the lawsuit. Indeed, the only procedural requirement in the statute is that an award of attorney fees and costs as a sanction may be imposed "only after notice to the party against whom the sanction is proposed to be imposed and opportunity for that party to be heard." (§271, subd. (b).) Further, as we have stated, section 271 is meant to "advance[] the policy of the law 'to promote settlement and to encourage cooperation which will reduce the cost of litigation.' " (*Petropoulos, supra,* 91 Cal.App.4th at p. 177.) As a matter of logic, to promote cooperation a trial court must be able to apply sanctions *during the course of the litigation* when the uncooperative conduct arises in order to encourage better behavior as the litigation progresses.

We accordingly conclude that based on the statutory language and the express purpose of section 271, a trial court may impose sanctions under section 271 before the end of the lawsuit.

2. *Aaron Has Waived the Argument That Elena's Attorney Fees Were Not Reasonable and Necessary*

Aaron argues that the trial court abused its discretion in setting the amount of attorney fees at $140,000, because those fees were not shown to be "reasonable and necessary."[22]

---

22. Aaron bases his argument for a "reasonable and necessary" standard by citing the attorney fee provision set forth in section 2032 and cases decided under that provision,

We reject Aaron's argument because he failed to raise a timely objection in the trial court. Elena submitted a series of declarations in support of her request for attorney fees as part of the sanctions motion. Although Aaron had ample opportunity to do so prior to or during the hearing on the sanctions motion, Aaron did not object to the amount of the fees that Elena was seeking. He did not argue that Elena had failed to show that the fees were reasonable or necessary, and he raised no other objection to the amount of the fees sought or to the documentation that Elena submitted in support of her fee request.[23] "'An appellate court will not consider procedural defects or erroneous rulings where an objection could have been, but was not, raised in the court below.'" (*Children's Hospital & Medical Center v. Bonta* (2002) 97 Cal.App.4th 740, 776; see also *Robinson v. Grossman* (1997) 57 Cal.App.4th 634, 648 [party that failed to object to the trial court that the opposing party's attorney fees were not sufficiently documented waived the right to object on appeal to the amount of the fee award].) We accordingly reject Aaron's challenge to the amount of the fees awarded to Elena.[24]

---

including *In re Marriage of Keech* (1999) 75 Cal.App.4th, 860, 869-870, and *In re Marriage of Braud* (1996) 45 Cal.App.4th 797, 827. We note that the trial court did not rely on section 2032 in awarding attorney fees, and Elena did not move for attorney fees based on that section.

23. At the trial court's request, after the trial court orally delivered its ruling, Elena submitted a proposed written order and findings (proposed order). Aaron subsequently objected to Elena's proposed order on the ground that it described the $140,000 fee award as "'attorney fees *for this Motion.*'" (Italics added.) Aaron argued that this wording was wrong because Elena had not sufficiently established that $140,000 in fees were incurred in litigating the sanctions motion. We do not believe that, through this objection, Aaron preserved for appeal the issue of whether Elena established that her attorney fees were reasonable and necessary. Aaron's objection was to the wording of Elena's proposed order, not to the substance of the trial court's decision, and Aaron was not, through the objection, seeking relief from the trial court's ruling. Moreover, the objection would not have been a *timely* objection to the amount of the fees claimed by Elena, as it was made *after* the fee application was litigated.

24. We note that Aaron makes no argument that the attorney fee award should be reversed because it imposed an unreasonable financial burden on him. Aaron does, however, take issue with the amount of the $250,000 sanction, arguing that it was excessive because "there is nothing in the evidence to establish that Aaron could reasonably pay this amount." We reject this argument based on evidence of Aaron's financial condition contained in the record, which shows, among other things, that as of November 2004 he had in excess of $50 million in assets, over $300,000 available to him in deposit accounts, over $3.5 million invested in the stock market, received over $2 million from dividends and loan repayments in 2004, and received on average over $150,000 per month from partnership distributions. Based on these facts, the trial court could reasonably conclude that Aaron had the means to pay the sanctions award, and an award of $250,000 was "in an amount sufficient to deter repetition of the conduct or comparable conduct." (§2107, subd. (c).)

F.   The Trial Court Was Not Required to Issue a Statement of Decision

At the conclusion of the trial court's oral ruling, Aaron made a request for a statement of decision under Code of Civil Procedure section 632. The trial court stated at the conclusion of the hearing that it did not think that Aaron was entitled to a statement of decision. In a minute order issued several days later, the trial court clarified that it was denying the request for a statement of decision because "[s]tatements of decision are not required for orders made after hearing on motions or orders to show cause."

In subsequent correspondence with the trial court, Aaron's attorney stated that "[Aaron] agrees that a statement of decision is not required," but he nevertheless asked the court to "exercise its discretion to issue a formal statement of decision." The trial court thereafter issued a six-page ruling, entitled "Findings and Order After Hearing," but it did not formally issue a statement of decision.

As Aaron properly concedes, the trial court was not required to issue a statement of decision. (See *Mechanical Contractors Assn. v. Greater Bay Area Assn.* (1998) 66 Cal.App.4th 672, 678 ["The general rule is that a trial court need not issue a statement of decision after a ruling on a motion"]; see also *Maria P. v. Riles* (1987) 43 Cal.3d 1281, 1294.)[25] Aaron argues, however, that even though a statement of decision was not required in this case, the trial court erred by refusing to exercise its *discretion* to issue a statement of decision. In support of his argument, Aaron points out that the trial court has the *discretion* to issue a statement of decision even in instances where it is not *required* to do so. (See *Khan v. Superior Court* (1988) 204 Cal.App.3d 1168, 1173, fn. 4 ["[Code of Civil Procedure] section 632 and [the corresponding rule of court] are directed to situations where a statement of decision is required; they do not limit situations where a statement of decision can be permitted"].)

We reject Aaron's argument. He has cited no authority *requiring* the trial court to exercise its discretion to issue a statement of decision in any specific instance. Further, we find no basis in statute or case law for a rule requiring the trial court to exercise its discretion to issue a statement of decision in instances where Code of Civil Procedure section 632 does not require it. Accordingly, we conclude that the trial court did not err in refusing to issue a statement of decision when it was not required by statute to do so.

DISPOSITION

The trial court's order is affirmed.

---

25.   No additional procedural rules requiring the issuance of a statement of decision appear in the Family Code in the context of a dissolution proceeding, except that section 2127 specifically requires a trial court to provide a statement of decision when it resolves controverted factual evidence in ruling on a request for relief from a judgment.

E. Joinder

The concept of joinder is not unique to family law nor is it of relatively recent vintage. *Joinder* refers simply to the act of a party "joining in" to ongoing litigation or a party being "joined in" to ongoing litigation by the litigants themselves. There are a variety of circumstances under which joinder might prove desirable. Most commonly, joinder is used where a full and complete resolution of the disputes between the parties to the litigation cannot be achieved without the participation of some other third party. In the family law context, issues of joinder typically arise in custody and visitation disputes and disputes relating to the division of community property, more specifically, disputes arising out of and pertaining to employee benefit pension plans.

The procedures used for invoking the concept of joinder are found primarily in the California Rules of Court, the Family Code, and the Code of Civil Procedure. C.C.P. section 389 provides that a party must be joined into a lawsuit if the failure to join that party will deprive the court of its ability to fully resolve the lawsuit. Section 389(a) states as follows:

> A person who is subject to service of process and whose joinder will not deprive the court of jurisdiction over the subject matter of the action shall be joined as a party in the action if (1) in his absence complete relief cannot be accorded among those already parties or (2) he claims an interest relating to the subject of the action and is so situated that the disposition of the action in his absence may (i) as a practical matter impair or impede his ability to protect that interest or (ii) leave any of the persons already subject to a substantial risk of incurring double, multiple, or otherwise inconsistent obligations by reason of his claimed interest. If he has not been so joined, the court shall order that he be made a party.

Section 389 is generally thought of as the "compulsory joinder" Code section for obvious reasons: The court is instructed to join in any parties whose absence will make the litigation incapable of being fully and finally resolved or significantly more expensive than it would otherwise be with his participation.

Similarly, the Code of Civil Procedure presents a statutory scheme for the joinder of persons on a permissive basis; that is, their presence in the action is not mandatory, but it might otherwise be allowed by the court upon proper request. Section 378 of the CCP provides

> (a) All persons may join in one action as plaintiffs if:
> (1) They assert any right to relief jointly, severally, or in the alternative, in respect of or arising out of the same transaction, occurrence, or series of transactions or occurrences and if any question of law or fact common to all these persons will arise in the action; or

(2) They have a claim, right, or interest adverse to the defendant in the property or controversy which is the subject of the action.

(b) It is not necessary that each plaintiff be interested as to every cause of action or as to all relief prayed for. Judgment may be given for one or more of the plaintiffs according to their respective right to relief.

The California Rules of Court also provide specific bases for the joinder of persons in Family Law matters. Rule 5.150 states: "Notwithstanding any other rule in this division, a person who claims or controls an interest subject to disposition in the proceeding may be joined as a party to the proceeding only as provided in this chapter. Except as otherwise provided in this chapter, all provisions of law relating to joinder of parties in civil actions generally apply to the joinder of a person as a party to the proceeding."

Rule 5.154 (a) provides an avenue by which the petitioner or respondent may apply to the court for an order joining a third party as a party to the litigation if that party "claims custody or physical control of any of the minor children of the marriage or visitation rights with respect to such children or who has in his possession or control or claims to own any property subject to the jurisdiction of the court in the proceeding." CRC 5.154 (b) expands on this rule by providing that the third party himself, to the extent he claims any interest in the custody or visitation of the minor children of the marriage, may move the court for an order allowing him to be joined into the litigation. An example of this might be grandparents or stepparents who would like to contend they should be awarded some participatory rights in the lives of the minor children. Note, however, that the joinder provisions only give these individuals an opportunity to *request* that they be joined into the litigation. This does not, of course, mean that they *will* be so joined.

Along this same vein, California Rule of Court 5.158 states that the court *must* join any party whom the court discovers has physical custody or claims custody or visitation rights of any minor children of the marriage into the proceeding. For example, if the court learns that a child's aunt does in fact have actual physical custody of the minor children, then the court must, under the authority of CRC 5.158, join the aunt as a party to any pending family law litigation between the parents of that child.

The general procedure for requesting joinder is set forth in California Rule of Court 5.156, which provides that applications for joinder are made by noticed motion followed by hearing on that motion less than 30 days from the date of filing the motion. The application need only state, in specific detail, exactly what the claimant's interest in the proceeding is and exactly what relief the claimant seeks in the proceeding. In addition, the claimant must set forth a pleading establishing his claim just as if he were going forward in a separate proceeding.

At the hearing on that motion, the court will consider the application of the claimant and will generally apply the factors set forth in CRC 5.158 in using its discretion of the subject of whether to allow him to be joined into the litigation or not. This Rule of Court establishes the following basic factors for the court's consideration:

1. Whether the determination of that issue will unduly delay the disposition of the proceeding;
2. Whether other parties would need to be joined to render an effective judgment between the parties;
3. Whether the determination of that issue will confuse other issues in the proceeding; and
4. Whether the joinder of a party to determine the particular issue will complicate, delay, or otherwise interfere with the effective disposition of the proceeding.

As indicated above, the issue of joinder is left to the discretion of the trial court. The determination of the trial court, therefore, will generally not be overturned on appeal unless, of course, the court abuses its discretion.

An example of the manner in which the compulsory provisions are examined by the court in the context of a family law matter is illustrated in the case of Jermstad v. McNelis, 210 Cal. App. 3d 528 (1989). In this case, Tom Jermstad (Father), who was in the merchant marine, was typically at sea for extended periods of time. His girlfriend, Nancy McNelis (Mother), became pregnant. She and Father were concerned about having a child because Father, a sailor, did not think he could care for the child. Additionally, the prospective mother, already a single mother, did not want another child. After discussion, Father agreed with Mother to place the baby up for adoption, although this agreement was never formalized. Mother thereafter chose adoptive parents, the Ellisons.

Prior to the baby's birth, however, Father started a new relationship with a woman whom he ultimately married (Wife). His prospective bride told Tom that she would assist with raising the child, which prompted him to file a complaint to establish parental relationship over the baby and to obtain custody. The prospective adoptive parents, the Ellisons, then filed a petition for adoption. At that time, the baby was living with the Ellisons. Mother made an attempt to join the Ellisons in Father's paternity proceeding under the permissive joinder provisions of the Code, but the trial court denied this request and awarded custody of the baby to Father. Mother appealed that determination, arguing that the failure to join the Ellisons in that litigation was reversible error. Interestingly, the court of appeal agreed with Mother and found that under Code of Civil Procedure section 389, the joinder of the adoptive parents was in fact compulsory.

However, the court of appeal affirmed the trial court's decision, finding instead that not only was the issue of compulsory joinder not raised by Mother at the trial level, but the Ellisons had actual knowledge of the proceedings and never attempted to intervene. Under those circumstances, the court determined that the failure of the trial court to join them did not constitute reversible error. It appeared to the trial court that the Ellisons had decided to allow Mother to act as their "surrogate" in the custody proceedings.

This result is interesting in that it demonstrates the absolute importance of seeking relief under the appropriate provisions of law. As indicated above, there are both permissive and compulsory joinder provisions in the law. The mother in this case sought to invoke the permissive joinder provision when all she really needed to do was cite Code of Civil Procedure section 389. Had the trial court denied a request under that section, its decision would indeed have been reversed and the appellate court would have remanded the case back to the trial court for further consideration following joinder of the adoptive parents in the litigation. Of course, the result might have been the same if the court had found that the interests of placing the child with its natural parent were more compelling than the child being with the adoptive mother. Unfortunately for Mother, however, and for the Ellisons, they were never given the opportunity to present their argument to the court.

Another example of the manner in which joinder has been used to facilitate the compelling goals of pending litigation is seen in the case of Marriage of Wilson, 209 Cal. App. 3d 720 (1989). In *Wilson*, the husband was a carpenter who obtained all of his jobs through the Carpenters' Union Hiring Hall. As a result, he had many different employers at any given time, and the district attorney was having trouble enforcing a child support wage assignment. The district attorney applied to the trial court for an order allowing joinder of the Union and an order requiring that the Union orally supply the name and address of each of the husband's employers within 24 hours of the husband being assigned to a new employer. The trial court granted this request.

Following the Union's appeal, the court of appeal held that joinder was appropriate on the ground that it was necessary to allow enforcement of a support judgment; the court further found that there was no "less restrictive" alternative to the measures employed in this case. As the reader will recall, one of the factors considered in allowing or not allowing joinder is the extent to which such an order would facilitate enforcement of the court's judgments and orders. In *Wilson*, the trial court found that it would facilitate enforcement, and its discussion in this regard was not disturbed on appeal.

F. Employment Benefits

In the family law context, joinder is perhaps most commonly used when litigating the division of property, especially pension plans. One of the more common benefits of employment today is an employee retirement plan, sometimes called a pension plan. Most larger companies offer some version of a pension plan, which provides for the accumulation of benefits over the period of time the employee works at the company. Upon retirement, the employee will have these funds available in order to fund his or her retirement.

There are many advantages to participating in such a plan, including significant tax benefits. Generally, when a company puts money away for its employees in a pension plan, under certain circumstances the employee does not have to recognize that money as income at the time it is earned so the employee does not have to pay tax on that money. For example, if an employee earns $60,000 per year, but his employer puts $10,000 per year away for his benefit in a pension plan, that employee is actually earning $70,000 per year. Because, however, he is not actually receiving the extra $10,000 on a current basis, under certain circumstances the employee can avoid paying taxes on that extra $10,000 at the time it is placed into the plan. Instead, all of this money accumulates in the pension plan over the life of the employee's employment; only upon retirement will the employee begin paying tax on the money as it is distributed to him. In addition, once the employee retires, he will fall within a lower tax bracket. Thus, the money he withdraws from the pension as a retiree will be taxed at a lower rate than the money he earned as an employee. Accordingly, an employee who is in a 50 percent tax bracket will only "net" $5,000 of the $10,000 placed into the retirement fund if he withdraws it while he is working. However if that same person withdraws the money as a retiree, he will "net" $8,000 of the $10,000 because he now falls in a 20 percent tax bracket.[4] The mechanics of the pension administration are somewhat complicated. Because the employer is usually dealing with a large number of employees and a large amount of money, the employer company will retain the services of a separate company whose job it is to administer the pension plan. Additionally, these pension plans typically became legal entities in and of themselves (usually trusts), which are capable of being treated as separate entities for many purposes, not the least of which is litigation.[5] In any event, the pension plan, which is charged with administering the plan funds, owes a fiduciary duty to its participants, the employees. Because the nonemployee spouse is not a direct participant in the plan, the pension plan does not owe the same level of duties to that person as it does to the employee spouse.

Over time circumstances have developed, especially in divorce litigation, where, either by manipulative scheming by the employed spouse or sometimes by sheer coincidence, the pension plan starts paying out the monies that it is holding for the benefit of the employee spouse to the employee without regard to the interest the nonemployee spouse may have in the plan funds. This obviously creates a problem for the non-employee spouse in a marital dissolution proceeding. The nonemployee spouse seeks to protect his interest in these plan funds and to ensure that he obtains his appropriate share. Naturally, if the plan pays the money out to the employee spouse without regard to the nonemployee spouse's interest, then the nonemployee spouse is at the mercy of the employee spouse for purposes of obtaining his fair share. This is where the concept of joinder has become prevalent.

Under appropriate circumstances, the pension plan can be put on notice or actually joined into the dissolution litigation in order to protect the non-employee spouse's interest in the retirement benefits. There are basically two ways in which a nonemployee spouse can place the plan administrator on notice of the nonemployee spouse's "adverse" interest in the pension plan funds. Family Code section 755 provides that the nonemployee spouse can simply send a letter to the plan administrator at its principal place of business putting that person on written notice that the nonemployee spouse claims entitlement to the payments that are being held for the benefit of the employee spouse. Pursuant to section 755, the nonemployee spouse would write a letter to the plan (1) advising the administrator that there is a pending marriage dissolution proceeding and the nonemployee spouse is claiming an interest in his spouse's retirement benefits, and (2) no benefits should be distributed to the employee spouse without the prior written agreement of the nonemployee spouse or a Qualified Domestic Relations Order. Although the Code section does not require that this notice be sent by certified mail, it is a good idea to do so because it provides the sending spouse with some proof that the plan administrator received the notice.

The other method by which a pension is put on notice of a nonemployee spouse's adverse claim is found in the Family Code at section 2021. Section 2021(b) provides: "An employee benefit plan may be joined as a party only in accordance with Chapter 6 (commencing with section 2060)." The procedures described in Family Code sections 2060 et seq. fully describe the joinder of an employee pension benefit plan as a party to a proceeding under the Family Code.

Section 2060 compels the clerk of the court to enter an order joining as a party to the proceeding any employee pension benefit plan in which either party claims an interest that is or may be subject to disposition by the court. All that is required is a "written application by a party." It thus becomes apparent that unlike applications for joinder discussed above, which are subject to the discretion of the trial court, joinder of the employee pension benefit plan as a party is virtually automatic once either party to the family law proceeding makes application for that joinder. Joinder of an employee's pension benefit plan becomes absolutely essential when one examines section 2060(b), which provides: "An order or judgment in the proceeding is not enforceable against an employee pension benefit plan unless the plan has been joined as a party to the proceeding." Accordingly, if a party does not join the employee pension benefit plan as a party, that plan is not required to comply with any court order that may come out of the family law proceeding compelling it to pay or not pay monies to particular individuals. This makes sense in light of the various jurisdictional issues discussed in this text. If the pension plan has not been made a party to the proceeding, the court cannot force it to comply with court orders arising out of the proceeding.

Utilizing the joinder provisions discussed in these sections of the Family Code, the nonemployee spouse may obtain joinder of the pension plan; he may also obtain a restraining order that prevents the plan from making any payment to the employee spouse that has not been approved by the court.

Once the clerk files the order of joinder discussed in section 2060, the requesting party must file an appropriate pleading that establishes her claim against the plan and sets forth the requested relief. These documents are then served on the administrator of the plan, who typically files a notice of appearance and a responsive pleading. The administrator of the plan is not *required* to file a responsive pleading; for all practical purposes, the plan usually does not have an interest in disputes between employee and nonemployee spouses. However, by being so joined, the pension is assured that it will not accidentally make the "wrong" payment, an event for which the plan might be found liable in the future. All of these pleadings (Application for Joinder, Joinder, responsive pleading, and so on) may be found on judicial council forms.

The pension plan need not file a response. Even if it merely files a notice of appearance, the court will presume that it contests the statements of fact and requests for relief contained in the nonemployee spouse's pleadings (section 2063). If the plan fails to file a notice of appearance, however, the court clerk, upon proper application, will enter a default judgment against the employee pension plan. This judgment will effectively terminate the plan's ability to contribute whatever facts or circumstances it deems pertinent to the proceeding.

The plan generally will not seek to participate in the hearing because it typically does not have an interest in the outcome of dissolution proceedings. The plan's sole concern is to distribute the funds in accordance with the court's order so it does not become liable for payment of these funds. After trial, the court's order governing the rights of the employee and nonemployee spouse must be served on the benefit pension plan; the order will become effective 30 days after service has been made. Thus, the pension plan has the opportunity to request that the orders be set aside or modified. Assuming the plan does not request the orders to be set aside or modified, they will become effective 30 days after service. The pension plan is charged with full compliance. If the plan does not comply with these orders, and it has been joined as party to the litigation, it will be subject not only to contempt of court, but perhaps more importantly, it may have to pay twice. For example, if the court orders the husband's pension plan to split the monthly payments 50 percent to husband and 50 percent to wife, but the plan pays 100 percent of the benefits to the husband, the wife may, through direct action against the pension plan, obtain an order that it pay her the 50 percent share.

The case of Marriage of Baker, 204 Cal. App. 3d 206 (1988) provides a valuable lesson about how joining a plan may protect the client's interests. In *Baker*, Wife joined Husband's pension (MEBA) as a party to the dissolution. The pension plan appeared and requested that any court order be stated in percentages rather than formulas. In the parties' judgment, the court reserved jurisdiction over Husband's pension plan pursuant to the "time rule," deferring the determination of Wife's interest in the plan until Husband retired. What neither Wife nor the court knew was that Husband applied for a lump sum distribution of his retirement benefits in early April of 1984. On April 5, 1984, Wife's attorney served the plan with a copy of the court order, which contained a stipulation between Husband and Wife regarding treatment of the plan. Approximately three months later, the plan paid Husband $400,000 in a lump sum distribution, which represented 100 percent of his interest in that retirement plan. Upon learning this, Wife obtained a court order requiring Husband to pay her the court-ordered portion of that sum, which was in excess of $165,000. Unfortunately, she was not able to collect from Husband. She then returned to court in the dissolution action and requested that the plan be ordered to distribute her full share in the plan, plus interest. This was affirmed on appeal. Had Wife's attorney *not* joined the plan into the dissolution proceedings, the result would not have been so favorable for Wife.

G. Discovery

The term *discovery* is used in litigation practice to describe the various procedures that parties use to learn as much as they can about the other side. In this text, we will focus on the basic forms of discovery used in family law practice. We will not describe in intimate detail the exact workings and rules with respect to these discovery devices. Generally speaking, the most common forms of discovery in family law practice (indeed in all areas of litigation) are: interrogatories, document production requests, depositions, and requests for admissions (although this latter discovery device does not find much use in family law matters).

1. Interrogatories

Interrogatories are a set of written questions that one party serves on the other. The responding party must answer each interrogatory under *penalty of perjury*. Thus, the responding party's responses have the same effect as testimony given in court. These responses constitute admissions that can be used as evidence against the responding party when the matter goes to trial. There are significant limitations with respect to the number of interrogatories that can be asked in a case, and there are severe restrictions with respect to the *form* in which these questions can be worded. The bulk of these rules are found in the Code of Civil Procedure at section 2030.

In the context of a family law proceeding, the judicial council has promulgated official form interrogatories and requests for admissions, which are quite complete and succinct. They are divided into 21 specific categories of inquiry as follows:

1. personal history
2. agreements
3. legal actions
4. persons sharing residence
5. support provided others
6. support received for others
7. current income
8. other income
9. tax returns
10. schedule of assets and debts
11. separate property contentions
12. property valuations
13. property held by others
14. retirement and other benefits
15. claims of reimbursement
16. credits
17. insurance
18. health
19. children's needs
20. attorney's fees
21. gifts

The full text of these judicial council form interrogatories are set forth in Figure 11-1 in the reproduction of Judicial Council form FL-145.

The party to whom the interrogatories have been served has 30 days (plus five if they were served by mail) to respond. As indicated above, this response must be made under oath; further, the original responses,

Figure 11-1
Judicial Council Form 145—Form Interrogatories

FL-145

ATTORNEY OR PARTY WITHOUT ATTORNEY *(Name, State Bar number, and address):*	TELEPHONE NO.:

ATTORNEY FOR *(Name):*

SUPERIOR COURT OF CALIFORNIA, COUNTY OF

SHORT TITLE:

FORM INTERROGATORIES—FAMILY LAW	CASE NUMBER:
Asking Party:	
Answering Party:	
Set No.:	

Sec. 1. Instructions to Both Parties

The interrogatories on page 2 of this form are intended to provide for the exchange of relevant information without unreasonable expense to the answering party. They do not change existing law relating to interrogatories, nor do they affect the answering party's right to assert any privilege or make any objection. **Privileges must be asserted.**

Sec. 2. Definitions

Words in **boldface** in these interrogatories are defined as follows:

(a) **Person** includes a natural person; a partnership; any kind of business, legal, or public entity; and its agents or employees.

(b) **Document** means all written, recorded, or graphic materials, however stored, produced, or reproduced.

(c) **Asset** or **property** includes any interest in real estate or personal property. It includes any interest in a pension, profit-sharing, or retirement plan.

(d) **Debt** means any obligation, including debts paid since the date of separation.

(e) **Support** means any benefit or economic contribution to the living expenses of another person, including gifts.

(f) If asked to **identify a person**, give the person's name, last known residence and business addresses, telephone numbers, and company affiliation at the date of the transaction referred to.

(g) If asked to **identify a document**, attach a copy of the document unless you explain why not. If you do not attach the copy, describe the document, including its date and nature, and give the name, address, telephone number, and occupation of the person who has the document.

Sec. 3. Instructions to the Asking Party

Check the box next to each interrogatory you want the answering party to answer.

Sec. 4. Instructions to the Answering Party

You must answer these interrogatories under oath within 30 days, in accordance with Code of Civil Procedure section 2030.260.

You must furnish all information you have or can reasonably find out, including all information (not privileged) from your attorneys or under your control. If you don't know, say so.

If an interrogatory is answered by referring to a document, the document must be attached as an exhibit to the response and referred to in the response. If the document has more than one page, refer to the page and section where the answer can be found.

If a document to be attached to the response may also be attached to the *Schedule of Assets and Debts* (form FL-142), the document should be attached only to the response, and the form should refer to the response.

If an interrogatory cannot be answered completely, answer as much as you can, state the reason you cannot answer the rest, and state any information you have about the unanswered portion.

Sec. 5. Oath

Your answers to these interrogatories must be under oath, dated, and signed. Use the following statement **at the end of your answers:**

I declare under penalty of perjury under the laws of the State of California that the foregoing answers are true and correct.

▶

_____ _____
(DATE)   (SIGNATURE)

Form Approved for Optional Use
Judicial Council of California
FL-145 [Rev. January 1, 2006]

FORM INTERROGATORIES—FAMILY LAW

Code of Civil Procedure,
§§ 2030.010–2030.410, 2033.710
www.courtinfo.ca.gov

Figure 11-1 (continued)

1. **Personal history.** State your full name, current residence address and work address, social security number, any other names you have used, and the dates between which you used each name.

2. **Agreements.** Are there any agreements between you and your spouse or domestic partner, made before or during your marriage or domestic partnership or after your separation, that affect the disposition of **assets, debts,** or **support** in this proceeding? If your answer is yes, for each agreement state the date made and whether it was written or oral, and attach a copy of the agreement or describe its contents.

3. **Legal actions.** Are you a party or do you anticipate being a party to any legal or administrative proceeding other than this action? If your answer is yes, state your role and the name, jurisdiction, case number, and a brief description of each proceeding.

4. **Persons sharing residence.** State the name, age, and relationship to you of each **person** at your present address.

5. **Support provided others.** State the name, age, address, and relationship to you of each **person** for whom you have provided **support** during the past 12 months and the amount provided per month for each.

6. **Support received for others.** State the name, age, address, and relationship to you of each **person** for whom you have received **support** during the past 12 months and the amount received per month for each.

7. **Current income.** List all income you received during the past 12 months, its source, the basis for its computation, and the total amount received from each. Attach your last three paycheck stubs.

8. **Other income.** During the past three years, have you received cash or other property from any source not identified in item 7? If so, list the source, the date, and the nature and value of the property.

9. **Tax returns.** Attach copies of all tax returns and tax schedules filed by or for you in any jurisdiction for the past three calendar years.

10. **Schedule of assets and debts.** Complete the *Schedule of Assets and Debts* (form FL-142) served with these interrogatories.

11. **Separate property contentions.** State the facts that support your contention that an asset or debt is separate property.

12. **Property valuations.** During the past 12 months, have you received written offers to purchase or had written appraisals of any of the assets listed on your completed *Schedule of Assets and Debts?* If your answer is yes, **identify the document.**

13. **Property held by others.** Is there any **property** held by any third party in which you have any interest or over which you have any control? If your answer is yes, indicate whether the property is shown on the *Schedule of Assets and Debts* completed by you. If it is not, describe and identify each such asset, state its present value and the basis for your valuation, and **identify the person** holding the asset.

14. **Retirement and other benefits.** Do you have an interest in any disability, retirement, profit-sharing, or deferred compensation plan? If your answer is yes, **identify** each plan and provide the name, address, and telephone number of the administrator and custodian of records.

15. **Claims of reimbursement.** Do you claim the legal right to be reimbursed for any expenditures of your separate or community property? If your answer is yes, state all supporting facts.

16. **Credits.** Have you claimed reimbursement credits for payments of community debts since the date of separation? If your answer is yes, **identify** the source of payment, the creditor, the date paid, and the amount paid. State whether you have added to the debt since the separation.

17. **Insurance. Identify** each health, life, automobile, and disability insurance policy or plan that you now own or that covers you, your children, or your assets. State the policy type, policy number, and name of the company. **Identify** the agent and give the address.

18. **Health.** Is there any physical or emotional condition that limits your ability to work? If your answer is yes, state each fact on which you base your answer.

19. **Children's needs.** Do you contend that any of your children have any special needs? If so, identify the child with the need, the reason for the need, its cost, and its expected duration.

20. **Attorney fees.** State the total amount of attorney fees and costs incurred by you in this proceeding, the amount paid, and the source of the money paid. Describe the billing arrangements.

21. **Gifts.** List any gifts you have made without the consent of your spouse or domestic partner in the past 24 months, their values, and the recipients.

together with the original *verification* form (stating that the responses were made "under penalty of perjury") must be sent to the propounding party. Of course, the responding party may object to the questions. However, as a practical matter, if these objections are not well-founded, the court will grant the propounding party an order compelling the other party to respond. Additionally, the Code of Civil Procedure provides that a party who is forced to bring this motion to compel is also entitled to recover the attorney's fees and costs incurred by making that motion.

2. Document Inspection Demands

Code of Civil Procedure sections 2031.010 et. seq. establish the statutory framework for a demand that the parties exchange and allow the inspection of documents. In essence, the propounding party will serve a demand for the inspection and copying of records pursuant to section 2031.010 on the other party. This demand requires a verified response (made under penalty of perjury) within 30 days of service of the demand (35 days if the demand was served by mail). The response must identify the documents in the responding party's possession that fall under one or more of the categories of documents requested; further, the response must indicate whether the responding party will make these documents available for inspection and copying. The document inspection request will establish the basic categories in which the requests are made. It is then incumbent upon the responding party to obtain all documents that fall within that category, identify them with specificity, and produce them for photocopying by the other side on the date specified in the demand. Set forth below are two examples of some of the basic categories in which a document request is very often made in the context of a family law proceeding.

Example 1:

FINANCIAL INFORMATION TAX RETURNS

1. Copies of all Federal and State income tax returns filed by you individually and/or jointly with any other person for each of the years commencing [insert starting point], to and including [insert ending point] and any amendments, adjustments and correspondence relating thereto.

PAYROLL RECORDS

2a. Copies of payroll check stubs for the period [insert starting point], to the present time, for all sources of employment.

2b. Any and all documents that reflect monies received by you as compensation either as an employee or independent contractor, as payroll, bonuses, severance pay, vacation pay, or any other item of compensation, for the period [insert starting point], to the present.

2c. All W-4 or 1099 forms received by you or on your behalf for the period [insert starting point], to the present.

INCOME

3. All pay records pertaining to any business entity in which you are or were affiliated or employed from [insert starting point], to the date of the production of documents pursuant to this matter which in any way reflect, evidence or refer to:

a. The annual gross income from all sources, including, but not limited to, regular pay, overtime, bonuses, cash profit sharing, commissions, expense accounts, reimbursement for personal expenses, payments on credit card accounts held by you or your employer and tips, identifying sources other than regular income.

b. The annual deductions from all income sources, identifying the nature of said deductions.

4. All pay records pertaining to any business entity in which you are or were affiliated from [insert starting point], to the date of production that reflect, evidence or refer to:

a. The monthly gross income from all sources, including but not limited to: regular pay, overtime, bonuses, cash profit sharing, commissions, expense accounts, reimbursement for personal expenses, payments on credit card accounts held by you or your employer and tips identifying sources other than regular income.

b. The monthly deductions from all income sources, identifying the nature of said deductions.

c. The number of exemptions claimed for both federal and state withholding tax purposes.

5. All W-2 forms, 1099 forms, statements of interest earned, of dividends paid, or other documents evidencing income earned by you for the period of [insert starting point], to the present time.

PENSION PLANS AND IRA ACCOUNTS

6. All records relating to or reflecting any retirement pension, profit sharing or any other IRA account or benefit plan in which you have had or presently have an interest during the duration of your marriage to your spouse to date of production, and the name in which said plan(s) or account(s) are maintained; state whether or not said interest(s) are vested; if not vested, state the terms and conditions under which said interest(s) will become vested, and the dates and amount of benefits payable.

7. All records that show contributions by you or your employer to retirement, pension, or profit sharing plans during the subject time period.

8. All records that show the contributions by you or your employer subject to retirement, pension or profit sharing plans from [insert starting point], to the date of the production of documents pursuant to this matter and the name in which said plan(s) is maintained.

9. All records that show your interest in the retirement, pension or profit sharing plan during the subject time period; state whether or not said interest is vested; if not vested, state the terms and conditions under which said interest will become vested, and the dates and amount of benefits payable.

10. All records that show the balance in the stock purchase plan, credit union, or any other benefits of employment during the period of [insert starting point], to the date of the production of documents pursuant to this request.

11. Records of all loans, loan accounts, or forgiveness of indebtedness to you from any business entity in which you are or were affiliated for the period of January 1, 1988, to the date of production of documents pursuant to this request.

12. Records of any and all payments made by any business entity in which you are or were affiliated, on behalf of debts or obligations incurred by you for the period of [insert starting point], to the date of service of this notice, including all records of reimbursements for said payments by you to any business entity in which you are or were affiliated.

13. Any and all records in your possession of trust accounts, escrow accounts, or any other interest bearing accounts in which you have or had any interest from the period of [insert starting point], to the date of production of documents pursuant to this deposition.

14. Any and all documents of any kind or nature whatsoever that show actual monies earned by you on an annual basis for the years [insert the years for which the information is requested], including without limitation federal and state tax returns (IRS Form 1040, FTB Form 540).

BANK RECORDS

15. Check registers or stubs, bank statements, passbooks, certificates of deposit, and all other documents reflecting deposits, withdrawals and exchanges of funds at any bank or financial institution having money in its possession, owned by you or standing in your name, individually or jointly with any person, and owned by or standing in the name of any corporation, partnership or joint venture in which you had any interest during the period of the following years: [insert starting point], through and including [insert ending point], and for each subsequent year through the date of production required herein.

FINANCIAL STATEMENTS

16. Financial statements including balance sheets and profit and loss statements, prepared by you or for you, individually and/or jointly with any person during the period from [insert starting point] to the date of production.

REAL PROPERTY

17a. Contracts, escrow instructions, deeds, promissory notes, trust deeds, escrow statements, and any other documents relating to real property reflecting ownership, acquisition cost, selling price, owned, or standing in your name, individually and/or jointly with any person or partnership, during the period from [insert starting point] to the date of production.

17b. The foregoing records set forth in sub-paragraph (a) hereof, shall include all records reflecting the source of the funds used by you in acquiring the real property interests set forth in sub-paragraph (a) during the period set forth in sub-paragraph (a) hereof.

17c. All records of the deposit and/or disbursements and/or the disposition of the funds received by you from the sale of real property and the interests therein mentioned in sub-paragraph (a).

PERSONAL PROPERTY

18. All documents reflecting purchase and ownership, acquisition cost of any jewelry, furs, furniture, furnishings, art works and automobiles, owned by or standing in your name individually and/or jointly with any person during the period from [insert starting point], to the date of production which item had an acquisition cost of over $500.

SAFE DEPOSIT BOX

19. Rental agreements and other records reflecting the rental, right of access to any safe deposit box by you, whether standing in your name or in the name of any person during the period from the date of your marriage to your spouse to the date of production.

CREDIT, CHARGE ACCOUNT RECORDS

20. Monthly statements and charge vouchers reflecting your use of charge accounts with American Express Company, Visa, MasterCard, department stores, and other credit or charge card organizations in your name, or in the name of any person, during the period from [insert starting point] to the date of production.

STOCK BROKERAGE ACCOUNTS

21. Monthly statements, purchase and/or sale confirmations, summary sheets and other records relating to securities purchased and/or sold or pertaining to any stock, commodity or other brokerage account owned by or standing in your name individually and/or jointly with any person during the period from [insert starting point] to and including the date of production requested herein.

OTHER BENEFITS

22. Any and all records and other documents reflecting obligations incurred by you or for your benefit and/or paid for by any person, firm or entity during the period from [insert starting point], to the date of production, for automobiles, travel, meals, lodging, insurance, entertainment, telephone and any other expenses paid for by cash or otherwise.

NOTES PAYABLE/RECEIVABLE

23a. Promissory Notes and any documents and any correspondence or other records relating to or reflecting monies owed to you individually and/or jointly with your spouse or any other person during the period from [insert starting point], to the date of production.

23b. All documents, records and materials reflecting the source of the funds used by you in connection with the loans evidenced by the Promissory Notes referred to in sub-paragraph (a) herein above.

23c. Promissory Notes and any documents and correspondence or other records reflecting monies owed by you, individually, during the period from [insert starting point], to the date of production.

23d. Promissory Notes and any correspondence and other records that relate to or reflect monies owed by you to any person or entity, and are still presently outstanding.

COPIES OF STOCKS, BONDS, ETC.

24. Copies of all certificates of stock, bonds, certificates of deposit and other securities presently in your name or that were owned by you at any time during calendar year [insert starting point] through the date of production requested herein.

GIFTS

25. Copies of all gift tax returns, federal and state, and any other documents and records reflecting gifts made by you to your spouse or to any third person during the period from the date of your marriage to your spouse to the date of production.

PARTNERSHIP TAX RETURNS

26. Copies of all partnership tax returns, federal and state, filed by any partnership and/or joint venture in which you, Respondent and/or your current spouse has or has had any interest during the period from the date of marriage to Respondent to the date of production.

ATTORNEY'S FEES AND COSTS

27a. Copies of any and all agreements that you have made as to attorney fees and costs with your present counsel, and any and all prior counsel, relating to the pending dissolution proceeding between yourself and your spouse.

27b. Records of all payments made to your present counsel and any and all prior counsel for and on account of services rendered in the dissolution proceeding between yourself and your spouse.

DEBTS AND LIABILITIES

28a. All records relating to or reflecting all current outstanding indebtedness, obligations or liabilities of you individually and/or jointly with your current spouse (if any) or any other person.

28b. All records and documents of any description that evidence your monthly expenses as set forth on your Income and Expense Declaration on file in the above-captioned action.

28c. All documents that reflect actual monthly living expenses for yourself and other persons with whom you reside, including, without limitation: residence payments (rent or mortgage, taxes, insurance and maintenance), food at home and household supplies, food eating out, utilities, telephone, laundry and cleaning, clothing, medical and dental care, insurance (life and accident), child care, education, entertainment, transportation and auto expenses (insurance, gas, oil and repair), and installment payments (credit cards, etc.).

Example 2:

A. All pay records from January 1, 2000 to the present that show:

1. The monthly gross income from all sources including, without limitation, regular pay, overtime, bonuses, amounts due you by reason of a contractual relationship, cash profit sharing, commissions, and expense accounts, identifying each source that is not regular income.

2. The deductions from all pay sources, identifying the nature of said deduction.

B. All personal records from January 1, 2000 to present showing the date and the amount of each pay increase.

C. All records that show contributions made by you to any 401(k), IRA, retirement, pension, profit sharing, or health plans, from January 1, 2000 to present.

D. All records that show money on deposit in any savings, checking, or any other type of account, as to this date and all activity in said account with deposits, withdrawals, loan transactions or otherwise, from January 1, 2000 to present, including any records evidencing a disbursement of moneys withdrawn to any individual(s), including, but not limited to Respondent, and whether that individual(s) acts as trustee or otherwise as to the account.

E. All records that show moneys expended by use of credit cards standing in the name [Responding Party] individually, or in conjunction with any other person(s). Said credit card statements are to include all credit card monthly statements from January 1, 2000, to present.

F. All records that show the contributions you made as an employee to any retirement, pension, profit sharing, or health plan from January 1, 2000 to present; state whether you made such contributions in your name individually or in conjunction with any other person.

G. All records that evidence your interest in any retirement, pension, profit sharing or health plan, whether or not said interest is vested; if not vested, state the terms and conditions under which said interest will become vested, and the dates and the amounts of benefits payable.

H. All records that evidence your interest in any stock purchase plan, credit union, or any other savings or employment benefit plan, whether or not said interest is vested at the present time.

I. All records that show moneys on deposit in a credit union account as of this date, and all activity in said account, whether deposits, withdrawals, loan transactions, or otherwise, from January 1, 2000 to present.

J. Any records that evidence or show the sale or liquidation of any stocks, bonds, money market accounts, IRA accounts, Keogh plans, or any other chattel or item of value, from January 1, 2000 to present.

K. All tax returns, including State and/or Federal Returns, filed by you separately or jointly with any other person, from tax year 1992 to present.

L. Any and all documents evidencing your interest in any business enterprise, including, but not limited to, any and all partnership agreements, whether limited or general partnerships; any and all shareholder certificates; any and all contracts; and any and all tax returns, whether individual or filed on behalf of any business entity in which you claim an interest, from January 1, 2000 to present.

M. Any and all documents showing your share of any profit and loss of any business you own or in which you claim an interest, from January 1, 2000 to present.

N. Any and all records, including but not limited to, statements, check registers, canceled checks, deposit receipts, withdrawal slips, transfer slips, passbooks, certificates of deposit, advice of interest earned, advice of interest paid, advice of loan status, advice of loan payments, and employee benefits statements, and any and all other documents relating to any and all checking, savings, money market, and credit union accounts in which you have a beneficial interest or on which your name appears, whether individually or with another person or entity, over which you have constructive custody or control, from January 1, 2000 to present.

O. Any and all deeds, certificates of ownership, certificate of registration, policies, agreements, contracts, bills of sale, bills of lading, or other evidence of ownership or prospective ownership of any property, whether such property is real, personal, or mixed; state whether it is claimed that such property is community, quasi-community, separate or held in trust for another; state whether such ownership is past, within the time specified herein, present or is an expectancy; and state whether such property is held in your name, alone or with another person, or in another's name but in which you have a beneficial interest. Said property includes, but is not limited to, real property; beneficial interest in trust deeds; beneficial interest in promissory notes; debts owned to you; cash held by you; certificates of deposit; stock certificates; bonds; commodities market certificates; gold certificates; silver certificates; mutual funds; GNMA and FNMA investments; pink slips on all vehicles; registration certificates on all vehicles, boats and/or aircraft; insurance policies; insurance interest expectancies; trusts; estates; gifts; winnings; awards; scholarships; works of art; jewelry; precious metals; royalties; patent rights; partnerships; joint ventures; tools; furniture, furnishings, and appliances; antiques; antiquities; collections and collector's items; and any other items of value, from January 1, 2000 to present.

P. Any and all documents and records reflecting the current market value of all property, real or personal, that you own or have an interest in, and any and all records and documents reflecting each and every encumbrance against each said property, including all documents that show the dates on which such encumbrances were incurred.

Q. Any and all records and documents indicating your personal monthly expenses, including, but not limited to, residence payments, whether mortgage or rent; maintenance expenses for your residence; taxes on your residence; food; household supplies; utilities, including gas, electricity, cable television, sewer, water, garbage, and telephone; laundry and cleaning; clothing; medical and dental expense; health and automobile insurance expense entertainment; incidentals; transportation and automobile expenses; payments made on secured and unsecured creditors, including any installment payments being paid; and any other expenses which you have incurred, and any advances on expense accounts.

R. Any and all records and documents indicating the name of the creditor, nature of the debt and amount of any and all community and/or separate obligations due and owing on the date of separation.

S. Any and all records that indicate each and every payment you have made, including the date and amount thereof, since the date of separation, on community and/or separate obligations.

T. Any and all documents that show, or tend to show, gifts you have made, loans you have made, and indebtedness you have forgiven, whether of money, personal items, or other assets, to any person, firm and/or entity, from January 1, 2000, to the present.

U. Any and all records and documents of any and all applications for credit and/or loans applied for in your name or in conjunction with any other person, from January 1, 2000 to the present.

V. Any and all records of each and every safety deposit box held in your name, to which you have access, or in which is deposited property belonging to you.

W. Any and all records, including, but not limited to, balance sheets, statements of revenue and expenses, cash flow statements, profits and loss statements, bank statements, and general ledgers, for any business you own or in which you claim any interest, whether a partnership interest (either limited or general), a sole proprietorship, dba, corporation, joint venture, and/or any other business entity, from January 1, 2000 to the present.

The inspection of the documents typically takes place at a location chosen by the propounding party. However, as is the case with all discovery requests, cooperation with the opposing party is encouraged by the courts and by statute. Accordingly, the inspection will usually take place in the location where the documents can be found if there are an unusually high number of documents or if for some other legitimate reason transporting the documents is unreasonable or impractical. In many cases, the responding party will photocopy the requested documents and mail them to the propounding party in compliance with the request. It is then up to the propounding party, of course, to decide whether he is willing to accept these photocopies as being accurate copies of the originals. It is generally good practice to inspect the *originals* of the documents produced.

3. Depositions

Code of Civil Procedure section 2025.010 establishes the framework for the conduct of oral depositions. A *deposition* is a proceeding whereby one party examines the other party under oath, in front of a court reporter who transcribes every word that is said. A party can compel the other to submit to deposition questioning by simply "noticing" him to appear at a specific place and time. A deposition is not entirely dissimilar to the question and answer "give and take" found at trial. Of course, depositions are typically conducted in the attorney's office and tend to be much less formal than testimony in court. In depositions, however, the witness (who can be a party to the litigation or a third-party witness) is placed under oath by the court reporter, the same oath he will take when he testifies in court, and questioned by the parties just as if he is testifying in court. After the deposition concludes, the court reporter will provide the parties with a transcript of the proceedings. The witness (or party) whose deposition was taken will have the opportunity to review the original transcript for accuracy; he or she must then sign it under penalty of perjury and return it to the party who noticed the deposition in the first place. Deposition testimony has the same effect as courtroom testimony, and it can be used in court to refresh the witness' recollection; preserve his testimony in the event something should happen to him between the time of deposition and the time of trial; and, *impeach* his testimony (show that it is untrustworthy) if it can be demonstrated that he has changed his story between the time of the deposition and the time of testimony.

In addition, the examining attorney may ask the deponent to bring various documents to his deposition. If the deponent brings such documents, the examining attorney can orally question the deponent about the documents. Oral questioning allows a significant level of "give and take" and follow-up questions, which are simply not available in the written form (document production requests and interrogatories).

Finally, it is possible to depose third-party witnesses (for example, expert witnesses, neighbors, teachers, and employers). Of course, each of these individuals must be personally served with a subpoena compelling him or her to appear and submit to deposition questioning.

4. Requests for Admissions

Requests for Admissions are discussed in Code of Civil Procedure section 2033.010. The procedure for serving requests for admissions is basically the same as for interrogatories. In fact, it can be said that the request for admission is simply a special type of interrogatory, specifically one that asks the responding party to admit that a particular fact as stated in the request is true. Additionally, the request can ask the responding party to admit the genuineness of certain documents. As with interrogatories, the responses to requests for admissions must be *verified* (signed under penalty of perjury). Furthermore, any fact that is established by admission pursuant to the request for admission process is deemed to be conclusively established against the responding party.

It has been this author's experience that the most effective use of these various discovery techniques involves an "initial volley" consisting of the form interrogatories, followed by (or coupled with) any specially prepared interrogatories as may be needed for the particular facts of the case. Once the interrogatory responses have been received, the propounding party is better equipped to prepare a request for inspection and photocopying of documents. Accordingly, the inspection demand should go out, followed by a notice of deposition of the responding party as well as any pertinent witnesses in the case. The deposition will be much more effective once the responses to the interrogatories and the request for production of documents have been fully analyzed. Finally, any holes in the evidence can usually be filled in through effective use of requests for admissions. Inasmuch as a request for admissions requires that the party admit the truth of facts as stated therein, one can also ask for a specially prepared interrogatory compelling the responding party to set forth all facts and evidence that support her denial or failure to unqualifiedly admit the request as framed by the request for admission.

This is not a text on civil discovery procedures: The foregoing is simply designed to familiarize the reader with the very basic concepts of discovery and their use in family law proceedings. Any inquiry beyond this cursory approach should be addressed by a text (of which there are many) addressing these topics in detail.

H. Bankruptcy

1. Generally

The concept of bankruptcy involves the use of those sections of the United States Code (U.S.C.) that establish the various forms of protection available to debtors in the bankruptcy court.[6] At its most basic, bankruptcy is a procedure by which a debtor (one who owes money) is given the opportunity to pay off his creditors (to the extent that is possible), and then obtain an economic "fresh start." As might be imagined, in this era of credit spending it is not uncommon for someone to incur a vast amount of debt and then find himself with little or no option for ever paying it off. For example, a man with an annual salary of approximately $30,000 might have a MasterCard with a credit limit of $3,000, a Visa card with a credit limit of $3,000, a Discover card with a similar credit limit, along with miscellaneous department store and gas station credit cards. Under these circumstances, he could run all of these cards up to the maximum amount allowable and suddenly find himself looking at approximately $20,000 in credit card debt. Inasmuch as most credit cards presently charge between 12 and 18 percent per annum interest, he could land in a precarious financial position. Indeed, to service only the interest on $20,000 of credit card debt (assuming 18 percent per annum) would require a minimum monthly payment of $300. Add to this the costs of rent (or mortgage) payments, utilities, food, school, child care, and so forth, and it is not difficult to see how an individual could find himself simply awash in debt with little or no hope of climbing out.

The role of bankruptcy in our legal system is designed to allow individuals who are in a precarious financial position an opportunity to pay off their creditors to the fullest extent possible (which might only be equal to 10 cents on the dollar) and then obtain a "fresh start" on their financial circumstance. Not so many years ago, the specter of filing bankruptcy was looked upon as a shameful event. Indeed, many people committed suicide or suffered a nervous breakdown at the prospect of being forced to "declare bankruptcy." As ridiculous as this may sound, it is a fear and a feeling still shared by many individuals today, individuals who would rather see their lives shattered than file for bankruptcy.

These days, this picture of bankruptcy is, for the most part, no longer present. Bankruptcy is gaining acceptance and is being seen as a legitimate, indeed honorable, alternative for rectifying a difficult financial situation. This is especially true when that financial situation has come about as a result of an untimely layoff, an unexpected illness, or a general downturn in the economy.

Of course, bankruptcy should still be avoided, if at all possible, because it will negatively impact one's credit. As the reader might well imagine, some lending institutions might be somewhat reluctant to loan money to an individual who has already demonstrated the willingness to file bankruptcy to avoid repaying his debts. As such, various alternatives to filing bankruptcy should be explored prior to taking this somewhat drastic step. For example, a so-called "workout" with creditors might be arranged. This involves negotiating with one's creditors a reduction of the debt or a payout over a greater time than was originally anticipated. The reader will be surprised to learn how many creditors (especially in this day and age) are willing to accommodate this type of arrangement and enter into such an agreement. There are also other forms of "pre-bankruptcy" negotiations and planning that can be undertaken with creditors to assist in a debt reduction plan. Assuming these do not work, of course, then resorting to bankruptcy may be unavoidable.

There are three different forms of bankruptcy available to a debtor. The differences among the three depend on the status of the debtor as well as the nature of the bankruptcy contemplated. The first is known as a *Chapter 7* bankruptcy, named so because it falls under Chapter 7 of the Bankruptcy Reform Act of 1978. In a Chapter 7 bankruptcy proceeding, the debtor's property is completely liquidated (sold) and his or her debts are paid off to the extent available by virtue of the proceeds of the liquidation. The Bankruptcy Code also provides a laundry list of items that the bankrupt debtor is allowed to keep, bankruptcy notwithstanding.

In practice, a Chapter 7 bankruptcy proceeds as follows: The nonexempt assets of the debtor are liquidated. Next, the trustee in bankruptcy (the person who oversees the sale and the payment to the creditors) determines how much money has been made available by the sale. The trustee then compares that figure to the amount of debt. At that point, all the creditors of the same class (that is, the same types of claims) share in accordance with the amount of money available. For example, if a debtor owes $10,000 to one class of creditors and the liquidation produces only $5,000 in cash, then each creditor will be paid off at the rate of 50 cents on the dollar. Accordingly, if Creditor *A* is owed $1,000, it will only receive $500, in full satisfaction of the debt as a result of this process. The balance of the debt owed after the liquidation will be discharged. Once a debt is discharged in this fashion, the creditor can take no further actions to collect from the debtor. The second type of bankruptcy proceeding is called a *Chapter 13* filing, sometimes called a plan of reorganization. A Chapter 13 proceeding does not involve liquidating the entire bankrupt debtor's estate. Rather, it contemplates a plan of paying off the creditors over an extended period of time. A successful Chapter 13 plan must provide that: (1) all creditors will receive at least what they would have received had the debtor liquidated under a Chapter 7 proceeding, and (2) the plan of reorganization will be completed within 36 months of its commencement. Additionally, the debtor must be an individual (as opposed to a partnership or a corporation); the debtor must be earning regular income; the debtor's unsecured debts, on the filing date, must total less than $100,000; and the debtor's secured debts, on the filing date, must total less than $350,000.

The third type of bankruptcy proceeding is found in Chapter 11 of the Bankruptcy Act. A *Chapter 11* reorganization is fundamentally the same as a Chapter 13 proceeding; Chapter 11 is unique, however, in that it is primarily designed for business entities (partnerships and corporations) rather than for individuals. It is not uncommon for a debtor to qualify for treatment under both Chapter 11 and Chapter 13. However, for reasons that are best left to a bankruptcy professional, individuals in this position are generally more apt to file for protection under Chapter 13.

One of the noteworthy aspects of a bankruptcy is that once the petition is filed, there "springs" into existence an automatic stay, which prevents all actions from being undertaken against the debtor until the stay is lifted. Specifically, all litigation in which the debtor is at that moment involved is automatically stopped (*stayed*) pending resolution of the bankruptcy action (or the receipt by one of the parties to the litigation of an order of "relief from stay" granted by the bankruptcy court). All actions being taken against the debtor to enforce the debt (collection, lawsuits, and things of that nature) must stop. Any act to create or enforce a lien against the debtor's property must stop. There are virtually no exceptions to the automatic stay. All actions being undertaken against the debtor must stop once the bankruptcy petition is filed. It is then up to the creditors to ask the bankruptcy court for permission to reconvene their proceedings and to get their "non-bankruptcy" cases back on track. This is accomplished by filing a motion for relief from automatic stay in the bankruptcy court.

As indicated above, once a bankrupt debtor emerges from the bankruptcy proceeding, virtually all of his or her debts are deemed discharged. For all practical purposes, those debts no longer exist. As regards a dissolution proceeding, if the court orders one spouse to pay the other spouse a payment to equalize the division of property, and then the spouse who is required to make this payment files for bankruptcy, he or she will be entitled to a discharge of that obligation.

Not all debts, however, are dischargeable. For example, any debt created as the result of a support obligation is not dischargeable in bankruptcy. What this means from a family law perspective is that the debtor will not be able to discharge amounts owed for child or spousal support or amounts that can be characterized as payments for child or spousal support obligations. The filing of the bankruptcy petition will, however, invoke the automatic stay. A party to a dissolution who wishes to continue the proceeding must seek relief from the bankruptcy court's stay; the court will almost always grant this relief.

2. Family Law Context

The potential of bankruptcy looms somewhat ominously over the field of family law primarily because it is such a specialized world unto itself. In any event, there are a few basic concepts that, once reviewed, will serve to somewhat "de-mystify" this area. These include the automatic stay, the general dischargeability of debts through bankruptcy, and the non-dischargeability of support obligations.

Once a party to a marital termination or legal separation files for bankruptcy, the other party may ask: "what happens to my divorce case?" Initially, the operation of the automatic stay contained in 11 U.S.C §362(a) will stay *all* legal proceedings brought against the debtor. Thus, to the extent that the dissolution or legal separation proceeding is seen as an "action against the debtor" (which it is), that action will be stayed by operation of law.

The other (nondebtor) spouse, however, may ask the bankruptcy court to lift (or terminate) the stay so that she can continue to litigate the family law matter. The court will not necessarily grant this request, and will base its decision on what the nondebtor party seeks in the underlying family law action. For example, because support orders are not discharged in bankruptcy, the bankruptcy court will not "keep" those actions in its venue. Accordingly, most actions involving support will not be stayed. If the nature of the underlying family law matter involves aspects of property division, the stay will generally *not* be lifted because resolving the debtor's property-related problems is what the bankruptcy system is all about.

By staying the underlying family law matter, the court does not adjudicate it. By issuing a stay, the court temporarily "freezes" the underlying family law action until the bankruptcy matter runs its course. Once the bankruptcy matter resolves, the family law court can complete the property aspect of the dissolution (subject, of course, to the determinations made by the bankruptcy court). For example, in the matter of *In re Willard*, 15 B.R. 898 (Bankr. 9th Cir. 1981), after the superior court issued its intended decision in the dissolution action, Husband filed for bankruptcy. Thereafter, the court entered a judgment of dissolution, which awarded certain real property to Wife. Wife then filed a request for relief from stay in the bankruptcy court to an order that Husband deed the property in question to her. The Bankruptcy Appellate Panel (BAP) found that the superior court judgment, while valid as between the parties, nevertheless did not affect the bankruptcy estate. The bankruptcy estate included the property in question (because Husband clearly had an interest in that property going into the bankruptcy). The BAP stated that "once the bankruptcy is filed, it is . . . clear that a superior court judgment does not affect the character or title of the property held in the debtor's estate. . . . Unless and until the bankruptcy court deflects such jurisdiction to another court, the property of the estate will be unaffected by the superior court decree."

Accordingly, until the bankruptcy court resolves all issues regarding the debtor and his estate, the superior court simply does not have jurisdiction to make orders relative to the debtor's property; only the bankruptcy court can make such orders.

Another common issue for family law litigants concerns support obligations and the extent to which, if at all, those obligations are affected by bankruptcy. Fortunately for recipients of support, as a general rule, support obligations are *not* affected by bankruptcy. 11 U.S.C. section 523 provides, in pertinent part:

> (a) A discharge [in bankruptcy] does not discharge an individual debtor from any debt . . . (5) for a domestic support obligation . . . [or] (15) to a spouse, former spouse, or child of the debtor and not of the kind described in paragraph (5) that is incurred by the debtor in the course of a divorce or separation or in connection with a separation agreement, divorce decree or other order of a court of record, or a determination made in accordance with State or territorial law by a government unit.

Accordingly, support obligations, whether spousal or child, will not be discharged in bankruptcy. A support obligation need not be payable directly to the support obligee; the obligation, however, must be properly characterized as a *support* obligation. Indeed, it is not uncommon for courts to characterize an award of attorney's fees, and even property, as "additional support." The court does this, of course, to prevent the award from being discharged in bankruptcy. In this regard, the case of Smalley v. Smalley, 176 Cal. App. 2d 374 (1959) is instructive. In *Smalley*, the parties' property settlement agreement and interlocutory judgment called for a payment by Husband to Wife of $3,000 to equalize the division of property between them. That amount was to be paid at the rate of $50 per month. Wife had waived spousal support, and the children had been adopted by grandparents. When Husband did not pay, Wife commenced collection efforts. Husband resisted on the ground that his payments had been discharged in bankruptcy. Wife contended that those payments were "in the nature of support" and thus were not dischargeable. The appellate court agreed with Husband, however, and found that the payments were *not* in the nature of support; therefore, they were dischargeable. The court stated:

> It is true . . . that an alimony judgment or a judgment which can properly be construed as being for alimony is not affected by a discharge in bankruptcy. However, . . . where the parties have entered into a property settlement agreement whereby payments are thereafter to be made to the wife, not for support but in settlement of property rights, the discharge in bankruptcy of the husband discharges the debt.

Similarly, the bankruptcy court in Forsdick v. Turgeon, 812 F.2d 801 (2d Cir. 1987), evaluated whether payments were "in the nature of support." Specifically, the court examined a Connecticut judgment that provided for payments of $100,000 to Wife over seven years with yearly stepdowns (found by state trial and appellate courts to be alimony); the judgment also provided for a $40,000 payment to Wife to be paid within six months (not characterized either way by the state courts). Both the bankruptcy court and the court of appeals found the payments that were specifically characterized by the state court as alimony to be "in the nature of support"; further, the courts agreed that the other payment was dischargeable as a payment relating to property. The court stated: "Although it is true that '[w]hat constitutes alimony, maintenance, or support, will be determined under the bankruptcy laws, not State law,' it is also true that 'Congress could not have intended that federal courts were to formulate the bankruptcy law of alimony and support in a vacuum, precluded from all reference to the reasoning of the well-established laws of the States.' [Citation.] Thus, while the characterization of the award by the [family law judge] is not determinative of the question, it is strongly indicative that the $100,000 was intended as, and constituted, alimony."

In this regard, the determination of whether a payment ordered by the state court constitutes a nondischargeable payment of support is left to the bankruptcy court; the label placed by the state court, while instructive, is not controlling. The controlling decision in this regard is Shaver v. Shaver, 736 F.2d 1314 (9th Cir. 1984). In *Shaver*, the dissolution judgment provided for payment of $150,000 over 75 months in settlement of the wife's "property rights." An amended judgment was later entered, which awarded the wife roughly $200,000 over a ten-year period as payment for her "marital and dower rights," with payments terminating on her death. The law of the state of the dissolution did not provide for alimony except in situations not applicable to that case. Nevertheless, the bankruptcy court found that those payments were nondischargeable as being in the nature of support. The court wrote:

> Because of the federal interests reflected in the Bankruptcy Act, the courts look to federal law to determine whether an obligation is "actually in the nature of . . . support" and is therefore nondischargeable. . . . "[R]egardless of how a state may choose to define 'alimony,' a federal court, for purposes of applying the federal bankruptcy laws, is not bound to a label that a state affixes to an award, and that, consistent with the objectives of federal bankruptcy policy, the substance of the award must govern." In determining whether an obligation is intended for support of a former spouse, the court must look beyond the language of the decree to the intent of the parties and to the substance of the obligation. . . . The courts that have considered this issue have used several factors to aid in the characterization of the debt. If an agreement fails to provide explicitly for spousal support, a court may presume that a so-called "property settlement" is intended for support when the circumstances of the case indicate that the recipient spouse needs support. . . . Factors indicating that support is necessary include the presence of minor children and an imbalance in the relative income of the parties. . . . Similarly, if an obligation terminates on the death or remarriage of the recipient spouse, a court may be inclined to classify the agreement as one for support. . . . A property settlement would not be affected by the personal circumstances of the recipient spouse; thus, a change in those circumstances would not affect a true property settlement, although it would affect the need for support. The court will look also to [the] nature and duration of the obligation to determine whether it is intended as support. Support payments tend to mirror the recipient spouse's need for support. Thus, such payments are generally made directly to the recipient spouse and are paid in installments over a substantial period of time.

Finally, of significant concern in the family law context is the extent to which a bankrupt spouse can be discharged from payment of debts that are assigned to that party by the state court. Generally speaking, under circumstances where a debtor spouse is discharged in bankruptcy from the payment of certain debts, that is the end of the discussion. That person will not be called on to "re-activate" that debt simply because the state court chooses to allocate it to the bankrupt. In this regard, the case of *In re* Marriage of Williams, 157 Cal. App. 3d 1215 (1984), is instructive. In *Williams*, after the judgment had been entered and the property divided in accordance, the wife filed for bankruptcy. She listed certain community debts assigned to her by the dissolution as well as a note regarding money she owed to her husband as an equalizing payment. In the subsequent litigation arising out of these acts, the trial court sought to fashion a remedy for Mr. Williams; specifically, it aimed to restructure the judgment in his favor to remedy the situation created by his wife. The appellate court, however, upheld the wife's "right" to have these debts discharged. The court held:

> Despite the obvious inequities of permitting one spouse who has assumed a share of the community property debts incident to a dissolution to subsequently discharge those debts and leave the non bankrupt spouse liable, in apparent derogation of the otherwise equal division of community property, the practice is well recognized and not one easily circumvented by the trial courts.

As inequitable a result as this may appear, the purpose of the Bankruptcy Act is clear: to provide, where appropriate, a "fresh start," free from the burdens of certain debts. The state court simply cannot substitute its opinion for the bankruptcy court on the subject of which debts should and should not be discharged. As such, if litigants are not careful, they may find themselves in the same position as Mr. Williams.

A reminder: Bankruptcy practice is an area of law fraught with malpractice traps for the unwary. It is best left to a specialist in the field. If the reader has any questions or is in any way contemplating entry into this field, he or she is most severely warned to seek out professional assistance. Dozens of volumes of text have been written on the subject of bankruptcy as it pertains to family law proceedings. Even more have been written on the subject of bankruptcy in general. Bankruptcy is not unlike family law in that it, too, is an area of the law in which it is "easy to practice poorly and difficult to practice well." Do not undertake any foray into this field without expert assistance.

I. Taxation

When parties to a marriage talk of divorce, at some point, the conversation turns to the subject of taxation. There are significant potential tax consequences involving the division of property as well as the payment of support and maintenance. From a tax perspective, the division of property between spouses is not unlike a sale of an asset (or at least half) from one to the other. Furthermore, the payment of support from one spouse to the other constitutes a transfer of money and can potentially be characterized as income. Both of these examples are situations in which the government has imposed taxes. The law in this area is constantly changing and the significance of the complexity of this area cannot be overstated. For purposes of this text, we shall simply touch on some of the more fundamental areas in which questions related to the tax consequences of certain transactions arise.

The first of these examples concerns spousal support, sometimes called alimony. As indicated in this book's chapter on support, this term describes a payment from one party to the other as a consequence of their marriage. Spousal support is, of course, contrasted with child support, which is made up of payments made from one party to another on account of, and for the support of, a child. Because spousal and child support payments carry different tax consequences, it is important to plan accordingly.

Perhaps the most significant inquiry in this regard is what constitutes alimony (or, from a California standpoint, spousal support), as that term is used in the United States Tax Code. Regardless of the definition under state law, from a tax standpoint, and from the IRS's perspective, for a payment to be construed as alimony it must meet all of the following requirements:

1. The payment must be made in cash or its equivalent;
2. The payment must be received by or on behalf of the payee spouse pursuant to a divorce or separation instrument;
3. Neither spouse may opt out of alimony treatment for purposes of federal income taxes;
4. Spouses cannot be members of the same household at the time the payment is made;
5. The obligation to make spousal support payments must terminate upon the recipient's death;
6. The payor and the recipient cannot file joint income tax returns; and
7. If any portion of the payment is considered to be child support, even if it is not actually designated as child support, that portion cannot be treated as alimony.

The term "divorce or separation instrument" makes general reference to a divorce decree. However, the divorce need not be final to invoke the treatment provided by the Internal Revenue Code. Thus, the "divorce or separation decree" does *not* need to be a divorce decree or a post-trial judgment. It need only be the result of a court-ordered legal obligation. In other words, alimony must be paid pursuant to a court order.

Assume that the payment is made in cash (or its equivalent) and it is made pursuant to a court order that specifically designates the payment as being for the support and maintenance of the recipient spouse, as a consequence of the marriage (and assume several other elements of the IRS test are met); now, will the payment be accorded treatment as alimony under the Internal Revenue Code? Basically, all payments constitute deductions to the payor; further, the recipient must include all payments in her income—and she must pay taxes on the payments.

In contrast, the payor cannot deduct child support payments; and the recipient need not include child support payments in her income. The distinction between the way alimony and child support is treated has left room for quite a bit of tax planning. It has been held that if the instrument by which the payment was made does not state that a specific amount must be paid for child support, then no portion of that payment is considered child support. The *"Lester rule"* basically states that if an order requires a party to pay $500 per month in support—but does not specifically designate any portion of the $500 as child support, the entire $500 can be treated as alimony; and the payments can be accorded the special tax treatment pertinent to that designation. As a consequence, individuals structured their support payments to include a greater portion of alimony and a lesser portion of child support. This process came to be known as "Lesterizing" (so named after the case that has lent its name to this concept: Commissioner v. Lester, 366 U.S. 299 (1961)).

"Lesterizing" is still viable today. Indeed, several computer programs make it simple to calculate the best ratio of spousal-to-child-support given the parties' respective tax positions. (The most notable programs, "DissoMaster" and "Supportax," are sold by California Family Law Report and The Rutter Group, respectively.) The ultimate calculation of spousal and child support is designated by the generic term "family support."

Another, often controversial, tax issue is the "dependency exemption." As the reader may be aware, a taxpayer may be entitled to a deduction for each dependent who lives with him during the tax year. There are basically five tests used to determine whether an individual qualifies as a dependent. These tests examine gross income, citizenship and residency; the nature of the relationship of the claimed dependent to the parties; and things of that nature. As a general rule, the parent having custody of the child for the greater portion of time during the calendar year in question is entitled to claim that child as a dependent—unless that parent signs a written waiver giving up the right to make that claim. Additional tax benefits are available to parents, including the child care credit and the earned income credit.

With respect to transfers of property between spouses, the current general law is rather uncomplicated: As long as the transfer between spouses occurs while they are married or incident to their divorce, no gain or loss will be recognized on the transfer. This nonrecognition provision is a very effective tool to transfer property between spouses; it allows them to effect an equitable property division of property and avoid the immediate tax consequences that would normally follow such a transfer. Of course, this is simply the general rule. The reader should consult other sources for an in-depth discussion on the subject.

The parties' filing status is another important tax issue. Parties may choose amongst the following status options when filing an income tax return: single, head of household/married living apart, married filing joint, and married filing separate. The most common of these are "married filing joint" and "single." If parties are separated (but not yet divorced) they may continue to file their income tax returns jointly.[7] Note, however, that when a joint income tax return is filed, both spouses are liable for the entire tax due on the return as well as any deficiencies, additions, and penalties that may be assessed at a later date on that return. This liability will continue even after the divorce unless a spouse can qualify for relief under the "innocent spouse" provisions of the Internal Revenue Code.[8]

In addition, a married taxpayer may file under the status "married filing separate." There is nothing particularly noteworthy about this filing status except that it is generally not as favorable from a tax payment standpoint as "married filing joint."

A party filing as "head of household" must file a separate tax return. To qualify for "head of household" status, the filing party cannot be married. This person must, therefore, actually be divorced from his or her spouse or qualify under the designation of "married living apart." Further, to qualify as "married living apart," the party's spouse cannot have been a member of the household at any time during the preceding six months of the tax year; the party must have paid at least one-half of the cost to maintain the household during the preceding tax year; and the household must have been the principal home of the party's child (or children) for more than six months of the preceding tax year. A party can benefit by filing as "head of household/married living apart" in two ways: he can enjoy a higher standard deduction and a preferential tax rate. The reader should note that this area of law is extremely complex. Many attorneys have fallen victims to malpractice suits simply because they did not take time to obtain expert advice. Only the most qualified tax professionals, whether they are lawyers or accountants, should venture into tax law. Under no circumstances whatsoever should a paralegal offer tax advice to a client. There are no exceptions to this rule.

J. Marital Agreements

A Marital Agreement can take several forms: a *premarital* agreement, a *postnuptial* agreement, or a *marital settlement* agreement. All three essentially effect the same thing: the contractual recitation of the rights and remedies of parties to a marital union. The three forms of marital agreements can be distinguished by the time of their creation. A *prem*arital agreement is entered into by parties to a marriage *before* they marry, the agreement becoming effective on the date of the marriage. A *post*nuptial agreement is entered into *after* the marriage. Finally, a *marital settlement* agreement is generally entered into in contemplation of dissolution (or legal separation). All three alter or define the parties' respective property rights incident to the marital union. While a thorough treatment of this subject is beyond the scope of this book, we will discuss some of the more fundamental concepts below.[9]

Generally speaking, marital agreements are governed by many of the same rules and regulations as "normal" contracts. Additionally, all three forms of marital agreements must comply with general principles of contract law. For example, the parties must have the capacity to enter into the contract, they must enter into the contract freely and without duress, and they must support their contractual promises with sufficient consideration.

There are a few worthy differences, however, between general contracts and marital agreements For example, specific statutes operate to prevent one spouse from waiving his or her rights to receive spousal support when such action violates public policy. These public policy restrictions generally do not apply, however, in instances where the waiver is given in the context of a marital dissolution or legal separation proceeding.

In general, parties sign a *premarital* agreement before marriage to protect their separate property and to limit the effect of community property law on their (future) community property. Premarital agreements can also affect the financial responsibilities of the parties to each other following marriage. The courts generally support these provisions, except when they violate public policy (by denying a spouse or child all means of support, for example).

The statutory scheme that operates to regulate these agreements is found at Family Code sections 1600 et seq. and is known as the Uniform Premarital Agreement Act (UPAA).[10] The court will uphold a marital agreement so long as it complies with the UPAA. According to the Act, marital agreements may affect a party's property rights in general as well as the various rights and obligations related thereto (for example, the right to lease property). The Act does not allow parties to enter into an agreement that promotes dissolution, however. Agreements that abrogate support rights are typically found to fall into that category and are thus not allowed.[11]

The second type of agreement in this area is the *marital* or *postnuptial* agreement. As its name implies, this is an agreement entered into by the parties *after* they have married. These agreements are very similar to premarital agreements and are generally governed by the same statutes. However, because the parties to marital and postnuptial agreements are husband and wife, they owe each other a much higher standard of care and fairness—a *fiduciary* duty. Therefore, marital and postnuptial agreements must meet a higher standard of fairness than premarital agreements.

Perhaps the most common type of postnuptial agreement is one that changes the status of community or separate property. As the reader will recall, parties are free to change the status of their various properties so long as they do so in writing. This is the writing to which that "rule" refers. Thus, the spouses may transmute an item of community property into the separate property of one spouse, so long as it is in writing and complies with the provisions relative to such agreements.

The third category of marital agreements—and by far the most common—is the *marital settlement* agreement. These agreements are in contemplation of dissolution or legal separation. Most dissolution cases ultimately settle, and most parties use the marital settlement agreement to memorialize the provisions of that settlement. In the context of this agreement, all outstanding issues between the parties are determined. These include provisions for property interests, allocations, and reimbursements; provisions for child custody, visitation and support; provisions for spousal support (or the waiver thereof[12]); and provisions for attorney's fees.

Great care should be taken in the negotiation and preparation of a marital settlement agreement. The following basic rules should be followed. First, make certain that the parties have completely and fully disclosed all items pertinent to the agreement. The importance of this rule cannot be overstated because a failure of disclosure can form the basis for setting aside a marital settlement agreement; and a "set aside" can prove embarrassing at the least and *extremely costly* at the worst. Second, if one of the parties to the agreement is operating without an attorney, care must be taken in every step of the negotiation to ensure that the unrepresented party is given every opportunity to have the agreement reviewed by an attorney prior to signing. In fact, many attorneys urge their clients to pay for an independent attorney to review the agreement on behalf of the unrepresented spouse. Without such a review, the unrepresented party can set aside the agreement if he decides that he is not happy with its terms. Third, the attorney should not offer advice that is beyond his scope of expertise—for example, that related to tax and estate planning.[13] Finally, remember that an oral agreement is only as good as the paper it is written on. If it is not in writing and signed by the party to be charged with its provisions, it is not a binding agreement.[14]

The terms of the marital settlement agreement typically constitute the basis of the judgment; in fact, a stipulated judgment is essentially a copy of the marital settlement agreement signed by the parties. Problems can arise, however, when one party changes his mind and tries to "get out of" the agreement to which he previously agreed. The reasons for this change of heart can come from many sources, including discovery of previously unknown facts, or simple spite.

Whatever the reason for a party's change of heart, it can cause a serious problem for the family law practitioner. In this context, the provisions of Code of Civil Procedure section 664.6 become very helpful. Code of Civil Procedure section 664.6 provides the basis for enforcing settlement agreements. It generally provides that the court may enforce the provisions of a settlement agreement between parties to litigation (in this case, a marital termination proceeding) if that agreement was entered into by the parties orally in open court, on the record in front of a judicial officer, or by the parties *in writing*. In any of these scenarios, if one party refuses to accept its provisions, the party who seeks to enforce the agreement must make a section 664.6 motion. As indicated above, this text is merely a brief introduction to the area of marital agreements. Sample premarital and marital settlement agreements are set forth below. Note, however, that these are simply *examples*; there is nothing inherently "right" or "wrong" in their provisions. The reader's agreements can, and most probably will, differ significantly as circumstances may require.

Sample Premarital Agreement*

PREMARITAL AGREEMENT

THIS AGREEMENT is made this _____ day of June 2009, by and between JOHN DOE, hereinafter referred as to "John," and MARY ROE, hereinafter referred to as "Mary," sometimes referred to in this Agreement collectively as "the parties." This Agreement is entered into freely and without duress or coercion as to each party and for valuable consideration, the receipt of which is hereby acknowledged.

1. RECITALS

1.1. John and Mary are contemplating marriage. They intend and desire by this Agreement to define their respective rights in the property of the other and to avoid such interests that, except for the operations of this Agreement, they might acquire in the property of the other as incidents of their marital relationship;

1.2. This Agreement is not and shall not be construed as a contract or a promise to marry by either party, and it shall be effective only in the event that the contemplated marriage is solemnized. If, for any reason, the marriage is not solemnized, this Agreement will be of no force and effect.

1.3. The parties hereby acknowledge that John has two children by a former marriage whose names and birth dates are as follows: Marshall Doe, born June 23, 2006, and Marta Doe, born September 26, 2008. Mary has two minor children by a former marriage whose names and birth dates are as follows: Ryan Roe, born August 9, 2004, and Lauren Roe, born January 11, 2006.

2. FULL AND COMPLETE DISCLOSURE

2.1. This agreement is entered into by and between John and Mary with the general knowledge of the extent and probable value of all their property, estate, and expectancies.

---

* *Note*: This sample is specifically tailored to meet the needs of a particular fact situation, and it is provided as an example *only*.

2.2. Each party further acknowledges an understanding of all rights that, but for this Agreement, would inure by law to the benefit of either or both of them by virtue of their marital relationship.

2.3. To ensure that both parties have a thorough knowledge of the nature and extent of the property owned by both or each of them, each party hereto has made to the other a full and complete disclosure of all property, estate, and/or expectancies that he or she owns.

2.4. The disclosures set forth herein are for courtesy only and are not an inducement to enter into this Agreement. John and Mary agree that each is willing to enter into this Agreement regardless of the nature or extent of the present or future assets, liabilities, income, or expenses of the other. To this end, John has substantially disclosed to Mary the nature, extent, and value of his property interest, including, without limitation, his various present and potential business and investment interests and his present and potential income from various sources, including, without limitation, his business and investments interests. Similarly, Mary has substantially disclosed to John the nature, extent, and value of her property interests, including, without limitation, her present and potential income from various sources.

2.5. Both John and Mary have had separate and independent counsel to advise them of their rights under this Agreement. Counsel has been fully advised and informed of previous and existing financial and marital facts of both parties and has apprised John and Mary of their rights under this Agreement with full knowledge of those facts.

2.6. The parties acknowledge that they have, prior to the execution of this agreement, fully and completely disclosed the nature of their respective estates and have, in that regard, executed an Acknowledgement of Disclosure of Assets, Liabilities, and Obligations pertinent thereto, the terms and provisions of which are incorporated fully herein.

3. AGREEMENTS REGARDING PROPERTY

3.1. John agrees that, except as otherwise specifically provided in this Agreement, the following described property is, shall remain, or shall become the separate property of Mary and shall be subject to her sole management and control and disposition as her separate property in the same manner as if no marriage had been entered into:

a. All property described in Exhibit "A," attached to this Agreement and incorporated into it, which property belonged to Mary at the commencement of the marriage.

b. Any and all property, both real and personal, acquired by Mary during the marriage by gift, devise, bequest, and inheritance.

c. Any and all earnings, accumulations, and profits from that property described in subsection "1" of this section accruing during the marriage of the parties.

d. Any and all property, both real and personal, acquired by Mary during the marriage either in whole or in part, through the sale, exchange, or hypothecation of that property described in subsection "1" of this section, or any of it, regardless of whether Mary is required to execute promissory notes, deeds of trust, continuing guarantees, or like documents of hypothecation or indebtedness, deeds, reconveyances, leases, assignments, or like documents of conveyance.

e. Any and all profits, increase, appreciation and income from Mary's separate property described in subsection "1" of this section by reason of any time, efforts, or skill expended by either of the parties in the maintenance, management, or ownership of that separate property.

f. Mary's earnings and income from all sources whatsoever after the date of marriage.

g. All debts, liens, and encumbrances on the assets described in subsection "a" of this section.

h. All debts, liens, and encumbrances, liabilities and contingent liabilities owed or incurred by Mary prior to the commencement of the marriage.

3.2. Mary agrees that, except as otherwise specifically provided in this Agreement, the following described property is, shall remain, or shall become the separate property of John and shall be subject to his sole management and control and disposition as his separate property in the same manner as if no marriage had been entered into:

a. All property described in Exhibit "B," attached to this Agreement and incorporated into it, which property belonged to John at the commencement of the marriage.

b. Any and all property, both real and personal, acquired by John during the marriage by gift, devise, bequest, and inheritance.

c. Any and all earnings, accumulations, and profits from that property described in subsection "2" of this section accruing during the marriage of the parties.

d. Any and all property, both real and personal, acquired by John during the marriage either in whole or in part, through the sale, exchange, or hypothecation of that property described in subsection "2" of this section, or any of it, regardless of whether John is required to execute promissory notes, deeds of trust, continuing guarantees, or like documents of hypothecation or indebtedness, deeds, reconveyances, leases, assignments, or like documents of conveyance.

e. Any and all profits, increase, appreciation and income from John's separate property described in subsection "2" of this section by reason of any time, efforts, or skill expended by either of the parties in the maintenance, management, or ownership of that separate property.

f. John's earnings and income from all sources whatsoever after the date of marriage.

g. All debts, liens, and encumbrances on the assets described in subsection "b" of this section.

h. All debts, liens, and encumbrances, liabilities and contingent liabilities owed or incurred by John prior to the commencement of the marriage.

3.3. The parties agree that a change in the form of the separate property of either spouse shall not constitute a change of characterization, and that such separate property shall remain the separate property of the owner spouse.

3.4. Each party has been advised as to the provisions of Family Code Section 2640 concerning rights to reimbursement for separate property used in the acquisition of community property. Each party waives any rights pursuant to Family Code Section 2640.

3.5. John and Mary acknowledge and agree that they have not previously entered into any other contract, understanding, or agreement, whether expressed, implied in fact, or implied in law with respect to each other's property or earnings, wherever or however acquired. Neither party now has, possesses, or claims any right or interest whatsoever, in law or equity, under the laws of any state, in the present or future property, income or estate of the other, or a right to support, maintenance, or rehabilitation payments of any kind whatsoever from the other by reason of the party's nonmarital relationship, if any. The parties acknowledge that they each have been advised by their respective counsel on California law respecting nonmarital relationships, and they each agree that neither has any rights and/or obligations arising out of their nonmarital relationship with each other.

3.6. John and Mary agree that the residence located at and commonly described as 111 North Hill Street, Los Angeles, California, 90012, and described in Exhibit "B" belonging to John at the beginning of the marriage, is his sole and separate property; *provided, however,* that, notwithstanding anything to the contrary set forth in this agreement, upon the parties' obtaining a Judgment of Dissolution of Marriage or Legal Separation, together with any other rights Mary may have pursuant to this agreement, Mary shall be entitled to receive from John's separate property estate a sum equal to one-half (1/2) of the principal paydown on the subject residence during the marriage, together with one-half (1/2) of the appreciation of the subject residence during the marriage of the parties. For purposes of this provision only, and the determination of principal pay-down and appreciation during marriage, the parties agree that the fair market value of the property (regardless of its actual value) as of the date of marriage shall be deemed to be $830,000.00. The parties further understand that the estimated outstanding debt on said property as of the date of the contemplated marriage is approximately $565,000.00. Until such time as the parties may live separate and apart, each shall have an equal right to use and occupy the residence.

3.7. Subject to the provisions of paragraph 3.6 herein, the parties understand that they may purchase a new residence within the next several years, although the parties make no promise to purchase such residence herein. In the event that the parties do purchase a new residence, the net proceeds of sale of the present residence, if any, located at 111 North Hill Street, Los Angeles, California, 90012, may be applied toward the purchase of the new residence. Title to the new residence may be taken in joint tenancy, provided that John shall retain a right of reimbursement in the new residence to the extent that proceeds of his present residence at 111 North Hill Street, Los Angeles, California, 90012, up to a maximum of $265,000.00, plus any other of his separate funds as are applied toward the purchase of the new residence. On the sale of the new residence, John shall be paid first from the net proceeds of sale (i.e., gross sales proceeds less all expenses of sale [e.g., fees, costs, commissions, etc.] and existing debt thereon) the amount of his right of reimbursement. The balance, if any, of the net proceeds shall be divided equally between the parties. For example, if the net proceeds of sale of John's residence at 111 North Hill Street, Los Angeles, California, 90012, were $150,000.00, and if those net proceeds were applied toward the purchase of a new residence, and if the new residence were sold, resulting in net proceeds of $250,000.00, John would receive $150,000.00 (the amount of this right of reimbursement) plus $50,000.00 (1/2 of the balance of the net proceeds), and Mary would receive $50,000.00 (1/2 of the balance of the net proceeds). Mary shall be reimbursed for any separate property contribution she may make toward the purchase of said property.

3.8. Notwithstanding anything to the contrary set forth in this agreement, so long as Mary is gainfully employed (for the purposes of this instant provision, defined herein as being eligible for and making contributions to her section 403(b) retirement plan), John agrees to credit to wife the sum of $1,250.00 per month ($15,000.00 per year) for a period not to exceed seventy-two (72) months, or separation of the parties, whichever shall first occur. Such credit will be paid by John directly to Mary within sixty (60) days of Mary's demand for same for John, in addition to those amounts payable to Mary pursuant to paragraph 3.6 hereinabove. During such periods as Mary is not gainfully employed (as defined herein), the payments contemplated herein to be made by John to Mary shall be in the sum of $1,750.00 per month.

3.9. Commencing with the first month of the seventh year of marriage (the seventy-third month of marriage) Mary's right, claim, title, and interest in and to the moneys and/or obligations referenced in paragraph 3.8 immediately above shall forever cease and terminate. Commencing with the first day of the seventy-third month, the parties agree that each party will acquire an interest in what would have been the community estate, as defined by statute, as if the parties had no premarital agreement, specifically excluding therefrom the residence discussed at paragraph 3.6 and the business interests discussed at paragraph 4.1, as determined by the schedule of vesting set forth herein below. In the event of separation of the parties, the parties shall calculate the value which a community estate of the parties would have acquired in the absence of this instant Agreement, not including the residence discussed at paragraph 3.6, or the business interests discussed at paragraph 4.1. This vesting schedule in that community estate is as follows:

At the commencement of year seven (7) of the marriage—twenty percent (20%)

At the commencement of year eight (8) of the marriage—forty percent (40%)

At the commencement of year nine (9) of the marriage—sixty percent (60%)

At the commencement of year ten (10) of the marriage—eighty percent (80%)

At the commencement of year eleven (11) of the marriage—one hundred percent (100%)

For example, if the parties separate after the commencement of year seven (7) of the marriage, then the parties shall determine what would have been the community estate acquired by the parties during the marriage. The parties will then determine what percentage of that community estate was generated by John, and what percentage of that community estate was generated by Mary, at which time Mary will be entitled to twenty percent (20%) of what would have been her fifty percent (50%) share of the community estate generated by John, and John will be entitled to twenty percent (20%) of what would have been his fifty percent (50%) share of the community estate generated by Mary. Similarly, if the parties separate during year ten (10) of the marriage (i.e., after nine full years of marriage), Mary will be entitled to eighty percent (80%) of what would have been her fifty percent (50%) interest in the community estate generated by husband and John will be entitled to eighty percent (80%) of what would have been his fifty percent (50%) interest in the community estate generated by Mary. When calculating Mary's share of the community estate for purposes of this paragraph, the parties shall not include the residence referred to in paragraph 3.6 above, inasmuch as Mary's entitlement to moneys therefrom shall be determined exclusively in accordance with the terms and provisions of said paragraph 3.6, and shall not include John's business interests as discussed in paragraph 4.1 below.

If the parties happen to separate during the middle of any particular year, the percentage interest of vesting will be determined on a pro-rata basis with the numerator being the number of months from the beginning of the year to the time of separation and the denominator being the number of months in a year. For example, if the parties separated six months into year seven, each party would have a thirty percent (30%) vesting interest in the community estate the twenty (20%) percent obtained at the commencement of year seven, plus one half (1/2) of the twenty percent vesting that would occur between year seven and year eight under the schedule set forth above.

Notwithstanding anything to the contrary in paragraph 3.8 above, if the parties separate during either years six (6) or seven (7) only, Mary shall be entitled to the greater of the amount of the payments payable pursuant to paragraph 3.8 up to the date of separation, or the amount payable under this instant paragraph, whichever is greater.

Each party shall have a right to disclosure and accounting of the financial records of the other party in order to ascertain or determine the assets, etc., that have been acquired by the parties during the marriage for purposes of the vesting calculation.

4. COMMUNITY EFFORTS IN MANAGING EACH PARTY'S OWN SEPARATE PROPERTY INTERESTS

4.1. The parties acknowledge and agree that John may devote considerable personal time, skill, service, industry, and effort during their marriage to the investment and management of his separate property and the income thereof, specifically including, without limitation, John's existing or future interest in the accountancy practice known as Doe, Roe & Joe, Certified Public Accountants, or any successor firm/business enterprise in which John is involved. The parties acknowledge and agree that even though the expenditure of John's personal time, skill, service, industry, and effort might constitute or create a community property interest, community property income, or community property asset in the absence of this Agreement, no such community property interest, income, or asset shall be created thereby, and any income, profits, accumulations, appreciation, and increase in value of the separate property of John during that marriage shall be and remain entirely John's separate property.

4.2. The parties acknowledge and agree that Mary may devote considerable personal time, skill, service, industry, and effort during their marriage to the investment and management of her separate property and income thereof. The parties acknowledge and agree that even though the expenditure of Mary's personal time, skill, service, industry, and effort might constitute or create a community property interest, community property income, or community property assets in the absence of this Agreement, no such community property interest, income, or asset shall be created thereby, and any income, profits, accumulations, appreciation, and increase in value of the separate property of Mary during marriage shall be and remain entirely Mary's separate property.

5. COMMUNITY EFFORTS IN MANAGING THE OTHER PARTY'S SEPARATE PROPERTY INTERESTS

5.1. The parties acknowledge and agree that during their marriage, one party may choose to contribute considerable personal time, skill, service, industry, and effort to the investment and management of the other party's separate property and the income thereof. The parties acknowledge and agree that even though any such contribution might constitute or create a community property interest, community property income, or a community property asset in the absence of this Agreement, no such community property interest, income, or asset shall be created thereby. The parties further agree that any such contribution shall not create any other claim, right, lien, or interest whatsoever, in favor of the party contributing the personal time, skill, service, industry, and effort, in or to the other party's separate property and any income, profits, accumulations, appreciation, and increase in value thereof during the parties' marriage.

6. SEPARATE PROPERTY EARNINGS, DEFERRED COMPENSATION, AND EMPLOYEE BENEFITS

6.1. The parties agree that any earnings, income, or benefits, no matter their nature, kind or source, from and after the marriage, including but not limited to salary, bonuses, stock options, deferred compensation, and retirement benefits, shall be the separate property of the party earning or acquiring such earnings, income or benefits as though the contemplated marriage had never occurred. There shall be no allocation made of any such earnings, income, or benefits between community property and separate property, and such earnings, income, or benefits shall be entirely the separate property of the party earning or acquiring the same. The parties acknowledge their understanding that in the absence of this Agreement any earnings, income or benefits resulting from the personal services, skills, industry, and efforts of either party during the contemplated marriage would be community property.

7. SEPARATE PROPERTY INTERESTS IN PREEXISTING RETIREMENT AND EMPLOYEE BENEFITS PLANS

7.1. Subject to the provisions of paragraph 3.9 above, John and Mary acknowledge that they each, independent of the other, presently own a substantial beneficial interest in various retirement plans, including, without limitation, a defined contribution pension plan as to John and a section 403(b) plan as to Mary. John and Mary acknowledge and agree that pursuant to the terms of this Agreement, all retirement benefits presently owned by or held for the benefit of John or Mary, together with any and all contributions, income, accumulations, appreciation, and increase of such retirement benefits during the parties' marriage because of John's or Mary's personal services, skills, industry, and efforts or otherwise, shall be and remain John's and Mary's separate property, and neither John nor Mary shall have any right, title, claim, or interest therein. The parties acknowledge their understanding that in the absence of this Agreement, contributions, income, accumulations, appreciation, and increase of retirement benefits attributable to John's and Mary's personal services, skills, industry, and efforts during the marriage would be community property.

8. RIGHTS UPON DEATH

8.1. Nothing contained herein shall constitute a waiver by either party of any bequest or devise that the other party may choose to make to him or her by will or codicil executed subsequent to this Agreement. However, the parties acknowledge that no promises of any kind whatsoever have been made by either of them about any such bequest or devise, except as may be set forth in this section.

8.2. John agrees to designate Mary as the sole beneficiary under a policy of life insurance to be acquired by him no later than September 1, 1998, with a death benefit of not less than $385,000.00. Such designation shall be deemed to be irrevocable as between John and Mary for so long as they are married and living together.

8.3. Upon John's death, provided the parties were still married and living together at the time of death, Mary shall be entitled to one hundred percent (100%) of John's "net estate" (as defined hereinbelow)—*provided, however*, that it is the intention of the parties to ensure that John's children (Marshall Doe, born 6/23/95, Marta Doe, born 9/26/97, share and share alike by right or representation in the event any of his children predecease John with living children of their own) shall receive not less than fifty percent (50%) of the value of the sum of (1) John's net estate, plus (2) all benefits payable to any beneficiary pursuant to any policy(ies) of life insurance of John's life in effect at the time of John's death. Item number 2 shall not include any death benefits that have already been included in John's net estate. The parties understand and agree that this instant provision is intended to operate as a third-party beneficiary contract for the benefit of said children, *provided, however*, that nothing contained herein shall operate to limit John's right to modify his children's rights created hereunder by operation of a document (testamentary or otherwise) executed subsequent hereto. If for any reason whatsoever, John's children do not receive their intended share as defined herein as set forth in items (1) and (2) herein, then an adjustment shall be made as to the amount payable so that the children, as a group, will receive the same amount as Mary.

By way of example only, notwithstanding anything to the contrary set forth in this Agreement, if, upon John's death, his net estate is zero and the only policy of life insurance in effect on his life is the policy discussed in paragraph 8.2 above, then John's children shall be entitled to receive (as above) and Mary agrees to pay them the sum of $192,500 (i.e., fifty percent (50%) of the death benefit payable pursuant to said insurance policy).

Similarly, by way of a second example, if upon John's death his net estate is valued at $400,000, exclusive of any life insurance death benefits in his net estate, and in addition, there are in effect two (2) policies of life insurance on John's life, to wit, the policy referenced in paragraph 8.2 above and a policy with a $500,000 death benefit payable to his children, then his children would be entitled to receive from all sources the sum of $642,500. Inasmuch as his net estate is, for purposes of this example, valued at $400,000, then under this example John's children would receive $142,500 therefrom (so as to bring their actual cash received from all sources to $642,500 [$500,000 in insurance proceeds plus $142,500 from the estate]) and Mary would receive the balance of the net estate (i.e., $257,500) in addition to the insurance benefits referenced in paragraph 8.2 above.

For purposes of this provision, the term "net estate" shall be defined as follows: as defined by the Internal Revenue Code and as reflected on Form 706 (of similar successor form) pertinent thereto; the term "net estate" shall also include any sums of money or assets payable directly or indirectly to either John's children (as defined hereinabove) or Mary upon John's death.

It is understood and agreed that the residence wherein the parties are residing at the time of John's death will not be sold against Mary's will (whether through probate or otherwise) so as to satisfy the claims of John's children hereunder. If, however, any other assets are available (in John's estate or otherwise) to so satisfy John's children's claims herein, then those assets shall be liquidated for the purpose of so satisfying the children's claims hereunder. If such assets do not exist, then John's children shall be paid from the proceeds of sale of the residence contemplated hereunder, or out of Mary's estate, or in any other manner not inconsistent herewith.

9. PROPERTY TRANSFERS BETWEEN PARTIES

9.1. The parties agree that nothing contained in this Agreement shall be construed as a bar to either party's transferring, conveying, devising, or bequeathing any property to the other. Neither party intends by this Agreement to limit or restrict in any way the right to receive any such transfer, conveyance, devise or bequest from the other made after the parties' marriage. However, the parties specifically agree that no promises of any kind have been made by either of them about any such gift, bequest, devise, conveyance, or transfer from one to the other, except as is set forth in this Agreement.

10. MANAGEMENT AND CONTROL OF SEPARATE PROPERTY INTERESTS; EXECUTING ARRAIGNMENTS

10.1. The parties agree that each shall retain and enjoy sole and exclusive management and control of his or her separate property, both during lifetime and upon death, as though unmarried. In order to accomplish the intent of this Agreement, each party agrees to execute, acknowledge, and deliver, at the request of the other, his or her heirs, executors, administrators, grantees, devisees, or assigns, any and all such deeds, releases, assignments, or other instruments (including, but not limited to, the retirement plan waiver and consent forms referred to in Article 7 of this

Agreement), and such further assurances as may be reasonably required or requested to effect or evidence the release, waiver, relinquishment, or extinguishment of the rights of the said party in the property, income or estate of the other under the provisions of this Agreement, and to assure that each party shall have sole and exclusive management and control of his or her separate property.

11. DEBT OBLIGATIONS ON SEPARATE PROPERTY INTERESTS

11.1. All obligations (including principal and interest) incurred due to or as a consequence of the purchase, encumbrance, or hypothecation of the separate property of either party, whether real, personal, or mixed, and all taxes, insurance premiums, and maintenance costs of said separate property, shall be paid from such party's separate property income or from such party's separate property funds, at such party's election. To the extent that either party uses his or her separate property to pay the foregoing obligations of the other party, there shall be no right to reimbursement for such expenditures.

12. UNSECURED DEBT RESPONSIBILITY

12.1. All unsecured obligations of each party, no matter when incurred, shall remain the sole and separate obligations of each such party, and each party shall indemnify and hold the other party harmless from liability therefor. Each party's unsecured obligations shall be paid from each respective party's separate property income or separate property funds, at such party's election. To the extent that either party uses his or her separate property to pay the unsecured obligations of the other party, there shall be no right to reimbursement for such expenditures.

13. DISCHARGE OF LIVING EXPENSES

13.1. The parties' joint living expenses shall be paid from a joint account to be established following the parties' marriage and to which each of the parties shall contribute such of their salaries from employment during marriage as they elect. The term "joint living expenses," as used in this paragraph, includes, but is not limited to: food; household supplies; utilities; telephone; laundry; cleaning; clothing; medical and dental expenses; medical, life, accident, and auto insurance; gasoline, oil, and auto repairs; automobile purchase and/or lease payments; entertainment; and joint gifts to third persons. The commingling of each party's separate property salaries in the aforesaid account shall not change the character of such salaries as the contributing party's separate property, and neither party shall acquire any right in the salary of the other by reason of such commingling.

14. SUPPORT LIABILITY

14.1. Nothing contained in this Agreement shall be construed as absolving either party of the statutory obligation to support the other during marriage or to effect in any way the obligation to support any children of the contemplated marriage. In the event of a separation or marriage dissolution, each party's obligation to support the other shall be determined and governed under the laws of the State of California.

15. FEDERAL AND STATE INCOME TAXES

15.1. During their marriage, the parties agree to file state and federal income taxes as follows:

a. The parties agree to file whatever state and federal income tax returns, or gift tax returns, or both, joint or separate, in order to minimize the combined total tax liabilities of the parties. If the parties decide that a joint return shall be filed, such return shall not constitute the creation of any community property or any other right or interest in contravention of this Agreement. Each party shall be responsible for and pay the taxes on his or her separate income and indemnify and hold the other party harmless therefrom.

b. If the parties file separate returns, each agrees to pay those taxes required by his or her separate return. Any taxes resulting from an audit or a claim from any taxing authority arising out of or in any way connected with the ownership or operation of the separate property of either party shall be paid by the party against whom such taxes are assessed from his or her separate property and the paying party shall hold the other harmless from any and all obligations pertaining thereto.

16. PARTIES AND PERSONS BOUND

16.1. This Agreement shall bind the parties to this Agreement, and their respective heirs, executors, administrators, representatives, assigns, and any other successors in interest.

17. VOLUNTARY ARM'S-LENGTH NEGOTIATIONS

17.1. The parties acknowledge and agree that this document is voluntarily entered into by and between them and that, as of the date of execution of the Agreement, there is no confidential or fiduciary relationship existing between them as defined under the laws of the State of California. The parties further acknowledge that they have had explained to each of them respectively, by their respective attorneys, the meaning of the terms "confidential relationship" and "fiduciary relationship." The parties specifically acknowledge that neither has ever offered business advice to the other, nor has either become dependant upon the other or relied upon the other for advice, and that their relationship as of the date of the execution of this Agreement is a purely personal relationship of two engaged individuals intending to be married to each other on August 22, 2012. Both parties specifically agree and understand that they are not acting under any pressure, duress, coercion, or influence of any kind whatsoever rising out of, pertinent to, or as a result of the presently pending and intended date of marriage, to wit, August 22, 2012.

18.   FORMALITIES OF EXECUTION

18.1. The parties specifically agree that forthwith upon their execution of this Agreement, their respective signature shall be acknowledged by a Notary Public in their presence. The parties further acknowledge that the date set forth on the first page of this Agreement is the actual date on which they and each of them are signing this Agreement. This Agreement or a memorandum of this Agreement may be recorded at any time and from time to time by either party in any place or office authorized by law for the recording of documents effecting title to or ownership status of property, real or personal, specifically including but not limited to any county in which either party resides during the marriage and any county in which either party owns or may own real or personal property.

19.   GOVERNING LAW

19.1. This Agreement is executed in the State of California and shall be subject to and interpreted under the laws of the State of California.

20.   ENTIRE AGREEMENT

20.1. This Agreement contains the entire understanding and agreement of the parties, and there have been no promises, representations, warranties, or undertakings by either party to the other, oral or written, of any character or nature, except as set forth herein.

21.   MODIFICATION/REVOCATION

21.1. This Agreement may be altered, amended, modified, or revoked only by an instrument in writing expressly referring to this Agreement, executed, signed, and acknowledged by the parties hereto, and by no other means. Each of the parties waives the right to claim, contend, or assert in the future that this Agreement was modified, canceled, superseded, or changed by an oral agreement, course of conduct, or estoppel.

22. INVALIDITY/SEVERABILITY

22.1. This Agreement has been prepared and negotiated by counsel for each of the parties and shall not be construed against either party. If any term, provision, or condition of this Agreement is held by a court of competent jurisdiction to be invalid, void, or unenforceable, the remainder of the provisions shall remain in full force and effect and shall in no way be affected, impaired, or invalidated.

23. CAPTIONS

23.1. The captions of the various paragraphs of this Agreement are for convenience only, and none of them is intended to be any part of the text of this Agreement, nor intended to be referred to in construing any of the provisions of it.

24. EXECUTION OF COUNTERPARTS

24.1. This Agreement shall be executed in four counterparts, any of which shall be deemed to be an original.

25. ATTORNEY'S FEES

25.1. Should it become necessary for either party to interpret or enforce the terms of this Agreement, whether by judicial or alternative (e.g., arbitration) dispute resolution, the prevailing party therein shall be entitled to their attorney's fees and costs incurred therein.

IN WITNESS WHEREOF, the parties have executed this Agreement on the day and year first above written.

_____   _____

JOHN DOE   MARY ROE

<u>ATTORNEY CERTIFICATION</u>

The undersigned hereby certifies that he is an attorney at law duly licensed and admitted to practice in the State of California; he has been employed by and compensated by John Doe, one of the parties to the foregoing Agreement; he has advised and consulted with John Doe in connection with his property rights and has fully explained to him the legal effect of the foregoing Agreement and the effect which it has upon his rights otherwise obtaining as a matter of law; John Doe, after being duly advised by the undersigned, acknowledged to the undersigned that he understood the legal effect of the foregoing Agreement; and John Doe executed the same freely and voluntarily in the presence of the undersigned.

Dated: _____ , 2011   _____

                                              MARSHALL W. WALLER

ATTORNEY CERTIFICATION

The undersigned hereby certifies that he is an attorney at law duly licensed and admitted to practice in the State of California; that he has been employed by and compensated by Mary Roe, one of the parties to the foregoing Agreement; that he has advised and consulted with Mary Roe in connection with her property rights and has fully explained to her the legal effect of the foregoing Agreement and the effect which it has upon her rights otherwise obtaining as a matter of law; that Mary Roe, after being duly advised by the undersigned, acknowledged to the undersigned that she understood the legal effect of the foregoing Agreement; and Mary Roe executed the same freely and voluntarily in the presence of the undersigned.

Dated: _____ , 2011   _____

                                              IMA GUD ATTORNEY

ACKNOWLEDGMENT OF DISCLOSURE OF ASSETS, LIABILITIES, AND OBLIGATIONS

This Acknowledgement of Disclosure is entered into this _____ day of June 2010, by and between, John Doe, hereinafter referred to as "John" and Mary Roe, hereinafter referred to as "Mary," sometimes collectively referred to herein as "the parties."

1. The parties hereto understand and acknowledge that they are contemplating marriage, specifically, it is intended that said marriage will take place between them on August 22, 2012.

2. In the context of that contemplated marriage, the parties hereto are contemplating entering into a Premarital Agreement, which agreement shall, by its terms, significantly alter the property rights of the parties otherwise obtainable pursuant to operation of law.

3. In the context of this pending marriage, as well as the execution of the Premarital Agreement referenced herein, the parties hereto have engaged in a full, complete, fair, and reasonable disclosure of the property

and/or financial obligations of the other party, and in that regard the parties hereto certify that we voluntarily and expressly waive, in writing, any right to disclosure of the property and/or financial obligations of the other party beyond the disclosure provided. The parties hereto further certify that we have had, or reasonably could have had, an adequate knowledge of the property or financial obligations of the other party, and in that regard, each party hereto expressly acknowledges and certifies that they are satisfied with the disclosure provided to date and have wither undertaken such independent investigation as we deem necessary and advisable, or have voluntarily chosen not to do so.

4. The parties further acknowledge that this instant certification of disclosure, and the legal effects and ramifications thereof have been fully and completely explained to them by their own separate and independent legal counsel, of their own choosing; to wit, Marshall W. Waller, Esq., acting as legal counsel for John Doe, and Ima Gud Attorney, Esq., acting as legal counsel for Mary Roe.

WITNESS, our signatures on the date and year first above written.

_____   _____

JOHN DOE   MARY ROE

In the context of premarital agreements, California has seen some significant changes to the law. Historically, prenuptial agreements were the subject of strict scrutiny as to fairness, and courts continue their careful examination today. Yet, in the past, courts were somewhat "undecided" on the propriety of spousal support waivers. Traditionally, courts did not enforce spousal support waivers because they were thought to violate public policy by promoting divorce. This has changed. To date, there is authority for the enforceability of spousal support waivers, and it is this author's opinion that such waivers will continue to be enforced. ,

The California Supreme Court has issued two very important decisions in this area. The first is *In re* Marriage of Bonds, 24 Cal. 4th 1 (2000). In *Bonds*, Wife tried to set aside the premarital agreement, in which she waived her community property rights. The trial court upheld the validity of the agreement, finding that Wife did not meet her burden to show that she did not voluntarily sign the agreement. The court of appeal reversed after determining that the agreement was subject to strict scrutiny because Wife not been represented by an attorney. The California Supreme Court reversed the court of appeal on the issue of voluntariness. Specifically, the State Supreme Court held that the court of appeal erred in holding that premarital agreements are subject to strict scrutiny where the less sophisticated party did not have independent counsel and did not waive counsel according to exacting waiver requirements. Such a holding was found to be inconsistent with Family Code section 1615, which governs the enforceability of premarital agreements. That statute provides that a premarital agreement will be enforced unless the party resisting enforcement can demonstrate that: (1) he or she did not enter into the contract voluntarily, or (2) the contract was unconscionable when entered into and he or she did not have actual or constructive knowledge of the assets and obligations of the other party and did not voluntarily waive knowledge of such assets and obligations. The California Supreme Court also held that substantial evidence supported the trial court's finding that Wife voluntarily entered into the agreement. Finally, the court stated that considerations applicable to commercial contracts do not necessarily govern the determination whether a premarital agreement was entered into voluntarily, and a premarital agreement is not to be interpreted and enforced under the same standards applicable to marital settlement agreements, or in pursuit of the policy favoring equal division of assets on dissolution.

Basically, *Bonds* stands for the proposition that if the parties made full disclosure of their assets, the court need not examine the agreement for unconscionability. The *Bonds* court was fundamentally concerned with whether or not Mrs. Bonds entered the agreement voluntarily, and its opinion is limited to the facts of the case. The court focused its inquiry on the following factors: (1) the amount of time that elapsed between the date that the agreement was presented and the date of marriage (in *Bonds*, one day), (2) whether the parties were (or could have been) surprised by the agreement (Mrs. Bonds was not), (3) whether each party had the opportunity to obtain counsel (Mrs. Bonds did), (4) the relative bargaining power of the parties, (5) whether each party fully disclosed his or her assets and liabilities to the other, (6) the extent to which the parties were aware of the terms of the agreement prior to its execution, (7) whether or not a confidential relationship existed between the parties (this would be likely if the parties had been living together at the time they signed the agreemen), and (8) other factors related to potential embarrassment of the parties.

Another important case in the area of premarital agreements is *In re Marriage of Pendleton and Fireman*, 24 Cal. 4th 39 (2000), decided the same day as *Bonds*. When drafting a premarital agreement, it is important for attorneys to establish a basis on which a waiver of spousal support is made that is consistent with the *Pendleton* court's reasoning. In *Pendleton*, the trial court ruled that the parties' premarital agreement, in which both parties waived spousal support, was unenforceable as against public policy. The court awarded the wife substantial spousal support. The court of appeal reversed and the California Supreme Court affirmed. The state supreme court held that the trial court erred in ruling that the parties' waiver of spousal support was unenforceable as against public policy. The court found that the common law policy was anachronistic; specifically, the court thought that it was outdated to assume that dissolutions of marriage are contrary to public policy and premarital waivers of spousal support may promote dissolution. The court held that when entered into voluntarily by parties who are aware of the effect of the agreement, a premarital waiver of spousal support does not offend contemporary public policy. Such agreements are, therefore, permitted under Family Code section 1612(a)(7), which authorizes the parties to contract in a premarital agreement regarding any matter, including their personal rights and obligations, that does not violate public policy or a statute imposing a criminal penalty. In *Pendleton*, the California Supreme Court held that no public policy is violated by permitting enforcement of a waiver of spousal support executed by intelligent, well-educated persons, each of whom is self-sufficient in property and earning ability, and both of whom had the advice of counsel regarding their rights and obligations as marital partners at the time of execution. The court further opined that permanency is no longer a dominant characteristic of marriage; thus, permanency should no longer be the standard by which factors are evaluated as promoting divorce.[15]

Sample Marital Settlement Agreement:

MARITAL SETTLEMENT AGREEMENT

THIS AGREEMENT is entered into as of this _____ day of _____ , 20 _____ , by and between JOHN DOE (hereinafter referred to as "Husband") and MARY DOE (hereinafter referred to as "Wife"), for the purposes and under the terms and conditions herein set forth.

1.   RECITALS

1.1 The parties were married on June 23, 2001, and ever since that time have been and now are Husband and Wife.

1.2 Irreconcilable differences have arisen and have led to the irremediable breakdown of the marriage, and there is no possibility of saving the marriage through counseling or other means and as a result thereof, the parties have lived separate and apart since June 30, 2008.

1.3 The minor child of the parties is: John Doe, Jr., born March 16, 2004.

1.4 Husband is currently employed by ABC Industries and has an approximate gross income from all sources of $7,500 per month. Husband currently has expenses of approximately $6,800 per month. Wife is currently employed by XYZ Development Corporation and has a gross income from all sources of approximately $3,500 per month. Wife currently has expenses of approximately $3,600 per month. The agreements set forth herein with respect to support are based on the circumstances set forth in this provision.

1.5 A proceeding for dissolution of marriage of the parties is now pending in the Superior Court of the County of Los Angeles, State of California, Case number BD 123 456, wherein Husband is the Petitioner and Wife is the Respondent.

2. PURPOSE OF AGREEMENT

2.1 The purposes of this Agreement are to effect a complete and final settlement with reference to each of the following:

a. The respective property rights of the parties.

b. The obligations of each party for the support of the other.

c. All past, present and future claims of any kind one party may have against the other, except as otherwise provided.

2.2 Provisions for payment an assumption of any debts and obligations.

2.3 The obligations of each party for the support, maintenance, custody and visitation of the minor child of the parties.

3. DIVISION OF PROPERTY

3.1 The parties agree that the items set forth in *Exhibit "A,"* attached hereto and by this reference made a part hereof, lists all of the separate and community property assets and liabilities of which Husband and Wife are now possessed. In order to achieve an equal and equitable division of the community property and liabilities, said items shall be distributed as follows:

(a) *TO HUSBAND:* Each and all of the items listed on *Exhibit "B,"* attached hereto and by this reference made a part hereof.

(b) *TO WIFE:* Each and all of the items listed on *Exhibit "C,"* attached hereto and by this reference made a part hereof.

3.2 Husband, except as otherwise provided by this Agreement, including any exhibits thereto, hereby transfers, assigns and conveys to Wife, as her sole and separate property, any and all right, title, interest, claim and/ or demand, which he has or may have or claim as her Husband or otherwise and does hereby waive any and all rights in or to each item of property and property interest set forth in *Exhibit "C,"* attached hereto.

3.3 Wife, except as otherwise provided by this Agreement, including any exhibits thereto, hereby transfers, assigns and conveys to Husband, as his sole and separate property, any and all right, title, interest, claim and/ or demand, which she has or may have or claim as his Wife or otherwise and does hereby waive any and all rights in or to each item of property and property interest set forth in *Exhibit "B,"* attached hereto.

3.4 All property transferred hereunder is transferred subject to all existing encumbrances and liens thereon. The transferee of such property agrees to indemnify and save harmless the other party from any claim or liability that the other party may suffer or may be required to pay on account of such encumbrances or liens.

3.5 The parties hereby agree to indemnify and save harmless each other from any and all liabilities and obligations assumed hereunder.

3.6 Each party has made a full disclosure to the other of his or her finances and assets as related to this proceeding, and each party hereto enters into this Agreement in reliance thereon. It is further understood and agreed by the parties hereto that neither Husband nor Wife have made any representations as to the value of any of the assets involved herein, and it is further understood and agreed that each party hereto is relying upon their own understanding and investigation with respect to such values. Furthermore, by executing this document, each party hereto warrants and represents to the other that they have been advised to so investigate the values of said assets and have satisfied themselves as to the results of said investigation.

3.7 Husband and Wife agree that each shall henceforth own and hold the property received by him or her, respectively, by the terms hereof, and likewise all salaries, earnings and other property hereafter acquired by each of them and acquired after the aforesaid date of separation respectively, as his or her sole and separate property, as the case may be, free from any claim of the other (except as specifically provided for herein) or of any creditor of the other by reason of the community property laws of the State of California, or by reason of any other law or fact.

3.8 The parties agree that the division of the parties' community property as set forth in Exhibits "B" and "C" includes the settlement of all reimbursement claims.

3.9 Husband, (hereinafter referred to as the "nonemployee spouse") specifically acknowledges and agrees that the employee spouse (in this case, Wife) may work past the first date that he or she is eligible to retire, that the employee spouse has unilateral control over the date that the nonemployee spouse's pension benefits begin, and that the employee spouse is not required to pay the nonemployee spouse his or her share of the pension payments until actual retirement. The nonemployee spouse further acknowledges that he or she has given up the right to receive the pension benefits (or their equivalent) until actual retirement of the employee spouse in exchange for valuable consideration, represented by the overall terms and conditions of this instant Marital Settlement Agreement.

4. ALLOCATION OF DEBTS

4.1 Basic Allocation. Each party shall be responsible for paying any and all obligations (whether known or unknown to either party) secured by property received by the party under the terms of this Agreement. Those debts, obligations, and liabilities known to both parties and incurred prior to the Separation Date (and not otherwise specifically assigned to a party under this Agreement), shall be the equal obligation of the parties. The court shall retain jurisdiction over any debt or claim against the parties, unknown to one or both parties and incurred prior to the Separation Date, unless the responsibility for the debt or claim has been specifically assigned to a party under this Agreement. Debts, known or unknown, incurred after the Separation Date shall be paid by the party incurring the debt.

4.2. Credit Card Accounts. All existing charge and credit accounts in the name of Husband and Wife, or in the name of either party, under which the other can make purchases or secure credit, shall immediately be closed or changed to the name of the party retaining that account without recourse against the other party. Any outstanding indebtedness on these accounts, not otherwise specifically scheduled to be paid by one party, shall be paid by the party incurring the debt, notwithstanding the general allocation of debts provided above.

4.3. Claims of Third Parties. Except as set forth in this Agreement, each party warrants that he or she has not incurred, and each agrees not to incur, any liability or obligation on which the other may be liable. Each party agrees that if any claim, action, or proceeding shall be brought seeking to hold the other liable on account of any such liability, obligation, act, or omission (other than those incurred for the support and maintenance of a party or a minor child for which a party is liable under this Agreement or under any order of a court of competent jurisdiction), the obligated party shall, at his or her sole expense, defend the other party against any such claim, liability, or obligation (whether or not well founded) and shall hold the other party free and harmless from it. This indemnification shall include any costs, including attorney's fees, reasonably incurred by the other party in defending any claim made against him or her. The parties acknowledge that they understand that any provisions of this Agreement requiring one party to assume the obligation of the community or post-separation debts of the other party may not be binding on creditors and that a creditor may have rights to seek payment against either party. The parties further acknowledge that they understand that their obligations to each other, and to third-party creditors, are subject to possible discharge in bankruptcy.

5. EQUALIZING PAYMENT

5.1 To equalize the division of community property, Husband shall pay to Wife the sum of $35,000 within thirty (30) days of execution by all parties of this agreement and the Judgment herein.

6.   PROPERTY WARRANTIES

6.1 Each of us hereby warrants to the other that neither of us is now possessed of or has any interest in any community property of any kind or description whatsoever, other than specifically listed in this Agreement and/or disclosed to the other party. If it shall hereafter be determined that one of us has an interest in an item of property which is determined to be community property, not set forth herein or otherwise disclosed to the other party, the warrantor agrees to give the other party, at the other's election, either one-half (1/2) of the fair market value of the warrantee's interest in said property, as of the date of this Agreement, or a one-half (1/2) interest in such community property. This Agreement shall not impair the availability of any other remedy.

7.   SPOUSAL SUPPORT

7.1 Having regard for the circumstances, health, employment history, education, achievements and/or abilities of the parties, together with the fact that both Husband and Wife are currently employed, Husband will pay to Wife for spousal support the sum of $643 per month, payable in advance, on or before the first day of each month for a period of 4 years (48 months), commencing January 1, 2008 and continuing until the death or remarriage of Wife, December 1, 2012 (the 48th payment being due at that time) or further order of court, whichever occurs first. Neither the amount nor the duration of spousal support is modifiable under any circumstances. No court will have jurisdiction to modify the amount of support or to extend the duration of support beyond the termination date specified above.

7.2 The court will have no jurisdiction of any kind to modify or extend its jurisdiction beyond the 48 month period ending December 1, 2012. As regards the issue of extension/modification of spousal support, the parties waive their rights under *Marriage of Vomaka*, 36 Cal. 3d 459, 204 Cal. Rptr. 568 (1984), and *Marriage of Jones*, 222 C.A.3d 505, 271 Cal. Rptr. 761 (1990).

7.3 Husband and Wife have carefully bargained in this agreement concerning all issues relating to their support, including the amount of spousal support, its duration, and whether or not it should be extendible. The December 1, 2012 termination date concerning spousal support specified in this agreement is absolute. As of December 1, 2012, this agreement cuts off forever: the right of either party to ask for support payments, the power of the court to order support payments, and the right of the other to receive support payments. No court has jurisdiction to extend or order any payments (except arrears) beyond that date. Counsel has advised the parties that this clause may work great and unexpected hardship on one or both of the parties, and the parties have considered that possibility in electing to fix a specific date after which there will remain no spousal support obligation.

8. CUSTODY AND VISITATION

8.1 The parties have carefully considered the question of custody of the minor child, JOHN DOE, JR., and being desirous of achieving a harmonious policy calculated to promote the best interest of the minor child, the parties agree that the legal custody of the minor child, John Doe, Jr., born March 16, 2004, shall be held jointly.

8.2 Subject to further agreement of the parties and/or further order of any court of competent jurisdiction, it is the parties' present intention that John Doe, Jr. shall reside with Wife, subject to Husband's rights of secondary custody as follows:

a. Alternating weekends from 6:00 p.m. Friday to 7:00 p.m. Sunday, commencing January 1, 2009, and continuing thereafter;

b. One mid-week overnight visit, from 6:00 p.m. to 9:00 a.m. the following morning. It is understood that the exercise of this option "b" is Husband's option, and that should he be so inclined he must first give not less than 48 hours notice of his intention to so exercise to Wife.

c. Holiday visitation as follows:

Holiday/Special Day	Odd Numbered Year	Even Numbered Year
Presidents' Day	Mother	Father
Easter Sunday	Father	Mother
Memorial Day	Mother	Father
July 4th	Father	Mother
Labor Day	Mother	Father
Veterans' Day	Father	Mother
Thanksgiving Day (4-day holiday)	Mother	Father
Christmas Day	Father	Mother
New Year's Day	Mother	Father
Child's Birthday (3/16)	Father	Mother
Mother's Day	Mother	Mother
Father's Day	Father	Father
Mother's Birthday (3/20)	Mother	Mother
Father's Birthday (6/23)	Father	Father

d. Husband shall be entitled to reasonable telephonic contact with the minor child between the hours of 8:00 a.m. to 8:00 p.m.

e. Two uninterrupted weeks in the summer time as per notice given by Husband no later than June 1.

8.3 Parental Cooperation. The parties recognize that frequent and continuing association between themselves and their children is in the best interests of the children, and they will work cooperatively toward that end. The parties agree to make reasonable efforts to foster a good relationship between the children and the other parent, which shall include honoring the other parent's privacy and authority. The parties shall consult with each other on matters materially affecting the education and welfare of the children, taking into account the best interests of the children, and where possible, the children's desires.

8.4 Access to Information and Records. Important information concerning the children, including medical condition, educational training, extracurricular activities, and moral and religious training shall be shared by the parents. Any significant change in the health, well-being, medical treatment (especially medical emergencies), or educational progress of the children, or any significant educational or other event, known to one parent shall be promptly communicated to the other parent. School notices sent to only one parent shall be copied by that parent and promptly sent to the other. School notices, as used in the preceding sentence, shall mean grade or performance reports, notices of parent-teacher conferences, disciplinary notices, and notices of other activities in which the other parent might normally participate. Upon request, each party shall execute any required authorization for the other party to obtain information concerning the health, welfare, and education of the children. The parties shall also share any other information concerning the children that would be reasonable to share.

8.5 Communication with Children. Each party shall have the right to communicate with the children while they are with the other party. This communication shall be reasonable, but otherwise without restrictions unless agreed to by the parties. Specifically, the children shall be allowed reasonable and private communication by telephone with a parent when they are absent from that parent.

8.6. Notice of Change of Address or Telephone. During any period a child is with a parent, that parent shall notify the other parent within forty-eight (48) hours of any change of address or telephone number of the child for any period that will exceed seven (7) days.

8.7 Relocation of Residence. Except by prior court order, Wife shall not relocate the residence of the minor children outside of the State of California without prior written notice to Husband. Notice shall be provided as soon as Wife becomes aware of the need to relocate, but in no event later than sixty (60) days prior to the proposed move. Except by prior court order, Husband shall not relocate his residence outside of the State of California without prior written notice to Wife. Notice shall be provided as soon as Husband becomes aware of the need to relocate, but in no event later than sixty (60) days prior to the proposed move.

9. CHILD SUPPORT

9.1 Having given extensive consideration to the parties' needs and abilities, coupled with the contemplated residence of the minor child, the parties agree that as and for child support, Husband shall pay to Wife the sum of Nine Hundred Twenty-Three ($923) dollars per month per child, for a total of Nine Hundred Twenty-Three ($923) dollars per month, payable one-half on the first and one-half on the fifteenth of each month, commencing January 1, 2009, and continuing thereafter as to each child until the child dies, reaches the age of majority (i.e., eighteen (18) years of age), becomes self-supporting, is no longer residing with Wife, marries, becomes otherwise emancipated, or until further order of court.

9.2 The parties further agree that all medical, dental and/or hospital (i.e., health care) expenses and/or related insurance deductions for the minor child, not otherwise covered by medical, dental and/or hospitalization (i.e., health care) insurance, provided to Husband, Wife, and/or the minor child, shall be divided equally by and between the parties.

9.3 Husband and Wife shall equally divide all extraordinary medical, dental and orthodontic expenses incurred for the benefit of the minor child, and not otherwise covered by medical (i.e., health) insurance provided to Husband, Wife, and/or the minor child. Husband shall be consulted concerning any expenditures except for when the expenditure arises out of an emergency and except those medical expenses that are covered by insurance. For the purposes of this paragraph, extraordinary expenses shall be defined as an aggregate medical bill of One Hundred Dollars ($100.00) or more resulting from any single occurrence or illness.

9.4 The parent having actual control (i.e., custody of or visitation with) of the minor child, when an emergency arises requiring immediate professional care, shall have authority to obtain that care without the consent of the other. The parent having control shall try to contact the other as quickly as possible, shall put the other in touch with all providers of care, and shall take the other party's suggestions into account in supervising the emergency. As soon as it is possible to restore joint decision-making, the parties shall do so. To be sure that the parties' intentions are clearly understood by others in the future, the parties shall sign separate authorizations for emergency care, of unlimited duration, and shall provide them to the other. The parties shall also sign other such institutional forms in the future and send copies to the other party.

9.5 Husband and Wife shall cooperate with each other in tendering medical bills or other insurance claims reasonably necessary to provide payment for the above-referenced insurance benefits covering the minor child.

9.6 Stay of Wage Assignment. The parties agree that Husband has consistently met the court-ordered support obligations in a timely manner and that no wage assignment is currently necessary to assure the continued timely performance of child support. In making its orders regarding support, the parties agree that there is good cause for the court to stay the service of the wage assignment to be issued pursuant to Family Code section 5260. For purposes of any support payment due under this Agreement, a payment made within five (5) days after the date it is due shall be considered timely. Husband understands that, in the event the child support obligations are not timely paid, Wife may, by filing a declaration under penalty of perjury attesting that Husband is in arrears in such payments, cause this stay to terminate. At the time the declaration is filed, the stay will automatically terminate and a wage assignment shall be served upon Husband's employer without notice to Husband. Husband shall notify Wife, within forty-eight (48) hours, of any change in employment. This notice shall include the name, address, and telephone number of the new employer.

9.7 Exchange of Income Information. Each party shall exchange income information by delivering to the other party a statement of his or her year-to-date income from all sources, and reasonable documentation to support the statement (including federal and state tax returns when filed). The statement shall be made quarterly not more than fifteen (15) days after the information and documentation is available. Within fifteen (15) days of a request, copies of all W-2s, 1099s, K-1s, and other reasonably necessary forms and data received by a party reflecting the prior period's income, which has not been previously provided, shall also be delivered to the party requesting them. The obligation to exchange income data shall terminate when there is no further jurisdiction of the court over child support.

10. RECONCILIATION

10.1 Should a reconciliation be effected, at such time, each party shall maintain his or her separate property, held by them, at the time, in their respective names as separate property and shall maintain bank accounts as his or her separate property. Neither shall commingle any such property, recognizing that if they do it may be deemed to be community property.

10.2 In the event of a reconciliation, this Agreement shall continue in full force and effect until modified, altered, or terminated by an agreement in writing to such effect, signed by each of us; and if such reconciliation fails, this Agreement and/or the provisions of the Judgment shall remain in full force and effect.

11. LEGAL REPRESENTATION

11.1 The parties hereto acknowledge and agree that each party has been represented by and/or consulted with legal counsel, of their own choosing, or have had an opportunity to be so represented in the negotiation and preparation of this Agreement; Husband has been represented by Mary Ellen Fisenne, Esq., and Wife has been represented by Marshall W. Waller, Esq., of Feinberg & Waller; each party has read the Agreement and has had an opportunity to have it explained to him or her; each party understands and is satisfied with its provisions and its legal effect; that this Agreement is made and entered into freely and voluntarily by both parties, free from any duress, menace, fraud or undue influence of any kind, character or nature upon the part of the other; and that it will be legally binding when signed by both of the parties.

12. ATTORNEY'S FEES AND COSTS

12.1 Neither party shall be liable to the other party nor his or her attorney(s) for any costs or legal fees whatsoever, incurred by the other in connection with the negotiation, preparation and execution of this Agreement and/or in connection with any action brought by any party for the purpose of obtaining a judgment of dissolution of marriage of the parties.

12.2 In the event of any default by Husband of any of the provisions of this Agreement, or of any court order, decree or judgment made pursuant to this Agreement or relating thereto or arising out of the subject matter of this Agreement, Wife shall be entitled to reasonable attorney's fees and other costs necessarily incurred by her in prosecuting any action or proceeding against Husband by reason hereof.

12.3 In the event of any default by Wife of any of the provisions of this Agreement, or of any Court order, decree or judgment made pursuant to this Agreement or relating thereto or arising out of the subject matter of this Agreement, Husband shall be entitled to reasonable attorney's fees and other costs necessarily incurred by him in prosecuting any action or proceeding against Wife by reason hereof.

12.4 If either party shall bring any action or proceeding relating to or arising out of the subject matter of this Agreement, the court in that action or proceeding shall have the power against either party to make whatever order it deems proper under all of the circumstances then present for attorney's fees and other reasonably necessary costs and shall defend, indemnify, and hold the other harmless therefrom including legal fees.

12.5 The arrangement for attorney's fees and costs specified in this agreement does not preclude either party, when it is appropriate, from seeking additional attorney's fees in the nature of a sanction from the other party under Family Code section 271 (or similar legislation).

13. RIGHTS AND MUTUAL COVENANTS

13.1 Except as otherwise provided in this Agreement, each party to this Agreement does hereby release the other from any and all liabilities, debts or obligations, of any kind or character, heretofore or hereafter incurred, and from any and all claims and demands, it being understood that this Agreement is intended to completely and fully settle all of the rights and duties of the parties in all respects.

13.2 Husband hereby warrants to Wife that he has not incurred, since the date of separation, and hereby covenants that he will not hereafter incur, any liability or obligation for which she is or will be liable. Husband hereby covenants and agrees that if any claim or action or proceeding shall hereafter be brought seeking to hold Wife liable on account of any debt, liability, act or omission of Husband (incurred subsequent to the date of separation) he will, at his sole expense, defend Wife against any such claim or demand (whether or not well founded) and that he will hold her free and harmless therefrom.

13.3 Wife hereby warrants to Husband that she has not incurred, since the date of separation, and hereby covenants that she will not hereafter incur, any liability or obligation for which he is or will be liable. Wife hereby covenants and agrees that if any claim or action or proceeding shall hereafter be brought seeking to hold Husband liable on account of any debt, liability, act or omission of Wife (incurred subsequent to the date of separation) she will, at her sole expense, defend Husband against any such claim or demand (whether or not well founded) and that she will hold him free and harmless therefrom.

13.4 All existing charge accounts and credit cards in the names of the Husband and Wife or in the name of either of them under which the other can make purchases, shall be allocated to the sole and exclusive use of the party receiving the assignment of debt thereon as set forth in *Exhibits B and C* hereto, and the other's right to use a card not so allocated to him/herself shall be terminated as of the date of execution of this Agreement and each party shall be solely responsible hereafter for any charges said party incurs on any joint credit card or charge account.

13.5 Each of the parties also releases the other and the other's heirs, representatives, successors and assigns of and from any and all other claims, demands, costs, expenses, liabilities, actions and causes of action based on, arising out of, or in connection with any matter, fact or theory occurring prior to the execution of this Agreement, except that nothing herein contained shall relieve or discharge either of the parties of or from any of his or her obligations under this agreement. Each of the parties agrees and understands that there is a risk that subsequent to the execution of this agreement either of them may incur or suffer loss, damage or injuries which are in some way caused by, or related to, the matters referred to above in this section, and which are unknown or unanticipated at the time of execution of this agreement. Each party hereby assumes said risk and the general releases contained herein shall apply to all unknown and unanticipated results, as well as those known and anticipated. Upon advice of their respective counsel, husband and wife each hereby waive all rights under California Civil Code, section 1542, which section reads as follows:

> SECTION 1542. GENERAL RELEASE. A GENERAL RELEASE DOES NOT EXTEND TO CLAIMS WHICH THE CREDITOR DOES NOT KNOW OR SUSPECT TO EXIST IN HIS FAVOR AT THE TIME OF EXECUTING THE RELEASE, WHICH IF KNOWN BY HIM WOULD MATERIALLY AFFECT HIS SETTLEMENT WITH THE DEBTOR.

13.6 The parties agree that from and after the date of separation, the earnings and accumulations thereafter accruing to or received by either of them and any and all property of any kind or description thereafter acquired by either of them shall be the sole and separate property of the one so acquiring it, and each party waives any and all property rights in or to such future earnings, income or acquisitions of property, and hereby grants the other all such future earnings, income and acquisitions of property as the sole and separate property of the one so acquiring same.

13.7 Husband further acknowledges that; (a) all negotiations leading to this agreement were carried on at arm's length; (b) the confidential relationship arising out of the marriage of the parties did not exist during such negotiations; and (c) his interests and Wife's interests were adverse during such negotiation.

13.8 Wife further acknowledges that: (a) all negotiations leading to this agreement were carried on at arm's length; (b) the confidential relationship arising out of the marriage of the parties did not exist during such negotiations; and (c) her interests and Husband's interests were adverse during such negotiation.

14. WAIVER OF RIGHTS

14.1 Each party hereby waives the right to receive any property or rights whatsoever on the death of the other, unless such right is created or affirmed by the other under a last will and testament or other written document executed after the effective date of this agreement. Each party acknowledges that he or she received a fair and reasonable disclosure of the property and the fiscal obligations of the other party before signing this agreement, and each party was represented by independent legal counsel at the time he or she signed this agreement. Each party's waiver of rights under this provision is entered into freely, voluntarily, and with full knowledge of the value of what each party is waiving, and constitutes an effective and binding waiver of that party's rights under Probate Code sections 140-147.

The rights waived include, but are not limited to, rights to any of the following:

(a) Property that would pass from the decedent by intestate succession;

(b) Property that would pass from the decedent by testamentary disposition;

(c) A probate homestead;

(d) The setting aside of exempt property;

(e) A family allowance;

(f) The setting aside of an estate;

(g) An election to take community or quasi-community property against the decedent's will;

(h) The statutory share of an omitted spouse;

(i) An appointment as executor or administrator of the decedent's estate, except as the nominee of a third party legally entitled to make such a nomination;

(j) Property that would pass from the decedent by nonprobate transfer, such as the survivorship interest under a joint tenancy, a Totten trust account, or a payable-on-death account;

15. TAX MATTERS

15.1 The parties recognize that the allocation between them of the responsibility for the payment of taxes on joint income tax returns (as set forth in this Agreement) is not binding on the Internal Revenue Service, the Franchise Tax Board (unless a tax clearance certificate under Revenue and Taxation Code section 19006 has previously been issued), or any other taxing authority. The parties are aware that if either party fails to pay the taxes for which he or she is responsible, the law may give the taxing authority power to collect these taxes from the other party.

15.2 If the anticipated deductibility, taxability, or tax allocation of any item in this Agreement is not accepted by a taxing authority, the party benefiting from that determination, to the extent of any benefit, shall indemnify and hold harmless the other party from all expenses and liabilities, including deficiencies, interest, penalties, and professional fees. If, however, the action by the taxing authority results from the indemnifying party's taking a position inconsistent with this Agreement, the indemnification in the preceding sentence shall not be limited to the benefit enjoyed. The parties shall report all income, losses, and deductions (or other taxable consequence) to the appropriate taxing authorities in a manner consistent with this Agreement. A party responsible for payment of taxes or filing a return who fails to perform those responsibilities or comply with the tax provisions of this Agreement shall indemnify and hold harmless the other party form all liabilities and expenses so incurred, including, without limitation, all deficiencies, interest, penalties, and professional fees. Each party also shall be solely responsible for, and shall indemnify and hold harmless the other party from, all such liabilities and expenses associated with his or her failure to report any separate property income or improper deductions claimed with respect to periods after the Separation Date. The parties agree that any indemnification payment from one party to the other, with respect to taxes, shall be deemed a tax-free interspousal transfer related to the cessation of marriage to effect a division of marital property under Internal Revenue Code section 1041 and comparable provisions of state law, regardless of the date on which payment is made. The court shall reserve jurisdiction to enforce the allocations set forth in this Agreement, including, without limitation, granting to either party a security interest in the property of the party who is responsible for the unpaid taxes.

15.3 The payments from Husband of child support set forth in Section 6.1 are tax free to Wife and are not deductible to Husband for federal or state income tax purposes. Current law does not allow for a deduction of child support from income.

15.4 Husband shall be entitled to claim the minor children of the parties as dependents on federal and state income returns filed hereafter. A party releasing an exemption to the other shall promptly execute, upon the other party's request, any documents necessary to confirm the allocation of the dependent's exemption according to this provision, including, without limitation, Internal Revenue Service Form 8332. The court shall retain jurisdiction to modify this provision.

15.5 The parties agree that under Internal Revenue Code section 1041, or the tax principles regarding interspousal division of community property, the allocation of property between the parties under this Agreement is not taxable, and the tax basis of each asset allocated under these provisions has not changed, and will not change, by reason of this division. Each party agrees not to seek a new tax basis for any asset grounded on any such change even though the transaction may otherwise appear to be a bona fide sale.

15.6 Husband and Wife shall each assume and pay (or defer under Internal Revenue Code section 1034 or shelter under Internal Revenue Code section 121) the federal and state capital gains tax attributable to the sale or other disposition of his or her share of the Residence. Basis shall be allocated in proportion to ownership. The court shall retain jurisdiction to make the orders necessary to effectuate the intent of the parties as expressed in this subsection in the event of subsequent tax assessments or if any taxing authority refuses to allow the allocations made by the parties.

15.7 In calculating the community property interest in any retirement, deferred compensation, or survivor rights, the gross amount of those payments, without regard to tax rate or deductions, shall be used. The party ultimately receiving an interest in any retirement or survivor benefits under this Agreement shall be liable for the income and employment taxes of both parties attributable to the benefits received. It is intended that the ultimate recipient of the benefit shall report and be responsible for these taxes, and that the other party shall have no responsibility for payment. Should the other party be required to pay such taxes, the party who is the ultimate recipient shall indemnify the other for the payment. Both parties agree to cooperate in making available to the other (or his or her agent) any information necessary to determine the amount of this tax liability. The court shall reserve jurisdiction to administer the provisions of this section, as needed.

15.8 The parties acknowledge that a joint tax return of the parties may not be filed for the year in which the judgment of dissolution of marriage terminating marital status is obtained. Each party will report on his or her own return one-half of any community property income (including earnings from personal services rendered prior to the Separation Date) and income or gain from separate property. Each party will be entitled to credits for one-half of any tax withholdings from the community income and for one-half of any estimated taxes paid from his or her respective community property (including overpayments from the prior year credited to taxes for such year), plus all estimated taxes paid from separate property, plus all estimated and withheld taxes from his or her separate property and separate income. Each party shall include all income from his or her separate property and all income from his or her earnings from personal services earned after the Separation Date. Each party shall take the deductions to which he or she is entitled; any deductions attributable to community investments or payments from community funds shall be divided equally. The parties shall exchange information with each other that is necessary or helpful to the other in preparing the separate returns on a prompt basis, but by no later than March 15th for the year following the tax year for which will be filed. Each party shall be solely liable for the taxes due on his or her respective returns, and each shall be solely entitled to any refunds paid.

15.9 With respect to periods during the marriage, the parties have filed (or will file) joint federal and state income tax returns. If any of those returns is audited, or if deficiencies or refunds arise for any other reason, the audit and allocation of deficiencies or refunds shall be governed by this section 15.9. Each party shall immediately provide written notice, and shall forward a copy, to the other party of any statutory notice of deficiency (90-day letter), or any other communication from any taxing authority regarding tax liabilities of either party attributable to joint returns for periods during the marriage. A tax preparer or tax attorney mutually agreeable to the parties shall be responsible for all communications and negotiations with the taxing authority. The parties shall execute necessary powers of attorney and disclosure authorizations designating this person to act as their agent in subsequent communications and negotiations. The parties shall make no direct communication with the taxing authority, except as required by law, in which case any communication shall be in the presence of or reviewed in advance by the agent. The parties shall cooperate fully with the agent, shall execute all documents reasonably requested by the agent, and shall furnish information and testimony necessary to respond to the action asserted by the taxing authority. If a deficiency is to be paid, or a refund to be received, the tax liability of both parties shall be shared equally by Husband and Wife, together with any interest, penalties, and expenses incurred (including professional fees) whether or not either party decides to contest any assessment. The parties shall likewise share equally any refunds arising from joint federal or state tax returns, after paying any professional fees and costs incurred in obtaining the refund.

15.10 The parties recognize that the allocation between them of the responsibility for the payment of taxes on joint income tax returns (as set forth in this Agreement) is not binding on the Internal Revenue Service, the Franchise Tax Board (unless a tax clearance certificate under Revenue and Taxation Code section 19006 has previously been issued), or any other taxing authority. The parties are aware that if either party fails to pay the taxes for which he or she is responsible, the law may give the taxing authority power to collect these taxes from the other party.

16.   EXECUTION OF FURTHER INSTRUMENTS

16.1 Husband and Wife each agree, on demand of the other, to execute or deliver any instrument, furnish any information, or perform any other act reasonably necessary to carry out the provisions of this Agreement without undue delay or expense. Notwithstanding the failure or refusal of either of us to execute any instrument necessary or convenient to transfer title or property conveyed to the other herein, this Agreement shall constitute a full and complete transfer and conveyance of the properties designated as being transferred, conveyed or assigned by each of us. Either of us who fails to comply with any of the terms of this Agreement shall reimburse the other for any expenses, including attorney's fees and court costs as designated in the *"Attorney's Fees"* Article, that as a result of this failure become reasonably necessary for carrying out this Agreement.

17.   WAIVER

17.1 It is mutually agreed between the parties that the failure of either party at any time to require the performance by the other party of any of the terms, provisions, and conditions hereof, shall in no way affect his or her rights thereafter to enforce same; nor shall a waiver of either party of any breach of any of the terms, conditions or provisions hereof be taken or held to be a waiver of any succeeding breach of any such term, provision and condition or as a waiver of the term, provision or condition itself.

18.   COMPREHENSION OF CONTENTS

18.1 Each party has read the foregoing Agreement and fully understands the contents thereof, and accepts same. There has been no promise, agreement or undertaking of either of the parties to the other, except as above set forth, relied upon by either as a matter of inducement to enter into this Agreement. Each party has had competent legal counsel represent him or her in the negotiations leading up to this instant agreement.

19.   MUTUAL REPRESENTATION AS TO EQUAL DIVISION

19.1 Any and all valuations set forth herein are approximate; are a reflection of the parties' personal beliefs; are not based on formal appraisals; and are not warranties, guarantees or representations of either party on which the other party relied. The designated amounts for the referenced liens, loans and/or financial obligations, if any so noted, of the parties are also approximate.

19.2 The parties represent, one to the other, that they have in good faith endeavored, where possible, to divide in kind community property of equal value where susceptible to such division. Each party is, therefore, satisfied on the whole that each has received a fair and equal division of the parties' community property.

20. NOTICES

20.1 Husband shall be given notice of Wife's address and she of his, and each party shall give the other written notification of any change of residence within a reasonable length of time.

21. FINALITY OF AGREEMENT

21.1 This Agreement contains the entire agreement of the parties and otherwise supersedes any previous agreements between the parties. No other agreement, statement or promise made by or to the other party, or the agent or representative of either of the parties shall be binding on the parties unless it is in writing and signed by both of them subsequent to the date of execution of this Agreement.

22. NOTICE OF FILING UNDER BANKRUPTCY LAWS

22.1 If either party decides to claim any rights under the bankruptcy laws, that party must notify the other of this intention in writing at least ten days before filing the petition. Such notice must include, but not necessarily be limited to, the name, address, and telephone number of the attorney, if any, representing the party in that proceeding and the Court in which the petition will be filed.

22.2 The party receiving notice will have five days in which to elect to participate jointly with the notifying party in a consolidated proceeding and to be represented by the same attorney, if any, representing the notifying party. If this election is made, the notifying party will pay all attorney's fees and related costs incurred by the other party with respect to the proceeding. If the party receiving notice elects joint representation in a consolidated proceeding and then fails to cooperate fully with the notifying party in that proceeding by failing adequately to complete court papers, failing to comply with court orders, or otherwise, the notifying party (a) will not be responsible for any of the attorney's fees and related costs incurred by the other party and (b) will be released from all obligations to the other party under this marital termination agreement relating to assumption of joint obligations of the parties or payments to the other party as part of the division of property.

23. GENERAL PROVISIONS

23.1 This Agreement shall be effective immediately as of the day and year first above written.

23.2 If a Judgment of Dissolution of Marriage is obtained by either party, the original of this Agreement shall be submitted to the court and the court shall be requested to receive said Agreement into evidence as an exhibit and to otherwise incorporate and merge any and all executory provisions of this Agreement into the Judgment and/or Final Decree of Dissolution of Marriage in said dissolution proceedings between the parties.

23.3 This Agreement shall survive its incorporation and merger into the Judgment and Final Decree of Dissolution of Marriage and shall take precedence over any inconsistent provisions of any such decree. The effectiveness of this Agreement is not dependent upon the approval of any court, the granting of any decree of dissolution of marriage, Judgment or Final, or upon any matter or thing.

23.4 This Agreement is entered into in the State of California and shall be construed and interpreted under and in accordance with the laws of said State. Should any of the terms or provisions of the Agreement or any clause or part thereof be held invalid, illegal or void, the terms, provisions, clauses or part held to be invalid, illegal or void shall be deleted from this Agreement, and the balance of the Agreement shall remain in full force and effect.

23.5 Each party hereby covenants and agrees not to harass, annoy or interfere with the other party in any way. The parties further agree not to interfere with the other's enjoyment or other business activities, or with the use, ownership or disposition of any property now owned or hereafter acquired by any other party.

23.6 Each party hereby waives findings of fact, conclusions of law, notice of intended decision, right to move for a new trial, right to move to set aside or vacate any Judgment of Dissolution of Marriage and/or the right to appeal any such judgment to the effect that a Final Decree of Dissolution of Marriage may be entered at the soonest possible time under the applicable California law.

23.7 Neither party shall request final entry of Judgment in the within matter until [insert appropriate date, if any].

23.8 If either party is in default for more than fifteen (15) days in the obligation described in the execution of further instruments, then upon five (5) days written notice to the defaulting spouse, all judges, commissioners and deputy court clerks of the court in which the pending action is filed and upon and pursuant to the court orders specifically therefor, shall have full authority to sign those instruments on behalf of the defaulting party.

23.9 The parties recognize that the law may change in the future regarding classification or distribution of property. Those changes in the law shall not apply to this Agreement.

23.10 The parties both acknowledge and agree that they have been advised by each of their counsel that there may be certain additional tax consequences as a result of the provisions of this Agreement, including but not limited to, capital gains tax consequences, real property tax consequences, state and federal income tax consequences, and local tax consequences. The parties both agree and acknowledge that their counsel have not given either party tax advice and each party has been advised by his counsel that they should each seek the advice of their own certified public accountant regarding any tax consequences of this Agreement, which may be substantial and might affect materially their entering into the terms of this Agreement.

23.11 Either party may submit a Judgment based upon this Agreement to the court, which court shall have full authority to execute a Judgment predicated thereon.

This *Marital Settlement Agreement* is executed on the day and year first above written.

_____   _____

JOHN DOE   MARY ROE

EXHIBIT A

COMMUNITY PROPERTY/DEBTS

ASSETS:

1.   Community property household furniture, furnishings, and appliances contained in the family residence.
2.   Personal belongings, clothing, and jewelry of Husband;
3.   Personal belongings, clothing, and jewelry of Wife.
4.   2008 Honda Accord, Lic. No. 123456;
5.   2004 Ford Bronco automobile, Lic. No. 7891011;
6.   Community interest in the single family residence located at and commonly described as 111 N. Hill Street, Los Angeles, CA 90012;
7.   Community interest in the single family residence located at and commonly described as 110 N. Grand Ave., Los Angeles, CA 90012;
8.   Husband's 401K plan benefits through his employment with ABC Industries; approximate date of separation value: $65,000.00;
9.   Husband's IRA accounts: approximate date of separation value: $8,000.00;
10.   Wife's 401(k) plan benefits through her employment with XYZ Development Corporation: approximate date of separation value: $25,000.00;
11.   Wife's IRA accounts: approximate date of separation value: $14,000.00;
12.   Cash in miscellaneous deposit accounts: approximate date of separation balance: $75,000.00;

DEBTS:

None.

EXHIBIT B

PROPERTY/DEBTS TO HUSBAND

PROPERTY:

    1. Personal belongings, clothing, furniture and jewelry of Husband.

    2. An equitable portion of the household furniture, furnishings, and appliances, as already divided between the parties.

    3. 2004 Ford Bronco automobile, Lic. No. 7891011;

    4. Community interest in the single family residence located at and commonly described as 110 N. Grand Ave., Los Angeles, CA 90012;

    5. Husband's 401(k) plan benefits through his employment with ABC Industries; approximate date of separation value: $65,000.00;

    6. Husband's IRA accounts; approximate date of separation value: $8,000.00;

    7. A portion of cash on hand in miscellaneous deposit accounts as already divided between the parties (to Husband, the approximate amount of $20,000.00);

DEBTS:

    N/A

EXHIBIT C

PROPERTY/DEBTS TO WIFE

PROPERTY:

    1.   Personal belongings, clothing, furniture, and jewelry of Wife.

    2.   An equitable portion of the household furniture, furnishings, and appliances, as already divided between the parties.

    3.   2008 Honda Accord, Lic. No. 123456;

    4.   Community interest in the single family residence located at and commonly described as 111 N. Hill Street, Los Angeles, CA 90012;

    5.   Wife's 401(k) plan benefits through her employment with XYZ Development Corporation: approximate date of separation value: $25,000.00;

    6.   Wife's IRA accounts: approximate date of separation value: $14,000.00;

    7.   A portion of cash on hand in miscellaneous deposit accounts as already divided between the parties (to Wife, the approximate amount of $55,000.00);

DEBTS:

    N/A

K. Collaborative Divorce

(*Author's note:* The following material on Collaborative Divorce, except where noted, is reprinted with kind permission from its author, Ronald Melin Supancic, Esq.)

Divorce is not an event; it is a process. It is a process through which we make the transition from being part of a couple to being single. It is a journey during the course of which one unit of two divides into two units of one. The goal of divorce should be to begin as two, end as one, and still feel whole.

This journey leads us through a maze of transitions: legal, emotional, and financial. If we are to successfully navigate this potentially treacherous and painful path, we must enlist the services of those who have expertise in specific areas of the divorce process. They will guide us along our path so that at the end of the journey we remain whole.

When we do this, we are doing something extraordinary called Collaborative Divorce. Divorce means to divide something into subparts that are less than the whole. Collaborative Divorce may be used as a transformative process. Collaborative Divorce is unique in that it stands for the possibility of growth, increased consciousness, enhanced skills, and new life strategies. It requires a new mindset that puts relationships ahead of financial considerations. When this happens, an opening is created for a new, reorganized family with great potential for satisfaction and self-fulfillment.

Collaborative Divorce is intended to help families reorganize in healthier ways. Our commitment is to family strength. We believe in the possibility of reorganized families in which relationships are healed, communication skills are mastered, and parenting strategies are in harmony. Conflict may then be recognized as a doorway through which we pass on a journey toward compassion and consciousness.

Services:

- Document Preparation
- Negotiation
- Mediation
- Collaborative Law
- Case Management
- Arbitration
- Rent-A-Judge & Mini-trials

Benefits to the Divorcing Parties:

- Save time and money
- Avoid court

- Client in charge, informed, and empowered
- Focus on well being of client and family
- Creative and flexible solutions to fit client needs
- Emotional agendas processed compassionately
- Divorce with dignity

Collaborative Divorce—Divorce without litigious lawyers. Divorce without black-robed judges who beat their gavels mercilessly, with each blow decimating income, disrupting visitation, and destroying any hope of an intact, if restructured family? Read on.

Who Qualifies for a Collaborative Divorce?

The bad news: not everyone qualifies for a Collaborative Divorce. The good news: anyone who is willing to put the emotional wholeness of their family before personal ill will, vendetta, and one-upmanship will qualify.

What Collaborative Divorce Is Not:

Collaborative Divorce is not marriage therapy or reconciliation counseling. It works on the assumption that the marriage is over and that the time has come to start building a restructured family. It is not appropriate for marriages in which one of the parties has hope that the marriage may continue. Divorce is usually a highly emotional event for all parties involved. *Collaborative Divorce* cannot magically alleviate the pain, guilt, and blaming. *Collaborative Divorce* is no panacea. It is a process. Like all procedures, it follows a series of orderly steps to completion. *Collaborative Divorce* can provide divorcing families with psychological completion, or closure, that litigation will never match.

May Any Attorney Do a Collaborative Divorce?

Attorneys, like most other professionals, are required to continue their education long after law school and passing the bar exam. California Certified Family Law Specialists must take at least twelve hours of specialized professional training each year.

If you have a broken leg, it should be set by an orthopedic doctor. If you need a root canal, go to an endodontist. Likewise with the law, a Personal Injury lawyer may process a divorce, but a Certified Family Law Specialist is preferred. As for *Collaborative Divorce*, it should only be undertaken by a Family Law Specialist trained in the collaborative process.

Collaborative Family Law is the newest approach to family law matters, including divorces. It is a method in which attorneys for both divorcing parties agree to assist to resolve the dispute using cooperation and prob-lem-solving strategies rather than adversarial approaches and litigation.

Collaborative divorce is always preferred for families with children. All negotiations are interest-based rather than positional, with each party's interests considered when crafting a resolution. Collaborative divorce differs from traditional litigation in several important ways. Each spouse and his or her lawyer sign a Collaborative Agreement outlining appropriate behavior throughout the process. In this document, the parties agree to avoid litigation and agree to negotiate in good faith. No court proceedings are permitted during the pendency of the collaborative law process. Should negotiations break down and one party decides to go to court, both attorneys will withdraw, and the clients must hire new attorneys.

By agreeing to this condition, the collaborative lawyer shares the risk of process failure that attorneys in litigation or mediation do not. The collaborative lawyer becomes responsible to manage and limit unreasonable positions in favor of a successful outcome in the family's best interest. Should a client fail to honor the Collaborative Agreement, both attorneys withdraw.

In another sensible economy, experts are retained jointly as neutrals within the collaborative process. Negotiations are informally handled, with each party attending a series of structured "4-Way" meetings in which both spouses and their attorneys sit down at a table and discuss the resolution of the divorce.

A major difference between collaborative family law and other approaches is that clients themselves craft the terms of their divorce and the final outcome. No third party (such as a judge) decides the outcome for them. This process only works when both parties agree to use it.

The Six Steps to Collaborative Divorce

Assessment
Intervention
Issue Identification
Process Selection
Initiation of the Legal Procedure
Closure

Assessment:

In the Assessment phase, the divorcing parties work with an attorney trained in collaborative law to identify the emotional profile of the family and determine effective interventions to assist the family as it is restructured. The parties meet and confer to review all options available, with the express goal being to design a strategy that will contribute to the family's reorganization rather than destroy the family by dissolving all family ties.

Intervention:

Based on the Assessment, the parties, with assistance from their lawyers, determine the Interventions appropriate to their case. The interventions may include, but are not limited to, Separation Therapy, Parenting classes, Rage Management, Personal Coaching, and individual psychotherapy. The children may benefit by becoming part of a group for children of divorcing families.

This may sound expensive, yet a family with average income, an owned home, two cars, and perhaps a pension plan, may conservatively expect to spend $60,000 on a litigated divorce. Much more will be spent if child custody is an issue. A Collaborative Divorce will cost a small fraction of this, even with all parties in therapy.

Divorcing parents do not become divorced from *each other—they become divorced* to *each other, for as long as their children live.* Why then should they not work together to achieve a healthy divorce, one in which mutual respect and concern for the best interests of the children prevail?

The collaborative approach offers great personal benefit to the family involved. It takes 300 hours of guided instruction to become a manicurist, 3000 hours of supervised training (plus a master's degree) to become a psychotherapist, and zero hours of schooling or training to marry or become a parent. Two of life's most important events are left to chance and luck. That's pretty scary. Family restructuring should not be similarly treated.

Issue Identification:

In this stage, the parties learn to apportion income streams, material assets and, with the assistance of a specialist, design an overall tax plan to facilitate a reorganization that contributes to the family rather than harms it. Insurance provisions may be addressed and a parenting plan designed with the help of a children's coordinator.

Process Selection:

Here the parties examine the options of negotiation, mediation, arbitration, or case management. The best method of settling any dispute is with negotiation. If both parties have willingly and honestly participated in Issue Identification, then negotiation is a good possibility. If, however, either party has a preponderance of power and the other feels even slightly coerced, negotiation cannot take place. Mediation is then preferred.

With Collaborative Divorce, mediation is accomplished with the assistance of a trained mediator and a collaborative lawyer to represent each party. Two lawyers and one mediator—sound expensive? Not compared to sitting in a backlogged court room for days, not-so-patiently awaiting an available courtroom and a busy judge. And then the judge decides, not you. Meanwhile, your lawyer and opposing counsel each bill on an hourly basis. While these attorneys wait with the parties to the action, they are unable to work on any other case. They must be responsible to the court, on hand and available. Their time adds up, even with good intentions.

If matters cannot be settled through mediation, arbitration is available, using an arbitrator or rent-a-judge. The presiding judge of the Family Law Department of the Los Angeles County Superior Court has instituted a program through which a retired judge or family law attorney may be hired by your lawyers to hear your case. This is more cost effective than traditional litigation because it eliminates the expensive wait. However, it is also the least preferable option. It still means that you give your power to decide to Someone Else. That Someone makes the decisions, not you.

Remember, the more you and your soon-to-be former spouse agree, the less costly your case. An important purpose of Collaborative Divorce is to avoid the debilitating financial and emotional expenses of litigation in favor of a healthier, more financially sensible alternative process for dispute resolution.

Initiation:

Initiation, the fifth step, is where typical courtroom divorces begin. The parties decide it is time to file the Petition for Dissolution. A joint petition may be filed, reinforcing the collaborative nature of the dissolution. This may eliminate any "I'm up—you're down," mind set, and help forestall adversarial tendencies. Temporary Orders, responses, and Case Management stipulations are filed, a Voluntary Settlement Conference may take place, and the parties participate in a joint resolution based on consensus.

Closure:

The process enters the final stage of completion when the judgment is prepared and entered. The final tax analysis is in order, insurance provisions are put in place, and, if desired, a ceremony may take place to mark the conclusion of the dissolution and reinforce the vision of the still viable, though restructured, family unit.

An insightful CPA with whom I work told me the advice he always gives his divorcing clients: *"It is as important to have a good divorce as it is to have a good marriage. You may have to live longer with the divorce than you lived with the marriage."* Those who, best efforts aside, find themselves walking the path of divorce would be wise to follow his advice. Collaborative Divorce provides healthier restructured families and stronger support for children, and may serve to mend and embellish co-parenting relationships for years to come.

How the Collaborative Process Can Help Save Your Marriage

(*Author's note:* The following article is reprinted with kind permission from its author, Veronika Melamed, CFLS.)

Most people are aware of the beneficial effects of using the Collaborative process for marriage dissolution: the reduced costs, the focus on family, the speed of resolution, and the lessening of trauma on the family.

What people may not know is that the Collaborative process is a highly effective tool in the preservation of one's union, decreasing the tensions that arise due to hardships in a marriage. The Collaborative process may be used in all of the following situations:

1.   A Prenuptial Agreement

Most Prenuptial agreements are entered into for the protection of one, or both, parties to a marriage. The goal for such an agreement is to ensure that, should the marriage result in divorce, the husband and wife have planned for their protection. Unfortunately, these agreements are often used as a way to financially diminish the other party, the "weaker" party, thus leading to the negative connotations of these agreements.

What many fail to realize is that these agreements lack the foresight necessary to achieve a harmonious transition from marriage to single life; they fail to foresee what the needs of all family members will be at the time that the marriage ends.

By incorporating Collaborative principles into the agreement, the spouses are assured that their divorce will consider the needs of the family as a whole, as well as each member individually, and that everyone will leave the marriage feeling whole and content.

Prenuptial agreements may be modified by including some of these provisions:

    a. The parties will meet with collaborative lawyers to review the agreement, which review will be conducted using the Collaborative Law principles.

    b. Once deciding on a divorce, the parties shall meet with Collaborative Lawyers to assess whether the agreement meets the needs of any children of the marriage. As the California courts have ruled that child support may not be waived in a prenuptial agreement, deciding in advance to use the Collaborative process will avoid the brutality of litigation.

   c. Any questions that may arise regarding child support and custody will be dealt with using a Collaborative team consisting of coaches, financial experts, parenting coaches, and either mediators or attorneys.

   d. Should the validity of this agreement be questioned, all settlement of that issue will be through the Collaborative process, using a full team approach with either a mediator or attorney.

   e. Any difficulties that may arise post-dissolution, which would normally require being handled by the courts through the use of an Order to Show Cause, will be handled using the Collaborative model.

2. *An Ante-nuptial Agreement*

An Ante-nuptial agreement is one entered into by husband and wife during their marriage. These usually arise when one spouse feels that there is a need for an agreement, even though the couple is not moving towards a divorce. These are often thought of as "just in case" agreements, usually arising after a significant financial change has happened, or is about to happen, for the couple. These are then used to plan the details of a division of assets, should a divorce actually occur.

These agreements, if improperly approached, may alienate the spouse rather than offering the reassurance sought. To avoid hurt feelings, and actually achieve the results wanted, the following provisions may be included:

   a. The parties will meet with collaborative lawyers to review the agreement, which review will be conducted using the Collaborative Law principles.

   b. Should the validity of this agreement be questioned, all settlement of that issue will be through the Collaborative process, using a full team approach with either a mediator or attorney.

   c. The divorce, should it occur, will be done in the Collaborative model, using the full Collaborative team to ensure that the family trauma is minimized.

   d. All actions taken during the dissolution of marriage will make the children, if any, the priority and will focus on preserving relationships.

   e. The parents agree that all of their actions will be geared towards what is the best for their children.

   f. Any impediments that may arise post-dissolution, which would normally require being handled by the courts through the use of an Order to Show Cause, will be handled using the Collaborative model.

3.   *Hardships That Arise During the Marriage*

All marriages face problems and hardships at one time or another. What sets an unsuccessful marriage apart from a successful one is how the couple deals with the inevitable trials and tribulations: whether the couple allows these difficulties to tear at the foundation of their marriage, or instead sees an opportunity for growth and the strengthening of the core of their marriage.

Many issues may lead to these troubles: money, child-rearing concerns, or disagreements over assets. By using the collaborative process, and a collaborative team, the couple can work through these problems, air their concerns, have their questions addressed and answered openly and honestly, and then may move on to continue their lives as one.

The collaborative process may be helpful in the following ways:

a.   In the current economy, it is a harsh reality that a family's income may be negatively impacted. As money becomes tighter, couples may notice that tension levels, and arguments, in their marriage tremendously increase. While the arguments may be about money, there are often deep-rooted emotional issues that underlie the disputes. By using the Collaborative process, all issues of the problem may be addressed. A collaborative neutral is brought in to guide the process and answer any legal or technical questions that may arise. The couple works with a team of coaches who help them cope with their concerns as a couple and as individuals. There may be a parenting coordinator involved, who will be the voice of the children during this difficult time. A Collaborative financial professional can guide and advise the family, helping to ensure that the needs of the family are still being met.

b.   Conversely, problems may arise when there is an unexpected bonus of money coming into a family. There may be disagreements as to how it is best spent, what amount to save, and how to make certain that the future needs of the family as a whole will be met. Again, the use of the Collaborative model is effective for lessening family anxiety. The couple may meet with a neutral, coaches, a parenting coordinator, and a financial specialist to deal with the visible concerns, the underlying worries, and the future stability of the family.

The collaborative model is effective for the myriad of dilemmas that arise during the course of a marriage. In all other instances where the friction rises, the Collaborative model is there to guide the family through rough waters into a safe harbor, where they may again prepare to sail once calm waters have arrived.

Collaborative Divorce as Part of the State's Statutory Scheme

The concept of collaborative divorce has now been adopted as part of the state's statutory scheme by inclusion of Section 2013 in the Family Code. Enacted in 2006 through the "Collaborative Family Law Act," Family Code §2013 states:

> (a) If a written agreement is entered into by the parties, the parties may utilize a collaborative law process to resolve any matter governed by this code over which the court is granted jurisdiction pursuant to Section 2000.
>
> (b) "Collaborative law process" means the process in which the parties and any professionals engaged by the parties to assist them agree in writing to use their best efforts and to make a good faith attempt to resolve disputes related to the family law matters as referenced in subdivision (a) on an agreed basis without resorting to adversary judicial intervention.

In keeping with the tenets of collaborative law and the legislature's support of an alternative means for parties to dissolve their marriage without the constant intervention of the judiciary, many counties have also adopted local court rules that accommodate collaborative law cases. The reader *must* review their local court rules to determine whether specific provisions have been made for collaborative divorce cases, because these provisions may have great impact on a pending dissolution action.

For example, Los Angeles County has Local Rule 14.26 addressing collaborative law cases, which discusses the designation of such cases, the filing of contested matters for cases designated as collaborative, and the termination of a case's designation as collaborative. In Los Angeles County, there is a direct mandate prohibiting the filing of a contested matter for a case designated as a "collaborative law case" and exempting these cases from case management proceedings.

As collaborative divorce plays a greater role in the dissolution process, and as more state and local provisions make accommodations for this alternative to a litigated divorce, the reader will have to keep abreast of the impact of this approach on family law.

L.   Same-Sex Marriage

As the reader is no doubt aware, same-sex marriage is a "hot topic" throughout the country, and it has raised strong emotions on both sides of the debate. It is arguably one of the most closely watched issues of this century to date. This text does not provide a comprehensive study of same-sex marriage. It does, however, summarize how the issue has been addressed in California.

On June 16, 2008, the California Supreme Court essentially cleared the way for same-sex marriage. The court found that by denying same-sex couples the opportunity to marry, the law treated one class of people differently and thus violated the Equal Protection Clause of the State Constitution. Yet, less than six months later, on November 5, 2008, California voters passed Proposition 8, an amendment to the State Constitution that restricted marriage to opposite-sex couples. On August 4, 2010, federal judge Vaughn R. Walker ruled that the ban on same-sex marriage was unconstitutional; Judge Walker, however, temporary stayed his ruling. To date (January 2011) proponents of same-sex marriage are working to promote a 2012 election ballot initiative that would allow California to once again grant marriage licenses to same-sex couples.

The following article provides an excellent framework for future research and analysis by interested readers. It explains the history of the same-sex marriage debate in California; it also examines the reasoning behind the state supreme court's June 16, 2008, decision in which it allowed same-sex marriage.

(*Author's note:* The following article on same sex marriage in California is reprinted with kind permission from its author, Veronika Melamed, CFLS.)

SAME SEX MARRIAGE IN CALIFORNIA, by Veronika Melamed © 2008

With the decision filed on May 15, 2008, in the six consolidated cases known as *In Re Marriage Cases* (2008) 43 Cal.4th 757, the California Supreme Court ruled that it was unconstitutional to deny same-sex couples the right to enter into a marriage. Stating that the current statutes that allowed marriage in California only between a man and a woman violated the equal protection and due process clauses of the California Constitution, and that the statutory scheme provided by the Legislature known as "Registered Domestic Partnerships" failed to accord the same level of Constitutional rights as did marriage, the Supreme Court made history by granting same-sex couples the right and privilege to enter into matrimony in California with *all* of the rights and responsibilities afforded to opposite-sex couples.

It had long been held as the law in California that only opposite-sex couples could marry, as defined both in statutory law and tradition. To address the growing numbers of same-sex couples in California and the change in current social mores and traditions, the California State Legislature developed a statutory scheme allowing same-sex couples, and opposite-sex couples where at least one person was over the age of 62, to enter into a "domestic partnership" that could be registered with the State of California, thereby creating, or at least attempting to create, a system akin to marriage while still protecting the concepts of marriage.

As first enacted in 1999, and amended in 2001 and 2003, finally becoming effective as of January 1, 2005, in its current form, Family Code Section 297 states that couples who meet the requirements established by the statute could enter into a Domestic Partnership that could then be Registered with the State, giving such Registered Domestic Partners "the same rights, protections, and benefits, and shall be subject to the same responsibilities, obligations, and duties under law, whether they derive from statutes, administrative regulations, court rules, government policies, common law, or any other provisions or sources of law, as are granted to and imposed upon spouses" (Family Code Section 297.5).

In a further attempt to create a situation *similar* to that of marriage, the State Legislature included provisions that the date of registration was equivalent to the date of marriage, that the rights of registered domestic partners with respect to a child of either of them would be the same as spouses, and that the registered partnership would have to be terminated in the same manner as a marriage, with the Superior Courts of this state having jurisdiction over the termination. While this was meant to appease the population—both those in favor of same-sex relationships by recognizing the legal validity of these relationships and those against same-sex relationships by withholding the actual state of matrimony, the attempt failed as same-sex couples still called for the right to marry.

The issue of same-sex marriage as was addressed by the Supreme Court in the *Marriage Cases* first arose as a result of the actions of the Mayor of the City of San Francisco, Gavin Newsom who, on February 10, 2004, wrote a letter to the county clerk, directing that official to determine what changes should be made to the forms and documents used to apply for and issue marriage licenses, so that licenses could be provided to couples without regard to their gender or sexual orientation. In response, the county clerk designed revised forms for the marriage license application and for the license and certificate of marriage, and on February 12, 2004, the City began issuing marriage licenses to same-sex couples. The next day, two separate lawsuits were filed seeking an order from the court prohibiting the City's issuance of marriage licenses to same-sex couples, claiming that the City's actions were in violation of the law and that the actions exceeded the scope of permissible conduct, as stated in the various applicable Codes and Statutes. The Court denied the request, and the City continued to issue marriage licenses to same-sex couples, eventually beginning to solemnize the marriages as well.

Following a denial of the request to stay the City's actions, two separate cases were filed that were eventually consolidated into one. The case of Lockyer v. City and County of San Francisco (2004) 33 Cal.4th 1055 was filed asserting that the City's actions were unlawful and warranted immediate intervention by the Court and its prohibition of these actions by the City. On March 11, 2004, the Supreme Court directed City officials to enforce the *existing* marriage statutes and to refrain from issuing marriage licenses other than those specifically authorized by those provisions. The basis of the ruling in the *Lockyer* case rested on the principle that the City's actions violated the law, rather than addressing the question of whether the law itself was valid.

Shortly after the court's March 11th decision, and with the *Lockyer* case still pending in the courts, the City filed its own lawsuit, challenging the constitutionality of the current law and asking the court to declare the laws allowing marriage only between a man and a woman to be unconstitutional. (City and County of San Francisco v. State of California (Super. Ct. S.F. City & County, No. CGC-04-429539 (CCSF).) It is this case, along with the multitude of county-wide cases filed simultaneously asking for the same relief, that became known as the *Marriage Cases*.

On August 12, 2004, while the *Marriage Cases* were in the process of being consolidated, the state Supreme Court issued its final ruling in the *Lockyer* case, concluding that the City officials had exceeded their authority in issuing marriage licenses to same-sex couples in the absence of a judicial determination that the statutory provisions limiting marriage to the union of a man and a woman were unconstitutional, and further concluding that the approximately 4,000 same-sex marriages performed in San Francisco prior to their March 11, 2004, order were void and of no legal effect. The Court also noted that its decisions addressed *only* the issue before it: whether City officials had acted appropriately and in keeping with current law. The Court went out of its way to state that this decision was in no way a ruling on the issue of whether the law allowing marriage only between a man and a woman was constitutional, as no one had raised that issue in this specific case.

To fully understand the impact and context of its decision in the Marriage Cases, and why the court ruled in favor of the Plaintiffs in *Lockyer* in 2004 yet seemingly ruled against them 4 years later in its decision in the *Marriage Cases*, one must look at what the issues were in each case, how they differed, and why the two rulings of the Supreme Court are actually both "correct."

As stated above, the question presented to the Court in the *Lockyer* case was only a question of whether the laws were being followed, rather than a question of whether the laws were "right" or "constitutional" or "correct." In that context, and without any challenge to the underlying laws, the Court could only look at the law as it existed at that time and determine whether City officials were complying with the law or breaking the law. In particular, the Supreme Court looked to Family Code section 308.5, which stated, "Only marriage between a man and a woman is valid or recognized in California," and Family Code section 300, which states, "(a) Marriage is a personal relation arising out of a civil contract between a man and a woman, to which the consent of the parties capable of making that contract is necessary. Consent alone does not constitute marriage. Consent must be followed by the issuance of a license and solemnization as authorized by this division, except as provided by Section 425 and Part 4 (commencing with Section 500). (b) For purposes of this part, the document issued by the county clerk is a marriage license until it is registered with the county recorder, at which time the license becomes a marriage certificate."

Enacted on March 8, 2000, Family Code Section 308.5 was added by Initiative Measure Proposition 22, and clearly defined "marriage" in this state as being *only* between a man and a woman, and was a further articulation of the definition of "marriage" in Family Code Section 300. Given that this was the law at the time the Court ruled in the *Lockyer* case, and that there were no challenges to the substance of the law pending before the state Supreme Court at that time, the Court ruled that the City's actions did, in fact, violate the laws of the State of California, and that its continued actions in issuing marriage licenses to same-sex couples and then performing solemnization ceremonies for these couples, would continue to be violative of the law. In essence, the Court stated that until such time as somebody actually challenged the law itself and presented that issue to the Court for its ruling, the City officials had to follow the law as written, irrespective of whether they personally agreed with it, believed in it, or wanted to follow it.

Whereas the *Lockyer* case was one of procedure, and the Court went out of its way to make that distinction, the *Marriage Cases* was one of substance, in which the Supreme Court was asked to rule on the question of whether the Family Code Sections that addressed and defined marriage in California were Constitutional because they treated same-sex and opposite-sex couples differently. That is, could the state limit marriage to be only between a man and a woman, or was that limitation actually unconstitutional because it treated these two types of couples differently? To be sure, the Legislature created a statutory scheme designed to *look* like and *act* like a "marriage"(Registered Domestic Partnerships), but that still denied same-sex couples the title and status of "marriage." So while the substantive issue before the Court pertained to the constitutionality of the statutes, the question was framed to draw the Court's attention to whether the same-sex couples were being treated the same as opposite-sex couples or whether same-sex couples were being denied their rights.

As the Supreme Court defined it, "the legal issue we must resolve is not whether it would be constitutionally permissible under the California Constitution for the state to limit marriage only to opposite-sex couples while denying same-sex couples any opportunity to enter into an official relationship with all or virtually all of the same substantive attributes, but rather whether our state Constitution prohibits the state from establishing a statutory scheme in which both opposite-sex and same-sex couples are granted the right to enter into an officially recognized family relationship that affords all of the significant legal rights and obligations traditionally associated under state law with the institution of marriage, but under which the union of an opposite-sex couple is officially designated a 'marriage' whereas the union of a same-sex couple is officially designated a 'domestic partnership.' The question we must address is whether, under these circumstances, the failure to designate the official relationship of same-sex couples as marriage violates the California Constitution." *Marriage Cases* at 779-780. At no time in its decision, or in the issue presented, was the court asked to decide whether marriage for same-sex couples was appropriate, and this was not the issue that the Court examined. Rather, the Court looked at whether the State should give these two different groups essentially the same rights, yet withhold the appellation of "marriage" from one of the groups.

While some readers may wonder at the importance of having a union labeled a marriage so long as the underlying rights and responsibilities are the same, the Court addressed this point in its ruling that the State could not create a system where people were treated "separate but equal" as it pertained to the fundamental right to be married:

> Upon review of the numerous California decisions that have examined the underlying bases and significance of the constitutional right to marry (and that illuminate *why* this right has been recognized as one of the basic, inalienable civil rights guaranteed to an individual by the California Constitution), we conclude that, under this state's Constitution, the constitutionally based right to marry people must be understood to encompass the core set of basic *substantive* legal rights and attributes traditionally associated with marriage that are so integral to an individual's liberty and personal autonomy that they may not be eliminated or abrogated by the Legislature or by the electorate through the statutory initiative process. These core substantive rights include, most fundamentally, the opportunity of an individual to establish—with the person with whom the individual has chosen to share his or her life—an *officially recognized and protected family* possessing mutual rights and responsibilities and entitled to the same respect and dignity accorded a union traditionally designated as marriage. As past cases establish, the substantive right of two adults who share a loving relationship to join together to establish an officially recognized family of their own—and, if the couple chooses, to raise children within that family—constitutes a vitally important attribute of the fundamental interest in liberty and personal autonomy that the California Constitution secures to all persons for the benefit of both the individual and society. . . . We therefore conclude that in view of the substance and significance of the fundamental constitutional right to form a family relationship, the California Constitution properly must be interpreted to

guarantee this basic civil right to all Californians, whether gay or hetero-
sexual, and to same-sex couples as well as to opposite-sex couples.

The Court reasoned that the right to marry, and to have one's union
carry the title of "marriage" is a person's fundamental right, their interest
in the personal liberty guaranteed to us individuals, such as one's right to
enter into an interracial marriage.

What exactly does the decision issued on May 15, 2008, and effective as
of 5:00 p.m. on June 16, 2008, mean to the California population? As established by the state Supreme Court, the State of California, until such time
as the decision is overruled by another state Supreme Court ruling or by
a newly-enacted law as voted on by the citizens of California, must issue
marriage licenses to same-sex couples and solemnize marriages between
same-sex couples. With the implementation of this ruling, same-sex couples now have the right to call each other "spouse" and to fully partake
in the social system of being married, giving their children the right and
privilege of saying their parents are married, and giving them the same.
Further, upon entering into their marriage, same-sex couples become entitled to the same state rights as opposite-sex couples, including the right to
file joint state income tax returns, and to receive all of the benefits afforded
opposite-sex couples under California state law; in essence, everything that
was provided for in the legal concept of Registered Domestic Partners, but
now with the state-recognized title of "marriage."

In the context of family law, same-sex couples fall within the full scope
of the Family Code as it pertains to dissolution and separation proceedings, and will be getting a divorce as opposite-sex couples have been doing
for years. With the creation of same-sex *marriage*, there will no longer be
any differentiation for the termination of same-sex unions and opposite-
sex unions, so long as the couples are married. Unlike with Registered
Domestic Partnerships, dissolution proceedings for same-sex couples
will entail the filing of the same Petition for Dissolution and/or Legal
Separation, and use the same forms, processes, procedures, and legal concepts and principles as are used and addressed in dissolution proceedings
for opposite-sex couples.

While the ruling in the *Marriage Cases* grants same-sex couples the right
to marry under the California Constitution and affords them the rights of
spouses, the Federal Government has enacted its own law that still prohibits the recognition of same-sex marriage. Signed into law on September 21,
1996, the Defense of Marriage Act (DOMA) explicitly defines marriage as
between a man and a woman for the purposes of federal law, bars federal
recognition by any federal agency or act of same-sex marriage, and grants
states the option to forego recognition of same-sex marriage or same-sex
unions as allowed by other states, and as would normally be recognized
under the principle of the Full Faith and Credit Clause of the United States

Constitution, which directs states to respect the public acts, records and judicial ruling of other states, which has traditionally included the solemnization of marriage. The impact of this on same-sex married couples is tremendous: according to the federal government's General Accounting Office, more than 1,138 rights and protections are conferred to U.S. citizens upon marriage by the federal government, (a complete list of which may be obtained from that federal agency).

One specific area where DOMA will affect California same-sex marriages is in the filing of federal income tax returns: while the state now allows couples to file joint returns as they would opposite-sex couples, DOMA forbids the Internal Revenue Service from recognizing these marriages and allowing these spouses to file joint tax returns. In a very real economic sense, same-sex couples will lose the financial benefit often associated with, and specifically created by, the filing of a "Married Filing Joint" tax return. In fact, given the existence of DOMA, same sex couples will likely still have to file tax returns as "single" individuals, losing out on the multitude of tax benefits and breaks afforded to married opposite-sex couples.

The question and issue of same-sex marriage in California is far from over and still has a ways to go before it is settled law. The ballot for the November 2008 election will once again give California voters the right to define marriage as "between a man and a woman" and override the state Supreme Court's decision in the *Marriage Cases*. One will have to wait and see what will be the end result of same-sex marriage in California.

[*Author's note:* Since this article was first published, California voters did indeed have the opportunity to revisit the concept of same sex marriage in the form of Proposition 8, a statutory amendment limiting "marriage" as between a man and a woman.]

M. Limited Scope Representation

(*Author's note:* The following article on limited scope representation is reprinted with kind permission from its author, Veronika Melamed, CFLS.)

In its attempt to help litigants in the family courts who are unable to afford an attorney to represent them, yet may nonetheless need an attorney's help, the Legislature has created Limited Scope Representation.

Limited Scope Representation allows a party going through dissolution proceedings to seek an attorney's services for certain aspects of their dissolution, and to be represented by that attorney in court, without requiring either the attorney or the client to commit to full representation of the client for all issues in the divorce. In the traditional understanding of representation in a divorce, the client will retain the attorney, and will have that attorney represent their interests in the entire divorce, making the attorney responsible for all of the outstanding issues: property, support, custody and visitation, and everything else that may arise. The high costs that may be associated with such full representation often limit a person's ability to seek attorney representation, even when they really need it. Sometimes, however, the client may only need an attorney's help on a specific issue, or for a specific period of time: to resolve the division of a pension, or address the question real property division, or to prepare, argue and follow-up on a request to modify child support, or any other single court appearance. For the attorneys, a different problem existed: even when the attorney wanted to help a client in only one area, perhaps where the client needed it most or because that was all the client could afford, there were no provisions in place to ensure that the attorney could help where it was needed most, without creating an obligation to represent the client's interests in all aspects of the divorce.

To solve these dilemmas for both the attorneys and the potential client, Limited Scope Representation was introduced into the California family law system, allowing the attorney and client to enter into a Limited Scope retainer that sets out the specific tasks and/or issues of the attorney's representation and responsibility, while the client continues to represent him or herself in the remainder of the dissolution. This allows the client to use the attorney's services only for these items that they believe they need an attorney, without incurring the fees for full representation, and without being forced to forego representation in an area where they may truly need it. At the same time, this allows the attorney to assist a person without becoming obligated to continue representation of an individual that may not be able to afford them. In this way, neither one is obligated to the other beyond the issues stated in the Limited Scope retainer.

One of the hallmarks of a Limited Scope retainer agreement is the provision within the Retainer that the client promises to execute a Judicial Council of California form MC-050, "Substitution of Attorney—Civil." Please note that there *must* be a written retainer agreement between the attorney and the client. The attorney must also be cognizant of the fact that they owe the client all of the duties and obligations as set forth by the State Bar and must perform the same services as they would in a full-representation situation. For instance, if the attorney is retained to assist the client in the area of establishing spousal support, they must perform the same services as they would in a case where they are responsible for the entire matter: propounding discovery, issuing subpoenas, taking depositions, asking for vocational evaluations, working with a forensic accountant, and all of the other tasks that one normally engages in when fully representing a client in a case that must resolve the question of spousal support. If, on the other hand, the attorney is hired to represent the client at a single proceeding, the attorney must still prepare fully for the proceeding: subpoena witnesses, ensure necessary documents are presented to the Court, prepare the appropriate moving papers and responses, and zealously represent the client at the appearance. Mistaking Limited Scope Representation for limited scope work may result in malpractice.

Once the attorney and client have come to an agreement as to the nature and scope of the representation, the attorney *must* file with the Court a Judicial Council of California form FL-950, "Notice of Limited Scope Representation."[See Figure 11-2.]

When completing and filing the Notice of Limited Scope Representation, the following items must be addressed:

1. The name of the attorney and client, stating that they have entered into a written limited scope retainer.
2. The nature of the attorney's representation, and how long it will last. It is here that the attorney will notify the court whether the representation is for a specific event or for a specific issue.
3. If the representation is for an issue(s) within the divorce, the Notice must reflect which ones. The Judicial Council form lists 7 specific areas that must typically be addressed within a divorce and has a space to be marked for an issue that may be specific to a particular dissolution proceeding.
4. The client reaffirms that they will execute a Substitution of Attorney at the completion of the limited representation.
5. Because the attorney is responsible for only a specific aspect or occurrence in the dissolution, and the client continues to represent him or herself in the remaining portions of the dissolution, and remains the person for service, the attorney must provide the client's contact information.
6. Both the attorney and the party must sign the Notice.
7. The Notice must be served on all other interest parties in the matter to notify them of the attorney's involvement in the case.

Upon filing the Notice of Limited Scope Representation, the attorney is now the attorney of record in the dissolution for those areas and/or proceedings identified in the Notice. As mentioned above, the attorney owes the Limited Scope client the same responsibilities as a full-representation client and must perform the same services with the same level of representation. For further guidance on this, please see the Professional Rules of Conduct and the various articles and publications from the State Bar of California. For assistance in the specific areas of representation, the reader is invited to review the substantive portions of this textbook.

Once the Limited Scope retainer has expired because the work for which the attorney was retained has been completed, there are now 3 options: the attorney and client may agree to continue their professional relationship,

Figure 11-2
Judicial Council Form FL-950—Notice of Limited Scope Representation

FL-950

ATTORNEY OR PARTY WITHOUT ATTORNEY *(Name, state bar number, and address):*	FOR COURT USE ONLY
Marshall W. Waller, CFLS SBN 101474 Feinberg & Waller, APC 23501 Park Sorrento, Suite 103, Calabasas, CA 91302 TELEPHONE NO.: (818)224-7900 FAX NO. *(Optional):* E-MAIL ADDRESS *(Optional):* ATTORNEY FOR *(Name):*	

SUPERIOR COURT OF CALIFORNIA, COUNTY OF Los Angeles
STREET ADDRESS: 111 North Hill Street
MAILING ADDRESS: Same
CITY AND ZIP CODE: Los Angeles, CA 90012
BRANCH NAME: CENTRAL

PETITIONER/PLAINTIFF: JANE DOE

RESPONDENT/DEFENDANT: JOHN DOE

OTHER PARENT/CLAIMANT:

NOTICE OF LIMITED SCOPE REPRESENTATION ☐ Amended	CASE NUMBER: BD 123 456

1. Attorney *(name):*
   and party *(name):*
   have a written agreement that attorney will provide limited scope representation to the party.

2. Attorney will represent the party
   ☐ at the hearing on: ☐ and for any continuance of that hearing
   ☐ until submission of the order after hearing
   ☐ until resolution of the issues checked on page 1 by trial or settlement
   ☐ other *(specify duration of representation):*

3. Attorney will serve as "attorney of record" for the party **only** for the following issues in this case:
   a. ☐   Child support: (1) ☐   Establish (2) ☐   Enforce (3) ☐   Modify *(describe in detail):*

   b. ☐   Spousal support: (1) ☐   Establish (2) ☐   Enforce (3) ☐   Modify *(describe in detail):*

   c. ☐   Restraining order: (1) ☐   Establish (2) ☐   Enforce (3) ☐   Modify *(describe in detail):*

   d. ☐   Child custody and visitation: (1) ☐   Establish (2) ☐   Enforce (3) ☐   Modify *(describe in detail):*

   e. ☐   Division of property *(describe in detail):*

   f. ☐   Pension issues *(describe in detail):*

Form Adopted for Mandatory Use
Judicial Council of California
FL-950 [New July 1, 2003]   **NOTICE OF LIMITED SCOPE REPRESENTATION**   www.courtinfo.ca.gov

Figure 11-2 (continued)

PETITIONER/PLAINTIFF: JANE DOE	CASE NUMBER:
RESPONDENT/DEFENDANT: JOHN DOE	BD 123 456
OTHER PARENT/CLAIMANT:	

g. ☐ Contempt *(describe in detail):*

h. ☐ Other *(describe in detail):*

i. ☐ See attachment 3i.

4. By signing this form, the party agrees to sign form MC-050, *Substitution of Attorney–Civil* at the completion of the representation as set forth above.

5. The attorney named above is "attorney of record" and available for service of documents only for those issues specifically checked on pages 1 and 2. For all other matters, the party must be served directly. The party's name, address, and phone number are listed below for that purpose.

Name:

Address *(for the purpose of service):*

Phone: Fax:

This notice accurately sets forth all current matters on which the attorney has agreed to serve as "attorney of record" for the party in this case. The information provided herein is not intended to set forth all of the terms and conditions of the agreement between the party and the attorney for limited scope representation.

Date:

▶ _____
(TYPE OR PRINT NAME)   (SIGNATURE OF PARTY)

Date:

▶ _____
(TYPE OR PRINT NAME)   (SIGNATURE OF ATTORNEY)

FL–950 [New July 1, 2003]   **NOTICE OF LIMITED SCOPE REPRESENTATION**   Page 2 of 3

American LegalNet, Inc.
www.USCourtForms.com

Figure 11-2 (continued)

PETITIONER/PLAINTIFF: JANE DOE	CASE NUMBER:
RESPONDENT/DEFENDANT: JOHN DOE	BD 123 456
OTHER PARENT/CLAIMANT:	

PROOF OF SERVICE BY ☐ **PERSONAL SERVICE** ☐ **MAIL**

1. At the time of service I was at least 18 years of age and **not a party to this legal action.**

2. I served a copy of the *Notice of Limited Scope Representation* as follows *(check either a. or b. below):*
   a. ☐ **Personal service.** The *Notice of Limited Scope Representation* was given to:
       (1) Name of person served:
       (2) Address where served:

       (3) Date served:
       (4) Time served:

   b. ☐ **Mail.** I placed a copy of the *Notice of Limited Scope Representation* in the United States mail, in a sealed envelope with postage fully prepaid. The envelope was addressed and mailed as follows:
       (1) Name of person served:
       (2) Address:

       (3) Date of mailing:
       (4) Place of mailing *(city and state):*
       (5) I live in or work in the county where the *Notice* was mailed.
3. Server's information:
   a. Name:
   b. Home or work address:

   c. Telephone number:

I declare under penalty of perjury under the laws of the State of California that the information above is true and correct.

Date:

_____ ▶ _____
(TYPE OR PRINT NAME)   (SIGNATURE OF PERSON SERVING NOTICE)

but with full representation; the attorney and client may agree to continue their Limited Scope representation on another issue or hearing; or, the attorney and client will end their professional representation because the Limited Scope retention has been completed. If the attorney and client choose to convert their professional relationship into full representation, then they must execute a Judicial Council form MC-050, "Substitution of Attorney," listing the attorney as the attorney of record for the entire case. If the decision is made to add another aspect to the Limited Scope representation, then another "Notice of Limited Scope Representation" must be filed with the Court setting forth the specifics of the new representation. It would also be advisable to prepare a new Limited Scope retainer setting forth the elements of this new representation, or, at the very least, to prepare an addendum to the previously executed Limited Scope retainer.

If the decision is made to end the representation because the Limited Scope issue has been resolved, the provisions for ending the relationship have already been set forth in both the Limited Scope retainer agreement and in the "Notice of Limited Scope Representation": the client has stated that they will sign a Judicial Council form MC-050, "Substitution of Attorney" at the end of the representation. The attorney must simply prepare and present the Substitution of Attorney to the client, ask them to execute it where indicated on the form, and then file the form with the Court, serving it on all interested parties in the dissolution proceedings.

Unfortunately, as sometimes happens in the day-to-day practice of law, a client may refuse to sign the Substitution of Attorney, despite having agreed to do so in both the retainer agreement and in the "Notice of Limited Scope Representation." If that happens, the attorney must file with the Court a Judicial Council of California form FL-955, "Application to Be Relieved as Counsel Upon Completion of Limited Scope Representation," set forth below. [See Figure 11-3.]

As it states on the form, the Application is filed with the Court in those circumstances when the attorney believes that the Limited Scope Representation has been completed but the client does not execute the requisite Substitution of Attorney to release the attorney from the representation. The attorney filing the Application with the Court must declare under penalty of perjury the nature of the Representation and that the Representation has been completed as per the terms of the agreement with the client. The attorney must also either describe in detail the nature of the Representation or attach a copy of the Notice of Limited Scope Representation, stating the original nature of the representation.

The attorney must serve the client with the Application and must include a blank Judicial Council of California form FL-956, "Objection to Application to Be Relieved as Counsel Upon Completion of Limited Scope Representation," filling out the appropriate Proof of Service for filing with the Court.

Figure 11-3
Judicial Council Form FL-955—Application to Be
Relieved as Counsel

FL-955

ATTORNEY OR PARTY WITHOUT ATTORNEY *(Name, State Bar number, and address)*:	**FOR COURT USE ONLY**

TELEPHONE NO.:   FAX NO. *(Optional)*:

E-MAIL ADDRESS *(Optional)*:

ATTORNEY FOR *(Name)*:

SUPERIOR COURT OF CALIFORNIA, COUNTY OF

STREET ADDRESS:

MAILING ADDRESS:

CITY AND ZIP CODE:

BRANCH NAME:

PETITIONER/PLAINTIFF:

RESPONDENT/DEFENDANT:

OTHER PARENT/CLAIMANT:

APPLICATION TO BE RELIEVED AS COUNSEL
UPON COMPLETION OF LIMITED SCOPE REPRESENTATION

CASE NUMBER:

1. I request an order to be relieved as counsel in this matter.

2. In accordance with the terms of an agreement between *(name)*: ☐ petitioner ☐ respondent
   ☐ other parent/claimant and myself, I agreed to provide limited scope representation.

3. I was retained as attorney of record for the following limited scope services *(describe in detail)*:

   ☐ see *Notice of Limited Scope Representation* (form FL-950).

4. I have completed all services within the scope of my representation and have completed all acts ordered by the court.

5. The last known address for the ☐ petitioner ☐ respondent ☐ other parent/claimant is:

6. The last known telephone number for the ☐ petitioner ☐ respondent ☐ other parent/claimant is:

NOTICE TO PARTY/CLIENT: Your attorney has filed this *Application to Be Relieved as Counsel Upon Completion of Limited Scope Representation* with the court stating that he or she no longer represents you in this action because the tasks that you agreed the attorney would perform for you have been completed.

If you do not agree that these tasks have been completed and you want the attorney to continue to represent you until the tasks are completed, you must file an *Objection to Application to Be Relieved as Counsel Upon Completion of Limited Scope Representation* (form FL-956) with the court within 15 calendar days of the date that this notice was served on you, asking the court to require the attorney to remain your attorney in the action until these tasks are completed. You must also serve this *Objection* on your attorney and the other party. If you do not file a form FL-956, the court will grant your attorney's request.

Please refer to the *Proof of Service* on page 2 of this form to determine the date that this notice was served on you (if this form was served by mail, the date of service is 5 days after the date of mailing).

This procedure may be used ONLY if you believe that the attorney has not completed the tasks that he or she agreed to perform for you. It is NOT to be used to resolve other disagreements you may have with the attorney, such as disagreements concerning fees.

I declare under penalty of perjury under the laws of the State of California that the foregoing is true and correct.

Date:

▶

_____
(TYPE OR PRINT NAME)

_____
(SIGNATURE OF ATTORNEY)

Page 1 of 2

Form Approved for Optional Use Judicial Council of California FL-955 [Rev. January 1, 2007]	**APPLICATION TO BE RELIEVED AS COUNSEL** **UPON COMPLETION OF LIMITED SCOPE REPRESENTATION**	Cal. Rules of Court, rule 5.71 www.courtinfo.ca.gov

Figure 11-3 (continued)

PETITIONER/PLAINTIFF:	CASE NUMBER:
RESPONDENT/DEFENDANT:	
OTHER PARENT/CLAIMANT:	

PROOF OF SERVICE BY ☐ **PERSONAL SERVICE** ☐ **MAIL**

1. At the time of service I was at least 18 years of age and **not a party to this legal action.**

2. I served a copy of the completed *Application to Be Relieved as Counsel Upon Completion of Limited Scope Representation* and all attachments as well as a blank *Objection to Application to Be Relieved as Counsel Upon Completion of Limited Scope Representation* as follows *(check either a. or b. below):*

   a. ☐ **Personal service.** I personally delivered the forms listed above and any attachments as follows:

   (1) Name of person served:

   (2) Address where served:

   (3) Date served:

   (4) Time served:

   b. ☐ **Mail.** I placed copies of the forms listed above in a sealed envelope with postage fully prepaid. The envelope was addressed and mailed as follows:

   (1) Name of person served:

   (2) Address:

   (3) Date of mailing:

   (4) Place of mailing *(city and state):*

   (5) I live in or work in the county where the forms were mailed.

3. Server's information:

   a. Name:

   b. Home or work address:

   c. Telephone number:

I declare under penalty of perjury under the laws of the State of California that the information above is true and correct.

Date:

_____
(TYPE OR PRINT SERVER'S NAME)

▶ _____
(SERVER TO SIGN HERE)

FL-955 [Rev. January 1, 2007]   **APPLICATION TO BE RELIEVED AS COUNSEL**   Page 2 of 2
UPON COMPLETION OF LIMITED SCOPE REPRESENTATION

If the client was personally served, the attorney must then wait 15 days to see if the client files the Objection with the Court; if service was by mail, the attorney must wait 15 days, plus whatever additional time period is mandated by law for service by mail.

If the client files no Objection to the attorney's Application, the attorney resubmits the Application along with Judicial Council of California form FL-958, "Order on Application to Be Relieved as Counsel upon Completion of Limited Scope Representation," noting in Item #2 that this is an uncontested Application and indicating the manner in which the client was served with the Application. The Court will then enter the Order releasing the attorney from the Limited Scope Representation. It is thereafter the attorney's responsibility to serve both the client and all interested parties with a copy of the Order, filing the appropriate Proof of Service with the Court.

If, however, the client does not agree with the attorney's Application to be relieved, then the client has 15 days—or more if service was by mail—to file the Objection with the Court, at which time the attorney's Application and the client's Objection will be set for hearing. Please note that unlike other family law filings that are set for hearing based on the Court's availability, an Objection to an Application to Be Relieved as Counsel Upon Completion of Limited Scope Representation *must* be calendared for hearing no later than 25 days from the date the Objection is filed.

In completing the Objection to the Application, the client must state the terms of the Limited Scope Representation and what remains to be completed, as well as the reasoning behind their belief that the terms of the Representation must still be fulfilled. The client must then serve the attorney with a copy of the Objection, including the date, time, and department for the Hearing.

At the Hearing, the Court will address both the Application and the Objection and determine whether the attorney has completed the Representation as agreed to between the parties. If it rules that the attorney *has not* completed the representation, the attorney remains responsible for that aspect of the case as was described in the original Notice of Limited Scope Representation filed with the Court. The attorney must then continue to represent the client until such time as the client signs a Substitution of Attorney, signifying his/her agreement with the end of the representation, or the attorney starts this entire process over again by filing a new Application to Be Relieved as Counsel Upon Completion of Limited Scope Representation with the Court, seeking an Order that the representation is complete at that future point.

If, however, the Court rules that the attorney *has* fulfilled his/her obligation as set forth in the Notice of Limited Scope Representation, it will enter an Order relieving the attorney as the attorney of record for the specific portion of the case. The Court will do so by completing the Order on Application to Be Relieved as Counsel upon Completion of Limited Scope Representation, noting in item 3 that the Application was contested by the client and the details of the Hearing, and noting in item 4 that the attorney is relieved as the attorney of record and setting the effective date of its Order. Regardless of the Court's Order, it is once again the attorney's responsibility to serve the Order on the client and all interested parties in the dissolution proceedings.

The procedure for terminating a Limited Scope Representation is set forth in California Rules of Court 5.71, and the reader is encouraged to review the Rules for any amendments or updates.

Summary

This chapter has explored many diverse subjects that have application in family law proceedings, from the availability of attorney's fees to the tax ramifications of marital termination practice. It has been stressed many times that the topics contained herein are very complex and extensive, and that it is prudent to consult an experienced professional in these areas prior to jumping in "feet first." As we have seen earlier in this book, malpractice looms precariously over any aspect of the practice of law. Family law is no exception to that rule. Because of the highly charged emotional and financial issues presented in a family law case, the chances of being sued for malpractice are probably even greater than in most other areas of civil litigation. Be careful.

We have seen in this chapter that, under appropriate circumstances, one party to a marital termination proceeding may be called upon to pay for the other party's attorney's fees. While this may seem unfair at first blush, it is not designed to punish a party (although there are provisions for that); rather, it is designed to equalize the litigating power between the parties in hopes of ensuring a more equitable result. We have also touched on the various methods of bankruptcy available to a beleaguered debtor and have reviewed several standard discovery procedures. Finally, this chapter has explored in somewhat greater detail aspects of injunctive relief, domestic violence prevention, employment benefits, joinder, and marital settlement.

We have taken a brief look into the future of family law in the United States, in the form of collaborative divorce, limited scope representation, and same-sex marriage. As the divorce process becomes more and more costly, both emotionally and financially, participants in that process are searching for a better way. Through these pathways, they just might find it.

Key Terms

The following is a list of key terms and phrases that you should be able to
define and use in context. Only then will you have demonstrated a command of the material in this chapter.

- attorney's fees
- costs
- prevailing party
- Case Management Plan
- sanctions
- discovery
- interrogatories
- discovery plan
- deposition
- impeach (testimony)
- requests for admissions
- bankruptcy
- dischargeable v. nondischargeable
- alimony
- deductible v. nondeductible
- Dissomaster; Supportax
- *Lester* rule; Lesterizing
- tax filing status
- Domestic Violence Prevention Act
- premarital agreement
- postnuptial agreement
- marital settlement
- Collaborative Divorce
- Limited Scope Representation

Questions for Discussion

1. What are the basic criteria for determination of an award of attorney's
fees in a family law matter?

2. What is a case management plan, and how is it used in the context of a
family law proceeding?

3. Under what circumstances might an award of attorney's fees as a *sanction* be appropriate?

4. Formulate and briefly discuss a discovery plan. Which discovery tools
do you use and in what order? Why?

5. Briefly describe/define the following discovery tools: interrogatories, requests for production of documents, depositions, and requests for admission.

6. What is the *Lester* rule, and how does it work? (Hint: The context of this question is the tax deductibility of spousal support.)

7. Briefly discuss the procedure used in obtaining an uncontested dissolution.

ENDNOTES

1. Note, however, that Family Code §2255 limits the availability of an award of attorney's fees in a nullity action to *putative spouses only*.

2. Various sections of the Family Code besides 2030 provide for the allocation of attorney's fees and costs between the parties. The Family Code makes an award of attorney's fees available to the *prevailing party* (the one who "wins") in child support proceedings, as do various provisions of URESA and other enforcement statutes. Family Code §2107 allows for attorney's fees in situations where one spouse fails to comply with the disclosure requirements discussed in that section. Family Code §7640 also makes these awards available in paternity proceedings. Sections 2030 et seq., however, are those sections typically used as the authority for these awards. An additional aspect of a §2030 award is that one need not be the "prevailing party" to obtain an award of fees and costs. This analysis is simply based upon *need* and *ability to pay*, concepts discussed in greater detail later in this chapter.

3. It is for this reason that the parties are generally best advised, if at all possible, to pool their resources and hire one objective evaluator or appraiser to arrive at a finding with which they both can live.

4. This is an extremely simplistic view and example of the financial mechanics in this area. This area also happens to be one of the most complicated in family law, if not in the law in general. Accordingly, the reader is encouraged to explore treatises devoted to the area of pension litigation for any information other than such as would scratch the surface as is done here.

5. Although this is not completely accurate, a good analogy of the pension plan in this context would be a corporation.

6. As a preface to this section of the text, the reader is cautioned that the subjects discussed herein are extremely complicated and the subject not only of several fine treatises in this area, but of an entire body of law unto itself. Additionally, as the current edition of this text is being written, the U.S. Congress in the process of amending many of these rules. This area, like that of taxation, is best left to a professional with experience. This material is provided simply to give the reader a flavor of this subject and an introduction to some of the more recurring themes associated therewith.

7. Remember, until such time as parties to a marital termination proceeding in California obtain a judgment of dissolution of marriage, and that judgment becomes final, they are in fact still *married*.

8. This is an extremely difficult thing to do. Reliance on the availability of "innocent spouse" treatment is, in all but the most rare cases, misplaced.

9. There are several good treatises that concentrate on this subject exclusively, including "Marital Settlement Agreements," published by California Family Law Report, and "California Civil Practice Guide, Family Law," by Hogoboom and King, published by The Rutter Group, the latter of which contains an excellent chapter devoted to this subject.

10. This Act applies to agreements entered into after January 1, 1986, the effective date of the statute. As a general rule, however, this Act codified existing law, thus making the basic provisions of the Act applicable by reference to that law.

11. The provision of the UPAA that disallows a support waiver does not specifically mention spousal support waivers, only child support. Accordingly, there is a school of thought that argues that because former law generally prohibited such waivers, and the UPAA does not specifically do so, then such waivers are permissible under the Act. The general consensus of thinking on this subject, however, is that these waivers will also be held to be unenforceable under the UPAA and should thus be entered into cautiously.

12. A spousal support waiver is allowed in the context of a marital termination proceeding because of the general public policy of the State of California to promote marriage and discourage marital termination. Such a waiver is not allowed in the context of a pre- or post-marital agreement because to do so is seen as an act that encourages dissolution (or at least makes it easier), a clear violation of this expression of public policy. In the context of a marital termination proceeding, however, this policy no longer has application.

13. Knowing when to say "I don't know" can very often be the best skill a new practitioner can develop.

14. This is not always technically correct, as in the case of valid oral contracts. For purposes of this discussion, however, the reader would be wise to adopt this as the "general rule."

15. The court's opinion is an interesting if not somewhat disturbing reflection on the American family in the 21st century.

Glossary

Ability to pay.   The actual earnings that a person enjoys at any given time inasmuch as those earnings will determine his or her ability to pay on any given order. *See also* Earning capacity.

Abstract of judgment.   A recapitulation of the court's orders, typically presented on a Judicial Council Form and recorded in the county in which the judgment debtor maintains property. This document is designed to give record notice of the existence of the debt such that the debt will automatically become a lien on all property of record in the county in which the abstract is filed.

Agnos Act.   A legislative attempt made in 1984 to close the gap between the amounts being paid by welfare agencies to parents with minor children and the amounts being ordered by the court as and for child support for those minor children. The Agnos Act established a two-level system of child support guidelines, which included a mandatory minimum statewide component and a discretionary component for making awards that were higher than the minimum amount. The goal of the Agnos Child Support Standards Act was to ensure that the amount of child support being ordered in any given case would in no event be less than the mandatory minimum contribution by the supporting parent under the welfare guidelines.

Alternate valuation date.   As a general rule, assets in a marital termination proceeding are valued as of the date of trial. Under certain circumstances, however, the court will allow an alternative valuation date to be employed, which is typically the date of separation.

Answer.   A pleading used to respond to the allegations contained in a Complaint in a litigated proceeding.

Apportionment.   The concept by which the separate property and community property components of an asset are established and dealt with.

Bankruptcy.   A procedure by which a debtor (one who owes money) is given the opportunity to pay off his creditors (to the extent that it is possible) and then obtain an economic "fresh start."

Bifurcation.   The "splitting out" or "splitting apart" of the issues arising out of and pertaining to the continuation of the marital status from all other issues in a litigated marital termination proceeding, including, without limitation, property and child-related issues.

Branch court.   An "arm" of the courts located outside of the county seat or central district of any given county. These branch courts service the outlying areas of the county.

California Rules of Professional Conduct.   Rules and regulations that have been promulgated to regulate the professional conduct of attorneys.

Chapter 7 Bankruptcy.   The debtor's property is completely liquidated and his or her debts are then paid off to the extent available by virtue of the proceeds of the liquidation.

Chapter 11 Bankruptcy.   Fundamentally the same as a Chapter 13 proceeding with the exception that it is primarily designed for business entities (partnerships and corporations).

Chapter 13 Bankruptcy.   Contemplates the plan of paying off the judgment debtor's (or bankrupt's) creditors over an extended period of time as opposed to the complete liquidation concept found in Chapter 7 proceedings.

Child custody evaluator.   Typically a mental health professional who specializes in evaluating questions of custody and placement of minor children.

Child support.   Support (usually in the form of money) typically paid by the noncustodial parent to the custodial parent for purposes of contributing to the expenses arising out of and related to the support of the parties' minor children.

Citation of contempt.   The document, typically in the form of an Order to Show Cause, by which an individual who is alleged to be in contempt of court is charged with the contempt and ordered to appear in court to defend those charges.

Citee.   In a family law contempt proceeding, the individual who is alleged to have violated the court's orders and is thus the responding party in the contempt proceeding.

Cohabitation.   More than two people simply living together as roommates. It typically arises out of a romantic or intimate relationship between two individuals, and where those individuals hold themselves out as "boyfriend/girlfriend,""husband/wife," or something similar thereto. The determination of cohabitation is a factual one, made on a case-by-case basis. It finds its genesis in nonmarital relationships.

Commingling. The act of "mixing up" assets of separate and community character to such a degree that the source thereof is no longer capable of ascertainment with specificity.

Common law. The law that has been handed down generation to generation over the years, typically through and by case decisions.

Community. The marital estate.

Community property. All property, real or personal, wherever situated, acquired by a married person during marriage while domiciled in California. *See also* Separate property.

Compensatory damages. Damages that are designed to compensate the victorious litigant for any loss that they suffered and proved up to the satisfaction of the trial court.

Complaint. A pleading used to initiate a litigated issue between parties.

Conciliation court. A service of the superior court wherein court-appointed mediators and family counseling professionals provide counseling and mediation services to litigants involved in matters arising out of and pertaining to the custody and visitation of their minor children.

Conclusive presumption. A matter that is presumed in law conclusively, that is, without the ability to rebut same. *See also* Presumption.

Contempt. In the family law context, a court proceeding typically initiated pursuant to an Order to Show Cause wherein a party who is the subject of court orders and who subsequently is alleged to have violated same is held accountable therefor. The contempt proceeding represents a potential to be punished for failing to obey a court order both civilly and criminally. The punishment is for violation of the court order, however, and is not designed to compensate the intended beneficiary of the court order.

Contract. A promise to perform an act or provide services, supported by consideration.

County seat. The headquarters for a county. This is typically the largest city in any given county and the headquarters of its civic operations (courthouse, county sheriff system, jail system).

Custody. Includes legal custody and physical custody and refers to the manner of exercising control and responsibility over minor children. *See also* Legal custody and Physical custody.

Debtor's examination. An examination of a judgment debtor taken under oath, at which time the judgment creditor (or the representative) is allowed to ask the judgment debtor a wide range of questions, the specific goal of which is to discover the location of the judgment debtor's assets and in so doing improve the chances that the judgment creditor will be able to collect on his judgment.

Defendant. The individual who is required to respond to and defend a Complaint. *See also* Respondent.

Deferred compensation. Compensation that is earned by an employee currently but paid out at some later date. *See also* Retirement benefits.

Deferred sale of home order. A court order given in the context of additional child support. It refers to the court authorizing a sale of the family home to be deferred for the benefit of the minor until such time as the minor child attains the age of majority or until the occurrence of some other terminating condition. This is sometimes called a *Duke* order in deference to the name of the case in which the concept was first espoused.

Defined benefit plan. In this type of deferred compensation or retirement plan, the known variable is the amount of the benefit to be received at retirement, and the required contribution over time is adjusted to meet that goal. *See also* Defined contribution plan.

Defined contribution plan. A retirement or deferred compensation plan whereby the ultimate amount of the benefits to be provided at retirement are not known until the date of retirement because they depend upon the future investment performance of the fund. The benefits are simply defined by a formula for contributions. In other words, the amount of the contribution made every month is the only element of the fund that is defined in advance. *See also* Defined benefit plan.

Dependency court. That branch of the superior court designed to handle matters arising out of and pertaining to incidents wherein a minor child's health, safety, and welfare are threatened.

Deposition. A proceeding whereby one party is allowed to examine the other party under oath, in front of a court reporter, in a question and answer session. Although relatively informal, the testimony elicited at these proceedings has the same force and effect as that given during a court proceeding.

Disaffirm. In the context of contracts, refers to an act whereby the contract is repudiated by one of the parties thereto.

Discovery. In litigation practice describes the various procedures utilized by parties to litigation that are designed to help them learn as much as they can about the other side. Included in the overall context of discovery are interrogatories, depositions, and requests for document production.

Dissolution.   Label given to the process by which a marital union is terminated.

Document production demand.   One of the various tools of the discovery process wherein the propounding party serves a demand for the inspection and copying of records to the responding party who must thereafter file a verified response identifying the documents in the responding party's possession that will be produced pursuant to the demand.

Domicile.   The place of a person's intended permanent residence.

Due process.   The level of constitutional and jurisdictional safeguards accorded to all litigants with regard to ensuring that they are not deprived of their property without first having been given the opportunity to participate in legal proceedings pertinent thereto.

Duke **order.**   *See* Deferred sale of home order.

Earning capacity.   The earning potential of a particular person. For example, an individual who has been trained and has experience as a medical doctor has the earning capacity typically associated with medical doctors. An individual who lacks this training and skill does not have this same earning capacity. A person's earning capacity will typically be defined by her level of education, skill, and experience. *See also* Ability to pay.

Emancipation.   Literally, to be "set free"; in the family law context, typically dealing with the emancipation of minors, this term refers to a minor obtaining freedom from the control of his or her parents and being treated, for all practical purposes thereafter, as an adult.

Epstein reimbursement credits.   The right of a spouse to be reimbursed for post-separation payments of separate property on community property assets. *See also* Watts reimbursement credits.

Equity.   In a property context, equity refers to the amount of value that an asset maintains over and above any amounts encumbering it. For example, if a home is worth $100,000 and $80,000 is owing on that home, then the amount of equity would be equal to $20,000.

Errors and omissions insurance.   Insurance designed to compensate a client for the negligence of the professional retained to represent him.

Exemplary damages.   *See* Punitive damages.

Ex parte.   The process undertaken when a party requesting certain relief does not (or cannot) give the responding party the usually required notice of his request.

Family law. That area of the law devoted to issues arising out of, pertaining to, and related to the familial relationship, including relationships by marriage and birth.

Family support. A combination of spousal support and child support designed to maximize the tax benefits of the deductibility of spousal support payments versus the nondeductibility of payments made for child support. *See also* Lesterizing.

Federal Parental Kidnapping Act. A federal law that provides rules and regulations arising out of and pertaining to acts of parental kidnapping of their own minor children.

Fiduciary. The designation of the person who is holding something in trust for another or who owes to another a duty of trust and confidence.

Forum non conveniens. One of the methods under which a litigant may seek to change the venue of a court proceedings. Literally, this term is Latin for "inconvenient forum." The litigant asserts the doctrine of forum non conveniens when he or she seeks to convince the court that the litigated matter should be moved to a more convenient venue.

***Freeman* order.** A basic standard visitation order, so named after the judge who first created it, which generally contemplates visitation by the secondary custodial parent along the lines of alternating weekends from Friday to Sunday, one midweek dinner, equal division of holidays, and two uninterrupted weeks during the summer for each parent.

Full disclosure. The level of disclosure that must be made in a legal context. It implies that no aspect of the matter can be left undisclosed.

Full faith and credit. A term typically used in the context of constitutional law, this describes the concept of "comity" wherein each state of the United States is required to give both full faith and credit (or recognition) to the judgments and orders of their sister states.

Garnishment. *See* Wage assignment.

Gift. An item of value that is transferred by one person to another gratuitously and without receiving anything in return for the transfer.

Goodwill. The portion of an ongoing business that represents the likelihood that it will have repeat patronage. Typically expressed in terms of "positive goodwill" or "negative goodwill." Keyed to the expectation of future earnings.

Gross income. Income received by an employed individual before any deductions are made (deductions for example, for state and federal taxes and state disability).

Independent adoptions.   Adoptions that are arranged and handled, typically by an attorney, outside of the context of the intervention and oversight of a county department or agency.

Informed written consent.   The level of consent necessary when same is being obtained in any legal proceeding. It implies that the person giving the consent is doing so after being fully informed of all of his rights in the context of the consent, typically in writing.

Inheritance.   A gift that takes place upon the death of the donor.

Injunction.   An order of court compelling that a party refrain from performing an act or that a party undertake an act, as the circumstances may require. *See also* Prohibitory injunction and Mandatory injunction.

Interrogatories.   A set of written questions that are mailed by one party to the other, which must be answered by the responding party under penalty of perjury.

Irreconcilable differences.   The basis of the "no fault" grounds for dissolution in California. For all practical purposes, any differences between married individuals can constitute "irreconcilable differences" and thus justify the granting of a dissolution of marriage so long as one of the parties is prepared to indicate to the court that the differences they are experiencing cannot be resolved.

Irremedial breakdown.   A statutory term used in conjunction with the "no fault" grounds for dissolution of marriage in California. This term refers to the fact that the marital relationship has broken down and that there is no possible remedy.

Joinder.   The concept by which a third party is "joined into" the marital litigation proceedings in order to allow the court to exercise jurisdiction or power over said third party.

Joint custody.   *See* Pure joint custody, Joint legal custody, and Joint physical custody.

Joint legal custody.   Arrangement whereby the parents will share equally the rights and responsibilities to make decisions regarding their minor child's health, education, and welfare. They do not, however, necessarily share the right to the child's physical presence.

Joint physical custody.   Arrangement whereby each parent has a significant period of physical custody with the minor child sometimes known as "shared physical custody." Under these circumstances the child will roughly split her time between the parents' respective homes.

Judgment creditor.   The individual in litigation in whose favor the judgment runs.

Judgment debtor. The individual required to pay under the terms of a judgment.

Judicial council form. Preprinted court forms that have been either adopted for use (wherein their use is mandatory) or approved for use (wherein their use is optional). These forms are used in the context of many civil actions, only one of which is a marital termination proceeding.

Jurisdiction. The nature of the power that is bestowed upon the court system.

Jurisdictional stepdown. This term, in the context of spousal support, is substantially similar to a "substantive step-down." In this context, however, the court limits its jurisdiction (or power) to award spousal support above a certain level rather than limiting the actual amount being ordered. *See also* Substantive stepdown.

Juvenile court. That branch of the superior court designed to handle fundamentally criminal matters wherein the defendants therein are minors.

Keeper. An individual used in debt collection. This individual is typically installed (that is, placed) on the business premises of a judgment debtor's business for the purpose of collecting the income of that business and applying same to the judgment.

Laches. An equitable concept that describes the situation that occurs when a party "sits on" his rights. In other words, when a party, notwithstanding his knowledge of his rights in a given situation, chooses to take no action to protect or preserve those rights, and by so doing (that is, failing to act) causes the other party who is [impacted] thereby to suffer some change in position as a result.

Lawful order. An order of court that is valid on its face in all respects and entitled to full recognition both by other jurisdictions as well as the parties to the litigation wherein the order was generated.

Legal custody. That aspect of custody wherein the right to exercise power, control, and responsibility over central issues arising out of and pertaining to the health, safety, and welfare of a minor child are involved. This includes decisions related to the minor child's religion, elective surgery, education, and the like.

Legal separation. Label given to the action by which the rights, duties, and responsibilities of the parties thereto (the spouses) are determined fully and finally while maintaining as intact the marital union.

Lengthy marriage. Typically defined (although not always) as a marriage of ten years or more.

Lesterizing. A term (derived from the *Lester* case) used to describe the creation of "family support," which seeks to capitalize on the fact that spousal support is deductible on one's income taxes while child support is not. The concept of Lesterizing is to shift some of the monies otherwise earmarked for child support into the category of spousal support for purposes of providing the paying parent a greater deduction than that to which they would be otherwise entitled. By so doing, the increased deduction will lessen the amount of his tax burden, thus providing him with additional after-tax income. In theory, at least, a portion of this additional income can then be paid over to the party who is receiving this support, thus increasing the overall amount of support being paid without actually costing the paying parent any more.

Mandatory injunction. A court order that compels a person to perform some act.

Minimum contacts. That amount of contact with the state seeking to obtain jurisdiction over a particular person, which that person must maintain prior to the court exercising its power over the litigant. In California the concept of "minimum contacts" means just that: the absolute bare minimum. Mere presence in the state for a brief period of time will often be sufficient to satisfy this requirement. This requirement is a constitutional requirement, finding support in the California and United States Constitutions.

Minor child. A child who is under the age of majority. In California this translates to a child who is under the age of 18. In some other jurisdictions, the age of majority may be higher, for example 21 years of age, in which case a minor child would be defined as one under the age of 21.

Moore/Marsden. Rule referring to apportioning separate property and community interests in real property containing elements of each.

Motion. A written request to a court to provide the applicant with relief requested therein. *See also* Order to Show Cause.

Net income. That amount of income obtained when standard deductions for federal and state taxes, state disability, social security, and so on, are deducted from gross income. Net income is sometimes referred to as "take-home pay."

Notice and opportunity to be heard. This refers to the constitutional requirement that, prior to granting orders with respect to a party litigant, that person must first be given notice of the action and the opportunity to be heard therein. *See generally* Due process.

Nullity. A legal action designed with the goal of declaring as invalid (or null) a marital union.

Order to Show Cause. A formal request of the court for the entry of orders based upon factual concerns and considerations. This is a vehicle typically used to obtain temporary orders in a family law context.

Passive income. Income derived from the investment of an asset, typically taking the form of interest or rents, issues, and profits.

Pendente lite. Literally, "pending litigation." Term used to describe an order given in the context of litigation that will expire at the termination of the litigation or upon further order of court on that subject.

Pereira/Van Camp rules. Methods of apportioning separate and community property interests in an asset containing elements of both.

Permanent spousal support. Sometimes referred to as a "long-term" award of spousal support. This is spousal support that is ordered to be paid posttrial in a marital termination proceeding and has as its purpose the maintenance of the supported party as well as the rehabilitation of said party with the intention of integrating the supported spouse back into the work force over a period of time. *See also* Temporary spousal support.

Personal jurisdiction. The jurisdiction (or power) that the court exercises over the person of the litigant.

Personal property. Items of property that do not fall into the category of "real property." *See generally* Real property.

Petition. This is the document used to initiate a marital termination proceeding whether by way of dissolution, legal separation, or nullity. *See also* Complaint.

Petitioner. The label given to the individual who is initiating the marital termination proceedings and is responsible for the filing of the Petition. *See also* Plaintiff.

Physical custody. That aspect of custody of a minor child arising out of and pertaining to where and with whom that child will physically reside.

Plaintiff. The label given to the individual who commences litigation by way of a complaint. *See also* Petitioner.

Preponderance of evidence. That level of evidence that is only "slightly more" in favor of one side than it is against the other. For example, 51 percent in favor as opposed to 49 percent against. *See also* Reasonable doubt.

Presumption. A matter of fact or law that is deemed established.

Prohibitory injunction. A court order that requires a person to refrain from undertaking an act.

Property. Items of tangible value, capable of being owned and valued.

Punitive damages. Monetary damages designed to punish a litigant rather than compensate the victorious litigant.

Pure joint custody. An arrangement whereby neither parent exercises exclusive control over the legal or physical custodial rights of a minor child. All decisions relating to the child's health, education, and welfare are shared jointly by both parents, and the child does not reside at any one parent's home for significantly more than 50 percent of the time.

Putative spouse. A party to a void or voidable marriage who, as a result thereof, is not entitled to the designation as "spouse," but who would be so entitled were it not for the bad acts of her spouse. To be a putative spouse is typically to enjoy many of the same benefits and protections afforded to "real" spouses, notwithstanding the fact that, through no fault of the putative spouse, the marriage was subsequently ruled invalid.

Qualified Domestic Relations Order (QDRO). Established under federal laws and guidelines for the preparation of orders designed to divide federal pension plans. The term refers to an order with regard thereto being "qualified" in the sense that it must meet the various requirements set out in the federal law.

Quasi-criminal. In the family law contempt context, refers to an action undertaken by the court which, while not purely of a criminal nature, carries with it punishments that could be considered "criminal" in nature (for example, jail time).

Quasi-community property. Property that would have been community property had it been acquired by the parties while they were married and domiciled in California. Typically refers to property acquired by individuals during their marriage while they are domiciled in some other state.

Quasi-marital property. Property acquired by parties to a putative marriage that would have been community or quasi-community property had the marriage been valid.

Real property. Land, real estate, and items permanently affixed thereto.

Reasonable doubt. That level of proof that must be overcome in a criminal or quasi-criminal matter before the responding party therein can be found guilty. For example, proof must be "beyond a reasonable doubt." There is no clear definition of this term. It is thought, however, to be comprised of proof to such an extent that reasonable persons would not disagree with regard to the matter sought to be proven. *See also* Preponderance of evidence.

Rebuttable presumption. A presumption capable of being overcome by reference to evidence tending to disprove the presumed fact. *See also* Presumption.

Receiver. An individual whose primary purpose is to manage and control property and assets for purposes of protecting their value and extracting sufficient funds from the property to ensure satisfaction of judgments.

Relocation. In the family law context, arising out of and pertaining to issues pertinent to the minor children, that situation created when one of the parents, typically the custodial parent, seeks to relocate her residence far enough away from the so-called visiting parent to create a problem with regard to visitation.

Request for admissions. One of the various discovery devices available to party litigants. The propounding party asks the responding party to admit the genuineness of certain documents and facts pertinent to litigation. The responding party must respond under oath.

Reservation of jurisdiction. The concept of the superior court agreeing to maintain, or "hold on to," its jurisdiction over any particular issue. This concept finds particular application with regard to spousal support.

Residence. That place where an individual maintains some level of habitation: a vacation home, for example. It is possible for an individual to maintain a residence at the same place in which he is domiciled. It is not, however, necessarily required that every residence must be located in that person's domicile.

Residency requirement. In the family law context, for the court to take jurisdiction over a litigated marital termination proceeding, the initiating party must meet a residency requirement.

Respondeat Superior. A legal theory upon which a person's employer may be held liable for the torts of their employee.

Respondent. The label given to the individual on whom a Petition for Dissolution of Marriage, Legal Separation, or Nullity has been served. This person is required to respond to the Petition and is therefore given this label. *See also* Defendant.

Response. The pleading used to respond to the Petition in a marital termination proceeding, including dissolution of marriage, legal separation, and nullity. *See also* Answer.

Retirement benefits. Refers to compensation that is earned by an employee currently but paid out at some later date. *See also* Deferred compensation.

Richmond **order.** Describes a court order with regard to spousal support that contemplates payments for a specific period of time at which point the payments will drop down to zero, placing the burden on obtaining an award for continuing support on the supported spouse, who must come back into court and give the court sufficient reasons to justify extending the period of spousal support.

Separate property. Separate property of a married person includes all property owned by that person before marriage, all property acquired by that person after marriage by gift, bequest, devise, or descent, and the rents, issues, and profits of said property. *See also* Community property.

Service of process. The manner in which a responding party litigant is brought "into the system." Service of process in its most general sense describes the function of notifying the responding party of the nature of the action being taken against him.

Sole legal custody. One parent only is the decision making parent concerning issues relating to the minor child's health, education, and welfare.

Sole physical custody. In this instance the child in question will primarily reside with and be supervised by one particular parent, while the other parent simply "visits." The visiting parent is sometimes known as the "secondary custodial parent."

Special appearance. An appearance that a responding party makes to a civil action whose primary purpose is to challenge the validity of the court's exercise of its power (or jurisdiction) over him. It is designed to allow for the appearance to contest jurisdiction without actually submitting to it in the context of the motion contesting the jurisdiction.

Spousal support. Support (typically money) paid by a person to his former spouse for purposes of providing rehabilitation and maintenance of the marital standard of living and status quo pending trial.

Statute of limitations. The period of time within which a legal action for the protection or preservation of an individual's rights must be brought. For example, an action for personal injury must be brought within one year that the injured party suffers the injury. It is therefore said that the statute of limitations on a personal injury matter is one year. There are many different statutes of limitations, depending upon the nature of the action and rights sought to be protected.

Statutory law. Laws that are created by statute.

Subject matter jurisdiction. The power that the court may exercise over the subject matter of the litigation.

Substantive stepdown. This term arises out of the concept of permanent spousal support and contemplates that the substance of the spousal support award (that is, the amount being paid every month) will be reduced at periodic intervals down to (usually) zero with an ultimate retention of jurisdiction component. *See also* Jurisdictional stepdown.

Summary dissolution. A quick and inexpensive process designed to provide for obtaining a marital dissolution easily and without participation by attorneys. This process is subject to strict statutory rules with regard to eligibility.

Summons. A document issued by the court clerk that acts as an officially issued document giving notice to the respondent that legal proceedings have been instituted against him and also so advises him to retain counsel to protect his interests.

Superior court. In California a county court with, for all practical purposes, no jurisdictional maximum. It is a branch of the judicial arm of government and is differentiated from the other courts (small claims and municipal) typically by its subject matter jurisdiction.

Support. *See* Child support, Spousal support, and Family support.

Temporary restraining order. Typically issued ex parte, an order of very brief duration designed to prohibit the restrained party from undertaking a particular and specified action during the restraining period (which is typically 15 to 25 days).

Temporary spousal support. Spousal support paid by one spouse to the other during the pendency of the litigation. Its purpose is to, as much as possible, ensure maintenance of the marital standard of living and status quo while the parties await trial of their marital termination proceeding. *See also* Permanent spousal support.

Title documents. Documents that establish ownership to particular assets wherein such ownership is set forth in such written document. For example, a grant deed with regard to a piece of real property or a "pink slip" with respect to an automobile or similar asset.

Tracing. Refers to the act of allowing the tracing party to rebut the general presumption contained in the Family Code that property acquired during marriage is community in nature if the source of the funds used to acquire that property can be traced to a separate property source. Similarly, a party seeking to establish a community property element in an item of separate property will be required to trace the source of some or all of the funds used in the acquisition of that asset to that community property source. *See also* Apportionment.

Transmutation. An agreement between spouses to change the status of an asset from either separate to community or community to separate.

Uniform Child Custody Jurisdiction Act. A uniform act, adopted generally throughout all 50 states, designed to provide guidance with regard to establishing a basis for a state's exercise of jurisdiction over issues arising out of and pertaining to minor children.

Venue. The location for the commencement or trial of a litigated matter.

Vesting. The extent to which actual ownership or the right to receive property has accrued to the benefit of the individual who is designated as the recipient thereof. Typically arises in the context of deferred compensation and retirement plans, and typically refers to a length of service that must be achieved by the employee prior to establishing ownership rights in the deferred compensation fund.

Visitation. Periods of secondary custodial time enjoyed by the parent who typically has less than 50 percent of the physical custody of the minor child. This parent is sometimes known as the "visiting parent" as opposed to the other "custodial parent."

Void marriage. A marriage that is invalid and of no force and effect from its very inception. *See also* Voidable marriage.

Voidable marriage. A marriage that is valid at its inception but subject to being set aside as void on some statutory basis. *See also* Void marriage.

Wage assignment. A document, issued by the court clerk, directing the employer of the judgment debtor to withhold a certain percentage of the judgment debtor's wages, paying same over to the judgment creditor, for purposes of satisfying the judgment.

Watts reimbursement credits. The reimbursement rights of a spouse who has been denied the use value of a community property asset postseparation when the rental value thereof exceeds its acquisition costs. *See also* Epstein reimbursement credits.

Writ of execution. A document issued by the clerk of the court directing the levying officer (typically a county marshal) to take possession of assets of the judgment debtor once their location has been ascertained. In a very simplistic sense, this can be referred to as a "license to take property."

Writ of possession or sale. Similar to a Writ of Execution, a document issued by the clerk of the court giving the levying officer the power to take possession of a piece of the judgment debtor's real property and, if necessary, sell same at auction for the purposes of satisfying the judgment.

Organization of Family Code

Index